TAMIL PROVERBS
WITH THEIR
ENGLISH TRANSLATION

TAMIL PROVERBS
WITH THEIR
ENGLISH TRANSLATION

CONTAINING
UPWARDS OF SIX THOUSAND PROVERBS.

BY THE
REV. P. PERCIVAL,
CHAPLAIN, MADRAS MILITARY FEMAL ORPHAN ASYLUM:
AUTHOR OF THE LAND OF THE VEDA, &C.

SECOND EDITION

GYAN

Published by

Gyan Publishing House
5, Ansari Road
Daryaganj, New Delhi-110002
Phone: 011-47034999, 9811692060
E-mail: books@gyanbooks.com

Distribution Network
gyanbooks.com
India, USA, Canada, UK, Australia, France

ISBN : 978-81-212-4087-1 (PB)
First Published, 1874

2nd Impression 2020

Printed at: Gyan Press, Delhi.

Tamil Proverbs with their English Translation
Author: Rev. P. Percival

TAMIL PROVERBS

WITH THEIR

ENGLISH TRANSLATION

CONTAINING
UPWARDS OF SIX THOUSAND PROVERBS

BY THE

REV. P. PERCIVAL,

CHAPLAIN, MADRAS MILITARY FEMALE ORPHAN ASYLUM.

AUTHOR OF THE LAND OF THE VEDA, &C.

SECOND EDITION

MADRAS:

PRINTED AND PUBLISHED AT THE *DINAVARTAMANI* PRESS.

LITTLE BOURNE, MYLAPORE.

1874.

PREFACE TO THE FIRST EDITION.

ADVERTISEMENT.

It is hoped that the following collection of Tamil Proverbs may be useful to those who are in any way connected with the interesting people who speak that language. Examples of concise and forcible expression are thereby furnished, which may tend to aid in the study of the language, and occasional allusions to national, social, and religious usages may suggest heads of valuable enquiry, while the modes of thinking, and the natural shrewdness of the Hindu mind may be seen through this medium. It is presumed that the translation generally conveys the sense of the original, although not always with its force, nor with the elegance that might be desired. Should it be called for, a future edition may remedy some of the existing faults, and also supply deficiencies, both as to the character of the translation, and the number of the examples.

P. PERCIVAL.

JAFFNA, *Christmas*, 1842.

PREFACE TO THE SECOND EDITION.

A FEW words on the history of the book now offered to the Public in an enlarged form may not be out of place in the Preface to the Second Edition.

Almost immediately after my arrival in this country in 1826, I entered on my Missionary work among the Tamil people, having acquired the rudiments of their language in England from a gentleman who had spent several years in the South of India and North Ceylon. Intercourse with the natives afforded me ample opportunities of becoming acquainted with their modes of thought and expression, and, noticing their predilection for proverbial sayings, I was led to an early study and use of Tamil proverbs.

In 1830 I was removed to Bengal. There I became acquainted with a clergyman who had, like myself, turned his attention to the proverbs of the people among whom he dwelt. He collected a considerable number of Bengali proverbs, and published them, with an English translation, in a small volume, printed at the Press connected with Bishop's College, Calcutta. When the Mission in Bengal with which I was connected was withdrawn, I returned to my former sphere of labor among the Tamil people. As opportunity offered, I collected and arranged proverbs that I found current among them; and in 1842 printed a collection of nearly nineteen hundred with an English translation.

The First Edition having become scarce, I was urged, by many whose judgment I felt bound to respect, to prepare matter for a second and enlarged edition. Various causes prevented me from immediately undertaking the work. For several years all my time was devoted to the revision of the Tamil Scriptures, in conjunction with Messrs. RHENIUS, KNIGHT, SPAULDING, HUTCHINGS, and others, and in passing the "Tentative Bible" through the Press. Subsequently a visit to England caused a further postponement of my plan, but, on my return to Madras in 1854, my attention was again directed to the subject of Tamil proverbs.

In the following year a Committee of gentlemen belonging to the Civil and Military Services of Government, Messrs. STOKES, SIM, CHAMIER, and Colonels BROWN, PEARS, and BELL resolved to start a Journal, for the purpose of diffusing, among the Tamil people, information social, political, and literary. The Committee invited my co-operation as Editor. This labor I at once accepted, the more readily because for several months I had been making arrangements to carry out the same idea, and had visited Calcutta to procure information on the subject, chiefly from Mr. MARSHMAN. In October 1855 the first number of the new journal, the *Dinavartamâni*, was published. Soon after this I also undertook the editing of a Telugu journal of the same scope, and bearing the same name. The circulation of these papers throughout the Madras Presidency afforded me a good opportunity of inviting the subscribers to assist me in the collection of Tamil and Telugu proverbs My request was met by contributions from all parts of the country. The former were added to a rapidly increasing collection, while a selection from the latter was published, from week to week, along with an

English translation, in the Telugu *Dinavartamâni*. When the late Major CARR informed me that he was preparing a volume of Telugu proverbs for the Press, I made over to him my collection, a service he thus acknowledged in the Preface to his work—"The Translator has to thank the Rev. P. PERCIVAL, Professor of Vernacular Literature, Presidency College, for kindly placing at his disposal a *MS.* containing a large number of Telugu proverbs."

In the year 1860 my collection of Tamil proverbs contained nearly five thousand examples translated into English and ready for the Press. At that time, however, I was so much engaged in preparing books and maps, in the Vernaculars, for the Director of Public Instruction, that I found it impossible to carry out my design of printing these proverbs, although I had announced it in the *Dinavartamâni*. Then followed an interval of ten years during which I was engaged in duties absorbing all my time and attention. I had the superintendence of the Public Instruction Press on my hands; and, aided by the Pundits of the Presidency College, and other competent native scholars, had the responsibility of editing, among the works that issued from the Press during this period, seven dictionaries, some of which have since been re-printed.

At the beginning of 1870, having been relieved from my heavy duties in connexion with the Presidency College and the University, I resolved to print the proverbs as they stood, and soon after this having met the Rev. G. FRYAR of Manargudi, Tanjore District, I learnt that he had for eight or nine years been also engaged in collecting Tamil proverbs, and that his collection then amounted to five thousand examples, and that he proposed eventually to publish it on the basis of my First Edition. On hearing of my own plan, Mr. FRYAR abandoned this purpose, and very generously placed his valuable *MS.* at my disposal, from which I obtained several hundred new proverbs.

Shortly after this, again, one of my compositors brought me an old-looking *MS.* containing over fifteen hundred examples. A volume printed in 1861 at Vepery, and containing nearly four thousand examples, was also put into my hands. But these collections yielded very few proverbs not already contained in my own *MS.* A Pundit of the Government Normal School furnished me with about a hundred fresh examples, and a small *MS.* belonging to a Native Christian lady of Tanjore contained a few curious proverbs that I had not seen before. These related to Christian character, and evidently originated in anything but a benign feeling.

Altogether my collections in 1872 exceeded fifteen thousand, but they only yielded the number contained in this volume. That the outcome of so large a gathering should be comparatively small may easily be accounted for by the fact that the several collections, in very many instances, contained the same proverbs. It must be borne in mind that my own collection, which eventually absorbed the others, was made during a period extending over forty years, and that, through the medium of the *Dinavartamâni*, I had received contributions from all parts of the Madras Presidency, as well from North Ceylon. Hence it was but natural that I should anticipate collectors who come into the field later.

But for the omission of many of the admired Aphorisms of the ancient Tamil matron, Avveyar, this collection would have been somewhat larger. Though these Aphorisms are compositions of unequalled brevity and beauty, I have, for the most part, omitted them, because they are generally taught in schools, and indeed regarded as part of a school course. *En passant* I may mention that seven or eight years ago I printed and published them, in a separate form, with an analysis and translation in English, and that a Second Edition of this work is now in the Press. Bible proverbs, and those obviously Sanskrit, are also omitted, because this collection is designed to be Dravidian. Translations from Western proverbs I have for the same reason left out.

In this edition, as in the First, the proverbs are arranged in alphabetical order. This of course is the easiest method. Some years ago I thought of classifying the subjects somewhat after the plan of *Amarakosha*, a Sanskrit Dictionary, wherein objects are divided into separate classes, as Supernals, Infernals, Men, Animals. &c. A division of subjects on the principle of a commonplace book was also thought of, and a friend whose judgment I greatly respect, suggested an index. Although each of the methods referred to has much to recommend it, at length I gave them all up, and resolved to adopt the easiest—the alphabetical arrangement. Had I decided otherwise, the work must have been delayed; and as in my case "the day is far spent," I might not have been able to accomplish my purpose.

On the analogy of the proverbial expressions current in all countries, many scraps of sentences, mere allusions, similitudes, and the like, are included in this collection, though not proverbs in the proper sense of the term. The objects of Nature, habits, and dispositions of animals, government, agriculture and commerce, domestic and religious usages supply a large number of proverbial expressions. The incidents of classical literature contribute many that prove highly acceptable to those who have any acquaintance with the sources of Hindu history. So largely do the stories of ancient writers contribute that the fact has originated a proverb universal among the people of Bengal.

What is there after Bhárata?

A glance at a few pages of this volume will suffice to show that the people among whom such proverbs are current cannot be ignorant of the laws of God.

Vox Populi, vox Dei,

may be applied to this aspect of many of the Dravidian proverbs

"The people's voice, the voice of God we call;
And what are Proverbs, but the people's voice?
Coined first and common made, by common choice;
Then sure they must have weight, and truth withal."

I may be permitted to say a few words on the utility of a volume like that now offered to the public. A foreigner destined to spend the best part of his life among the Tamil people will find their proverbs of inestimable value. In these pithy and instructive sayings a vast fund of information will be found, not to be obtained from ordinary books, and not at all from books designed for Western minds;—practical maxims, resulting from the experience of many generations, maxims that will be sought in vain in books of modern origin.

The translation will, I hope, be generally approved. In some instances I have found it difficult to ascertain the meaning; and in many the application has equally puzzled both myself and others to whom I have applied for information. In some cases I may have been misled by those who might be more disposed to hazard a conjecture than to acknowledge ignorance. For the benefit of foreigners the occasional notes might have been advantageously increased in number, but usages differ so much that great caution is required in this matter. So varied is the operation of race, language, religion, and climate, upon the character and social usages of the Hindus who occupy the vast area of India that it is unsafe to assume generally that what is common in one Province is so in others.

In conclusion, any one interested in this work will oblige by sending me proverbs not found in the collection, or any suggestions for improving the next Edition. Though I may not hope to see another edition, my son-in-law, Mr. W. A. Symonds, who has long studied Tamil proverbs with great interest, will, should it be called for, undertake the editing.

Little Bourne, Madras,
February 13, 1874.

P. PERCIVAL.

TAMIL PROVERBS,

WITH THEIR TRANSLATION IN

ENGLISH.

அ.

1. அகங்கையிற் போட்டுப் புறங்கையை நக்கலாமா?

    Having placed the thing on the palm, why lick the back of the hand?

---

2. அகடவிகடமாய்ப் பேசுகிறான்.

    He speaks artfully.

---

3. அகதிக்கு ஆகாயம் துணை.

    Heaven is the help of the helpless.

---

4. அகதிக்குத் தெய்வமே துணை.

    God Himself is the help of the helpless.

---

5. அகதி சொல் அம்பலம் ஏறாது.

    The word of the destitute does not reach the assembly.

    An assembly of learned men or men in power. The words of the poor, whether they relate to oppression, or to other injuries, or to opinion, are not likely to find admission where alone they can avail.

---

6. அகதி தலையிற் பொழுது விடிகிறது.

    Light breaks on the head of the destitute.

    Blame, or suspicion, will fall on the head of the unprotected and friendless The poor are at work by break of day.

---

7. அகதி பெறுவது பெண்பிள்ளை, அதுவும் வெள்ளி பூராடம்.

    The destitute brings forth a female child, and that on Friday under the star Púrádam.

Used of one suffering from an accumulation of evils. The condition of the parent, the sex of the child, the day of its birth and its ruling star are alike inauspicious.

8. அகதியைப் பகுதி கேட்கிறதா?

What! is tribute demanded of the destitute?

9. அகத்தில அழகு முகத்தில் தெரியும்.

The beauty of the mind appears in the face.

10. அகத்தி ஆயிரம் காய் காய்த்தாலும் புறத்தி புறத்தியே.

Though the Agatti—*Coronilla grandiflora*,—brings forth by thousands, its fruit remains ungathered.

Spoken of the beneficent acts of one not held in estimation, and whose kindness is not therefore appreciated. The proverb is also used of a miser whose treasures are useless.

11. அகப்பட்டுக்கொள்வேன் என்றோ கள்ளன் களவெடுக்கிறது?

Does the thief steal in expectation of being caught?

12. அகப்பட்டவனுக்கு அஷ்டமத்துச்சனி, ஓடிப்போனவனுக்கு ஒன்பதாம் இடத்து ராஜா.

He who was caught was under the influence of Saturn in the eighth sign, and he who escaped, did so, under the influence of Saturn in the ninth.

Saturn situated in the eighth sign from that of one's birth is supposed to exercise a most malignant influence. This opinion o the Hindus appears in many of their Proverbs.

Hindu Astronomy is made the foundation of a vast system of Astrology. The *real movements* and *the relative positions* of the planets are wrought into a systematic connection with a great variety of arbitrary divisions of the signs of the Zodiac, and of the twenty-seven Lunar Mansions. To these bodies are added various Mythological appendages, as beasts, birds, trees, &c., all of which, of course, being a part of the fine-spun theory, help to form in the view of the people generally, a more recondite and imposing system than that of Astronomy itself.

The Astrological dogmas of India have an important bearing on all the domestic arrangements and practices of the people. They extend to a great variety of popular superstitions which run out into every department of life. This is seen in the lucky and unlucky months, days and other divisions of time, in the horoscope, which has a powerful controlling influence in marriage, and in other matters relating to the settlement of families and in the more general prognostics for the year as given in the Hindu Calendar. Astrology in its popular developments exerts a powerful influence on all classes of Hindu Society.

---

13. அகப்பை பிடித்தவன் தன்னவனானால், அடிப்பந்தியில் இருந்தாலென்ன, கடைப்பந்தியில் இருந்தாலென்ன?

If he who has the ladle be one's own servant, what matters it whether one be seated first or last at the feast?

The Agappai—ladle—here referred to is made of a piece of cocoanut shell with a suitable wooden handle. The shell being very hard and not porous is well suited for the purposes of a spoon or ladle. It is easily cleaned, and well adapted for earthen cooking vessels. It may be seen in every cooking room or shed throughout the Tamil country.

---

14. அகம் ஏறச் சுகம் ஏறும்.

As grain becomes cheaper, enjoyment increases.

---

15. அகம் மலிந்தால் அஞ்சும் மலியும், அகம் குறைந்தால் அஞ்சும் குறையும்.

If grain abound, the five also will abound; if grain be scarce, the five will be so.

---

16. அகம் மலிந்தால் எல்லாம் மலியும், அகம் குறைந்தால் எல்லாம் குறையும்.

If grain abounds, all *things* abound, if grain be scarce, all *things* are scarce.

---

17. அகல இருந்தால் நீள உறவு, கிட்ட இருந்தால் முட்டப் பகை.

If apart, long friendship, if together, the least touch will provoke hatred.

---

18. அகல இருந்தால் பகையும் உறவாம்.

When apart, even enmity becomes friendship.

19. அகல இருந்தால்ப் புகல உறவு.

Separation secures manifest friendship.

20. அகலவட்டம் பகல் மழை.

A large halo—a rainy day.

21. அகவிலை அறியாதவன துக்கம் அறியான்.

He who knows not the price of grain, knows not sorrow.

22. அகழிலே விழுந்த முதலைக்கு அதுவே வைகுண்டம்.

The moat into which the alligator has plunged is to itself Vaikundam. (*Paradise.*)

23. அகா நாக்காய்ப் பேசுகிறான்.

He speaks glibly.

24. அகிர்த்தியம் செய்கிறவன் முகத்தில் விழிக்கிறதா?

Is it to see the face of one who acts improperly!

25. அகோர தபசி விபரீத சோரன்.

A terrible ascetic, an atrocious cheat.

26. அகோர தபசி, விபரீத நிபுணன்.

In austerity, severe; in perversity, an adept.

Prone to extremes.

27. அக்கரை மாட்டுக்கு இக்கரை பச்சை.

Green *pasture* on this shore for the cattle on that.

28. அக்காடு வெட்டிப் பருத்தி விதைக்கிறேன் என்றால், அப்பா எனக்கொரு துப்பட்டி என்கிறான் பிள்ளை.

If I say that I am about to clear away the jungle to sow cotton seed, my child exclaims, O father, *give me* a cloth.

Sanguine and very anticipatory

29. அக்காடு வெட்டிப் பருத்தி விதைத்தால, அப்பா முழச்சிற்றாடை என்கிறதாம் பெண்.

If I clear away the jungle and sow cotton seed, it is said that the girl exclaimed, O father, a cubit of cloth.

30. அக்காள் இருக்கிறவரையில் மச்சான் உறவு.

The friendship of a brother-in-law lasts while one's sister lives.

31. அக்காள் உண்டானால், மச்சான் உண்டு.

If one has a sister, *he may have* a brother-in-law.

32. அக்காள் உடைமை அரிசி, தங்கைச்சி உடைமை தவிடா?

Is the property of the elder sister rice, and that of the younger bran?

Said of one who is extremely chary about his own property, and indifferent about that of another.

33. அக்காள் உறவும் மச்சான் பகையுமா?

Whilst cherishing friendship for the sister, are you at enmity with the brother-in-law?

34. அக்காளைக் கொண்டால், தங்கையை முறை கேட்பானேன்?

Having taken in marriage the elder sister, why inquire after the rank of the younger?

35. அக்காளைப் பழித்துத் தங்கை அபசாரியானாள்.

Having reproached her elder sister, the younger played the harlot.

36. அக்காள்தான் கூடப்பிறந்தாள், மச்சானும் கூடப்பிறந்தானா?

My sister was indeed born of the same mother: was my brother-in-law also?

37. அக்கிராரத்தில் பிறந்தாலும், நாய் வேதம் அறியுமா?

Will a dog understand the Vedas, although born in a Brahman village?

38. அக்கிராரத்துக்கு ஒரு ஆடு வந்தால், ஆளுக்கு ஒரு மயிர்.

Should a sheep come into a Brahman village, each person will get but a hair.

After a sheep has been sacrificed in a Brahmanical village and the carcass consumed, the Brahmans may use the hair when performing pûja; this interpretation is disputed.

39. அக்கிராரத்து நாய் பிரதிஷ்டைக்கு விரும்பினதுபோல.

As a dog longed for the consecrated *things* of a Brahman village.

Said when great expectations are entertained of something that is likely to prove illusory: an amusing story is told about this proverb.

---

40. அக்கினி மலைமேல் கர்ப்பூரபாணம் பிரயோகித்ததுபோல.

As one discharged a camphor arrow at a burning mountain.

Spoken of an act done to injure another, fruitless or inadequate, d possibly destructive of the means employed.

---

41. அக்கினி தேவனுக்கு அபிஷேகம் செய்ததுபோல் இருக்கிறான்.

He is as if a libation had been poured out to the god of fire.

Used of one naturally very black, who on hearing the proverb if he understands its purport, is of course very angry. When water is poured on burning charcoal the cinders appear exceedingly black. The intended reflection is not the less insulting because of the complimentary way in which it is conveyed.

---

42. அக்கினியாற் சுட்ட புண் விஷமிக்காது.

A cauterized wound will not fester much.

---

43. அக்குத்தொக்கு இல்லாதவனுக்குத் துக்கம் என்ன?

Whence sorrow to him who has no connections?

Said of one who is so obscure and isolated as to have no one whose griefs he can share or assuage.

---

44. அங்கத்தை ஆற்றில் அலைசொணாதா?

Is it improper to bathe in a river!

---

45. அங்கத்தைக் கொண்டுபோய் ஆற்றில் அலைசினாலும், தோஷம் இல்லை.

Although he take his body and wash it in the river, no fault will be found

---

46. அங்கத்தைக் கொன்று ஆற்றில் சேர்க்கவொண்ணாது.

A body that has been deprived of life (murdered) may not be put into a river.

---

47. அங்காங்கு வைபோகமாயிருக்கிறான், இங்கே பார்த்தால அரைக் காசு முதலும் இல்லை.

He is seen everywhere enjoying himself: when looked at in his homestead, he is not worth half a cash

Said of one who, when out, affects to be well off, whereas he has nothing at all to depend upon.

The word (காசு) Cash, is used for several kinds of coin, also for money.

---

48. அங்காடி விலையை அதிர அடிக்காதே.

Do not beat down the market price.

Do not contravene the established opinions and practices of the people with whom you are associated.

---

49. அங்காடிக்காரியைச் சங்கீதம் பாடச்சொன்னால், வெங்காயம் கருவேப்பிலை என்பாள்.

If a song be demanded of a woman going along with her market basket, she will exclaim venkaiyam, karuvéppilai, (*Unions curry leaves.*)

---

50. அங்கிடுதொடுப்பிக்கு அங்கிரண்டு குட்டு, இங்கிரண்டு சொட்டு.

One who frequently changes his party will receive two slaps here and three cuffs there.

---

51. அங்கும் தப்பி இங்கும் தப்பி அகப்பட்டுக்கொண்டான் தும்மட்டிப்பட்டன்.

Tummattippattan, who had escaped here and there, was caught.

Referring to the adventures of a sorcerer.

---

52. அங்கும் இருப்பான் இங்கும் இருப்பான், ஆக்கின சோற்றுக்குப் பங்கும் இருப்பான்.

He is here and there and has a share also in the boiled rice.

---

53. அங்கேண்டி மகளே கஞ்சிக்கு அழுகிறாய்? இங்கே வந்தால், காற்றாய்ப் பறக்கலாம்.

Why, my daughter, are you crying there for kanji? come hither and you may fly as the wind.

Spoken of a proffered change which may be for the worse.

---

54. அசல வாழ்ந்தால், ஐந்து நாள் பட்டினி கிடப்பாள்.

If her neighbour prospers, she will starve herself for five days.

---

55. அசல் வீடு வாழ்ந்தால் பரதேசம் போகிறதா?

Is one to go to a foreign country, because his neighbour prospers!

56. அசலும் விசலும் அறியாமல் அடுத்தவனைக் கெடுக்கப் பார்க்கிறான்.

Regardless of circumstances, he aims to destroy his neighbour.

57. அசவாப் பயிரும் கண்டதே உறவும்.

Stunted grain—friendship at sight.

Both valueless.

58. அசைந்து தின்கிறது மாடு, அசையாமல் தின்கிறது வீடு.

A cow eats moving; a house eats standing.

59. அச்சம் இல்லாதவன் அம்பலம் ஏறுவான்.

The fearless goes into the assembly.

Used of those who have more courage than discretion.

60. அச்சாணி இல்லாத தேர் முச்சாணும் ஓடாது.

A car without a linch-pin will not move even three spans.

Intimating that appliances however trivial cannot be dispensed with, and that the best instruments and weapons require due management.

61. அச்சிக்குப் போனாலும், அகப்பை அரைக்காசு.

Though taken to Achchi, a wooden ladle will fetch only half a cash.

Achchi being a prosperous place, cooking utensils are there in great demand, yet even there this inferior article will bring no more than its value.

Spoken of the intrinsic value of a thing.

62. அச்சியிலும் பிச்சைக்காரர் உண்டு.

There are beggars even in Achchi.

See the preceding proverb.

63. அஞ்சனக்காரன் முதுகில் வஞ்சனைக்காரன் ஏறினான்.

The cheat has got on the shoulders of the conjurer.

Said when one deceiver has got the better of another.

64. அஞ்சலிவந்தனம் ஆருக்கும் நன்மை.

Deferential respect is agreeable to every one.

65. அஞ்சா நெஞ்சு படைத்தால ஆருக்கு ஆவான?

Who will tolerate a presumptuous or impudent man!

---

66. அஞ்சாவது பெண் கெஞ்சினாலும் கிடையாது.

A fifth born female cannot be obtained though earnestly sought.

A fifth born female is regarded as the special favourite of fortune; an eighth,—as the very opposite

---

67. அஞ்சிலே வளையாதது ஐம்பதிலே வளையுமா?

Will that which was not bent at five, bend at fifty

---

68. அஞ்சினவனைக் குஞ்சும் வெருட்டும்.

Even a fledgeling may scare the timid.

---

69. அஞ்சில் அறியாதவன் ஐம்பதில் அறிவானா?

Will one ignorant at five understand at fifty?

Early instruction essential to future knowledge. The proverb may also suggest that growth in years will not make one, that is naturally dull, bright.

---

70. அஞ்சினவனைப் பேய் அடிக்கும்.

Demons strike the timid.

---

71. அஞ்சி ஆண்மை செய்.

Act manfully, but modestly.

---

72. அஞ்சினாரைக் கெஞ்சுவிக்கும், அடித்தாரை வாழ்விக்கும்.

Those who were once feared may be made to beg; and they who were once oppressed may be made prosperous.

---

73. அஞ்சினவன் கண்ணுக்கு ஆகாயமெல்லாம் பேய்.

To the timid the sky is full of demons.

---

74. அஞ்சு காசுக்குக் குதிரையும் வேண்டும், அதுவும் ஆற்றைக் கடக்கப் பாயவும் வேண்டும்.

A horse is required for five cash, and he must be able to leap over a river.

Used in derision when great results are expected from inadequate means.

75. அஞ்சு குஞ்சும் கறியாமோ? அறியாப் பெண்ணும் பெண்டாமோ

Are five young birds a curry? Is a young girl a wife?

76. அஞ்சுக்கு இரண்டு பழுதில்லை.

Of the five *senses* two are uninjured.

Used with reference to some, of several desiderated objects that have been accomplished, or of some things that remain uninjured.

77. அஞ்சு பணம் கொடுத்தாலும், இத்தனை ஆத்திரம் ஆகாது.

Even if you were to give away five fanams, such haste or precipitation will not do.

Precipitance in judgment is worse than actual loss.

78. அஞ்சும் மூன்றும் உண்டானால், அறியாப் பெண்ணும் கறி சமைக்கும்.

If possessed of five and three, even a young girl may make a curry.

The five are acid pepper, salt, mustard and cumin; the three, are water, fuel and fire.

This proverb is used by a man when his wife has prepared a curry that does not please him.

79. அஞ்சுருத்தாலி நெஞ்சுருவக் கட்டிக்கொண்டு வந்தாற்போல வலக்காரமாய்ப் பேசுகிறாய்.

Thou speakest ostentatiously as a matron who has come having her bosom adorned with a táli ornamented with five figures.

The táli is a marriage symbol used as a wedding ring is in Europe. Various astrological observances attend the melting of the gold &c. The five forms referred to are the five weapons of Vishnu. Viz. the discus, the club, the conch, the bow and the sword

The Romanists ornament the táli with the figure of a dove.

80. அஞ்சு வயது ஆண்பிள்ளைக்கு ஐம்பது வயதுப் பெண் கால் முடக்கவேண்டும்.

A woman of fifty must bend the knee before a boy of five.

Referring to the deference paid to the male sex by the Hindus.

81. அஞ்சுவோரைக் கெஞ்சடிக்கப் பார்க்கிறான்.

He aims to humble the timid by force.

82. அஞ்சூர்ச்சண்டை சுண்டநங்கி, ஐங்கல அரிசி ஒரு கவளம்

Conflict in five villages is but curry, five maracals of rice is only a mouthful.

Spoken of one who delights in the misfortunes of others.

83. அஞ்செழுத்தும் பாவனையும் அவனைப்போல இருக்கிறது.

The five letters and the sentiment are like him.

Spoken of a child who in feature and disposition resembles its father.

84. அடக்கத்துப் பெண்ணுக்கு அழகேன்?

Of what use is beauty to a damsel living in retirement?

85. அடக்கமுடையார் அறிஞர், அடங்காதார் கல்லார்.

The well-ordered are wise; the disorderly are fools.

86. அடக்கமே பெண்ணுக்கு அழகு.

Modesty is the ornament of a woman.

The proverb may be used of moderation generally and self-restraint.

87. அடக்குவாரற்ற கழுக்காணியும் கொட்டுவாரற்ற மேளமுமாய்த் திரிகிறான்.

A dwarf without restraint—an unused tomtom—he wanders about.

Used of one irrecoverably worthless

88. அடங்காத பாம்பிற்கு ராஜா மூங்கில்த்தடி.

A bamboo staff is the king of a vicious snake.

89. அடங்காத பெண்சாதியினாலே அத்தைக்கும் நமக்கும் பொல்லாப்பு.

A disobedient wife is an evil both to her mother and to one's self.

Spoken of a person inimical alike to two parties.

90. அடங்காத மனைவியும் ஆங்கார புருஷனும்.

A disobedient wife and a self-willed husband.

Said of uncongenial society.

91. அடங்கின பிடி பிடிக்கவேண்டும், அடங்காத பிடி பிடிக்கலாகாது.

Seize that which can be grasped, not that which cannot.

Aim at the practicable.

92. அடம்பங்கொடியும் திரண்டால் மிடுக்கு.

Even tender creepers when united are strong.

93. அடா என்பான், வெளியே புறப்படான்.

He will speak abusively, but will not come out.

94. அடாது செய்தவர் படாது படுவார்.

They who do what they ought not, will suffer what they might have avoided.

It serves him right.

95. அடி அதிரசம் குத்துக் கொழுக்கட்டை.

A slap is a cake, a cuff is sweetmeat.

Spoken of one who is beyond ordinary discipline.

96. அடி உதவுகிறதுபோல அண்ணன் தம்பி உதவுவார்களா?

Will an elder or younger brother aid one as effectually as discipline or punishment?

97. அடிக்க அடிக்கப் பந்து விசைகொள்ளும்.

The more a ball is struck, the more it rebounds.

98. அடிக்கிற காற்றுக்கும் பெய்கிற மழைக்கும் பயப்படவேண்டும்.

Beware of a beating wind and of falling rain.

Beware of things beyond human control.

99. அடிக்கிற காற்று வெயிலுக்குப் பயப்படுமோ?

Does the beating wind fear the sunshine?

Spoken of irrelevant means to subdue an evil.

100. அடிக்கும் காற்றிலே எடுத்துத் தூற்றவேண்டும்.

Winnow while the wind blows.

101. அடிக்கும் ஒரு கை, அணைக்கும் ஒரு கை.

One hand smites, the other embraces.

Discipline regulated by love; used sometimes of Divine chastisements.

102. அடிச்சட்டிக்குள்ளே கரணம் போடலாமா?

Can one make a somersault in the bottom of a chatti?

103. அடித்த ஏருக்கும் குடித்த கூழுக்கும் சரி.

What he received for his labour (ploughing) only paid for the kanji he drank.

104. அடித்துப் பழுத்ததும் பழமா ?

Is that which ripens by force fruit ?

(A favour done under constraint is no favour.)

105. அடித்துப் பால் புகட்டுகிறதா ?

Is a child to be beaten *in order* to pour milk into its mouth ?

106. அடித்து வளர்க்காத பிள்ளையும் முறுக்கி வளர்க்காத மீசையும் செவ்வையாகா.

Neither the child that is unchastised, nor the mustache that is untwirled will be right.

Implying that due care must be exercised to secure a desiderated result.

107. அடித்துவிட்டவன்பின்னே போனாலும், பிடித்துவிட்டவன்பின்னே போகலாகாது.

Though you may trust one who has administered correction, you may not trust one who has betrayed you.

108. அடிநாக்கிலே நஞ்சும் நுனிநாக்கிலே அமிர்தமுமா ?

What! is it nectar at the tip of the tongue while poison is at the root ?

Said of one, or to one whose professions are at variance with his intentions.

109. அடி நொச்சி நுனி ஆமணக்கா ?

Is the stem nochchi, and the top a castor plant ?

Intimating that the same characteristics will prevail in a family or tribe.

110. அடிப்பானேன் பிடிப்பானேன் ? அடக்குகிற வழியில் அடக்குவோம்.

Why beat him, why seize him ? we will subdue him by proper means.

111. அடிமேல் அடி அடித்தால், அம்மியும் நகரும்.

Even a grindstone will move under repeated strokes.

112. அடிமை படைத்தால் ஆள்வது கடன்.

It is the duty of one who has a slave to employ him.

113. அடியற்ற பனைபோல் விழுந்தான்.

He fell as a palmira tree severed from its root.

So perfect was his prostration. This may be used of obeisance or ruin.

114. அடியற்ற மரம்போலே.

As a tree without root.

115. அடியற்றால் நுனி விழாமலிருக்குமா?

If the root fail, will not the top fall?

116. அடியா நாடு படியாது.

A province in which authority is not enforced will not submit.

117. அடியாத மாடு படியாது.

An unchastised bullock will not obey

118. அடியிலுள்ளது நடுவுக்கும் முடிவுக்கும் உண்டு.

That which exists in the bottom is likewise in the middle and top.

119. அடியும் பட்டுப் புளித்த மாங்காயா தின்னவேண்டும்?

And besides being beaten, must (one) also eat sour mangoes?

Spoken of something imposed on one who is already suffering from questionable inflictions.

120. அடியென்று அழைக்கப் பெண்டீர் இல்லை, ஆண் எத்தனை பெண் எத்தனை என்கிறதுபோல.

Like saying to a man how many boys have you, and how many girls, when he has not a wife to whom he can say, Adi.

121. அடிவானம் கறுத்தால், ஆண்டை வீடு வறுக்கும்.

If the horizon becomes black, the household of the farmer will begin to parch.

122. அடுக்களைக் கிணற்றிலே அமுதம் எழுந்தாற்போல.

Like the springing up of nectar in a kitchen well.

123. அடுக்களைக்கு ஒரு பெண்ணும் அம்பலத்துக்கு ஒரு ஆணும் இருக்கிறதென்கிறான்.

He says, to cook, there is a woman; for outdoor work, a man.

Spoken of needful help already at hand.

---

124. அடுக்குகிற அருமை தெரியுமா உடைக்கிற நாய்க்கு?

Does the dog that breaks (*the cooking pots*) know how difficult it is to arrange them?

Used when a heedless clumsy person has disarranged or spoiled some cherished work on which great pains had been bestowed.

---

125. அடுத்த கூரை வேவுங்கால் தன் கூரைக்கு மோசம்.

When a neighbour's roof is in flames one's own is in danger.

---

126. அடுத்தவனைக் கெடுக்கலாமா?

Is it right to destroy one's neighbour?

---

127. அடுத்தவன் வாழப் பகலே குடி எடுப்பான்.

Because his neighbour prospers he removes in the day-time i. e., at once.

---

128. அடுத்தாரைக கெடுத்து அன்னம் இட்டாரைக் கன்னம் இடுகிறான்.

He destroys those about him and robs those who fed him.

---

129. அடுத்து அடுத்துச் சொன்னால் தொடுத்த காரியம் முடியும்.

By continually urging, the work undertaken may be completed.

---

130. அடுத்துக் கெடுப்பான் கபடன், தொடுத்துக் கெடுப்பாள் வேசி.

A deceiver destroys when near, a harlot in contact.

---

131. அடுத்து வந்தவர்க்கு ஆதரவு சொல்லுவோன் குரு.

He is a teacher or spiritual guide who gives wholesome counsel to those who resort to him.

---

132. அடுப்பருகில் வெண்ணெயை வைத்த கதை.

A story about butter being placed near the hearth,

133. அடுப்புக் கட்டிக்கு அழகு வேண்டுமா?
Is ornamentation requisite in a hearth or fireplace?
The needful is sufficient in common things

134. அடுப்பு நெருப்பும் போய் வாய்த்தவிடும் போச்சுது.
No fire in the hearth, no bran in the mouth.

135. அடுப்பு எரிந்தால் பொரி பொரியும்.
Should the fire burn, you may parch grain.

136. அடைந்தோரை ஆதரி.
Take care of those who are under your protection.

137. அடைப்பைப் பிடுங்கினால் பாம்பு கடிக்கும்.
A snake will bite him who removes a fence.

138. அடைமழைக்குள்ளே ஓர் ஆட்டுக்குட்டி செத்ததுபோல.
As a lamb died in heavy rain.
Said of one coming to grief from want of due care.

139. அடைமழை விட்டும் செடிமழை விடவில்லை.
Though the heavy rain is over, the dropping from the trees continues.
Though the greater evils have passed away, the lesser remain. Though the spoiler is not upon us, the ordinary imposts are demanded by men in power

140. அட்டமத்துச் சனி கிட்ட வந்ததுபோல.
As Saturn in the eighth sign approached.
Some person or thing ominous of evil.

141. அட்டமத்துச் சனி நட்டம் வரச் செய்யும்.
Saturn in the eighth sign will bring loss.
See the preceeding.

142. அட்டமத்துச் சனி பிடித்து, அரைத் துணியும் உரிந்துகொண்டது.
Saturn in the eighth sign seized, and stripped off even the waist-cloth.

143. அட்டமத்துச் சனியை வட்டிக்கு வாங்கினாற்போல.
Like borrowing Saturn in the eighth sign on interest.

---

144. அட்டைக்கும் திருத்தியில்லை, அக்கினிக்கும் திருத்தியில்லை.
The leech is not satisfied, nor is fire.

Inordinate desire is never satisfied.

---

145. அட்டையைப் பிடித்து மெத்தையில் வைத்ததுபோல.
As a reptile caught and placed on a cushion.

Said of a person in an unnatural situation.

---

146. அட்டையை எடுத்து மெத்தையில் வைத்தாலும் செத்தையையே நாடும்.
Although you take a reptile and place it on a cushion, it will seek a heap of dried leaves.

---

147. அணில் ஏறவிட்ட நாய் பார்ப்பதுபோல.
As a dog looks up at a squirrel that has ascended and escaped his grasp.

A despairing look after a thing irrecoverably lost.

---

148. அணிற்பிள்ளைக்கு நுங்கு அரிதோ? ஆண்டிச்சி பிள்ளைக்குச் சோறு அரிதோ?
Does the squirrel lack the pulp of the young palmyra fruit, or the child of a Saiva mendicant, rice?

To give to religious mendicants is held, by the Hindus generally, to be meritorious.

---

149. அணு மகாமேருவாமா?
Is an atom the great Meru?

The sacred mountain *Meru*, forming the centre of the seven continents according to the Mythological geography of the *Hindus*; it appears to mean the highland of *Tartary* north of the Himálaya.

---

150. அணுவும் மலையாச்சு, மலையும் அணுவாச்சு.
An atom is become a mountain, a mountain an atom.

---

151. அணை கடந்த வெள்ளம் அழுதாலும் வருமா?
Though one cry after it, will the flood that has burst its bund return?

As a premonition, this proverb is used to inculcate caution, and as a remark on misfortune, it suggests the uselessness of regret.

152. அணை கடந்த வெள்ளத்தை மறிப்பவர் ஆர்?
Who can stop a flood that has burst its bund?
Spoken of insuperable evils.

153. அண்டத்திற்கு உள்ளது பிண்டத்திற்கும் உண்டு.
Whatever exists in the universe exists in the human body.

154. அண்டத்தில் இல்லாததும் பிண்டத்தில் உண்டா?
Does that exist in the body which does not exist in the universe?
The greater includes the lesser This and the preceeding proverb really relate to the dialectics of the learned and philosophic schools.

155. அண்டத்தைச் சுமக்கிறவனுக்குச் சுண்டைக்காய் பாரமா?
Will a fruit be burdensome to Him who bears the universe?
Used when some favour is sought of one who is known to possess ample resources.

156. அண்டமும் பிண்டமும் அந்தரங்கமும் வெளியரங்கமும்.
Of the universe and the body, the former is hidden, the latter open.

157. அண்டாத பிடாரி ஆருக்கு அடங்குவாள்?
Whom will the unapproachable demoness obey?
The term Pidári is generally applied to a village goddess who is regarded as an evil being.

158. அண்டை வீட்டுச் சண்டை கண்ணுக்குக் குளிர்ச்சி.
A quarrel in a neighbouring house is refreshing.
Spoken of envious persons who may be supposed to delight in a neighbour's shortcomings or misfortunes

159. அண்டை வீட்டுப் பார்ப்பான் சண்டை மூட்டித் தீர்ப்பான்.
The neighbouring Brahman will breed a quarrel and settle it.
Said of one who promotes evil in order that he may gain by it.

160. அண்டையிற் சமர்த்தன் இல்லாத ராஜாவுக்கு அபகீர்த்தி வரும்.
Disgrace will attach to a king who has not a competent person near him.

161. அண்ணனார் அரண்மனையில் அள்ளி உண்ணப் போகிறாள்.
She is going to eat rice in her elder brother's house.

---

162. அண்ணனிடத்தில் ஆறு மாதம் வாழ்ந்தாலும், அண்ணியிடத்தில் அரை நாழிகை வாழலாமா?
Although one may live six months with an elder brother, one cannot abide with his wife even half an hour.

The first condition is proverbially difficult, how much more so the second?

---

163. அண்ணனுக்குப் பெண் பிறந்தால், அத்தை அசல் நாட்டாள்.
If my elder brother has a daughter, my paternal aunt becomes an alien.

---

164. அண்ணனும் தம்பியும் சென்மப் பகைவர்.
An elder and younger brother are natural (*birth*) enemies.

They are supposed to be subject to envy, jealousy and hatred on account of the rights they inherit.

---

165. அண்ணனைக் கொன்ற பழி, சந்தையிலே தீர்த்துக்கொள்ளுகிறது போல.

Like taking revenge in the market-place, or in the place where the Vedas are read, on account of an elder brother who has been murdered.

---

166. அண்ணன் பெரியவன், அப்பா நெருப்பு ஊது.
My elder brother is superior, father, blow the fire.

Said when an inferior is treated with greater deference than one really entitled to distinction.

---

167. அண்ணன் கொம்பு பம்பழ பளாச்சு.
The horn of my elder brother is as soft (harmless) as a shivered stick.

The foxes of a certain region familiar with the hare had, for a long time, an idea that its fine long ears were formidable horns, and therefore kept aloof from it. At length an old fox proposed that they should try to ascertain the nature of the extraordinary excrescences on its head; and suggested that some of their neighbours should be invited to a feast. This was done; and when all things were ready the foxes led their guests into the festive hall and they were seated a fox and a hare alternately at table. During the feast one of the foxes professing great admiration for the fine horns of their guests, laid his hand upon one and looking round uttered the Proverb. On hearing this, each fox seized and devoured the hare next to him.

---

168. அண்ணன் உண்ணாதது எல்லாம் மைத்துனிக்கு லாபம்.

Whatever is left uneaten by my elder brother is an advantage to my sister-in-law.

---

169. அண்ணன் தம்பி வேண்டும் இன்னம் தம்பிரானே.

Elder brother and younger brother are still wanted, O God.

---

170. அணாவியார் விழுந்தால் அடைவுமுறை.

Should a teacher make a slip, it is attributed to his art.

---

171. அண்ணாவி பிள்ளைக்குப் பணம் பஞ்சமா, அம்பட்டன் பிள்ளைக்கு மயிர் பஞ்சமா?

Is the child of an artist (a dancing-master) without money, is the son of a barber in want of hair?

---

172. அண்ணாக்கும் தொண்டையும் அதிர அடைத்தது.

It obstructed the throat and the uvula so as to cause them to quake.

---

173. அண்ணாமலையார் அருளுண்டானால் மன்னார்சாமி மயிரைப் பிடுங்குமா?

If the favour of Annámalai (Siva) be obtained, will the god Mannár pull out a hair?

Safe as regards an inferior, if protected by a superior.

---

174. அண்ணாமலையாருக்கு அறுபத்துநாலு பூசை, ஆண்டிகளுக்கு எழுபத்துநாலு பூசை.

The forms of worship prescribed for Siva are sixty-four; whereas the seasons for feeding religious mendicants are seventy-four.

---

175. அதிக ஆசை அதிக நஷ்டம்.

Excessive desire *entails* excessive loss.

---

176. அதிக ஆசை அஷ்டதரித்திரம்.

Excessive desire or greed *ends in* eight *forms of* poverty.

The eight forms of poverty are the absence or negation of the eight sources of fruition or enjoyment. These are பெண் women; ஆடை apparel; அணிகலன் jewels; போசனம் food; தாம்பூலம் betel; பரிமளம் perfumes; பாட்டு songs; பூவமளி reclining on flowers.

---

177. அதிகாரியும் தலையாரியும் ஒன்றானால், விடியுமட்டும் திருடலாம்.

If the chief and headman are united, stealing may be carried on till day-break.

---

178. அதிகாரி வீட்டில் திருடித் தலையாரி வீட்டில் வைத்ததுபோல.

As one placed in the house of the headman what he had stolen in the house of the chief.

Said of a thing done unwittingly.

---

179. அதிகாரி வீட்டுக் கோழிமுட்டை குடியானவன் வீட்டு அம்மியை உடைக்கும்.

An egg obtained from the house of the chief will break the grind-stone in the house of the peasant.

Implying that authority imparts to the insignificant overwhelming power.

---

180. அதிஷ்டம் தொட்ட கழுக்காணி.

A short thick person favoured by fortune.

---

181. அதிஷ்டம் ஆறாய்ப் பெருகுகிறது.

Fortune flows as a river.

---

182. அதிஷ்டம் இருந்தால் அரசு பண்ணலாம்.

When fortune smiles one may reign as a king.

---

183. அதிஷ்டம் இல்லாதவனுக்குக் கலப்பால் வந்தாலும், அதையும் பூனை குடிக்கும்.

Although the unfortunate gets a large measure of milk, the cat will lap it all up.

Destiny prevails to thwart benefits when one is unfortunate.

---

184. அதிஷ்டவான் மண்ணைத் தொட்டாலும் பொன்னாகும்.

When touched by the fortunate even earth becomes gold.

185. அதிர அடித்தால், உதிர விளையும்.

If thoroughly ploughed, the yield will be abundant.

186. அதிலும் இது புதுமை, இதிலும் அது புதுமை.

This is stranger than that, and that is stranger than this.

187. அதிலே குறைச்சல் இல்லை ஆடட்டா பூசாரி.

O, priest there is no lack, proceed with the ceremony.

Said to a Pujáchári by way of encouragement.

188. அது அதற்கு ஒரு கவலை, ஐயாவுக்கு எட்டுக் கவலை.

Each object is attended by a single anxiety, whereas the master has eight.

189. அது எல்லாம் உண்டிட்டு வா என்பான்.

He will eat it all and say come.

190. அதுக்கு இட்ட காசு பினக்கெட்டு அரிவாள்மணைக்குச் சுருக்கிட்டதா?

Did the money, diverted from the object for which it was given, avail for the purchase of a sickle?

191. அதுவும் போதாதென்று அழலாமா இனி?

May you hereafter weep because that also is too little?

192. அதைரியமுள்ளவனை அஞ்சாத வீரன் என்றாற்போல்.

Like calling a coward a fearless hero.

Said of false adulation.

193. அதைவிட்டாலும் கதியில்லை, அப்புறம்போனாலும் வழியில்லை.

If that is renounced there is no help, if you go further there is no way.

Spoken of evils from which there is no escape.

194. அத்தம் மிகுதியினால் அல்லவோ அம்பட்டன் பெண் கேட்கிறான்?

It is by reason of his great wealth, is it not, that the barber asks a maiden in marriage?

195. அத்தனையும் சேர்ந்தாள், உப்பிட மறந்தாள்.

Although she put in so many ingredients, she omitted salt.

Said of something complete in all but one essential.

196. அத்தான் செத்தான் மயிராச்சு, கம்பளி மெத்தை நமக்காச்சு.

My brother-in-law's death has not affected me any more than the loss of a hair: but his blanket and mattress have become mine.

197. அத்திக்காயைப் பிட்டுப்பார்த்தால், அங்கும் இங்கும் பொள்ளல்.

If you break open a fig, you will see cavities here and there.

198. அத்தி பூத்ததுபோல் இருக்கிறது அவன் வந்தது.

His coming is like the flowering of the fig-tree.

Something that never happens.

199. அத்திப் பழத்தைப் பிட்டுப்பார்த்தால், அத்தனையும் புழுத்தான்.

The more a fig is opened, the greater will be the number of worms found.

200. அத்திப்பூவை ஆர் அறிவார்கள்?

Who ever saw the flower of a fig-tree?

201. அத்திப்பூவைக் கண்டவர்கள் உண்டா? ஆந்தைக் குஞ்சைப் பார்த்தவர்கள் உண்டா?

Are there any who have seen the blossom of the fig-tree? are there any who have seen the young of an owl?

Said of things that rarely or never happen.

202. அத்திமரத்தில் தொத்திய கனிபோல.

Like fruit sticking to a fig-tree.

203. அத்து மீறிப்போனான், பித்துக்கொள்ளி ஆனான்.

He transgressed and became mad.

204. அத்தைக்கு மீசைமுளைத்தாற் சிற்றப்பா என்கலாம்.

Should the mustache of *one's* aunt grow we may call her uncle.

Referring to improbable contingencies.

205. அந்தம் சிந்தினவனுக்கு அழகு ஒழுகுமா?
Will beauty emanate from one void of symmetry?

206. அந்தணர்க்குத் துணை வேதம்.
The Veda is the staff of the Brahman.

207. அந்தணர் மனையிற் சந்தனம் மணக்கும்.
The house of the Brahman is perfumed.

It being a requisite for ceremonial usages.

208. அந்தரத்தில் கோல் எறிந்த அந்தகன்போல.
Like a blind man who has thrown his staff into the air.

209. அந்தி ஈசல் பூத்தால், அடைமழை அதிகரிக்கும்.
If white-ants take wing in the evening, it prognosticates excessive rain.

210. அந்தி மழை அழுதாலும் விடாது.
The evening rain will not cease even if one should weep.

211. அந்தூது நெல்லானேன்.
I am become as useless as a grain of paddy eaten by insects.

212. அப்பச்சி குதம்பையைச் சூப்பப் பிள்ளை முற்றின தேங்காய்க்கு அழுகிறதுபோல.
While the father is sucking the husk of the cocoanut his son is crying for the kernel or pulp.

Indicating desires beyond one's means.

213. அப்பச்சி கோவணத்தைப் பருந்து கொண்டோடுகிறது, பிள்ளை வீரவாளிப் பட்டுக்கு அழுகிறது.
While the hawk snatches away the father's waist-cloth his daughter is crying for a silk dress.

Said in reproof when wishes are entertained beyond one's means.

214. அப்பத்தை எப்படிச் சுட்டீர்கள்? தித்திப்பை எப்படி நுழைத்தீர்கள்?
How did you bake the cake? how did you sweeten it?

215. அப்பம் சுட்டது சட்டியில், அவல் இடித்தது திட்டையில்.

Cakes are baked in a chatty, steeped rice is flattened in a mortar.

Means must be suited to the end.

216. அப்பம் என்றாற் பிட்டுக்காட்ட வேண்டுமா?

If bread, is it necessary to break and prove it?

217. அப்பன் அருமை அப்பன் மாண்டால் தெரியும், உப்பின் அருமை உப்புச் சமைந்தால் தெரியும்.

The value of a father is known after his decease, that of salt when exhausted.

218. அப்பன் சோற்றுக்கு அழுகிறான், பிள்ளை கும்பகோணத்தில் கோதானம் செய்கிறான்.

The father is crying for rice and his son is performing the ceremony of giving a cow at Kumbhakónam.

219. அப்பன் பெரியவன், சிற்றப்பா சுருட்டுக்கு நெருப்புக் கொண்டு வா என்கிறதுபோல.

Like saying, my father is a great person, uncle, bring fire to light my cigar.

Pride of wealth leads one to neglect the observance of established social rules.

220. அப்பா என்றால் உச்சி குளிருமா?

If one exclaim, alas! alas! will the crown of the head become cool!

Expressions of sympathy are unavailing if not associated with real help

221. அப்பியாசம் கூசாவித்தை.

Experience is knowledge that maketh not ashamed.

222. அப்பியாச வித்தைக்கு அழிவு இல்லை.

Thoroughly acquired knowledge does not fail.

Said in commendation of obvious efficiency.

223. அமஞ்சி உண்டோ குப்புநாய்க்கரே என்பானேன்?

Why ask of the military officer if there is any compulsory service?

Why gratuitously seek avoidable evil?

224. அமரபட்சம் பூர்வபட்சம், கிஷ்ணபட்சம் சுக்கிலபட்சம்.
The latter and former halves of the moon—its dark and bright sides.

These symbolize the light and darkness, the gladness and sadness of human life.

---

225. அமரிக்கை ஆயிரம் பெறும்.
Quietness is worth thousands of gold

---

226. அமர்த்தனுக்கும் காணி வேண்டாம், சமர்த்தனுக்கும் காணி வேண்டாம்.
An oppressor and a clever man need no landed property.

---

227. அமாவாசைக் கருக்கலிலே பெருச்சாளி போனதெல்லாம் வழி.
In the darkness of the new moon the bandycoote finds a way wherever he goes.

---

228. அமாவாசைப் பருக்கை என்றைக்கும் அகப்படுமா?
Is the food peculiar to the new moon to be had every day?

---

229. அமுதம் உண்கிற வாயால் விஷம் உண்பார்களா?
Will poison be received by the mouth accustomed to nectar?

---

230. அம்பட்டக்கிறுதும் வண்ணார ஒயிலும்.
The arrogance of a barber and the affectation of a washerman.

Said when inferiors give themselves airs of importance.

---

231. அம்பட்டன் குப்பையைக் கிளறினால் மயிர் மயிராய்ப் புறப்படும்.
If the rubbish heap of the barber be stirred, nothing but hair turns up.

The more you examine an inferior thing, the viler will it appear.

---

232. அம்பட்டன் பிள்ளைக்கு மயிர் அருக்காணியா?
Is hair a rare sight to the child of a barber?

---

233. அம்பலக் கழுதை அம்பலத்திற் கிடந்தால் என்ன, அடுத்த திருமாளிகையிற் கிடந்தால் என்ன?
What matters it whether the helpless ass lies in an open place or in the adjoining palace.

234. அம்பலத்தில் ஏறும் பேச்சை அமசடக்கம் பண்ணப் பார்க்கிறான்.

He is aiming to conceal the rumour which is to be brought before the public assembly (for discussion.)

---

235. அம்பலத்தில் கட்டுச்சோறு அவிழ்க்கிறாப்போல்.

As boiled rice tied up for a journey is untied in an open place.

---

236. அம்பலத்தில் பொதி அவிழ்க்கல் ஆகாது.

It is not good to unpack in an open place

Unnecessary exposure of one's personal affairs is to be avoided.

---

237. அம்பாணி தைத்ததுபோலப் பேசுகிறான்.

He speaks like piercing arrows.

---

238. அம்பிகொண்டு ஆறு கடப்போர், நம்பிக்கொண்டு நரிவால கொள்ளுவார்களா ?

Will those who cross the river on a raft entrust themselves to the tail of a jackal?

---

239. அம்மணமும் இன்னலும் ஆயுசுபரியந்தமா ?

Are nakedness and misery to continue to the end of life?

---

240. அம்மா கெட்ட கேட்டுக்கு முக்காடு ஒன்றா ?

Is a veil necessay for a woman in a bad condition?

---

241. அம்மானும் மருமகனும் ஒரு வீட்டுக்கு ஆள் அடிமை.

The father-in-law and son-in-law are slaves in the same house.

---

242. அம்மான் மகளுக்கு முறையா ?

Why enquire after the relationship of the daughter of one's maternal uncle?

---

243. அம்மான் வீட்டு வெள்ளாட்டியை அடிக்க அதிகாரியைக் கேட்க வேண்டுமா ?

Having to chastise a maid-servant in a father-in-law's house, is it necessary to ask the chief permission to do so?

---

244. அம்மி மிடுக்கோ அரைப்பவள் மிடுக்கோ ?

Whether is stronger, the grindstone or she who grinds?

245. அம்மி மிதித்து அருந்ததி பார்த்ததுபோல.

Like one standing on a grindstone and looking at Arundathi.

Arundathi is a star in the Great Bear regarded as the wife of Vasishta, a pattern of chastity. This star is pointed out to the bride at the marriage ceremony.

---

246. அம்மியிருந்து அரசனை அளிப்பாள்.

She will bring forth a king on the grindstone.

During the time of child-birth it is not uncommon for the mother to be seated on a grindstone.

---

247. அம்மியும் குழவியும் ஆகாயத்தில் பறக்கச்சே, எச்சிற் கல்லை எனக்கு என்ன புத்தி என்றாற்போல.

As a leaf-plate sought advice when the grindstone and its roller were flying in the air.

---

248. அம்முக்கள்ளி ஆடையைத் தின்றால் வெண்ணெய் உண்டா?

If a thievish woman eat the cream will there be any butter ?

---

249. அம்மைக்கு அமர்க்களம் பொங்கிப் படையுங்கள்.

The strife of Ammai, (a village goddess) has begun, boil and present (rice.)

---

250. அம்மையார் எப்பொழுது சாவாள்? கம்பளி எப்பொழுது நமக்கு மிச்சமாகும்?

When will my mistress die ? when shall I get her blanket ?

---

251. அம்மையார் நூற்கிற நூலுக்கும், பேரன் கட்டுகிற அரைஞாட் கயிற்றுக்கும் சரி.

The yarn spun by the old dame will only just suffice to form waist-string for her grandson.

---

252. அம்மையார் பெறுகிறது அரைக்காசு, தலை சிரைக்கிறது முக்காற் காசு.

Three fourths of a cash is demanded for shaving the head of an old woman worth only half a cash.

---

253. அம்மையார்க்கு என்ன துக்கம், கந்தைத் துக்கம்.

What sorrow has the old dame ? that of raggedness.

254. அம்மையாரே வாரும், கிழவனைக் கைக்கொள்ளும்.

Come, old lady, and receive the old man.

---

255. அயலார் உடமைக்குப் பேயாய்ப் பறக்கிறான்.

He flies at his neighbours' property as a demon.

---

256. அயலார் உடைமையில் அந்தகன்போல இரு.

Be blind as regards your neighbours' property.

---

257. அயன் இட்ட கணக்கு ஆருக்கும் தப்பாது.

No one escapes the decree of Brahma.

---

258. அயன் இட்ட எழுத்தில் அணுவளவும் தப்பாது.

The writing of Brahma will not fail in the least.

---

259. அயிரையும் சற்றே அருக்குமாம் பிட்டுக்குள் போட்டுப் பிசறாமல்.

Even the Airai (small as it is) will give itself airs if it be not mixed with the food.

---

260. அயோக்கியர் அழகு அபரஞ்சிச் சிமிழில் நஞ்சு.

Beauty in the unworthy is poison in a casket of fine gold.

---

261. அய்யன் அளந்தபடி.

As God measured.

---

262. அய்யாவையர் கூழுக்கு அப்பையங்கார் தாதாவா?

Is Appaiyangar the dispenser of Aiyavaiyar's gruel?

---

263. ஹர ஹர என்பது பெரிதோ, ஆண்டிக்கு இடுவது பெரிதோ?

Whether is greater as regards merit, to say Hara, Hara, or to give to the mendicant?

---

264. அரக்கன் ஆண்டால் என்ன, மனிதன் ஆண்டால் என்ன?

What matters it whether a demon or a man rules?

---

265. அரங்கின்றி வட்டாடலும், நூலறிவின்றிப் பேசலும் ஒன்று.

To play draughts without a board and to speak without a knowledge of the shastras are alike.

266. அரசன் அளவிற்கு ஏறிற்று.
It reached even the king.

267. அரசன் இல்லாத நாடு, புருஷன் இல்லாத வீடு.
A country without a king, a family without a head.

268. அரசன் உடைமைக்கு ஆகாயம் சாக்ஷி.
The sky is the witness regarding the king's property.

269. அரசன் அன்று கொல்லும், தெய்வம் நின்று கொல்லும்.
The king kills at once, God delays and kills.

270. அரசன் கல்லின்மேல் கத்தரி காய்க்கிறது என்றால், கொத்து ஆயிரம் குலே ஆயிரம் என்பார்கள்.
If it be reported that brinjals are growing on a stone in the king's courtyard they will say that the outcome is thousands of bunches and thousands of clusters.

271. அரசன் எப்படியோ அப்படியே குடிகள்.
As is the king such are his subjects.

272. அரசன் எவ்வழி குடிகளும் அவ்வழி.
The people follow the lead of their ruler.

273. அரசன் வழிப்பட்டது அவனி.
It is the earth i. e., *its inhabitants* that follows the king.

274. அரசன் வழிப்படாதவன் இல்லை.
No one is exempt from duty to the king.

275. அரசனுக்கு ஒரு சொல் அடிமைக்குத் தலைசுமை.
As regards the king it is a word, to the subject it is a burden.

276. அரசனுக்கு வலியார் அஞ்சுவது எளியார்க்கு அனுகூலமாயிருக்கிறது.
The fear of the king among those in power operates auspiciously as regards the poor.

277. அரசனுக்குத் துணை வயவாள்.
The help of a king is *his* mighty sword.

278. அரசனும் அரவும் சரி.
A king and a snake are alike.

279. அரசனும் அழலும் சரி.
A king and fire are alike.

280. அரசனும் நெருப்பும் பாம்பும் சரி.
A king, fire, and snake are alike.

281. அரசனை நம்பிப் புருஷனைக் கைவிட்டதுபோல.
Like losing a husband through trusting in a king.

282. அரசுக்கு இல்லைச் சிறுமையும் பெருமையும்.
A king observes not the distinction between little and great.

283. அரசுடையானை ஆகாயம் காக்கும.
The heavens guard the king.

284. அரண்டவன் கண்ணுக்கு இருண்டது எல்லாம் பேய்.
To the eye of the timid every thing obscure is a demon.

285. அரத்தை அரம் அறுக்கும், வயிரத்தை வயிரம் அறுக்கும்.
A file will cut a fi e, diamonds cut diamonds.

286. அரபிக் குதிரையிலும் ஐயம்பேட்டைத் தட்டுவாணி நல்லது
An Aiyampettah pony is preferable to an Arab steed.

287. அரவத்தைக் கண்டால் கீரி விடுமா?
If a mungoose see a snake will it let it escape?

288. அரவுக்கு இல்லைச் சிறுமையும் பெருமையும.
The distinction of big and little does not apply to snakes.

289 அரன் அருளில்லாமல் அணுவும் அசையாது.
Not an atom will move without the permission of God.

290. அரன் அருள் அற்றால், அனைவரும் அற்றார்.
Should the favour of God fail, every one will come to nought.

291. அரி அரி என்றால், ராமா ராமா என்கிறான்.
If I say Ari, Ari, he cries Rama, Rama.

292. அரி என்கிற அக்ஷரம் தெரிந்தால் அதிகாரம் பண்ணலாம்.
If one understand the import, of the word Ari, he may exercise regal power.

293. அரி என்கிற அக்ஷரம் தெரிந்தால் அதிக்கிரமம் பண்ணலாமா?
May one transgress the bounds of propriety if he comprehends the purport of the syllable Ari!

294. அரி என்றால் ஆண்டிக்குக் கோபம், அர என்றால் தாதனுக்குக் கோபம்.
If one says Ari the Saiva mendicant is angry, if one says Ara the Vaishnava mendicant is angry.

295. அரிசி அள்ளின காக்காய்போல.
Like a crow that has taken up rice.

296. அரிசி ஆழாக்கானாலும், அடுப்புக்கட்டி மூன்று வேண்டும்.
Though there be only one álak of rice, three supporting points in the hearth are required.

Alak—a small measure of capacity.

297. அரிசி உண்டானால் வரிசையும் உண்டு, அக்காள் உண்டானால் மச்சானும் உண்டு.
If there be rice there will be order—honour also, if a sister exist a brother-in-law may.

298. அரிசி உழக்கானாலும் அடுப்பு மூன்று.
Though there be only one ulak of rice, three supporting points in the hearth are required.

An ulak is two álaks or the fourth of a measure.

299. அரிசி என்று அள்ளிப் பார்ப்பாரும் இல்லை, உமி என்று ஊதிப் பார்ப்பாரும் இல்லை.
No one takes up rice to examine it, nor does any one blow upon chaff.

300. அரிசி கொண்டு உண்ண அக்காள் வீட்டுக்குப் போவானேன்?
Seeing you have to pay for the rice you eat why go to the house of your elder sister?

301. அரிசிக்குத் தக்க உலையும் ஆமுடையானுக்குத் தக்க விருப்பும்.

Water in a pot proportioned to the rice, and a display of authority in a husband suited to his condition.

302. அரிசிப் பகையும் ஆமுடையான் பகையும் உண்டா?

Does hatred against rice or a husband exist?

303. அரிசிப் பொதியுடன் திருவாரூர்.

Tiruvaroor with a bag of rice.

Spoken of a double benefit—the grain is valuable, and a visit to a sacred place is auspicious.

304. அரிசி மறந்த உலைக்கு உப்பு என்ன?

Of what use is salt in a pot of boiling water without rice?

305. அரிச்சந்திரன் வீட்டுக்கு அடுத்த வீடு.

His house is next to Harischandra's.

Used ironically of a notorious liar. Harischandra, a king famed for veracity.

306. அரிது அரிது அஞ்செழுத்து உணர்தல்.

It is difficult indeed to compreh nd the purport of the five letters.

The famous five lettered incantation called the மூலமந்திரம் as being the foundation of all spiritual wisdom and all religion, and the means prescribed and proper for obtaining emancipation from births and all the evils thereunto belonging, and union with the supreme.

307. அரித்து எரிக்கிற சுப்பிக்கு ஆயம் தீர்வை உண்டா?

Is tax levied on dry twigs scraped together for fuel?

308. அரிய சரீரம் அந்தரத்தெறிந்த கல்.

The precious body is a stone thrown into the air;

309. அரியது செய்து எளியதுக்கு ஏமாந்து திரிகிறான்.

Having performed difficult things he wanders about alarmed at that which is easy.

310. அரியும் சிவனும் ஒன்று, அல்ல என்கிறவன் வாயில் மண்.

Vishnu and Siva are one; let sand be put into the mouth of him who denies it.

311. அரிவாளும் அசையவேண்டும், ஆண்டை குடியும் கெடவேண்டும்.

The sickle must be moved, and the landlord's family must be ruined.

312. அரிவாள் சூடடைப்போலக் காய்ச்சல் மாற்றவோ?

Is it attempted to remove the heat of a burning fever as if it were that of a sickle?

313. அரிவாள் சுறுக்கே அரிவாள்முனை கருக்கே.

Was it the dexterity of the reaper, or the sharpness of the sickle.

Success in an enterprise is mainly owing to the means employed.

314. அரிவை மொழி கேட்டால் அபத்தன் ஆவான்.

He who listens to the words of a woman will be accounted worthless.

315. அருகாகப் பழுத்தாலும், விளாமரத்தில் வௌவால் சேராது.

Although the fruit of the wood-apple tree (Feronia elephantum) close by ripens, bats will not approach it.

316. அருக்காணி நாச்சியார் குரங்குப்பிள்ளைப் பெற்றுவாம்.

The haughty dame is said to have brought forth a monkey child.

317. அருக்காணிமுத்துக் கரிக்கோலமானாள்.

She who was a precious pearl has become black as coal.

318. அருக்காமணியா முருக்கம்பூவா?

Is it a rare gem or a Murukkam flower!

319. அருங்கோடைத் துரும்பு அற்றுப்போகுது.

Through severe drought every blade has perished.

320. அருட்செல்வம் ஆருக்கும் உண்டு, பொருட்செல்வம் ஆருக்கும் இல்லை.

Divine favour is common to all, material wealth is not.

321. அருணம்பரமே கருணமபரம.

A cloth tinged red *indicates* the divine favour.

Refers to the dress of religious mendicants.

322. அருமை அறியாதவன் ஆண்டு என்ன, மாண்டு என்ன?

What matters it whether he who has no discrimination rules or dies?

323. அருமை மருமகன் தலைபோனாலும் போகட்டும், ஆதிகாலத்து உரல் போகல் ஆகாது.

If it must be so, let the head of my son-in-law go; but the old mortar must not go.

Said of things which long possession has made peculiarly precious.

324. அருமையற்ற வீட்டில் எருமையும் குடியிராது.

Even a buffalo will not abide in a house where it is not regarded.

325. அரும் சுனை நீர் உண்டால், அப்பொழுதே ரோகம்.

The drinking of water from a hill reservoir will at once produce disease.

326. அருள் வேணும், பொருள் வேணும், அடக்கம் வேணும.

Kindness, wealth and self-restraint are essentials.

327. அரைக்காசுக்கு அழிந்த கற்பு ஆயிரம்பொன் கொடுத்தாலும் கிடையாது.

Chastity forfeited for half a cash, cannot be recovered though one should give thousands of gold.

328. அரைக்காசுக்குப் போன மானம் ஆயிரம் கொடுத்தாலும் வாராது.

The honour that has been forfeited for half a cash, will not return though one give thousands.

329. அரைக்கினும் சந்தனம் அதன் மணம் அறாது.

Though sandal wood be rubbed, its fragrance will not be destroyed.

330. அரைக்குடம் ததும்பும் நிறைகுடம் ததும்பாது.

The water in a pot half full wabbles, if full it wabbles not.

331. அரைசசல்லியை வைத்து எருக்கு இலையைக் கடந்ததுபோல.

As one leaped over an Erukku leaf, *Calotropis gigantea,* under which he had concealed half a challi.

A challi is a small copper coin, a fractional part of a larger coin.

332. அரைச்சீலை கட்டக் கைக்கு உபசாரமா?

Is the hand to be complimented for tying the waist-cloth?

---

333. அரைச்சொற் கொண்டு அம்பலம் ஏறலாமோ?

Can one go before an assembly with half a word?

---

334. அரைச்சொற் கொண்டு அம்பலம் ஏறினால், அரைச்சொல் முழுச்சொல்லாகும்.

Half a word admitted into the assembly becomes a whole word.

---

335. அரைத்த பயறு முளைத்தாற்போல.

As if macerated gram should sprout.

---

336. அரைத்து மிஞ்சுது அம்மி சிரைத்து மிஞ்சுது குடுமி.

After grinding the stone remains; after shaving the head, the kudumi tuft of hair) remains.

A tuft of hair left on the head of a boy or man with a knot at the end 'It is considered becoming; and is usually about a foot in length.

---

337. அரைப்பணம் கொடுத்து அழச்சொல்லி ஒருபணம் கொடுத்து ஓயச்சொல்லுவானேன்?

Having given half a fanam to weep, why give a fanam to cease?

Fanam—a small coin of gold or silver.

---

338. அரைப்பணச் சேவகம் ஆனாலும் அரண்மனைச் சேவகம்போல் ஆகுமா?

Though the service bring half a fanam, will it be equal to service in the king's house?

---

339. அரைப்பணம் கொடுக்கப் பால்மாறி, ஐம்பது பொன் கொடுத்துச் சேர்வை செய்த கதை.

A story of one who gave fifty gold pieces for a compound medicine after having hesitated to give half a fanam.

---

340. அரையிற் புண்ணும் அண்டைவீட்டுக் கடனும் ஆகாது.

Sores about the waist, and debt to one's neighbour are both bad.

363. அவசாரிக்கு வாய் பெரிது, அஞ்சு ஆறு அரிசிக்குக் கொதி பெரிது.

The mouth of the harlot is large, and the bubbling of five or six grains of rice when boiling is excessive.

364. அவசாரிக்கு ஆணை இல்லை, திருடிக்குத் தெய்வம் இல்லை.

The harlot has no oath, the thief has no god.

Spoken of one wholly derelict.

365. அவசாரி ஆடினாலும் அதிஷ்டம் வேண்டும் திருடப் போனாலும் திறமை வேண்டும்.

If one plays the harlot fortune is wanted, and when one goes to steal ability is needed.

366. அவசாரியென்று ஆனைமேல் ஏறலாம் திருடியென்று தெருவில் வரலாமா?

As an abandoned woman one may ride on an elephant, but can one go along a street as a thief?

367. அவதந்திரம் தனக்கு அந்தரம்.

Chicanery ends in one's ruin.

368. அவதிக்குடிக்குத் தெய்வமே துணை.

God himself is the help of a family in extremities.

369. அவத்தனுக்கும் சமர்த்தனுக்கும் காணி கவை இல்லை.

The worthless and the cheat have no need of land.

370. அவப்பொழுதிலும் தவப்பொழுது நல்லது.

Time is better spent in austerities than in vanity.

371. அவமானம்பண்ணி வெகுமானம் பேசுகிறான்.

Having acted reproachfully he speaks flatteringly.

372. அவரா சுறுக்கே அரிவாண்மணை கருக்கே.

He is surely as sharp as the edge of a sickle.

Spoken ironically of a man of vain pretensions.

373. அவருடைய சிறகு முறிந்துபோயிற்று.

His wing is broken.

374. அவர் அவர் மனசே அவர் அவர்க்குச் சாட்சி.

Each one's mind is the witness *that acquits or condemns.*

375. அவர் அவர் எண்ணத்தை ஆண்டவர் அறிவார்.

The supreme Ruler knows the purposes of every one.

376. அவலட்சணம் உள்ள குதிரைக்குச் சுழி சுத்தம் பார்க்கிறதில்லை.

The circular curls of an ugly horse are not examined.

377. அவலமாய் வாழ்பவன் சவலமாய்ச் சாவான்.

He who leads a useless life will die a miserable death.

378. அவலை நினைத்து உரலை இடித்தாற்போல.

As if one beat an empty mortar thinking it contained unhusked steeped rice.

Spoken of absence of mind.

379. அவள் பாடுகிறது குயில் கூவுகிறதுபோல் இருக்கிறது.

Her singing is like the voice of the kuyil (an Indian cuckoo.)

380. அவள் சமர்த்துப் பானை சந்தியில் உடைந்தது.

Her best cooking-pot was broken in the middle of the road.

381. அவனுக்கு இவன் எழுந்திருந்து உண்பான்.

This person will rise and eat before him.

382. அவனுக்குக் கப்படாவும் இல்லை வெட்டுக்கத்தியும் இல்லை.

He has neither a cloth nor a knife.

Said of one utterly destitute.

383. அவனுக்குள்ளே அகப்பட்டிருக்கிறது என் பிழைப்பு.

That which is in his keeping is my livelihood.

384. அவனுக்குச் சுக்கிரதிசை அடிக்கிறது.

He is now under the auspicious influence of the planet Venus.

Spoken of one who is the favourite of fortune.

385. அவனுக்கும் இவனுக்கும் எருமைச்சங்காத்தம்.

The intimacy or friendship of these two persons is that of the buffalo.

386. அவனுடைய பேச்சு காற்சொல்லும் அரைச்சொல்லும்.

His speech consists of quarters and halves of words.

Undecisive.

387. அவனுடைய வாழ்வு நண்டுக்குடுவை உடைந்ததுபோல் இருக்
கிறது.

His prosperity is *scattered* like crabs from a broken vessel.

388. அவனே இவனே என்பதைவிடச் சிவனே சிவனே என்கிறது நல்லது.

It is better to cry Siva, Siva, than opprobriously to reproach others.

389. அவனே வெட்டவும் விடவும் கர்த்தன்.

He has authority both to behead and to release.

390. அவனை அவன் பேச்சிட்டுப் பேச்சு வாங்கி; ஆமை மல்லாத்து கிறதுபோல் மல்லாத்திப்போட்டான்.

Having fished out his secrets by cunning he turned him upside down as a turtle is turned.

391. அவனோடே இவனை ஏணிவைத்துப் பார்த்தாலும் காணாது.

He cannot equal him though he raise himself to the top of a ladder.

Said of one who is far inferior to another either socially or intellectually.

392. அவன் நா அசைய நாடு அசையும்.

When his tongue moves the country moves.

393. அவன் அருள் அற்றால் அனைவரும் அற்றார், அவன் அருள் உற்றால் அனைவரும் உற்றார்.

Without his favour all are destitute, if he favour, all are prosperous.

Said of God's grace and displeasure

394. அவன் ஒரு குளிர்ந்த கொள்ளி.

He is a cold firebrand.

Said of a person really dangerous though apparently not so.

395. அவன் மிதித்த இடத்தில் புல்லும் சாகாது.

Even the grass under his footsteps will not die.

Used when speaking of one remarkable for gentle habits.

---

396. அவன் மிதித்த இடம் பற்றியெரிகின்றது.

The place whereon he treads bursts into flames.

Spoken of the reckless and violent

---

397. அவன் மெத்த அத்துமிஞ்சின பேச்சுக்காரன்.

His words exceed all bounds.

Said of one who delights in abusing others.

---

398. அவன் காலால் இட்ட வேலையைக் கையால் செய்வான்.

The work that was indicated by the foot he will perform by the hand.

---

399. அவன் சாதி எந்தப் புத்தி குலம் எந்த ஆசாரமோ அதுதான் வரும்.

The devices of his caste and habits of his tribe will predominate.

---

400. அவன் காலால் முடிந்ததைக் கையால் அவிழ்க்கக்கூடாது.

That which he tied with his foot cannot be loosened by the hand.

Spoken of one of superior skill

---

401. அவன் அசையாது அணுவும் அசையாது.

Unless he move not an atom will move

---

402. அவன் அவன் எண்ணத்தை ஆண்டவன் ஆக்கினாலும் ஆக்குவான், அழித்தாலும் அழிப்பான்.

Every man's purpose will be either effectuated or frustrated by the Supreme Ruler.

---

403. அவன் கழுத்துக்குக் கத்தி தீட்டுகிறான்.

He is sharpening a knife for another's throat.

---

404. அவன் உள்ளெல்லாம் புண் உடம்பெல்லாம் கொப்புளம்.

His mind is full of sores, his body is covered with blisters.

405. அவன் எனக்கு அட்டமத்துச்சனி.
To me he is Saturn in the eighth sign.

The most malignant of enemies.

---

406. அவன் தொத்தி உறவாடித் தோலுக்கு மன்றாடுகிறான்.
He seeks friendship and prays for a skin.

---

407. அவன் தன்னாலே தான் கெட்டால் அண்ணாவி என்ன செய்வான்?
What can his teacher do if he ruin himself?

---

408. அவன் காலால் கிறினதை நான் நாவால் அழிக்கிறேன்.
What he has scored with his feet I efface with my tongue.

---

409. அவன் உனக்குக் கிள்ளுக்கீரையோ?
Do you consider him as a green-herb nipped off!

---

410. அவன் கையைக்கொண்டே அவன் கண்ணில் குத்துகிறான்.
He took another's hand and struck his eyes

---

411. அவன் சிறகில்லாப் பறவை.
He is a bird without wings

---

412. அவன் என் தலைக்கு உலை வைக்கிறான்.
He is preparing to cook my head.

---

413. அவன் அவன் செய்த வினை அவன் அவனுக்கே.
Every one is responsible for his own actions.

---

414. அவன் என்னை ஊதிப் பறக்கடிக்கப் பார்க்கிறான்.
He aims to scatter me to the winds.

---

415. அவன் எரிபொரியென்று விழுகிறான்.
He breaks out saying burn *him*, fry *him*.

Said of one who suddenly bursts into a rage

---

416. அவன் ஓடிப்பாடி நாடியில் அடங்கினான்.
Having run and sung, he at length sank like the pulse,

---

417. அவன் வல்லாளகண்டனை வாரிப்போரிட்டவன்.
He is the man who encountered and fought the champion.

418. அவன் கொஞ்சப்புள்ளியா?
Is he a man of limited wealth?
Spoken of a slovenly miser.

419. அவாந்தரத்தில் அக்கினி பற்றுமா?
Can fire be kindled in mid-air?
No, except by the Almighty "who holds the lightning in his hand and tells it whom to strike."

420. அவித்த பயறு முளைத்த கதைபோல.
Like the story of the germination of boiled peas.

421. அவிவேகி உறவிலும், விவேகி பகையே நன்று.
Better is the hatred of the wise than the friendship of fools.

422. அவிழ் என்ன செய்யும் அஞ்சு குணம் செய்யும் பொருள் என்ன செய்யும் பூவை வசம் செய்யும்.
What can rice do? it can work the five senses, what can wealth do? it can subdue the world.

423. அவையிலும் ஒருவன் சவையிலும் ஒருவன்.
One who *belongs* to this convention and to that convention.

424. அவ்வளவு இருந்தால் அடுக்கிவைத்து வாழேனே.
If I had so much should I not arrange my chatties *earthen cooking vessels* and prosper.
Spoken regretfully of succour which ought to be and is not afforded.

425. அழகிலே பிறந்த பவளக்கொடி அகத்திலே பிறந்த சாணிக்கூடை.
In beauty equal to natural coral, at home a cow-dung basket.

426. அழகிற்கு மூக்கை அறுப்பார் உண்டா?
Are there any who cut the nose for the sake of beauty.

427. அழகு இருந்து அழும், அதிஷ்டம் இருந்து உண்ணும்.
Beauty will sit and weep, fortune will sit and eat.

428. அழகுப்பெண்ணே காற்றாடி உன்னை அழைக்கிறாண்டி கூத்தாடி.
O beautiful maid, frail kite, the comedian calls you.
Spoken of a female whose demeanour is inconsistent with modesty.

429. அழகுக்கு இட்டால் ஆபத்துக்கு உதவும்.

A jewel worn as an ornament may aid in adversity.

Gold ornaments are often given as security for money borrowed to trade with, as well as to serve in pressing emergencies.

---

430. அழச்சொல்லுகிறவர் தமர், சிரிக்கச்சொல்லுகிறவர் பிறர்.

They who advise weeping are one's friends, those who advise laughing are strangers.

Spoken with reference to the character of advisers

---

431. அழச்சொல்லுகிறவன் பிழைக்கச்சொல்லுவான், சிரிக்கச்சொல்லுகிறவன் கெடச்சொல்லுவான்.

He who counsels *us* to weep does so to favour life; he who counsels mirth seeks our ruin.

---

432. அழிக்கப்படுவானைக் கடவுள் அறிவீனன் ஆக்குவார்.

God dements him who is to be destroyed.

---

433. அழிந்தவள் ஆரோடு போனால் என்ன?

What matters it with whom an abandoned *woman* goes?

---

434. அழிந்த நந்தவனத்தில் அசுவம் மேய்ந்து என்ன, கழுதை மேய்ந்து என்ன?

What matters it whether a horse or an ass grazes in a garden that lies waste?

---

435. அழிவழக்குச் சொன்னவன் பழிபொறுக்கும் மன்னவன்.

One who seeks to maintain an unjust claim and a king who extenuates crime.

Both are injurious to society.

---

436. அழுகள்ளர் தொழுகள்ளர் ஆசாரக்கள்ளர்.

Weeping hypocrites, canting sycophants and religious formalists.

---

437. அழுகிற ஆணையும் சிரிக்கிற பெண்ணையும் நம்பககூடாது.

A weeping man and a smiling woman are not to be trusted.

438. அழுகிற வீட்டில் இருந்தாலும் இருக்கலாம், ஒழுகுகிற வீட்டில் இருக்கலாகாது.

Though one may abide in a house of mourning, it is not possible to remain in one that is leaky.

---

439. அழுகிற பிள்ளைக்கு வாழைப்பழம் காட்டுகிறதுபோல.

Like showing a ripe plantain to a crying child.

A premium on naughtiness.

---

440. அழுகிற வேளை பார்த்து அக்குள் பாய்ச்சுகிறான்.

He tickles when one is weeping.

Spoken of something that is obtruded at an inconvenient time.

---

441. அழுகிறதற்கு அரைப்பணம் கொடுத்து, ஓய்கிறதற்கு ஒரு பணம் கொடு.

Having given half a fanam for weeping, give a fanam to cease.

---

442. அழுகையும் ஆங்காரமும் சிரிப்புக் கெலிப்போடா?

Are grief and self-will things to be made sport of?

---

443. அழுக்குச் சீலைக்குள்ளே மாணிக்கம்.

A ruby in a dirty rag.

---

444. அழுக்கை அழுக்குக் கொல்லும் இழுக்கை இழுக்குக் கொல்லும்.

Dirt will remove dirt, reproach will overcome reproach.

---

445. அழுக்கைத் துடைத்து மடிமேல் வைத்தாலும் புழுக்கைக் குணம் போகாது.

Though cleaned and placed on one's knee, the mean disposition of a slave or low person will not leave him.

---

446 அழுத கண்ணும் சிந்திய மூக்கும்.

A weeping eye and a running nose.

---

447. அழுதவனுக்கு அகங்காரமில்லை.

He who is weeping has no pride.

---

448. அழுதபிள்ளை பால்குடிக்கும்.

A crying child obtains milk.

449. அழுத பிள்ளை உரம் பெறும்.
The weeping child will gain strength.

450. அழுதும் பிள்ளை அவளே பெறவேண்டும்.
Although she may weep, she herself must bare the child.

451. அழுத்த நெஞ்சன் ஆருக்கும் உதவான், இளகின நெஞ்சன் எவர்க்கும் உதவுவான்.
The hard-hearted will be of use to none, the tender hearted will be of use to all.

452. அழுவார் அற்ற பிணமும் ஆற்றுவார் அற்ற சுடலையும்.
A corpse unwept and a funeral pyre unquenched.
An affair or person forsaken by all.

453. அழுவார் அழுவார் தம் தம் துக்கமே திருவன்பெண்டிருக்கு அழுவாரில்லை.
All weep on account of their own griefs, none on account of Tiruvan's wife.
Spoken of feigned sympathy and also of that outward expression of sorrow which is occasioned by surrounding circumstances.

454. அழையா வீட்டிற்கு நுழையாச் சம்பந்தி.
The mother of a bride or bridegroom will not visit their new relations unless invited.

455. அளகாபுரியிலும் விறகுதலையன் உண்டு.
There are firewood carriers even in Alagapuri, (the city of Kuvéra.)
Kuvéra a wealthy king; now regent of the North and the guardian of riches.

456. அளகாபுரி கொள்ளையானாலும், அதிஷ்டஈனனுக்கு ஒன்றும இல்லை.
Although Alagapuri be given up to plunder, the unfortunate gains nothing thereby.

457. அளகேசன் ஆனாலும் அளவு அறிந்து செலவு செய்யவேண்டும்.
Though as wealthy as Kuvéra you must keep your expenses within due bounds.

458. அளக்கிற நாழி அகவிலை அறியுமா?

Does the measure know the price of grain?

---

459. அளந்த நாழிகொண்டு அளப்பான்.

He will measure in the accustomed measure.

---

460. அளந்தால் ஒரு சாணில்லை அரிந்தால் ஒரு சட்டிகாணாது.

When measured it is not a span long, when chopped up it does not fill a chatti.

---

461. அளந்து அளந்த நாழி ஒழிந்து ஒழிந்து வரும்.

By repeated measurement articles will be diminished.

Constant use wears out a thing.

---

462. அளவளாவில்லாதவன் வாழ்க்கை குளவளாக் கோடின்றி நீர் நிறைந்தற்று.

The prosperity of him who does not cultivate sociality is like the filling of a tank without a bank.

---

463. அளவுக்கு மிஞ்சினால் அமிர்தமும் நஞ்சு.

If in excess even nectar is poison.

---

464. அள்ளாது குறையாது சொல்லாது பிறவாது.

That of which no part is taken out will not lessen, that which is not uttered will not get out.

---

465. அள்ளிக் கொடுத்தால் சும்மா, அளந்துக் கொடுத்தால் கடன்.

If taken up and given in handsful it is free, if measured out it is charged for.

---

466. அள்ளிப் பால் வார்க்கையிலே சொல்லிப் பால் வார்த்திருக்குது.

Whilst teeming milk already laded, the quantity is given.

---

467. அள்ளுகிறவன் இடத்தில் இருக்கல் ஆகாது கிள்ளுகிறவன் இடத்தில் இருந்தாலும்.

One cannot afford to live with a plunderer though he might live with a pilferer.

438. அள்ளுவது எல்லாம் நாய் தனக்கென்று எண்ணுமாம்.

It is said that a dog imagines every thing taken up by the hand is intended for himself.

469. அறக்காத்தான் பெண்டிழந்தான் அறுகாதவழி சுமந்து அழுதான்.

An over-suspicious man lost his wife and carried her sixty miles weeping.

Some mischievous persons having concealed her in a box employed him to carry it to the sea-shore.

470. அறக்குழைத்தாலும் குழைப்பாள் அரிசியாய் இறக்கினாலும் இறக்குவாள்.

She will over-boil the rice ; or she will boil it imperfectly.

471. அறக்கூர்மை மழுமொட்டை.

Excessive sharpness is perfect bluntness.

472. அறச்செட்டு முழுநஷ்டம்.

Hard dealing *ends* in loss.

473. அறணை அலகு திறவாது.

The streaked lizard opens not its mouth.

474. அறணை கடித்தால் மரணம்.

If a streaked lizard bite, death ensues.

475. அறத்தால வருவதே இன்பம்.

That is happiness which springs from virtue.

476. அறநனைந்தவருக்குக் கூதல் என்ன!

No cold to them that are completely wet.

477. அறப்பேசி உறவாடவேண்டும்.

On a full understanding of the party admit to friendship.

478. அறப்படித்தவர் அங்காடிபோனால் விற்கவுமாட்டார் கொள்ளவு மாட்டார்.

When the hypercritical go to market they neither buy nor sell.

479. அறப்படித்தவர் கூழ்ப்பானையில் விழுந்தார்.
One highly learned fell into a pot of gruel.

80. அறப்பத்தினி ஆமுடையானை அப்பா என்று அழைத்த கதை.
The story of a scrupulousy chaste wife who addressed her husband as Appa, *father*.

481. அறப்படித்த மூஞ்சூறு கழுநீர்ப்பானையில் விழுந்ததுபோல்.
As the thoroughly practised musk-rat was drowned in the refuse-pan.

482. அறமுறுக்கினால் கொடுமுறுக்காகும்.
When twisted to excess, fibres snap.

483. அறமுறுக்கினால் அற்றுப்போகும்.
If over-twisted it will snap.

484. அறமுறுக்குக் கொடும்புரி கொண்டு அற்றுவிடும்.
When excessively twisted, strands break.

485. அறம் பொருள் இன்பம் எல்லாருக்கும் இல்லை.
Virtue, wealth and pleasure are not common to all.

486. அறவடித்த முன்சோறு காடிப்பானையில் விழுந்தாற்போல.
As when being thoroughly strained the uppermost portion of the boiled rice fell into the refuse-pan.

487. அறவும் கொடுங்கோலரசன்கீழ்க் குடியிருப்பிற் குறவன்கீழ்க் குடியிருப்பு.
(Better) to live in subjection to a mountaineer than to be the subject of a cruel tyrant.

488. அறிஞர்க்கழகு அகத்துணர்ந்து அறிதல்.
It is the merit of the wise to gain knowledge by meditation.

489. அறிந்த ஆண்டையென்று கும்பிடப் போனால், உங்கள் அப்பன் பத்துப் பணம் கொடுக்கவேண்டும் கொடு என்றான்.
When I went to a master whom I knew, to pay my respects, he said, your father owes ten fanams, give it me.

490. அறிந்த பார்ப்பான் சிநேகிதன் ஆறு காசுக்கு மூன்று தோசையா?

A known brahman is a friend; are there only three pancakes for six cash?

Said of taking advantage of previous acquaintance in a bargain.

---

491. அறிந்தும் கெட்டேன் அறியாமலும் கெட்டேன் சொறிந்து புண் ஆயிற்று.

Knowingly and unknowingly I have been ruined; scratching has caused sores.

---

492. அறிந்தவனென்று கும்பிட அடிமை வழக்கிட்ட கதை.

The story of one who claimed as his slave the man who had paid his respects to him because he was an acquaintance.

---

493. அறிய அறியக் கெடுவார் உண்டா?

Do any become vicious by increasing knowledge!

---

494. அறியாத நாள் எல்லாம் பிறவாத நாள்.

All the days before the age of discretion are as the days before birth.

---

495. அறியாமல் தாடியை வளர்த்து அம்பட்டன் கையிற் கொடுக்கவா?

Have I grown my beard not knowing that it would fall into the hands of the barber!

Said with reference to the loss of a cherished object.

---

496. அறியாப் பிள்ளைப் புத்தியைப்போல.

Like the idea of an innocent child.

---

497. அறிவீனனிடத்தில் புத்தி கேளாதே.

Do not ask advice of the ignorant.

---

498. அறிவீனர் தமக்கு ஆயிரம் உரைக்கினும் அவம்.

Though fools are told a thousand times the thing is useless.

---

499. அறிவு ஆர் அறிவார்? ஆய்ந்தார் அறிவார்.

Who possesses information? Those who have examined *a thing* thoroughly.

500. அறிவு இல்லாதவன் பெண்டுகளிடத்திலும் தாழ்வுபடுவான்.

An ignorant man is despised even by women.

501. அறிவு இல்லாச் சயனம் அம்பரத்திலும் இல்லை.

So to sleep as to be incapable of feeling is an impossibility.

502. அறிவு பெருத்தோன் நோய் பெருத்தோன்.

He that increaseth knowledge increaseth sorrow.

503. அறிவு இல்லார்க்கு ஆண்மையும் இல்லை.

The ignorant are not manly.

504. அறிவு புறம்போய உலண்டதுபோல.

As a chrysalis destitute of intelligence.

505. அறிவுடன் ஞானம் அன்புடன் ஒழுக்கம்.

Wisdom is regulated by knowledge, good conduct by love.

506. அறிவு மனதை அரிக்கும்.

Conscious *guilt* will fret the heart.

507. அறிவு தரும் வாயும் அன்பு உரைக்கும் நாவும்.

A mouth that instructs and a tongue uttering words of love.

Spoken of one characterized by wisdom and love.

508. அறிவுடையானை அரசனும் விரும்பும்.

Even a king will approve of wise men.

509. அறிவுடையானை அடுத்தாற் போதும்.

To obtain the favour of the wise is enough.

510. அறிவேன் அறிவேன் ஆலிலை புளியிலைபோல் இருக்கும்.

I know, I know (i. e., I know it well) the leaf of the banyan tree is like that of the tamarind tree.

511. அறுக்கமாட்டாதவன் அரையில் ஐம்பத்தெட்டு அரிவாள்.

Fifty-eight sickles on the hip of one that cannot reap.

Used in contempt of mere show and parade.

512. அறுதலி மகனுக்கு அங்கம் எல்லாம் சேட்டை.

The son of a widow has evil gestures throughout his body.

Said of persons irreclaimably and naturally vicious.

---

513. அறுத்த கோழி துடிக்குமாப்போல.

Fluttering as a fowl with its throat cut.

---

514. அறுத்தவள் ஆண்பிள்ளை பெற்ற கதை.

The story of a widow who gave birth to a son.

---

515. அறுபது நாளைக்கு எழுபது கந்தை.

Seventy rags for sixty days.

---

516. அறுபத்துநாலு அடிக் கம்பத்தின்மேல் ஆடினாலும், கீழே வந்து தியாகம் வாங்கவேண்டும்.

Although one may balance himself on a pole sixty-four feet high, he has to descend to receive gifts.

---

517. அறுபத்தெட்டுக் கோரம்பலம்.

Sixty-eight tricks.

Said of the various impediments which one meets with in carrying out a scheme.

---

518. அறுப்புக் காலத்தில் எலிக்கும் ஐந்து பெண்சாதி.

In harvest time even a rat has five wives.

---

519. அறுவாய்க்கு வாய் பெரிது, அரிசிக்குக் கொதி பெரிது.

The mouth of the rice-pot being enlarged by fracture, the rice must be boiled the longer.

---

520. அறையில் ஆடி அல்லவோ அம்பலத்தில் ஆடவேண்டும்?

One must appear in the assembly, must he not, after having practised privately!

---

521. அறையில் இருக்கிறவர்களை அம்பலத்தில் ஏற்றுகிற புரட்டன்.

One who leads private persons into a place of justice and perverts judgment.

---

522. அற்ப ஆசை கோடி தவத்தைக் கெடுக்கும்.

The least unlawful desire destroys a myriad acts of austerity.

523. அற்பத்திற்கு அழகு குலைகிறதா?

Is beauty (self-respect) to be forfeited for a mere trifle ?

524. அற்பத் துடைப்பமானாலும் அகத்தூசியை அடக்கும்.

Although the broom is inferior it will lay the dust in the house.

525. அற்பர் சிநேகிதம் பிராண கண்டிதம்.

The friendship of the mean will issue in fatal results.

526. அற்பர் சிநேகம் பிராண சங்கடம்.

The friendship of the base is dangerous.

527. அற்பனுக்கு ஐஸ்வரியம் வந்தால் அர்த்தராத்திரியில் குடைபிடிப்பான்.

If a low-bred man obtain wealth, he will carry an umbrella at midnight.

528. அற்பன் பணம் படைத்தால் வைக்க வகை அறியான்.

When a mean person acquires wealth he knows not how to take care of it.

529. அற்றத்துக்கு உற்றதாய்.

Fitted to the opportunity.

530. அனல் குளிர் வெதுவெதுப்பு இம்மூன்று காலமும் ஆறு காலத்திற்குள் அடக்கம்.

Three kinds of weather, hot, cold and temperate are included in the six seasons.

A year is divided into six seasons of two months each, beginning with August The names of the seasons are 1. கார், cloudy. 2 கூதிர், cold 3. முன்பனி, evening dew. 4. பின்பனி, morning dew. 5. இளவேனில், mild heat. 6. முதுவேனில், very hot.

531. அனுபோகம் தொலைந்தால் அற்ப அவிழ்தமும் பலிக்கும்.

Even a common medicine may prove effectual after a disease has passed the crisis.

532. அன்பற்ற மாமியாருக்குக் கால் பட்டாலும் குற்றம், கை பட்டாலும் குற்றம்.

The touch whether of the foot or the hand is an offence to one's unkind mother-in-law.

533. அன்பற்ற மாமியாருக்குக் கும்பிடும் குற்றந்தான்.

Even obeisance is an offence to an unloving mother-in-law.

534. அன்பற்றார் வாசலிலே பின்பற்றிப் போகாதே.

Don't enter the portal of the uncharitable.

535. அன்பான சிநேகிதனை ஆபத்திலே அறி.

Know a loving friend in adversity.

536. அன்பில்லார் தமக்கு ஆதிக்கம் இல்லை.

They who are destitute of love are void of influence.

537. அன்புள்ள குணம் அலையில்லா நதி.

A loving disposition is a river without a ripple.

538. அன்பு இருந்தால் ஆகாதும் ஆகும்.

Where love reigns the impossible may be attained.

539. அன்புடையானைக் கொடுத்து அலையச்சே அசல் வீட்டுக்காரன் வந்து அழைத்த கதை.

The story of a neighbour who invited a woman in distress at the loss of her husband.

540. அன்பே பிரதானம் அதுவே வெகுமானம்.

Love is all-important, and it is it's own reward.

541. அன்றற ஆயிரம் பொன்னிலும், நின்றற ஒரு காசு பெரிது.

A single cash saved is greater than thousands of gold spent as soon as acquired.

542. அன்றிறுக்கலாம் நின்றிறுக்கலாகாது.

Pay at once, delay is bad.

543. அன்று கண்ட மேனிக்கு அழிவு இல்லை.

The body we then saw has suffered no decay.

The word மேனி is also used for beauty, freshness.

544. அன்றும் இல்லைத் தையல், இன்றும் இல்லைப் பொத்தல்.

There was no stitching then, nor is there any hole now.

545. அன்றுகொள், நின்றுகொள், என்றும் கொள்ளாதே.

Buy when you require, be slow to make purchases, do not make daily purchases.

546. அன்று தின்ற சோறு ஆறு மாதத்திற்கு ஆமா?

Will the boiled rice eaten then suffice for six months?

547. அன்று தின்ற ஊண் ஆறு மாசத்துப் பசியை அறுக்கும்.

The food which was then eaten will keep one free from hunger for six months.

548. அன்று எழுதினவன் அழித்து எழுதுவானா?

Will he who wrote then, erase and write again?

Referring to the changeless preordination of God.

549. அன்றைக்குக் கிடைக்கிற ஆயிரம் பொன்னிலும் இன்றைக்குக் கிடைத்த அரைக்காசு பெரிது.

The half cash obtained to-day is greater than thousands of gold to be got hereafter.

550. அன்றைக்குத் தின்கிற பலாக்காயைவிட இன்றைக்குத் தின்கிற களாக்காய் பெரிது.

The Kalà fruit, *carissa diffusa*, of to-day is better than the jack fruit of the future.

551. அன்னப் பிடி வெல்லப் பிடி ஆச்சுது.

A handful of boiled rice has become as precious as a handful of sugar.

552. அன்ன மயம் பிராண மயம்.

The property of food is the support of life.

The supporting, nourishing quality of grain is its special property, without which, as life is now conditioned, it cannot exist.

553. அன்ன மயம் இன்றிப் பின்னை மயம் இல்லை.

There is no physical virtue in aught but food.

The same as the preceding.

---

554. அன்னம் மிகக் கொள்வானும் ஆடை அழுக்கு ஆவானும் பதர்.

The glutton and the sloven are alike worthless.

---

555. அன்னம் இட்டார் வீட்டில் கன்னம் இடலாமா?

May we break through the wall of the house of those who fed us?

---

556. அன்னம் ஒடுங்கினால் அஞ்சும் ஒடுங்கும்.

When food fails, the five *senses* fail.

Referring to the exercise of the senses as dependent on the health of the body and its dependence on food.

---

557. அன்ன நடை நடக்கப்போய்த் தன் நடையும் கெட்டாற்போல.

As in attempting to walk like a swan, *the crow* lost even its natural gait.

---

558. அன்னம் முட்டானால் எல்லாம் முட்டு.

When food or grain is scarce, all is scarce.

---

559. அன்னப்பாலுக்குச் சிங்கியடித்தவள் ஆவின் பாலுக்குச் சர்க்கரை தேடுகிறாள்.

She who was wandering about for rice water, is seeking sugar to mix in cow's milk.

---

560. அன்னதானத்திற்குச் சரி என்ன தானம் இருக்கிறது?

What gift is *there that* equals the gift of food?

---

561. அன்னிய மாதர் அவதிக்கு உதவார்.

Strange women will not avail in adversity.

---

562. அன்னைக்கு உதவாதான் ஆருக்கு உதவுவான்?

Whom will he help that does not help his mother?

---

563. அஸ்த செம்மானம் அடைமழைக்கு லக்ஷணம்.

A crimson sunset betokens abiding rain.

564. அஸ்திமசகாந்தரம் என்றதுபோல் இருக்கிறது.

The difference is as great as that between an elephant and a mosquito.

ஆ.

565. ஆகடியக்காரன் போகடியாய்ப் போவான்.

A scoffer will be destroyed.

---

566. ஆகாத நாளையில் பிள்ளை பிறந்தால், அண்டை வீட்டுக்காரனை என்ன செய்யும்?

If a child be born at an inauspicious time what evil will it occasion to a neighbour?

---

567. ஆகாத பஞ்சாங்கத்துக்கு அறுபது நாழிகையும் தியாச்சியம்.

In a false almanac, the sixty hours are to be rejected.

In astrological calculations a time of three and three quarters to four Indian hours (நாழிகை 24 minutes) for the asterism that rules the day is considered unlucky: it is called தியாச்சியம் rejected.

An imperfect or uncertain formula should be wholly rejected.

---

568. ஆகாதவன் குடியை அடுத்துக் கெடுக்கவேண்டும்.

The family of the wicked must be destroyed by associating with it.

---

569. ஆகாதவற்றை ஏற்ருல் ஆராய்ந்து ஏற்றுக்கொள்.

If about to undertake a difficult work do so after due inquiry.

---

570. ஆகாத்தியக்காரனுக்குப் பிரமகத்திக்காரன் சாட்சியா?

Is a brahmanicide a suitable witness for an abandoned wretch?

---

571. ஆகாயத்துக்கு மையம் காட்டுகிறதுபோல.

Like pointing out the middle of the sky.

An impossibility.

---

572. ஆகாயத்தைப் பருந்து எடுத்துக்கொண்டு போகுமா?

Can a hawk carry away the sky?

573. ஆகாயத்தில் பறக்க உபதேசிப்பேன், என்னைத் தூக்கி ஆற்றுக்கு அப்பால் விடு என்கிறான் குரு.

The spiritual guide observed, I will teach you how to fly through the air, take me up and convey me to the other side of the river.

---

574. ஆகாய வல்லிடி அதிர இடிக்கும்.

A powerful thunder-clap will occasion tremor.

---

575. ஆகாயமட்டும் அளக்கும் இருப்புத்தூணைச் செல்லரிக்குமா?

Will white ants destroy an iron pillar that reaches to the clouds?

The proverb was used by Sita when speaking to Ravana.

---

576. ஆகாயம் பார்க்கப்போயும் இடுமுடுக்கா?

Is there not sufficient space for one to go and look at the sky?

---

577. ஆகாயத்தை வடுப்படக் கடிக்கலாமா?

Can the air be bit so as to leave a mark?

---

578. ஆகாயம் பெற்றது, பூமி தாங்கினது.

The sky brought forth, the earth supported.

---

579. ஆகிறகாலத்தில் அவிழ்தம் பலிக்கும்.

If favoured by fortune medicine will take effect in due time.

---

580. ஆகுங்காலத்தில் அடியாளும் பெண் பெறுவாள்.

In times of prosperity, even a slave woman may bring forth a female child.

---

581. ஆகுங்காய் பிஞ்சிலே தெரியும்.

A sound fruit may be known when it begins to set.

---

582. ஆகுங்காலம் ஆகும், போகுங்காலம் போகும்.

In auspicious times it succeeds, in inauspicious times it fails.

---

583. ஆக்கப் பொறுத்தவன் ஆறப் பொறானா?

Will he who waited till it was cooked, not wait till it cools?

---

584. ஆக்கிற் குழைப்பேன், அரிசியாய் இறக்குவேன்.

Should I cook I shall spoil the rice, either by under or over-doing it

585. ஆக்கினையும் செங்கோலும் அற்றது அரை நாழிகையில்.

Rule will last but half an hour where discipline and authority do not exist.

586. ஆக்குகிறவள் சலித்தால் அடுப்புப் பாழ், குத்துகிறவள் சலித்தால் குந்தாணி பாழ்.

If the cook be weary, the hearth will be useless; if she who pounds the rice be weary the mortar will be useless.

587. ஆங்காரிகளுக்கு அதிகாரி.

The chief of the proud.

588. ஆங்காலம் எல்லாம் அவசாரி ஆடிச் சாங்காலம் சங்கரா சங்கரா என்கிறாள்.

She exclaims Sangará, Sangará at death having through life been given up to lewd behaviour.

589. ஆசரித்த தெய்வம் எல்லாம் அடியோடே மாண்டது.

All the deities that were venerated have entirely perished.

590. ஆசாரம் இல்லா அசடருடன் கூடிப் பாசாங்கு பேசிப் பதி இழந்துபோனேன்.

By being associated with the base and by speaking hypocritically I have forfeited my dwelling-place.

591 ஆசீர்வாதமும் சாபமும் அறவோர்க்கு இல்லை.

The virtuous are not affected by blessing and cursing.

592. ஆசை அவள் மேலே ஆதரவு பாய் மேலே.

His mind is fixed upon her, his body is on the mat.

593. ஆசை அறுபது நாள், மோகம் முப்பதுநாள், தொண்ணூறு நாளும் போனால் துடைப்பக்கட்டை.

Sixty days of excessive desire, thirty of enjoyment; when the ninety are over, the remaining time is as useless as a worn-out broom.

594. ஆசை அண்டாதாகில், அழுகையும் அண்டாது.

If evil desire spring not sorrow will not approach.

595. ஆசை உண்டானால் பூசை உண்டு.
If there be heartfelt love, there will be deferential regard

Spoken of a devoted wife who has a cruel husband.

596. ஆசை உள்ளளவும் அலைச்சலும் உண்டு.
As long as desire continues, there will be anxiety also.

597. ஆசைகொண்டபேருக்கு ரோசம் இல்லை.
Persons of *inordinate* desire have no shame.

598. ஆசைக்கு அளவில்லை.
Desire has no limits.

599. ஆசை சொல்லி மோசம் செய்கிறதா?
Is it to deceive after using enticing words!

600. ஆசை நோவுக்கு அவிழ்தம் ஏது?
What remedy is there for love-sickness!

601. ஆசை பெருக அலைச்சலும் பெருகும்.
As desire increases, anxiety increases.

602. ஆசை பெரிதோ, மலை பெரிதோ?
Which is greater, (human) desire or a mountain!

603. ஆசைப்பட்டது ஊசிப்போயிற்று.
What was desired is now disgusting.

604. ஆசையெல்லாம் தீர அடித்தாள் முறத்தாலே.
She beat him with the winnowing fan to banish all his desires.

605. ஆசை வெட்கம் அறியாது.
Desire knows not shame

606. ஆசை வைத்தால் நாசம்.
Cherished desire *ends* in ruin.

607. ஆச்சி ஆச்சி மெத்தப் படித்துப் பேசாதே.
O mother, mother, do not speak so much.

ஆச்சி is a provincialism for ஆயி.

608. ஆடப் பாடத் தெரியாது இரண்டு பங்கு உண்டு.
Neither able to sing nor dance, but *he* has two shares.

609. ஆடமாட்டாத தேவடியாள் கூடம் போதாது என்றாள்.
The temple girl who could not dance said that the hall was not large enough.

610. ஆடவிட்டு நாடகம் பார்க்கிறதா?
Is it to look at the drama after having encouraged a profligate course?

Spoken ironically.

611. ஆடாஜாதி கூடாஜாதியா?
Are those unfit for the drama unfit for every thing.

612 ஆடாது எல்லாம் ஆடி அவரைக்காயும் அறுத்தாச்சுது.
All is done and the avarai fruit is cut!

Indicating decayed circumstances.

613. ஆடி அறவெட்டை அகவிலை நெல்விலை.
July harvest having failed, the price of dry grain is that of paddy

614. ஆடி அமர்ந்தது கூத்து ஒரு நாழிகையில்.
The comedy began and ended in an hour.

615. ஆடி ஓய்ந்த பம்பரம்.
A top that spins no longer.

616. ஆடிக் கரு அழிந்தால் மழை குறைந்துபோம்.
If the embryo clouds of July fail rain will be scant.

617. ஆடிக்கறக்கிற மாட்டை ஆடிக் கறக்கவேண்டும், பாடிக் கறக்கிற மாட்டைப் பாடிக் கறக்கவேண்டும்.
A restless cow must be milked by force, and a gentle cow must be milked with kindness.

Treatment to be regulated by circumstances.

618. ஆடிக்காற்றில் உதிரும் சருகுபோல.
As dry leaves falling in the winds of July.

619. ஆடிக்காற்றில் எச்சிற் கல்லைக்கு வழியா ?

Is there any way *of escape* for a leaf-plate before the wind of July !

620. ஆடிக்காற்றிலே இலவம்பஞ்சு பறந்ததுபோல.

Like silk-cotton scattered by the wind of July.

621. ஆடிக்கு அழைக்காத மாமியாளைத் தேடி மயிரைப் பிடித்துச் செருப்பால் அடி.

Seek, seize her by the hair, and slipper a mother-in-law who does not invite you in July.

The parents of a newly married woman separate her from her husband, that she may be under their care during the first year of marriage, in the month of July. This is necessary to prevent conception in that month and delivery in the following April. The birth of a first child in April if a son is believed to bring ruin upon a family.

622. ஆடிமாசத்தில் குத்தின குத்து ஆவணிமாசத்தில் உளைவு எடுத்ததாம்.

They say that the cuff was given in July, and the pain felt in August.

623. ஆடிய காலும் பாடிய மிடறும்.

A dancing foot and a singing throat.

624. ஆடி விதை தேடிப்போடு.

Provide seed-corn and *sow* in July.

625. ஆடு இருக்க இடையனை விழுங்குமா ?

While there are sheep will it (the tiger or wolf) swallow the shepherd.

626. ஆடு எடுத்த கள்ளனைப்போலே விழிக்கிறான்.

He stares like a thief who has stolen a sheep.

627. ஆடு கடிக்கிறதென்று இடையன் உறியேறிப் பதுங்குகிறான்.

The shepherd is trembling aloft fearing the sheep may bite him.

628. ஆடு காற்பணம் வால் முக்காற்பணம்.

The price of the sheep is a quarter of a fanam that of its tail three fourths of a fanam,

629. ஆடு கிடந்த இடத்திலே மயிர்தானும் கிடையாமற் போயிற்று.
Not even hair is found where sheep were penned

630. ஆடு கிடந்த இடமும் அகம்படியான் இருந்த இடமும் உருப்படாது.
A place where sheep were penned and a place once occupied by an Agambadyan are profitless.

631. ஆடுகிடந்த இடத்தில் பழுப்புத்தானும் கிடையாது.
Not a leaf will be found where the sheep lay.

632. ஆடு கொழுக்கிறது எல்லாம் இடையனுக்கு லாபம்.
The fattening of the sheep is an advantage to the shepherd.

633. ஆடு கொண்டவன் ஆடித்திரிவான், கோழி கொண்டவன் கூவித்திரிவான்.
He that has bought a sheep will wander about; he that has bought fowls will go about crying them for sale.

634. ஆடு கொடாத இடையன் ஆவைக் கொடுப்பானு?
Will the shepherd who refused to give a sheep give a cow?

635. ஆடு கோனுனின்றித் தானுய்ப் போகுமா?
Will a sheep lead itself when the shepherd is absent.

636. ஆடுங்காலம் தலைகீழாய் விழுந்தாலும் கூடும் புசிப்புத்தான் கூடும்.
Though he may fall headlong when dancing, he will not thereby meet with greater success.

637. ஆடுங்காலத்துத் தலைகீழாக விழுந்தால் ஓடும் கப்பரையும் உடையவன் ஆவான்.
If one should fall headlong when he ought to be active, he will be so impoverished as to possess only broken pots and an alms-dish.

Indolence in youth leads to poverty in old age.

638. ஆடுதவுமா குருக்களே என்றால், கொம்பும் குளம்பும் தவிரச் சமூலமும் ஆகும் என்கிறார்.
If one say, O my teacher, can the sheep be of any use to you, he replies yes, all except the horns and the hoofs.

639. ஆடு தழை தின்பதுபோலே.

Like a goat cropping leaves.

640. ஆடு நனைகிறதென்று கோனாய் அழுகிறதாம்.

It is said that the wolf wept because the sheep were wet,

641. ஆடு நினைத்த இடத்தில் பட்டி போடுகிறதா?

Will the pen be put up where the sheep may wish?

642. ஆடு பிழைத்தால் மயிர்தானும் கொடான்.

If the sheep should recover, he will not give even a hair.

Said where benefits are not requited.

643. ஆடு வீட்டிலே ஆட்டுக்குட்டி காட்டிலே.

The dam at home, the lamb in the jungle.

644. ஆடை இல்லாதவன் அரை மனிதன்.

He who is naked is but half a man.

Self-respect essential.

645. ஆடையைத் தின்றால் வெண்ணெய உண்டா?

If the cream be consumed, can butter be obtained?

646. ஆட்காட்டி சொந்தக்காரனையும் திருடனையும் காட்டிக்கொடுக்கும்.

The lapwing will *by it's cries* betray whether he who approaches be the owner or a thief.

647. ஆட்காட்டி தெரியாமல் திருடப்போகிறவன் கெட்டிக்காரனோ, அவன் அறியாமல் அவன் காலடிபிடித்துப் போகிறவன் கெட்டிக்காரனோ?

Which is the cleverer, the thief that goes out to steal taking care that the lapwing does not see him, or he that follows the track of that thief?

648. ஆட்டாளுக்கு ஒரு மோட்டாள்.

A stupid servant to a shepherd.

649. ஆட்டில் ஆயிரம், மாட்டில் ஆயிரம், வீட்டிலே கரண்டி பால் இல்லை.

Possessed of sheep by the thousand, of cattle by the thousand, *he has* not a spoonful of milk at home.

---

650. ஆட்டுக்கு வால் அளவறுத்து வைத்திருக்கிறது.

The tail of the sheep is proportioned to its size.

---

651. ஆட்டுக்கும் மாட்டுக்கும் இரண்டு கொம்பு, ஐயம்பிடாரிக்கு மூன்று கொம்பு.

Sheep and oxen have two horns, an Aiyam-pidári has three.

---

652. ஆட்டுக்குத் தோற்குமா கிழப்புலி?

Can an old tiger be overcome by a sheep?

---

653. ஆட்டுக்கும் மாட்டுக்குமுறையா, காட்டுக்கும் பாட்டுக்கும் வரையா?

Are relationships observed among sheep and oxen? have woods and uncultivated tracts any line of demarkation?

---

654. ஆட்டுக்கிடையிலே கோனாய் புகுந்ததுபோல.

As the wolf entered the sheepfold.

---

655. ஆட்டுக்குத் தீர்ந்தபடி குட்டிக்கும் ஆகிறது.

The fate of the lamb is that of its dam.

---

656. ஆட்டுத்தலைக்கு வண்ணான் பறக்கிறதுபோல.

As the washerman flies at the sheep's head.

---

657. ஆட்டு வெண்ணெய் ஆட்டு மூளைக்கும் காணாது.

The butter the sheep yields is not enough (to stew) the marrow with.

---

658. ஆட்டுவித்துப் பம்பை கொட்டுகிறான்.

He causes them to dance and beats the drum.

---

659. ஆட்டுக் குட்டிமேல் ஆயிரம் பொன்னா?

What, thousands of gold for a young sheep?

660. ஆட்டுக்குட்டிக்கு ஆனையைக் காவுகொடு.

Sacrifice an elephant for the sake of a kid.

661. ஆட்டுக்குட்டியைத் தோளிலே வைத்துக் காடெங்கும் தேடின கதை.

The story of one who wandered through the jungle in search of a lamb that he had on his shoulder.

662. ஆட்டைக் காட்டி வேங்கை பிடிக்கப் பார்க்கிறான்.

He aims to catch the leopard by exposing the sheep.

663. ஆட்டைத் தேடி அயலாள் கையிற் கொடுப்பதைப்பார்க்க, வீட்டைக் கட்டி நெருபபு வைப்பது நல்லது.

It is better to build a house and set fire to it, than to buy sheep and place them under the care of others.

664. ஆட்டைக்கொருமுறை காணச் சோட்டை இல்லையோ?

Have you no desire to see *us at least* once a year!

665. ஆணமும் கறியும் அடுக்கோடே வேண்டும்.

Broth and curry ought to be prepared with all their ingredients.

666. ஆணவத்தால் அழியாதே.

Do not destroy yourself by pride.

667. ஆணிக்கு இணங்கின பொன்னும் மாமிக்கு இணங்கின பெண்ணும் அருமை.

Standard gold, and a woman at one with her mother-in-law are rare.

668. ஆணுக்கு அவகேடு செய்தாலும் பெண்ணுக்குப் பிழைகேடு செய்யலாகாது.

Although one may injure a man, a woman may not be injuriously treated.

669. ஆணை அடித்து வளர், பெண்ணைப் போற்றி வளர்.

Train a boy strictly, but a girl kindly.

670. ஆணையும் வேண்டாம் சத்தியமும் வேண்டாம் துணியைப்போட்டுத் தாண்டு.

Neither swearing nor oaths are required, put down the cloth and stride over it.

671. ஆண்ட பொருளை அறியாதார் செய்த தவம் மாண்ட மரத்துக்கு அணைத்த மண்.

The austerity of those who are ignorant of the Supreme is as profitless as soil at the foot of a dead tree.

672. ஆண்டாருக்குக் கொடுக்கிறையோ சுரைக்குடுக்கைக்குக் கொடுக்கிறையோ?

Do you give to mendicants, or to the hard shell of the bottle-gourd?

673. ஆண்டார் இருக்குமட்டும் ஆட்டும் கூத்தும்.

While the head of a family lives, prosperity may be enjoyed.

674. ஆண்டிகள்கூடி மடம் கட்டினாற்போல.

Like mendicants combining to build a choultry.

675. ஆண்டி கிடப்பான் மடத்திலே சோளி கிடக்கும் தெருவிலே.

The mendicant lies in the choultry and his bag in the street.

676. ஆண்டிக்கு இடச்சொன்னால் தாதனுக்கு இடச்சொல்லுகிறான்.

When told to give *rice* to the Saiva mendicant, he says give it to the Vaishnava mendicant.

677. ஆண்டிக்கு வாய்ப்பேச்சு பார்ப்பானுக்கு அதுவும் இல்லை.

To the religious mendicant a word, to the brahman not even that.

678. ஆண்டிச்சி பெற்ற அஞ்சும் அவம்.

The five *children* borne by the mendicant's wife are all weaklings.

679. ஆண்டி மகன் ஆண்டியானால் நேரம் அறிந்து சங்கு ஊதுவான்.

When the son of a mendicant assumes a mendicant's profession, he will blow his conch at the proper time.

680. ஆண்டியை அடித்தானாம் குடுவையை உடைத்தானாம்.

It is said that he beat the mendicant, and broke his alms-dish.

681. ஆண்டியும் தாதனும் தோண்டியும் கயிறும்.

The Saivite and the Vaishnavite mendicants are sa a water-pot and its cord.

United or separate

682. ஆண்டியைக் கண்டால் லிங்கன் என்கிறான், தாதனைக் கண்டால் ரங்கன் என்கிறான்.

When he meets a Saiva mendicant he is a Lingan, and when he meets a Vaishnava mendicant he is a Rangan.

683. ஆண்டியும் ஆண்டியும் கட்டிக்கொண்டால் சாம்பலும் சாம்பலும் ஒட்டிக்கொள்ளும்

When two mendicants embrace each other, the ashes of the one cleave to the other.

684. ஆண்டி வேஷம்போட்டும் அலைச்சல் தீரவில்லை.

Though he assumed the guise of a mendicant, his troubles did not cease.

685. ஆண்டி குண்டியைத் தட்டினால் பறப்பது சாம்பல்.

If a mendicant be struck on his posteriors, ashes fly.

686. ஆண்டு மாறின காரும் அன்று அறுத்த சம்பாவும் ஆளன் கண்ணுக்கு அரிது.

Kár *rice* a year old, and newly reaped Samba (superior rice) are rare to the eye of a cultivator.

687. ஆண்டு மறுத்தால் தோட்டியும் கும்பிடான்.

If the year withhold her increase, even the menial servants will neglect to do obeisance

688. ஆண்டைமேற் கோபம் கடாவின்மேல் ஆறினான்.

He wreaked his anger against his master on the male buffalo.

689. ஆண்பிள்ளைகள் ஆயிரம் ஒத்திருப்பார்கள், அக்காள் தங்கைச்சி ஒத்திரார்கள்.

A thousand men may live together in harmony, whereas two women are unable to do so although they be sisters.

690. ஆண்மையற்ற வீரன் ஆயுதத்தின்மேற் குறைசொல்லுவான்.
The coward blames his weapon.

691. ஆதரவற்ற வார்த்தையும் ஆணிகிடாவாத கைமரமும் பலன் செய்யாது.
A comfortless word, and a palmira rafter without a bolt are of no use.

692. ஆதாயமில்லாத செட்டி ஆற்றோடே போவானா?
Will a chetty (a merchant,) take his departure by a river without gain?

693. ஆதாயமில்லாத செட்டி ஆற்றைக் கட்டி இறைப்பானா?
Will a chetty dam up a river and drain out its waters for nothing.

694. ஆதீனக்காரனுக்குச் சாதனம் வேண்டுமா?
Is a man possessed of landed property without a legal instrument?

695. ஆத்திரக்காரனுக்குப் புத்தி மட்டு.
The over-hasty is wanting in sense.

696. ஆத்திரக்காரன் கோத்திரம் அறிவானா?
Will the over-hasty be nice about family pedigrees?

697. ஆத்திரப்பட்டவனுக்கு அப்போது இன்பம்.
The hasty is gratified at the instant.

698. ஆத்தை படுகிற பாட்டுக்குள்ளே மகன் மோருக்கு அழுகிறான்.
While his mother is in extremity, her grown up son is crying for butter-milk.

699. ஆஸ்தியில்லாதவன் அரைமனிதன்.
He who possesses no property is but half a man.

700. ஆஸ்தியுள்ளவன் ஆஸ்திக்கு அடிமை.
A man of wealth is the slave of his possessions.

701. ஆஸ்தியுள்ளவனுக்கு நாசம் இல்லை.
The wealthy are not *exposed to immediate* ruin.

702. ஆந்தை சிறிது கூச்சுப் பெரிது.
The owl is small, its screech is loud.

703. ஆபத்திற் காத்தவன் ஆண்டவன் ஆவான்.
He who helps another in his misfortune becomes his master.

704. ஆபத்தும் சம்பத்தும் ஆருக்கும் உண்டு.
Prosperity and adversity are common to all.

705. ஆபத்துக்குப் பாவம் இல்லை.
A thing done through necessity is no crime.

706. ஆபத்துக்கு உதவினவனே பந்து.
He is a friend who aids in adversity.

707. ஆப்பாத்தாள் கலியாணம் போய்ப்பார்த்தால் தெரியும்.
The condition of one's elder sister may be ascertained by attending her wedding.

708. ஆப்பைப் பிடுங்கின குரங்கு நாசம் அடைந்ததுபோல.
As the monkey perished by drawing out a wedge.

709. ஆமணக்கு விதைத்தால் ஆச்சா முளைக்குமா ?
If castor seed (palma christi) be sown will Achoha (ebony) spring up?

710. ஆமணக்கு முத்து ஆணிமுத்தாமா ?
Are the nuts of the castor plant pearls?

711. ஆமணக்கும் பருத்தியும் அடர விதைப்பானா ?
Will he sow castor and cotton seeds in close proximity?

712. ஆமை கிணற்றிலே அணில் கொம்பிலே.
The tortoise or a turtle is in the well, the squirrel is on a branch.

Said of two things or persons not found together.

713. ஆமை பிடிப்பார் மல்லாத்துவார் நாம் அது சொன்னாற் பாவம்.
They will catch the turtle, they will turn it on its back, for me to say so would be a crime.

Indicating that it is more dangerous to speak of the crime of another than to commit it.

714. ஆமுடையானைக் கொன்ற அறநீலி.

A most abandoned woman who murdered her own husband.

715. ஆமுடையான் செத்தபின்பு அறுதலிக்குப் புத்தி வந்தது.

The woman became wise after the death of her husband.

716. ஆமுடையானுக்கு அழுதவளுக்கு அந்துக்கண்ணன் வந்து வாய்த்தான்.

A blear-eyed man became the husband of a woman who had been crying for one.

717. ஆமுடையான் அடித்ததற்கு அழவில்லை, சக்களத்தி சிரிப்பாளென்று அழுகிறேன்.

I do not weep because my husband has beaten me, but because my rival will laugh at me.

718. ஆமுடையான் செத்து அவதிப்படுகிறபோது, அண்டைவீட்டுக்காரன் வந்து அக்குளில் குத்தினனும்.

When in great extremity she was mourning the death of her husband, a neighbour came and *attempted* to tickle her under the arm.

719. ஆமுடையான் கோப்பில்லாக் கூத்தும், குருவில்லா ஞானமும் போல் இருக்கிறுன்.

The husband resembles a merry, making without food and knowledge without a competent teacher.

720. ஆமுடையான் வடடமாய் ஓடினுலும் வாசலால் வரவேண்டும்.

No matter what the circumambulation of a husband may be, he enters his house by the door.

721. ஆமுடையானுக்குப் பொய் சொன்னுலும் அடுப்புக்குப் பொய் சொல்லலாமா?

True, you may utter a falsehood to your husband, but can you deal falsely with the hearth?

722. ஆமுடையானை வைத்துக்கொண்டல்லோ அவசாரியாடவேண்டும்?

It is while she has a husband, is it not, that a woman should play the harlot?

723. ஆமுடையான் செத்தவளுக்கு மருத்துவிச்சி தயவேன்?
Of what use is the favor of a midwife to her who has lost her husband?

724. ஆமுடையான் பலம் இருந்தால் குப்பை ஏறிச் சண்டை செய்ய லாம்.
If your husband be a powerful man, you may ascend the dunghill to fight

725. ஆமை திடரில் ஏறினாற்போல.
As if a tortoise or turtle crept up a hillock.

726. ஆமையுடனே முயல் முட்டையிடப்போய்க் கண்பிதுங்கிச் செத் ததாம்.
It is said that when the hare went with the tortoise to lay eggs it strained its eyes out and died.

727. ஆய உபாயம் அறிந்தவன் அரிதல்ல வெல்வது.
It is not difficult for one to win who understands the tricks of dice.

728. ஆயக்காரனுக்குப் பிரமகத்திக்காரன் சாட்சி.
The brahmanicide is the witness of the custom officer.

729. ஆயக்காரன் அஞ்சு பணம் கேட்பான் அதாவெட்டுக்காரன் ஐம் பது பணம் கேட்பான்.
The under-hand extortioner demands fifty fanams whilst the custom officer demands five.

730. ஆயத்திலும் நியாயம் வேண்டும்.
Even in gain justice is required.

731. ஆயத்துக்குக் குதிரை கியத்துக்குக் குட்டி.
Hire for the horse, nothing for its colt.

732. ஆயத்துக்குப் பயந்து ஆற்றில் நீந்தினதுபோல.
Like swimming the river to avoid the tax.

733. ஆயத்துறையில் அநியாயம் செய்யாதே.
Do not commit injustice at the custom-house.

734. ஆயிரக்கலம் நெல்லுக்கு ஓர் அந்துப்பூச்சி போதும்.
One *grain destroying insect* will consume a thousand grains of rice.

735. ஆயிரம் காக்கைக்குள் ஒரு அன்னம் அகப்பட்டதுபோல.
As a swan in the midst of a thousand crows.

736. ஆயிரம காக்கைக்கு ஒரு கல்லுப்போல.
Like a single stone thrown at a thousand crows.

737. ஆயிரம் கட்டு அண்டத்தைத் தாங்குமா.
Can a thousand props support the universe?

738. ஆயிரம் கட்டு ஆனைப்பலம்.
A thousand bonds may equal the strength of an elephant.

739. ஆயிரம் சொன்னாலும் அவசாரி சமுசாரியாகாள்.
Though a thousand *times* admonished, a faithless woman will not become a faithful wife.

740. ஆயிரத்திலே பிறந்து ஐஞ்ஞூற்றிலே கால் நீட்டினதுபோல.
Like one born with a thousand stretched out his legs with five-hundred.

741. ஆயிரத்தில் ஒருவனே அலங்காரபுருஷன்.
Beauty is found only in one of a thousand.

742. ஆயிரம் நட்சத்திரம் கூடினாலும் ஒரு சந்திரன் ஆகாது.
The combined light of a thousand stars is not equal to a single moon.

743. ஆயிரம் மாகாணி அறுபத்திரண்டரை.
A thousand sixteenths make sixty-two and a half.

744. ஆயிரம் உடையார் அமர்ந்திருப்பார் துணிபொறுக்கி தொந்தோம் தொந்தோம் என்று கூத்தாடுவான்.

He whose fortune amounts to thousands is quiet, while the rag-gatherer leaps for joy.

Dignity is characteristic of the worthy, and levity of the worthless

745. ஆயிரம் வந்தாலும் ஆயத்தொழில் ஆகாது.

Though it may bring in thousands, the occupation of a tax-gatherer is bad

746. ஆயிரம் வருஷம் சென்று செத்தாலும் அநீதச்சா ஆகாது.

Although one may live a thousand years an unnatural death is bad.

747. ஆயிரம் வித்தைகள் கற்றாலும் உலகத்தில் ஆடம்பரங்கள் வேண்டும்.

Although one has acquired a thousand arts, he will still feel the necessity of earthly show.

748. ஆயிரம் பெயரைக் கொன்றவன் அரைவைத்தியன்.

He who has killed a thousand persons is half a doctor.

749. ஆயிரம் வந்தாலும் ஆத்திரம் ஆகாது.

Though a thousand may thereby be obtained, impetuosity is not good.

750. ஆயிரம் பெயர் கூடினாலும் ஒரு அந்துப்பூச்சியைக் கொல்லக்கூடாது.

Though a thousand persons unite, they cannot kill a single grain-insect

751. ஆயிரம் பொன் போட்டு யானை வாங்கி அரைப்பணத்து அங்குசத்துக்குப் பால்மாறுகிறதா?

After laying out thousands for an elephant why hesitate to give half a fanam for a goad?

752. ஆயிரம் அரைக்காறபணம்.

A thousand eighths of a fanam.

753. ஆயிரம் சொல்லுக்கு அரை எழுத்து.

Half a letter *is equal* to a thousand words.

754. ஆயிரம் பசுக்களில் ஒரு பசு உதைத்துக்கொண்டால் நஷ்டமா?

Will it prove a loss if one of a thousand cows kicks?

755. ஆயிரம் பனையுள்ள அப்பனுக்குப் பிறந்தும் பல்லுக் குத்த ஒரு ஈர்க்கும் இல்லை.

Although born of a father possessed of a thousand palmira trees, he has not a fibre with which to pick his teeth.

756. ஆயிரம் பாம்பினுள் ஒரு தேரை அகப்பட்டாற்போல.

Like a toad among a thousand serpents.

757. ஆயிரம் பொன் பெற்ற குதிரைக்கு அரைப்பணத்துச் சவுக்கு.

Half a fanam to buy a whip for a horse worth thousands of gold.

758 ஆயிரம் நற்குணம் ஒரு லோபகுணத்தால் கெடும்.

A single avaricious desire will destroy a thousand good qualities.

759. ஆயிரம் பொன்பெற்ற குதிரைக்கும் சவுக்கடி வேண்டும்.

Even a horse worth thousands of gold may require a whip.

760. ஆயிரம் பொய் சொல்லிக் கோயிலைக் கட்டு.

Tell lies by the thousand and build a temple.

761. ஆயுதபரீக்ஷை அறிந்தவன் நூற்றில் ஒருவன்.

One of a hundred makes a skilful swords-man.

762. ஆயுதம் இல்லாரை அடிக்கிறதா?

What! strike the unarmed?

763. ஆயோதன முகத்தில் ஆயுதம் தேடுகிறதுபோல.

Like seeking a weapon in the face of battle.

764. ஆய்ச்சலாய்ச்சலாய் மழை பெய்கிறது.

It rains in successive torrents.

765. ஆய்ந்து பாராதான் காரியம் தான் சாந்துயரம் தரும்.

An ill-considered undertaking may occasion the agony of death.

766. ஆரக்கழுத்தி அரண்மனைக்கு ஆகாது.

A female with an inauspicious mark on the neck will prove an evil in a king's palace.

767. ஆரடா விட்டது மானியம் நானே விட்டுக்கொண்டேன்.

Sirrah! who invested you with a free tenure, I did it myself.

A long continued favour is regarded as a right.

768. ஆராகிலும் படியளந்து விட்டதா?

Has any one measured out *my* daily allowance?

769. ஆராருக்கு ஆளாவேன் ஆகாத உடம்பையும் புண்ணையும் கொண்டு.

How many shall I serve with this debilitated and ulcerated body!

770. ஆராற் கெட்டேன் நாராற் கெட்டேன்.

By whom was I ruined, by twisted hemp.

771. ஆரியக் கூத்தாடினாலும் காரியத்திற் கண் வேண்டும்.

Although engaged in a mere puppet-show, one ought to keep the eye on the main chance.

772. ஆருக்கும் அஞ்சான் ஆர்படைக்கும் தோலான்.

He is fearless and shrinks not in the presence of any foe.

773. ஆருக்கு ஆர் சதம்?

Who is really true to another?

774. ஆருக்குப் பிறந்து மோருக்கு அழுகிறாய்?

To whom were you born! you cry for butter-milk.

775. ஆருக்காகிலும் துரோகம் செய்தால் ஐந்தாறு நாட்பொறுத்துக் கேட்கும், ஆத்துமத்துரோகம் செய்தால் அப்போதே கேட்கும்.

Treachery against any man will be slowly requited, but treachery against one's self will meet with immediate retribution.

776. ஆருமற்றதே தாரம் ஊரில் ஒருவனே தோழன்.

A wife who has no connections *is to be preferred* and so the friendship of one.

777. ஆரும் ஆரும் உறவு? தாயும் பிள்ளையும் உறவு.

Who are related to each other! the mother and her child.

778. ஆரும் இல்லாத ஊரிலே அசுவமேதயாகம் செய்தானும்.

He is said to have performed Ashwamedha, (the sacrifice of a horse) in an uninhabited country.

---

779. ஆரை நம்பித் தோழா காருக்கு ஏற்றம் போட்டாய்?

My friend, on whom did you depend *for assistance* when you put up a picotta *to irrigate the* kár rice !

An efficient picotta is worked by two, frequently by three men.

---

780. ஆரோ செத்தான் எவனோ அழுதான்.

Some one died : some one cried.

---

781. ஆர் ஆத்தாள் செத்ததும் பொழுது விடிந்தால தெரியும்.

In the morning it will be known whose mother is dead.

---

782. ஆர் கடன் வைத்தாலும் மாரிகடன் வைக்கக்கூடாது.

Whomsoever you delay to pay, the debt of Mári must be at once discharged.

Mári is the Goddess who presides over pestilence, &c.

---

783. ஆர் குடியைக் கெடுக்க ஆண்டிவேஷம் போட்டாய்?

Whose family did you intend to ruin when you assumed the guise of a religious mendicant !

---

784. ஆர் குத்தினாலும் அரிசியானால் சரி.

No matter who pounds it if we obtain the rice.

---

785. ஆலகால விஷம் போன்றவன் அந்தரமாவான்.

He who is as dangerous *to society* as the poison of a serpent will be ruined.

---

786. ஆலசியம் அமிர்தம் விஷம்.

Indolence changes nectar into poison.

---

787. ஆலமரம பழுத்ததென்று பறவைக்கு ஆர் சீட்டனுப்பினர்?

Who informed the birds that the banyan tree was in fruit ?

---

788. ஆலின்மேற் புல்லுருவி.

A parasite on a banyan tree.

789. ஆலும் வேலும் பல்லுக்கு உறுதி நாலும் இரண்டும் சொல்லுக்கு உறுதி.

As the banyan and the acacia strengthen the teeth, so Náladiyàr and Kural give force to speech.

Náladiyar and Kural two celebrated poetic works on moral subjects.

790. ஆலைக் கரும்பும் வேலைத்துரும்புமானேன்.

I am become a bruised reed tossed on the waves.

791. ஆலயம் அறியாது ஓதிய வேதம்.

The temple understands not the hidden meaning of the Vedas.

792. ஆலையில்லா ஊரிலே இலுப்பைப்பூச் சர்க்கரை.

The flowers of the olive, *Bassia*, are regarded as sugar in a place without a *sugar cane* mill

793. ஆலை விழுது தாங்குகிறாப்போலே.

As the pendulous roots of its branches support the banyan tree.

794. ஆல் பழுத்தால் அங்கே அரசு பழுத்தால் இங்கே.

If the banyan be in fruit, thither, if the arasu, hither, *the birds flock.*

795. ஆலபோல் விழுதுவிட்டு, அறுகுபோல வேரோடி மூங்கில்போற் சுற்றம் முசியாமல் வாழ்ந்திருக்க.

May you prosper as the banyan with its daughter-stems, take root like the wide-spreading arugu grass, and as the bamboo amid unfailing friends.

A congratulatory expression to a newly married couple.

796. ஆவணிமாதம் அழுகல் தூற்றல்.

The month of August is attended with incessant drizzling.

797. ஆவத்தை அடரான் பாவத்தை தொடரான்.

He is not subject to calamity who pursues not a sinful course.

798. ஆவல்மாத்திரம் இருந்தால் என்ன, அன்னம் இறங்கினால் அல்லவோ பிழைப்பான்?

What avails mere desire, he will live, will he not, if he swallows rice!

799. ஆவாரை இலையும் ஆபத்துக்குதவும்.

Even the leaves of the àvárai may be useful in misfortune.

---

800. ஆவென்று போனபிறகு அள்ளி இடுகிறது ஆர்?

After his last gasp who will distribute *our food*?

---

801. ஆவேறு நிறமானாலும், பால்வேறு நிறமாமோ?

Will the colour of the skin of a cow affect that of its milk?

---

802. ஆழமறியும் ஓங்கில் மேளம் அறியும் அரவம்.

The ónkil fish is acquainted with depth, and the snake knows the sound of a drum.

This reference to the instincts of animals serves to indicate the aptitude &c., of individuals.

---

803. ஆழம் அறியாமல் காலை விடாதே.

Do not step down unless you know the depth.

---

804. ஆழாக்கு அரிசி மூழாக்குப்பானை முதலியார் வருகிற வீறுப்பைப் பாரும்.

With an àlak of rice in hand and a pot that will suffice to boil only three fourths of it look at the ostentation the Mudáliar displays.

---

805. ஆழியெல்லாம் வயலானால் என்ன அவனியெல்லாம் அன்னமயமானால் என்ன?

What if the great deep were an extended field and all the world standing corn?

Even then each could enjoy only what he might consume.

---

806. ஆளமாட்டாதவனுக்குப் பெண்டேன்?

Of what use is a wife to him who cannot govern her?

---

807. ஆளனில்லாத் துக்கம் அழுதாலுந் தீராது.

The grief occasioned by the death of a husband will not be removed by a flood of tears.

808. ஆளன் இல்லாதவள ஆற்று மணலுக்குச் சரி.
She who has no husband is like sand in the bed of a river.
Uncertain as to position.

809. ஆளான ஆட்களுக்கு அவிழ் அகப்படாக் காலத்திலே காகா பிசாசு கஞ்சிக்கு அழுகிறது.
The raven demon crying for kanji when the well-to-do cannot obtain a grain of boiled rice.

810. ஆளுக்கு ஒரு குட்டுக் குட்டினலும் அவனுக்குப் புத்தி வராது.
Although each of you may cuff the fellow, he will not thereby become wiser.

811. ஆளுக்கு ஒரு குட்டுக் குட்ட அடியேன் தலை மிடாப்போல.
Being buffeted by every one, my head has become as large as a water-pot.

812. ஆளுக்குள்ளே ஆளாயிருப்பான்.
He may escape recognition in a crowd.

813. ஆளை அறிந்துதான் அறுக்கிறான்.
After ascertaining the character of the person he undermines his interests.

814. ஆளை ஆள் அறியவேண்டும் மீனைப் புளியங்காய் அறியவேண்டும்.
Man must be tested by man and fish by tamarind acid.

815. ஆளை ஆள் குத்தும் ஆள்மிடுக்குப் பத்துப் பேரைக் குத்தும்.
Personal valor enables one to encounter an enemy, but outward show will scare away ten.

816. ஆளைச் சுற்றிப்பாராமல் அளக்கிறதா?
What, do you take your measure of a person without eyeing him all around?

817. ஆளைப் பார் முகத்தைப் பார்.
Look at the person, look at his face.
Spoken in derision of a boaster.

818. ஆளைப் பார்த்து வாயால் ஏய்த்தான்.
He eyed the man and deceived him by his talk.

819. ஆள் ஆளைக் குத்தும், பகடம் பத்துப் பேரைக் குத்தும்.
One man may stab one, threatening may stab ten.

820. ஆள் இல்லாமல் ஆயுதம் வெட்டுமா?
Will a sword cut *unwielded* ?

821. ஆள் இருக்கக் கொலை சாயுமா?
Is he who is yet alive, murdered ?

822. ஆள் இல்லாப் படை அம்பலம்.
Mere weapons are ineffective.

823. ஆள் இளந்தலை கண்டால தோணி மிதக்கப் பாயும்.
When a dhony finds her steersman unskilful she pitches.
Spoken of something going wrong from want of skill.

824. ஆள் ஏற நீர் ஏறும்.
As men embark, the *surrounding* water rises.

825. ஆள் கொஞ்சமாகிலும் ஆயுதம மிடுக்கு.
Though feeble in person, his weapon is powerful.

826. ஆள் மெத்தக் கூடினல் மீன் மெத்தப் பிடிக்கலாம்.
When numerous fishermen combine together, multitudes of fish may be caught.

827. ஆறல்ல நூறல்ல ஆகிறது ஆகட்டும்.
Neither six nor a hundred *are required,* let that be which will be.

828. ஆரும் பேறு பெண்ணுய்ப் பிறந்தால் ஆருன குடித்தனம் நீருய் விடும்.
If the sixth-born be a female, a family of overflowing wealth will be reduced to powder.

829. ஆறிலும் சாவு நூறிலும் சாவு.
Death may occur at six, or at a hundred years of age.

830. ஆறின கஞ்சி பழங்கஞ்சி.

Cold kanji is old kanji.

831. ஆறின புண்ணிலும் அசடு நிற்கும்.

There will be a scab even after the wound is healed.

Interrupted amity though restored will occasion suspicion.

832. ஆறினல் அச்சிலே வார் ஆருவிட்டால் மிடாவிலே வார்.

If cool pour it into the mould, if not pour it into the large *earthen* pot.

833. ஆறு கடக்குமளவும் அண்ணன் தம்பியெனல், ஆறு கடந்தால் நீயார் நானர்.

To avow fraternal relationship until the river is crossed; and to ignore it on arriving at the opposite bank.

834. ஆறு கலியாணம் மூனறு பெண்கள் மாரோடு மார் தள்ளுகிறது.

Where six marriages *are being celebrated* three women are pressing and pushing.

835. ஆறு காதம் என்கிறபோதே கோவணத்தை அவிழ்ப்பானேன்?

Why loose your waist-cloth on mentioning that the river is yet ten miles off?

836. ஆறு கெட நாணல் இடு ஊர்கெட நூலை இடு.

Plant reeds to destroy a river, to destroy a country introduce yarn.

Weavers who neglect tillage, and foul the water by dying processes &c are here referred to.

837. ஆறு கொண்டது பாதி தூறு கொண்டது பாதி.

The river has destroyed one half and the jungle the other.

838. ஆறு நிறையச் சலம் போனாலும் பாய்கிறது கொஞ்சம் சாய்கிறது கொஞசம்.

Though the river is in full flood part of it flows on *in its course*, and part diverges.

839. ஆறு நிறையப் போனாலும் நாய்க்கு நக்குத் தண்ணீர்.

Though the river is full to overflowing, a dog laps.

Amid the greatest abundance one can only enjoy what is required.

840. ஆறு நீந்தின எனக்குக் குளம் நீந்துவது அரிதோ?

Having swum a river, will it be difficult for me to swim over a tank?

841. ஆறு நீந்தினவனுக்கு வாய்க்கால் எவ்வளவு?

What is a mere channel to him who has swum a river?

842. ஆறு நேராய்ப் போகாது.

A river never flows straight.

843. ஆறு நேரான ஊர் நிலை நில்லாது.

A town in the course of a river will not endure.

844. ஆறு பார்க்கப் போக ஆய்ச்சிக்குப் பிடித்தது சலுப்பு.

The old dame caught a cold by going to look at the river.

845. ஆறு போவதே போக்கு அரசன் சொல்வதே தீர்ப்பு.

The flow of a river is its course, the utterance of a ruler is his decision.

846. ஆறு மாசப் பயணம் அஞ்சி நடந்தால் முடியுமா?

Can a six months journey be accomplished *if the party* walks hesitatingly?

An arduous enterprize requires unremitted exertion.

847. ஆறு மாதம் காட்டிலே, ஆறு மாதம் வீட்டிலே.

Six months in the jungle and six at home.

848. ஆறு மாதத்துக்குச் சனியன் பிடித்தாற்போல.

As Saturn seized one for six months *together*.

849. ஆறும் கடன் நூறும் கடன் பெருக்கச் சுடடா பணிகாரத்தை.

Debt is debt whether it amounts to six or a hundred; you fellow bake the cakes large.

850. ஆறு வடிவிலேயும் கரிப்புத் தெளிவிலேயும் வருத்தம்.

Their severity is most felt, when a flood subsides, and a famine terminates.

---

851. ஆறெல்லாம் கண்ணீர் அடி எல்லாம் செங்குருதி.

All the way is bedewed with tears, and the foot-prints are red with blood.

---

852. ஆற்றித் தூற்றி அம்பலத்தில் வைக்கப் பார்க்கிறான்.

He aims to expose me, after comforting and abusing me.

---

353. ஆற்றிலே போகிற தண்ணீரை அப்பா குடி, ஐயா குடி.

Drink sir, and drink the water that is flowing in the river.

Spoken of apparent generosity which in reality costs nothing.

---

854. ஆற்றிலே ஒரு காலும் சேற்றிலே ஒரு காலுமாய் இருக்கிறான்.

He has one foot in the river and one in mud.

Said of one involved in inextricable difficulty.

---

855. ஆற்றிலே போட்டாலும் அளந்துபோட வேண்டும்.

Although you are throwing it into the river, measure it first.

---

856. ஆற்றிலே கணுக்கால் தண்ணீரிலும் அஞ்சி நடப்பது உண்டு.

Though water in a river is up to one's ankle only, some will wade with hesitation.

---

857. ஆற்றிலே ஊருகிறது மணலிலே சுவறுகிறது.

Creeping along a river and sinking in the sand.

---

858. ஆற்றிலே விட்ட தெர்ப்பைபோல் தவிக்கிறேன்.

I am tossed about like a *tuft* of sacred grass that has been thrown into a river.

---

859. ஆற்றிற் கரைத்த புளியும் அங்காடிக்கிட்ட பதருமாயிற்று.

It is the pulp of the tamarind fruit dissolved in a river, and chaff sent to the bazaar.

Said of things useless and unavailing.

860. ஆற்றிற் பெருவெள்ளம் நாய்க்கென்ன சளப்புத் தண்ணீர்.

The river is in flood, but what of that to a dog? it is only a fordable stream.

861. ஆற்றுக்குப் பார்ப்பான் துணையா, சோற்றுக்குப் பயற்றங்காய் கறியா?

Will a Brahman be of any use when one crosses a river, or pulse in pod serve for a curry!

862. ஆற்றுக்கும் பயம் காற்றுக்கும் பயம்.

Both the river and weather are dreaded.

863. ஆற்றுக்குப் போனதும் இல்லை செருப்புக் கழற்றினதும் இல்லை.

I neither went to the river, nor put off my shoes.

864. ஆற்றுப்பெருக்கும் அரசும் அரை நாழி.

The flood of a river and the reign of a king last but half an hour.

865. ஆற்று மணலை அளவிடக்கூடாது.

The sands of a river cannot be counted.

866. ஆற்று நீரை நாய் நக்கிக் குடிக்குமோ எடுத்துக் குடிக்குமோ?

How does a dog drink the water of a river, by lapping or by lading?

867. ஆற்றைக் கடந்தல்லோ அக்கரை ஏறவேண்டும்?

Before ascending its opposite bank it is necessary first, is it not, to cross the river?

868. ஆற்றைக் கடந்தால் ஓடக்காரனுக்கு ஒரு சொட்டு.

After crossing the river the boatman gets a cuff.

869. ஆற்றைக் கடத்திவிடு ஆகாசத்திற் பறக்கக் குளிகை தருகிறேன் என்கிறான்.

He says, carry me over the river and I will give you a pill that will enable you to fly through the air.

870. ஆனதல்லாமல் ஆவதறிவாரோ?

Can one comprehend the future as well as the past?

871. ஆன தெய்வத்தை ஆறு கொண்டுபோகிறது அனுமந்தராயனு க்குத் தெப்பத்திருவிழாவா?

After the river has carried away every imaginable deity, do you stay to celebrate an aquatic festival in honour of Hanuman!

Said of one seeking the lesser aid when the greater has failed.

---

872. ஆனமட்டும் ஆதாளியடித்துப்போட்டு, ஆந்தைபோல் விழிக் கிறான்.

Having spent all he stares like an owl.

---

873. ஆனமுதலை அழித்தவன் மானம் இழப்பது அரிதல்ல.

Having lost his capital, it will not be difficult for him to lose his reputation.

---

874. ஆனவன் ஆகாதவன் எல்லாத்திலும் உண்டு.

The good and the bad exist among all.

---

875. ஆனால் அச்சிலே வார்க்கிறேன் ஆகாவிட்டால் மிடாவிலே வார்க் கிறேன்.

If I succeed I will pour it into a mould, if not, into a large pot.

Accommodating one's conduct to circumstances.

---

876. ஆனி அடியிடாதே கூனி குடிபோகாதே.

Do not begin to build in June; nor set out to occupy a house in March.

---

877. ஆனி அரை ஆறு, ஆவணி முழு ஆறு.

In June half a river, in August a full river.

---

878. ஆனி ஆனை வாலொத்த கரும்பு.

In June sugar-cane is like an elephant's tail.

---

879. ஆனை அசைந்து தின்னும் வீடு அசையாமல் தின்னும்.

An elephant moves when eating, a house eats without moving.

---

880. ஆனை ஆசாரவாசலைக் காக்கும், பூனை புழுத்த மீனைக் காக்கும்.

An elephant waits before the outer hall of a king's court; a cat watches the putrid fish.

881. ஆனை ஆயிரம் பெற்றால் அடியும் ஆயிரம் பெறுமா?

If an elephant fetch a thousand, will the mark of his footstep be worth so much?

882. ஆனை இருந்து அரசாண்ட இடத்திலே பூனை இருந்து புலம்பி அழுகிறது.

A cat sits and mews in the place once occupied by the royal elephant.

883. ஆனை இலைக்கறி பூனை பொரிக்கறி.

An ordinary curry for an elephant and a superior curry for a cat.

884. ஆனை உண்ட விளாங்கனி போல.

Like a blighted wood-apple swallowed by an elephant.

885. ஆனை ஏறியும் சந்துவழி நுழைவானேன்?

Why enter by a corner when mounted on an elephant?

886. ஆனை ஏறித் திட்டிவாயில் நுழைவாரா?

Will one mounted on an elephant enter through a wicket?

887. ஆனை ஒரு குட்டிபோட்டும் பலன், பன்றி பல குட்டிபோட்டும் பயன் இல்லை.

It is of value though an elephant brings forth a single young one; but the many young ones of a pig are of no value.

One good thing is better than ten bad ones.

888. ஆனை கட்டத் தூர் வானமுட்டப் போர்.

The stalks *of the grain* are so strong that an elephant may be tied to them, and the stacks are as high as the heavens.

Said in exaggeration of an abundant harvest.

889. ஆனை கண்ட பிறவிக்குருடர் அடித்துக்கொள்ளுகிறதுபோல.

As the blind quarrelled about an elephant they had examined.

890. ஆனை கறுத்திருந்தும் ஆயிரம் பொன் பெறும்.

Though black, an elephant will fetch a thousand gold pieces.

891. ஆனை காணுமற்போனாற் குண்டுச்சட்டியில் தேடினால் அகப்படுமா ?
If an elephant be lost, is it to be sought in an earthen pot ?

892. ஆனை குண்டுச் சட்டியினும் குழிசியினும் உண்டோ ?
Is the elephant in the rice-pot or in the water-pot ?

893. ஆனை கேட்ட வாயால், ஆட்டுக் குட்டி கேட்கிறதா ?
What, does the mouth that asked for an elephant ask for a lamb ?

894. ஆனை கொடுத்தும் அங்குசத்திற்குப் பிணக்கா ?
Having given the elephant is there a dispute about the goad ?

895. ஆனை கொடிற்றில் அடக்குகிறதுபோல எந்தமட்டும் அடக்குகிறது ?
How long shall I conceal *it* as an elephant incloses *a thing* in his jaws ?

896. ஆனைக் கவடும் பூனைத் திருடும்.
The deceit of an elephant and the thievishness of a cat.

897. ஆனைக்கு அறுபது முழம் அறக்குள்ளனுக்கு எழுபது முழம்.
Keep away from an elephant sixty cubits, and from a dwarf seventy cubits.

898. ஆனைக்கும் பானைக்கும் சரி.
The same reason is applicable alike to elephants and earthen pots.

899. ஆனைக்கும் புலிக்கும் நெருப்பைக் கண்டால் பயம்.
The elephant and tiger are afraid of fire.

900. ஆனைக்கும் அடி சறுக்கும்.
Even an elephant may slip.

901. ஆனைக்குத் தீனியிடும் வீட்டில், ஆட்டுக்குட்டிக்குப் பஞ்சமா ?
Will a lamb be famished in a place where elephants are fed ?

902. ஆனைக் கூட்டத்திற் சிங்கம் புகுந்ததுபோல.
As if a lion had entered a herd of elephants.

903. ஆனைக்குத் தேரை உணவோ?
Are toads fit for elephant's food?

904. ஆனைக்குத் துறடும் அன்னத்துக்கு மிளகாயும் வேண்டும்.
An elephant requires a goad, and boiled rice a chilli (condiment.)

905. ஆனைக்கு இல்லை கானலும் மழையும்.
An elephant is not affected by sunshine or rain.

906. ஆனைக்கு ஒரு காலம் பூனைக்கு ஒரு காலம்.
The elephant has its time, the cat also has its time.

907. ஆனை செத்தாலும் ஆயிரம் பொன்.
Although dead, an elephant will fetch a thousand gold pieces.

908. ஆனை தழுவிய கையாலே ஆடு தழுவுகிறதோ?
What! does the hand that has caressed an elephant caress a sheep?

909. ஆனை தன் தலையில் தானே மண்ணைப் போட்டுக்கொள்ளும்.
The elephant will put sand on its own head.

To see this done by wild elephants when travelling through a jungle is very interesting.

910. ஆனை தன்னைக் கட்டச் சங்கிலியைத் தானே கொடுத்ததுபோல.
As an elephant gives the chain to tether himself.

Said of one who, whether consciously or not, supplies means to his own disadvantage

911. ஆனை துரத்திவந்தாலும் ஆலயத்தில் நுழையலாகாது.
Though chased by an elephant, it is not right to enter a temple.

912. ஆனை நிழலைப் பார்க்கத் தவளை கலங்கினாற்போலே.
As a frog trembled at the shadow of an elephant.

913. ஆனை படுத்தால் ஆள்மட்டம்.
When an elephant lies down its height will equal the stature of a man.

914. ஆனை படுத்தால் ஆட்டுக்குட்டிக்குத் தாழுமா?
When an elephant lies down, will he be lower than a lamb?

915. ஆனை பார்க்க வெள்ளெழுத்தா?

Are your eyes too dim to see an elephant?

You must be blind indeed.

---

916. ஆனை போன வீதி.

The street by which an elephant passed.

---

917. ஆனைமிதிக்கப் பிழைப்பார்களா?

Has any survived after being trodden under foot by an elephant?

---

918. ஆனை முட்டத் தாள் வானமுட்டப் போர்.

Stubble as high as an elephant, stacks towering to the skies.

---

919. ஆனை மேயும் காட்டில் ஆட்டுக்குட்டி மேய இடம் இல்லையா?

Is there not room for a lamb to crop its food in a jungle where elephants feed?

---

920. ஆனைமேலே போகிறவனைச் சுண்ணாம்பு கேட்டாற்போல.

Like asking chunam (lime) of one who is going along on an elephant.

---

921. ஆனைமேல் இட்ட பாரம் பூனைமேல இட்டாற்போல.

As if an elephant's load was transferred to a cat.

---

922. ஆனையும் அறுகம்புல்லினால் தடைபடும்.

Even an elephant may be impeded by arugu, *Agrostis linearis*, grass.

This grass is sacred to Ganèsa.

---

923. ஆனையும் ஆனையும் முட்டும்போது இடையில் அகப்பட்ட கொசுகுபோல.

As a gnat between two elephants that are brought into collision.

---

924. ஆனையை வித்துவானுக்கும் பூனையைக் குறவனுக்கும் கொடு.

Give an elephant to a pundit, and a cat to a mountaineer.

---

925. ஆனையைக் கொன்றவன் பூனையை வெல்லமாட்டானா?

Is he who slew an elephant unable to overcome a cat?

926. ஆனையை ஆயிரம் பொன்னுக்கு வாங்கி இருப்பு அங்குசத்திற்கு ஏமாந்து நிற்பானேன்?

After having paid a thousand gold pieces for an elephant, why hesitate to buy an iron goad?

---

927. ஆனையைக் குத்திச் சுளகாலே மூடுவாள்.

She willl stab the elephant and cover it with a sieve.

---

928. ஆனையைக் கட்டிச் சுளகாலே மறைப்பாள்.

Having tied the elephant she will cover it with a winnowing fan!

---

929. ஆனையைத்தேடக் குடத்துக்குள் கை வைத்ததுபோல

Like putting one's hand into a water-pot in search of a missing elephant.

---

930. ஆனையை விற்றுத் துறட்டிக்கு மன்றாடுகிறான்.

Having sold the elephant he begs for the goad.

---

931. ஆனையைத் தண்ணீரில் இழுக்கிற முதலை, பூனையைத் தரையில் இழுக்குமா?

Can an alligator which can draw an elephant in water, drag a cat on dry ground?

---

632. ஆனை வரும் பின்னே மணி ஓசை வரும் முன்னே.

The sound of the bell is heard before the elephant makes its appearance.

Spoken of events which cast their shadows before.

---

933. ஆனை வால் பிடித்துக் கரையேறலாம் ஆட்டுக்குட்டியின் வால் பிடித்துக் கரையேறலாமா?

One can cross a river by holding the tail of an elephant can one do so by holding the tail of a sheep?

---

931. ஆனை விழுந்தால் கொம்பு, புலி விழுந்தால் தோல்.

On the death of an elephant the tusk remains, on the death of a tiger the skin.

935. ஆனை விழுங்கிய அம்மையாருக்குப் பூனை சுண்டாங்கி.

A cat will be a small thing to an old dame who swallowed an elephant.

936. ஆனை விழுந்தாற் குதிரை மட்டம்.

When down, an elephant is as high as a horse.

937. ஆனை வேகம் அடங்கும் துறட்டியால்.

The force of an elephant is subdued by the goad.

இ.

938. இகழ்ச்சியுடையோன் புகழ்ச்சியடையான்.

The contemptible will not be praised.

939. இக்கரையில் பாகலைப் போட்டு அக்கரையில் கொழுகொம்பு நடுகிறான்.

He puts down the seed pagal (a creeper) on this side of the river and erects a supporting pole on that.

940. இங்கு இருந்த பாண்டம்போல.

Like a vessel that contained assafœtida.

941. இச்சித்த காரியம் இரகசியம் அல்லவே.

A thing that is greatly desired is not secret.

942. இஞ்சி தின்ற குரங்குபோல.

Like a monkey that has eaten green ginger.

943. இடக்கனுக்கு வழி எங்கே? கிடக்கிறவன் தலைமேலே.

Where is the way of the perverse? on the head of the man that is lying down.

944. இடங்கொடுத்தால் மடம் பிடுங்குவான்.

If permitted he will pull down the choultry.

Intimating that persons of violent tendencies must be at once repressed.

945. இடதுகைக்கு வலதுகை துணை வலதுகைக்கு இடதுகை துணை.

The right hand helps the left and the left the right.

946. இடம் வலம் தெரியாதவனோடு இணக்கம் பண்ணக்கூடாது.

One may not make friendship with him who does not know the right side from the left.

Intimating that one must have nothing to do with fools.

947. இடி ஓசை கேட்ட பாம்புபோல.

Like a snake that has heard thunder.

948. இடிக்குக் குடை பிடிக்கலாமா?

Will an umbrella be of any use in a thunder-storm?

949. இடுகிற தெய்வம் எங்கும் இடும்.

A liberal deity will give every where.

950. இடுப்பு வைத்த இடமெல்லாம் அடுப்பு வைத்தான்.

In every place on which he reclined he constructed a hearth.

Spoken of one who takes care of himself.

951. இடுப்பு ஒடிந்த கோழிக்கு உரற் குழியே கதி.

The mortar hole is the asylum of the fowl with a broken back.

952. இடும்பு செய்வார்க்கு இராப் பகல் நித்திரை இல்லை.

Oppressors sleep not day or night

953. இடுவது பிச்சை பெறுவது மோக்ஷம்.

Alms-giving secures heavenly bliss.

954. இடுவார் பிச்சையைக் கெடுவார் கெடுப்பார்.

The evil-disposed will destroy the good deeds of the beneficent.

955. இடுவாள் இடுவாளென்று ஏக்கற்று இருந்தாளாம், நாழி நெல்லுக் கொடுத்து நாலாசையும் தீர்த்தாளாம்.

It is said that she waited patiently for her mistress assured she would be rewarded; and at length she got a measure of rice, and her four desires were met.

956. இடைக்கணக்கன் செத்தான், இனிப் பிழைப்பான் நாட்டான்.

The curnam of the shepherd caste is dead, henceforth the peasant may prosper.

---

957. இடை சாய்ந்த குடம் கிடை.

The water-pot remains aslant as when put down.

---

958. இடைத்தெருவில் கோலம் வரும்போது குசத்தெரு எங்கே என்கிறாள்?

When the *marriage* procession comes along the shepherd's street she asks where the potter's street is.

---

959. இடைப்பிறப்பும் கடைப்பிறப்பும் ஆகாது.

Middle and lower ranks in life are not good.

960. இடைப் புத்தி பிடரியிலே.

The sense of the shepherd is in his neck.

---

961. இடையன் கெடுத்தது பாதி மடையன் கெடுத்தது பாதி.

The shepherd destroyed half, and the simpleton destroyed !

---

962. இடையன் கலியாணம் விடியும்பொழுது.

A shepherd's marriage *takes place* at day-break.

---

963. இடையாண்டியும் குசத்தாதனும் இல்லை.

Among shepherds there are no Saiva mendicants, among potters there are no Vaishnava mendicants.

---

964. இடையூறு செய்தோன் மனையில் இருக்கலாது பேய்முதலாய்?

Even a demon will not haunt the dwelling of him that defeats the hopes of another.

---

965. இட்ட எழுத்திற்கு ஏற ஆசைப்பட்டால் கிடைக்குமா?

If one's desires are in excess of destiny, will they be obtained?

---

966. இட்டதன்மேல் ஏறுசைப்படுகிறதா?

Is it fit to wish for more than what is already given!

967. இட்டவன் இடாவிட்டால் வெட்டுப்பகை.

If the giver cease to give, mortal hatred will ensue.

968. இட்டார்க்கு இடு, செத்தார்க்கு அழு.

Give to those who have given, weep for the dead.

969. இட்டு வைத்தால் தின்னவும் எடுத்து வைத்தால் சுமக்கவும் தெரியும்.

He knows how to eat if food be set before him, and he knows how to carry if the burden be laid upon him.

970. இணங்காரோடு இணங்குவது இகழ்ச்சி.

To associate with the obstinate will bring disgrace.

971. இது என்ன வெள்ளரிக்காய் விற்ற பட்டணமா?

What! is this a town in which water-melons were sold?

972. இத்தனை பெரியவன் கையைப் பிடித்தால் எப்படி மாட்டேன் என்கிறது?

When so great a personage takes one by the hand, how can one say nay!

973. இத்தனை அத்தனை ஆனால் அத்தனை எத்தனை ஆகும்?

If this amouts to that how much will that come to?

974. இந்த அடிக்கு எந்த நாயும் சாகும்.

Such a blow would kill any dog.

975. இந்த எலும்பைக் கடிப்பானேன் சொந்தப்பல்லும் போவானேன்?

Why gnaw this bone, and why lose one's own teeth!

976. இந்தக் கூழுக்கோ இத்தனை திருநாமம்?

Is it for this gruel that so many sacred namams *are used*?

977. இந்தக் கூழுக்கா இருபத்தெட்டு நாமம்?

What, is it for this gruel that I have made twenty-eight námams *sectarial marks*

978. இந்தக்கரிப்பிற் செத்தால், இன்னம் ஒரு கரிப்பு மயிரைப் பிடுங்குமா?

If one die during this famine will another famine pull off his hair?

979. இந்தப் பூனையும் பால் குடிக்குமா என்றாற்போல் இருக்கிறான்?

He is as if one said of a cat, will this also drink milk?

980. இந்தப் பெருமையும் பந்தல் அழகும் பார்த்தையா பண்ணைக்காரா?

O, headman, hast thou noticed this greatness, and the beauty of the Pandal?

981. இந்த நாயை ஏன் இப்படிச் செய்கிறாய்?

Why do you treat this dog in this way?

982. இந்திரனைச் சந்திரனை இலையாலே மறைப்பாள், எமதருமராஜனைக் கையாலே மறைப்பாள்.

She will conceal Jupiter and the moon with a leaf, and Yama, the *regent of the dead,* with her hand.

983. இமைக் குற்றம் கண்ணுக்குத் தெரியாது.

The defects in the eye-lashes are not apparent to the eye.

984. இயமன் ஒருவனைக் கொல்வான், ஏற்றம் மூவரைக் கொல்லும்.

Yama *the regent of the dead,* kills one *at a time,* a picotta may kill three *at once.*

985. இயற்கை வாசனையோ செயற்கை வாசனையோ?

Is the habit natural or acquired?

986. இரக்கம் இல்லாதான் நெஞ்சம் இரும்பிலும் கடிது.

The heart of one void of compassion is harder than iron.

987. இரக்கப் போனாலும் சிறக்கப் போகவேண்டும்.

Though you go a-begging, go decently attired.

988. இரங்காதவர் உண்டா? பெண் என்றால் பேயும் இரங்கும்.

Are there those who have no pity? If the word woman be uttered even a demon will be moved with compassion.

989. இரண்டு ஆட்டிலே ஊட்ட விட்ட குட்டிபோல.
Like a lamb allowed to suck two sheep.
Spoken of a youth full of strength and activity.

990. இரண்டு பட்ட ஊரில் குரங்கும் குடி இராது.
Even a monkey will not stay in a village divided against itself.

991. இரண்டு தோணியில் கால வைக்கிறதா?
Is it to plant your feet on two dhonies.

992. இரண்டு பெண்டாட்டிக்காரன் வீட்டில் நெருப்பேன்?
Why fire in the house of a man that has two wives!

993. இரண்டு வீட்டிலும் கலியாணம இடையிலே செத்ததாம நாய்க் குட்டி.
It is said that the pup died between two houses where marriage festivities were going on.

994. இரண்டு நாய்க்கு ஒரு எலும்பு போட்டதுபோல.
As a bone thrown to two dogs.

995. இரந்தும் பரத்துக்கு இடு.
Though you have to beg them, make your offerings to God.

996. இரந்தோர்க்கு ஈவது உடையார் கடன்.
It is the duty of the rich to give *alms* to beggars.

997. இரப்பவனுக்கு வெண்சோறு பஞ்சமா?
Is it difficult for a beggar to get fine rice?

998. இரப்பவனுக்கு எங்கும் பஞ்சம் இல்லை.
A beggar nowhere suffers from famine.

999. இரவல் உடைமை இசைவாய் இருக்கிறது, என் பிள்ளை ஆணை நான் கொடுக்கமாட்டேன்.
The thing borrowed suits; I swear by my child that I will not return it

1000. இரவல் சதமா, திருடன் உறவா?
Is a *thing* borrowed a durable possession, is a thief a friend!

1001. *இரவற் சோறு பஞ்சம் தாங்குமா?*

Will borrowed rice prove a security against famine?

1002. *இரவற் சீலையை நம்பி இடுப்புக் கந்தையை எறிந்தாளாம்.*

It is said, that relying on a borrowed cloth, she threw away her tattered cloth.

1003. *இராகு திசையில் வாழ்ந்தவனும் இல்லை, ராஜ திசையிற் கெட்டவனும் இலலை.*

None ever prospered under Ràhu, nor was any one ever ruined under Jupiter.

Rahu is the name of a monstrous serpent or dragon, the ascending node, and regarded as one of the nine planets, which, with Kèthu the descending node, is said to grasp the sun and moon periodically, and thus to cause eclipses. When the supernals assembled at a feast to drink the water of immortality obtained from the churning of the milky ocean Rahu and Kethu, two *Asuras*, clandestinely got admission. The sun and moon saw them and at once informed Vishnu of their presence Vishnu dispatched his marvellous disc and decapitated them just as the coveted nectar was about to enter their throats They to avenge themselves resolved periodically to swallow the sun and moon.

1004. *இராக் கண்ட சனி மிடாப்போல வீங்கின கதை.*

The story of one who in a dream of the night saw Saturn swelling as a large pot.

1005. *இராசன் ஏறிய குதிரையைப்போல்.*

Like a horse ridden by a king.

1006. *இராசமுகத்துக்கு எலுமிச்சம் பழம்போல.*

As a lemon offered to a king.

A gift to procure his favour: a hindu when offering a lemon or fruit of any kind invariably does so with the right hand.

1007. *இராச கீரியைக் காவுகிறதுபோல.*

Like carrying a royal mongoose.

1008. *இராசன் ஆனாலும் தன் தாய்க்கு மகனே.*

Though a king, he is the son of his mother.

1009. இராசன் செங்கோல் தன் நாடுவரையில்.

A king's sceptre extends to the limit of his territory.

1010. இராசா மகள் ஆனாலும் கொண்டவனுக்குப் பெண்டுதான்.

Though a princess, she is the wife of the man who has taken her in marriage.

1011. இராசாளியைக் கண்ட கொக்குப்போல

Like a heron which saw a falcon.

1012. இராசா கடன்பட்ட புளுககை காடித்தண்ணீர் குடித்ததுபோல.

As a slave lived on gruel because the king was in debt.

1013. இராப்பட்டினி கிடந்தவன் உரித்த வாழைப்பழம் விற்கிறதா என்று விசாரித்தானாம்.

It is said that he who starved the whole night inquired if peeled plantains could be obtained.

1014. இராப்பட்டினி கிடப்பவன் அகவிலை கேட்பானோ ?

Does he who lies down at night fasting, enquire after the price of grain ?

1015. இராப்பட்டினி பாயோடே.

The sense of hunger *ends* on the mat.

1016. இராப்பகல கண்ணிலே.

In the eye night and day.

1017. இராமர் இருந்த இடம் அயோத்தி.

Ayodhya was the city of Ràma.

1018. இராமன் மங்கையோடு இணங்கியது அவம.

Acquiescence with the wishes of his wife was fatal to Ràma.

1019. இராமனைப்போல ராஜா இருந்தால் அனுமானைப்போலச் சேவகனும் இருப்பான்.

If the king be equal to Ráma, his servant may be equal to Hanumàn.

Hanumán was the monkey chief, ally of Rama in his expedition against *Lanka.*

1020. இரா முழுதும் ராமாயணம் கேட்டுச சீதைக்கு ராமன் என்ன என்ற கதை.

The story of one who having listened to the reading of the Rámayana a whole night, asked what relationship existed between Síta and Ráma.

1021. இராமேசுரத்துக்குப் போயும் சனீசுரன் தொலையவில்லை.

Though he went on a pilgrimage to Ràmèswaram, Saturn has not left him.

1022. இராவணன் குடிக்கு மகோதரன் போலும், சுயோதனன குடிக்குச் சகுனிபோலும்.

He is what Mahódharan was to the family of Rávana and what Sakuni was to Suyodhana.

Said of one who under professions of friendship secretly plots one's ruin.

1023. இராவண சந்நியாசிபோல் இருக்கிறான்.

He is as Ràvana in the guise of a hermit.

1024. இராவுத்தனைத் தள்ளினதும் அல்லாமல் குழியும பறித்ததாம் குதிரை.

It is said that the horse not only threw his rider, but dug his grave also.

1025. இருக்கிற அன்றைக்கு எருமைமாடு தின்றாற்போல.

Like a buffalo he consumes the day's supply.

1026. இருக்கிறவன் செவ்வையாய் இருந்தால் சிரைக்கிறவன் செவ்வையாய்ச் சிரைப்பான்.

If he who is being shaved sits properly, the barber will shave well.

1027. இருக்க வேண்டும் என்றால் இரும்பைத் தின்.

If you wish to live *long*, eat iron.

1028. இருக்க இருக்க எல்லாம் இசைவாகும்.

In time all will be in harmony.

1029. இருக்கும் இடம் ஏவுமா?

Will the place on which we sit, incite?

1030. இருசி உடைமை இராத்தங்கல் ஆகாது.

Oblations made to a demoness must not be kept till the morning.

1031. இரு சுழி, இருந்து உண்டாலும் உண்ணும், இரந்து உண்டாலும் உண்ணும்.

He who has a double twirl *of hair*, may live either on his own resources or by begging.

1032. இருட்டு வேலையோ குருட்டு வேலையோ?

Was the work done in the dark or by the blind?

1033. இருட்டு வீட்டுக்குள் போனால் திருட்டுக்கை நிற்குமா?

Will his thievish hand be restrained when he enters a dark room?

1034. இருட்டுக் குடிவாழ்க்கைத் திருட்டுக்கு அடையாளம்.

It is a sign of thievishness for a family to live in obscurity.

1035. இருதலை மணியன் பாம்பைப்போல.

Like a snake that has a head at both ends.

1036. இருதலைக்கொள்ளி எறும்புபோல் ஆனேன்.

I have become like an ant on a fire-brand lighted at both ends.

Spoken when in danger from opposite quarters.

1037. இருந்தல்லோ படுக்கவேண்டும்?

Must one not sit before lying down?

1038. இருந்த நாள் எல்லாம் இருந்துவிட்டு ஊர்ப்பறையனுக்குத் தாரைவார்த்த கதை.

The story of one who after leading an unexceptionable course of life gave his daughter in marriage to the village Pariah.

1039. இருந்தவன் தலைமேலே இடி விழுந்ததுபோல.

As the thunder-bolt fell on the head of the one who remained.

1040. இருந்த கால் மூதேவி நடந்த கால் சீதேவி.

The sluggish foot is Múdévi *the goddess of adversity*, the active foot is Shrídèvi *the goddess of prosperity*.

These two personages were produced when the milky ocean was churned to obtain ambrosia. They play an important part in the economy of the Hindus.

1041. இருந்தவனுக்குப் போனவன் குணம்.

He that went away was better than he who stayed.

1042. இருந்தவன் எழுந்திருக்கிறதற்குள்ளே நின்றவன் ஒரு காதம போவான்.

Whilst he who was seated was rising, the man who was standing had gone ten miles.

1043. இருந்தால் பூனை, பாய்ந்தால் புலி.

While squatting, a cat, when springing, a tiger.

1044. இருந்தால இருப்பீர், எழுந்திருந்தால் நிற்பீர்.

If sitting you sit, if you rise you stand.

1045. இருந்து பணம் கொடுத்து நடந்து வாங்கவேண்டியதாய் இருக்கிறது.

One must walk a long way to get back the money lent when seated.

1046. இருபத்தொரு மழையும் எண்ணி ஊற்றியது.

The twenty-one kinds of rain were enumerated and poured out.

1047. இருப்புக் கதவு இடித்துத் தவிட்டுக் கொழுக்கட்டை எடுக்கிறதா?

What! knocking down an iron door to obtain a bran cake?

1048. இருப்புச் சலாகையை விழுங்கிப்போட்டு இஞ்சிச்சாறு குடித்தால் தீருமா?

If one has swallowed a bar of iron, will its effects be removed by drinking a decoction of ginger?

1049. இருப்புக் கோட்டையும் கற்கதவும்போல.

Like an iron fort and a stone door.

1050. இரு மனது மங்கையோடு இணங்குவது அவம்.

To associate with a double minded woman is fatal.

1051. இரும்பு செம்பானால் துரும்பும் தூணாம்.

If iron becomes copper, a straw may become a pillar.

One impossibility is as like as another.

1052. இரும்புத்தூணைச் செல் அரிக்குமா?

Can white-ants eat an iron pillar!

1053. இரும்பு செம்பானால் திரும்பிப் பொன் ஆகும்.

If iron can be converted into copper, copper may be reconverted into gold.

1054. இரும்புக்கட்டியைக் காற்றடிக்கிறபோது இலவம்பஞ்சு எனக்கு என்ன புத்தி என்கிறதாம்.

It is said that when the wind was driving along a piece of iron, the silk-cotton asked what was best for him to do.

1055. இரும்புக்கட்டி பறக்கிறபோது இலவம்பஞ்சுக்கு இருப்பிடம் எங்கே?

When a piece of iron is flying away, where will silk-cotton find a resting place?

1056. இரும்பு அடிக்கிற இடத்தில் நாய்க்கு என்ன வேலை?

What has a dog to do in a smith's shop?

1057. இரும்பு பிடித்த கையும் சிரங்கு பிடித்த கையும் சும்மா இராது.

The hand that has taken up an iron tool and the hand affected by the itch will not be still.

1058. இரும்பு அடிக்கிற இடத்தில் நாய்க்கு என்ன கிடைக்கும்?

What will a dog get in a smith's shop?

1059. இரும்புத்தூணை எறும்பு அரித்தாற்போல.

As if an ant had gnawed an iron pillar.

1060. இரும்பு துறட்டிக்கு அசையாத புளியங்காய் திருப்பாட்டுக்கு அசையுமா?

Will the tamarind fruit that has resisted an iron hook shake at a sacred song.

In illustration of this proverb the following may not be considered irrelevant. In the year 1826 when I went to my first Missionary station, Trincomalee on the Eastern coast of Ceylon, I called on the chief Mudaliar to pay my respects. and to urge the claims of Christianity. The old gentleman who remembered the coercive system adopted by the Dutch for the propagation of Christianity, and well knowing too that Missionaries under the mild sway of Great Britain can use no weapon but the Gospel, uttered with great animation the above proverb. In view of the youthful character of his visitor he seemed to feel like Goliath in the presence of David

---

1061. இரும்பை எறும்பு அரிக்குமா?

Can an ant gnaw iron?

1062. இரும்பை எலி தின்னுமா?

Can a rat eat iron?

1063 இரும்பை எலி கவ்விற்று என்கிறான் படுக்காளி.

The infamous liar says that the rat took the iron in its mouth.

1064. இரும்பைக் கறையான் அரித்தால் பிள்ளையைப் பருந்து கொண்டு போகாதா?

If the white-ants can eat iron, why cannot a hawk carry off a child?

1065. இருவரும் ஒத்தால் இணக்குவார் ஏன்?

If the two agree what need of arbitrators?

1066. இருவராலே ஆகாத காரியம் ஒருவராலே ஆகுமா?

Can an affair be effected by one that could not be accomplished by two?

1067. இருவர் நட்புக்கு ஒருவர் பொறுமை.

The friendship of two *depends on* the forbearance of one.

1068. இருளன் பிள்ளைக்கு எலிக்குஞ்சு பஞ்சமா?

Does the son of an Irulan, *a wild tribe*, suffer from a scarcity of young rats?

1069. இருளன் ராஜவிழி விழிப்பானா?

Can a savage put on the look of a king?

1070. இருளும் ஒரு காலம் நிலவும் ஒரு காலம்.

A time of darkness, a time of moonshine

1071. இரெட்டியாரே இரெட்டியாரே என்றால், கலப்பையைத் திட்டென்று போட்ட கதை.

The story of one who dropped his plough when accosted O Reddy, O Reddy.

1072. இலக்கணம் கற்றவன் கலக்கம் அற மன்னர் சபை காண்பான்.

The learned will appear undismayed in a royal assembly.

1073. இலக்ஷணம் அவலக்ஷணம் முகத்திலே.

Beauty and ugliness are in the face.

1074. இலங்கணம் பரம ஔஷதம்.

Abstinence is the best medicine.

1075. இலங்கையில் பிறந்தவன் எல்லாம் இராவணன் ஆவானா?

Are all that are born in Ceylon, Ràvanas?

1076. இலங்கையைச் சுட்ட குரங்கு.

The monkey that set fire to Lanka.

1077. இலவு காத்த கிளி ஆனேன்.

I am like the parrot that waited for the silk-cotton pod.

Spoken of one who has been sadly disappointed in his expectations. The proverb is said to refer to a parrot that on seeing a green pod on a silk-cotton tree believed it would ripen into fruit, whereas it eventually burst and the cotton was scattered to the winds

1078. இலுப்பைப்பூவைத் திருப்பினால் இருபுறமும் பொத்தல்.

If the flower of ilupai (Bassia Longifolia) be turned, it will be found hollow on both sides.

1079. இலை தின்னி காய் அறியான்.

He who feeds on leaves knows not the flavor of fruit.

1080. இலையும் பழுப்பும் எங்கும் உண்டு.

Leaves green and sear are found every where.

1081. இலௌகிகம் வைதீகம் இரண்டும் வேண்டும்.

The secular and the sacred are both necessary.

1082. இல்லது வாராது உள்ளது போகாது.

That which is not will not come, that which is, will not go.

1083. இல்லறம் பெரிது துறவறம் சிறிது.

Domestic life is better than that of the ascetic.

1084. இல்லறம் பெரிது துறவறம் பழிப்பு.

Domestic life is honourable, that of the ascetic is disgraceful.

1085. இல்லாதவன் பொல்லாதவன்.

He that is destitute is wicked.

1086. இல்லாதது பிறவாது அள்ளாதது குறையாது.

That which is not, will not come out; that from which nothing is taken, will not lessen.

1087. இல்லாது சொல்லி அல்லற் படுதல்.

Uttering a falsehood and suffering the evil thereof.

1088. இல்லாளை விட்டு வல்லாண்மை பேசுகிறதா?

What! is it to speak manfully after deserting *thy* wife?

1089. இல்லாதும் இல்லன் இருப்பதும் இல்லன்.

He lacks nothing, nor does he possess any thing.

1090. இல்லாதவன் பெண்சாதி எல்லாருக்கும் தோழியா?

Is the wife of the destitute the friend or companion of all?

1091. இல்லை என்ற வீட்டில் பல்லியும் சேராது.

Even a lizard will not enter a house occupied by the niggardly.

1092. இல்லோர் இரப்பது இயல்பு.

It is natural for the destitute to beg.

1093. இவள் விலைமோரில் வெண்ணெய் எடுத்துத் தலைமகனுக்குக் கலியாணம் பண்ணுவாள்.

She will make butter out of the butter milk-given for sale, and make provision for the marriage of her first-born son.

1094. இவனுக்கும் அவனுக்கும் ஏழாம் பொருத்தம்.

There are seven *points* of agreement between this person and that.

1095. இவனுக்குச் சொல்லும் புத்தி கடலிற் பெருங்காயம் கரைத்தது போல் இருக்கிறது.

The advice given to him is like assafœtida dissolved in the sea.

1096. இவன் ஊராருக்குப் பிள்ளை.

He is the child of the whole village.

Said of a self-willed wandering youth

1097. இவன் மகா பெரிய கள்ளன், காலாலே முடிந்ததைக் கையாலே அவிழ்க்கிறது அரிது.

He is a clever rogue, what he ties with his feet it is difficult to untie with the hand.

1098. இவன் கல்லாது கற்றவன், உள்ளங்கையில் வைகுண்டம் காட்டுவான்.

He has attained the unattainable; he can show Vaikundam *Paradise* in the palm of his hand.

1099. இவன் புத்தி உலக்கைக்கொழுந்து.

His wit is as sharp as a wooden pestle.

1100. இழவுக்கு வந்தவள் தாலி அறுப்பாளா ?

Will she who attends a funeral remove her marriage symbol!

1101. இழுக்குடைய பாட்டிற்கு இசை நன்று.

Harmony sets off a faulty stanza.

1102. இழுவை கண்டால அடி பார்ப்பானேன் ?

When the trail marks are before you, why look for footprints ?

1103. இழை ஆயிரம் பொன் பெற்ற இந்திரவர்ணப்பட்டு.

A scarlet cloth each thread of which is worth a thousand gold pieces.

1104. இழையத் தீட்டிக் குழைய வடித்தல்.

Thoroughly pounded and properly boiled.

1105. இளகின இரும்பைக் கண்டாற் கொல்லன் குண்டியைத் தூக்கி அடிப்பான்.

When the smith perceives that the iron is soft, he will raise himself to the stroke.

The Indian smith squats at the forge, and rises to his feet only when he uses a two-handed hammer.

1106. இளங்கன்று பயம் அறியுமா ?

Does a young calf know fear !

1107. இளமையிற் சோம்பல் முதுமையின் மிடிமை.

Indolence, in youth will bring poverty in old age.

1108. இளமையில் முயற்சி முதுமையிற் காக்கும்.

Industry in youth will support one in old age.

1109. இளமையிற் பழக்கம் எப்போதும் மறவாது.

The habits of early life will never be forgotten.

1110. இளமையும் முதுமையும் சரியான வயதல்ல.

Youth and senility do not properly belong to a man's age.

1111. இளவெயில் காயாத நீயா தீ பாயப்போகிறாய் ?

Do you who cannot endure the early beams of the sun presume to walk over fire !

1112. இளைஞன் ஆனாலும் ஆடுவான் மூப்பு.

Although young he will play the man.

1113. இளைத்தவள் தலையில் ஈரும் பேனும்.

In the tresses of a poor woman are found nits and lice.

1114. இளைத்தவன் சினேகிதனைச் சேர்.

Associate with the friend of the poor.

1115. இளைத்தவனே எள்ளை விதை.

O you weak fellow, sow the sessamum seed.

1116. இளையாள் இலைதின்னி மூத்தாள் காய்அறிவாள்.

The younger sister feeds on leaves, the elder is accustomed to fruit.

1117. இளையாளே வாடி மலையாளம் போவோம், மூத்தாளே வாடி முட்டிக்கொண்டு சாவோம்.

Come my younger sister, we will proceed to Malayalam; come my elder sister, we will strike our heads together and die.

1118. இறகு முற்றிப் பறவை ஆனல், எல்லாம் தன் வயிற்றைத் தான் பார்க்கும்.

When mature and on the wing, *all* birds will look after their own food.

1119. இறக்கும் காலம் வந்தால் பிறக்கும் ஈசலுக்குச் சிறகு.

When death approaches, white-ants take wing.

1120. இறக்கும் காலம் வராமல் பிறக்குமா ஈசலுக்குச் சிறகு?

Will white-ants take wing except on the approach of death!

1121. இறங்கும் துறையிலே நீந்தானல, இந்த ஆற்றை எப்படிக் கடக்கிறது?

If on stepping into the river one is obliged to swim, how will he get across?

1122. இறங்கு பொழுதிலே மருந்து குடி.

Take medicine at sun-set.

1123. இறந்தவன் இருப்பவனுக்கு வழிகாட்டி.

The dead is the pilot of the living.

1124. இறந்தவன் பிள்ளை இருந்தவன் அடைக்கலம்.
The child of the dead is the ward of the living.

1125. இறந்தவனுக்கு எள்ளும் தண்ணீரும்.
Sessamum and water *offered* to the dead.

1126. இறுதத குடிககு அனர்த்தம் இல்லை.
A family out of debt is out of danger.

1127. இறுப்பானுக்குப் பணமும் கிடையாது, உழைப்பானுக்குப் பெண்ணும் கிடையாது.
He who pays his debts cannot obtain money, nor can the labourer obtain a wife.

1128. இறைச்சி தின்கிறவர் கடுப்புக்கு மருந்து அறிவார்.
They who live on flesh are acquainted with the medicine for tooth-ache.

1129. இறைச்சி தின்றாலும் எலும்பைக் கோத்துப் போட்டுக்கொள்ளலாமா?
Is one to wear a neck-lace of bones because he eats flesh?

This and the preeeding proverb are somewhat singular but not unnatural among a vegetarian people.

1130. இறைத்த கிணறு ஊறும், இறையாத கிணறு நாறும்.
The water of a well always drawn, is fresh, that of a well not drawn is fetid.

1131. இறைத்த கிணறு சுரக்கும.
The water of a well always drawn springs up a-fresh.

1132. இனம் பிரிந்த மான்போல.
Like a deer separated from its herd.

1133. இனிமேல் ஒரு தெய்வத்தைக் கையெடுக்கிறதா?
Hereafter is it to lift up the hands to a god?

1134. இனிமேல் எமலோகபரியந்தம் சாதிக்கலாம்.
Hereafter he may effect his purpose as far as the realms of Yama.

1135. இன்பமும் துன்பமும் பொறுமையிலே.

Joy and grief must be regulated by moderation.

1136. இன்பத்தில் ஆசை எவர்க்கும் உண்டு.

Happiness is desired by all.

1137. இன்பமும் துன்பமும் எடுத்த உடலுக்கு.

The body it is that is affected by pleasure and pain.

1138. இன்று இருப்பார் நாளைக்கு இல்லை.

Those who are alive to-day may not be on the morrow.

1139. இன்றைக்கு இலை அறுத்தவன் நாளைக்குக் குலை அறுப்பான்.

He who cut off the leaves to-day may possibly cut off the bunch to-morrow.

1140. இன்றைக்கு ஆகிறது நாளைக்கு ஆகட்டும்.

That which is practicable to-day may be so on the morrow.

1141. இன்றைக்குச் செத்தால் நாளைக்கு இரண்டு நாள.

If one die to-day, to-morrow will be the second day.

1142. இன்றை என்பதும நாளை என்பதும் இல்லை என்பதற்கு அடையாளம்.

To say to-day, to-morrow, indicates refusal.

ஈ.

1143. ஈ கலையாமல் தேன் எடுப்பார்கள், எடுக்காமற் பிடிப்பார்கள்.

They will take the honey without dispersing the bees, they will take it without raising it up.

1144. ஈகை உடையவன் எக்களிப்பு அடைவான்.

The liberal giver will be happy.

1145. ஈக்கு விடம் தலையில், தேளுக்குக் கொடுக்கில்.

In a fly, the head is the seat of poison, in a scorpion, the tail.

1146. ஈசலுக்கு எல்லாம் பகை.

All are against the winged white-ants.

1147. ஈசல் இறகு எல்லாவற்றிலும் மிருது.

The wing of a white-ant is the softest of all things.

1148. ஈசல் மடிந்தாற்போல் மாண்டதே சேனை.

The army perished like winged white-ants.

1149. ஈசற் பெரும்போக்கில் தவளை தத்தி விழுங்குகிறது.

The frog leaps and swallows the swarming winged white-ants.

1150. ஈசனுக்கு ஒப்பு இங்கு ஒன்றும் இல்லை.

Nothing here is equal to God.

1151. ஈச்சங்கள்ளு எதிலும் குளிர்ச்சி.

Date-palm toddy is the coolest of beverages.

1152. ஈச்சம் காட்டில் எருமை குடியிருந்த கதை.

The story of a buffalo that lived in a date-palm grove.

1153. ஈடன் பாடஞ்சான் கூழையெருது நுளம்பஞ்சாது.

A strong man fears not hardship, nor does a bullock with a stunted tail fear gnats.

1154. ஈடாகாதவனை எதிராக்காதே.

Do not oppose your inferior.

1155. ஈடுள்ள குடிக்குக் கேடு இல்லை.

A wealthy family is not exposed to danger.

1156. ஈட்டிய பொருளினும் எழுத்தே உடைமை.

Learning is more substantial than accumulated riches.

1157. ஈட்டி எட்டியமட்டும் குத்தும், பணம் பதின்காதமும் குத்தும்.

A spear wounds as far as it reaches, the effect of money reaches ten kathams (100 miles).

1158. ஈட்டுக்கு ஈடும் சோட்டுக்குச் சோடுமாய் இருந்தால் வாசி

Like for like, and equality in a pair are desirable.

1159. ஈட்டுக்கும் பாட்டுக்கும் இருந்தாள் இடுகுமரி.
The maiden who was given *in marriage* was equal to all the exigencies of life.

1160. ஈந்து பார்த்தால் இம்மி வெளி ஆகும்.
The smallest fraction will come out by division.
இம்மி=1,075,200th part of a unit.

1161. ஈப்பிசினி இரப்பதுகூடக் கக்கிசம்.
A miser will find even begging difficult.

1162. ஈயத்தைக் காய்ச்சலாம் இரும்பைக் காய்ச்சலாமா ?
Lead may be melted, can iron ?

1163. ஈயம் பிடித்தவன் எது சொல்லினும் கேளான்.
He who has taken up lead will not listen, no matter what is said to him.

1164. ஈயாத புலலனை எவ்விடத்திலும் காணோம்.
A niggardly savage is nowhere found.

1165. ஈயார் தேட்டைத் தீயார் கொள்வார்.
The wicked obtain *by rapacity* what the miserly accumulate

1166 ஈயார் பொருளுக்குத் தீயார்.
The wicked enjoy the property of the miser.

1167. ஈயும் எறும்பும் எங்கும் உண்டு.
Flies and ants abound every-where.

1168. ஈயைப் பிடித்தால் கை வேறு கால் வேறு.
If you catch a fly, its limbs will be separated.

1169. ஈயைப்போலே சுத்தமும் எறும்பைப்போலே பலமும்.
Clean as a fly and strong as an ant.

1170. ஈரச்சீலையைப்போட்டுக் கழுத்து அறுப்பான்.
He will cut the throat after tying a wet cloth round it.

1171. ஈர நாவிற்கு எலும்பு இல்லை.
There is no bone in a slanderous tongue.

1172. ஈரம் அற்ற இடத்திலே ஈ மொய்க்குமா, ஈரம்
லே ஈ மொய்க்குமா?

Do insects swarm in a dry place or in a wet place?

1173. ஈரவெங்காயத்திற்கு இருபத்தெட்டுப் புரை.

In an onion there are twenty-eight coats.

1174. ஈரை நினைப்பான் பேரை மறக்கான்.

He who thinks of a nit will not forget its name.

1175. ஈரைப் பேனாக்கிப் பேனைப் பெருமாள் ஆக்கினேன்.

I magnified the nit into a louse, and the louse into Perumál.

1176. ஈர் உருவப் பேன் அகப்படுமா?

Will lice be obtained when drawing nits between the finger and the thumb.

1177. ஈ விஷ்டித்ததும் நாய் திருடித்தின்றதும்.

That which a bee ejects and that which a dog has stolen.

1178. ஈ விழுந்த சாதம் எடுத்தாலொழியப் போமா?

Will a fly that has fallen into the boiled rice go unless it be taken out?

1179. ஈவோனுக்கு ஒரு போசனம், இரப்போனுக்கு ஏராளம்.

To the giver a meal, to the beggar plenty.

1180. ஈழத்திற் செக்காட இங்கே பதம் பார்க்க.

The press is turned in Lanka, and the material under pressure is examined here.

1181. ஈனவும் தெரியாது நக்கவும் தெரியாது.

It knows not how to bring forth nor how to lick.

1182. ஈன்றவள் தாய் பாட்டி, இவள் தாயின் தாய் பீட்டி.

The mother of one's mother is his grand-mother, her mother is his great grand mother.

1183. ஈன்றோர் நஞ்சிற் சான்றோர் இல்லை.

Indulgence in the parent is not good *for the child.*

உ.

. உகமுடிய மழை பெய்தாலும் ஓட்டாங்கிளிஞ்சில் பயிர் ஆகுமா ?

Though it should rain to the end of the world, would broken oyster shells vegetate ?

85. உகிர்ச்சுற்றின்மேல் அம்மி விழுந்ததுபோல்.

As a grind-stone fell on the whitlow.

6. உங்கள் உறவிலே வேகிறதைப்பார்க்கிலும் ஒரு கட்டு விறகிலே வேகிறது நல்லது.

It is better to be consumed by a faggot than by your friendship.

1187. உங்கள் பெண்டுகள் கொண்டல் அடித்தால் கண்கள் கொள்ளாது.

The eyes will be over-powered by the dancing of your women.

1188. உங்களைக் கடலிலே கைகழுவினேன்.

I have washed my hands of you in the sea.

1189. உசு பிடி என்றால் நீ பிடி என்கிறதாம் நாய்.

It is said that when he urged his dog to seize, it replied, you do so.

1190. உச்சந்தலையிற் செருப்பால் அடித்தாலும் உச்சி குளிருமா ?

If slippered on the head, will the crown of the head become cool ?

1191. உடம்பு எல்லாம் புழுத்தவன் அம்மன் கோவிலைக் கெடுத்த கதை.

The story of a man who defiled Amman covil by his ulcerated body.

1192. உடம்புளைந்த கழுதை உப்புகளத்திற்குப் போனதுபோல.

As the wearied ass went to the salt-pit.

1193. உடம்பு எடுத்தவன் எல்லாம் ஓடு எடுத்தான்.

All who have taken a body have taken an alms-dish.

1194. உடம்பு தேற்றிக்கொண்டு அல்லவா யோகத்தில் போகவேண்டும் ?

Must one not invigorate the body and then proceed to meditation ?

1195. உடம்பு எங்கும் சுடுகிற தழலை மடியிலே கட்டுகிறாய்.

Thou huggest up in thy bosom the embers that warm every part of the body.

1196. உடம்பு முழுதும் நனைந்தவருக்குக் கூதல் என்ன?

Of what consequence is cold to him whose whole body is drenched?

1197. உடலுக்கோ பால் வார்த்து உண்பது, ஊருக்கோ பால் வார்த்து உண்பது?

Do we feed on milk for the benefit of the body, or that our neighbours may know it?

1198. உடல் இரண்டு உயிர் ஒன்று.

Divided *as regards* body, one in soul.

1199. உடல் ஒருவனுக்குப் பிறந்தது நா பலருக்குப் பிறந்தது.

The body is born for one, the tongue for many.

1200. உடல் உள்ளவரைக்கும் கடல் கொள்ளாத கவலை.

Anxieties which the ocean cannot contain attend the body as long as it exists.

1201. உடன்பிறப்பு இல்லா உடம்பு பாழ்.

The body of one who has no kindred *is exposed to* desolation.

1202. உடாப்புடைவை பூச்சிக்கு இரை.

A garment not worn is a prey to moths.

1203. உடுத்த புடைவைதானே பாம்பாய்க் கடிக்கிறது.

The cloth one has put on bites as a snake.

1204. உடும்பு போனாலும் போகிறது கையைவிட்டால் போதும்.

The guana may go, it is enough if the hand be free.

1205. உடும்புக்கு இரண்டு நாக்கு மனிதனுக்கு ஒரு நாக்கு.

The guana has two tongues, man only one.

1206. உடும்புக்கு இரண்டு நாக்கு உண்டு, மனிதனுக்கு இரண்டு நாக்கு உண்டா?

The guana has a double tongue, has man the same?

1207. உடைமுள்ளுக்கு எதிரோ உதைக்கலாமா?
Can you kick against the thorns of the Acacia?

1208. உடைமை என்பது கல்வியுடைமை.
Learning is real wealth.

1209. உடைமையும் வறுமையும் ஒரு வழி நில்லா.
Wealth and poverty are not abiding.

1210. உடைமையும் கொடுத்து அருமையும் குலைகிறதா?
What! give one's property and sacrifice one's reputation!

1211. உடையவன் பாராப் பயிர் உருப்படுமா?
Will a crop not looked after by the owner flourish?

1212. உடையவன் சொற்படி உரலைச்சுற்றிக் களைபறி.
Pluck up the weeds about the mortar as your master bids you.

1213. உடையவனிற் கைப்பற்றினவன் மிடுக்கன்.
An embezzler is more obstinate than the owner.

1214. உடையவன் சொற்படி கமுகடி களைபறி.
Weed around the areca tree at thy master's biding.

1215. உடையவன் இல்லாச் சேலை ஒரு முழம் கட்டை.
The cloth whose owner is absent is a cubit too short

1216. உடையார் வீட்டு மோருக்கு அகப்பைக் கணக்கு என்ன?
What necessity is there for estimating the quantity of butter-milk by the ladle in the homestead of the chief?

1217. உட்கார்ந்து அல்லவோ படுக்கவேண்டும்?
You must sit before lying down, must you not!

1218. உட்கார்ந்தவனைக் கட்ட மாட்டாதவன் ஓடுகிறவனைக் கட்டு வானா?
Can he tie a man that is running who cannot tie one that is sitting?

1219. உடசுவர் இருக்கப் புறச்சுவர் பூசலாமா?
What! beautify the outside of a wall while the inside is neglected!

1220. உடசுவர் தீற்றிப் புறச்சுவர் தீற்று.
Garnish the inside of the wall and then the outside.

1221. உட்புறத்துக்கு வெளிப்புறம கண்ணாடி.
A mirror reflects whatever is before it.

1222. உணர்வில்லாக் கருவியும் உப்பில்லாச் சோறும் சரி.
A mere instrument void of feeling and food without salt are alike.

1223. உண்கிற சோற்றிலே நஞ்சைக் கலக்கிறதா ?
What, is it to mix poison with the rice one is eating !

1224. உண்ட உடம்பிற்கு உறுதி, உழுத புலத்தில் நெல்லு.
There is strength in a body well fed, and grain in the ploughed field.

1225. உண்ட பிள்ளை உரஞ்செய்யும்.
A child that eats well thrives.

1226. உண்ட வயிற்றுக்குச் சோறும் மொட்டைத்தலைக்கு எண்ணெயுமா ?
Is rice required for a full stomach, or oil for a baldhead !

1227. உண்டதுதான் ஏப்பம் வரும.
That which has been eaten will be evidenced in the belching.

1228. உண்ட வீட்டுக்கு இரண்டகம் பண்ணலாமா ?
May hospitality be requited by treachery !

1229. உண்ட உடம்பு உருகும் தின்ற பாக்குச் சிவக்கும்.
The body nourished by another's bounty will melt, arecanut when chewed turns red.

1230. உண்ட சுற்றம் உருகும்.
Friendship cemented by food will compassionate.

1231. உண்டார் மேனி கண்டால் தெரியும்.
The body shews who is well fed.

1232. உண்டால் தீரும் பசி, கண்டால் தீருமா !
Hunger is appeased by eating, will it be so by looking *at food* !

1233. உண்டால் தின்றால் உறவு, கொண்டால் கொடுத்தால் உறவு.

Friendship is promoted and strengthned by hospitality and also by intermarriage.

1234. உண்டாலும் உறுதிப்பட உண்ணவேண்டும்.

When you eat, do so to keep up your strength.

1235. உண்டாற் கொல்லும் விஷம்.

Poison destroys when taken.

1236. உண்டி சுருங்குதல் பெண்டிர்க்கு அழகு.

Moderation *in food* becomes women.

1237. உண்டு தின்று உள்ளே இருவென்றால் உயர எழும்பி ஏன் குதிக்கிறாய்?

When you are told to eat heartily and remain in-doors, why do you rise up and jump?

1238. உண்டு உறியில் இரு என்றால் உருண்டு தரையில் விழுகிறாய்.

If I say eat and sit on the hanging-shelf, you fall to the ground.

1239. உண்டு கொழுத்தால் நண்டு வளையில் இராது.

If a crab gets fat, it will not stay in its hole.

1240. உண்டு தின்று உயரம் ஆனால் ஊரிலே காரியம் என்ன?

What business has he in the village seeing that he is grown up?

1241. உண்ணக் கை சலித்து இருக்கிறான்.

His hand is weary with eating

1242. உண்ண வா என்றால் குத்த வருகிறாய்.

When I call you to eat, you come to strike me.

1243. உண்ணாக்கை அறுத்துச் சுண்ணாம்புக்குறி இடுவேன்.

I will cut your uvula and smear it with chunam-*lime*.

1244. உண்ணாச் சொத்து மண்ணாய்ப் போகும்.

Property not enjoyed comes to nought.

1245. உண்ணுமல் ஊர் எல்லாம் திரியலாம் உடுக்காமல் ஒரு வீட்டுக்கும் போகலாகாது.

One may wander over the whole country without eating, but one may not go to a single house without dressing.

1246. உண்ணுமல் ஒன்பது வீடு போகலாம், உடுக்காமல் ஒரு வீடும் போகல் ஆகாது.

One may go to nine houses without eating, but not to one without garments.

1247 உண்ணும் கீரையிலே நண்ணும் புல்லுருவி.

Mistleloe attached to edible greens.

1248. உண்பது இருக்க ஒரு கருமம் செய்யேல்.

Do not go to work without eating.

1249. உண்பான் தின்பான் சிவப்பிராமணன், குத்துக்கு நிற்பான் வீரமுஷ்டி.

The Saiva Brahman will freely eat, the ferocious mendicant will show fight.

1250. உண்பாரைப் பார்த்தாலும் உழுவாரைப் பார்க்கல் ஆகாது.

Though you look at those who are eating, you may not look at those who are ploughing.

1251. உண்மை சொல்லிக் கெட்டாரும் பொய் சொல்லி வாழ்ந்தாரும் இல்லை.

None ever perishes by speaking the truth, none flourishes by uttering falsehood.

1252. உதடு மன்றுடப் போய் உள்ளிருந்த பல்லும் போனற்போல.

As if the teeth also went out when the lips had gone to beg.

1253. உதட்டிலே உள்ள வாழைப்பழத்தை உள்ளே தள்ளுவார் உண்டோ?

Are there any who push into the mouth the plantain that is already between the lips?

1254. உதட்டுக்கு மிஞ்சின பல்லும் திருட்டுக்கு மிஞ்சின கையும் ஆகாது.

Protruding teeth and a hand given to thieving are bad.

1255. உதட்டிலே புண் ஆனால் பால் கறக்காதா?

Will the cow not yield its milk because it has sore lips?

1256. உதட்டுத் துரும்பு ஊதப் போகாது?

A small particle adhering to the lip cannot be removed by blowing

1257. உதர நிமித்தம் வெகு கிர்தவேஷம்.

Divers disguises for the sake of the belly.

1258. உதவாப் பழங்கலமே ஓசை இல்லா வெண்கலமே!

Thou art a useless vessel, a piece of brass without sound!

1259. உதவாத செட்டிக்குச் சீட்டு எழுதினதுபோல.

Like writing a chit to a thrifty merchant.

1260. உதவி செய்வார்க்கு இடையூறு ஏது?

What, accident can harm those who help others?

1261. உதறுகாலி வந்தாள் உள்ளதும் கெடுத்தாள்.

A woman with a bustling gait came and destroyed what there was.

1262. உதாரிக்குப் பொன்னும் துரும்பு.

Even gold is a thing of nought to the generous.

1263. உதிரத்துக்கு அல்லோ உருக்கம் இருக்கும்?

Sympathy arises, does it not, from consanguinity?

1264. உதைத்த கால் புழுக்கிறபோது அல்லவோ புழுக்கும்?

Worms will breed in due course, will they not, in a foot accustomed to kick?

1265. உதைத்த கால் புழுக்கிறதற்குமுன்னே அடிவயிறு சீழ்கட்டுகிறது.

Before his kicking feet were eaten of worms his abdomen had ulcerated.

1266. உதைப்பானுக்கு வெளுப்பான் சாதிவண்ணான்.
He that washes for him who kicks him is a first-rate washerman.

1267. உத்தமனுக்கும் தப்பிலிக்கும் உடன்படிக்கை வேண்டாம்.
Contracts are needless as regards honest men and cheats.

The one needs no binding, and the other admits no obligations.

1268. உத்தமச்சேவகன் பெற்றதாய்க்கு அதிகம்.
A faithful servant is more than a mother.

1269. உத்தமனுக்கு எத்தாலும் கேடு இல்லை.
The good are exposed to no danger.

1270. உத்தியோகம் புருஷ லக்ஷணம்.
Exertion is a manly quality.

1271. உத்தியோகத்துக்குத் தக்க சுகம்.
Facilities suited to one's office.

1272. உபகாரத்துக்கு அபகாரம் வருவது துரதிஷ்டம்.
It is unfortunate when evil is returned for good.

1273. உபசரியாத வீட்டிலே உண்ணாதிருப்பதே ஒரு கோடி தனம்.
It is a crore of wealth to abstain from entertainment in a house void of civility.

1274. உபசாரம் செய்தவர்க்கு அபசாரம் பண்ணுகிறதா?
What! are the civil to be requited by incivility!

1275. உபசாரவார்த்தை காசாகுமா, உண்டாலொழியப் பசி தீருமா?
Will mere ceremony pass for money, will hunger be appeased otherwise than by eating!

1276. உபாயத்தால் ஆகிறது பராக்கிரமத்தால் ஆகுமா?
Can that which may be realized by cunning be obtained by force!

1277. உப்பு இருந்த பாண்டமும் உபாயம் இருந்த நெஞ்சமும் தட்டி உடையாமல் தானே உடையும்.
A salt-cup and a deceitful heart will of themselves come to destruction.

1278. உப்பு இருந்த பாண்டமும் உண்மை இல்லா நெஞ்சும் தட்டி உடையாமல் தானே உடையும்.

A vessel impregnated with salt, and a mind without truth need none to destroy them, they destroy themselves.

1279. உப்பு இல்லாப் பண்டம் குப்பையிலே.

Unsalted food *is fit only* for the rubbish heap.

1280. உப்பு இட்டவர்களை உள்ளளவும் நினை.

Remember through life those who have given you salt.

1281. உப்பு முதல் கர்ப்பூரம் வரைக்கும் வேண்டும்.

Every thing from salt to camphor is required.

Said of things domestic and sacred

1282. உப்புத் தின்றவன் தண்ணீரைக் குடிப்பான்.

He who has eaten salt will drink water.

1283. உப்புக்கண்டம் பறிகொடுத்த பார்ப்பாத்திபோல விழிக்கிறாய்.

Thou starest as the Brahmanee who had lost her salted mutton.

In her bewilderment she had no remedy because she dared not make known the loss of a thing she ought not to have had in her possession.

1284. உப்பு வாணிகன் அறிவானா கர்ப்பூர விலை?

Does the salt merchant know the price of camphor?

1285. உப்புக் கட்டினால் லோகம் கட்டும்.

If there be a supply of salt the world will be sustained.

1286. உப்பும் கர்ப்பூரமும் ஒன்றாய் வழங்குமா?

Are salt and camphor used together?

1287. உப்பு நீர் மேகம் உண்டால் உலகிற் பிரவாகம்.

If the ocean were to become clouds, the world would be flooded.

1288. உப்புத் தண்ணீருக்கு இலாமிச்சம் வேர் போடவேண்டுமா?

Must the root of cusa grass be added to sea-water to make it fragrant?

1289. உப்பு மிஞ்சினால் தண்ணீர், தண்ணீர் மிஞ்சினால் உப்பு.
Excess of salt calls for water, excess of water requires salt.

1290. உப்பைச் சிந்தினையோ துப்பைச் சிந்தினையோ?
Did you spill the salt or the food?

1291. உப்பைத்தொட்டு உப்பைத் தின்னாதே.
Do not use salt both as food and condiment.

1292. உப்பைத் தொட்டுக்கொண்டு உரலை விழுங்கலாம்.
Using salt as a condiment you may swallow a mortar.

1293. உப்போடு ஒன்பதும் பருப்போடு பத்தும் வேண்டும்.
Nine things are required with salt, ten with pulse.

1294. உமக்கு என்ன, வயதுக்கு நரைத்ததோ மயிருக்கு நரைத்ததோ?
Have you grown grey by age, or is your hair prematurely grey?

1295. உமியைக் குற்றிக் கைசலித்ததுபோல.
As the hand was wearied by beating husks in a mortar.

1296. உயரப் பறந்தாலும் ஊர்க்குருவி கருடன் ஆகுமா?
Though it may fly high, will a common bird become a hawk?

1297. உயிரும் உடலும்போல.
Like soul and body.

1298. உயிரை வைத்திருக்கிறதிலும் செத்தாற் குணம்.
It is more natural to die than to continue in life.

1299. உயிரோடு திரும்பிப் பாராதவர் செத்தால் முத்தம் கொடுப்பாரா?
Will he who would not turn to look at me when alive kiss me when dead?

1300. உயிரோடு ஒரு முத்தம் தராதவள் செத்தால் உடன்கட்டை ஏறுவாளா?
Will she who would not kiss me when alive ascend my funeral pyre when I am dead?

1301. உயிர் இருந்தால் உப்புமாறித் தின்னலாம்.
If one is alive, he may subsist by bartering salt.

1302. உரலில் அகப்பட்டது உலக்கைக்குத் தப்புமா?
Will that which is in the mortar escape the pestle?

1303. உரலிலே தலையை மாட்டிக்கொண்டு உலக்கைக்குப் பயப்பட்டால் தீருமா?
Will your fear of the pestle avail aught after your head has become fast in the mortar?

1304. உரலுக்கு ஒரு பக்கம் இடி மத்தளத்துக்கு இரண்டு பக்கமும் இடி.
The mortar is beaten at one end the drum at both.

1305. உரல் பஞ்சம் அறியுமா?
Does the *rice* mortar know what a famine is?

1306. உரல் போய் மத்தளத்தோடே முறையிட்டதுபோல.
As the mortar went to the tomtom with its complaints.

Used when one complains of his misfortunes to another who is in greater distress The mortar is beaten at one end only, whereas the tomtom is beaten at both ends.

1307. உரு ஏறத் திரு ஏறும்.
Supernatural power increases according to the intensity of the incantations.

1308. உருக்கம் உள்ள சிற்றாத்தை ஒதுக்கில் வாடி கட்டி அழ.
O my loving aunt, come with me apart that we may embrace each other and weep.

1309. உருசி கண்ட பூனை உறியைத் தாவும்.
The cat that has tasted *nice things* will leap on the swinging-tray.

1310. உருட்டப் புரட்ட உள்ளதும் உள்ளுக்கு வாங்கும்.
When one deals fraudulently, even that which he has diminishes.

1311. உருட்டும் புரட்டும் ஒடுக்கும் சிறப்பை.
Frauds and tricks will destroy reputation.

1312. உருட்டும் புரட்டும் மிரட்டும் சொல்லும்.
Tricks and frauds and threats.

1313. உருத்திராக்ஷப் பூனை ஒன்றும் தெரியாதுபோல் இருக்கும்.
Like a beaded cat he appears as if he knew nothing.

1314. உருத்திராக்ஷப் பூனை உபதேசம் பண்ணினதுபோல.
As a beaded cat gave divine instruction.

1315. உருப்படத் திருப்படும்.
As the figure is formed, beauty will become manifest.

1316.* உருவத்தை அல்ல குணத்தைப்பார், பணத்தையல்ல சனத்தைப்பார்.
Look to the temper, not beauty, to the connections not at money, *when choosing a wife.*

1317. உருவத்தினால் அல்ல, இன்பப் பேச்சினால் கிளி நன்குமதிக்கப்படும்.
It is not for its form, but for its sweet prattling that a parrot is esteemed.

1318. உருவிய வாளை உறையில் இடாத வீரன்.
A hero who does not sheath *his* sword.

1319. உலகத்துக்கு ஞானம் பேய், ஞானத்துக்கு உலகம் பேய்.
To the world wisdom is folly, to wisdom the world is folly.

1320. உலகம் பல விதம்.
The world has many forms

1321. உலகிலே கள்ளனுக்கு ஊரார் யாவரும் பகை.
The whole country is at enmity with the thief who dwells there

1322. உலக்கைப்பூசைக்கு அசையாதது திருப்பாட்டுக்கு அசையுமா?
Will that which has resisted the strokes of the pestle shake at a sacred chant?

1323. உலக்கைதேய்ந்து உளிப்பிடி ஆயிற்று.
The pestle by wearing away has become the handle of a chisel.

1324. உலக்கை பெருத்து உத்திரம் ஆயிற்று.

The pestle grew and became a beam.

1325. உலுத்தன் விருந்திற்கு ஒப்பானது ஒன்றும் இல்லை.

Nothing can be compared to the banquet of a miser.

1326. உலைவாயை மூடினாலும் ஊர்வாயை மூடலாமா?

You may cover the mouth of a rice-pot, but can you cover the mouth of the country!

1327. உலோபிக்கு இரு செலவு.

The avaricious are subject to double expense.

1328. உல்லாசநடை மெலுக்குக்குக்கேடு மினுக்கு எண்ணெய் தலைக்குக் கேடு.

An affected gait is injurious to graceful movement, and varnish is bad for the head.

1329. உழக் குளிர் அடித்தால் நாற்றுப்பிடுங்கப்படாதா?

If it be too cold to plough, why not put out the young plants?

1330. உழக்கு உற்றார்க்குப் பதக்குப் பரதேசிக்கு.

A quarter of a measure to one's friends, and sixteen measures to a religious mendicant.

1331. உழக்கிலே கிழக்கு மேற்கா?

Is the distinction of east and west observable in an ullak *a small measure of capacity*?

1332. உழக்கிலே வழக்கு.

A dispute about an ullak.

See the preceding.

1333. உழக்கு மிளகு கொடுப்பான் ஏன், ஒளித்திருந்து மிளகுநீர்குடிப்பான் ஏன்?

Why give a measure of pepper, why drink the pepper water in a corner?

1334. உழவிற்கு ஏற்ற கொழு.

A plough share adapted to the tillage.

1335. உழவின் மிகுத்த ஊதியம் இல்லை.
Nothing more advantageous than tillage.

1336. உழவு ஒழிந்த மாடு பட்டிப்புறத்திலே.
Cattle unfit for the plough are kept outside.

1337. உழவு மாடு ஆனால் ஊருக்குள்ளே விலைப்படாதா?
If the ox be fit for the plough, will it not fetch a price in its own village?

1338. உழவுக்கு ஒரு சுற்றும் வராது, ஊணுக்கு முன்னே வரும்.
At the plough it will not go a single round, at foddering time it comes first.

1339. உழவுக்குப் பிணைத்துவிடுகிற மாடும், கூட்டுக்குப் பிடித்துவிடு கிற ஆளும் உதவாது.
The bullock yoked to the plough by force, and a man acting as a subsitute are alike useless.

1340. உழுகிறதைவிட்டு நழுவுகிறவன் தெய்வம் ஆடினாற்போல.
Like one who, to avoid ploughing, feigned to be demonized.

1341. உழுகிற நாளையில் ஊருக்குப் போய், அறுக்கிற நாளையில அரிவாள் கொண்டுவந்தாற்போல.
As if one retired into the interior in the ploughing season, and returned with a sickle at the approach of harvest.

1342. உழுகிறமாடு பரதேசம் போனால், அங்கு ஒருவன் கட்டி உழுவான இங்கு ஒருவன் கட்டி உழுவான்.
If a ploughing bullock go astray, it will be yoked wherever found.

1343. உழுகிற மாட்டை நுகத்தால் அடித்தாற்போல.
Like beating the ploughing ox with the yoke.

1344. உழுகிற மாட்டை எருது நக்கினதுபோல.
As an ox licked a yoke of oxen when ploughing.

1345. உழுகிறவன் இளப்பமானால் எருது மச்சினமுறை கொண்டாடும்.
The ox treats the unskilful ploughman as his brother-in-law.

1346. உழுதவனுக்கு ஊர்க்கணக்குப்பண்ணத் தெரியாது.

A ploughman is unable to keep village accounts.

1347. உழுதவன் கணக்குப் பார்த்தால் உழக்கேனும் மிஞ்சாது.

When a ploughman balances his accounts, not even an ullak *of grain* remains.

1348. உளவன் இல்லாமல் ஊர் அழியுமா?

Can a country be destroyed if there be no spy?

1349. உளவு இல்லாமல் களவு இல்லை.

No spy, no theft.

1350. உளைவழியும், அடைமழையும், பொதி எருதும், ஒருவனுமாய் அலைகிறான்.

He wanders alone after a pack-bull, through deep mud and incessant rain.

1351. உள்வீட்டுக் கடனும், உள்ளங்கைச் சிரங்கும் கெட்டது.

To be in debt to an inmate and to have the itch in the palm of the hand are intolerable evils.

1352. உள்ள பிள்ளை உரலை நக்கிக்கொண்டிருக்க, மற்றொரு பிள்ளை கருத் திருப்பதிக்கு நடக்கிறாள்.

While her child licks the mortar, she goes on a pilgrimage to Tirupati in expectation of another.

1353. உள்ளங்கைப் பாற்சோற்றை விட்டுப் புறங்கை நக்கியதுபோல.

Like putting rice-milk in the palm and licking the back of the hand.

1354. உள்ளதைக் கொண்டு இல்லதைப் பாராட்டலாம்.

With what we have we may pretend to have that which we have not

1355. உள்ளதைச் சொன்னால் உடம்பெல்லாம் புண்ணாம்.

It is said that the whole body breaks out into ulcers when the truth is told.

1356 உள்ளதை விற்று நல்லதைக் கொள்ளு.

Sell what you have and buy what is *really* good.

1357. உள்ளானும் கள்ளனுமாய் இருக்கிறான்.

He is both an inmate and a thief.

1358. உள்ளங்கையில் ஒன்பது கொண்டை முடிப்பேன்.

I will tie nine knots of hair in the palm of the hand.

1359. உள்ளங்கையில் நெல்லிக்கனிபோல.

Like the Nelli berry (Phyllanthus simplex) in the palm of the hand.

Said of something unmistakably evident.

1360. உள்ளங்கையில் உரோமமுளைத்ததாயின், அறிவிலான் அடங்குவான்.

If it be that hair has sprung up in the palm of the hand, a fool may yield to discipline.

1361. உள்ளானும் கள்ளனும் கூடினால் விடிகிறமட்டும் திருடலாம்.

When an inmate of a house joins the thief, stealing may be carried on till day-break.

1362. உள்ளதைச் சொன்னால் நொள்ளைக்கண்ணிக்கு நோப்பாளம.

If the truth be told, the blind woman will be greatly afflicted.

1363. உள்ளதை எல்லாம் கொடுத்து நொள்ளைக்கண்ணியைக் கொண்டானும்.

It is said that he took to wife a blind girl having given away all he had.

1364. உள்ளவன் பிள்ளை உப்போடு உண்ணும், இல்லாதவன் பிள்ளை சர்க்கரையோடு உண்ணும்.

The child of the wealthy takes salt with his food, the child of the poor, sugar.

1365. உள்ளக்கருத்து வள்ளலுக்குத் தெரியும்.

Our inmost thoughts are known to God.

1366. உள்ளதைச் சொன்னால் எல்லாருக்கும் பகை.

When the truth is told, every one takes it ill.

1367. உள்ளதையும் கெடுத்தான் கொள்ளிக் கண்ணன்.
The evil-eyed destroyed even what there was.

1368. உள்ளதைச் சொன்னவன் ஊருக்குப் பொல்லாதவன்.
He who speaks the truth is regarded as a wicked person by the country.

1369. உள்ளாளும் கள்ளாளும் கூட்டமா?
Is association between an inmate and a thief to be tolerated!

1370. உள்ளிருந்தார்க்குத் தெரியும் உள்வருத்தம்.
Internal distress is known to the inmates.

1371. உள்ளூர் மருமகனும் உழுகிற கடாவும் சரி.
A son-in-law of the same village and a ploughing buffalo are overwrought.

1372. உள்ளே கொட்டின தேளே ஒரு மந்திரம் சொல்லுகிறேன் கேளே.
O thou scorpion thou hast thrust thy sting into me, listen, I will utter an incantation.

1373. உள்ளே பகையும் உதட்டிலே உறவுமா?
What! is it enmity at heart and friendship on the lips!

1374. உள்ளே வயிறெரிய உதடு பழம் சொரிய.
Bowels burning within, lips shedding ripe fruit.

1375. உறவிலே நஞ்சு கலக்கிறதா?
What! is poison to be mixed with friendship?

1376. உறவுபோல இருந்து குளவிபோலக் கொட்டுகிறதா?
What! to feign friendship and to sting as a wasp!

1377. உறவு உறவுதான் பறியிலே கை வைக்காதே.
No doubt about friendship, but do not put your hand into my basket.

1378. உறவுக்கும் பகைக்கும் பொருளே துணை.
Wealth may aid both in friendship and enmity.

1379. உறவுக்கு ஒன்பது படி ஊருக்குப் பத்துப் படி.

Nine measures for your friends and ten for the country.

1380. உறி அற மூளிநாய்க்கு வேட்டை.

The snapping of the cord of the swinging-tray is like a hunting excursion to the cropped dog.

1381. உறியிலே தயிர் இருக்க ஊர் எங்கும் போனாற்போல்.

As if one sought curds throughout the village when a supply was on his own tray.

1382. உறியிலே வெண்ணெய் இருக்க நெய்க்கு அலைவானேன்?

Why go about in quest of ghee when you have butter on *your own* tray?

1383. உறியிற் பணம் போய்த் தெருவிற் சண்டையை இழுக்கிறது.

The money on the swinging-tray goes out and picks a quarrel in the public road.

Money is not infrequently put on a swinging tray in a cup or small basket.

1384. உறுதியான காரியம் ஒருபோதும் கெடாது.

An affair firmly settled will never fail.

1385. உறுதிக்கு உதவாதவன் உறவனா?

Is he a friend who helps not in adversity?

1386. உற்சாகம் செய்தால் மச்சைத் தாண்டுவான்.

If encouraged, he will jump over the house top.

1387. உற்ற சிநேகிதன் உயிர்க்கு அமிர்தம்.

A true friend is the nectar of life.

1388. உற்றது சொன்னால் அற்றது பொருந்தும்.

When the truth is told, a breach between friends may be healed.

1389. உற்றது சொல்ல ஊரும் அல்ல, நல்லது சொல்ல நாடும் அல்ல.

This is not the village in which a man may speak the truth, nor the country in which, to give advice.

1390. உற்றார் தின்றால் புற்றாய் விளையும், ஊரார் தின்றால் போராய் விளையும்.

If friends consume *one's grain* an ant hole, if strangers consume it, fame.

1391. உற்றாருக்கு ஒன்றும் கொடான், நமனுக்கு நாலும் கொடுப்பான்.

He will give nothing to friends, but to Yama *the regent of the dead* he will give even four i. e., all.

1392. உற்றார் உதவுவாரோ அன்னியர் உதவுவாரோ?

Will friends help or will strangers?

1393. உனக்கும் பேபே உன் அப்பனுக்கும் பேபே.

Pè, pè to you, and pè pè to your father also.

The following story is told about this proverb:—a debtor had two creditors. One of them said if you will pay me I will suggest an expedient for getting rid of the other creditor He then instructed him when again applied to for payment, to feign madness, and to say Pé, Pé a demon, a demon. The creditor not satisfied had him summoned before a Magistrate where he did as before. The Magistrate thinking the debtor mad, decided that he was not amenable to a court of justice.

The other creditor then went to the debtor expecting to be paid according to promise To his surprise the man said Pé, Pé, whereupon he said, do you deal with me also in this way, when, the debtor replied as the proverb stands.

1394. உனக்கு யான் அபயம் எனக்கு நீ உபயம்.

I am under your protection, you are my patron.

1395. உன் சமர்த்திலே குண்டு பாயாது.

Bullets will not fly by your strength.

1396. உன் சொல்லிலே உப்பும் இல்லை புளியும் இல்லை.

In your words there is neither salt nor acid.

1397. உன் முறுக்குத் திருக்கு எல்லாம் என் உடுப்புக்குள்ளே.

Your petulance and fraud are all in my dress.

1398. உன்னை வஞ்சித்தவனை ஒருபோதும் நம்பாதே.

Never trust one who has deceived you.

1399. உன்னைக் கொடுப்பேனோ சென்னைக் கூனி, நீ சுமை சுமந்தல்லோ கூனிப்போனாய்.

O thou hunch-backed woman of Madras, how can I give thee up, hast thou not become crooked by bearing burdens!

ஊ.

1400. ஊசல் ஆடியும் தன் நிலையில் நிற்கும.

Though the swing oscillates, it will resume its proper centre

1401. ஊசி ஒரு முழத்துணியையாவது கொடுக்கும் உற்றார் என்ன கொடுப்பார்?

A needle will give a cubit of cloth, what will your friends give?

1402. ஊசி கொள்ளப் போய்த் துலாம் கணக்குப் பார்க்கிறதா?

When going to buy a needle, is the weight to be regarded!

1403. ஊசி கோக்கிறதற்கு ஊரில் துளாவாரம் ஏன்?

Why such a stir in the village about threading a needle?

1404. ஊசிக்குக் கள்ளன் உடனே இருப்பான்.

Where there is a needle there will be a thief.

1405. ஊசிக்கு ஊசி எதிரேறிப் பாயுமா?

Can one needle penetrate another when brought point to point!

1406. ஊசி பொன்னானால் என்ன பெறும்?

Though made of gold what will a needle fetch!

1407. ஊசி போகிறது கணக்குப் பார்ப்பான் பூசனிக்காய் போகிறது தெரியாது.

He notes the loss of needles, but not that of pumpkins.

1408. ஊசிபோல மிடறும் தாழிபோல வயிறும்.

A throat like a needle, a belly like a caldron.

1409. ஊசி மலிவென்று சீமைக்குப் போகலாமா?
May one go to a foreign country to buy needles because they are there cheap?

1410. ஊசி முனையில் தவம் செய்தாலும் உள்ளதுதான் கிடைக்கும்.
Though penance be performed by standing on the point of a needle, that which is predestined only will be obtained.

1411. ஊசியின் காதில் ஒட்டகம் நுழையுமா?
Can a camel pass through the eye of a needle?

1412. ஊசியை ஊசிக்காந்தம் இழுக்கும், உத்தமனைச் சினேகம் இழுக்கும்.
A magnet attracts a needle, friendship, the good.

1413. ஊணன் கருமம் இழந்தான், உலுத்தன் பெயர் இழந்தான்.
The glutton failed in his object, and the miser lost his fame.

1414. ஊணினால் உறவு பூணினால் அழகு.
Friendship is promoted by entertainments, and beauty is set off by ornaments

1415. ஊணினால் புத்தி பூணினால் சாதி.
Good sense *is indicated* by food, and rank by ornaments.

1416. ஊணுக்கு முந்தவேண்டும் கோளுக்குப் பிந்தவேண்டும்.
Be first at a feast, and the last to slander.

1417. ஊணும் இல்லை உறக்கமும் இல்லை.
Neither food nor sleep.

1418. ஊண் அற்றபோதே உறவு அற்றுப்போம்.
When entertainment is discontinued, friendship ceases.

1419. ஊண்பாக்கு ஒழிய வீண்பாக்கு ஆகாது.
Betel is not good except after food.

1420. ஊத அறிந்தவன் வாதி உப்பு அறிந்தவன் யோகி.
He is an alchemist who knows how to infuse metals, and he is a Yogi who knows the quality of salt.

1421. ஊதாரிக்குப் பொன்னும் துரும்பு.

Even gold is a mere rush to the spendthrift.

1422. ஊதினற் போம் உறிஞ்சினல் வரும்.

If blown it will fly off, if sucked it will go in.

1423. ஊதுகிற சங்கு ஊதினல் விடிகிறபோது விடிகிறது.

If you blow the conch, the day will break as it is wont.

1424. ஊத்தைவாயன் தேட நாற்றவாயன் தின்ன.

Acquired by the filthy mouthed and consumed by the fetid mouthed.

1425. ஊத்தை திரண்டு அச்சாணி ஆகுமா?

Will the dirt on one's body when collected form a linch-pin?

1426. ஊத்தைவாயன் தேடக் கர்ப்பூரவாயன் தின்ன.

Accumulated by the foul mouthed and consumed by a mouth fragrant with camphor.

1427. ஊத்தை போகக் குளித்தவனும் இல்லை பசிபோகத் தின்றவனும் இல்லை.

No one performs ablutions so as not to repeat them, nor does any one eat so as not again to suffer hunger.

1428. ஊமை ஊரைக் கெடுக்கும் ஆமை கிணற்றைக் கெடுக்கும்.

The dumb destroys a viliage, a tortoise or turtle destroys a well.

1429. ஊமை ஊரைக் கெடுக்கும் பெருச்சாளி வீட்டைக் கெடுக்கும்.

A community is injured by the dumb, and a house by bandycootes.

1430. ஊமை கண்ட கனப்போல் இருக்கிறது.

It is like the dream of the dumb.

He is unable to relate his dream and therefore cannot obtain its interpretation.

1431. ஊமைக்கு உளறுவாயன் உற்பாதபிண்டம்.

The dumb regards a babbler as a wonder.

1432. ஊமையன் பேச்சு பழகின பேருக்குத் தெரியும்.

The speech—*gesticulation*—of the dumb is known to those accustomed to it.

1433. ஊமையாயிருந்தால் செவிடும் உண்டு.

If one is dumb he is deaf also.

1434. ஊமையும் ஊமையும் மூக்கைச் சொறிந்தாற்போல.

As the dumb on meeting the dumb scratch their noses.

If a person on meeting a dumb man scratches his own nose the dumb man becomes very angry.

1435. ஊமையும் அல்ல செவிடும் அல்ல.

Neither dumb nor deaf.

1436. ஊராரைப பகைத்து உயிரோடு இருந்தவர் இல்லை.

No one at enmity with the whole community ever preserved his life.

1437. ஊரார் கணக்கு உடையவன் பிடரியிலே.

The liabilities of a village are on the neck of its chief.

1438. ஊரார் உடைமைக்குப் பேயாய்ப் பறக்கிறான்.

He flies on the property of others like a demon.

1439. ஊரார் எருமை பால் சுறக்கிறது நீயும் ஊட்டு நானும் உண்ணுகிறேன்.

The buffalo of the village is in milk, you suck and I will also suck.

1440. ஊரிலே கல்யாணம் மார்பிலே சந்தனம்.

Marriage ceremonies in the village and sandal paste on the breast.

1441. ஊரில் ஒருவனே தோழன் ஆரும் அற்றதே தாரம்.

Have one only of the community as a friend, and a woman without ties as a wife.

1442. ஊரில் எளியாரை வண்ணான் அறிவான் சாதிப்பொன் பூண்டாரைத் தட்டான் அறிவான்.

The washerman knows the poor of a village, the goldsmith knows whose ornaments are made of fine gold.

1443. ஊருக்கெல்லாம் ஒரு வழி உனக்கு ஒரு வழியா ?

While all the people of the village have one road in common, do you expect one for yourself ?

1444. ஊருக்குப் பால்வார்த்து உண்ணுகிறாயா உடம்புக்குப் பால்வார்த்து உண்ணுகிறாயா ?

Do you take milk on account of the community or to promote your own health ?

1445. ஊருக்கெல்லாம் சாஸ்திரம் சொல்லுகிற பல்லி கூழ்ப்பானையில் விழுந்தாற்போல.

As if a lizard, the oracle of the whole village, should fall into a pot of gruel

Spoken reproachfully, when a person remarkable either by position or profession, has done something injurious to his reputation.

The lizard—பல்லி a newt—here referred to, is seen on the walls of houses in India and Ceylon, and its chirp may be frequently heard. Its voice is never disregarded since it may bear a message of great consequence to the family or individual concerned. A small book called the *Shaster of the Lizard* contains all needed information regarding its chirping. On hearing it the facts *to be observed are* the point of the compass, the hour of the day &c These being known the party has recourse to his formula and ascertains whether the omen is auspicious or not. The premonitions of this little domestic monitor derive their significance from the character of the preternatural regent who may at the time preside over the region indicated by the chirp. Thus it appears that the shaster of the domestic lizard is based on the dogmas of Astrology.

1446. ஊருக்கு ஆகாதவன் வீட்டுக்கும் ஆகான்.

He who is useless abroad is useless at home.

1447. ஊருக்கு ஆகாத பிள்ளை தாய்க்கு ஆகுமா ?

Is a child injurious to the community, of any use to its mother ?

1448. ஊருக்கு ஓமல் வீட்டுக்கு வயிற்றெரிச்சல்.

Fame abroad and famine at home.

1449. ஊருக்கு இளைத்தவன் பிள்ளையார்கோயில் ஆண்டி.

He who was too feeble for the service of the community became a devotee in the temple of Genèsha.

In Sanskrit a similar proverb exists: "The dancing girl being old has become a devotee" It is a case not of breaking away from sinful habits, but the power of sinning is gone.

1450. ஊருடன் பகைக்கில் வேருடன் கெடும்.

If one is hated by the whole community he will be rooted out.

1451. ஊரெங்கும் பேர் வீடு பட்டினி.

Fame throughout the country, at home starvation.

1452. ஊரெல்லாம் வாழ்கிறதென்று வீடெல்லாம் புரண்டு அழுதால் வருமா?

Can you gain anything by wallowing and weeping because the village is prosperous?

1453. ஊரெல்லாம் சுற்றி எனக்கு என்ன புத்தி என்கிறான்.

Having wandered all over the country he says, what advice do you give.

1454. ஊரெல்லாம் உற்றார் அந்திபட்டால் பொதி சந்தியிலே.

He has friends in every part of the village, yet his bundle is left in the public road after sun-set.

1455. ஊரென்று இருந்தால் பறைச்சேரியும் இருக்கும்.

Wherever there is a village there is a *Parachéri*.

A Parachery is a hamlet of Pariahs—non caste Natives. Pariahs are employed in the lowest offices, as beaters of the tomtom or Native drum on festive and mournful occasions. They are employed to publish proclamations &c, as a bell-man in Europe.

1456. ஊரை உழக்கால் அளக்கிறாள் நாட்டை நாழியால் அளக்கிறாள்.

She measures the village with an ulak and the province with a nàli.

The உழக்கு is a quarter of a படி. உழக்காழாக்கு three eighths of a measure. A நாழி is a measure, of which there are eight in a மரக்கால், marcàl.

1457. ஊரைப் பார்க்கச்சொன்னால் பறைச்சேரியைப் பார்க்கிறான்.

When told to visit the village, he goes to the Pariah quarter.

1458. ஊரைப் பிடித்த சனி பிள்ளையாரையும் பிடித்தது.

Saturn that seized the village seized also Ganesha.

One thing happens to all.

1459. ஊரை வளைத்தாலும் உற்ற துணை இல்லை, நாட்டை வளைத்தாலு
ம் நல்ல துணை இல்லை.

Though one goes round the village he finds no help, though he goes round the country no real aid can be got.

1460. ஊரோட ஒக்க ஓடு நாடோட நடு ஓடு.

If the people of the village flee, join them, if the whole country flee, flee in their midst.

1461. ஊரோர்ச்சம் வீடு பட்டினி.

Distinguished abroad, starving at home.

1462. ஊர் ஆளுகிறவன் பெண்டு பிடித்தால் ஆருடன் சொல்லி முறை
யிடுகிறது?

When the ruler of a village forcibly takes away another man's wife, to whom is be to make his complaint!

1463. ஊர் இருக்கிறது ஓடு இருக்கிறது.

The village still exists and also the alms-dishes.

1464. ஊர் இரண்டுபட்டால் கூத்தாடிக்குக் கொண்டாட்டம்.

If the village be divided into two parties, it will be advantageous to the commedians.

1465. ஊர் இளப்பம் வண்ணானுக்குத் தெரியும்.

That which is bad or exceptionable in a village is known to its washerman.

The clothes of all pass through his hands, he has therefore the opportunity of inferring much from their condition.

1466. ஊர் உண்டு பிச்சைக்கு, குளம் உண்டு தண்ணீருக்கு.

There is a village for alms, and a tank for water.

1467. ஊர் ஓரத்திற் கொல்லை உழுதவனுக்குப் பயிர் இல்லை.

He that cultivates a field on the outskirts of a village loses its produce.

1468. ஊரா கூடிச் செக்குத் தள்ளினுற்போல.

As if a whole village united to put an oil-press in motion

1469. ஊர்க்குருவிமேல் ராமபாணம் தொடுக்கிறதா ?

What, discharge Ráma's arrow at a sparrow ?

Why lavish means so precious on objects so mean !

1470. ஊர்க்கோழியும் நாட்டுக்கோழியும் கூடி உரலிற் புழுங்கல் அரிசிக்குச் சேதம்.

When the poultry of the village and the poultry of the country at large come together, the rice in the mortar is spoiled.

1471. ஊர் நஷ்டம் ஊரிலே தேர் நஷ்டம் தெருவிலே.

Loss occurring in a village affects the community, injury occasioned by a temple car is apparent in the street.

1472. ஊர் நல்லதோ வாய் நல்லதோ ?

Is the village good or your description ?

1473. ஊர்ப்பிள்ளையை முத்தமிட்டால், உதட்டுக்குக் கேடு.

To kiss the child of another is bad for the lips.

1474. ஊர்வாயைப் படலிட்டு மூடலாமா ?

Is it possible to shut the mouth of a village by a hurdle.

1475. ஊர் வாழ்ந்தால் ஓட்டுப்பிச்சைக்கும் வழி இருக்கும்.

If the village be prosperous—there will be an opening for alms-dishes.

1476. ஊழிக்காய்ச்சல அதிகம் ஆனல சூனியக்காரன் கொள்ளை.

When epidemic fever prevails, sorcerers abound.

1477. ஊழி பேரினும் ஊக்கமது கைவிடேல்.

Though the world come to an end do not remit your efforts.

1478. ஊழிற் பெருவலி ஒன்று உண்டோ?

Is there any power greater than destiny?

1479. ஊழும் உற்சாகமும் ஒத்துக்கொள்ளவேண்டும்.

Destiny and exertion must go together.

1480. ஊன்றக் கொடுத்த தடி உச்சியை உடைக்கிறது.

The staff I gave for his support breaks the crown of my head.

எ.

1481. எங்களால் ஒன்றும் இல்லை எலலாம் உங்கள் கர்மம்.

Nothing lies in our might, all must be done by you.

1482. எங்கும் மடமாய் இருக்கிறது இருக்கத்தான் இடம் இல்லை.

Choultries everywhere, but no place of accommodation.

1483. எங்கே அடித்தாலும் நாய் காலைத் தூக்கும்.

No matter where hit, a dog when struck, lifts up his leg.

1484. எங்கே புகை உண்டோ அங்கே நெருப்பு உண்டு.

Wherever there is smoke there is fire.

1485. எச்சிலைத் தின்று ஏப்பம் இட்டாற்போல.

Like belching after eating leavings.

1486. எச்சிலைத் தின்று பசி தீருமா?

Can hunger be appeased by eating leavings?

1487. எச்சிற்கல்லைக்கு மண்ணாங்கட்டி ஆதரவு மண்ணாங்கட்டிக்கு எச்சிற்கல்லை ஆதரவு.

A clod is the support of the leaf-plate, and the leaf-plate is the support of the clod.

1488. எச்சில் இரக்க அடிக்கும், பற்று பறக்க அடிக்கும்.

Spitting *about* will drive one to beggary, and ceremonial impurity will scatter a family.

1489. எச்சிற்கையால் காக்கை ஓட்டமாட்டான்.

He will not scare away a crow with an unwashen hand.

1490. எச்சில் எடுக்கச் சொன்னார்களா எத்தனைபேர் சாப்பிட்டதென்று கணக்குப்பார்க்கச் சொன்னார்களா?

Did they order the leavings to be removed, or an account to be taken of the number who had eaten?

1491. எச்சில் தின்றாலும் வயிறு நிறையத் தின்னவேண்டும், ஏச்சுக் கேட்டாலும் பொழுது விடிகிறமட்டும் கேட்கவேண்டும்.

If you eat offal eat heartily, if you listen to abusive language, listen till day-break.

1492. எச்சிலிலைக்கு நாய் அடித்துக்கொண்டு நிற்கிறதுபோல.

As dogs impatiently wait for leaf-plates.

1493. எச்சிலைக் கழுவி உன் சுத்தத்திலே வார்.

Wash off the refuse and pour *the water* on your clean *person*.

Spoken in derision of affected cleanliness.

1494. எடுக்குமுன்னம் கழுதை இடுப்பு ஒடிந்து விழுந்ததாம்.

It is said that the ass fell down with a broken hip as soon as it was loaded.

1495. எடுக்கப் போன சீமாட்டி இடுப்பு ஒடிந்து விழுந்தாளாம்.

It is said that the wealthy matron, whom one had gone to take *in marriage*, fell down, her waist having *broken*.

1496. எடுத்தாலும் பங்காருப்பெட்டியை எடுக்கவேண்டும் இருந்தாலும் சிங்காரக்கழுவில் இருக்கவேண்டும்.

If you steal, take away a golden casket; if you are impaled, endure the punishment on an ornamented stake.

1497. எடுத்த சுமை சுமந்தல்லவோ இறக்கவேண்டும்?

A burden must be first carried, must it not, before it is put down!

1498. எடுத்து ஆளாத பொருள் உதவாது.

Things unused, spoil.

1499. எடுத்த அடி மடங்குமா ?

Will the lifted foot be drawn back ?

1500. எடுத்துவிட்ட எருது எத்தனை நாள் உழும் ?

How long can an ox plough that requires to be lifted up ?

1501. எடுப்பது பிச்சை ஏறுவது பல்லக்கு.

His occupation is begging, his conveyance a palanquin.

1502. எடுப்பாரும் பிடிப்பாரும் உண்டானால் இளைப்பும் தவிப்பும் உண்டு.

Where many are in attendance to lift up and support, there will be weariness and fainting.

1503. எடுப்பார் கைக் குழந்தை.

A baby in the arms.

1504. எடுப்பார் மழுவைத் தடுப்பார் புலியைக் கொடுப்பார் அருமை.

There are who take up the battle axe, and there are who stop tigers. but givers are scarce.

1505. எடுப்புண்ட கலப்பை இருந்து உழுமா ?

Will a worn out plough last long ?

1506. எட்டாப் பழத்தைப் பார்த்துக் கொட்டாவி விட்டதுபோல.

As one gazed and gaped at a fruit beyond his reach.

1507. எட்டாப் பூ தேவர்க்கு எட்டும் பூ தங்களுக்கு.

Flowers beyond reach are sacred to God, but those within reach are for themselves.

1508. எட்டிக் குட்டி இறங்கிக் காலைப் பிடித்துக்கொள்ளுகிறதா ?

What ! is it to reach up and cuff, and cower and cling to the feet !

1509. எட்டி பழுத்து என்ன, ஈயாதார் வாழ்ந்து என்ன ?

What if the fruit of the etti tree (strychnos nux vomica) ripens ; of what use is the prosperity of the niggardly ?

1510. எட்டிமரமானாலும் பச்சென்று இருக்கவேண்டும்.

Though a *poisonous* tree, it should be green.

1511. எட்டிமரமானாலும் வைத்த மரத்தை வெட்டாதே.

Cut not down the tree you planted though it is the (strychnos nux vomica.)

I have observed among many natives a remarkable disinclination to cut down trees: though not rational creatures they are said to have one sense அறிவு.

1512. எட்டிக்குப் பால்வார்த்து வளர்த்தாலும் தித்திப்பு உண்டாகுமா?

Although you may nourish an etti tree by pouring milk at its root, will it become sweet?

1513. எட்டியிலே கட்டுமாம்பழம் உண்டாமோ?

Will an etti tree bear graft-mangoes?

1514. எட்டியுடனே சேர்ந்த இலவும் தீப்படும்.

Even the silk-cotton tree growing by the etti will also be consumed by fire.

Evil association brings destruction.

1515. எட்டினால் குடுமியைப் பிடிக்கிறது எட்டாவிட்டால் காலைப் பிடிக்கிறது.

If it can be reached, seizing by the kudumi *knot of hair*, if not, clinging to the feet.

1516. எட்டி எட்டிப் பார்த்துக் குட்டிச்சுவரிலே முட்டிக்கொள்ளலாமா?

Can you strike your head against a dwarf wall when peeping on tiptoe?

1517. எட்டி எட்டிப் பார்ப்பாரும் ஏணி வைத்துப் பார்ப்பாரும் குட்டிச்சுவராலே குனிந்து நின்று பார்ப்பாரும் உண்டு.

There are who peep on tiptoe, there are who peep on a ladder, there are those who peep over a dwarf wall crouching.

1518. எட்டிமரமானாலும் வைத்தவர்க்குப் பக்ஷம்.

Though an etti tree, he who planted it will like it.

1519. எட்டிப்பழத்தை இச்சிக்கிறதா ?

What, is an etti fruit to be desired !

1520. எட்டுக் கிழவரும் ஒரு மொட்டைக்கிழவியைக் கட்டிக்கொண்டார்கள்.

Eight old men conjointly took to wife a bald-headed old woman.

1521. எட்டுக் குஞ்சு அடித்தாலும் சட்டிக்கறி ஆகாது.

Eight chickens are not sufficient for a chatty of curry.

1522. எட்டு வருஷத்து எருமைக்கடா ஏரிக்குப் போக வழி தேடுகின்றது.

A buffalo eight years old is at a loss to find its way to the tank.

1523. எண்சாண் உடம்பும் ஒரு சாணுனேன்.

My eight-span body is reduced to one span.

1524. எண்சாண் உடம்பிலே எள்ளத்தனை நாணம் இல்லை.

There is not a grain of modesty in *his* eight-span body.

1525. எண்சாண் உடம்பிற்கும் சிரசே பிரதானம்.

The head is the chief part of the eight-span body.

1526. எண்ணம் எல்லாம் பொய் எமன் ஓலை மெய்.

All *our* thoughts are vain, the ola of Yama is real.

Ola is the name of the Palmyra palm leaf. On this material, books, accounts, correspondence &c., are written with an iron pen. Several of the Tamil books I first read were written on ola. Yama, the regent of the dead, is graphically represented as stretching out his hand to deliver the order for departure

1527. எண்ணம் எல்லாம் பொய் ஏளிதம் மெய்.

Expectations are all unreal, a despicable condition is a reality.

1528. எண்ணறக் கற்று எழுத்தற வாசித்தாலும் பெண் புத்தி பின் புத்தியே.

No matter how skilled a woman may be in numbers and letters, her judgment will be second rate.

Many modern Hindus of the day 1873 though themselves earnest about University honors, evince but very little interest regarding the intellectual and moral culture of their daughters The Rev K. M. Banerjee, a learned brahman of Calcutta, very recently gave a sad account of the disabilities to which native ladies in that city are subject.

1529. எண்ணப்பட்ட குதிரை எல்லாம் மண்ணைப் போட்டுக்கொள்ள, தட்டுவாணிக்குதிரை வந்து கொள்ளுக்கு அழுகிறதாம்.

Whilst horses of the first blood lick the ground, the miserable tattoo is neighing for gram.

1530. எண்ணம் அற்ற இராசன் பன்றிவேட்டை ஆடினாற்போல்.

As an incautions king went to hunt wild hog.

1531. எண்ணம் எல்லாம் பொய் எழுதிய எழுத்து மெய்.

All imaginations may be false, that which is written is true, *certain*.

1532. எண் இல்லாதவர் கண் இல்லாதவர், எழுத்து இல்லாதவர் கழுத்து இல்லாதவர்.

Those who are ignorant of figures have no eyes, those who are ignorant of letters have no head.

1533. எண்ணிச் செய்கிறவன் செட்டி எண்ணாமற் செய்கிறவன் மட்டி.

He who acts after due consideration is a chitty *a superior man*, he who acts without consideration is a matti *a fool*.

1534. எண்ணிச் செய்வது செட்டு எண்ணாமற் செய்வது வேளாண்மை.

Trade requires forethought, agriculture requires none.

1535. எண்ணிய எண்ணம் என்னடி அண்ணா என்று அழைத்த முறை என்னடி?

What was our expectation, and what led you to call me elder brother?

1536. எண்ணித் துணிவது கருமம், துணிந்தபின் எண்ணுவது இழுக்கு.

An action undertaken after due consideration *may prove successful*, consideration after action may end in disgrace

1537. என்னிய குடிக்கு ஒரு மின்னிய முடி.

A brilliant crown for an illustrious family.

1538. எண்ணெய் முந்துகிறதோ திரி முந்துகிறதோ?

It is questionable which will be *first consumed*, the oil or the wick.

1539. எண்ணெய் போக முழுகினாலும் எழுத்துப் போகத் தேய்ப்பார் உண்டா?

Although oil may be washed off, can the writing *of Brahma* be rubbed off?

1540. எண்ணெய்ச் செலவொழிய பிள்ளை பிழைத்தபாடு இல்லை.

As regards the child's recovery, nothing has resulted but an expenditure of oil.

1541. எண்ணெய்க் குடத்தைச் சுற்றும் எறும்புபோல.

Like ants round a pot of oil.

1542. எண்ணெய்ப் பிள்ளையோ வண்ணப் பிள்ளையோ?

Is the beauty attributable to oil, or is it real?

1543. எண் மிகுத்தவனே திண் மிகுத்தவனே.

He who excels in figures excels in strength.

1544. எதாகுதல பேசினால் அகப்பைச் சூனியம் வைப்பேன்.

If you speak a word, I will place *before you* an empty ladle.

1545. எதார்த்தவாதி வெகு சன விரோதி.

He who is truthful *may be* the enemy of many.

1546. எதிரி இளைப்பமானால் கோபம் சண்டப்பிரசண்டம்.

If the opposite party be inferior in position, the anger of his enemy will rage like a tempest.

1547. எதிரிக்கு இளக்காரமாய்ச் சொல்லுகிறதா?

What, is it to yield to an opponent?

1548. எதிர்த்த வீடு ஏகாலி வீடு, அடுத்த வீடு அம்பட்டன் வீடு.

The house opposite is the washerman's. and my next door neighbour is a barber.

1549. எதிர்வீடு ஏகாலி வீடு, பக்கத்து வீடு பணிசெய்பவன் வீடு, அடுத்த வீடு அம்பட்டன் வீடு.

The opposite house is the washerman's, the adjoining house is the goldsmith's, and the next to mine is that of the barber.

1550. எதிர்த்தவன் ஏழை என்றால் கோபம் சண்டாளம்.

When the opposed is poor, the anger of his opponent ends in cruelty.

1551. எது எப்படிப் போனாலும் தன் காரியம் தனக்கு.

No matter how any thing may go, each should mind his own business.

1552. எத்தனைதான் துலக்கினாலும் பித்தளை நாற்றம் போகுமா?

No matter how frequently it may be polished, the bad odour of brass will not leave it.

1553. எத்தனை புடம் இட்டாலும் இரும்பு பசும்பொன் ஆகாது.

Though iron may be heated never so much, it will not become gold.

1554. எத்தனை ஏழை ஆனாலும் எலுமிச்சங்காய் அத்தனை பொன் இல்லாமற்போமா?

However poor one may be, will he not possess gold, at least of the value of a lemon?

1555. எத்தாற் பிழைக்கலாம் ஒத்தாற் பிழைக்கலாம்.

How may we subsist? if united we may subsist.

1556. எத்திலே பிள்ளை பெற்று இரவலிலே தாலாட்டுகிறது.

Bringing forth a child without cost, and rocking it in a borrowed cradle.

1557. எத்தேச காலமும் வற்றாப் பெருஞ் சமுத்திரம்.

An ocean that knows no ebb anywhere at any time.

1558. எந்த ஆயுதமும் தீட்டத்தீட்டக் கூரும்.

The more an instrument is whetted, the sharper it becomes.

1559. எந்த இலை உதிர்ந்தாலும் ஈச்சம் இலை உதிராது.
Though the leaves of other trees may fall off, those of the date-palm will not.

1560. எந்தப் புற்றிலே எந்தப் பாம்பு இருக்கிறதோ தெரியாது.
It is not known what species of snake may be found in any particular hole.

1561. எந்த வாக்குப் பொய்த்தாலும் சந்தவாக்குப் பொய்யாது.
Whatever else may fail the words, *marks*, of low breeding will not fail.

1562. எந்நேரமும் அவள்பேரில் கண்ணாய் இருக்கிறான்.
His eye is always upon her.

1563. எமனுக்கு வழிகாட்டுவான்.
He can pilot Yama, *the regent of the dead.*

1564. எமன் பிள்ளையைப் பேய் பிடிக்குமா?
Will a demon seize the child of Yama, *the regent of the dead*?

1565. எய்கிறவன் எய்தால் அம்பு என்ன செய்யும்?
What can the arrow do if discharged by a skilful archer?

1566. எய்தவன் இருக்க அம்பை நோவானேன்?
Why blame the arrow, letting the archer go free?

1567. எரிகிற கொள்ளியை ஏறத் தள்ளினதுபோல.
As a burning firebrand was pushed into the hearth.

1568. எரிகிற கொள்ளியில் எந்தக் கொள்ளி நல்ல கொள்ளி?
Which of the burning firebrands is the best?

1569. எரிகிறதைப் பிடுங்கினால் கொதிக்கிறது அடங்கும்.
If the burning fuel be removed, the bubbling will cease.

1570. எரிகிற நெருப்பை எண்ணெய் விட்டு அவிக்கலாமா?
May a burning fire be extinguished by pouring oil on it?

1571. எரிகிற நெருப்பிலே நெய் விட்டதுபோல.
As if ghee were poured on a flaming fire.

1572. எரிகிற வீட்டை அவிக்கக் கிணறு வெட்ட நாள் பார்த்தது போல.

Like seeking an auspicious day, to dig a well in order to quench the flames of a house on fire.

1573. எரிகிற வீட்டிற் பிடுங்குகிறது லாபம்.

Whatever is abstracted from a burning house is a gain.

1574. எருதின் புண்ணிற்குச் சாம்பல் மருந்து.

Ashes are medicine for the sores of a bull.

1575. எருதுக்கும் தன் புண் அழற்சி காக்கைக்கும் தன் பசி அழற்சி.

The buffalo suffers from the smarting of its sores, and the crow *that picks them* suffers from the smarting of hunger.

1576. எருது கொழுத்தால் தொழுவத்தில் இராது, பறையன் கொழுத்தால் பாயில் இரான்.

If an ox grow fat, it will not remain in a stall; if a Pariah becomes rich, he will not sit on a mat.

1577. எருது நோயை நினைக்கும், காக்கை பசியை நினைக்கும்.

The ox feels the pain, the crow its hunger.

1578. எருது நோய் காக்கைக்குத் தெரியுமா?

Is a crow aware what pain *it occasions when picking the sore* of an ox?

1579. எருது ஈன்றது என்றால் தொழுத்திலே கட்டு என்கிறது.

If it be reported that the bull has a calf, he will say, O, tie it up in the stall.

1580. எருது கெட்டார்க்கும் எட்டே கடுக்காய். இளம்பிள்ளைத்தாய்ச்சிக்கும் எட்டே கடுக்காய்.

Giving eight gall nuts to him who has lost a bull, and eight to a woman in the first stage of pregnancy.

1581. எருது வாங்குமுன்னே புன்செய்க்கு உழு என்கிறாய்.

You bid me plough the dry land before the ox is bought.

1582. எருது நினைத்த இடத்திலே தொழும் கட்டுகிறதா ?

Is its shed put up where the bull may think fit ?

1583. எருது கோபங்கொண்டு பரதேசம் போனதுபோல.

As a bull went away in a rage to a foreign country.

1584. எருது மறைவிற் புல்லுத் தின்கிறாயா ?

Dost thou eat grass screened by a bull ?

1585. எருதுக்கு நோய் வந்தால் கொட்டாயைச் சுடுகிறதா ?

Is its shed to be burnt down because the ox is sick ?

1586. எருதும் வண்டியும் ஒத்தால் மேடு பள்ளம் ஏது ?

What matters the ruggedness *of the road* if the bullocks and bandy-*a country cart*-hold together ?

1587. எருமைக்கடா என்றாலும் குழந்தைக்குப் பால் ஒரு பீர் இல்லையா என்கிறாய்.

Though it is a male buffalo, you ask me if there be not a drop of milk for the child.

1588. எருமை வாங்குமுன் நெய்விலை கூறுகிறாய்.

You publish the price of ghee before buying a buffalo.

1589. எருமைக் கொம்பு நனைகிறதற்குமுன்னே எழுபது தரம் மழை வருகிறது.

It will rain seventy times before a buffalo's horns will be wet.

1590. எருமைக் கோமயம் எக்கியத்திற்கு ஆகுமா ?

Will the dung of the buffalo serve for sacrificial purposes ?

1591. எருமை மாட்டின்மேல் மழை பெய்ததுபோல.

As it rained on a buffalo.

1592. எருமை மாட்டின்மேல் எத்தனை சூடு இருந்தாலும் தெரியாது, பசுமாட்டில் ஒரு சூடு இருந்தாலும் தெரியும்.

Brands on a buffalo however numerous will scarcely appear, but a single brand on a cow will be visible.

1593. எருமை இருந்தல்லோ பால் கறக்கவேண்டும்?

We may milk may we not, provided there be a buffalo?

1594. எருமையிலும் வெள்ளாடு ஏறக்கறக்குமா?

Will a goat yield more milk than a buffalo?

1595. எருவுக்குப் போனவன் இளையாளைக் கைப்பிடித்தாற்போல.

As he who went in search of manure, seized the hand of a maiden.

1596. எருவுக்குப் போனவன் எலுமிச்சம்பழம் எடுத்ததுபோல.

As he who went to pick up cow-dung, gathered lemons.

1597. எலி அம்மணத்தோடே போகின்றது என்கிறான்.

He says that the rat goes naked.

1598. எலி அழுதால் பூனை விடுமா?

Will the cat leave its hold on the crying of the rat?

1599. எலி அழுது புலம்பினாலும் பூனை பிடித்தது விடாது.

Although the rat may cry and lament, the cat will not relinquish its hold.

1600. எலி அறுக்கும் தூக்கமாட்டாது.

The rat nibbles the grain, but it does not carry off *the basket.*

1601. எலி இருக்கிற இடத்தில் பாம்பு இருக்கும்.

Where there is a rat, there will also be a snake.

1602. எலிக்குப் பயந்து வீட்டைச் சுட்டதுபோல.

Like burning down the house for fear of rats.

1603. எலிக்குப் பிராணவஸ்தை பூனைக்குக் கொண்டாட்டம்.

The death-struggle of a rat is the sport of a cat.

1604. எலிக்கு அனுகூலம் பாம்பு பிடாரனுக்கு அஞ்சுதல், எளியார்க்கு அனுகூலம் வலியார் இராசனுக்கு அஞ்சுதல்.

The snake's fear of him who catches it, is favourable to the rat; when the strong fear the king, the weak are benefited.

1605. எலிக்கு மணியம் சுவரை அறுக்கிறதுதான்.
The business of the rat is to burrow in the wall.

1606. எலி தலையிலே கோடாலி விழுந்ததுபோல.
As an axe fell on the head of the rat

1607. எலி தலையிற் கோபுரம் இடிந்து விழுந்தாற்போல.
As if the tower of the temple should fall on the head of a rat.

1608. எலி பூனையை வெல்லுமா?
Can a rat overcome a cat?

1609. எலி பூனைக்குச் சலாம்பண்ணுவதுபோல.
As a rat makes salaam to a cat.

1610. எலிப்பிழுக்கை இறப்பில் இருந்து என்ன, வரப்பில் இருந்து என்ன?
What matters it whether the droppings of a rat are in the inside of a sloping roof, or on the ridge of a cornfield?

1611. எலியும் பூனையும்போல இருக்கிறது.
Living like a rat and a cat.

1612. எலியும் பூனையும் இணைந்து விளையாடினதுபோல.
As the rat and the cat united in sport.

1613. எலியைக் கண்டு பூனை ஏக்கம் அடையுமா?
Will the cat be alarmed at the sight of a rat?

1614. எலியைக் கண்டு பூனை ஏங்கி ஏங்கிக் கிடக்குமோ?
Will a cat be greatly alarmed at the sight of a rat?

1615. எலிவளை ஆனாலும் தனிவளை வேண்டும்.
A separate hole is to be preferred though it be a rat-hole.
One's own cot is desirable however humble.

1616. எலி வீடு கட்டப் பாம்பு குடிகொள்ளும்.
A rat makes the hole, a snake inhabits it.

1617. எலிவேட்டைக்குத் தவில் அடிப்பாரா?
Do they beat a tomtom when hunting rats?

1618. எலுமிச்சங்காய்க்குப் புளி ஏற்றுகிறதுபோல.

Like infusing acidity into a lemon.

1619. எலுமிச்சஞ்செடிக்கு எருப் போட்டாற்போல.

Like manuring a lemon tree.

1620. எலும்பு கடிக்கிற நாய்க்குப் பருப்புச்சோறு ஏன்?

Why give pulse to a dog that gnaws bones?

1621. எலும்பு கடிக்கிற நாய் இரும்பு கடிக்குமா?

Can a dog that gnaws bones bite iron?

1622. எலும்பு இல்லா நா எல்லாம் பேசும்.

A boneless tongue may say any thing.

1623. எல்லாம் அறிந்தவனும் இல்லை, ஒன்றும் அறியாதவனும் இல்லை.

No one knows everything, nor is any one ignorant of everything.

1624. எல்லாம் இருக்கிறது பெட்டியிலே இலைக்கறி கடையச் சட்டி இல்லை.

Everything wanted is in the box, but there is no chatty in which to macerate the vegetable curry.

1625. எல்லாத் தலையிலும் எட்டு எழுத்து, என் தலையிலே பத்து எழுத்து.

On all heads there are eight letters, on mine there are ten.

1626. எல்லாருக்கும் சொலலுமாம் பல்லி, தான் போய்க் காடிப்பானை யில் விழுமாம்.

It is said that the lizard which uttered prognostications, will go and fall into the refuse pan.

1627. எல்லா மசகமும் சாயந்தரத்திற்முன் வருகிறது.

It is in the evening that all the mosquitos come.

1628. எல்லாருக்கும் சனி துரும்புபோல, எனக்குச் சனி மலைபோல.

Saturn who is a mere straw to all other men, to me is as a mountain.

1629. எல்லாரும் பாக்கு இவன் ஒரு தோப்பு.

All other men are areca-nuts, but this man is a grove of areca-trees.

1630. எல்லாரும் தடுக்கின்கீழ் நுழைந்தால் அவன் கோலத்தின்கீழ் நுழைவான்.

If all can hide themselves under a small mat, he can conceal himse'f und r the ornamental drawing on the floor.

The கோலம் here mentioned is a floor ornament very commonly formed at the entrance of a native house: the form is circular. These ornaments are renewed every morning They contain various devices In some a temple car as delineated, in others trees, birds, flowers They are generally striking because the combinations indicate considerable skill. It may be that they are connected with the prevalent ideas regarding the evil eye.

1631. எல்லாத் தாட்டோட்டும் குல்லாவுக்குள்ளே இருக்கிறது.

All the skill in steering centres in the out-rigger.

Out-rigger boats or canoes are common on the south western coast of Ceylon. They are very swift and most safe. In 1848 when at Colombo duty called me daily to a large ship at the time out in the offing anchored in seven fathoms of water. On the occasion under notice I went on board in an ordinary Cingalese out-rigger canoe. In the evening after having completed the berths, for my two daughters who were going home for education, I betook myself to the boat, and soon after we got clear of the ship the boat was struck in the stern, filled, and went down. When I emerged from the waves I found myself near one of the two brackets of the out-rigger. The canoe was submerged but could not sink lower than the ends of the brackets tied to her side. The out-rigger at the other end of the brackets was floating on the surface of the sea, the canoe being suspended by it like a pair of scales from a beam. Aided by one of those brackets, which I pressed to my bosom, and a Chubb's Palanquin box, I gained the rocks soon after sünset and escaped to land.

1632. எல்லா ஓட்டும் குல்லாவிலே.

All *our* progress depends on the outrigger.

1633. எல்லாரும் நல்லாரா, கல் எல்லாம் மாணிக்கமா?

Are all men good men, are all stones rubies?

1634. எல்லா வேலையும் செய்வான், செத்தால் பிழைக்கமாட்டான்.

He can do all things, but when dead he cannot resuscitate himself.

1635. எலலாரும் கப்பல் ஏறியாயிற்று இனி அம்மானுர் பொற்பட்டம் கட்டப்போகிருர்.

All have embarked, my uncle is about to receive a golden mark of distinction.

Spoken of aspirations beyond one's merits.

1636. எல்லாரும் ஏறி இளைத்த குதிரையில் சாஸ்திரியார் ஏறிச் சறுக்கி விழுந்தார்.

On mounting a jaded horse that all had ridden, the astrologer slipped and fell down.

1637. எல்லாம் அறிந்தும், கழுநீர்ப்பானையில் கையிடுகிறதா?

What, is one who knows all things, to put his hand into filthy water!

1638. எல்லை பாழ்பட்டாலும் கொல்லைக்கடமை விடார்.

Though the landmarks be destroyed, they will not remit the ground-rent.

1639. எவன் ஆகிலும் தான் சாக மருந்து உண்பானு?

Will any one take medicine to poison himself!

1640. எழுதாக் கடனுக்கு அழுதால் தீருமா?

Will crying avail for money lent of which no account has been kept?

1641. எழுதி வழங்கான் வாழ்க்கை கழுதை புரண்ட களம்.

The condition of the man who keeps no accounts is like the place in which an ass has rolled itself.

1642. எழுதிய விதி அழுதால் தீருமா?

Will destiny be averted by weeping

1613. எழுதுவது அருமை எழுதினதைப் பழுதற வாசிப்பது அருமை.
Writing is important, reading correctly what is written, is more so.

1644. எழுதுகிறது பெரிது அல்ல, இனம் அறிந்து சேர்க்கிறது பெரிது.
To be able to write is no great matter; to compose harmoniously is great.

1645. எழுத்து அறிந்த வண்ணான் குறித்து எறிந்தான் ஓலை.
The washerman who had learnt his letters threw away his ola.

1646. எழுத்து அறிந்த மன்னன் கிழித்து எறிந்தான் ஓலையை.
The king who had learnt his letters tore and threw away his ola.

It would appear that the two preceding proverbs relate to persons who suppose that ability to read supercedes all records.

1647. எழுத்துக்குப் பால்மாறின கணக்கனும் உடுக்கைக்குப் பால்மாறின தாசியும் வருத்தம் அடைவார்.
The curnum who neglects *his accounts*, and the dancing girl who is careless about her dress, will come to grief.

1648. எழுந்திருப்பான் கால் இல்லை.
He would rise, but he has no feet.

1649. எழுபது சென்றாலும் பறை ஏவினாற்றான் செய்யும்.
Though seventy years old, a Pariah will do nothing unless he is prompted.

1650. எழுபது பேரைக் கொன்ற படுநீலி.
A *cruel* Nili-*woman*-who killed seventy persons.

1651. எழைக்கும் பேழைக்கும் காடுகாள் அம்மை.
The mother of Vairavi is the patroness of the poor and of boats.

1652. எளியவள் பிள்ளை ஆனாலும் செய்யும் சடங்கு செய்யவேண்டும்.
Though the child of a poor woman, the accustomed rites must be performed.

1653. எளியவனை அடித்துப் புளியங்காய் பறித்தாற்போல.

Like beating a poor man, and plucking his tamarind fruit.

1654. எளியவனுக்குப் பெண்டாய் இருக்கிறதிலும் வலியவனுக்கு அடிமை ஆகிறது நல்லது.

It is better to be the slave of the wealthy, than the wife of the indigent.

1655. எளியவனைக் கண்டு வாயால் ஏய்க்கிறான்.

Seeing that the man is poor, he deceives him by fair words.

1656. எளியவன் பெண்டாட்டி எல்லாருக்கும் மைத்துனிச்சி.

The wife of a poor man is sister-in-law to all.

1657. எளியாரை வலியார் அடித்தால் வலியாரைத் தெய்வம் அடிக்கும்.

If the powerful oppress the weak, God will punish them in return.

1658. எளியாரை எதிர் இட்டுக்கொண்டால் பிராணஹானி.

Inferiors if opposed become mortal enemies.

1659. எள் அத்தனையை மலை அத்தனை ஆக்குகிறது.

Magnifying a rape seed into a mountain.

1660. எள்ளுக்காய் பிளந்த விவகாரம்.

A dispute *as easy* to decide as the splitting of a rape seed.

1661. எள்ளுக்காய் பிளந்தாற்போலப் பேசவேண்டும்.

One ought to speak as evenly as a rape-pod splits.

1662. எள்ளுக்குத் தக்க எண்ணெய், எள்ளுக்குத் தக்க பிண்ணாக்கு.

Oil is proportioned to the *sessamum*, refuse proportioned to the *pressed* seed.

1663. எள்ளுக்குப் புள்ளு வரும் எச்சிற்கு எறும்பு வரும்.

Birds are attracted by rape seed, ants by leavings.

1664. எள்ளுக்குள் எண்ணெய்போல.

As oil in sessamum seed.

1665. எள்ளுக்குள் எண்ணெய்போல் எங்கும் நிறைந்திருக்கும்.

Everywhere present as oil throughout the sesamum seed.

1666. எள்ளுக்கு ஏழு உழவு கொள்ளுக்கு ஓர் உழவு.

Ploughing seven times for sesamum seed, once for gram.

1667. எள்ளுத்தான் எண்ணெய்க்கு உலருகிறது, எலிப்பிழுக்கை என்னத்துக்கு உலருகிறது?

Sesamum seed is dried for oil; but why dry rat-dung ?

1668. எள்ளும் பச்சை அரிசியும்போல இருக்கவேண்டும்

It must be as sesamum seed and raw rice.

1669. எள்ளும் கரும்பும் இறுக்கினால் பயன் தரும்.

Sesamum seed and sugarcane yield a profit when pressed

1670. எள்ளுக்கு ஏழு உழவு உழுகிறவேளா வெள்ளாளா கொள்ளுக்கு ஓர் உழவு உழுது பயிர்செய்.

O, Vellala who ploughest seven times to sow rape-seed, plough once for horse-gram and thus cultivate the ground.

1671. எறிகிறது முயலுக்குப் படுகிறது புற்றைக்கு.

Throwing at a hare and hitting a bush.

1672. எறிவானேன் சொறிவானேன் ?

Why throw, why scratch !

Why provoke a nuisance !

1673. எறும்பு கடிக்கப் பொறுக்காதா ?

Canst thou not bear the bite of an ant.

1674. எறும்பின் கண் அதன் அளவுக்குப் பெரிது, ஆனையின் கண் அதன் அளவுக்குச் சிறிது.

The eyes of an ant are large in proportion to its size, the eyes of an elephant are small for its size.

1675. எறும்புக்குக் கொட்டாங்கச்சித் தண்ணீர் சமுத்திரம்,

A cocoanut shell-full of water is an ocean to an ant.

1676. எறும்புப் புற்றில் பாம்பு குடிகொள்வதுபோல.

As a snake occupies an ant-hole

1677. எறும்புக்கும் தன் கையால் எண்சாண் உடம்பு.

Even an ant is eight spans long *as measured* by its own hand.

1678. எறும்பு ஊரக் கல் தேயும்.

By the *continual* creeping of ants a stone will wear away.

1679. எறும்பின் கண்ணுக்கு எருமை மூத்திரம் ஏகப்பெருவெள்ளம.

The urine of the buffalo is as a perfect deluge in the eye of an ant.

1680. எறும்பு ஊரக் கல் குழியும்.

By the *continual* creeping of ants a stone will become hollow.

1681. எறும்பு ஊர இடங்கொடுத்தால எருதும் பொதியும் உள்ளே செலுத்துவான்.

If room be given sufficient for ants to creep in, he will drive a loaded bullock that way.

1682. எறும்பு எடுத்துப் போவதற்குத் தடி எடுத்து நிற்கிறது, பெரிய பூசனிக்காய் போகிறது தெரியாதா?

You stand armed with a club to watch that which may be carried away by ants, are you unable to see when a large pumpkin has been taken away?

1683. எறும்பு முதல் எண்ணுயிரம் கோடிக்கும் தெரியும்.

It is known to the eighty thousand millions *of creatures* from an ant upwards.

1684. எறும்பு முட்டை கொண்டு திட்டை ஏறின் மழைபெய்யும்.

If ants carry their eggs to a higher place, it will rain.

1685. எனக்கு அட்டமத்துச் சனி.

With me Saturn is in the eighth sign.

1686. எனக்கு ஊணும் இல்லை உறக்கமும் இல்லை.

I have neither food nor sleep.

1687. எனது நாட்கள் எல்லாம் ஊமை கண்ட கனுப்போல் ஆயின

My days are like the dream of the dumb.

1688. என் ஈரலைக் கருக்கு அரிவாள்கொண்டு அறுக்கிறது.

It cuts my liver with a sharp sickle.

1689. என் காரியம் எல்லாம் நந்தன் படைவிடாய்ப் போயிற்று.

My affairs are like Nandan's camp.

The name of a shoemaker who is reputed to have reigned as a king for three hours, and to have issued leather coin.

1690. என் குடி கெட்டதும் உன் குடி கெட்டதும் பொழுது விடிந்தால் தெரியும்.

It will be known at day-break whether my family or your's has been ruined.

1691. என்னைத் தின்று சதையைக் கொடுத்து வளர்த்தாள்.

Eating bones *herself*, she has brought up *her children* on flesh.

1692. என் மகள் வாரத்தோடே வாரம் முழுகுவாள், என் மருமகன் தீபாவளிக்குத் தீபாவளி முழுகுவான்.

My daughter bathes once a week, my son-in-law bathes at dèpàveli.

1693. என் மருமகனுக்கு வேப்பெண்ணெயாம் நாக்கெண்ணெய்.

Superior oil is said to be Margosa oil to my son-in-law.

1694. என் முகத்திற் கரிபூசினையே.

Thou hast smeared my face with charcoal.

1695. என் முதுகின் தோல் உனக்குச் செருப்பாய் இருக்கும்.

The skin of my back will serve you for shoes

1696. என் வீட்டுக்கு வந்தால் என்ன கொண்டு வருகிறாய், உன் வீட்டுக்கு வந்தால் என்ன கொடுக்கிறாய்?

When you come to my house, what do you bring, when I come to yours, what do you give?

1697. என்றும் மறைந்திருப்பதிலும் எதிரே போதல் உத்தமம்.

It is better to come to the front at once than to be always concealed.

1698. என்று நின்றும் பொன்றுவர் ஓர் நாள்.

No matter how long one may live, the day of death will come.

1699. என்ன சொன்னாலும் என் புத்தி போகாது.

Say what you may, I will not change my mind.

1700. என்னடா தாதா புரட்டாசிமாதம் முப்பதும் ஒரு கந்தாயம்.

O! mendicant, the thirty days of September are all days of receipt.

1701. என்னடா குச்சுக் கட்டிப் பேசுகிறாய்.

You fellow, you affect to speak in an elegant style.

1702. என்னமாய்ச் சொல்லி இதமாய் உரைத்தாலும் கழுதைக்கு உபதேசம் காதில் ஏறாது.

No instruction however explicit or agreeable will enter the ear of an ass.

1703. என்ன மாயம் இடைச்சி மாயம், மோரோடு தண்ணீர் கலந்த மாயம்.

What is the deception practised by the dairy maid? It is mixing water with butter-milk.

1704. என்னடா கெட்டுப்போகிறாய் என்றால், இன்னமும் கெட்டுப் போகிறேன் பந்தயம் போடு என்கிறான்.

If one say, fie on thee, thou art destroying thyself, he replies, I will take a bet that I will exceed my former course.

1705. என்ன தின்றாலும் அதற்குமேலே நாலு பேரீச்சம்பழம் தின்ன எல்லாம் அடிபடும்.

No matter what may be eaten; if four dates be taken afterwards, the whole will be digested.

1706. என்னுடைய வீட்டிற்குப் பூவாய் வரப் பொன்னும் துரும்பாச்சு.

Since the woman came to my house, even gold has become a common thing.

1707. என்னைப்போலக் குரலும் என் அக்காளைப்போல ஒயிலும் இல்லை என்கிறதாம் கழுதை.

The ass boasted that there was no voice equal to his, and no gait equal to that of his elder sister.

1708. என்னைக் கண்டால் சணலுக்குள்ளே ஒளிக்கிறாய், என் பெண்சாதியைக் கண்டால் சட்டிக்குள்ளே ஒளிக்கிறாய்.

On seeing me, thou hidest among the hemp, and on seeing my wife, thou hidest in a chatty.

ஏ.

1709. ஏகாதசிக்கு மா இடித்தாற்போல.

Like pounding flour for Ekàdasi.

Ekàdasi, the eleventh of December which is observed by the Hindus as a fast and therefore the preparation of food is not required. Said of something irrelevant.

1710. ஏகாதசித் திருடியை ஏற்றடா ரதத்தின்மேலே.

O fellow, put the pretended observer of Ekádasi on the car.

1711. ஏகாலி வாகனம் பொதி சுமந்தாற்போல.

As a washerman's vehicle (a donkey) carries its load.

1712. ஏச்சிலும் பேச்சிலும் வல்லவனே.

He is indeed clever in abuse and empty talk.

1713. ஏடா கூடக்காரனுக்கு வழி எங்கே என்றால், போகிறவன் தலை மேலாம்.

If it be asked where is the way for the stubborn, it is replied, on the head of the way faring man.

1714. ஏடு அறியாதான் பீடு பெறாதான்.

The ignorant man is not held in estimation.

1715. ஏட்டுச் சுரைக்காய் கறிக்கு ஆகுமா?

Will the word suraikai *a gourd* serve as a curry?

1716. ஏணிக்கொம்புக்கு கோணக்கொம்பு போடலாமா?

Is a crooked pole fit for a ladder?

1717. ஏணைக்கழிக்குக் கோணற்கழி வெட்டுகிறதா?

Do you cut a crooked stick for a litter.

1718. ஏண்டா தென்னமரத்தில் ஏறினாய் என்றால், கன்றுக்குட்டிக்குப் புல் பிடுங்க என்றான்.

You fellow! why did you go up the Cocoanut tree! when thus addressed, he replied, I went to get grass for the calf.

1719. ஏண்டா கருடா சுகமா? இருக்கிற இடத்தில் இருந்தால் சுகம் தான்.

O Garuda, are you well? I should be well enough if I were in the place where I ought to be.

1720. ஏண்டா பட்டப்பகலில் திருடுகிறாய்? என் அவசரம் உனக்குத் தெரியுமா?

What! do you steal in broad day light? *He replies*, do you know how pressing my necessities are?

1721. ஏண்டா புளியமரத்தில் ஏறினாய்? பூனைக்குட்டிக்குப் புல் பறிக்க.

Why, man, have you got up into the Tamarind tree! he replied, to pluck grass for my kitten.

1722. ஏண்டா முடிச்சு அவிழ்க்கிறாய்? என்பசி உனக்குத் தெரியுமா?

Why, you fellow, do you untie the knot? Do you know how hungry I am!

1723. ஏண்டி சிறுக்கி புல்லு ஆச்சா? ஒரு நொடிக்குமுன் கட்டாச்சே.

Well, my girl, have you cut the grass? *she replied*, it was tied up before one could snap his fingers.

1724. ஏண்டி பெண்ணே சோர்ந்திருக்கிறாய்? சோறு பத்தியம்.

Why, my girl, do you faint? I have not had rice enough.

1725. ஏண்டி பெண்ணே குந்தியிருக்கிறாய்? சோறு பற்றாமல்.

Why my girl do you squat? For want of sufficient rice.

1726. ஏது பிரியம்? இல்லாதது பிரியம்.

What do you wish? That which I have not.

1727. ஏதும் அற்றவனுக்கு ஏன் இரண்டு பெண்டாட்டி?

Why two wives to one who has nothing?

1728. ஏதென்று கேட்பாரும் இல்லை, எடுத்துப் பிடிப்பாரும் இல்லை.

None to enquire, none to help.

1729. ஏரி உடைகிறதற்குமுன்னே அணை போடவேண்டும்.

Before the bund bursts, it must be strengthened.

1730. ஏரி நிறைந்தால் கரை கசியும்.

If the tank be full, its bank will be moist.

1731. ஏரி பெருகில் எங்கும் பெருக்கு.

When the tank overflows, the flood will spread all around.

1732. ஏரி மிதந்தால் இடையனை மதியாது.

If the hunch *of the ox* grow high, he will not fear his keeper.

1733. ஏரியின் நீரைக் கட்டுதல் அரிது உடைத்தல் எளிது.

It is difficult to confine the water of a tank, but easy to break the bund.

1734. ஏரியின் தண்ணீர் இதோ சூரியதேவா?

O divine sun, behold the water of the tank?

1735. ஏரியோடு பகைகொண்டு சவுசம் செய்யாதிருக்கிறதா?

Do you abstain from ablution because you are dissatisfied with the tank?

1736. ஏர் உழுகிற பிள்ளை இளைத்துபோனால் போகிறது; பரியம் போட்ட பெண்ணைப் பார்த்து வளர்.

Never mind, should the youth at the plough become lean, take care of the girl who has received the nuptial presents.

1737. ஏர் பிடித்தவன் என்ன செய்வான் பானைபிடித்தவள் பாக்கியம்.
Comfort depends on her who has charge of the cooking pots, not on the ploughman.

1738. ஏலவே தொலைந்தது எங்களைத் தொட்ட கர்மம்.
The sin which affected us is already removed.

1739. ஏலேலம்! ஏலேலம்! எருமைச்சாணி காய்கிறது.
Elélam, Elélam, the buffalo dung is drying.

The sound élélam is uttered by boatmen and others on the Coromandel coast when pulling together, as savas is, by boatmen on the Hoogly: some derive it from ஏலிக்கிறது.

1740. ஏலேலசிங்கன்பொருள் ஏழு கடலிற் போனாலும் திரும்பும்.
The property of Elélasingam, though it pass over seven seas, will return.

Elélasingam a wealthy merchant, the disciple of Tiruvalluvar.

1741. ஏவற்பேய் கூரையைப் பிடுங்கும்.
The excited demon will take off the thatch.

1742. ஏவா மக்கள் மூவா மருந்து.
Children *who do their duty* unprompted are as a life-preserving remedy.

1743. ஏவுகிறவனுக்கு வாய்ச்சொல், செய்கிறவனுக்குத் தலைச்சுமை.
To the taskmaster a word, to the servant a burden on the head.

1744. ஏழை அழுத கண்ணீர் கூரியவாளை ஒக்கும்.
The tears of the poor are as sharp swords.

1745. ஏழை பாக்குத் தின்ன எட்டு வீடு அறியவேண்டுமோ?
Because the poor man uses betel-nut, is it to be made known at eight houses?

1746. ஏழை பேச்சு அரண்மனைக்கு ஏறுமா?
Will the speech of the poor go up to the palace?

1747. ஏழைப்பிள்ளைக்குத் தெய்வமே துணை.
God is the helper of the helpless child.

1748. ஏழைப் பிள்ளைக்கு எவர்களும் துணை.

Every one is a helper to a helpless child.

1749. ஏழையைக் கண்டால் மோழையும் பாயும்.

Even a beast without horns will attack the poor.

1750. ஏறச் சொன்னால் எருதுக்குக் கோபம், இறங்கச் சொன்னால் நொண்டிக்குக் கோபம்.

When told to mount, the bull is angry, when told to dismount, the lame man is dissatisfied.

1751. ஏறப்படாத மரத்திலே எண்ணப்படாத மாங்காய்.

Innumerable mangoes on a tree no one can climb.

1752. ஏற விட்டு ஏணியை வாங்குகிறதா?

What! remove the ladder after allowing one to mount!

1753. ஏறின கொம்பால் இறங்க வேண்டும்.

One must come down on the branch by which he ascended.

1754. ஏறுகிற குதிரையிலும் உழவுமாடு அதிக உத்தமம்.

A plough bull is superior to a saddle horse.

1755. ஏறுநெற்றி சூறுதலை எதிர்க்க வந்தால் ஆகாது.

It is a bad omen to meet *one with* a high forehead or curly hair.

1756. ஏறுமாறாய்ப் பேசுகிறதா?

What, is it to speak at random!

1757. ஏறும் தேமல் இறங்கும் படர்தாமரை கூடும் புருவம் குடியைக் கெடுக்கும்.

Ascending cutaneous spots, descending ring-worm and eyebrows contiguous are ominous.

1758. ஏற்கவே மாமி பேய்க்கோலம் அதிலும் கொஞ்சம் மாக்கோலம்.

The mother-in-law is frightfully ugly already, and the flour on her face makes her more so.

1759. ஏற்கனவே வருகிற விக்கினங்களைத் தடுக்கவேண்டும்.

Approaching evils should be provided against in due time.

1760. ஏற்றக்கோலுக்குப் பிடித்தால் அரிவாட்பிடிக்கு வரும்.

If you measure sufficient for a well-bucket pole, it may suffice for the handle of a sickle.

1761. ஏற்றப்பாட்டுக்கு எதிர்ப்பாட்டா?

Is the song of the picotta responsive?

1762. ஏன் கொழுக்கட்டை சவுக்கிட்டாய்? ஒரு காசு வெல்லம் இல்லாமற் சவுக்கிட்டேன்!

Cake! why so insipid? Because I lack a cash-worth of sugar.

ஐ.

1763. ஐங்கலக் கப்பியில் நழுவின கப்பி இவன்.

He is a broken grain fallen out of five kalams.

One of a large number of insignificant persons.

1764. ஐங்காதம் போனாலும் அகப்பே அரைக்காசு கிடையாதே.

Though you may go fifty miles, you will not fetch half a cash.

1765. ஐங்காதம் போனாலும், அகப்பை அரைக்காசு.

Although it may go fifty miles, an agappai will fetch but half a cash.

1766. ஐங்காதம் போனாலும் அறிமுகம் வேண்டும்.

Though one goes fifty miles off, an acquaintance is needed.

1767. ஐங்காதம் போனாலும், தன் பாவம் தன்னோடே.

Though he may go fifty miles, his own sin will still cleave to him.

1768. ஐங்காயம் இட்ட காரம் இட்டாலும் தன் நாற்றம் போகாதாம் பேய்ச்சுரைக்காய்க்கு.

Though cooked with five ingredients, the wild gourd will not lose its odour.

1769. ஐதது நெல், அடர்ந்தது சுற்றம்.

In rice plants, distance is required, in kindred, closeness.

1770. ஐந்து சிட்டுக்கு இரண்டு காசு விலை.

The price of five chits *a small bird* is two cash.

1771. ஐப்பசி மாதம் அழுகைத் தூறல் கார்த்திகை மாதம் கன மழை.

In October drizzling, in November heavy rain.

1772. ஐப்பசி மாதத்து வெய்யலில் அன்று உரித்த தோல் அன்று காயும்.

In the sunshine of October a skin dries the day it is stript off.

1773. ஐப்பசிக்கும் கார்த்திகைக்கும் மழை இல்லாவிட்டால் அண்ண னுக்கும் சரி தம்பிக்கும் சரி.

If the rains of October and November fail, the elder and younger brother will be on a par.

1774. ஐப்பசி மாதத்து எருமைக்கடாவும் மார்கழி மாதத்து நம்பி யானும் சரி.

A buffalo in the month of October and a Vaishnava brahman in December are alike.

1775. ஐம்பதிலே அறிவு, அறுபதிலே அடக்கம், அறுபதுக்குமேல் ஒன்றுமில்லை.

At fifty discrimination, at sixty moderation, after sixty no distinguishing characteristic

1776. ஐம்பது வயதானவனுக்கு ஐந்து வயதுப் பெண்ணோ ?

Is a girl of five fit to be the wife to a man of fifty ?

1777. ஐயங்காரும் தொத்துக் கொடுப்பார்.

Even the Aiyangar may communicate contagious disease.

1778. ஐயப்பட்டால் பைய நட.

If in doubt, advance slowly.

1779. ஐயப்பன் குதிரையை வையாளி விட்ட கதை.

Like the story of one who rode Aiyanàr's horse.

1780. ஐயமான காரியத்தைச் செய்யல் ஆகாது.

To do a doubtful thing is bad.

1781. ஐயம் ஏற்றும் அறிவே ஓது.

Though reduced to beggary, learn to be wise.

1782. ஐயர் என்பவர் துய்யர் ஆவர்.

Those who are *entitled to be* called brahmans are holy.

1783. ஐயர் வருகிறவரையில் அமாவாசியை நிற்குமா ?

Will the new moon await the brahman's arrival ?

1784. ஐயர் கதிர்போல அம்மாள் குதிர்போல.

The husband is like an ear of corn, the wife is like a rice bin or grain receptacle.

1785. ஐயனர் படையிற் குயவனர் பட்டதுபோல.

As the potter perished in the army of Aiyanar.

1786 ஐயனர் கோவில் செங்கல் அத்தனையும் தெய்வம்.

The bricks of Aiyanar's temple are so many gods.

1787. ஐயனர் கோவில் மண்ணை மிதித்தவர் அத்தனையும் பிடாரி.

Those who have trodden the ground of Aiyanar's temple are so many Pidaris.

1788. ஐயனரே வாரும் கடாவைக் கைக்கொள்ளும்.

Come, Aiyanar, and accept a goat, *a sacrifice.*

1789. ஐயன் அமைப்பை ஆராலும் தள்ளக்கூடாது.

No one may dispute the pre-ordination of god.

1790. ஐயோ என்றால் இவனுக்கு ஆறு மாசத்துப் பாவம் சுற்றும்.

The man who expresses commiseration for him will incur six months sin.

ஒ.

1791. ஒக்கப் பிறந்த தங்கை ஓலமிட்டு அழச்சே ஒப்பாரித் தங்கைக் குச்சிற்றுடையாம்?

When one's sister is weeping for a cloth, is it to be given to a woman who resembles her?

1792. ஒச்சியம் இல்லாத ஊரிலே பெண் வாங்கின கதை.

The story of a man taking a girl to wife in a village inhabited by the shameless.

1793. ஒடிந்த கோல் ஆனாலும் ஊன்றுகோல் இருக்கவேண்டும்.

Though a broken one, a walking stick is necessary.

1794. ஒட்டிக்கொண்டு வந்தும் தட்டிக் கழிக்கிறான்.

Though I cling to him, he repels me.

1795. ஒட்டினால் தொட்டிலும் கொள்ளும் ஒட்டாவிட்டால் கட்டிலும் கொள்ளாது.

If compressed the crib will hold it, but if not even a bedstead will not contain it.

1796. ஒட்டினாலும் உழக்குப்பீர்ச் சொன்கிறதா?

Is it to say draw one ulak of milk though the *animal* is lean?

1797. ஒட்டைக்குப் பளுவு ஏற்றுகிறதுபோல.

As a camel is loaded.

1798. ஒதி பெருத்துத் தூணுமா?

Though the odina tree grow large, will it do for a pillar?

1799. ஒதி பெருத்தால் உரலாமா?

Though the odina tree grow large, will it serve for a mortar?

1800. ஒதி பெருத்து என்ன, உபகாரம் இல்லாதவன் வாழ்ந்து என்ன?

What avails the growth of an odina tree? Of what use is the prosperity of the ungenerous?

1801. ஒதியமரம் தூணுமோ? ஓட்டாங்கிளிஞ்சில் காசாமோ?

Will an odina tree do for a pillar? will a broken oyster-shell pass as a coin?

1802. ஒதியமரமும் ஒரு சமயத்துக்கு உதவும்.

Even an odina tree may prove useful on an emergency.

1803. ஒய்யாரக்கொண்டையாம் தாழம்பூவாம் உள்ளே மேயுமாம் ஈரும் பேனும்.

Her tresses are graceful and ornamented with the flowers of the screw pine, but nits and lice breed therein.

1804. ஒரு உறையிலே இரண்டு கத்தியா?

Are two swords contained in one sheath?

1805. ஒரு ஊருக்கு ஒரு வழியா?

Is there but one way to a village?

1806. ஒரு கட்டு வைக்கோலைத் தண்ணீரிற் போட்டு எட்டு ஆள் கூடி இழுத்தாற்போல.

As a bundle of straw that had been dipped in water was dragged along by eight persons.

1807. ஒரு கம்பத்தில் இரண்டு ஆனை கட்டுகிறதா?

What, to tie two elephants to one pole?

1808. ஒரு காசு அகப்படுகிறது குதிரைக் கொம்பு.

To earn one cash is as difficult as to find a horse with horns.

1809. ஒரு காசு பேணின் இரு காசு தேறும்.

One cash saved is two cash got.

1810. ஒருகாற் செய்தவன் இருகாற் செய்வான்.

He who has done a thing once, may do it again.

1811. ஒரு காசு கொடாதவன் ஒரு வராகன் கொடுப்பானா?

Will he who refuses to give a cash, give a pagoda?

A Pagoda is a gold coin worth about seven shillings.

1812. ஒரு காசு என்ற இடத்தில் அழுகிறுன்.
He weeps when the word money is uttered.

1813. ஒருகுடம் பாலுக்கு ஒரு துளி புரை.
One drop of butter-milk to a pot of milk.

1814. ஒரு குண்டிலே கோட்டை பிடிக்கலாமா?
Can a fort be taken with one ball?

1815. ஒரு குளத்திற் பிறந்த தாமரையும் அலலியும் ஒரே தன்மை யுடையதல்ல அதுபோல ஒரு தாயின் வயிற்றில் பிறந்த சகோதரர் இருப்பார்கள்.
The lotus flowers of a tank are not all of the same species, so the children of the same mother are not all alike.

1816. ஒரு கூடு முடைந்தவன் ஒன்பது கூடு முடைவான்.
He who has platted one basket may plat nine.

1817. ஒரு கூடை கல்லும் தெய்வமானுல், கும்பிடுகிறது எந்தக்கல்லே!
If all the stones in a basket be gods, which shall I worship!

1818. ஒரு கை தட்டினுல் ஓசை எழும்புமா?
Can clapping be effected by one hand!

1819. ஒரு கை தட்டினுல் ஓசை எழும்புமா, இருகை தட்டினுல் ஓசை எழும்புமா?
Can clapping be effected with one, or with both hands!

1820. ஒரு கை முழம் போடுமா?
Can cubits be measured with *only* one arm!

1821. ஒரு கோபம் வந்து கிணற்றில் விழுந்தால் ஆயிரம் சந்தோஷம் வாந்தாலும் எழும்பலாமா?
When one has fallen into a well in a fit of anger, will a thousand joyous *considerations* help him out?

1822. ஒரு சட்டியிலே இரண்டு தைலம்.
Two kinds of oil in one chatty.

1823. ஒரு சந்திப்பானை நாய் அறியாது.

A dog does not know the vessels used on fast-days.

Separate vessels are kept for special occasions, and also for different purposes on ordinary days, as for boiling milk &c.

1824. ஒரு சாண் காட்டிலே ஒரு முழத்தடி வெட்டலாமா?

Can a stick a cubit long be cut in a grove a span high?

1825. ஒரு தரம் விழுந்தால் தெரியாதா?

Having fallen once are you not wiser?

1826. ஒருதலை வழக்கு நூலிலும் செவ்வை.

An ex parte statement is straighter than a line.

1827. ஒரு தலைக்கு இரண்டு ஆக்கினையா?

Are there two punishments for one head?

1828. ஒரு தாய் அற்ற பிள்ளைக்கு ஊரெல்லாம் தாய்.

The whole village is mother to the motherless.

1829. ஒரு நன்றி செய்தவரை உள்ள அளவும் நினை.

Think of those who have done you even one favour as long as you live.

1830. ஒரு நாட் கூத்துக்குத் தலையைச் சிரைத்ததுபோல்.

Like shaving the head for a single day's dance.

1831. ஒரு நாளைக்கு இகழ்ச்சி ஒரு நாளைக்குப் புகழ்ச்சி.

One day blame, another day praise.

1832. ஒரு நாளைக்கு இறக்கிறது கோடி பிறக்கிறது கோடி.

Ten millions are born, and ten millions die, daily.

1833. ஒரு நாளும் சிரிக்காதவன் திருநாளிலே சிரித்தான், திருநாளும் வெறுநாளாயிற்று.

A man who had never laughed before, laughed on a festival day, consequently it became a common day.

1834. ஒரு நாளாகிலும் திருநாள்.

Although only one day, it is a festival day.

1835. ஒரு பனை இரண்டு பாளை ஒன்று நுங்கு ஒன்று கள்ளு.

One palmyra has two spathes, one yields fruit, the other toddy.

1836. ஒரு பானைச் சோற்றுக்கு ஒன்றே மாதிரி.

One grain suffices to test a whole pot of boiled rice.

1837. ஒரு பிள்ளை பெற்றவளுக்கு உறியிலே சோறு, நாலு பிள்ளை பெற்றவளுக்கு நடுத்தெருவிலே சோறு.

The rice for a woman who has borne one child, is on the swinging tray, that of the woman who has borne four, is in the middle of the street.

1838. ஒரு பிள்ளையென்று ஊட்டி வளர்த்தாளாம், அது செரியாக் குணம் பிடித்துச் செத்ததாம்.

It is said that having only one child she fed it well, but that it died of indigestion.

1839. ஒரு புத்திரன் ஆனாலும் குரு புத்திரன் ஆவானா?

Although he is an only son, will he become an obedient disciple

1840. ஒரு பொருள் ஆகிலும் எழுதி அறி.

Though only one item, note it.

1841. ஒரு மரத்துப் பழமா ஒருமிக்க?

What! did one tree yield all this fruit?

1842. ஒரு மரத்துப் பட்டை ஒரு மரத்திலே ஒட்டுமா?

Will the bark of one tree stick to another?

1843. ஒரு மரத்துக் கொம்பு ஒரு மரத்தில் ஒட்டாது.

The branch of one tree will not stick to another.

1844. ஒரு மனப்படு, ஓதுவார்க்கு உதவு.

Be single-minded, assist those that teach the Vedas.

1845. ஒரு மிளகுக்கு ஆற்றைக் கட்டி இறைத்த செட்டி.

A merchant who dammed up and drained a river to recover a grain of pepper.

1846. ஒரு மிளகும் நாலு உப்பும் போதும்.

One grain of pepper and four grains of salt will suffice.

1847. ஒரு முழுக்கிலே மண் எடுக்கிறதா ?

What ! is it to take up the soil by diving once ?

1848. ஒருமைப்பாடு இல்லாத குடி ஒருமிக்கக் கெடும்.

A family divided against itself will perish together.

1849. ஒருவன் அறிந்தால் உலகம் அறியும்.

If known to one, the world *may* know it.

1850. ஒருவன் அறிந்த ரகசியம் உலகத்தில் பரவும்.

A secret known to one may spread through the world.

1851. ஒருவனுக்கு இருவர் துணை ஒருவனை அறிய இருவர் வேண்டும்.

Two men may help one, two are necessary that one may be known.

1852. ஒருவரும் அறியாத உச்சித நாமன்.

One of illustrious name unknown to any.

1853. ஒருவனைக் கொன்றவன் உடனே சாவான் பல பேரைக் கொன்றவன் பட்டம் ஆளுவான்.

He who kills one person immediately suffers death, he who kills many is rewarded with a crown.

1854. ஒருவனாய்ப் பிறப்பது ஒரு பிறப்பாமா, ஒன்றி மரம் தோப்பாமா ?

Is it worth being to be an only offspring ? Is a single tree a tope *a grove* ?

1855. ஒருவன் தலையில் மாணிக்கம் இருக்கிறதென்று வெட்டலாமா ?

May you cut off a man's head because there is a ruby in it ?

1856. ஒருவனாய்ப் பிறந்தால் தனிமை, இருவராய்ப் பிறந்தாற் பகைமை.

When only one is born there is loneliness, when two enmity.

1857. ஒருவர் அறிந்தால் இரகசியம் இருவர் அறிந்தால் பராசியம்.

If known to one only it is a secret, if to two it is public.

1858. ஒருவனைப் பற்றி ஓரகத்திரு.

Attach yourself to one person, and dwell in one house.

1859. ஒரு விரல் நொடி இடாது.

A single finger cannot snap.

1860. ஒவ்வாக் கூட்டிலும் தனிமை அழகு, ஒவ்வாப் பேச்சு வசை யோடு ஒக்கும்.

Solitude is preferable to disagreeable society, an unpleasant expression may be felt as a reproach.

1861. ஒழுகாத வீடு உள்ளங்கை அத்தனை போதும்.

If only as large as the palm of the hand a house that does not leak will suffice.

1862. ஒழுக்கம் உயர் குலத்தில் நன்று.

Virtue is superior to rank.

1863. ஒழுக்கு வீட்டிலே வெள்ளம் வந்ததுபோல.

As a flood came into a leaky house.

1864. ஒழுக்குக்கு வைத்த சட்டிபோல.

As a chatty placed under a leak.

1865. ஒழுங்கு ஒரு பணம சளுக்கு முக்காற் பணம்.

Propriety *is worth* a fanam, pride, three fourths of a fanam.

1866. ஒளிக்கும் சேவகனுக்கு முகத்தில் ஏன் மீசை?

Of what use is a mustache to a sneaking soldier?

1867. ஒளிக்கப் போயும் தலையாரி வீட்டிலா?

When trying to conceal one's self, is it fit to do so in the house of the chief?

1868. ஒளிக்கப் போயும் இடம் இடைஞ்சலா?

Is the place too narrow for one who has gone to hide himself?

1869. ஒள்ளியர் தெள்ளியர் ஆயினும் ஊழ்வினை பைய நுழைந்து விடும்.

However enlightened and clear-headed one may be, his destiny will quietly creep in.

1870. ஒற்றியும் சீதனமும் பற்றி ஆளவேண்டும்.

Property received under mortgage, or as a dowry, must be taken into immediate possession.

1871. ஒன்ற வந்த பேய் ஊரைக் கெடுத்ததுபோல்.

As the demon that came for shelter destroyed the village.

1872. ஒன்ற வந்த காகம் உரம் பெற்றாற்போல.

As if a crow that came for shelter was strengthened in his position.

1873. ஒன்ற வந்த பிடாரி ஊர்ப் பிடாரியை ஓட்டினதுபோல்.

As a demoness that came for shelter drove away the demoness of the village.

1874. ஒன்ற வந்த பிடாரி ஊர்ப் பிடாரி ஆனதுபோல.

As a demoness that came for shelter became the de.noness of the villlage.

1875. ஒன்றான பிரபு உறங்கிக் கிடைக்கையில் பிச்சைக்கு வந்தவன் தத்தியோதனத்திற்கு அழுகிறானாம்.

It is said that whilst a peerless nobleman was lying hungry and exhausted, a beggar cries for rice and curds.

1876. ஒன்றால் ஒன்று குறை இல்லை, முன்னாலே கட்டத் துணி இல்லை.

Not a single want, yet no cloth to put on.

1877. ஒன்று நினைக்க ஒன்றாயிற்று.

One thing meditated, another effected.

1878. ஒன்றும் அறியாளாம் கன்னி அவளைப் பிடித்ததாம் சன்னி.

It is said that the virgin is innocent, and is seized with lock-jaw.

1879. ஒன்று தெரிந்தவனுக்கு எல்லாம் தெரியாது.

He who knows one thing does not know all things.

1880. ஒன்றும் இல்லையென்று ஊதினான் அதுதானும் இல்லையென்று கொட்டினான்.

He blew a conch to report that there was nothing; and beat a drum to intimate that there was not even that.

1881. ஒன்றும் அற்றவனுக்கு ஒன்பது பெண்டாட்டி.

Nine wives to him who has nothing.

1882. ஒன்றும் அற்ற தங்காளுக்கு ஒன்பது நாள் சடங்கா?

Is a ceremony of nine days to be performed for a destitute woman?

1883. ஒன்றே குதிரை ஒன்றே ராவுத்தன்.

One horse, one horseman.

1884. ஒன்றே ராஜா ஒன்றே குதிரை.

One king, one horse.

1885. ஒன்றைப் பெற்றால் நன்றே பெறவேண்டும்.

If one thing only be obtained, it ought to be good.

1886. ஒன்றைப் பிடித்தாற் சாதிக்க வேண்டும்.

The thing asserted must be maintained.

1887. ஒன்றைப் பெற்றாலும் கடுகப் பெறு.

Though you get only one thing, get it quickly.

1888. ஒன்றைப் பெற்றாலும் கன்றைப் பெறு.

If you get only one *as your hire,* take a calf.

1889. ஒன்றைத் தொடினும் நன்றைத் தொடு.

Though you touch but one thing, touch what is good.

Most likely referring to the choice of a wife.

ஓ

1890. ஓ கொடுப்பானுக்கு வாழ்க்கைப் பட்டு ஓட்டம் ஒழிய, நடை இல்லை.

Having become the wife of the wretch, I am *compelled* to run instead of walking.

1891 ஓங்கில் அறியும் உயர் கடலின் ஆழம், பாங்கி அறிவாள் தன் பத்தாவின் வலிமை.

An onkil fish knows the depth of the ocean, a wife knows her husband's strength.

1892. ஓசை காட்டிப் பூசை செய்.

Ring the bell, and perform pujá.

1893. ஓசை பெறும் வெண்கலம், ஓசைபெறா மட்கலம்.

Sounding brass, a soundless earthen vessel.

1894. ஓடம் விட்டு இறங்கினால் ஓடக்காரனுக்கு ஒரு சொட்டு.

On landing, a cuff for the boatman.

1895. ஓடம் விட்ட ஆறும் அடி சுடும்.

Even a navigable river may burn the feet when dry.

1896. ஓடம் கட்டின தூலம்.

A block of wood to which a boat is moored.

1897. ஓடம் கடந்தால் ஓடக்காரனுக்கு ஒரு சொட்டு.

After crossing, a cuff for the boatman.

1898. ஓடம் வண்டியிலும் வண்டி ஓடத்திலும் காணவும்படும்.

A boat may be sesen in a cart, and a cart in a boat.

1899. ஓடம் விட்ட இடம் அடி சுடும் அடி சுட்ட இடம் ஓடம் விடப்படும்.

The foot may be burnt in a navigable river, and a boat may float where the foot was burnt.

1900. ஓடவும் மாட்டான் பிடிக்கவும் மாட்டான், ஓயாமல் பேசுவான்.

He can neither run nor overtake, but he can talk continually.

1901. ஓடவும் மாட்டேன் பிடிக்கவும் மாட்டேன்.

I can neither run nor catch.

1902. ஓடி ஒரு கோடி தேடுவதிலும் இருந்து ஒரு காசு தேடுவது நலம்.

It is better to acquire a cash in quiet than a lak by running about.

1903. ஓடி ஒன்பது பணம் சம்பாதிப்பதிலும் உட்கார்ந்திருந்து ஒரு பணம் சம்பாதிப்பது நன்று.

Better earn one fanam where you are, than nine fanams by running hither and thither.

1904. ஓடி ஓடி உள்ளங்காலும் வெளுத்தது.

The sole of the foot has become white by constant running.

1905. ஓடிப்போன புருஷன் வந்து கூடிக்கொண்டான், உடைமைமேல் உடைமை போட்டு மினுக்கிக்கொண்டாள்.

The husband that ran away has returned and is reconciled, therefore she has adorned herself with jewels to excess.

1906. ஓடிப்போன ஊரில் ஆதரித்தவன் கவுண்டன்.

He who entertained the man that fled from his own village was a Koundan-*a man of that tribe.*

1907. ஓடிப்போகிறவன் பாடிப் போகிறான்.

He who is running away, does so singing.

1908. ஓடிய முயல் பெரிய முயல் அல்லவோ?

The hare that ran away was a large one, was it not?

1909. ஓடியம் ஆகிலும் ஊடுருவக் கேள்.

Though it is obscene, hear it out.

1910. ஓடியும் கிழவிக்குப் பிறகேயா?

Having set out to run will it do for him to be behind an old woman?

1911. ஓடுகிற பாம்பைப் பிடிக்கிற பருவம்.

Old enough to seize a running snake.

1912. ஓடுகிறவனைக் கண்டால் துரத்துகிறவனுக்கு இலேசு.

Seeing him who retreats, makes the efforts of his pursuer easy.

1913. ஓடுகிற வெள்ளம் அணையில நிற்குமா?

Will a rolling flood stay at the anicut?

1914. ஓட்டைச் சட்டி ஆனாலும் கொழுக்கட்டை வெந்தாற் சரி.
The chatty may be cracked, what matters that if it bakes the cakes.

1915. ஓட்டை நாழிக்குப் பூண் கட்டினது போல.
Like adorning a cracked measure with a metal rim.

1916. ஓட்டைப் பானையிலே சர்க்கரை இருக்கும்.
A cracked pot will hold sugar.

1917. ஓட்டைப் பானைச் சர்க்கரை கசக்குமா?
Will sugar, because put in a cracked pot, taste bitter?

1918. ஓட்டை மணி ஆனாலும் ஓசை நீங்குமா?
Though the bell may be cracked will it be void of sound?

1919. ஓணான் விழுங்கிய கதைபோல.
Like the story relating to the swallowing of a bloodsucker.

1920. ஓதாதார்க்கு இல்லை உணர்வொடு ஒழுக்கம்.
The unlettered have neither good sense nor virtue.

1921. ஓதுவன் எல்லாம் உழுவான் தலைக்கடையில்.
All poets may be found at the entrance of the ploughman's house

1922. ஓதுவானுக்கு ஊரும் உழுவானுக்கு நிலமும் இல்லையா?
Has the poet no country, has the ploughman no land?

1923. ஓதுவார்க்கு உதவு.
Assist instructors-*the brahmans.*

1924. ஓந்தி வேலிக்கு இழுக்கின்றது, தவளை தண்ணீருக்கு இழுக்கின்றது.
The blood-sucker draws *its prey* to a hedge, the frog to water.

1925. ஓமபிண்டத்தை நாய் இச்சித்தாற்போலே.
As if a dog longed for consecrated food.
Spoken by Sita to Râvanâ

1926. ஓயா மழையும் ஒழியாக் காற்றும்.
Continual rain, and ceaseless wind.

1927. ஒய்விலா நேசமே யோலமே சரணம்.
Thou, the object my unceasing love, take me under thy protection.

1928. ஓரம் சொன்னவன் ஆருக்கு ஆவான்?
Will any employ a person who is given to one-sided statements?

1929. ஓரம் சொன்னவன் குடித்தனம்போலே.
Like the family of him who makes partial statements.

1930. ஓர் ஆண்டி பசித்திருக்க உலகம் எல்லாம் கிறுகிறென்று சுற்றுகிறதா?
Is the whole world so giddy through famine as to allow a religious mendicant to suffer from hunger?

1931. ஓர் ஆறு தாண்ட மாட்டாதவன் ஒன்பது ஆறு தாண்டுவானா?
Will he who cannot cross one river, cross nine!

1932. ஓர் ஊருக்குப் பேச்சு மற்றோர் ஊருக்கு ஏச்சு.
That which is polite in one country may be abusive in another

1933. ஓர் ஊருக்கு ஒரு பேரிட்டுக் கொள்ளலாமா?
May one assume a different name in every village!

ஔ.

1934. ஔவை சொல்லுக்கு அச்சம் இல்லை.
No fear about Avvai's sayings.

1935. ஔவையார்மேலும் குற்றம் உண்டு அண்ணாவியார்மேலும் பழுது உண்டு.
Even Avvai may be charged with blame, a *religious* teacher also may have his defects

க.

936. கங்கையிலே முளைத்தாலும் பேய்ச்சுரை நல்லசுரை ஆமா?
Will a wild gourd become a good gourd by growing on the Ganges?

1937. கங்கையில் முழ்கினாலும் காக்கை அன்னம் ஆகுமா?
Will a crow become a swan by bathing in the Ganges?

1938. கங்கையில் ஆடினாலும், கணமும் விடாமற் செய்த பாவம் தீராது?
Though you wash in the Ganges, sin repeated again and again will not be expiated.

1939. கங்கையில் ஆடினாலும் பாவம் தீருமா?
Will sin be expiated by bathing in the Ganges.

1940. கங்கையிலே படிந்தாலும் பேய்ச்சுரைக்காய் நல்லசுரைக்காய் ஆகாது.
Though a wild gourd be dipped in the Ganges, its inferiority will remain.

1941. கங்கையிலே பிறந்த நத்தை சாலக்கிராமம் ஆகாது.
A snail of the Ganges is not a Shalgram

The Shalgram is a flinty stone, containing the impression of one or more ammonitæ, supposed by the Hindus to represent Vishnu.

1942. கசக்கி மோரலாமா?
Can the fragrance of a flower be appreciated after bruising it?

1943. கசடருக்கு இல்லைக் கற்றோர் உறவு.
The base do not enjoy the friendship of the learned.

1944. கசடறக் கல்லார்க்கு இசை உறல் இல்லை.
Persons of imperfect learning have no reputation.

1945. கசடான கல்வியினும் கல்வியீனம் நலம்.
Ignorance is better than imperfect knowledge.

1946. கசிந்து வந்தவன் கண்ணைத் துடை.
Wipe off the tears of him who comes weeping.

1947. கச்சற் கருவாடு மோட்சத்திற்குப் போனாலும், பிச்சைக்காரர் மோட்சத்திற்குப் போகமாட்டார்கள்.
Though dried fish may attain final emancipation-*heaven*-beggars cannot.

1948. கஞ்சி வரதப்பா என்ருல், எங்கே வரதப்பா என்கிருன்.

If I say, O Varathappa *give me some* kanji, he replies, O Varathappa where.

1949. கடலிலே ஏற்றம் போட்ட கதை.

The story relating to a picotta on the sea-side.

1950. கடலில் இட்ட பெருங்காயம்போல.

Like assafœtida cast into the ocean.

1951. கடலிலே துரும்பு கிடந்தாலும் மனதிலே ஒரு சொல் கிடவாது.

A rush may remain in the sea, but a secret will not remain in the mind.

1952. கடலில கரைத்த புளிபோல.

Like tamarind acid dissolved in the sea.

1953. கடலைத் தூர்த்தும் காரியம் முடிக்க வேண்டும்.

You must accomplish your undertaking, though you may have to fill up the ocean.

1954. கடலைத் தூர்த்தாலும் காரியம் முடியாது.

Though the sea be filled up, the thing cannot be effected.

1955. கடல் கொதித்தால் விளாவ நீர் எங்கே ?

Should the sea boil, whence water to cool it ?

1956. கடல்நீர் நிறைந்து ஆவது என்ன, காஞ்சிரை பழுத்து ஆவது என்ன ?

What benefit arises from the water of the ocean, what good comes from the ripening of the kànjirai, *strychnos nux vomica*, fruit ?

1957. கடல் தாண்ட ஆசை உண்டு, கால்வாய் தாண்டக் கால் இல்லை.

He wishes to cross the ocean, but has no feet to cross a small drain.

1958. கடல் மீனுக்கு நுளையன் இட்டதே சட்டம்.

As regards the fish of the sea, whatever name the fisherman gives is final.

1959. கடல் வற்றிக் கருவாடு தின்னலாமென்று உடல் வற்றிச் செத்ததாம் கொக்கு.

It is said that the stork died while waiting for the ocean to dry, in the hope of getting a supply of dried fish.

1960. கடல் பெருகினால் கரையும் பெருகுமா ?

Will the shore extend when the sea flows ?

1961. கடல் பெருகினால் கரை ஏது ?

What avails the shore when the sea flows ?

1962. கடற் கரைத் தாழங்காய் கீழ் தொங்கி என்ன மேல் தொங்கி என்ன ?

What matters it whether the wild pine fruit on the sea-shore hangs high or low ?

1963. கடனோடு கடன் கந்தப் பொடி காற்பணம்.

Though my debt be increased, let me have a quarter of a fanam worth more of fragrant powder.

1964. கடன் இல்லாத கஞ்சி கால் வயிறு.

One fourth supply of kanji for the stomach *is better than* debt.

1965. கடன்காரனுக்குக் கடனும், உடன்பிறந்தானுக்குப் பங்கும் கொடுக்கவேண்டும்.

One must pay one's creditor and give to a relation the portion due to him.

1966. கடன் வாங்கிக் கடன் கொடுத்தவனும்கெட்டான் ; மரம் ஏறிக் கை விட்டவனும் கெட்டான்.

He who borrowed to lend was ruined; and he who let go his hold of the tree he had climbed also perished.

1967. கடன் வாங்கியும் பட்டினி கல்யாணம் பண்ணியும் சந்நியாசி.

Famished though he has borrowed, an ascetic though he is wedded.

1968. கடன் வாங்கியும் பட்டினியா !

What to famish after having borrowed *money* !

1969. கடன்காரனுக்குக் கடனும் பழிகாரனுக்குப் பழியும் கொடுக்க வேண்டும்.

Debt to the creditor and retaliation to the wrong-doer are due.

1970. கடன்காரனை வைக்கக் கழு உண்டா?

Is there a stake for impaling debtors ?

1971. கடன் பட்டார் நெஞ்சம்போற் கலங்கினான்.

He was as disquieted as the mind of a debtor.

1972. கடா கடா என்றாலும் மருந்துக்கு ஒரு பீர் என்கிறான்.

Though informed that it is a he-goat, he persists in asking a drop of milk for a medicinal purpose.

1973. கடா பின்வாங்குகிறது பாய்ச்சலுக்கு அடையாளம்.

The drawing back of the he-goat shows that he is about to butt.

1974. கடா மேய்க்கிறவன் அறிவானோ கொழுப் போனவிடம்.

Does the cowherd know where the ploughshare has passed ?

1975. கடாவின் சந்திற் புல்லைத் தின்கிறதுபோல.

Like eating grass screened behind a bull.

1976. கடாவும் கடாவும் சண்டை போடுகிறபோது உண்ணி நசுங்கினாற்போல.

As the tick was crushed to death when the goats fought.

1977. கடிகோலிலே கட்டின நாய்.

A dog tied to a stick.

1978. கடிக்க ஒரு எலும்பும் இல்லை, காதில் மினுக்க ஓலையும் இல்லை.

She has not even a single bone to pick, nor has she an ear-ornament to polish.

1979. கடிக்கிற நாகம கலந்து உறவாகுமா?

Will the cobra be affected by friendly intercourse ?

1980. கடிக்கிற நாய்க்குக் கழுத்தில் குறுங் கயிறு.

A short rope round the neck of a biting dog.

1981. கடினமான பிள்ளை பெற்றாருக்கு உதவுமா?

Will an obdurate child prove helpful to its parents?

1982. கடிதான சொல் அடியிலும் வலிது.

A harsh word is more painful than a blow.

1983. கடித்த பாக்கும் கொடாத சிற்றப்பன் கடைத்தெரு வரையில் வழிவிட்டானாம்.

It is said that *his* uncle who would not give even a bite of an areca-nut, bore *him* company to the bazaar.

1984. கடித்த வாய் துடைத்தாற்போல

Like wiping the mouth after biting.

1985. கடித்த பாம்புக்கு பாலவார்த்தால் விஷத்தைத் தரும் அது போலப் பொல்லாதவர்க்குச் செய்யும் உபகாரம் இருக்கும்.

When milk is placed before a biting snake, *in return* it gives poison, and such is the return for the favours done to the wicked.

1986. கடித்த மூட்டையும் சரி, கடியாத மூட்டையும் சரி.

Bugs are all the same whether they bite or not.

1987. கடித்த நாய்க்குக் காடியைக் கொடு.

Give vinegar to the dog that bit *you*.

1988. கடித்தாலும் கடிக்கட்டும் நீ கொல்லாதிரு.

No matter if *it* bite *you*, do not kill *it*.

1989. கடித்த நாயைப் பயித்தியம் கொண்டது என்று சொல்வார்கள்.

They will call that a mad dog which has bitten *some one*.

1990. கடிந்த சொல்லிலும் கனிந்த சொல்லே நன்மை.

A kind word is better than a harsh one.

1991. கடியாத மூட்டையென்று விட்டு விடுவார்களா?

Will they let a bug escape because it did not bite?

1992. கடியும் சுறுக்குத்தான் அடியும் சுறுக்குத்தான்.

Both the bite and the stroke were quickly effected.

1993 கடுகிச்சு முடுகிச்சு வடுகச்சி கலியாணம்.

The Vaduga woman's wedding is come nigh.

1994. கடுகு போகிற இடத்தில் தடி எடுத்துக்கொண்டு திரிவான், பூசனிக்காய் போகிற இடம் தெரியாது.

He walks about with a staff in a place that will admit a mustard seed, and yet he is ignorant of the place where a pumpkin might easily pass.

1995. கடுகு சிறுத்தாலும் காரம் போகாது.

Though small, the mustard seed is not without pungency.

1996. கடுகு போன இடம் ஆராய்வார் பூசனிக்காய் போன இடம் தெரியாது.

They search for a grain of mustard seed, but not for a missing pumpkin.

1997. கடுகு போன இடம் ஆராய்வார் மிளகு போன இடம் ஆராயார்.

They search for a grain of mustard seed but not for a grain of pepper.

1998. கடுகுக் களவும் களவுதான் காப்பூரக் களவும் களவுதான்.

Theft is theft whether as regards a mustard seed or camphor.

1999 கடுக்காய்க்கு அகணி நஞ்சு, சுக்கிற்குப் புறணி நஞ்சு.

The kernel of the gall-nut and the skin of ginger are poisonous.

2000. கடுங்காற்று மழை காட்டும், கடுசிஞ்னேகம் பகை காட்டும்.

Strong wind foretells rain, excessive friendship foreshows hatred.

2001. கடுஞ்சினேகம் கண்ணுக்குப பகை.

Excessive intimacy will prove unfriendly to one's eyes.

2002. கடுஞ்செட்டுக் காரியக்கேடாம்.

It is said that hard dealing fails in its object.

2003. கடுஞ்செட்டுக் கண்ணைக் கெடுக்கும்.

Unfair dealing destroys the eyes.

2004. கடுஞ்சொற் கேட்டால் காதுக்கு அருவருப்பு.

It is shocking to the ears to hear harsh words.

2005. கடுமுடுக்கடா சேவகா கம்பரிசி அடா சம்பளம்.

Peon, my fellow, you are too strict, you have kamboo rice only as wages.

2006. கடும்பசி கல் மதில் உடைத்தும் களவுசெய்யச் சொல்லும.

Extreme hunger will induce a man to break through a stone wall and steal.

2007. கடை கெட்ட வாழ்வு தலை கட்ட நேரம் இல்லை.

Labouring in menial offices *she has* not leisure to put up her tresses.

2008. கடைக்குக் கடை ஆள் இருப்பார்கள்.

Each bazaar will have its attendant.

2009. கடைசிச் சோற்றுக்கு மோரும், கால் மாட்டிற்குப் பாயும் வேண்டும்.

Buttermilk for the last *distribution of* rice, and a mat for the foot of the bed are indispensable.

2010. கடைத் தேங்காய் எடுத்து வழிப் பிள்ளையாருக்கு உடைத்தாற் போல்.

Like taking up a cocoanut in the bazaar and breaking it to Ganésa.

2011. கடையிலே கொண்டு மனையிலே வைக்கிறான்.

He buys in the bazaar, and bestows at home.

2012. கடையில் அரிசி கஞ்சிக்கு உதவுமா, அபிசாரி புருஷன் ஆபத்துக்கு உதவுவானா?

Will the rice in the bazaar serve for kanji, will the paramour of an adulteress be of service to her in distress!

2013. கடையில் வந்ததும் அரிசியோ நடையில் வெந்ததும் சாதமோ?

Is that which comes to the bazaar rice? Is boiled rice cooked by the way *desirable*?

2014. கடையிலே கட்டித் தூக்கினுலும் அழுகற் பூசணிக்காய் அழு கலே.

Although rotten pumpkins are tied up in the bazaar, they are still rotten.

2015. கட்டப்பாரையை விழுங்கிச் சுக்குக் கஷாயம் குடித்ததுபோல.

Like drinking a decoction of dry ginger after swallowing a crow-bar.

2016. கட்டாந்தரை அட்டைபோல.

Like a wood-louse on dry ground.

2017. கட்டிக்கொண்டு வரச்சொன்னல் வெட்டிக்கொண்டு வருவான்.

When told to tie and bring, he cuts and brings.

2018. கட்டி அழுகிறபோது கையும் துழாவுகிறதே.

When she embraces and weeps, her hand is groping *to steal.*

2019. கட்டில் உள்ள இடத்தில் பிள்ளை பெற்றுச் சுக்குக் கண்ட இடத்தில் காயம் தின்பாள்.

She brings forth her child where she sees a bedstead, and takes the prescribed tonic where she sees dry ginger.

2020. கட்டி வழி விட்டால் வெட்டி அரசு ஆளலாம்.

If he organize *an army* and lead it, he may cut down *the enemy* and reign as a king.

2021. கட்டி அழுகையிலே என் மகளே உனக்குப் பெட்டியிலே கை என்ன ?

My daughter, why is your hand in the basket while you embrace and weep ?

2022. கட்டி அடித்தால என்ன விட்டு அடித்தால் என்ன ?

It makes no difference whether you flog one bound or unbound.

2023. கட்டின வீட்டுக்குப் பழுது சொல்லுவார் பலர்.

Many will find fault with a house newly built.

2024. கட்டின வீட்டுக்குக் கருத்துச் சொல்லுவார் பலர்.

Many will express an opinion respecting a house just built.

2025. கட்டினவனுக்கு ஒரு வீடானால், கட்டாதவனுக்குப் பல வீடு.
He who has built a house has only one, whereas he who has not built makes use of many.

2026. கட்டிவைத்த பூனையை அவிழ்த்து விட்டு வாபூஸ் வாபூஸ் என்றால் வருமா?
On untying a cat and calling puss, puss, will it come?

2027. கட்டிலைத் திருப்பிப்போட்டால் தலைவலி போமா?
Will head-ache go by turning the bedstead?

2028. கட்டிவைத்த பணத்தைத் தட்டிப் பறித்தாற்போல.
As if one displaced and carried away money carefully tied up.

2029. கட்டி விதை வெட்டி விதை.
Provide seed-corn, and sow having tilled the ground.

2030. கட்டு அறிந்த நாயும் அல்ல, கனம் அறிந்த கப்பரையும் அல்ல.
He is not a dog accustomed to restraint, nor a mendicant's dish that knows what self-respect is.

2031. கட்டுக்குக் கட்டு மாறிக் கட்டவேண்டும்.
Every time you have to tie, you must tie it in a different way.

2032. கட்டுப்பட்டாலும் கவரிமான் மயிரால் கட்டுப் படவேண்டும். குட்டுப்பட்டாலும் மோதிரக் கையால் குட்டுப்பட வேண்டும்.
When bound, it should be by the hair of the roe, and if cuffed, it should be by a hand ornamented with jewels.

2033. கட்டுச்சோற்று மூட்டையும் இளம் பிள்ளையும் எடுப்பது வருத்தம்.
It is difficult to carry, besides a child, boiled rice tied up *for a journey*.

2034. கட்டைக்குப் போகும்போது காலாழி பீலியா?
Are toe-rings necessary when a *woman* goes out to get the firewood?

2035. கட்டோடே போனால் கனத்தோடே வரலாம்.
If one sets out auspiciously, he may return with honour

2036. கணக்கதிகாரத்தைப் பிளக்கும் கோடாலி.
He is an axe splitting the tree of arithmetic.

2037. கணக்கன் கணக்கு அறிவான், தன் கணக்கைத் தான் அறியான்.
The accountant is clever at numbers, but he is ignorant of his own accounts.

2038. கணக்குக் குஞ்சையும் காக்கைக் குஞ்சையும் கண்ட இடத்திலே கண்ணைக் குத்து.
Bore through the eyes of a young kurnum and a young crow wherever you find them.

2039. கணக்கைப் பார்த்தால் பிணக்கு வரும்.
When accounts are examined, difficulties arise.

2040. கணக்கனுக்குப் பட்டினி உடன் பிறப்பு.
To suffer hunger is natural to an accountant.

2041. கணக்கு அறிந்த பிள்ளை வீட்டில் இருந்தால் வழக்கு அறாது.
There will be constant disputes in a house should one of its inmates be a skilful accountant.

2042. கணக்கன் வீட்டுக் கலியாணம் விளக்கெண்ணெய்க்குக் கேடு.
A marriage ceremony in the house of an accountant is a waste of oil.

2043. கணக்கப்பிள்ளை எல்லாம் எழுத்துப்பிள்ளை அல்ல.
All accountants are not learned.

2044. கணபதி பூசை கை மேலே பயன்.
The pooja of Ganèsa has immediate effect.

2045. கணவனைப் பிரிந்தும் அயல் வீட்டில் இருக்கிறதா?
What! in a neighbour's house, separated from your husband!

2046. கணுக்கால் பெருத்தால் கணவனைத் தின்பாள்.
If her ankle grow big, she will be deprived of her husband.

2047. கண் கண்டது கை செய்யும்.
What the eye has seen the hand may do.

2048. கண்குத்திப்பாம்புபோலப் பார்த்திருந்தேன்.

I was waiting like an eye-snake.

2049. கண் குருட்டுக்கு மருந்து இட்டால் தெளியுமா?

Is blindness curable by an external application?

2050. கண் குருடு ஆனாலும் நித்திரையில் குறையா?

Though blind, does he sleep the less?

2051. கண் கெட்ட பின்பு சூரிய நமஸ்காரம் செய்து என்ன பலன்?

What benefit can you expect from the worship of the sun if you have lost your eyesight?

2052. கண்ட பாவனையாய்க் கொண்டை முடிக்கிறது.

Tying one's lock of hair in imitation of other's.

2053. கண்ட கண்ட கோயில் எல்லாம் கை எடுத்துக் கும்பிட்டேன்.

I worshipped with raised hands in every temple I visited.

2054. கண்டது பாம்பு கடித்தது மாங்கொட்டை.

That which was seen was a snake, that which bit was the stone of a mango fruit.

2055. கண்டது காட்சி பெற்றது பேறு.

Whatever is seen is a sight, whatever is received is a gift.

2056. கண்டதைக் கேளாவிட்டால் உண்டு உறங்க மாட்டான்.

He will neither eat nor sleep without asking whatever he sees.

2057. கண்டதைக் கேளாவிட்டால் கொண்டவன் அடிப்பான்.

If she does not attend to the affairs of her *family*, her husband will beat *her*.

2058. கண்டறியாதவன் பெண்டு படைத்தால் காடு மேடு எல்லாம் இழுத்துத் திரிவானாம்.

It is said that if an inexperienced man marries, he will wander about dragging his wife, through jungles and over hills.

2059. கண்டதைக் கற்கப் பண்டிதன் ஆவான்.

By learning what he sees, a person becomes a pundit.

2060. கண்டது கேட்டது சொல்லாதே காட்டுமரத்திலே நில்லாதே.

Never utter what you have seen and heard, nor stand under a wild tree.

2061. கண்டது பாம்பு கடித்தது கருக்குமட்டை.

That which he saw was a snake, but he was bit by the rough points of the palmyra stem.

2062. கண்டதைக் கற்றுக்கொண்டு கரையேறு.

Acquire what you can, and go ashore.

2063. கண்டவன் எடானு ?

Will he who finds, not take up ?

2064. கண்டால் தெரியாதா கம்பளியாட்டு மயிர் ?

May not sheep-hair be known as soon as seen ?

2065. கண்டால் முறை சொல்லுகிறது காணுவிட்டால் பெயர் சொல்லுகிறதா ?

If present, do you call mentioning the relationship of the party, and when absent, his name only ?

2066. கண்டால் ஆயம் காணு விட்டால் மாயம்.

If seen, duty, if not seen, fraud.

2067. கண்டு செத்த பிணம் ஆனால் சுடு காட்டிற்கு வழி தெரியும்.

If one die under *human* observation, his corpse will find its way to the place of cremation.

2068. கண்டு பேசக் காரியம் இருக்கிறது முகத்தில் விழிக்க வெட்கமாய் இருக்கிறது.

I have something to speak of in person, but I am ashamed to look at his face.

2069. கண்டும் காணவில்லை, கேட்டும் கேட்கவில்லையென்று இருக்கவேண்டும்.

Behave as though seeing, you see not, and hearing, you hear not.

2070. கண்டு எடுத்தவன் கொடுப்பானா?

Will he who finds and takes a thing give it up?

2071. கண்ணால் கண்டதற்குச் சாட்சியும் வேண்டுமோ?

Is a witness needed to prove that which one has seen with his own eye?

2072. கண்ணாற் கண்டது பொய் அகப்பைக்குறி மெய்.

That which one has seen is false, the sign of agappai is true.

2073. கண்ணாற் கண்டதற்கு ஏன் அகப்பைக்குறி?

Why the sign of an agappai in proof of that which one has seen?

2074. கண்ணாரக் காணாதது மூன்றில் ஒரு பங்கு.

That one has not seen with his own eye amounts to one third.

2075. கண்ணாலே சீவன் கடகட என்று போனாலும் வண்ணான் கழுதை சுமந்தே தீரவேண்டும்.

The ass of a washerman must carry the pack through, though its life may depart with a rattling noise through the eyes.

2076. கண்ணான பேர்களை மண்ணாக்குகிறான்.

He treats as common earth those who are precious as the eyes.

2077. கண்ணான மனதைப் புண்ணாக்குகிறான்.

He wounds the heart which is as tender as the eye.

2078. கண்ணாலே சீவன் கடகடவென்று போனாலும் வண்ணானுக்கு மழை நஞ்சு.

Though the life of the washerman is *forced* through his eyes by reason of drought, rain to him would be poison.

2079. கண்ணாடி நிழலிற் கண்ட பணம் கடனுக்கு உதவுமா?

Will the money reflected in a mirror avail for the payment of a debt?

2080. கண்ணான பேர்களைப் புண்ணாக்கினாய்.

You have wounded your dearest friends.

2081. கண்ணிமை கைநொடி அளவே மாத்திரை.

The twinkling of the eye, or the snapping of the fingers, is the measure of a moment of time.

2082. கண்ணியில் அகப்பட்ட மான்போல் கலங்குகிறான்.

He is dismayed like a deer caught in a snare.

2083. கண்ணியில் அகப்பட்ட கரிக்குருவிபோல் கலங்குகிறான்.

He is agitated as an ensnared blackbird.

2084. கண்ணிற் பட்டாற் கரிக்குமா, புருவத்திற் பட்டாற் கரிக்குமா?

When will it give pain, when it hits the eye or the eye-brow?

2085. கண்ணினால் எண்ணுவான்.

He can count with his eyes—*at sight.*

2086. கண்ணிற் புண் வந்தால் கண்ணாடி பார்க்கல் ஆகாது.

When the eyes become sore, one cannot see them reflected in a mirror.

2087. கண்ணின்முன்னே ஒன்று சொல்லிக் காணாத இடத்திலே இரண்டு சொல்லுகிறது.

To assert a thing when in sight and to contradict it when out of sight.

2088. கண்ணிலே எண்ணெய் பட்டாற் கரிக்குமோ பிடரியில் பட்டால் கரிக்குமோ?

Will oil give pain when it falls into the eye, or on the back of the neck?

2089. கண்ணிற் பட்ட கையைத் தறிப்பார் இல்லை.

No one cuts off the hand because it has struck the eye.

2090. கண்ணிலே பட்டால் விரலைத் தறிக்கிறதா?

Should it strike the eye is the finger to be cut off.

2091. கண்ணிலே வருகிறது புருவத்திலே.

The eye brow has received that which threatened the eye.

2092. கண்ணில் கண்டது கோடி காணாதது அனந்தம் கோடி.

That which was seen was a crore, and that not seen many crores.

2093. கண் உள்ளபோதே காட்சி.

One has the pleasure of seeing as long as the eyes are *unimpaired.*

2094. கண் ஊனன் கைப்பொருள் இழப்பான்.

The blind will lose his wealth.

2095. கண்ணுக்குப் புருவம் காதாமா?

Is the brow ten miles in advance of the eye?

2096. கண்ணுக்குப் புண்ணும் அல்ல, காண்பார்க்கு நோயும் அல்ல.

It is neither an eye-sore, nor painful to beholders.

2097. கண்ணும் கருத்தும் உள்ளபோதே காணேம் அதன் பின்பு என்ன கிடைக்கும்?

We do not realize it when the eye and mind are unimpaired; what may we expect to gain afterwards?

2098. கண்ணுக்கு இமை காதாமா?

Is the eye-lid far apart from the eye?

2099. கண்ணுக்குட் சம்மணம் கொட்டுவாள் கம்பத்தில் ஐந்தானை கட்டுவாள்.

She will sit in one's eye cross-legged, and tether five elephants to the pole *of a dancer.*

2100. கண்ணை இமை காத்ததுபோல்.

As the eye-lash preserved the eye.

2101. கண்ணைக் கெடுத்த தெய்வம் மதியைக் கொடுத்தது.

The deity that deprived him of sight gave him superior mental endowments.

2102. கண்ணைக் கொண்டு நடந்ததுபோல உன்னைக் கொண்டு நடந்தேன்.

I guarded you as I did my own eyes.

2103. கண்ணைக் கட்டிக் காட்டில் விட்டதுபோல.

As one was left in the jungle blindfolded.

2104. கண்ணைக் காட்டி அழைத்தால் வராதவள் கையைப் பிடித்து இழுத்தால் வருவாளா?

Will she who would not come when called by the expression of your eyes, obey when taken by the hand?

2105. கண்ணைக் கெடுத்த தெய்வம் கோலைக் கொடுத்தது.

The deity that destroyed the eyes gave a *supporting* staff.

2106. கண்ணைமூடிக் குட்டுகிறதா?

Is it to strike the head after covering the eyes?

2107. கண்ணோ புண்ணோ.

Is it an eye, or a sore?

2108. கண் தெரிந்து நடப்பவர்கள் பள்ளத்தில் விழமாட்டார்கள்.

They who walk with their eyes open will not fall into the pit.

2109. கண்தெரிந்து வழி நடக்கும்படி நினை.

Take care that you walk with your eyes open.

2110. கண் பார்த்தால் கை செய்யும்.

If the eye have seen it, the hand may perform it.

2111. கதவைச் சாத்தினால் நிலை புறம்பு.

When the door is shut, the door-frame is outside.

2112. கதிரவன் சிலரைக் காயேன் என்குமோ?

Will the sun say, I will not burn certain persons?

2113. கதிரைக் களைந்தும் களையைப் பிடுங்கு.

Weed the corn even at the risk of destroying the ears.

2114. கதிர் நூல் குறைந்தாலும் கள்ளச்சி கழுத்து நூல் குறையாது.

Though the thread on the spindle diminishes, that on the neck of a kalla woman does not.

2115. கதைக்குக் காலும் இல்லை தலையும் இல்லை.

Mere rumours have neither head nor foot.

2116. கதைக்குக் கால் இல்லை பேய்க்குப் பாதம் இல்லை.

Rumours have no legs, nor have demons feet.

2117. கதையோ பிராமணா கந்தையோ பொத்துகிறாய், அல்லடீ பேய் முண்டாய் சீலைப்பேன் குத்துகிறேன்.

O brahman, do you repeat a story or mend old clothes? No, you foolish widow, I crush the lice in my clothes.

2118. கத்தரிக்காய் சொத்தை என்றால் அரிவாள் மணைக் குற்றம் என்கிறாள்.

When it is said that the brinjal is worm eaten, she imputes it to a defect in the knife.

2119. கத்தரிக்காயிலே காலும் கையும் முளைத்தாற்போல.

As if feet and hands shot forth in the brinjal.

2120. கத்தரிக்காய் விரை சுரைக்காய் காய்க்காது.

The seed of a brinjal will not produce gourds.

2121. கத்தரிக்காய் வாங்கப் பூசணிக்காய் கொசுறா?

When you buy a brinjal, will the bazaar people give you a pumpkin in at the bargain?

2122 கத்தியும் கடாவும் போலே.

Like a knife and a he-goat.

2123. கத்தியைப் பார்க்கிலும் கன கோபம் கொலை செய்யும்.

Great anger is more destructive than the sword.

2124. கத்திகட்டி பெண்சாதி எப்போதும் கைம்பெண்சாதி.

The wife of a swordsman is at any moment *liable to become* a widow.

2125. கத்தி இருக்கும் இடத்துக்கு மரை காவுகிறதா?

Is the elk to be carried to the knife?

2126. கத்துமட்டும் கத்திப்போட்டுக் கதவைச் சாத்திவிட்டுப் போ.

Bawl out as long as you like, and shut the door when you go.

2127. கத்து கத்து என்ருல் கழுதையும் கத்தாது, சொல்லு சொல்லு என்ருல் புலவனும் சொல்லான்.

When repeatedly urged to bray, even an ass will not do so, when asked to sing, eveu a poet will refuse.

2128. கந்தபொடிக் கடைக்காரனுக்கு வாசனை தெரியுமா?

Does the perfumer appreciate the distinction of scents ?

2129. கந்தைக்குத் தக்க பொந்தை.

The hole is in proportion to the rag.

2130. கந்தைக்குச் சரடு ஏறுகிறது எல்லாம் பலம்.

The more it is stitched and the stronger does the rag become.

2131. கந்தை ஆனாலும் கசக்கி உடு, கூழ் ஆனாலும் குளித்துக் குடி.

Though only a rag, wash it and put it on, and if but kanji, drink it after ablution.

2132. கபட இன் சொல்லினும் கடிய சொல்லே நலம்.

Better is a harsh word than one smooth and feigned.

2133. கபாலக் குத்து கண்ணைச் சுழித்தது.

Severe head-ache caused the eyes to sink.

2134. கப்பலிலே பாதிப்பாக்குப் போட்டதுபோலே.

Like dropping a bit of areca-nut in a ship.

2135. கப்பல் ஏறிப் பட்ட கடன் கொட்டை நூற்றுத் தீர்க்கவேண்டும்.

Debt incurred by the sea-faring merchant must be discharged by spinning cotton.

2136. கப்பல் ஓடிப் பட்ட கடன் கொட்டை நூற்றுத் தீருமோ?

Can a debt incurred on account of a sea-faring life be discharged by spiuning ?

2137. சப்பற்காரன் பெண்டாட்டி தொப்பைக்காரி, கப்பல் உடைந்தால் பிச்சைக்காரி.

The ship owner's wife is in good condition as long as the ship is safe, but if that be lost she is a beggar.

2138. கப்பற்காரன் வாழ்வு காற்று அடித்தால் போச்சு.

The prosperity of the ship-owner is at the mercy of the wind.

2139. கமரிற் கவிழ்ந்த பால் அமரர்க்கு இட்ட அன்னம்.

Milk poured into a crevice, rice offered to enemies.

2140. கம்பப் பிச்சையோ கடைப் பிச்சையோ?

Are not alms obtained by pole-dancing the lowest species of alms?

2141. கம்பளியிலே ஏற்றசோற்றை மயிர் மயிர் என்கிறதா?

Is it to say that the boiled rice received in a cumbly is full of hair?

2142. கம்பளி விற்ற பணத்துக்கு மயிர் முளைத்து இருக்கிறதா?

Does hair grow in the money for which cumblies have been sold?

2143. கம்பளியில் ஒட்டின கூழைப்போல.

Like food sticking to a cumbly.

2144. கம்பளிமேல் பிசின்.

Gum on a cumbly.

2145. கம்பன் வீட்டுக் கட்டுத் தறியும் கவி பாடும்.

Even the peg to which a cow is tied at Kamban's house will sing.

2146. கம்புக்குக் களை வெட்டினாற்போலும் இருக்கவேண்டும், தம்பிக்குப் பெண்கொண்டாற்போலும் இருக்கவேண்டும்.

Arrange it so that when he goes to weed the rye, he may also engage a wife for his younger brother.

2147. கம்மாளன் பசுவைக் காது அறுத்துக் கொள்ளவேண்டும்.

One must buy a smith's cow after cropping her ears.

2148. கம்மாளன் வீட்டில் பிள்ளை பிறந்தால் தேவடியாள் தெருவில சர்க்கரை வழங்கவேண்டும்.

When a child is born in a smith's family, sugar must be dealt out in the street of the dancing girls.

2149. கம்மாளன் நாய் சம்மட்டித் தொனிக்கு அஞ்சுமா?

Will the smith's dog be alarmed at the sound of a hammer?

2150. கயிறு இல்லாப் பம்பரம்போல.

Like a top without a string.

2151. கயிற்றைப் பாம்பென்று எண்ணிக் கலங்குகிறது.

Trembling at a bit of rope thinking it to be a snake.

2152. கரகத்து நீர் காதங் காக்கும்.

Water in a hand-pot will avail for a katham.

2153. கரடி பிறை கண்டதுபோல.

As a bear saw the new moon.

2154. கரடி துரத்தினாலும் கைக்கோளத் தெருவில் போக வழி இராது.

Though one be pursued by a bear, he may not escape through weavers' street.

2155. கரடியால் துரத்தப்பட்டவனுக்குக் கம்பளிக்காரனைக் கண்டாற் பயம்.

He who has been kicked by a bear, fears the sight of one who sells cumblies.

2156. கரடி புற்றிலே வாய் வைத்தாற்போல், கருடன் காலிற் சதங்கை கட்டியதுபோல்.

As the bear puts its nose into the anthill, as small bells were tied to the legs of a kite.

2157. கரணம் தப்பினால் மரணம்.

To fail in a somersault may be fatal.

2158. கரம்மாறிக் கட்டினால் கனம் குறையாது.

Excessive cording will not diminish the weight of a package.

2159. கரிப்புக்கு இருந்து பிழை, கலகத்துக்கு ஓடிப் பிழை.

In famine, save your life where you are, in war, by flight.

2160. கரிப்பிலே பிள்ளை விற்றாற்போலே.

Like selling a child in famine.

2161. கரு இல்லாத வித்தையும் குரு இல்லா சிஷனும்போல்.

Like an art without ingenuity *to comprehend it,* and a disciple without a teacher.

2162. கருக்கி உருக்கி நெய்வார்த்தாலும் கண்ட நியாயந்தான் சொல்லுவான்.

Though you give him fried meat and pour melted ghee *on his rice,* he will say nothing but what he saw.

2163. கருங்கண்ணி பட்டால் களையான் கண்ணாலும் திரும்பிப் பாரான்.

When the karunkanni fish is caught, the fisherman dces not even turn to look at it.

2164. கருங்கல்லிலே நார் உரிப்பான்.

He will strip fibre from a piece of granite.

2165. கருங்காலி உலக்கைக்கு வெள்ளிப் பூண் கட்டினதுபோல.

As a silver ferrule fastened to an ebony pestle.

2166. கருங்காலிக் கட்டைக்கு வாய் நாணாக் கோடாலி இள வாழைத் தண்டுக்கு வாய் நாணுமா ?

Will an axe whose edge is not blunted by cutting a piece of ebony, be made dull by cutting a stem of a plantian tree ?

2167. கருடன் காலில் கெச்சை கட்டினதுபோல.

As a string of small bells was tied to the leg of a kite.

2168. கருடனைக் கண்ட பாம்புபோல.

Like a snake in sight of a kite.

2169. கருப்பங்கட்டியிலும் கல்லு இருக்கும்.

Stones may be found even in sugar candy.

2170. கரும ஒழுங்கு பெருமைக்கு அளவு.

Consistency of action is the measure of greatness.

2171. கருமத்தை முடிக்கிறவன் அருமை ஒன்றும் பாரான்.

A resolute man cares nothing about difficulties.

2172. கருமான் இருந்த இடமும் கழுதை புரண்ட களமும் சரி.

A blacksmith's shop, and the place in which asses roll themselves are alike.

2173. கரும்பிலும் தேன் இருக்கும் கள்ளியிலும் பால் இருக்கும்.

There is honey in sugarcane, there is sap in milk-hedge.

2174. கரும்புக்கட்டிக்கு எறும்புதானே வரும்.

Ants will of course be attracted by a lump of sugar-candy.

2175. கரும்பு முறித்துக் கழுதையை அடித்த கதை.

The story of one striking an ass with a sugar-cane.

2176. கரும்பைக் கழுதைமுன் போட்டால் கழுதைக்குத் தெரியுமோ கரும்பு ருசி?

Does the ass enjoy the flavor of the sugar-cane that is placed before it?

2177. கரும்பு தின்னக் கூலியா?

What, a reward for eating sugar-cane!

2178. கரும்பும் வேம்பு ஆயிற்றே.

Even sugar-cane has become a margosa tree.

2179. கரும்புக்கு உழுத புழுதி காய்ச்சின பாலுக்குச் சருக்கரை ஆமா?

Will earth pulverised by the plough for sugar-cane, answer for sugar to be mixed with boiled milk?

2180. கரும்பு கசக்கிறது வாய்க்குற்றம்.

If sugar-cane prove bitter to the palate, it is the fault of the mouth.

2181. கரும்பு ருசியென்று வேரோடு பிடுங்கலாமா?

May sugar-cane be plucked up by the root because it is of fine flavor?

2182. கரும்பை விரும்ப, அது வேம்பு ஆயிற்று.

If taken to excess sugar-cane becomes bitter as margosa.

2183. கரும்பு கட்டோடே இருக்க எறும்பு தானே வரும்.

Where bundles of sugar-cane are, there ants will come of themselves.

2184. கருவு இல்லாத முட்டையும் குரு இல்லாத வித்தையும்.

An egg without yolk, an art without a teacher.

2185. கருவேலமரத்திற்கு நிழல் இல்லை, கன்னானுக்கு முறை இல்லை.

The karuvél *Acasia* casts no shade, smiths observe no relationship *in marrying*.

2186. கரை காணாத தோணிபோல.

As a doney out of sight of land.

The common name of a country vessel, some of which are of considerable size. They have no deck and are thatched with palm leaves.

2187. கரை தட்டின கப்பல்போல.

Like a stranded vessel.

2188. கரைப்பக்கம் பாதை இருக்கக் கப்பல் ஏறினவனும், சொல்லாததை மனையாளுக்குச் சொன்னவனும் பட்ட பாடுபோல.

Like the misery endured by him who embarked when there was a way by land, and by the husband who revealed to his wife that which he ought not.

2189. கரைப்பார் கரைத்தாற் கல்லும் கரையும்.

Under the management of the skilful, even a stone may be dissolved.

2190. கலகத்திலே புளுகாதவன் நரகத்திலே போவானும்.

It is said that he who does not exaggerate when a tumult occurs will go to hell.

2191. கலகத்திலே பேயும் கால்மாடு தலைமாடா?

In regard to a bed is the distinction of head and foot *observed* in a battle-field?

2192. கலகம் கலந்தால் உலகம் கலங்கும்.

In a general insurrection universal consternation prevails.

2193. கலகம் பிறந்தால் நியாயம் பிறக்கும்.

Popular agitation leads to justice.

2194. கலகமே மெய்யானுற் புளுகாதவன் பாவம்.

If an insurrection exists, it is wrong not to make it known.

2195. கலக்கந்தை கட்டிக் காணப் போனல் இருகலக் கந்தை கட்டி எதிரே வந்தாள்.

When I went in rags to see her, she appeared enveloped in double the quantity.

2196. கலக் கம்பு தின்றாலும் காடை காட்டிலே.

Though it may consume a kalam of grain, the quail *lives* in the jungle.

2197. கலக்கினும் கடல் சேறுகாது.

Though never so troubled, the sea does not become muddy.

2198. கலத்திலே சோற்றை இட்டுக் கையைப் பிடித்தாற்போல.

Like holding the hand after putting rice on the plate.

2199. கல நெல்லுக்குக் கல உமி இருக்குமா?

Will a kalam of paddy yield a kalam of husks?

2200. கலப் பணத்தைப் பார்க்கிலும் ஒரு கிழப் பிணம் நல்லது.

The corpse of an old person is better than immense wealth.

2201. கலப் பால் கறக்கலாம் துளிப் பால் முலைக்கு ஏற்றலாமா?

A kalam of milk may be drawn; can a drop be infused into the teat?

2202. கலப் பாலுக்குத் துளிப் புரை.

A drop of butter-milk or curds to a kalam of milk.

2203. கலப்பானாலும் பூசப்பூசப் பொன்னிறம்.

Though not pure, repeated gilding *will give it* the colour of gold.

2204. கலப் பாலில் ஒரு துளி விஷம் கலந்தாற்போலே.

Like putting a drop of poison in a kalam of milk,

2205. கலப் பால் குடித்த பூனை ஆழாக்குப் பால் குடியாதா?

Will not a cat that has drunk a kalam of milk drink an álak?

2206. கல மா இடித்தவள் பாவியும், கப்பி இடித்தவள் புண்ணியவதியுமா?

Is she who pounded a kalam of flour vicious, and she who pounded rolong virtuous?

2207. கலம் கலந்தால் குலம் கலக்கும்.

When plates are interchanged, tribal marriages interchange.

2208. கலம் குத்தினாலும் பதர் அரிசி ஆகாது.

Though a kalam of chaff be pounded, it will not become rice.

2209. கல உமி தின்றால் ஒரு அரிசி தட்டாதா?

If a kalam of chaff be eaten may not a grain of rice turn up!

2210. கலியாணச் சந்தடியில் தாலி கட்ட மறந்தானாம்.

It is said that he forgot to tie the táli owing to the bustle at the wedding.

2211. கலியாணத்திலும் பஞ்சம் இல்லை, களத்திலும் பஞ்சம் இல்லை.

No scarcity at a wedding, nor in the threshing floor.

2212. கலியாண வீட்டில் பந்தற்காலைக் கட்டி அழுகிறவள் செத்த வீட்டில் சும்மா இருப்பாளா?

Will the woman who wept as she clung to the post of a marriage pandal at be silent when she attends a funeral!

2213. கலியாண வீட்டிற்குப் போய் அறியான், மேளச் சத்தமும் கேட்டு அறியான்.

He has never been at a wedding, nor has he heard the sound of a tom-tom.

2214. கலியாணம் செய்தும் சன்னியாசியா?

What, though married yet a Sanyási-*ascetic*?

2215. கல் ஆகிலும் கணவன், புல் ஆகிலும் புருஷன்.

Though *in heart* hard as a stone, and worthless as a blade of grass, he is your husband.

2216. கல் எறிக்குத் தப்பினாலும் கண் எறிக்குத் தப்பக்கூடாது.

Though one may escape the cast of a stone, he cannot escape the glance of an *evil* eye.

The evil eye கண்ணேறு and the evil tongue நாவூறு are feared very generally. To avert their influence as regards fruits &c, in a garden, it is common to put up some object of attraction as a water-pot whitewashed, inverted on a stump, and dotted with black spots &c. In some enclosures grotesque images are seen.

2217. கல்லடிச்சித்தன் போகிற வழி, காடு மேடு எல்லாம் தவிடு பொடி.

All the rough and rugged ground before the stone-cutter will be reduced to powder.

2218. கல்லாடம் படித்தவனோடு மல் ஆடாதே.

Do not contend with him who has studied kalladam.

Kalladam a work on the third part of grammar is said to be extremely dry.

2219. கல்லாதார் செல்வத்திலும் கற்றார் வறுமை நலம்.

The poverty of the learned is better than the wealth of the unlearned.

2220. கல்லாத ஒருவன் குலநலம் பேசுதல் நெல்லுடன் பிறந்த பதராகுமே.

The illiterate who boast of high rank may be compared to the dust mixed with paddy-*unhusked rice*.

2221. கல்லார் உறவிலும் கற்றோர் பகை நலம்.

The enmity of the learned is better than the friendship of the illiterate.

2222. கல்லார் உறவகல் காமக் கடல் கட.

Keep at a distance from the unlettered; cross the sea of passion.

2223. கல்லிலும் வன்மை கனமூடர் நெஞ்சம்.

The heart of a great fool is harder than a stone.

2224. கல்லிலே நார் உரிக்கிறதுபோல.

Like stripping fibre from a stone.

2225. கல்லும் தேங்காயும்போலப் பேசுகிறான்.

He speaks as effectively as the hitting of a stone on a cocoanut.

2226. கல்லும் காவேரியும் உள்ளமட்டும் வாழ்க.

May you live as long as the rocks and the Cauveri exist.

The river Cauveri rises in the western ghauts and flows into the bay of Bengal. It is the source of the great fertility of Tanjore and the adjacent districts. According to the legend it originated in the following manner. In ancient times when the people of southern India suffered from drought, Ganésa became incarnate in the form of a crow. As such he visited the abode of an ascetic on one of the western hills. He there alighted on the waterpot of a hermit and upset it. The water thus spilt, by reason of the hermit's merit, became a river: the current spelling would make the name the lake of the crow: the legend requires the word to be spelt காவேறி crow mounting, whereas காவேரி lake of the crow is common.

2227. கல்லு வருகிற விசையைக் கண்டால் பல்லைச் சிக்கென மூட வேண்டும்.

On seeing the rapid approach of a stone press your teeth and shut your mouth.

2228. கல்லை ஆகிலும் கரைக்கலாம், மூர்க்கன் மனதைக் கரைக்கல் ஆகாது.

Even stones may be dissolved, but the mind of a fool cannot.

2229. கல்லைக் கண்டால் நாயைக் காணோம், நாயைக் கண்டால் கல்லைக் காணோம்.

On finding a stone we see no dog, on seeing a dog we find no stone.

2230. கல்லைக் குத்துவானேன் கை நோகிறது என்று அழுவானேன்?

Why beat a stone and then weep, exclaiming it has pained my hand!

2231. கல்லைப்போலக் கணவன் இருக்கக் கஞ்சிக்கு அழுவானேன்?

Why weep for kanji while you have a husband as *hard* as a stone!

2232. கல்லைக் கிள்ளிக் கை இழந்தது போலாம்.

Like losing the hand by pinching a stone.

2233. கல்வி இல்லான் செல்வம் கற்பில்லாள் அழகு.

Wealth without learning is like beauty without chastity.

2234. கல்வி என்ற பயிருக்குக் கண்ணீர் என்ற மழைவேண்டும்.

Plants of learning flourish in the rain of tears.

2235. கல்வியும் குலமும் வெல்வது வினவில்.

When inquiring what will prevail, *one's* learning and rank *naturally occur.*

2236. கல்வி உள்ள இளைஞன் கன கிழவன்.

A well instructed youth is an old man.

2237. கல்வியைப் பங்குபோட ஏலாது.

Learning cannot be allotted in portions-*to persons.*

2238. கவணெறி நெறியில் நில்லாதே, கண்டவன் தலையை உடைக்கும்.

Do not stand in the way of *a stone* from a sling, it may break the head of the beholder.

2239. கவி கொண்டார்க்குக் கீர்த்தி, அதைச் செவிகொள்ளார்க்கு அவகீர்த்தி.

Praise to those who approve of a poem, and blame to those who will not listen to it.

2240. கவிக்கொண்டார்க்கும் கீர்த்தி கலைப்பார்க்கும் கீர்த்தியா?
Are those who accept a poem and those who reject it alike praiseworthy?

2241. கவிந்திராணம் கஜேந்திராணம் ராஜாவே நிற்பயே வகி.
O king, manage a poet laureate and a superior elephant without fear.

2242. கவையைப்பற்றிக் கழுதையின் காலைப் பிடி.
To effect your object, *if necessary*, cling to the legs of an ass.

2243. கழுதை காணவேண்டினுல் குட்டிச்சுவரிலே காணலாம்.
If an ass be wanted, it may be found *feeding* near a ruinous wall.

2244. கழுதைக் கெட்டால் குட்டிச்சுவர்.
If an ass be out of condition, it will be as useless as a ruinous wall.

2245. கழுதைக்கு ஏன் கடிவாளம்?
Why a bridle for an ass?

2246. கழுதைப் புண்ணுக்குப் புழுதி மருந்து.
Dust is medicine for the sores of an ass.

2247. கழுதையும் குதிரையும் சரி ஆமா?
Are an ass and a horse equal?

2248. கழுதையும் குதிரையும் பிணைத்தாற்போல.
Like yoking an ass and a horse together.

2249. கழுதை அறியுமா கந்தப்பொடி வாசனை?
Can an ass appreciate fragrant powder?

2250. கழுதைக்குச் சேணம் கட்டினுலும் குதிரை ஆமா?
Does an ass become a horse by being saddled?

2251. கழுதை தேய்ந்து கட்டெறும்பு ஆயிற்று.
The ass by wearing away has become an ant.

2252. கழுதைக்கு ஏன் கவினம், அல்லது கடிவாளம்?
Why a bit or a bridle for an ass?

2253. கழுதையைக் கட்டி ஓமம் வளர்த்ததுபோல.

Like tying an ass and feeding a sacrificial fire.

This proverb relates to the following story. A certain Mahárája had a barber who had evinced great skill in shaving his royal master when he was asleep. To reward him the King resolved to elevate him in the social scale. The brahmans were called and ordered to make a brahman of the barber. They set to work, kindled a sacred fire and the barber was led round it, whilst the priests uttered the required incantations for accomplishing their purpose.

The prime minister being of a somewhat facetious temperament determined to metamorphose an ass. As the proverb intimates he kindled a fire and led the animal round it. When the King saw him thus engaged he asked him what he was doing. The prime minister replied by stating that if the brahmans could make a brahman of a barber he thought an ass might be made into a horse, and he was therefore engaged in the ceremony.

2254. கழுதைக்கு உபதேசம் காதிலே சொன்னாலும் அபயக் குரல் அன்றி அங்கு ஒன்றும் இல்லை.

Though religious instruction be whispered in the ears of an ass nothing will come of it but the accustomed braying.

2255. கழுதைக்கு வாழ்க்கைப்பட்டு உதைக்கு அஞ்சலாமா?

Having married an ass, do you fear his kicking!

2256. கழுதைமேல் ஏறி என்ன, இறங்கி என்ன?

What matters it whether you mount an ass, or alight from one?

2257. கழுதைமேல் ஏறியும் பெருமை இல்லை, இறங்கியும் சிறுமை இல்லை.

Though you may ride on an ass, you gain no honour, nor are you disgraced by dismounting.

2258. கழுதை உழுது வண்ணான் குடி ஆனானா?

Did the washerman become a farmer by ploughing with an ass?

2259. கழுதை உழுது குறவன் குடி ஆனானா?

Has the forester become a farmer by ploughing with an ass!

2260. கழுதை மயிர் பிடுங்கினால் இலாபம் என்ன நஷ்டம் என்ன?
What profit or loss will arise from plucking off the hair of an ass?

2261. கழுதை மயிர் பிடுங்கித் தேசம் கட்டி ஆள்வானா?
Can one reign as a king by selling ass-hair?

2262. கழுதைக்குத் தெரியுமா கஸ்தூரி வாசனை?
Does an ass appreciate the odour of musk?

2263. கழுதைக்குப் பரதேசம் குட்டிச்சுவர்.
The foreign country of an ass is a ruinous wall.

2264. கழுதை தப்பினால் குட்டிச்சுவரிடத்தில் இருக்கும்.
If an ass goes astray, it may be found near a ruinous wall.

2265. கழுதைப்பொதியில் ஐங்கல மாறாட்டமா?
Are there five kalams of fraud in the pack on an ass?

2266. கழுதை விட்டை ஆனாலும் கை நிரம்ப வேண்டும் என்கிறாய்.
You say get a handful, although it be but ass dung.

2267. கழுத்திலே கரிமணி இல்லை பெயர் முத்துமாலை.
Her name is pearl necklace, yet on her neck she has not a black bead.

2268. கழுவிக் கழுவிப் பின்னும் சேற்றை மிதிக்கிறதா?
What! is it to tread in the mud every time you wash your feet?

2269. கழுவுக்கு ஏற்ற கோமுட்டி.
A kómutti exactly fitted to the stake.

2270. களம் சாறுகிறவளை மிரட்டுவானாம் போர் பிடுங்குகிறவன்.
It is said that he who steals *grain* from the stack, will frighten away the women who may sweep the threshing floor.

2271. களையக் கூடாததைக் கண்டால் அடி பெயர்ந்து அப்புறம் போ.
If you cannot pluck up, pass by on the other side.

2272. களையக் கூடாததைக் கண்டியாமல் சகித்துக்கொள்.
Do not fret yourself about that which cannot be avoided.

2273. கள் விற்றுக் கலப்பணம் சம்பாதிப்பதை விடக் கற்பூரம் விற்றுக் காற்பணம் சம்பாதிப்பது மேல்.

It is better to gain a quarter of a fanam by selling camphor than a kalam by selling toddy.

2274. கள்ளனும் ஆகி விளக்கும் பிடிக்கிறான்.

He plays the thief and also holds the lamp.

2275. கள்ள விசுவாசம் கழுத்தெல்லாம் செபமாலை.

The neck of the hypocrite is covered with rosaries.

2276. கள்ளனையும் வெள்ள அணையும் கட்டிவிடு.

Secure a thief by tying, and a flood by damming it up.

2277. கள்ளப் பிள்ளையிலும் செல்லப்பிள்ளை உண்டா?

Are there any indulged ones among the children of kallars?

2278. கள்ளனை ஆரு நள்ளார் என்றும்.

No one will ever approve of a thief.

2279. கள்ளனுக்கு ஊரெல்லாம் விள்ளாப் பகை.

The whole country owes implacable hatred to a thief.

2280. கள்ள மாடு சந்தை ஏறாது.

A vicious bullock will not be brought to market.

2281. கள்ளனை நம்பினாலும் குள்ளனை நம்பலாகாது.

A rogue may be trusted, but not a dwarf.

2282. கள்ளன் பின்போனாலும் குள்ளன் பின்போகப்படாது.

One may follow a rogue *without risk*, but not a dwarf.

2283. கள்ளன் அச்சம் காடு கொள்ளாது.

The jungle is not large enough to contain the fear of robbers.

2284. கள்ள மாடு துள்ளும்.

An unwilling bullock is restless.

2285. கள்ள மனம் துள்ளும்.

A guilty mind is agitated.

2286. கள்ளன் உறவு உறவும் அல்ல, காசா விறகு விறகும் அல்ல.

The friendship of a rogue is not friendship, nor is kásá wood fuel.

2287. கள்ளன் புத்தி திருட்டுமேலே.

The mind of a rogue is set on thieving.

2288 கள்ளன் பிள்ளைக்கும் கள்ளப் புத்தி.

Even the child of a thief is characterized by thievish propensites.

2289. கள்ளன் மனைவி கைம்பெண் என்றும்.

The wife of a thief is at any moment *liable to become* a widow.

2290. கள்ளன் மனையாளைக் களவுப் பொருளைக் காணும் குறி கேட்கலாமா?

Can the wife of a thief be consulted as an augur for the recovery of stolen property?

2291. கள்ளனும் வெள்ளமும் ஒன்று.

A thief and a flood are alike.

2292. கள்ளனுக்குப் பாதி வெள்ளனுக்குப் பாதி.

One half to the rogue, and one half to the honest.

2293. கள்ளனும் தோட்டகாரனும் ஒன்று.

A gardener is another term for a thief.

2294. கள்ளனும் தோட்டக்காரனும் ஒன்று கூடினால் விடியுமட்டும் திருடலாம்.

If the thief and a gardener are united, one may steal till day-break.

2295. கள்ளன் கொண்ட மாடு எத்துறை போயென்ன?

What matters it to what ferry the bull may go that has been bought by a thief?

2296. கள்ளனுக்குக் காண்பித்தவன் பகை.

He who points out a thief is hated by him.

2297. கள்ளி பெருத்து என்ன? காய் உண்டா நிழல் உண்டா?

What if the kalli grow large! Has it any fruit or any shade!

2298. கள்ளிக்கு நாடு எல்லாம் காடு.

The whole country is a wild *fit for the growth of* the kalli.

2299. கள்ளிக் கொம்புக்கு வெள்ளிப்பூண் கட்டினதுபோல.

Like attaching a silver ferrule to a kalli stick.

2300. கள்ளி என்னடி கல் இழைப்பது? காதில் இருப்பது பித்தளை.

Why you hypocrite, inlay with gems? that which is in the ear is *made of* brass.

2301. கள்ளிக்கும் வெட்டிக் கற்றாழைக்கும் வெட்டுகிறது.

After cutting the kalli to cut the kattalai.

2302. கள்ளிக்குத் தண்ணீர் கண்ணிலே, நீலிக்குத் தண்ணீர் நிமையிலே.

The tears of a thievish woman are in her eyes, those of an abandoned woman are in her eyebrows.

2303. கள்ளிக்கு கலநீர் கண்ணிலே.

A thievish woman has a kalam of tears in her eyes.

2304. கள்ளிக்கு வேலி ஏன், சுள்ளிக்குக் கோடாலி ஏன்?

What avails a fence against a thievish woman, or an axe for cutting twigs?

2305. கள்ளும் சூதும் இருக்கிற இடத்தில் கூத்திக் கள்ளனும் இருப்பான்.

Where there is theft and gambling, there will also be a whoremonger.

2306. கள்ளைக் குடித்தால் உள்ளதைச் சொல்வான்.

Should he drink toddy, he will tell the truth.

2307. கறக்கிறது உழக்குப் பால், உதைக்கிறது பல்லுப் பறக்க.

Yielding an ulak of milk, and kicking out the teeth.

2308. கறந்த பாலும் எச்சில் பிறந்த பிள்ளையும் எச்சில்.

First drawn milk is unclean, and so is a first-born child.

2309. கறந்த பால் முலைக்கு ஏறுமா?

Will the milk that has been drawn, again enter the udder?

2310. கறந்த பாலைக் காய்ச்சாமற் குடித்தால் காச வியாதி தானே எடுபடும்.

If fresh drawn milk unboiled be drunk, consumption may be cured.

2311. கறுத்தது எல்லாம் தண்ணீர் வெளுத்தது எல்லாம் பால் என்கிறான்.

Whatever is black he calls water, and whatever is white he calls milk.

2312. கறுப்பு வெளுப்பு ஆகாது, கசப்பு இனிப்பு ஆகாது.

Black will not become white, nor bitter sweet.

2313. கறுப்பு நாய் வெள்ளை நாய் ஆகுமா?

Will a black dog become white!

2314. கறுமுறுகாந்தப் படலம் வாசிக்கிறார் கவிராயர்.

The poet is reading the section on grumbling.

2315. கறையான் புற்றில் அரவம் குடிகொண்டதுபோல.

Like a snake that occupied an ant-hill.

2316. கறையான் புற்றுப் பாம்புக்கு உதவுகிறது.

An ant-hill is useful to a snake.

2317. கற்கண்டாற் செய்த எட்டிக்கனி கசக்குமா!

Will etti fruit made of sugar-candy taste bitter?

2318. கற்கையில் கல்வி கசப்பு, கற்றபின்பு அதுவே இனிப்பு.

Learning when being acquired is bitter, but when possessed it is sweet.

2319. கற்பகதருவைச் சார்ந்த காகமும் அமுதம் உண்ணும்.

Even a crow that lives in the kalpaka tree feeds on ambrosia.

2320. கற்பித்தவன் கண்ணைக் கொடுத்தவன்.

He who gave the eye is he who taught.

2321. கற்பித்தவன் காப்பாற்றுவான்.
He who preordained will protect or guide.

2322. கற்பில்லா அழகு வாசனை இல்லாப் பூ.
Beauty without chastity, a flower without fragrance.

2323. கற்ற இடத்திலா வித்தையைக் காட்டுகிறது?
To practise a trick on him who taught it?

2324. கற்றவரது கோபம் நீரின் பிளவுபோல் மாறும்.
The anger of the learned passes away as water recovers its surface after being divided.

2325. கற்றது கையளவு கல்லாதது உலகளவு.
What he has learnt is a handful, and what he has still to acquire is wide as the world.

2326. கற்றது சொல்லான் மற்று என்ன செய்வான்?
What other service will he do for you who would not tell you what he has learnt!

2327. கற்றவனுக்கு வித்தை கால் நாழி.
To the artist *his* art is but a quarter of a náli.

2328. கற்ற வித்தையைக் காய்ச்சிக் குடிக்கிறவன்போலே.
Like one who boils and drinks his learning.

2329. கற்றறி மோழையாய் இராதே.
Be not a learned fool.

2330. கற்றவனும் உண்பான், பெற்றவளும் உண்பாள்.
A learned man and a fruitful woman will not suffer from want of food.

2331. கற்றாழை நாற்றமும் பித்தளை வீச்சமும் போகாது.
The ill odour of the karráli and the bad smell emitted from brass will not leave them.

2332. கற்றாழை சிறுத்தாலும் ஆனை அடி வைக்காது.
Though the karràlai be small, the elephant will not tread upon it.

2333. கற்றுக் கொடுத்த பேச்சும் கட்டிக் கொடுத்த சாதமும் எத்தனை நாள் நிற்கும்?

How long will words put into one's mouth, and rice prepared for a journey, last?

2334. கற்றுக் கற்றுப் பேசாதே.

Do not speak in a studied way.

2335. கற்றும் கற்றறிமோழை.

Though he has learnt, he continues a learned fool.

2336. கற்றும் கற்றறிமோழையா?

What, to be a learned fool?

2337. கற்றோர் அருமை கற்றோர் அறிவர்.

The learned know the worth of the learned.

2338. கன ஆசை கன நஷ்டம்.

Excessive desire entails great loss.

2339. கன எலி வளை எடாது.

When rats are numerous, they do not burrow.

2340. கனக மாரி பொழிந்ததுபோலே.

As it rained gold.

2341. கனஞ் செய்தால் இஷ்டம், கனவீனத்தால் நஷ்டம்.

Dignity gains approval, meanness entails loss.

2342. கனத்த உடமைக்கு அனர்த்தம் இல்லை.

Solid jewels are invaluable.

2343. கனத்தால் இனமாகும் பணத்தால் சனமாகும்.

Dignity or worth increases relatives, wealth secures society.

2344. கனத்திற்கு நற்குணம் சுமைதாங்கி.

Virtue is the support of dignity.

2345. கனத்தைக் கனம் அறியும் கருவாட்டுப் பானையை நாய் அறியும்.

Dignity is appreciated by dignity, the pot of dried fish is known to the dog.

2346. கன மூடன் கைப்பொருள் இழப்பான்.

A great fool loses his substance.

2347. கனவிலும் காக்கைக்கு மலம் தின்கிறதே நினைவு.

Even in its dreams the crow's thoughts turn on eating filth.

2348. கனவில் கண்ட பணம் செலவிற்கு உதவுமா ?

Will the money seen in a dream meet one's expenses ?

2349. கனவில் கண்ட பொருள் கானலில் கண்ட புனல்.

The wealth seen in a dream, the water observed in a mirage.

2350. கனவில் உண்ட சோறு பசி தீர்க்குமா ?

Will the rice consumed in a dream appease hunger ?

2351. கனவிலே கண்டவனுக்குப் பெண் கொடுத்த கதை.

The story of a woman given in marriage to a man seen in a dream.

2352. கனிந்த பழம் தானே விழும்.

Ripe fruit falls of itself.

2353. கனிந்த பழம் நீர் தின்றீர் காயை உலுக்கிவிட்டீர்.

You have eaten the ripe fruit, and you have shaken off the unripe.

2354. கனியை விட்டுக் காயைத் தின்கிறதா ?

What, to leave ripe fruit and to eat *unripe* ?

2355. கன்மத்தினாற் சாதியன்றிச் சென்மத்தினால் இல்லை.

Caste arises from action, it is not from birth.

2356. கன்மழை பெய்தாலும் கருங்கல் கரையுமா ?

Will granite be dissolved by any amount of hail ?

2357. கன்மத்தினால் வந்தது தன்மத்தினால் போகவேண்டும்.

That which has come of action-*sin*-must go by alms giving *religious merit*.

2358. கன்று இருக்கக் காசத்தனை பால் கறவாப் பசு கன்று செத்த பிறகு கலப்பால் கறக்குமா?

Will a cow that gave milk worth a small coin while its calf lived, give a kalam after her calf is dead?

2359. கன்றுக்குட்டியை அவிழ்க்கச் சொன்னார்களா கட்டுத்தறியைப் பிடுங்கச் சொன்னார்களா?

Did they tell you to loose the calf or to pull up the peg?

2360. கன்றும் பசுவும் காடேறி மேய்ந்தால் கன்று கன்று வழியே பசு பசு வழியே.

When the calf and cow go out to graze, each takes its own way.

2361. கன்றுகளாய்க் கூடிக் களை பறிக்கப் போனால் வைக்கோல் ஆகுமா செத்தை ஆகுமா?

If a herd of calves weed the corn, wili there be any straw, or even dry stubble?

2362. கன்றைக் கண்டு ஓடிவரும் பசுவைப்போலே.

Like a cow that comes running on seeing her calf.

2363. கன்னான் நடமாடக் குயவன் குடிபோவான்.

When the brazier begins to move, the potter will abandon his dwelling-place.

2364. கன்னானுக்கு முன்னே கழுதை பரதேசம் போனாற்போலே.

As an ass went on a pilgrimage before a copper-smith.

2365. கன்னி இருக்கக் காளை மணம் போகலாமா?

When a virgin is yet unmarried, may the youth-*her brother* marry?

கா.

2366. காகத்திலே வெள்ளை உண்டா?

Are there any white crows?

2367. காகத்தின் கண்ணுக்குப் பீர்க்கம்பூ பொன் நிறம்.

To the eye of a crow the flower of the gourd is tinged with gold.

2368. காகம் கர் என்றால் கணவனை அப்பா என்று கட்டிக்கொள்ளு வாளாம்.

It is said that when a crow caws she will exclaim, alas, and cling to her husband.

2369. காகம் ஏறிப் பனங்காய் உதிருமா?

Will palmyra fruit fall because a crow alights on the tree?

2370. காகம் இல்லாத ஊர் பாவி இல்லாத ஊர்.

Vicious persons are not found in a village which has no crows.

2371. காகம் இருக்கப் பழம் விழுந்ததுபோல.

Like the dropping of the fruit when a crow alighted on the tree.

2372. காகம் இல்லாத ஊர் சோனகன் இல்லாத ஊர்.

The country in which crows do not exist is without mussalmans.

2373. காகம் காலமே கா கா என்று கத்தும்.

Crows will caw at day-break.

2374. காக்கனுக்கும் பூக்கனுக்கும் பூத்தாயோ புன்னை கண்ணாளர் வருந்தனையும் பொறுக்கலையோ புன்னை?

O punnai tree, *Alexandrian laurel*, hast thou blossomed for Kakan and Pookan, couldst not thou have waited till the arrival of my husband!

2375. காக்காய்க் குஞ்சு ஆனாலும் தன் குஞ்சு பொன் குஞ்சு.

Though but a young crow, it is a golden one to its mother.

2376. காக்கையிற் கரிது களாம்பழம்.

Kalà fruit, *carissa*, is blacker than a crow.

2377. காக்கையும் குயிற் குஞ்சைத் தன் குஞ்சுபோல் வளர்க்கும்.

Even a crow will bring up a young kuyil-*Indian cuckoo*-as her own.

2378. காக்கைக்கு அஞ்சு குணம்.

The crow has five characteristics.

2379. காக்கை ஏறினதும் பனம்பழம் விழுந்ததும்.

The alighting of the crow, and the falling of the palmyra fruit.

2380. காக்கையும் கத்திக் கத்திப் போகிறது கருவாடும் உலர்ந்து போகிறது.

The crow continues to caw whilst the karuvadu, (salted fish) dries.

2381. காக்கையும் காற்றும் போக்கு உண்டானால் வரும்.

Crows and winds go but to return.

2382. காக்கையைக் கண்டு அஞ்சுவாள், கரடியைப் பிடித்துக் கட்டுவாள்.

She is afraid on seeing a crow, and yet she will capture a bear.

2383. காக்கை ஏறின கொம்பு அசையாதா?

Will not the branch shake on which a crow alights?

2384. காசி இரண்டு எழுத்துத்தான் காண எத்தனை நாட்செல்லும்?

Kàsi is formed of two letters only, how many days will it take to reach it?

2385. காசிக்குப் போயும் கருமம் தொலையவில்லை.

Though one has gone to Benares his sins are not removed.

2386. காசிக்குப் போனாலும் அகப்பை அரைக்காசு.

Though taken to Benares, a wooden ladle will fetch but half a cash.

2387. காசிக்குப் போனாலும் கதி பெற வழி இல்லை.

Although he may go to Kàsi, he will not find the way to heaven.

2388. காசிக்குப்போயும் முடத்தவசி காலில் விழுகிறதா?

What! having gone to Kàsi is it to fall at the feet of a lame ascetic?

2389. காசியில் இருக்கிறவன் கண்ணைக் குத்தக் காஞ்சிபுரத்திலிருந்து கையை நீட்டிக்கொண்டு போகிறதா?

If you wish to strike the eyes of one at Kási, do you go, for that purpose, with outstretched hand from Conjevaram!

2390. காசு இல்லாதவனுக்கு வராகன் பேச்சு என்ன?

Why should a penniless man talk about pagodas?

2391. காசு கொடுத்தால் வேசி வருவாள், கல நெல்லைக் கொடுத்தால் அவள் அக்காளும் ஆத்தாளும் கூட வருவார்கள்.

If you are free with your money a harlot will come, if you give also a kalam of rice, her sister and her mother will come.

2392. காசுக்கு ஒரு குஞ்சு விற்றாலும் கணக்கக் குஞ்சு ஆகாது.

Though young birds are sold a cash each, an accountant's young bird is not good.

2393. காசுக்கு ஒரு குஞ்சு விற்றாலும் கம்மாளக் குஞ்சு ஆகாது.

Though sold for a single cash, never buy a smith's bird.

2394. காசுக்கு ஒரு புடைவை விற்றாலும் நாயின் சூத்து அம்மணம்.

Though cloth may be cheap, dogs go naked.

2395. காசுக்கூடு கரிக்கூடாய்ப் போயிற்று.

The money basket has become a charcoal basket.

2396. காசுக்குப் போன மானம் கோடி கொடுத்தாலும் வராது.

Chastity lost for a cash will not be recovered by a crore.

2397. காசைக் கொடுத்துக் குத்து மாடு தேடுகிறதா?

Will you buy a vicious cow at a high price!

2398. காஞ்சிபுரத்திற்குப் போனால் கால் ஆட்டி உண்ணலாம்.

If you go to Conjeveram, you may eat without labour.

2399. காடிக்குப் போய்த் தயிர் கொண்டுவந்ததுபோல.

Like going for vinegar and bringing curds.

2400. காடு காத்தவனும் கற்சேரி காத்தவனும் பலன் அடைவான்.

Both will be benefited, he who watches the jungle and he who waits at the cutchery.

2401. காடு வா என்கிறது வீடு போ என்கிறது.

Home bids *me* go, and the place of incremation says come.

2402. காடு விளைந்தாலும் ஒரு மேடு விளைந்தாலும் கடன் கழிந்து போம்.

The debt will be discharged in either case, whether the jungle or highland yield a *good crop*.

2403. காடு விளையாவிட்டாலும் கடமை போகுமா?

Though the waste land has yielded nothing, will the tax be remitted?

2404. காடு வெந்தாற் சந்தன மரமும் வேகாதோ?

Should the jungle be consumed, would the sandal wood tree escape?

2405. காடை இடம் ஆனால் நாட்டை ஆளலாம்.

If a quail crosses one's path to the left, he will govern a province.

2406. காட்டிக் கொடுத்துக் கடக்கப் போய் நிற்கலாமா?

Is it proper to betray one, and then stand aloof?

2407. காட்டில் ஆனையைக் காட்டி வீட்டில் பெண்ணைக் கொடுக்கிறதா?

Is it to give a girl in marriage when an elephant in the jungle is shown *as dower*?

2408. காட்டிலே செத்தாலும் வீட்டிலேதான் தீட்டு.

Though a man dies in the jungle, ceremonial uncleanness will attach to his house.

2409. காட்டுப் பூனைக்குச் சிவராத்திரி விரதமா?

Does the wild cat observe the fast of Sivaratri?

2410. காட்டுக்கு எறித்த நிலாவும் கானலுக்குப் பெய்த மழையும்.

Moonlight in the jungle and rain in the plains.

2411. காட்டு வாழை வந்தால் வீட்டு வாழ்வு போகும்.

When wild plantains come, domestic prosperity will vanish.

2412. காட்டுப் பேய்ச்சுரைக்காய் கறிக்கு ஆகுமா?

Is a wild gourd fit for curry?

2413. காட்டுக் கோழிக்கு உரற் குழியே கைலாசம்.

The hole in a mortar is paradise to a jungle fowl.

2414. காட்டுப் பூச்சிகள் எதிர்த்த கதை ஆச்சு.

It has become the story of wild insects offering resistance.

2415. காணக் கிடைத்தது கார்த்திகைப் பிறைபோல.

That which was seen was like the new moon of November.

2416. காணப்பட்டன எல்லாம் அழியப்பட்டன.

All that is seen is temporary.

2417. காணாமல் கண்டேனா கம்பங்கதிரே சிந்தாமல் குத்தடி சில்லி மூக்கே?

Have I seen kambu-millet for the first time, pound it without scattering thou nose bleeding woman?

2418. காணி ஆளன் வீடு வேகச்சே காலைப் பிடித்து இழுத்த கதை.

The story of one pulling by the feet the landlord whose house was on fire.

2419. காணி ஏறக் கோடி அழியும்.

While $\frac{1}{80}$ is added a crore is destroyed.

2420. காணி கவிழ்ந்துபோகிறதா?

Does land turn upside down?

2421. காணி காணியாய்ச் சம்பாதித்துக் கோடி கோடியாய்ச் செலவழிக்க வேண்டும்.

We must acquire by eightieths and spend by crores.

2422. காணிக்கு ஒத்தது கோடிக்கு.

The profit or loss on an eightieth part of a unit, will determine that on a crore.

2423. காணி சோம்பல் கோடி வருத்தம்.

A little indolence creates great trouble.

2424. காணி மந்தம் கோடி துக்கம்.

A little indolence will bring great sorrow.

2425. காதம் விட்டு இருகாதம் சுற்றுகிறதுபோல.

Like ranging over the distance of two kathams instead of one.

2426. காதம் கொடுத்து இருகாதம் வாங்குகிறதுபோல.

Like giving a katham and getting two.

2427. காதவழி போய் அறியாதான் மாதம் எல்லாம் நடந்தானும்.

He who never walked a katham is said to have walked a whole month.

2428. காதவழி போய் அறியான் கழுதைப் பிறப்பு.

He who never walked a katham is an ass.

2429. காதவழி பெயர் இல்லான் கழுதையோடு ஒக்கும்.

He whose reputation does not reach a katham is like an ass.

2430. காதிலே நாராசம் ஏற்றினாற் போல.

Like an iron wire passed into the ear.

2431. காதில் சிலந்தி ஓதடி ஆனந்தி.

O Ananti, I have a boil in my ear, utter an incantation.

2432. காது அறுத்த கூலி கைமேலே.

The hire for tearing the ear is readily paid.

2433. காது அறுத்தாலும் அறுக்கும் பேனைப் பார்த்தாலும் பார்க்கும் குரங்கு.

A monkey may tear the ears or hunt lice if he choose.

2434. காது காது என்றால் நாதி நாதி என்கிறான்.

If one says, my ear, my ear, he replies it is mine, it is mine.

2435. காது காது என்றால் செவிடு செவிடு என்கிறான்.

If one cry an ear, an ear, he cries deafness deafness.

2436. காது குத்தப் பொறுக்காதா?

Can you not bear the boring of your ears?

2437. காதுக்கு இட்டால் முகத்துக்கு அழகு.

If worn in the ears, they will add beauty to the face.

2438. காதுக்குக் கடுக்கன் இட்டு ஆட்டிக்கொண்டு திரிகிறான்.
Having put on ear-rings he walks about shaking them.

2439. காதும் காதும் வைத்தாற்போல இருக்கவேண்டும்.
It should be as if an ear, and an ear, were brought in contact.

2440. காதை அறுத்தவன் கண்ணையும் குத்துவானோ ?
Will he who cut off the ear strike the eye also ?

2441. காத்திருந்தவன் பெண்டாட்டியை வேற்று மனிதன் பிடித்துக்கொண்டான்.
A stranger took possession of the wife of him who was watching her.

2442 காந்தமும் ஊசியும்போல்.
Like a magnet and needle.

2443. காப்பானுக்குக் கள்ளன் இல்லை.
He who takes care *of his property* will not be robbed.

2444. காயம் பட்ட குரங்குபோல்.
Like a wounded monkey.

2445. காயும் புழுவிற்குச் சாயும் நிழல் போல.
Like a falling shadow on a sun-striken worm.

2446. காய்த்த மரத்தில் கல் எறிபடும் காயாத மரத்தில் கல் எறிபடுமா?
Stones are thrown at a fruit bearing tree ; are they thrown at that which does not bear !

2447. காய்த்த மரத்திலே கல் எறியும் சில் எறியும்.
Stones and other missiles are thrown at a fruit-bearing tree.

2448. காய்த்த மரம் வளைந்து நிற்கும் நற்குணம் உடையவர் தணிந்து நிற்பார்.
A fruit-bearing tree bends ; the virtuous are lowly.

2449. காய்ந்த மரம் தளிர்க்குமா ?
Will a dry tree bud !

2450. காய்ந்த மாடு கம்பிலே விழுந்தாற்போல.
Like a starving cow falling in the kambu-millet.

2451. காய்ந்த புலி ஆட்டு மந்தையிலே விழுகிறதுபோல.
Like a hungry tiger falling on a flock of sheep.

2452. காய்ந்த புலி ஆவிலே விழுகிறது.
A lean tiger falls on a cow.

2453. காய்ந்தாலும் வெந்நீர் அவம் போமோ?
Is water useless because it is boiled?

2454. காய்ந்த வானம் பெய்ந்தால் விடாது?
Rain after drought will not soon cease?

2455. காய்ந்தும் கெடுத்தது பெய்ந்தும் கெடுத்தது.
It was destroyed by the sun and by the rain.

2456. காராம்பசுவுக்குப் புல்லானால் நந்தவனத்துக்குக் களையுமாம்.
Grass serves as food for kine, and as an ornament to a flower garden.

2457. காரிகை கற்றுக் கவி சொல்லுவதிற் பேரிகை கொட்டிப் பிழைப்பது நன்று.
It is better to live by beating a drum than by composing verses according to the rules of prosody.

2458. காரியக்காரன் கொல்லையிலே கழுதை மேய்கிறது.
The ass grazes in the grounds of the industrious.

2459. காரியத்திலே கண் அல்லாமல் வீரியத்திலே இல்லை.
His eye is on the object, not on the attendant applause.

2460. காரியத்துக்குக் கழுதையின் காலைப் பிடி.
If necessary, secure your purpose by clinging to the feet of an ass.

2461. காரியம் பெரிதோ வீரியம் பெரிதோ?
Which is the greater, success or boasting?

2462. கார் அறுக்கட்டும் கத்தரி பூக்கட்டும்.
Wait till the kár paddy is reaped, and the brinjal blossoms.

2463. கார்த்திகைக்கு மேல் மழையும் இல்லை, கர்ணனுக்கு மேல் கொடையும் இல்லை.

No rain like that of November, no liberality superior to that of Karnan.

Karnan, one of the seven princes distinguished for great generosity.

2464. கார்த்திகைப் பிறைபோலக் கண்டேன்.

I saw it like the third-day moon of November.

2465. காலஞ் செய்கிறது கோலம் செய்யாதே.

Time will effect that which mere parade cannot.

2466. காலஞ் செய்கிறது ஞாலம் செய்யாது.

The world cannot accomplish that which time effects.

2467. காலத்தினல் செய்த நன்றி.

A benefit conferred opportunely.

2468. காலத்திற் பெய்த மழைபோல.

Like seasonable rain.

2469. காலத்துக்கு ஏற்ற கோலம்.

Equipage suited to the occasion.

2470. காலமே எழுந்திருந்து காக்கை விழிக்கல் ஆகாது.

The sight of a crow on rising of a morning is ominous of evil.

The crow being regarded as the vehicle of Saturn the sight of a single crow is inauspicious; two are not so regarded. The cawing of a crow may excite apprehension. When this is the case the following formula may be used.

Measure the length of your shadow by the foot and add 12 to the number of feet ascertained. Then divide by 7 and the remainder will determine the import of the bird's note (1) Good luck, (2) Gain, (3) Rain, (4) Conflict, (5) Feasting, (6) Victory. If on dividing by 7 there is no remainder the cawing of the crow is ominous of death.

2471. காலம் அறிந்து ஞாலம் ஒழுகு.

Regulate your affairs *with due reference* to the times *in which you live.*

2472. காலம் கெட்டுக் கைப்பிச்சை எடுத்தாற்போல.

Like receiving alms when in distress.

2473. காலம் அறிந்து பிழையாதவன் வால் அறுந்த குரங்கு ஆவான்.

He who does not live according to the times will become an ape.

2474. காலம் போம் வார்த்தை நிற்கும், கப்பல் போம் துறை நிற்கும்.

Time goes, words remain, a ship goes, the shore remains.

2475. காலம் போன காலத்தில் மூலம் வந்து குறுக்கிட்டதுபோல.

As one is subject to piles in his riper years.

2476. காலம் அல்லாத காலத்திலே கப்பல் ஓட்டி.

A mariner in unfavourable weather.

2477. காலாலே நடந்தால் காதவழி, தலையாலே நடந்தால் எவ்வளவு தூரம்?

If on foot it is a katham; how much more distant if one walk on the head?

2478. காலால் முடிந்ததைக் கையால் அவிழ்க்கக்கூடாது.

What he tied with his feet others cannot untie with the hands.

2479. காலிலே பட்டபிறகா கிரகசாரம் போதாது?

After having hurt the foot is it to be attributed to planetary influence?

2480. காலில் விழுகிறது நல்லது மேலில் விழுகிறது கெட்டது.

To fall at the feet is good, to fall on *another* is bad.

2481. காலில் பட்டது கண்ணில் பட்டதுபோல.

That which struck the feet was felt as if it had struck the eye.

2482. காலுக்குப் போட்டால் தலைக்குப் போடுகிறான்.

If he puts *ornaments* on his legs, he will put *ornaments* on his head.

2483. காலுக்குக் கடுப்பே தவிர, கண்ட பலன் ஒன்றும் இல்லை.

No benefit accrued but the trouble of walking.

2484. காலுக்குக் கை உதவி கைக்குக் கால் உதவி.

The hand helps the legs and the legs help the hands.

2485. காலுக்குத் தக்க செருப்பும் கூலிக்குத் தக்க உழைப்பும்.

A slipper suited to the foot, and labour suited to the hire.

2486. காலுக்கு ஆகிற செருப்பு தலைக்கு ஆகுமா?

Will a slipper that fits the foot do for the head?

2487. காலைச் சுற்றின பாம்பு கடித்தால் ஒழிய விடாது.

The snake that has coiled round the leg will not leave without biting.

2488. காலைச் செல் பூத்தால் அடுத்த மழை அடங்கும்.

Should winged white-ants come out in the morning the heavy rain will cease.

2489. காலை துயில்வானும் மாலை இருப்பானும் பதர்.

He who sleeps after day-break, and he who keeps awake in the fore part of the night are worthless.

2490. காலைப் பிடித்த சனியன் ஊரைச் சுற்றி அடிக்கும்.

If Saturn seize the feet, he will drive one round the village.

2491. காலைப் பனிக்கும் கண்விழிக்கும் ஒத்தது செல்வம்.

Wealth is comparable to the morning dew, and the twinkling of an eye.

2492. காலை மோட்சமும் வாலை ஞானமும் நிலைக்காது.

Dreams of bliss and premature wisdom are not lasting.

2493. கால் அளவே ஆகுமாம் கப்பலின் ஓட்டம் நூல் அளவே ஆகுமாம் துண்சீலை.

The speed of a vessel is proportioned to the force of the wind, the quality of cloth will be as the yarn *used in its manufacture.*

2494. கால் ஆடக் கோல் ஆடும் கோல் ஆடக் குரங்கு ஆடும்.

The foot puts the stick in motion, as that moves, the monkey dances.

2495. கால் சிறிதாகில் கனல் ஊரும் கன்னியர்மேல் மால் சிறிதாகில் மனம் ஊரும்.

Where there is a little wind fire will spread, where there is lust the affections will be fastened on women.

2496. கால் நடைக்கு இரண்டு காசு கை வீச்சுக்கு ஐந்து காசு.

Two cash for walking on foot, five cash for the swing of the arms.

2497. கால் மாறிக் கட்டினால் கனம் குறையுமா ?

If one be tied cross-legged, will his weight diminish ?

2498. கால்வாயைத் தாண்டாதவன் கடலைத் தாண்டுவானா ?

Can he who cannot leap over a channel leap over the sea ?

2499. காவடிப் பாரம் சுமக்கிறவனுக்குத் தெரியும்.

The weight of a burden is felt by the bearer.

2500. காவல் தானே பாவையர்க்கு அழகு.

Chastity is a feminine grace.

2501. காவேரி ஆற்றை மறிப்பாய் கார்த்திகை மாதத்துக் கற்கடக சங்கிரமணயும் மறிப்பாயா ?

You may stay the Cauvery, but can you hinder the full moon of November if he be in Cancer ?

2502. காவேரி கஞ்சியாய்ப் போனாலும் நாய் நக்கித்தான் குடிக்க வேண்டும்.

Should the Cauvery become kanji, the dog would partake thereof by lapping.

2503. காவோலை விழுந்ததென்று குருத்தோலை சிரித்ததாம்.

The green leaves of the palm laughed because the dry ones fell off.

2504. காளிதோட்டத்துக் கற்பக விருக்ஷம் ஆருக்கும் உதவாது.

Even the katpaka tree in the garden of Durga is of no use to mankind.

The katpaka tree is said to yield whatever a suppliant may require.

2505. காளிப்பட்டம் போனாலும் மூளிப்பட்டம் போகாது.

The name Kali may become obsolete, but not the (nickname) Mooli, *the earless.*

2506. காற் காசுப் பூனை முக்காற் காசுத் தயிரைக் குடித்தது.

A cat worth a quarter of a cash consumed curds worth three quarters of a cash.

2507. காற்றில் அகப்பட்ட கப்பல்போல் அலைகின்றது மனம்.

The mind is agitated like a ship in a storm.

2508. காற்றுக்கா மழைக்கா போர்த்துக்கொள்ள துணிக்கா?

Is it as a security against the wind and rain that you are thus clad?

2509. காற்றுக்கு எதிரிலே துப்பினால் முகத்திலே விழும்.

If one spit against the wind-*the spittle*-will strike his own face.

2510. காற்றுக்குத் தோணி எதிர்த்து ஓடாது.

A dhony cannot sail against the wind.

2511. காற்றும் சிலரை நீக்கி வீசுமோ?

Will the wind blow so as to avoid certain persons?

2512. காற்று உள்ளபோது தூற்றிக்கொள் கரும்பு உள்ளபோது ஆட்டிக்கொள்.

Winnow when the wind blows, work the sugar-mill when the cane is ripe.

2513. காற்றைப் பிடித்துக் கரகத்தில் அடைக்கலாமா?

Can one seize the wind and confine it in a small vessel?

2514. காற்றைப் பார்த்துக் கப்பல் நாட்டு.

Anchor a ship with reference to the wind.

2515. கானலை நீரென்று எண்ணி மான் ஓடி இளைத்ததுபோல.

Like the deer that wearied itself in pursuit of a mirage imagining it to be water.

கி

2516. கிடக்கிறது கிடக்கட்டும் கிழவனை எடுத்து மணையிலே வை.

Leave the things as they are, and take the old man and put him on the stool *to bathe*.

The first thing done before a corpse is removed from the homestead is to bathe it.

2517. கிடக்கிறது குட்டிச்சுவர் கனாக் காண்கிறது மச்சுவீடு.

Dwelling in a ruinous hut and dreaming of a palace.

2518. கிட்ட வா நாயே என்றால் மூஞ்சியை நக்குகிறது.

When called, the dog licks the face.

2519. கிட்டாத ஒன்றை வெட்டென மற.

Forget at once what cannot be obtained.

2520. கிணறு வெட்டப் பூதம் புறப்பட்டாற்போல் ஆயிற்றே.

It has happened as if a demon had sprung out of a well just dug.

2521. கிணறும் வெட்டித் தவளையும் பிடித்து விடுகிறதா?

What! is it to dig a well and supply it with frogs!

2522. கிணறு கிடக்க மலை கல்லாதே.

Whilst there is a well do not excavate a mountain *for water*.

2523. கிணறு வெட்டித் தாகம் தீர்க்கலாமா?

Must one dig a well to quench his thirst!

2524. கிணறு மெத்தினாற் கீழ்வளை பொசியும்.

If there be water the undermost ring of the well will be wet.

2525. கிணறு இறைக்க இறைக்கச் சுரக்கும்.

The more a well is drawn, the better the spring.

2526. கிணறு தப்பித் துரவில் விழலாமா?

Having escaped falling into the well, shall we fall into a tank!

2527. கிணற்றைத் தூர்த்தால் வயிற்றைத் தூர்க்கும்.

If the well is to be filled up, the belly must be filled up.

2528. கிணற்றுத் தவளை தண்ணீர் குடித்ததைக் கண்டது ஆர், குடியாததைக் கண்டது ஆர்?

Who knows whether the frog in the well did or did not drink water?

2529. கிணற்றுத் தவளைக்கு ஏன் நாட்டு வளப்பம்?

What has the frog in the well to do with the news of the country?

2530. கிணற்றுக்குத் தப்பித் தீயிலே பாய்ந்தான்.

Having escaped falling into the well he jumped into the fire.

2531. கிணற்றைக் கண்டு கடல் ஒதுங்கிப்போகுமா?

Will the sea shrink at the sight of a well?

2532. கிணற்றுத் தண்ணீரை வெள்ளம் கொண்டுபோகுமா?

Will the flood carry away the water of the well?

2533. கிணற்றிலே தண்ணீர் உதித்தது.

Water sprang up in the well.

2534. கிணற்று ஆழமும் கயிற்று நீளமும் பார்க்கவேண்டும்.

The depth of the well and the length of the cord must be ascertained.

2535. கிணற்றில் விழுந்தவன் மறுபடியும் விழுவானா?

Will he who has fallen into a well once fall in again?

2536. கிணற்றில் கல் போட்டதுபோல.

Like dropping a stone into a well.

2537. கிண்டக் கிண்ட அம்பட்டன் குப்பை மயிரே புறப்படும்.

The more you dig in the refuse heap of the barber, the more will hair turn up.

2538. கிண்டக் கிண்டக் கீரையும் மயிரும்.

The more you dig, the more will greens and hair appear.

2539. கிரக சாந்திக்குச் சவரம்பண்ணிக் கொள்ளுகிறதா?

Will shaving counteract the evil influence of a planet?

2540. கிரியை அற்றோன் மறை சாற்றுவது ஏன்?

What! is it for an evil-doer to teach religious precepts?

2541. கிருபா நதியே சருவா நிதி.

The stream of grace is *the source of* all treasures.

2542. கிழக் குடலுக்குச் சோறும் இடிச் சுவருக்கு மண்ணும் இடு.

Give rice to the aged and add mud to a ruinous wall.

2543. கிழப் பேச்சு சபைக்கு ஏறுமா?

Will the words of an old man go up to the assembly?

2544. கிழவன் ஆனாலும் கெட்டை ஆனாலும் கட்டிக்கொண்டவள் பிழைப்பாள்.

She who marries will do well whether *her husband* be old or poor.

2545. கிழவனுக்கு வாழ்க்கைப்படுகிறதிலும் கிணற்றில் விழலாம்.

It is better to fall into a well than to marry an old man.

2546. கிழவி பேச்சைக் கின்னரக்காரன் கேட்பானோ?

Will a musician listen to the speech of an old woman?

2547. கிழவியும் காதம் குதிரையும் காதம்.

The old woman is a katham from the horse, and the horse a katham from the old woman.

2548. கிழவி இருந்த வீடும் கிளி இருந்த காடும் ஈடேற மாட்டாது.

Neither the house of an old woman, nor the grove in which there are parrots, will be saved from ruin.

2549. கிழிந்த சீலை காசுக்கு இரண்டு.

Two rags for a cash.

2550. கிழிந்த பம்பரம் காசுக்கு இரண்டு.

Two split tops for a cash.

2551. கிளியை வளர்த்துப் பூனை கையில் கொடுக்கலாமா?

Is it proper to train a parrot and give it into the paw of a cat?

2552. கிளியைப்போலப் பேச்சும் மயிலைப்போல நடையும்.

Speech like that of a parrot, gait like that of a peacock.

2553. கிள்ளப் பழுக்குமாம் கிளி இருந்து கொஞ்சுமாம்.

It is said that it ripens by being pinched, and that parrots will nibble it leisurely.

2554. கிள்ளுவார்கீழ் இருப்பதிலும் அள்ளுவார்கீழ் இருக்கலாம்.

One may endure those who rob, but not those who pilfer.

கீ.

2555. கீரி கடித்த பாம்புபோலே.

Like a snake bit by a mungoose.

2556. கீரிக்கும் பாம்புக்கும் தீராப் பகை.

Inveterate enmity exists between the mungoose and snakes.

2557. கீரியும் பாம்பும்போல.

Like a mungoose and a snake.

2558. கீரைக் கடைக்கும் எதிர்கடை வேண்டும்.

An opposition shop is good even among green grocers.

2559. கீரைக்குப் புல்லுருவி கீழே முளைத்தாற்போலே.

As if a parasite should spring from the lower part of a vegetable.

2560. கீரைக் கட்டை வெட்டச் சொன்னால் தோரணம் கட்டுகிறதா?

When I order the greens to be pruned, is a garland put up?

2561. கீரைத் தண்டு பிடுங்க ஏலேலப்பாட்டு ஏன்?

Why sing elela when plucking up greens?

2562. கீரையை இரண்டு கறி பண்ணாதே.

Do not make two curries of a vegetable.

2563. கீர்த்தியால் பசி தீருமா?

Will hunger be appeased by fame?

2564. கீர்த்தி பெற்றும் கிலேசம் என்ன?
Whence sorrow *to him* who has obtained praise?

2565. கீழே பாம்பு என்றால் மேலே பார்க்கிறான்.
If it is said that a snake is below, he looks up.

2566. கீழ்குலத்தான் ஆனாலும் கற்றவன் மேல்குலத்தான்.
Though of low origin, the learned ranks with the highest class.

2567. கீழ்க்காது மேற்காது மூளி, சண்டைக்கு ரணபத்திரகாளி.
Her ears are rent at both ends; in an affray she is equal to Durga.

2568. கீறி ஆற்றினால் புண் ஆறும்.
If lanced, the sore will heal.

கு.

2569. குங்கிலியத் தூபம் காட்டிச் சன்னதம் குலைந்தால் கும்பிடு எங்கே?
If indeed the incense has expelled the demon, where is the sign of uplifted hands.

2570. குங்குமம் சுமந்த கழுதை பரிமளம் அறியுமா?
Can the ass which carried the kungumam-*a fragrant resin*-appreciate scents?

2571. குங்குமக் கோதைக்கு அஞ்சு பணம், குருட்டுக் கண்ணிக்கும் அஞ்சு பணமா?
The donation to the perfumed dame being five fanams, is five fanams to be assigned to the blind woman also?

2572. குஞ்சிரிப்புக்கு மருந்து சாப்பிட உள்ள சிரிப்பும் போனாற் போல.
As if one lost his natural smile by taking medicine to induce a simpering expression.

2573. குடத்தில் ஏற்றிய விளக்கு.
A lamp lit in an earthen pot.

2574. குடத்திற் பொன் கூத்து ஆடுமோ?

Will gold in a pot dance?

2575. குடப்பால் கறந்தாலும் குதிரை ஓட்டம் ஓடமாட்டாது.

Though *the cow* gives a large pot of milk, it is not equal to the horse in speed.

2576. குடப்பால் கறந்தாலும் கூரை பிடுங்குகிற மாடு ஆகாது.

Though it may yield a large pot of milk, a cow that destroys the roof is not desirable.

2577. குடம் தண்ணீரிற் கொள்ளி வைத்தாற்போல.

As if a firebrand were put into a pot of water.

2578. குடலும் கூந்தலும் கொண்டது கொள்கை.

Habit is the rule of the stomach and the hair.

2579. குடல் கூழுக்கு அழுகிறதாம் கொண்டை பூவுக்கு அழுகிறதாம்.

It is said that the stomach cries for gruel, and the tresses for flowers.

2580. குடல் அறுந்த நரி எந்தமட்டும் ஓடும்?

How far can a jackal run after its bowels are dislodged?

2581. குடல் அறுந்த கோழி எங்கே போகும்?

Whither will a fowl go after its entrails have been exposed?

2582. குடி இருந்து அறி வழி நடந்து அறி.

Learn the character *of a person* by dwelling with him, and the *condition* of a road by walking in it.

2583. குடி இருந்து பார் கூட்டுப்பயிர் இட்டுப் பார்.

Test *his social qualities* by living with him, *and his honesty* by joint tillage.

2584. குடி இருப்பது குச்சுவீடு, கனாக் கண்டது மச்சுமாளிகை.

He who dwells in a humble cottage dreams of ceiled apartments.

2585. குடி இல்லா வீட்டிற் குண்டுப்பெருச்சாளி உலாவும்.

Bandycootes will run about in an uninhabited house.

2586. குடி இல்லா ஊரிலே அடி இட ஆகாது.

It is a risk to set a foot in an uninhabited village.

2587. குடி இல்லா ஊருக்கு நரி இராசன்.

A jackal is king in a deserted village.

2588. குடி உடையானே முடி உடையான்.

He is fit for kingship who is approved by the people.

2589. குடிக்கிறது கூழாம் கொப்பளிக்கிறது பன்னீராம்.

He has gruel to drink, and washes his mouth with rose water.

2590. குடிக்கிற பாலை வெடிப்பிலே வார்க்கிறதா?

What, is it to pour down the drinkable milk iuto a crevice!

2591. குடிக்கிறது காடி நீர், அதற்குத் தங்கவட்டிலா?

What you drink is sour gruel; do you require a cup of fine gold for it?

2592. குடிக்கிறது கூழாம் இருக்கிறது சிங்காசனமாம்.

Living on gruel and sitting on a throne.

2593. குடிக்கிற வீடு விடியுமா?

Will the family of a drunkard prosper!

2594. குடித்தனமோ துரைத்தனமோ எது பெரிது?

Whether is greater, the government of a family or of a state?

2595. குடித்தனம் மேவிட வேண்டி பிடாரியைப் பெண்டுவைத்துக் கொண்டான்.

Wishing to elevate his family he married a Pidari-*village goddess.*

2596. குடித்தனமென்று பண்ணினல் நன்மையும் வரும் தீமையும் வரும்.

If one becomes a householder, he must expect both good and evil.

2597. குடிபோன வீட்டிலே வறட்டு நாய் காத்ததுபோல.

As a lean dog watched a deserted house.

2598. குடிமதம் அடிபடத் தீரும்.

The madness of a drunkard may be cured by beating.

2599. குடியனும் வெறியனும் சரி.

A drunkard and a mad man are alike.

2600. குடியாத வீடு விடியாது.

The family of a drunkard is always benighted.

2601. குடியிற் பெண் வயிறு எரிந்தால் கொடியிற் சேலை நின்று எரியும்.

If the bowels of the house-wife burn, her cloth hanging on the line will burn also.

2602. குடியில்லா ஊரிலே ஒற்றைப் பணக்காரன்.

He is the only wealthy man in a deserted village.

2603. குடியிற் பிறந்து குரங்கு ஆட்டம் ஆடுதல்.

Born in a good family, and playing the monkey.

2604. குடியிற் பிறந்து செடியில் விழுந்தான்.

Born in a good family and falling into a bush.

2605. குடி வைத்துக் கொண்டாயோ கொள்ளி வைத்துக் கொண்டாயோ?

Have you taken a family *to dwell with you*! Or have you taken firebrands?

2606. குடி வைத்த வீட்டிற் கொள்ளி வைக்கலாமா?

Is it proper to burn down a house after admitting a family!

2607. குட்டிக் கிடையிலே ஓனாய் புகுந்ததுபோல்.

As a wolf entered a fold of lambs.

2608. குட்டிக் கலகம் பண்ணுகிறவன் குட்டுப்பட்டுச் சாவான்.

He who breeds divisions *in a family* shall be cuffed to death.

2609. குட்டிக் கரணம் போட்டாலும் லோபன் கொடான்.

The miser will give nothing though you tumble heels overhead.

2610. குட்டிச் சுவரிலே தேள் கொட்ட, கட்டுத் தறியிலே நெறி இடுமோ?

If a scorpion sting in a ruinous dwarf wall, will the glandular swelling appear in the stall?

2611. குட்டிச் சுவரிலே தேள் கொட்டத் தண்ணீர் மிடாவிலே நெறி கட்டுமோ?

Does the sting of a scorpion in a ruinous wall, produce a glandular swelling in a water-pot?

2612. குட்டிச் சுவரை முட்ட வெள்ளெழுத்தா?

Is he so dim-sighted as to stumble against a ruinous wall?

2613. குட்டி போட்ட பூனைபோல் அலைகிறான்.

He wanders about like a cat that has kittened.

2614. குட்டின குட்டும் குண்டிற் பாய்ந்த தண்ணீரும் வருமா?

Can a cuff already inflicted and water that has run into a pit be recalled?

2615. குட்டி ஆடு கொழுத்தாலும் வழுவழுப்புப் போகாது.

Though it become fat, the flesh of a kid is always clammy.

2616. குட்டி குலைத்து நாய்பேரில் வைக்கிறதுபோல.

Like pups barking and creating a quarrel among dogs.

2617. குட்டி நாய்கொண்டு வேட்டை ஆடினதுபோல.

Like hunting with pups.

2618. குட்டு மானம் தப்பிக் குசவனோடே பேசினால், சட்டையும் பண்ணான், சட்டியும் கொடான்.

If yon speak familiarly with a potter, he will not respect you, nor will he supply you with chatties.

2619. குணத்தை மாற்றக் குரு இல்லை.

No guroo-a *religious teacher*-can change a man's temperament.

A Guru among the Hindus is regarded as a spiritual parent from whom the youth receives the initiatory *mantra* or prayer, and who conducts the ceremonies necessary at various seasons of infancy and youth, up to the period of investiture with the sacred thread or string: this person may be the natural parent or the religious preceptor. The word Guru is also used for a teacher or preceptor generally.

2620. குணத்திற்கு அழுகிறதா, பிணத்திற்கு அழுகிறதா?

Is the weeping on account of the virtue of the *deceased* or does it relate to his corpse?

2621. குணம் உற்றவன் மணம் உற்றவன், குணம் அற்றவன் மணம் அற்றவன்.

A good-natured man has an engaging exterior, an ill-natured man has a repulsive aspect.

2622. குணம் பாதி கொண்ட நோவு பாதி.

His suffering is due partly to his faint-heartedness, and partly to a disease.

2623. குண்டாக் கரணம் போட்டாலும் பிண்டாச் சோற்றுக்கு வழி இல்லை.

Though he makes somersaults *to all he sees,* he has no food to eat.

2624. குண்டி காய்ந்தால் குதிரையும் வைக்கோல் தின்னும்.

If starved even a horse will eat straw.

2625. குண்டி எத்தனை கோணற் கோணினாலும் சுமை வீட்டிற் போய்ச் சேர்ந்தாலே சரி.

No matter how the body may be bent if the burden be carried home.

2626. குண்டி அறுந்த பருந்துபோல.

Like a kite with a broken tail.

2627. குண்டுச் சட்டியிலே குதிரை ஓட்டுகிறான்.

He displays his horsemanship in an earthen pot.

2628. குண்டு பட்டுச் சாகாதவன் வண்டு கடித்துச் செத்தானாம்.

It is said that he who survived a gunshot wound, died of the bite of an insect.

2629. குண்டுச் சட்டியிற் கரணம் போடலாமா?

Can one turn a somersault in an earthen pot?

2630. குண்டுப் பெருச்சாளியும் வண்டுபோல.

The bandycoote is also like a beetle.

2631. குண்டுணி சொல்லுகிறவனுக்கு இருநாக்கு கட்டுவிரியனுக்கும் இருநாக்கு.

A slanderer and a snake of deadly poison have each two tongues.

2632. குண்டை பலத்தால் குடி பலக்கும்.

As kine increase, a household increases.

2633. குதி குதி என்பார்கள் எல்லாரும், கூடக் குதிப்பார் இல்லை.

They will all say leap, leap *into the pyre*, but there is none willing to leap with me.

2634. குதித்துக் குதித்து மா இடித்தாலும் புழுக்கைக்கு ஒரு கொழுக்கட்டையே.

Though she may leap joyously and pound the grain, the slave woman gets but one cake.

2635. குதிரை குருடானாலும் கொள்ளுத் தின்கிறதிற் குறைச்சல் இல்லை.

Though blind, the horse does not eat the less grain.

2636. குதிரை கொண்டால் கவினத்துக்கு வழக்கா?

When you have bought the horse, is there any occasion for disputing about its bit?

2637. குதிரையின் குணம் அறிந்தல்லவோ தம்பிரான் கொம்பு கொடுக்கவில்லை?

Was it not because the Creator knew the nature of the horse that he did not provide him with horns!

2638. குதிரை செத்ததல்லாமற் சேணம் சுமக்க வேலை ஆயிற்று.

Besides the death of the horse there is the saddle also to be carried.

2639. குதிரைக்கும் நாய்க்கும் குடிபோகச் சந்தோஷம்.

The horse and the dog like a change of place.

2640. குதிரை ஏற அதிஷ்டம் இருந்தாற் குண்டியின் கீழ் வந்து நுழை யாதா ?

If it be your good fortune to ride, will not your horse come and place itself under your seat !

2641. குதிரை நல்லதுதான் சுழி கெட்டது.

It is certainly a good horse, but its circular marks are bad.

The circlets of hair on a horse are generally observed by dealers and owners very carefully.

2642. குதிரை ஏறி என்ன, கோணக் கொம்பு ஊதி என்ன, வீணர்க் கும் கீர்த்திக்கும் வெகு தூரம்.

What if you do ride a horse, and have a horn blown before you ? There is a great distance between the worthless and reputation.

2643. குதிரை பாகனைத் தள்ளுவதும் அல்லாமல் குழியும் தோண்டு கிறதாம்.

It is said that the horse has not only thrown its rider, but is digging his grave.

2644. குதிரை செத்தது அல்லாமல் குழி தோண்ட மூன்று பணமா ?

Besides losing the horse, have I to pay three fanams to bury him ?

2645. குதிரையும் காதம் கிழவியும் காதம்.

The horse is ten miles *before you*, and the old woman is *ten* miles *behind you.*

2646. குதிரை பிடிக்கச் சம்மட்டி அடிக்க கூப்பிட்டக் குரலுக்கு ஏனென்ன.

You will attend to my horse, ply the sledge hammer and answer my calls.

2647. குதிரை இருப்பு அறியும் கொண்ட பெண்டாட்டி குணம் அறி வாள்.

The horse knows his rider, and a wife her husband.

2648. குத்தி வடித்தாலும் சம்பா குப்பையிலே போட்டாலும் தங்கம்.

Though pounded and boiled it is samba-*superior rice*-though cast on the rubbish heap it is gold.

2649. குத்துப்பட்டுப் பொறுத்தாலும் குறைவயிறு பொறுக்குமா?
A cuff may be borne, can hunger?

2650. குந்தி இருந்து தின்றால் குன்று மாளும்.
If you eat properly seated you may consume a heap of rice.

2651. குபேரன் பட்டணத்திலும் விறகு சுமக்கிறவன் உண்டு.
Even in the city of Kubèran there were firewood carriers.

2652. குபேரன் பட்டணம் கொள்ளைபோனாலும் அதிஷ்டவீனனுக்கு அகப்பைக் காம்பும் அகப்படுமா?
Though the city of Kubèran be despoiled, will the unfortunate obtain even the handle of a wooden spoon?

2653. குப்புற விழுந்து தவம் செய்தாலும் குருக்களுக்கு மோட்சம் இல்லை.
Though they may prostrate themselves and perform penance, religious teachers do not attain heaven.

2654. குப்புற விழுந்தும் மீசையிலே மண் படவில்லை என்கிறான்.
Though he fell flat on his face, he says that his mustache did not touch the ground.

2655. குப்பையில் முளைத்த கீரை கப்பலுக்குக் காலாகுமா?
Will a plant grown on a dunghill answer for the mast of a ship?

2656. குப்பையில் முளைத்த கொடி கூரையில் ஏறினதுபோல.
As a creeper springing on a dunghill climbed on a roof.

2657. குப்பையின்றிப் பயிர் விளையாது.
Without manure the growing grain will not yield a good crop.

2658. குப்பையிற் கிடந்தாலும் குன்றிமணி குன்றிமணிதான்.
Though it lies on the dunghill the kunrimani-*abrus precatorius*-remains unchanged.

2659. குப்பையிற் புதைத்தாலும் குன்றிமணி நிறம் போகாது.
Though the kunr'mani be buried in the dunghill its colour will not change.

2660. குப்பை உயர்ந்தது கோபுரம் தாழ்ந்தது.

The rubbish heap has risen, the tower has sunk.

2661. குப்பை உயர்ந்ததென்ன கோபுரம் தாழ்ந்ததென்ன ?

How is it that the rubbish heap has risen, and the tower sunk ?

2662. குப்பையும் கோழியும்போலக் குருவும் சிஷனும்.

The teacher and his disciple are like the dunghill and the fowl.

2663. குமரி ஒரு பிள்ளை கோடி ஒரு வெள்ளை.

A woman is young till she bears a child, and cloth is new till it is washed.

2664. குமரி தனிவழியே போனாலும் கொட்டாவி தனிவழியே போகாது.

Though a young woman may go on her way alone, yawning is never alone.

2665. குமரியாய் இருக்கையிற் கொண்டாட்டம் கிழவியாய் இருக்கிறபோது திண்டாட்டம்.

When young, a woman is full of hilarity, when old her portion is vexation.

2666. கும்பிட்டுக் கடன் கொடாதே கும்பிட்டுக் கடன் வாங்காதே.

Neither lend nor borrow beseechingly.

2667. கும்பிடப் போன இடத்தில் கோயில் இடிந்து விழுந்தது.

When I went to worship the temple fell.

2668. கும்பிடப் போன தெய்வம் குறுக்கே வந்ததுபோல்.

As the deity one went to worship came to meet one cross wise.

2669. கும்பிட்ட தெய்வம் குலதெய்வம்.

The deity I worship is my hereditary deity.

2670. கும்பிடும் கள்ளர் குழைந்திடும் கள்ளர்.

Obsequious rogues, deceitful friends.

2671. குயவனுக்குப் பல நாளை வேலை, தடி அடிகாரனுக்கு ஒரு நிமிஷ வேலை.

That which cost the potter many days labour, is but the labour of a moment to the breaker.

2672. குயவா கலசம் கொண்டுவா, இடையா பால் கொடு என்றாற் போல.

Like saying to the potter bring a vessel, and to the shepherd fill it with milk.

2673. குயில் கூவினாற்போல.

Like the warbling of the Indian cuckoo.

2674. குயிற் குரலும் மயில் அழகும்போல.

Like the voice of the Indian cuckoo, and the beauty of the peacock.

2675. குரங்கின் கைப் பூமாலை.

A garland of flowers in the hand of a monkey.

2676. குரங்குக்குப் புத்திசொல்லித் தூக்கணங்குருவி கூண்டு இழந்தது.

The advice which the pendulous bird *Loxia*, gave to the monkey ended in the destruction of its own nest.

2677. குரங்குக்கும் தன்குட்டி பொன்குட்டி.

Even to the monkey its own young is precious.

2678. குரங்குப் புண் ஆறாது.

A sore on a monkey never heals.

2679. குரங்குப் புண் பிரமாண்டம்.

A sore of the monkey is enormously large.

2680. குரங்குப் பிணமும் குறப் பிணமும் கண்டவர் இல்லை.

No one ever saw the dead body of a monkey, or the corpse of a kuravan-*a mountaineer*.

2681. குரங்கு தன் குட்டியின் கையைக்கொண்டு பதம் பார்க்கிறது போலப் பார்க்கிறான்.

He tests it *by another* as a monkey tests an object by the hand of its young.

2682. குரங்குப் பிடிபோல் பிடிக்கவேண்டும்.

Lay hold of a thing *as firmly* as a monkey.

2683. குரங்கின் பீயை மருந்துக்குக் கேட்டால் கொப்பு கிளை எல்லாம் தத்திப்பாயும்.

If a monkey be asked for his droppings for medicinal purposes, he will leap from branch to branch.

2684. குரங்கு எல்லாம் ஒரு முகம்.

All monkeys have faces alike.

2685. குரங்கு ஆனாலும் குலத்தில் கொள்ளவேண்டும்.

Though she be a mere monkey, one should take a wife in one's own tribe.

2686. குரங்கு ஏறாத கொம்பு உண்டா?

Is there a branch the monkey has not climbed?

2687. குரங்கு எல்லாம் கூட்டம் கூட்டமாக இருக்கும்.

All monkeys *go about* in troops.

2688. குரங்கின் கையில் கொள்ளி அகப்பட்ட கதை.

The story of a firebrand in the hand of a monkey.

2689. குரு இல்லாத சிஷன் உண்டா?

Is there a disciple without a Guru-*teacher*?

2690. குரு இல்லார்க்கு வித்தையும் இல்லை முதல் இல்லார்க்கு லாபமும் இல்லை.

There is no art without a teacher, and no profit without capital.

2691. குரு என வந்தான் திரு உரை தந்தான்.

He came as a Guru; he gave sacred instruction.

2692. குருக்கள் பிழைத்தது மறுபிறப்பு.

The escape of the *religious* teacher was *as it were* a second birth

2693. குருடன் கையில் விலாங்கு அகப்பட்டதுபோல.

As an eel was caught in the hand of a blind man.

2694. குருடனுக்கு வேண்டியது கோல்.

The need of a blind man is a staff.

2695. குருடனுக்கு வேண்டியது கண்.

What the blind want is eye-sight.

2696. குருடனுக்குக் குருடன் கோல் பிடிக்கலாமா?

Can the blind lead the blind with a staff?

2697. குருடன் ஆடு மேய்க்க எட்டாளுக்கு வேலையா?

Is it a work for eight men *to help* a blind man to feed sheep?

2698. குருடன் கூத்துப் பார்க்கப் போனால் பயன் என்ன?

What advantage will the blind man gain by attending a comedy?

2699. குருடனுக்குப் பால் கொக்குப் போன்றது.

To the blind milk was like a heron.

2700. குருடன் பெண்டாட்டி கூனனோடு உறவாடினாள்.

The wife of a blind man became intimate with a hunch-backed man.

2701. குருடன் பெண்டினை அடித்தாற்போல.

As if a blind man beat his wife.

2702. குருடனைப் பார்த்து இராச விழி விழிக்கச் சொன்னால் விழிப்பானா?

If requested to assume the looks of a king, can a blind man do so?

2703. குருடனை கோட்டம் பார்க்கச் சொன்னாற்போல.

As if a blind man was asked to assay metals.

2704. குருடன் கைக் கோலைப் பிடுங்கினதுபோல.

Like snatching away the staff of the blind.

2705. குருடனுக்கு குருடன் வழி காட்டினால் இருவரும் குழியிலே விழுவார்.

If the blind lead the blind, both will fall into the pit.

2706. குருடி தண்ணீர்க்குப் போக எட்டாள் வினைகெட்டதுபோல்.

As the work of eight persons was stopped by reason of a blind woman going to fetch water.

2707. குருடும் செவிடும் கூத்துப் பார்த்ததுபோல.

As the blind and the deaf attended a comedy.

2708. குருட்டுக் குதிரைக்குச் சறுக்கினது சாக்கு.

The excuse of a blind horse was his stumbling.

2709. குருட்டுப் பூனை விட்டத்திற் பாய்ந்ததுபோல.

As a blind cat leaped on the cross beam.

2710. குருட்டுக்கொக்கிற்கு ஊர்க்குளமே சாட்சி.

The village tank is the witness of the blind crane.

2711. குருட்டுக் கோழி தவிட்டுக்கு விங்கியதுபோல.

As a blind fowl was over-anxious to feed on bran.

2712. குருட்டுக் கண்ணுக்குக் குறுணி மை இட்டு ஆவது என்ன?

Why adorn blind eyes with collyrium?

2713. குரு மொழி கேளாதவனும் தாய் வார்த்தைக்கு அடங்காதவனும் சண்டி.

He who will not hear the words of his Guru-*religious teacher*-and he who disobeys his mother, are worthless.

2714. குரு மொழி மறந்தோன் திருவழிந்து அழிவான்.

He who forgets the words of his Guru will forfeit the divine *favor* and perish.

2715. குருவியின் கழுத்திலே பனங்காயைக் கட்டித் தூக்கலாமா?

Can a palmyra fruit be suspended from the neck of a small bird?

2716. குருவிக்குத் தக்க இராம அத்திரம் அல்லவோ?

Is not the weapon of Rama suited to the bird?

2717. குருவிக்குத் தக்க ராமேசுரம்.

Raméswaram suited to the bird.

This is I think a perversion of the foregoing proverb An aged or feeble person may say, my Raméswaram, pilgrimage, efforts, must be moderate.

2718. குருவிக்குத் தக்க பாரம்.

A burden suited to the bird.

2719. குருவிக் கூட்டைக் கோலாற் கலைக்காதே.

Never disturb the nest of a bird with a stick.

2720. குருவுக்கு மிஞ்சின சிஷனு?

Is there a disciple who is above his Guru!

2721. குருவுக்கு நாமம் குழைத்துப்போடுவான்.

He will deceive his own Guru.

2722. குருவுக்குத் துரோகம் செய்தாலும் குடலுக்குத் துரோகம் செய்யக்கூடாது.

Though a Guru may be deceived, the stomach cannot.

2723. குரு வேஷம் கொண்டவன் எல்லாம் குரு ஆவானு?

Are all religious teachers who have assumed the garb?

2724. குலத்தைக் கெடுத்த கோடாலிக்காம்பு.

The handle of an axe that destroyed its own species.

The tree from which its handle was taken, was felled by the axe.

2725. குலத்தைக் கெடுக்குமாம் குரங்கு.

It is said that a monkey will destroy its own species.

2726. குலமகட்கு அழகு தன் கொழுநனைப் பேணுதல்.

It becomes a lawful wife to honour her husband.

2727. குலமகன் குலத்துக்கு அழுவான், மூக்கறையன் மூக்குக்கு அழுவான்.

The high-born mourns the loss of caste, and the man who has lost his nose, his nose.

2728. குலமும் ஒன்று குறியும் ஒன்று.

Birth and *external* sign are at *variance*.

2729. குலம் புகுந்தும் குறை தீரவில்லை.

Though he has entered another tribe he is still in want.

2730. குலம் குலத்தோடே வெள்ளம் ஆற்றோடே.

Tribe goes with tribe, the flood with the river.

2731. குலம் குலத்தோடே வெள்ளாடு தன்னோடே.

A tribe associates with its own tribe, and goats follow their own kind.

2732. குலம் குப்பையிலே பணம் பந்தியிலே.

High birth lies on the dunghill, while wealth is at the festive board.

2733. குலவித்தை கற்றுப் பாதி கல்லாமற் பாதி.

Arts appropriate to a family are partly intuitive and partly acquired.

2734. குலைக்கிற நாய் கடிக்க அறியாது.

A barking dog does not bite.

2735. குலைக்கிற நாய்க்கு எலும்பைப் போட்டாற்போல.

Like throwing a bone to a barking dog.

2736. குலைக்கிற நாய் வேட்டை பிடிக்குமா?

Will a barking dog avail in hunting!

2737. குலைக்கிற நாயின் வாயிலே கோலைக் கொடுத்தால் ஊர் எங்கும் கொண்டோடிக் குலைக்கும்.

If a staff be put into the mouth of a noisy dog, it will carry it through the village barking.

2738. குலையாத நாய் குதிங்காலைக் கடிக்கும்.

A silent dog will bite the heels.

2739. குழந்தை பட்டினியும் கோயில் பட்டினியும் இல்லை.

Infants and temple servants do not suffer from hunger.

2740. குழந்தைக்கும் நாய்க்கும் குடிபோகச் சந்தோஷம்.
Children and dogs are pleased with a change of place.

2741. குழந்தையும் தெய்வமும் கொண்டாடின இடத்திலே.
Children and gods best agree with their admirers.

2742. குழந்தைக் காய்ச்சலும் குண்டனி காய்ச்சலும் பொல்லாது.
The fever of children and the spite of a slanderer are bad.

2743. குழந்தை தூங்குகிறது எல்லாம் அம்மையாருக்கு இலாபம்.
The sleep of a child is advantageous to the mother.

2744. குழந்தையின் தேகம்போல்.
Tender as the body of an infant.

2745. குழந்தாய் குழியில் அமிழ்ந்தாதே.
My child, do not sink into the pit.

2746. குழப்படி கண்டு திரைகடல் ஏங்குமா ?
Has the stormy weather set the whole sea in motion ?

2747. குழம்புப் பால் குடிக்கவும் குமரா கண்டவலியா ?
O my youthful son, is your throat pained by drinking thick milk ?

2748. குழியிற் பயிரை எடுத்துக் கூரைமேல் இடலாமா ?
Is it right to train a parasite to the roof ?

2749. குழியிற் பிள்ளையை நரி சுற்றுகிறதுபோலே.
Like a jackal going round the grave of a child.

2750. குளத்தைக் கலக்கிப் பருந்துக்கு இரை இடலாமா ?
Is it proper to agitate the tank to supply prey for kites ?

2751. குளத்துக்கு மழை குந்தாணியா ?
Are rain drops the weight of a mortar to a tank ?

2752. குளத்திற் போட்டுக் கிணற்றில் தேடலாமா ?
Having put it into the tank, do you seek it in the well ?

2753. குளத்தோடு கோபித்துக் கால் கழுவாதவன்போல்.

Like the man who would not wash his feet in the tank because he was angry with it.

2754. குளப் படி நீர் இறைத்தாலும் கடற் பள்ளம் நிரம்புமா ?

Will the hollow of the sea be filled by draining a tank down to the lowest step ?

2755. குளம் உடைந்து போகும்போது முறைவிதமா?

When a tank bursts, do they dispute about turns ?

2756. குளம் காக்கிறவன் தண்ணீரைக் குடியானோ ?

Will not he who watches the tank drink ?

2757. குளம் வற்றியும் முறைவீதம் உண்டா ?

Why dispute about your turn *for drawing water* seeing that the tank is dried up ?

2758. குளம் வெட்டுமுன்னே முதலை குடி இருக்குமா ?

Before the tank is dug will the alligator go to dwell therein ?

2759. குளவிக் கூட்டைக் கோலால் குலைத்தாற்போல.

Like poking a wasp's nest with a stick.

2760. குளவிக் கூட்டிலே கல்லு விட்டு எறிகிறதா ?

What ! throw a stone at a wasp's nest !

2761. குளவிக்குப் பச்சைப் புழு பிள்ளை.

A green caterpillar is the offspring of a wasp.

2762. குளவி புழுவைத் தன் நிறம் ஆக்குவதுபோல.

Like a wasp changing worms to its own colour.

2763. குளிக்கப்போய்ச் சேற்றைப் பூசிக்கொண்டதுபோல.

As one smeared himself with mud after bathing.

2764. குளிர்ந்த கொள்ளியாய் இருந்து குடியைக் கெடுக்கலாமா ?

Pretending to be an extinguished firebrand, is it proper to destroy the house ?

2765. குள்ளப் பார்ப்பான் பள்ளத்தில் விழுந்தான் தண்டு எடு தடி எடு.

The dwarf Brahman has fallen into a pit, take a staff, take a stick.

2766. குள்ளனைக் கொண்டு ஆழம் பார்க்கிறான்.

He sounds the depth by means of a dwarf.

2767. குள்ளன் குடி கெடுப்பான் குள்ளன் பெண்சாதி ஊரைக் கெடுப்பாள்.

A dwarf will destroy a family; his wife will destroy the whole village.

2768. குறத்தி பிள்ளை பெற்றால் குறவன் காயம் தின்பான்.

If the wife of a mountaineer is brought to bed, her husband takes the prescribed stimulant.

2769. குற வழக்கும் இடை வழக்கும் கொஞ்சத்தில் தீராது.

Disputes among mountaineers and shepherds are not easily settled.

2770. குற வழக்குக்குச் சக்கிலி வழக்கு இலேசு.

Disputes among chakliyars are more easily settled than those among mountaineers.

2771. குறுணிப் பால் கறந்தபோதிலும் கூரை பிடுங்கப் பார்த்திருக்கலாமா?

May one suffer his cow to destroy his roof although she yields a kuruni of milk at a meal?

2772. குறுணி மைதான் இட்டாலும் குருடு குருடே.

Though a kuruni of collyrium be applied to the eyes of the blind, the blindness remains.

2773. குறும்பியுள்ள காது தினவு தின்னும்.

A ceruminous ear will itch.

2774. குறும்பைத் தவிர்க்கும் குடிதாங்கி.

The supporter who puts an end to inhuman acts.

2775. குறை அறக் கற்றவன் கோடியில் ஒருவன்.

A thoroughly learned man is one of a lac.

2776. குறை குடம் தளம்பும் நிறை குடம் தளம்பாது.

A water pot not full is agitated, a full pot is not.

2777. குறையச் சொல்லி நிறைய அள.

Give more than you profess to sell.

2778. குறையுள்ளோர்க்கு உண்டு குறுகுதல் கறையுள்ளோர்க்கு உண்டு கரவு.

The guilty are dejected, those that have a tarnished reputation elude observation.

2779. குறை வேலையைக் குருக்களுக்கும் காட்டல் ஆகாது.

An unfinished work ought not to be shown even to a Guru-*master*.

2780. குறை வேலையை அம்பலத்திற் கொண்டுவரலாமா?

Is it proper to expose an unfinished work *for sale or otherwise*?

2781. குற்றமுள்ள நெஞ்சு குறுகுறு என்னும் குறும்பியுள்ள காது தினவு தின்னும்.

A guilty conscience is agitated, a foul ear itches.

2782. குற்றம் மறைப்பதில் மற்றொரு குற்றமும் நேரும்.

By concealing one fault another may arise.

2783. குற்ற மனச்சாட்சி கூடி வாழ் சத்துரு.

A guilty conscience is an enemy that lives with its possessor.

2784. குற்றம் அடைந்த கீர்த்தி குணங்கொள்வது அரிது.

Distinction attained by wrong makes reformation difficult.

2785. குற்றத் தண்டனையிலும் சுத்த தண்டனை நல்லது.

Undeserved punishment is better than deserved punishment.

2786. குற்றம் பார்க்கிற் சுற்றம் இல்லை.

If every fault be noticed, all intercourse must cease.

2787. குன்றிமணிக்கும் குண்டியிற் கறுப்பு.

Even a kunrimani seed-*abrus precatorius*-has a black spot on it.

கூ.

2788. கூகைக்குப் பகலில் கண் தெரியாது.

An owl cannot see in the day-time.

2789. கூகை விழித்தாற்போல விழிக்கிறான்.

He stares like an owl.

2790. கூடக் குடி இருந்துகொண்டு கொள்ளி சொருகலாமா?

Whilst residing with one shall we thrust a firebrand into his house?

2791. கூடத்தைக் கொடுத்தாலும் மாடத்தைக் கொடுக்கல் ஆகாது.

Although you may give an outer room, it is not proper to give an inner one.

2792. கூடம் ஒன்று போடுமுன்னே, சுத்தி இரண்டு போடும்.

Before the big hammer strikes one, the little hammer strikes two.

2793. கூடம் இடித்தால் மாடம்.

If the party-wall be broken down, one room only will remain.

2794. கூடி இருந்து குலாவுவார் வீட்டில் ஓடி உண்ணும் கூழும் இனிதே.

Gruel served in the house of a united family is enjoyable.

2795. கூட்டத்திற் கட்டுச்சோறு அவிழ்த்ததுபோல.

As food prepared for a journey was untied in a crowd.

2796. கூட்டோடே போச்சுது குளிரும் காய்ச்சலும்.

Shivering and fever left with the body.

2797. கூண்டிலே குறுணி நெல் இருந்தால் மூலையிலே முக்குறுணித் தெய்வம் கூத்தாடும்.

When there is a kuruni of paddy in the bin, three kurunies of gods will be dancing in a corner.

2798. கூத்தரிசி குத்துகிற வீட்டில் வாய்க்கு அரிசிக்கு வழி இராது.

In the house where rice is pounded for sale, there is not enough to put into the mouth *of a corpse.*

Before a corpse is removed the females of the family place a little raw rice near the mouth, the males do the same in the cemetry before the body is laid on the pyre.

2799. கூத்தாட்டுச் சிலம்பம் படைவெட்டுக்கு ஆகுமா?

Will the art of fencing avail in a battle-field?

2800. கூத்தாடிக்குக் கீழே கண் கூலிக்காரனுக்கு மேலே கண்.

A rope-dancer directs his eye downwards, one who bears a burden upwards.

2801. கூத்திக்கு இட்டுக் குரங்கு ஆனான் வேசிக்கு இட்டு விறகு ஆனான்.

By wasting his substance on concubines he has become spare as a monkey, and by giving to common women he has become as dry as a stick.

2802. கூத்திப் பிள்ளைக்குத் தகப்பன் ஆர்?

Who is the legal father of the child of a concubine?

2803. கூத்தியார் ஆத்தாள் செத்தால் கொட்டும் முழக்கும் கூத்தியார் செத்தால் ஒன்றும் இல்லை.

When the mother of one's concubine dies, there will be beating of drums, but when the concubine dies, there will be no such display.

2804. கூத்தியார் செத்தால் பிணம், அவள் தாய் செத்தால் மணம்.

When a concubine dies she is a mere corpse, whereas if her mother dies, her remains are honoured.

By honouring the remains of her mother it is supposed that a man secures greater respect from his concubine.

2805. கூத்தியார் வீட்டுக்கு நாய்போல் அலைகிறான்.

He frequents his concubine's house as a dog wandering about.

2806. கூத்துப் பார்க்கப் போன இடத்தில் பேய் பிடித்ததுபோல.

As one was seized by a demon when he went to see a comedy.

2807. கூரிய சொல்லான் ஆரிலும் வல்லன்.

He whose words are keen, is of all the most powerful.

2808. கூருக்கு எதிர் உதைத்தல் சூரெழ வருத்தும்.

Kicking against thorns will cause pain.

2809. கூரை ஏறிக் கோழி பிடிக்கமாட்டாத குருக்கள் வானம் கீறி வைகுண்டம் காட்டுவாரா ?

If a guru is not able to go to the house-top to catch a fowl, how can he rend the heavens and show vikundam *to his disciple* !

2810. கூரைமேலே சோறு போட்டால் ஆயிரம் காகம் வரும்.

If rice is thrown on the roof, a thousand crows will come.

2811. கூர்மையாளனே நேர்மையாளன்.

The acute man is the upright man.

2812. கூலி குறைத்தால் வேலை கெடும்.

If the hire be diminished, the work will be spoiled.

2813. கூலி குறைத்தாயே குறை மரக்கால் இட்டாயே.

Thou hast reduced my wages, and used false measures when paying me.

2814. கூலிக்காரன் பெண்டாட்டி பிள்ளை பெறப்போகிறாளாம் குப்பையிலே ஆமணக்கு முளைக்கப் போகிறதாம்.

It is said that the wife of a labourer is about to be confined, and that a castor plant will spring upon the midden.

2815. கூலிக்கு நாற்று நட வந்தவனுக்கு எல்லைக்கு வழக்கோ ?

Does he who came on hire to transplant grain institute a boundary suit ?

2816. கூலிக்குப் பாவி குறுக்கே வந்தானே.

A vicious fellow prevented the payment of my wages.

2817. கூலிக்குக் கழு ஏறுவார்களா?

Will they hire themselves to be impaled?

2818. கூலிப் படை வெட்டுமோ?

Will mere hirelings conquer?

2819. கூழ் ஆனாலும் குப்பை ஆனாலும் குடித்துக்கொண்டவன் பிழைப்பான்.

Whether gruel or refuse, he who has drunk it will live.

2820. கூழுக்கு மாங்காய் தோற்குமா?

Will an unripe mango fail before gruel?

2821. கூழுக்கு மாங்காய் கொண்டாட்டம் குரங்குக்குத் தேங்காய் கொண்டாட்டம்.

An unripe mango improves the gruel, the kernel of a cocoanut is a feast to a monkey.

2822. கூழுக்கும் ஆசை மீசைக்கும் ஆசை.

He wishes to drink the gruel, and he also wants a nice mustache.

Spoken of things incompatible.

2823. கூழுக்குக் கொறடா மிளகாய்.

A chilly serves as a whip to gruel.

It makes it pungent.

2824. கூழ் என்றாலும் வாழ்வுக்குத் தக்கதாக குடிக்கத்தான் வேண்டும்.

Though only gruel, it must be drunk agreeably to one's circumstances.

2825. கூழ் என்றாலும் குடித்தவன் பிழைப்பான்.

If only gruel, he who drinks it will live.

2826. கூழ் குடிக்கிலும் கூட்டு ஆகாது.

Fellowship is undesirable even in drinking gruel.

2827. கூழ் புளித்ததென்றும் மாங்காய் புளித்ததென்றும் உணராமற் சொல்லலாமா?

Is it proper to say thoughtlessly that the gruel was sour, and then again that it was the mango that was sour!

2828. கூனனைக் கொண்டு குழப்படி மாமி காணிக்குப் பிள்ளை பெற.

O, mother-in-law, incite a quarrel through the hunchbacked that an heir may be born.

2829. கூனன் குறை தீர்ந்தான் கொடியோன் வினை பெயர்ந்தான்.

The hunchbacked is relieved, the cruel man has escaped.

2830. கூனி ஆனாலும் கூடை சுமந்துதான் கூலி பெறவேண்டும்.

Although her back is crooked, she will have to carry the basket before she gets her hire.

2831. கூனி வாயாற் கெட்டாற்போல.

As she (Kaikesi) was demoralized by *listening to* the words of Kuni.

கெ.

2832. கெடு காலத்துக்குக் கெட்டோர் புத்தியைக் கேட்பார்.

They will listen to the advice of the wicked when their star is not favourable.

2833. கெடு குடி சொற் கேளாது.

A decaying family will not listen to advice.

2834. கெடுக்க நினைக்கில் அடுக்கக் கெடும்.

When you mediate *another's* ruin, your own will soon follow.

2835. கெடுக்கினும் கல்வி கேடுபடாது.

Learning can suffer no damage.

2836. கெடுப்பாரைத் தெய்வம் கெடுக்கும்.

The deity will destroy those that injure others.

2837. கெடுப்பதும் வாயால் படிப்பதும் வாயால்.

It is with the mouth we injure others; it is with the mouth we read.

2838. கெடுமதி கண்ணுக்குத் தோன்றாது.

One is blind to his own imprudence.

2839. கெடுமதிக்குப் படுகுழியை வெட்டு.

Make a pitfall for imprudence.

2840. கெடுவாய் கேடு நினையாதே.

Thou wilt be ruined, think not of destroying *another*.

2841. கெடுவான் கேடு நினைப்பான்.

He who is on the way to ruin, will mediate *another's* ruin.

2842. கெட்ட காலத்துக்கு நாரை கெளிற்றை எடுத்து விழுங்கினது போல.

As a crane in an evil time seized and swallowed a keliru fish.

2843. கெட்ட நாய்க்குப் பட்டது பிரீதி.

The wretched dog feels satisfied with the beating he received.

2844. கெட்ட ஊருக்கு எட்டு வார்த்தை.

A village doomed to ruin profits not by repeated precaution.

2845. கெட்ட கேட்டுக்கு வட்டம் காற்பணமா?

Is a premium of half a fanam demanded of one who is reduced in circumstances?

2846. கெட்ட பால் நல்ல பால் ஆகுமா?

Will curdled milk become sweet again?

2847. கெட்டதும் பட்டதும் கீரைக்கு இறைத்ததும் போதும்.

I have had enough of loss, sufferings and toil in watering the vegetable *garden*.

2848. கெட்ட குடிக்கு ஒரு துஷ்டப் பிள்ளை.

A vicious child in a poor family.

2849. கெட்ட குடிக்கு ஒரு கேட்டை பிறந்தது.

A child is born under the star kèttai in a poor family.

2850. கெட்ட கழுதைக்குத் துஷ்டபுத்தி.

A vicious donkey has mischievous propensities.

2851. கெட்டவன் குடி கெட்டது வட்டி நஷ்டம் இல்லாமல் வாங்கவே வாங்கு.

The family is ruined, do not fail to get the interest without reduction.

2852. கெட்டவன் குடி கெட்டும் நீ குடி மிளகுசாற்றை.

No matter whose family is ruined, you drink the pepper water.

2853. கெட்ட குடியே கெடும் பட்ட காலிலே படும்.

The decaying family will be ruined It will hit the leg which is already struck.

2854. கெட்ட மாடு தேடுமுன்னம் எட்டு மாடு தேடலாம்.

You may procure eight cows before you can recover one that has strayed.

2855. கெட்ட மார்க்கத்திலே இருக்கிற ஒருவன் மற்றவர்களையும் அதில் இழுக்கப் பிரயாசப்படுவான்.

He who pursues a vicious course will try to lead others into the same.

2856. கெட்டார்க்கு உற்றார் கிளையிலும் இல்லை.

The impoverished have no friends even among their own kindred.

2857. கெட்டார் வாழ்ந்தால் கிளைகிளையாய்த் தளிர்ப்பார் வாழ்ந்தார் கெட்டால் வறையோட்டுக்கும் ஆகார்.

When the ruined in circumstances flourish they cast out innumerable branches; when the prosperous are reduced to poverty they are not worth a potsherd.

2858. கெட்டான் பயல் பொட்டலிலே, விழுந்தான் பயல் சறுக்கலிலே.

The boy suffered *by walking* in the arid tract, he fell in the slippery ground.

2859. கெட்டாலும் செட்டி செட்டியே கிழிந்தாலும் பட்டு பட்டே.

Though reduced *in circumstances* a chetty is a chetty; silk is silk though never so torn.

2860. கெட்டிக்காரன் புளுகு எட்டு நாளுக்குள் தெரியும்.

The deception of the clever will be manifest in eight days.

2861. கெட்டிக்காரனுக்குப் பயம் இல்லை மட்டித்தனனுக்கு நயம் இல்லை.

The clever fear nothing; the fool gains nothing.

2862. கெட்டிக்காரன் பொட்டு எட்டு நாள் அளவும்.

The reputation of the adroit lasts only eight days.

2863. கெட்டும் பட்டணம் சேர்.

Though you are ruined, cling to the city.

2864. கெட்டுப்போகிற காலம் வந்தால் துஷ்ட புத்தி தோன்றாதா?

When the time of destruction comes will not evil devices operate?

2865. கெட்டுப்போன பார்ப்பானுக்குச் செத்துபோகிற பசுவைத் தானம் பண்ணினதுபோல.

Like giving a dying cow to a poor Brahman.

2866. கெட்டுக் கெட்டுக் குடி ஆகிறதா?

Can a family survive repeated misfortunes!

2867. கெண்டையைப்போட்டு வராலை இழுக்கிறதுபோல.

Baiting with a small fish and catching a large one.

2868. கொரடி கற்றவன் இடறி விழுந்தால் அதுவும் ஒரு வரிசை என்பான்.

If the fencer fall, he will pretend he did so according to the rules of his art.

2869. கெவியன் பாற் சோறு கண்டதுபோல.

As the greedy saw milk and rice.

கே.

2870. கேடது இல்லான் பாடது இல்லான்.

One free from loss, free from suffering.

2871. கேடு காலத்துக்கு ஓடு கப்பறை.

A bad time is followed by an alms-dish.

2872. கேடு கெட்ட நாயே வீடு விட்டுப் போவேன்.

You worthless dog quit *my* house.

2873. கேடு வரும் பின்னே மதி கெட்டு வரும் முன்னே, ஆனைவரும் பின்னே மணி ஓசை வரும் முன்னே.

Indigence follows indiscretion, the elephent makes its appearance after the sound of its bells reaches *the ear*.

2874. கேட்டது எல்லாம் நம்பாதே நம்பினது எல்லாம் சொல்லாதே.

Believe not all you hear, tell not all you believe.

2875. கேட்டில் உறுதி கூட்டும் உடைமை.

Fortitude under privations will *tend to* restore lost fortune.

2876. கேட்பார் சொல்லைக் கேட்டுக் கெடாதே.

Be not deceived by hearsay reports.

2877. கேண்மைத் தானவா வாய்மைக் கானவா.

Thou the self-existent, thou art the powerful.

2878. கேளும் கிளையும் கெட்டோர்க்கு இல்லை.

Friends and relations are denied to the ruined.

2879. கேள்விச் செவியன் ஊரைக் கெடுத்தான்.

He who acted on hearsay destroyed the village.

2880. கேள்வி உடமை கீர்த்தியே கல்வி.

Instruction is wealth, and learning is fame.

2881. கேள்விப் பேச்சில் பாதிதான் நிசம்.

But half of what one hears is true.

2882. கேள்வி முயல்.

Endeavour to obtain instruction.

கை.

2883. கை அழுத்தமானவன் கரையேற மாட்டான்.

The miser will not prosper.

Literally will not "get ashore." The marriage of a girl is phrased in the same way.

2881. கை இல்லாதவன் கரணம் போடலாமா, கால் இல்லாதவன் ஓடலாமா ?

Can one who has no hands turn a somersault, can one who has no feet run about ?

2885. கை உண்டாவது கற்றவர்க்கு ஆமே.

It is the learned that have hands.

2886. கை ஊன்றிக் கரணம் போடவேண்டும்.

One has to fix his hands *on the ground* before he makes a somersault.

2887. கை காய்த்தாற் கமுகு காய்க்கும்.

If the palm of the hand becomes callous *by drawing water*, the areca will bear.

2888. கைக்கு எட்டினது வாய்க்கு எட்டவில்லை.

That which reaches the hand does not *always* reach the mouth.

2889. கைக்கோளனுக்குக் காற்புண்ணும் நாய்க்குத் தலைப்புண்ணும் போல.

Like a sore on the leg of a weaver, and one on the head of a dog.

2890. கை தப்பிக் கண்ணிலே பட்டாற் கையைத் தறித்துப் போடுவார்களா ?

If the hand by accident strike the eye, will they cut it off ?

2891. கை தப்பினூற் கரணம்.

If the hand missess its hold, a somersault.

2892. கை நிறைந்த பொன் இல்லா விட்டாலும் கண் நிறைந்த கணவன் இருக்கவேண்டும்.

Though not possessed of a handfull of gold, one should have a husband that fills the eye.

2893. கை பட்டால் கண்ணுடி.

Handling makes *a thing shine as* glass.

2894. கைப்பழத்தைக் கொடுத்துத் துறட்டிப் பழத்துக்கு அண்ணுந்து நிற்பானேன்?

Why give the fruit in your hand and stand gazing at that which can only be reached by a hook?

2895. கைப்பொருள் தன்னில் மெய்ப்பொருள் கல்வி.

Learning is better than riches.

2896. கைப்பொருள் இல்லா வழிப்போக்கன் கள்வர் முன் படலாம்.

The wayfaring man who has no money may encounter thieves *with impunity*.

2897. கைப்பொருள் அற்ருல் கட்டுக்கழுத்தியும் பாராள்.

If destitute of wealth, even one's own married wife will not regard *him*.

2898. கைம்பெண்டாட்டி பெற்ற கழிகடை.

The refuse that the widow has brought forth.

2899. கைம்பெண்சாதி எருமையில் கை பழக வந்தான்.

He came to the buffalo of the widow to learn to milk.

2900. கையாற் கிள்ளி எறியும் வேலைக்குக் கனத்த கோடாலி வேண்டுமோ?

Is a heavy axe required for a work that may be easily effected by the hand?

2901. கையாற் கிழிக்கும் பனங்கிழங்கிற்கு ஆப்பும் வல்லீட்டுக்குற் றியும் ஏன் ?

Why a wedge and a mallet to split the edible root of the palmyra?

2902. கையிலும் இல்லை செட்டியார் பையிலும் இல்லை காசு.

There is no money either in the hands or purse of the chetty.

2903. கையிலும் மடியிலும் இல்லாதவனைக் கள்வன் என்ன செய்ய லாம் ?

What *harm* can a thief do to him who has nothing in hand or in his belt?

2904. கையிலே மஞ்சள் ஆனால் காரியம் மஞ்சூர்தான்.

If the hands are dipped in turmeric water, the undertaking will prove successful.

2905. கையில் இருக்க நெய்யிலே கையிடுவானேன் ?

When it (the stolen thing) is in the hand, why put the hand in (hot) ghee?

2906. கையில் இல்லாதவன் கள்ளன்.

He who has nothing in hand is a thief.

2907. கையில் அரிசியும் கமண்டலத்தில் தண்ணீரும்.

Rice in the hand and water in the pot.

2908. கையில் எடுக்குமுன்னம் கோழி மோசமென்று அறியாது.

The fowl is not aware of its danger before it is caught.

2909. கையிற் புண்ணுக்குக் கண்ணாடி வேண்டுமோ ?

Is a mirror required for a sore in the hand?

2910. கையிற் பறவையை விட்டுக் காட்டுப் பறவைக்குக் கண்ணி வைக் கலாமா ?

Why let a bird in the hand go and snare one in the jungle?

2911. கையிற் பிள்ளையோடு கடலில் விழுந்தேன்.

I have fallen into the sea with the child in my arms.

2912. கையிற் குடையும் காலிற் சோடும் வேண்டும்.

One must have an umbrella in the hand, and shoes on the feet.

2913. கையிற் கிடைத்த அமுதைக் கமரில் ஊற்றலாமா?

May one pour into the cracked ground the nectar he has in his hand!

2914. கையிற் காசு வாயில் தோசை ஆமா?

Will the money in the hand become a cake in the mouth?

2915. கையும் கணக்கும் சரி.

The *money* in hand is just sufficient for current expenses.

2916. கையைப் பார் முகத்தைப் பார் என்று இருந்தாற் காரியம் ஆகுமா?

If you say look at the hands and look at the face, will the work be accomplished!

2917. கைவினை கரவேல்.

Neglect not a work in which you are skilful.

கொ.

2918. கொக்கரிப்பார்க்குச் சுவர்க்கமோ நெருப்பிற் குதிப்பார்க்குச் சுவர்க்கமோ?

Which attains swerga the mere boaster, or the self-immolated?

2919. கொக்கு இளங்குஞ்சும் கோணாத தெங்கும் கண்டது இல்லை.

No one has seen a young crane, nor a straight cocoanut tree.

2920. கொக்குக்கு உண்டா வீர சைவம்?

Does the stork observe the rules of Linga-worship!

The strict Saivite is a rigid vegetarian.

2921. கொக்குக் கூட்டத்தில் ராஜாளி விழுந்தாற்போல.

As if a falcon fell among herons.

2922. கொக்குத் தின்னப் பெருச்சாளி பாய்ந்தாற்போல.

As if a bandycoote rushed on to prey on a stork.

2923. கொக்குக்குத் தெரியுமா கோழிக்குஞ்சைக் கொண்டுபோக?

Does the crane know how to carry away a chicken?

2924. கொக்கென்று நினைத்தாயோ கொங்கணு?

O devotee, did you mistake *me* for a stork?

2925. கொங்கிலே குறுணி விற்கிறது, இங்கு என்னத்திற்கு.

Why remain here when grain sells cheap in the Kongu country.

2926. கொசுகின் முதுகிலே பிளவை வந்ததுபோல.

As a carbuncle appeared on the back of a mosquito.

2927. கொசுகிலே குறுணி பால் கறக்கலாமா?

Can you draw from a mosquito a kuruni of milk?

2928. கொசுகிலே பிளவை அதிலே நீரழிவு, அறுக்கிறது எங்கே அட்டை விடுகிறது எங்கே?

A mosquito suffering from a carbuncle, has also diabetes: where shall we put in the lancet, and how apply leeches?

2929. கொசுகே கொசுகே தலை முழுகு நான் மாட்டேன் சனிக்கிழமை.

O mosquito, mosquito, bathe your head; I will not, it is Saturday.

2930. கொசுகைப் பொருட்டாய் எண்ணிக் கருடன் எதிர்த்தாற்போல.

As if a hawk assailed a mosquito imagining it to be a rival.

2931. கொசுகை வடிகட்டி ஒட்டகத்தை விழுங்குகிறதா?

What! do you strain out a gnat and swallow a camel?

2932. கொசுகை வடிப்பார், அசுகைப்படுவார்.

Those who strain out gnats are *naturally* suspected.

2933. கொச்சிக்குப் போனவன் செய்தியைப் பார், தன் குருவை விற்றவன் செய்தியைப் பார்.

See the result of his having gone to Cochin, and of one who betrayed his Guru.

2934. கொஞ்சத்தில் இருக்கிறதா குரங்கு மிளகுநீர் குடிக்கிறது?

What, is it a small thing for a monkey to drink pepper water?

2935. கொஞ்சத்தில் உண்மை இல்லாதவன் கோடியிலும் இருக்கமாட்டான்.

Not one even of ten millions is unfaithful in a little thing.

2936. கொடிகள் அருகான மரத்திலே படரும்.

Creepers spread over the trees that grow near them.

2937. கொடிக்குக் காய் கனத்திருக்குமா?

Is its fruit burdensome to the creeper?

2938. கொடி சுற்றிப் பெண் பிறந்தால் கோத்திரத்திற்கு ஆகாது.

It is an evil omen to a tribe for a girl to be born with her navel-string round *the body*.

2939. கொடுக்கிறான் பழனியாண்டி, தின்கிறான் சுப்பனாண்டி.

Palaniándi gives and Subbanándi eats.

2940. கொடுக்க மாட்டாதவன் கூத்தைப் பழித்தான்.

He who was not disposed to contribute to the drama spoke disparagingly of it.

2941. கொடுக்கிறதையும் கொடுத்துக் குஷ்டரோகி காலில் விழுவானேன்?

Whilst bestowing gifts why fall prostrate at the feet of a leper?

2942. கொடுக்காத இடையன் சினையாட்டைக் காட்டினதுபோல.

As a niggardly shepherd pointed to a sheep that was with young.

2943. கொடுங்கோல் மன்னன் ஆளும் நாட்டிற் கடும்புலி வாழும் காடு நன்று.

A jungle inhabited by fierce tigers is better than a country ruled by a cruel tyrant.

2944. கொடுங்கோல் அரசன்கீழ் குடியிருக்கல் ஆகாது.

It is not good to live under a tyrant king.

2945. கொடுத்ததைக் கேட்டால் அடுத்து வரும் பகை.

If that which has been given be demanded hatred ensues.

2946. கொடுத்தவனைப் புகழ்வார் கொடாதவனை இகழ்வார்.

They praise the liberal, but reproach the niggard.

2947. கொடுத்தவன் அப்பன் கொடாதவன் சப்பன்.

The liberal are fathers, niggards are useless.

2948. கொடுத்ததைக் கொடுக்கும் குறளிப் பிசாசு.

The dwarf demon returns only that which had been given to it.

Jugglery is generally attributed by the common people to the power of a dwarf demon which, retaining the materials entrusted to it, gives them one by one to the juggler as he may want them.

2949. கொடுத்தவருக்கு எல்லாம் உண்டு கொடாதவருக்கு ஒன்றும் இல்லை.

The liberal have all things, the niggardly nothing.

2950. கொடுத்து உறவுகொள், கோளன் என்று இரேல்.

Be liberal and friendly, avoid being called a talebearer.

2951. கொடுப்பாரைத் தடுக்காதே.

Do not check the liberal.

2952. கொடுமை அற்றவன் கடுமை அற்றவன்.

The kind-hearted is yielding.

2953. கொடும் பாவி ஆனாலும் கொண்ட மாமியார் வேண்டும்.

However cruel a mother-in-law may be, she is nevertheless desirable.

2954. கொட்டிக்கிழங்கு வெட்டுகிறவளுக்குக் கோயிலில் வந்து ஆடத் தெரியுமா?

Can the woman who digs up roots dance before a temple *idol?*

2955. கொட்டிக் கொட்டி அளந்தாலும் குறுணி பதக்கு ஆகாது.

Though measured again and again, a kuruni will not become a pathakku.

2956. கொட்டினால் தேள் கொட்டா விட்டாற் பிள்ளைப்பூச்சியா?

If it stings it is scorpion, if it does not sting is it only a gryllus?

2957. கொண்டவன் சீறினல் கண்டவனுக்கு எல்லாம் இளக்காரம்.
If despised by her husband, all will slight her.

2958. கொண்டவனுடைய பலத்தைக் கண்டால் குப்பைமேடு ஏறிச் சண்டை செய்வாள்.
If she finds out the strength of her husband, she will get on the rubbish heap and fight.

2959. கொண்டார் முனியிற் கண்டார் முனிவர்.
If husbands treat *their wives* angrily, others will do so too.

2960. கொண்டு குலம் பேசுகிறதா?
Do you speak lightly of a family into which you have chosen to marry!

2961. கொண்டைக்குப் பூ சூடிச் சண்டைக்கு நிற்கிறது.
To stand up to quarrel with a chaplet of flowers on the tresses.

2962. கொண்டைக்குப் பூ சூடுகிறதா தாடிக்குப் பூ சூடுகிறதா?
Are flowers for the tresses, or for the beard?

2963. கொண்டோர் எல்லாம் பெண்டீர் அல்ல.
All that are betrothed are not *real* wives.

2964. கொய்சகத்தில் கொள்ளி வைத்துக்கொண்டதுபோல.
Like keeping a firebrand in the border of her own cloth.

2965. கொல்லன் தெருவில் ஊசி விலைபோமா?
Can needles be sold in a street of smiths?

2966. கொல்லன் எளிமை கண்டு குரங்கு காலுக்குப் பூண் கட்டச் சொன்னதாம்.
It is said that a monkey seeing the weakness of a blacksmith urged him to adorn his legs with rings.

2967. கொல்லன் பிணம் விறைத்தாற்போல.
As the smith's corpse became stiff.

2968. கொல்லுகிறதும் சோறு பிழைப்பிக்கிறதும் சோறு.
Rice kills and it makes alive.

2969. கொல்லைக் காட்டு நரி பல்லைக் காட்டினதுபோல.

Like a wild jackal showing his teeth.

2970. கொல்லைக் காட்டில் நரியைக் குடிவைத்துக்கொண்டதுபோல்.

Like encouraging jackals in a field.

2971. கொல்லைக்குப் பல்லி குடிக்குச் சகுனி.

He is a palli plant,-*Bachnera Asiatica*-to a garden, and a Saguni to a family.

Both are injurious.

2972. கொல்லையில் குற்றியை அடைந்த புல்லு உழவர் உழுபடைக்குக் கெடுமோ?

Will the ploughshare destroy the grass at the foot of scarecrows in the field?

2973. கொல்லை பாழானலும் குருவிக்கு இரை பஞ்சமா?

Are small birds famished because the fields lie waste?

2974. கொழுக்கட்டைக்குத் தலையும் இல்லை குடியனுக்கு முறையும் இல்லை.

The steamed cake has no head, nor has a drunkard sense to regard the rules of relationship.

2975. கொழுக்கட்டைக்குத் தலையும் இல்லைக் காலும் இல்லை, குறவருக்கு நெறியும் இல்லை முறையும் இல்லை.

The kolukkattai has neither head nor foot, foresters are neither virtuous nor mannerly.

2976. கொழுத்தவன் கைக்கு இளைத்தவன் துரும்பு.

He who is thin is a mere straw to him who is fat.

2977. கொள் என்றால் வாயைத் திறக்கிறது, கடிவாளம் என்றால் வாயை மூடுகிறதா?

What! opening the mouth when one says gram, and covering it when one says bridle!

2978. கொள்வாரும் இல்லைக் கொடுப்பாரும் இல்லை.

There are neither buyers nor sellers.

2979. கொள்ளி கொண்டு தலை சொறிகிறதா?

Do you scratch your head with a firebrand?

2980. கொள்ளிக்கு எதிர் போனாலும், வெள்ளிக்கு எதிர் போகல் ஆகாது.

Though you may encounter a firebrand, you must not appear before the planet Venus.

2981. கொள்ளிக் கட்டையால் சுட்டால் கொப்பளிக்குமென்று வாழைப்பழம் கொண்டு வடுவடுவாய்ச் சுடுகிறாய்.

Because burning with a firebrand will produce blisters, you are branding me with a plantain fruit.

2982. கொள்ளும்வரையில் கொண்டாட்டம் கொண்டபிறகு திண்டாட்டம்.

Great pleasure till attained, great misery afterwards.

2983. கொள்ளைக்குப் போனாலும் கூட்டு ஆகாது.

Even when going to plunder association is bad.

2984. கொள்ளைக்கும் ஊழிக்கும் தப்பு.

Escape from plunder and pestilence.

2985. கொற்றவன் தன்னிலும் கற்றவன் மிக்கோன்.

The learned are more than kings.

2986. கொன்றாற் பாவம் தின்றால் தீரும்,

The sin arising from killing is expiated by eating the flesh so killed.

கோ.

2987. கோடாலிக்காம்பு குலத்துக்கு ஈனம்.

The handle of the axe is the enemy of its kind.

2988. கோடி சீமானும் கோவண ஆண்டியும் சரியா?

Are the wealthy and mendicants on a par!

2989. கோடி சீமான் துணியவேண்டும், அல்லது கோவண ஆண்டி துணியவேண்டும்.

An attempt is to be made either by the wealthy, or by a beggar that has only a span-long cloth.

2990. கோடி தனம் இருந்தாலும் குணம் இல்லா மங்கையை மணம் முடிக்கல் ஆகாது.

It is not good to marry a girl, no matter how great her wealth, if her natural temper is exceptionable.

2991. கோடீசுவரன் ஆகவேண்டுமோ, அல்லது லக்ஷாதிபதி ஆகவேண்டுமோ?

Which is to be preferred as a possession, ten millions, or a hundred thousand?

2992. கோடை இடி இடித்தாற்போல.

As it thundered in summer.

2993. கோட் சொல்பவனைக் கொடும் தேள் என நினை.

Treat him who carries tales, as a scorpion.

2994. கோட் சொல்லும் வாய் காற்றுடன் நெருப்பு.

The mouth of the slanderer is as fire exposed to the wind.

2995. கோட்டானை மடியிற் கட்டிக்கொண்டதுபோல.

Like concealing an ominous owl in the lap.

2996. கோட்டுச் சம்பா ஆக்கிவைத்தால் போட்டுச் சாப்பிட வருவார்கள்.

If samba rice is boiled, they will come and eat.

2997. கோட்டையில் பெண் பிறந்தாலும் போட்ட எழுத்துப் போகுமா?

Will destiny be averted because the female was born in a fort?

2998. கோட்டைக்குள்ளே குத்தும் வெட்டுமா?

Can a great battle be fought in a fort?

2999. கோணக் கொம்பு ஏறி என்ன குதிரை ஏறி என்ன வீணர்க்கும் கீர்த்திக்கும் வெகு தூரம்.

Whether they mount a palanquin or a horse, the distance between the vain and reputation is very great.

3000. கோணி கொண்டது எருது சுமந்தது.

That which the sack contained the buffalo carried.

3001. கோணிக் கோணிக் கோடி கொடுப்பதிலும் கோணாமற் காணி கொடுப்பது நல்லது.

It is better to bestow a small gift freely than lacs with a wry face.

3002. கோத்திரம் அறிந்து பெண் கொடு, பாத்திரம் அறிந்து பிச்சை இடு.

Having ascertained the character of the family give your daughter *in marriage*, and knowing the worthiness *of the applicant* give alms.

3003. கோத்திரவீனன் சாத்திரம் பார்ப்பான்.

One of low birth consults a fortune-teller.

3004. கோபம் இல்லாத துரையும் சம்பளம் இல்லாத சேவகனும்.

A master without anger, a servant without wages.

3005. கோபம் பாபம், நித்திரைச் சத்துரு.

Anger is sin, sleep is an enemy.

3006. கோபம் சண்டாளம்.

Anger *ends in* cruelty.

3007. கோபம் அற்றுற் குரோதம் அறும்.

When anger ceases, revenge ceases.

3008. கோபம் உள்ள இடத்தில் குணம் உண்டு.

Where there is anger, there may be excellent qualities.

3009. கோபி குதிரைமேல் கடிவாளம் இல்லான்.

The irascible is like a man on horseback without a bridle.

3010. கோபுரம் தாங்கிபோல் நடக்கிறான்.

He walks as if supporting a tower.

3011. கோபுரம் தாங்கிய பூதம்போல் சுமக்கிறான்.

He carries like a goblin that bears a tower.

3012. கோமுட்டிப் புத்திக்கு மோசம் இல்லை.

The foresight of a komutti-*merchant*-never fails.

3013. கோயிலையும் குளத்தையும் அடுத்து இருக்கவேண்டும்.

One should reside near a temple and a tank.

3014. கோயில் இல்லா ஊரிலே குடியிருக்கலாமா?

May one dwell in a village in which there is no temple?

3015. கோயில் மணியம் என்று கூப்பிட்டால் போதும்.

It is enough to be called the manager of the temple.

3016. கோயிற் பூனை தேவருக்கு அஞ்சுமா?

Will the temple cat reverence the deity?

3017. கோயிற் பூனைக்குப் பயம் ஏன்?

Why should a temple cat fear?

3018. கோரக்கர் வைத்தியம் குணத்துக்கு ஏற்குமா?

Will the medical work by Korakkar assist one to find out the symptoms of disease?

3019. கோரை குடியைக் கெடுக்கும்.

Course grass is ruinous to the cultivator.

3020. கோரைக் கிழங்கு ஒருவேளைக்கு உதவும்.

Even the root of the korai grass will be of use sometime or other.

3021. கோல் ஆடக் குரங்கு ஆடும், அதுபோல மனம் ஆடும்.

As the staff moves the monkey moves, in like manner the mind moves.

3022. கோல் இழந்த குருடன்போல.

Like a blind man who has lost his staff.

3023. கோல் எடுத்த பிள்ளை குருட்டுப்பிள்ளை.
The child that handles a stick is *in danger of becoming* blind.

3024. கோழிக்கு அழகு செங்கோல் முறைமை.
A sceptre of justice is the beauty of royalty.

3025. கோழி அடிக்கிறதற்குக் குறுந்தடி வேண்டுமோ?
Is a club needed to kill a fowl?

3026. கோழி களவுபோக ஆடு வெட்டிப் பொங்கல் இடுகிறதா?
Do you attempt to recover a stolen fowl by sacrificial offerings?

3027. கோழி கூவி விடிகிறதா நாய் குலைத்து விடிகிறதா?
Does the day dawn at the crowing of a cock, or at the barking of a dog?

3028. கோழிக்குஞ்சுக்குப் பால் கொடுத்ததுபோல.
As one fed a chicken with milk.

3029. கோழிக் காய்ச்சலும் குண்டுணி காய்ச்சலும் விடாது.
The fever of fowls and the jealousy of a spiteful woman have no remedy.

3030. கோழிக்கறி என்றதும் கொண்டாடிக் கொண்டதும் கீரைத்தண்டாணம் அடா சுப்பா கீரைத்தண்டாணம் அடா.
All that ado about the fowl curry, Subba, ends in a mess of greens.

3031. கோழி சிறகால் குஞ்சுகளைக் காப்பதுபோல.
As a hen keeps her chickens under her wings.

3032. கோழி திருடியும் கூட அழுகிறாள்.
Having herself stolen the fowl she weeps *with the owner on account of its loss.*

3033. கோழி தின்ற கள்ளனும் கூட நின்று உலாவுகிறான்.
The thief who has stolen the fowl, walks about *with the owner in search of it.*

3034. கோழி போனதும் அல்லாமல் குரலும் போச்சுது.
Not only is the fowl gone, but her voice also is gone *by calling it.*

3035. கோழி மிதித்துக் குஞ்சு முடம் ஆகுமா?

Will a chicken become lame if the mother hen treads on it?

3036. கோழி முடத்துக்குக் கடா வெட்டிப் பலி இட்டதுபோல்.

Like sacrificing a sheep for the recovery of a lame fowl.

3037. கோழி முட்டையில் மயிர் பிடுங்கலாமா?

Can hair be plucked off a hen's egg?

3038. கோழியைக் கேட்டோ ஆணம் காய்ச்சுகிறது?

Is the fowl to be consulted when it is to be prepared for the table?

3039. கோளுக்கு முந்தேன் கூழுக்குப் பிந்தேன்.

Be not first at slander nor last at meals.

3040. கோளும் சொல்லிக் கும்பிடுவானேன்?

Why professions of respect regarding one about whom you are always telling tales?

கௌ.

3041. கௌசிகத்து ஒளியில் எவர்க்கும் ஒளிரும்.

Near the candle-stick it will be clear to all.

3042. கௌவை உடையார் காலைத் தொடு.

Touch the feet of those with whom you have aught to do.

3043. கௌவை கருதேன்.

Be mindful of your business.

3044. கௌவைச் சொல்லில் எவர்க்கும் பகை.

Abusive words will create enmity.

3045. கௌவைப்பட்டால் காயத்தில் ஒரு முழம் நீளுமா?

Can anxiety add length to one's body?

3046. கௌவையதில்லான் திவ்விய சொல்லான்.

He who has no concern will not say any thing favourable.

ந.

3047. நப்பன் பிறந்தது வெள்ளிமலை, நாயி பிறந்தது பொன்மலை.

My father was born in a silver mountain, and my mother was born in a golden mountain.

3048. நப்போல் வளை.

Bend yourself like the letter ந-*be humble.*

ச.

3049. சகதியிலே கல்லை விட்டு எறிந்தால் தன் துணி என்றும் அசலார் துணி என்றும் பாராது.

If one throws stones into mud, his own cloth and those of others will be spattered.

3050. சகலன் உறவில் சாண்கொடி பஞ்சமா?

Is there such a dearth of span-long-creepers that you are obliged to stay at your sister's husband's house?

3051. சகலமும் கற்றவன்றன்னைச் சார்ந்திரு.

Associate with a person who is versed in every thing.

3052. சகல தேசத்து வார்த்தையும் கற்றுக்கொள்ளுகிறதே யாவருக்கும் நல்லது.

To study the different dialects of each country is useful to all.

3053. சகோதரன் உள்ளவன் படைக்கு அஞ்சான்.

He who has a brother does not fear to fight.

3054. சக்குச் சக்கு என்று பாக்குத் தின்பான் சபைமெச்ச, வீட்டிலே வந்து கடைவாயை நக்குவான் பெண்டுகள் மெய்ச்ச.

When out he chews betel to attract public notice, when he returns home he licks the corners of his mouth to secure the admiration of women.

3055. சங்கனும் புங்கனும் சந்நியாசிக்கு உதவியா?

Are fools and blockheads of service to the religious mendicant?

3056. சங்கிலே வார்த்தால் தீர்த்தம், சட்டியிலே வார்த்தால் தண்ணீர்.

If poured into a conch, water becomes sacred, if into a chatty, it is what it is.

3057. சங்கு ஆயிரம் கொண்டு காசிக்குப் போனாலும் தன் பாவம் தன்னோடே.

Though one carries a thousand conchs to Benares, his sin sticks to him.

3058. சங்கு வாயும் ஆண்டி வாயும்.

The mouth of the conch, the mouth of the religious mendicant.

3059. சங்கோசம் விட்டால் சங்கையும் இல்லை.

When deprived of modesty, there will be no *sense of* honour.

3060. சடைத் தம்பிரான் சாற்றுக்கு அழுகிறானும், லிங்கம் பஞ்ச அமிர்தத்திற்கு அழுகிறதாம்.

It is said that the religious mendicant with matted hair cries for pepper water, and the linga *he worships* cries for the five delicacies, viz., milk, curds, ghee, sugar and honey.

3061. சடைத் தம்பிரான் சாதம் என்கிறபோது மொட்டைத் தம்பிரானுக்கு மோர் எங்கே கிடைக்கும்.

When a religious mendicant with matted hair finds it difficult to obtain rice, where will the bald headed obtain butter milk.

3062. சடைத்தம்பிரான் தவிட்டுக்கு அழுகிறபோது லிங்கம் பரமானந்தத்துக்கு அழுகிறதா?

When a religious mendicant is crying for bran, will the linga ask for delicacies?

3063. சடையைப் பிடித்து இழுத்தால் சந்நியாசி கிட்டவருவான்.

If dragged by his matted hair, the religious mendicant may be brought near one.

3064. சட்டி சுட்டதும் கை விட்டதும்.

The chatty burnt, the hand left it.

3065. சட்டுவம் கறிச்சுவை அறியுமோ?

Can a ladle appreciate the flavour of curry?

3066. சணப்பன் வீட்டுக் கோழி, தானே விலங்கு பூட்டிக்கொண்டது போல.

As a flax-dresser's fowl fettered itself.

3067. சணம் பித்தம் சணம் வாதம்.

One moment he is bilious and the next rheumatic.

3068. சண்டமாருதத்திற்கு எதிர்ப்பட்ட சருகுபோல.

Like dry leaves before a strong wind.

3069. சண்டிக்கு ஏற்ற மிண்டன்.

A stubborn *person* well suited to the self-willed.

3070. சண்டை முகத்திலே உறவா?

Is relationship recognised in a battle field?

3071. சண்ணி அண்ணுமலை என்று பெயர் இடுவாள்.

She will call him Annamalai the gormandizer.

3072. சதகோடி சங்கத்திலே மொட்டைத் தாதனைக் கண்டாயா என்கிறதுபோல.

Like asking one in a crowd, if the bald headed devotee has been seen.

3073. சதுரக்கள்ளியில் அகில் உண்டாகும்.

The eaglewood-*acquilla* grows with the prickly pear.

3074. சதைக் கண்டு கத்தி நாடவேண்டும்.

The *surgeon's* knife must be judiciously applied.

3075. சதை இல்லாமற் கத்தி நாடுமா?

Will the knife operate where there is no flesh?

3076. சதை உள்ள இடத்திலே கத்தி நாடும்.

The *surgeon's* knife seeks the fleshy parts.

3077. சத்த மேகங்களும் கூடி நெருப்பு மழை பெய்தாற்போல.

As if seven clouds simultaneously rained fire.

3078. சத்திரத்துக் கூழுக்கு நாயக்கர் அப்பணையா?

Is the order of the Naidu required in order to procure gruel at the choultry?

3079. சத்திரத்துப் பாட்டுக்குத் திருப்பாட்டு மேலா?

Is a divine hymn superior to that sung in a choultry?

3080. சத்திரத்திலே போசனம், மடத்திலே நித்திரை.

Eating in a choultry and sleeping in a monastery.

3081. சத்தியத்திலே சாமி சாட்சி என்கிற சத்தியம் பெரிது.

To say God is the witness *of what one testifies*, is the highest of all forms of oath.

3082. சத்தியத்திற்கு இல்லாத பிள்ளை துக்கப்பட்டப்போது அழப் போகிறதா?

Will the child that has no regard for truth go to weep with one when in sorrow?

3083. சத்தியம் நன்னிலை, சாவைத் தினம் நினை.

Truthfulness is the best condition, daily think of death.

3084. சத்தியமே வெல்லும் அசத்தியமே கொல்லும்.

Truth prevails, falsehood kills.

3085. சத்தியமே கொல்லும் சத்தியமே வெல்லும்.

Truth kills *falsehood*, truth prevails.

3086. சத்திய வாசகன் சமஸ்த சற்குணன்.

The truthful man has all other virtues.

3087. சத்திரத்துச் சாப்பாட்டுக்குத் தலத்து ஐயங்கார் அப்பணையோ?

To eat rice at the choultry, is the permission of the head brahman necessary?

3088. சத்துக்கள் ஓடி சத்துக்கள் சேர்வார், சந்தனத்தோடு கருப்பூரம் சேரும்.

The powerful associate with the powerful, sandal paste mixes with camphor.

3089. சத்துருக்களையும் சித்தமாய் நேசி.

Love even your enemies heartily.

3090. சத்துரு பொறுமை தனக்கே தண்டனை.

An enemy's envy is his own punishment.

3091. சந்திரனைப்பார்த்து நாய் குலைத்தாற்போல.

As a dog barked at the moon.

3092. சந்திரன் சண்டாளன் வீட்டிலும் பிரகாசிக்கிறான்.

The moon shines even in the house of the outcast.

3093. சந்தையில் அடிபட்டவனுக்குச் சாட்சி ஆர்?

Who is the witness of him that has been flogged in the bazaar?

3094. சந்தைக் கூட்டம் பொம்மல் ஆட்டம்.

A crowd of people in a market-place is *like* a puppet-show.

3095. சந்தைக்கு வந்தவர்கள் துணை ஆவாரா?

Will those who frequent the same market aid *as friends*?

3096. சந்நியாசி வீடு திண்ணையிலே.

The pial-*open verandah*-is the home of the ascetic.

3097. சந்நியாசி பயணம் திண்ணை விட்டுக் குதிப்பதுதான்.

The pilgrimage of the mendicant is to jump off a pial.

3098. சந்நியாசிக்குப் பழைய குணம் போகாது.

The old temper of the ascetic will not leave him.

3099. சந்நியாசி கோவணத்துக்கு இச்சித்துச் சமுசாரம் மேலிட்டது.

As an ascetic became a householder when he coveted a cloth.

3100. சந்நியாசியைக் கடித்த நாய்க்குப் பின்னாலே நரகமாம் சந்நியாசிக்கு முன்னாலே மரணம்.

They say that the dog that bites an ascetic will go to hell eventually; the ascetic will die before.

3101. சந்நியாசியை நிந்தித்தவனுக்குப் பின்னாலே நரகமாம்.

It is said that hell awaits him who reproaches an ascetic.

3102. சந்நியாசிக்கும் சாதிமானம் போகாது.

Even an ascetic feels proud of *his* caste.

3103. சபைக்கோழை ஆகாது.

Timidity before an assembly is bad.

3104. சபையிலே நக்கீரன் அரசிலே விற்சேரன்.

In the assembly of the learned he is a nakkíran-*a sage*, in a royal council a chèran-*a king skilled in archery*.

3105. சப்பாணிக்கு நொண்டி சண்டப்பிரசண்டம்.

A lame man is a hero before a cripple.

3106. சமண சந்நியாசிக்கும் வண்ணானுக்கும் சம்பந்தம் என்ன?

What has a naked mendicant to do with a washerman?

3107. சமயம் வாய்த்தால் நமனையும் பலகாரம் செய்வான்.

When opportunity offers he may eat even Yama as a cake.

3108. சமயம் வாய்த்தால் களவு செய்வான்.

He will steal if opportunity offer.

3109. சமர்த்தனுக்கு ஏதும் பெரிதல்ல.

Nothing is too great for a clever man.

3110. சமர்த்திலே குண்டு பாயுமா?

Do cannon balls fly with intelligent force?

3111. சமர்த்தி என்ன பெற்றாள் சட்டிச்சோறு தின்னப் பெற்றாள்.

What did the clever matron get, she got rice in chatty fulls.

3112. சமர்த்துள்ள சேவகனுக்குப் புல்லும் ஆயுதமாம்.

Even a blade of grass is a weapon in the hands of a skilful warrior.

3113. சமர்த்துள்ள சேவகனுக்கு வாள் பழுதானாலும் கேடு இல்லை.

Though his sword is injured, the skilful soldier suffers no loss.

3114. சமர்த்துக்குச் சனியன்.

In power, *equal to* Saturn.

3115. சமிக்கை அறியாதவன் சதுரன் அல்ல.

He who cannot comprehend a sign is not clever.

3116. சமிக்கை காட்டிச் சண்டைக்கு அழைக்கிறான்.

He is inciting to fight by shewing signs.

3117. சமுசாரக்குட்டு வெளி இட்டால் நஷ்டம்.

It is a loss for family broils to get abroad.

3118. சமுத்திரமும் சாக்கடையும் சரியா?

Are the ocean and a ditch alike?

3119. சமுத்திரத்திலே ஏற்றம் போட்டதுபோல் இருக்கிறது.

Like planting a picotta on the sea-*side*.

3120. சமுத்திரத்திற்கும் சாண் குண்டுக்கும் எம்மாத்திரம்?

How vast the difference between the ocean and a span-wide ditch?

3121. சமுத்திர வன்கணன் சண்டாளன்.

A deep treacherous fellow is a wretch.

3122. சமையல் வீட்டிலே நாய் நுழைந்தாற்போல.

As a dog crept into the cooking room.

3123. சமையல் வீட்டிலே முயல் தானே வந்ததுபோல.

As a hare of its own accord came into the cook room.

3124. சம்பத்தும் விபத்தும் கூடவே இருக்கிறது.

Abundance and straitness are closely allied.

3125. சம்பளம் அரைப்பணமானாலும் சலுகை இருக்கவேண்டும்.

Though one's income is only half a fanam, an air of respectability must be preserved.

3126. சம்பளம் அரைப்பணமானாலும் நம்பினவரைக் காக்கவேண்டும்.

Though one's hire is but half a fanam dependents must be protected.

3127. சம்பன்ன கிரகஸ்தன் வந்தான், செம்பு தவலையை உள்ளே வை.

Our rich and honest neighbour is come, remove the copper vessels out of sight.

3128. சயினன் கையில் அகப்பட்ட சீலைப்பேன் போல.

Like lice in a cloth that had been in the hands of a Jaina mendicant.

3129. சரக்குக் கண்ட இடத்திலே பிள்ளை பெறுகிறது.

Bringing forth a child where the required conveniences are found.

3130. சரக்குக் கண்ட இடத்திலே பிள்ளைக்கு அவிழ்தம் கொடுக்க நினைக்கிறது போல.

Like intending to give medicine to her child where conveniences are found.

3131. சருகு அரிக்க நேரம் அன்றி குளிர் காய நேரம் இல்லை.

He has only just time to collect dry leaves; he has not time to warm himself.

3132. சருக்கரை என்றால் தித்திக்குமோ?

Is the word sugar sweet?

3133. சருக்கரைப் பந்தலிலே தேன்மாரி பெய்ததுபோல.

A honey-fall in a sugar pandal-*an open shed.*

3134. சருக்கரையும் மணலும் சரியா?

Are sugar and sand alike?

3135. சருக்கரையும் மாவும் சரியா?

Are sugar and flour alike?

3136. சருக்கரை தின்று பித்தம் போனால், கைப்பு மருந்து ஏன் தின்னவேண்டும்.

If bile can be removed by taking sugar, why take bitter medicine.

3137. சலம் நுழையாத இடத்தில் எண்ணெயும், எண்ணெய் நுழையாத இடத்தில் புகையும் நுழையும்.

Oil gets in where water cannot, and smoke enters where oil cannot.

3138. சல்லிய சாரத்தியம் செய்யாதே.

Drive not the coach by magic.

3139. சவாதிலே மயிர் வாங்கினதுபோல.

Like pulling out hair from civet.

3140. சளி பிடித்ததோ சனியன் பிடித்ததோ?

Are you suffering from catarrh, or has Saturn seized you!

3141. சளுக்கன் தனக்குச் சத்துரு, சவளிக்காரனுக்கு மித்துரு.

The fop is his own enemy, but a friend of the cloth merchant.

3142. சற்சனர் உறவு சருக்கரைப் பாகு போல.

The friendship of the good is agreeable as molases of sugar.

3143. சனத்தோடு சனம் சேரும் சந்தனத்தோடு கர்ப்பூரம் சேரும்.

Men associate with men, camphor and sandal paste blend together.

3144. சனப் பலம் இருந்தால் மனப் பலம் வரும்.

When a man has a strong party he will act with decision.

3145. சனி நீராடு.

Bathe on Saturdays.

This proverb is regarded by the people among whom I have lived as equivalent to a command, and is obeyed as such, by observing Saturday as a bathing day.

Some interpreters put another construction upon it, making the word, usually translated Saturday, a verb, meaning to spring as water, and render it, bathe in springing, fresh, cool water. In some parts of the country, men bathe on Saturday, while women bathe on Friday. or Monday. To bathe on Tuesday is regarded as fatal if repeated again and again.

3146. சனி பிடித்ததோ சனியன் பிடித்ததோ?

Has Saturn seized, or one possessed by him, seized?

3147. சனிப் பிணம் தனிப்போகாது.

A Saturday corpse goes not alone.

To avert evil as far as possible, it is not uncommon, with reference to the prevailing opinion expressed in this proverb, for Hindus to bury a fowl when a death happens on Saturday. A Native friend informed me that he saw a chicken put into the coffin of a deceased Native Christian. I have been informed that on some occasions the fowl is carried alive to the place of incremation or burial, the people scattering various kinds of grain on the way. In this case the fowl is killed near the corpse and its blood is sprinkled upon it.

3148. சனியனை விலைக்கு வாங்கினதுபோல.

Like procuring Saturn at a price.

3149. சனியன் பிடித்தவளுக்குச் சந்தையிலும் கந்தை அகப்படாது.

A woman seized by Saturn will not find a rag even in the market.

3150. சனியன் பிடித்தவளுக்குச் சந்தையிற் போனாலும் புருஷன் அகப்படமாட்டான்.

A woman seized by Saturn will not obtain a husband though she may go to the market.

3151. சன்னதம் குலைந்தால் விருப்பு எங்கே?

If oracular power has failed, whence the ground of exultation?

சா.

3152. சாகத்திரிகிருன் சண்டாளன் சாப்பிட்டுத்திரிகிருன் பெண்டாளன்.

The vicious wanders about famished; the householder is in the enjoyment of plenty.

3153. சாகத் துணிந்தவனுக்குச் சமுத்திரம் நீச்சு.

The sea is but swimming depth to one that braves death.

3154. சாகப் பொழுதன்றி வேகப் பொழுது இல்லே.

There is time to die, but none to be consumed by fire.

3155. சாகிறவரையில் வைத்தியன் விடான், செத்தாலும் விடான் பஞ்சாங்கக்காரன்.

A physician will not leave one till death, an astrologer will not leave even then.

3156. சாகிறவரையில் மருந்து கொடுக்கவேண்டும்.

Medicine must be given to the very last.

3157. சாகிறதுபோல் இருந்து வியாதி தீருகிறதும் உண்டு.

They who were apparently dying have recovered.

3158. சாகிறவனுக்குச் சமுத்திரம் முழங்கால் ஆழம்.

The ocean is but knee-deep to him who is dying.

3159. சாகிறவன் சனியனுக்குப் பயப்படுவானு?

Will one who is dying be afraid of Saturn!

3160. சாகிற வரைக்கும் சஞ்சலமானுல் போகிறது எந்தக் காலமோ?

If anxieties attend us till death, when will they be removed?

3161. சாகிறவரைகும் சங்கடமானுல் வாழுகிறது எக்காலம்?

If we are to be troubled till death, when shall we enjoy prosperity!

3162. சாகிற நாய் வீரத்தைக் காட்டினுற்போல.

As a dying dog showed courage.

3163. சாகிற நாய் வீட்டின்மேல் ஏறினாற்போல.

As a dog about to die ascended the house top.

For a dog to get on the roof of a house is regarded as an omen of some great calamity, and therefore the dog should be destroyed.

3164. சாக்கடைச் சேறு என்றாலும் சக்களத்தி என்றாலும் சரி.

The mud of a ditch and a rival wife are alike.

3165. சாக்கடைப புழு என்றாலும் சக்களத்தியை வெல்லப்போகாது.

Though *despicable* as a worm in a ditch, it is difficult to overcome a rival wife.

3166. சாக்கடைப் புழுவிற்குப் போக்கிடம் எங்கே?

Where shall the worm that was born and bred in the ditch go?

3167. சாக்கும் போக்கும் ஏற்காது ஐயன் முன்.

Excuses are of no avail before God.

3168. சாக்கோ நோக்கோ அம்மையார் வாக்கோ?

Is it *the result of* excuse, *planetary* influence or the matron's word?

3169. சாடிககு மூடி வாய்த்ததுபோல.

As a lid fitted to a jar.

3170. சாட்சிக்காரன் காலில் விழுவதிலும் சண்டைக்காரன் காலில் விழலாம்.

Better to fall at the feet of an opponent than at the feet of witnesses.

3171. சாட்டு இல்லாமற் சாவு இல்லை.

No death occurs without an ostensible cause.

3172. சாட்டை இல்லாப் பம்பரம் ஆட்டிவைக்க வல்லவன்.

He is able to spin a top without a string.

3173. சாட்டை இல்லாப் பம்பரம் ஆடுமோ?

Will a top spin without a string?

3174. சாணான் எச்சில் கருப்புக்கட்டி, சர்க்கரை வெல்லம் உழவன் எச்சில.

Course sugar is defiled by a chanan's-*tree climber*-saliva, and sugar by that of a ploughman.

3175. சாணிக் குழியும் சமுத்திரமும் சரியாய் நினைக்கலாமா ?

Can you imagine the ocean and a dung-pit to be of equal *magnitude* ?

3176. சாணிச் சட்டியும் சருவச்சட்டியும் சரியாமா ?

Can you compare a cow-dung chatty with a brass pan ?

3177. சாணியும் சவாதும் சரியாகுமா ?

Are dung and civet alike ?

3178. சாணுக்குச் சாண் வித்தியாசம்.

It differs at every span-length.

3179. சாணோ வயிறு சரீரம் எல்லாம் வயிறோ ?

Is your stomach a span-long, or are you all stomach ?

3180. சாண் ஏற முழம் சறுக்குகிறது.

To advance a span, and slide back a cubit.

3181. சாண் கற் கழுவினால் முழச்சேறு.

In every span of pavement I wash, there is a cubit of deep mud.

3182. சாண் குருவிக்கு முழ வாலாம்.

It is said that a span-long bird has a cubit-long tail.

3183. சாண் சடைக்கு முழக் கயிறா ?

What, a cubit of string for a span of matted hair ?

3184. சாண் செடியிலே முழத் தடி வெட்டலாமா ?

Can a stick a cubit long be cut in a span-long copse ?

3185. சாண் பறைக்கு முழத் தடி.

A cubit stick for a span drum.

3186. சாண் பாம்பானாலும் முழத் தடி வேண்டும்.

Although the snake may be only a span-long, a stick a cubit long is required to kill it.

3187. சாண் பிள்ளையோ ஆண்பிள்ளையோ?

Is it a span-long child or a *bold* man?

3188. சாதி அந்த புத்தி குலம் அந்த ஆசாரம்.

Ideas suited to caste, manners suited to rank.

3189. சாதிமானமும் சமயமானமும் சந்நியாசிக்கு உண்டு.

Caste and religious distinctions obtain even among religious mendicants.

3190. சாது மிரண்டாற் காடு இடம் கொள்ளாது.

When the meek are enraged, even a forest will not hold *their wrath*.

3191. சாதுரியப் பூனை மீன் இருக்கப் புளியங்காயைக் கொண்டு போய்விட்டது.

The cunning cat left the fish, and carried off the tamarind fruit.

3192. சாதுரியப் பூனை தயிர் இருக்கச் சட்டியை நக்கிற்று.

The artful cat left the curds, and licked the chatty.

3193. சாத்தானி குடுமிக்கும் சந்நியாசி பூணூலுக்கும் முடி போடுகிறாய்.

Thou art tying the knot of Sattàni's hair to the sacred thread of the religious mendicant.

3194. சாஸ்திரம் பொய் என்றால் கிரகணத்தைப் பார்.

If the shasters are false, look at the eclipse.

3195. சாஸ்திரம் பார்த்துப் பெண்ணைக் கொள் கோத்திரம் பார்த்துப் பெண்ணைக் கொடு.

Take a wife after consulting the shasters and give a daughter in marriage after ascertaining the character of the family into which she is going.

3196. சாஸ்திரம் பாராத வீடு சமுத்திரம், பார்த்த வீடு தரித்திரம்.
The family that regards not the shasters has an ocean *of wealth*, whilst the one that regards them is in poverty.

3197. சாஸ்திரம் கற்றவன் தானே காசு.
He who is learned in the shasters is himself money.

3198. சாந்துப்பெட்டி பாம்புப்பெட்டி ஆயிற்று.
The scent box has become a box of snakes.

3199. சாப்பிள்ளை பெற்றுத் தாலாட்டவா?
Can you dandle a still-born child?

3200. சாப்பிள்ளை பெறுவதிலும் தான்சாவது நலம்.
Better die than bear a still-born child.

3201. சாப்பிள்ளை பெற்றவளுக்குச் சந்தோஷம் வருமா?
Will she have joy who has borne a still-born child?

3202. சாப்பிள்ளை பெற்றாலும் மருத்துவிச்சிகூலி தப்பாது.
Though a still-born child is brought forth, there is no escape from the midwife's fee.

3203. சாமி வரம் கொடுத்தாலும் பூசாரி இடம் கொடுக்கமாட்டான்.
Though God may bestow the gift, the priest will not suffer you to enjoy it.

3204 சாமைப்பயிரும் சக்கிலியப்பெண்ணும் சமைந்தால் தெரியும்.
Sámi rice when boiled, and a girl of the shoe-maker class when matured, appear to advantage.

3205. சாம்பலைக் கிண்டிக் கோழி தானே விலங்கு இட்டுக்கொண்டதுபோல,
As a hen fettered herself whilst scratching a rubbish heap.

3206 சாம்பலைத் தின்று வெண்ணெய்யைப் பூசினதுபோல.
Like rubbing the mouth with butter after having eaten ashes.

3207. சாராயத்தை வார்த்துப் பூராயத்தைக் கேளு.
Pour in liquor and draw out the secret.

3208. சாலாய் வனைந்தால் என்ன சட்டியாய் வனைந்தால் என்ன?

What matters it whether the potter makes a large or a small chatty !

3209. சாலோடே தண்ணீர் சாய்த்துக் குடித்தாலும் தாய் வார்க்கும் தண்ணீர் தாகம் தெளியும்.

Though one may drink water out of a large pot, the water that one's mother pours out allays one's thirst.

3210. சாவாமற் கற்பதே கலவி, பிறர் இடத்தில் ஏகாமல் உண்பதே ஊண்.

That is learning which teaches us to escape death, and that is food which is obtained without dependence on others.

3211. சான்றோர் இல்லாச் சபை குறவர் சேரி.

A community without learned men is a hamlet of mountaineers.

சி.

3212. சிங்கம் பசித்தால் தேரையைப் பிடிக்குமா ?

When hungry will a lion prey on frogs !

3213. சிங்கம் பசிக்கு ஆனையையே தேடிக் கொல்லும்; அதுபோல், பெரியோர் அக்கறைப்பட்டால் பெரிய காரியத்தையே செய்வார்கள்.

When lions are hungry they go in search of elephants to prey on, in like manner, when the great are reduced to poverty they achieve great things-*to relieve their wants.*

3214. சிங்கத்துக்குப் பங்கம் இல்லை.

A lion knows no danger.

3215. சிட்டுக்குருவிமேல் பனங்காய் வைத்ததுபோல்.

As a palmyra fruit was placed on a small bird.

3216. சிட்டுக்குருவிமேல் பிரம்மாஸ்திரம் தொடுக்கலாமா ?

Do you discharge heavy arrows at small birds ?

3217. சிணுக்கு எல்லாம் பிணக்குக்கு இடம்.

Hesitancy and delay lead to disagreeables.

3218. சிதம்பரத்திலே பிறந்த பிள்ளைக்குத் திருவெம்பாவை கற்றுக் கொடுக்கவேண்டுமா ?

Is it necessary to teach venba-*holy verses*-to a child born and brought up at Chilambaram?

3219. சிதம்பர சக்கரத்தைப் பேய் பார்ப்பதுபோல.

As a demon looks at the circle of Chilambaram.

This proverb refers most likely to magical diagrams generally.

3220. சித்தன் போக்குச் சிவன் போக்கு ஆண்டி போக்கு அதே போக்கு.

The manner of Chittan is like the manner of Siva, the manner of religious mendicant is like itself.

3221. சித்திரை மாதத்திற் செல்வன் பிறந்தால் சீரும் சிறப்பும் கெடும்.

If a son is born in Chittirai-*April*-the state and reputation of the family will be ruined.

3222. சித்திரை மாதத்திற் பிறந்த சீர் கேடனும் இல்லை, ஐப்பசி மாதத்திற் பிறந்த அதிஷ்டவானும் இல்லை.

None born in Chittirai-*April*-is unfortunate, none born in Aipasi-*October*-is fortunate.

3223. சித்தி பெருத மருந்தும் மருந்தோ பெற்றுப் படையாத பிள்ளையும் பிள்ளையோ ?

Is that medicine which does not take effect, is that which *a woman* has not brought forth and reared, her child?

3224. சித்திராங்கி பொம்மா சின்ன வெங்கிட்டம்மா.

Little Vengadamma is a hypocritical lady.

3225. சிநேகம் செய்யுமுன் ஆராய்தல் செய், செய்தபின் ஐயப்படாதே.

Form friendships after due deliberation, having done so do not give place to doubt.

3226. சிநேகம் செய்தபின் சோதி தெளிந்தபின் நம்பு.

On forming friendship try it, and on being convinced of its sincerity, rely on it.

3227. சிந்த அறுந்துபோகிற மூக்கு எந்தமட்டும் இருக்கும்?

How long will the nose last that breaks off on blowing!

3228. சிப்பியிலே விழுந்த மழைத்துளி முத்தாகும்; அதுபோல, நல்லவர்க்குச் செய்த உதவி நிலைநிற்கும்.

A rain drop that falls on an oyster-shell will become a pearl, so a benefit conferred on the virtuous will endure.

3229. சிம்பிலே வளையாதது தடித்தால் வளையப்போகிறதா?

If when it is a twig it cannot be bent, will it bend when it has become a large tree?

3230. சிரைத்தால் மொட்டை வைத்தாற் குடுமி.

If shaven-bald, if kept, kudumi

3231 சிரைத்தால் கூலி சேவித்தாற் சம்பளம்.

If you shave, hire, if you serve, wages.

3232. சில்வானக் கள்ளி செலவு அறிவாளா?

Is a woman who pilfers aware what expense means!

3233. சிவபூசை வேளையில் கரடி புகுந்ததுபோல.

As a bear entered at the time of Siva puja.

3234. சிவபூசை வேளையிலே கரடியை விட்டு ஆட்டுகிறதா?

Is a dancing bear produced at the time of Siva puja!

3235. சிவலிங்கத்தின்மேல் எலி.

A rat on Siva linga.

3236. சிவியானுக்கு அடிமைப்பட்டால் காவவும் வேண்டும் சுமக்கவும் வேண்டும்.

If subject to a palanquin bearer, one must bear both palanquins and burdens.

3237. சிறகிலும் மெல்லிசாய்ப் பொன் அடிப்பான்.
He will beat out gold even thinner than a feather.

3238. சிறகு இல்லாப் பறவைபோல.
Like a bird without wings.

3239. சிறகு பறிகொடுத்த பறவைபோல.
Like a bird deprived of its wings.

3240. சிறியாரோடு இணங்காதே சேம்புக்குப் புளி விட்டு மசியாதே.
Do not associate with the mean, do not macerate chambu greens with acid.

3241. சிறியார்க்கு இனியதைக் காட்டாதே சேம்புக்குப் புளி விட்டு ஆக்காதே.
Do not offer sweets to children, nor mix acid with chambu greens.

3242. சிறியோர் செய்த சிறு பிழை எல்லாம் பெரியோர் ஆனவர் பொறுப்பது கடனே.
It is the duty of the great to forgive the faults of inferiors.

3243. சிறியோர் எல்லாம் சிறியர் அல்ல.
All that are little are not inferiors.

3244. சிறுகச் சிறுகத் தின்றால் மலையையும் தின்னலாம்.
If you eat little by little, you may consume a mountain.

3245. சிறுகக் கட்டிப் பெருக வாழு.
Build a small house, and live thriftily.

3246. சிறுக விதைத்தவன் சிறுக அறுப்பான்.
He that sows little will reap little.

3247. சிறு குழிகள் கொஞ்சம் தண்ணீரால் நிரம்பும்.
But little water is required to fill a small hole.

3248. சிறு குழந்தை இல்லாத வீடும் வீடு அல்ல, சீரகம் இட்டு ஆக்காத கறியும் கறி அல்ல.
A house without an infant is not a house, nor is a curry without seerakam-*cummin*-a real curry.

3249. சிறுக்கி சின்னப் பணம், சிறுக்கி கொண்டை மூன்று பணம்.
The young lady is worth a small fanam, and she requires three fanams to adorn her tresses.

3250. சிறு துரும்பும் பல்லுக் குத்த உதவும்.
Even a small fibre may serve as a tooth-pick.

3251. சிறுத்திருக்கையில் வளையாதது பருத்திருக்கையில் வளையுமா?
Will that which did not bend when small, do so when it becomes large?

3252. சிறு பிள்ளை செய்த வேளாண்மை விளைந்தாலும் வீடு வந்து சேராது.
The harvest of little children will never be housed.

3253. சிறு பெண் கட்டின சிற்றுடையா?
Is it a small cloth worn by a little girl?

3254. சிறுபோது படியாத கல்வி அழுக்குச் சேலையில் சாயம் ஏற்றினதுபோல.
Learning not acquired in early life is like a cloth dyed when dirty

3255. சிறு மீன் எல்லாம் பெரு மீனுக்கு இரை.
Little fish are the prey of great fish.

3256. சிறுமையும் பெருமையும் தான் தர வரும்.
The lower and higher stations in society, *are the result* of each one's exertions.

3257. சிறு ரூபத்தை உடைய பேரும் அரும்பொருளைச் செய்வார்; அதுபோல, சிறு விதை ஆகிய ஆலமரம் பெரு நிழலைக் கொடுக்கும்.
Those who are of inferior stature may accomplish difficult things: the seed of the banyan is small, but the tree affords a large shade.

3258. சிறு வயதில் கல்வி சிலையில் எழுத்து.
Learning acquired in youth, is an inscription on stone.

3259. சிறைச்சாலைக்கு அறை இல்லை, தேவடியாளுக்கு முறை இல்லை.
A prison has no apartments, a temple girl observes no relationships.

3260. சிற்ருள் எட்டு ஆளுக்குச் சரி.

A young hireling is equal to eight grown up servants.

3261. சிற்ருத்தை பிள்ளையும் பிள்ளையோ செத்தையிற் பல்லியும் பல்லியோ ?

Is the child of a maternal aunt a child ? Is a lizard on the rubbish heap a lizard ?

This refers to a species whose chirp is not regarded in augury.

3262. சிற்றின்பம் எண்ணூர் மற்றின்பம் கண்டவர்.

Those who have tasted real happiness, will not regard inferior pleasures.

3263. சிற்றுணர்வோர் என்றும சிலுசிலுப்பர்.

Persons of little learning are always talkative.

3264. சிற்றூரிலே பாரக்கூத்தா ?

Will an extended comedy be performed in a mere hamlet ?

3265. சிற்றூண் இனிது.

Moderate refection is sweet.

3266. சிற்றெறும்பைச் சிற்றெறும்பும் கட்டெறும்பைக் கட்டெறும்பும் தேடும்.

Little ants seek small ants; big ants seek great ones.

3267. சினத்தால் அறுத்த மூக்குச் சிரித்தால் வருமா ?

Will the nose cut off in anger, be restored by laughing ?

3268. சினத்தாலும் சீர் அழியப் பேசாதே.

Dot not speak reproachfully though provoked.

3269. சின்ன சின்னப் பேச்சுச் சிங்காரப்பேச்சு வன்னவன்னப் பேச்சு மெத்த வழக்கமான பேச்சு.

Short expressions, beautiful expressions; florid expressions, colloqual expressions.

சீ.

3270. சீ என்ற வீட்டிலே பேயும் நுழையாது.

Even a demon will not enter a house that has pooh-poohed him.

3271. சீ என்ற காட்டிலே செந்நாய் சேருமா?

Will a dog enter a jungle that is looked down upon?

3272. சீக்கிர புத்தி பல ஈனம்.

A hasty mind is feeble.

3273. சீட்டாளுக்கு ஒரு மூட்டாள் செருப்புத் தூக்கிக்கு ஒரு அடப்பக்காரனு?

Does a letter-carrier, require a helper, or a shoeboy employ one to carry his betel pouch?

3274. சீதை பிறக்கவும் இலங்கை அழியவும்.

The birth of Sita was the ruin of Lanka.

3275. சீபுரத்துப் பள்ளி செத்தும் கெட்டான் இருந்தும் கெட்டான்.

A Palli of Sîpuram is ruined when dead, as well as when alive.

3276. சீப்பு எடுத்து ஒளித்தால் கலியாணம் நிற்குமா?

If the comb be concealed, will the marriage ceremony be delayed?

3277. சீரங்கத்துக் காகமானாலும் கோவிந்தம் பாடுமா?

Though hatched at Shrirangam, will a crow sing the praises of Govinda?

3278. சீரங்கத்துக்குப் போகிறவன், வழியிலே பாரியைப் பறிகொடுத்ததுபோல.

As a man lost his wife on his way to Shrirangam.

3279. சீரங்கத்தில் உலக்கை கொடுத்ததுபோல.

As a pestle was given at Shrirangam.

3280. சீரங்கத்துக்குப் போகிறவன் ஓரியை மாராப்புப் போட்டதுபோல.

As one going to the shrine of Shrirangam concealed an old jackal in his bosom.

3281. சீர் அற்றூர் கையிற் செம்பொன் விலை பெரு.
Fine gold in the hands of the unthrifty is of no value.

3282. சீரியர் கெட்டாலும் சீரியரே.
Though reduced to poverty, the virtuous are still virtuous.

3283. சீரியர்க்கு அன்பு செய்.
Be kind to the virtuous.

3284. சீலைப்பாய் ஈழம் போய்ச் சீனி சருக்கரை கட்டுமா?
Will a ragged cloth go to Ceylon to tie up sugar?

3285. சீவனம் செய்ய நாவினை விற்கேல்.
Do not make merchandise of your tongue for a livelihood.

3286. சீவன் போனல் கீர்த்தியும் போமா?
Will fame go when life goes?

3287. சீனி என்று எழுதி நக்கினல் இனிக்குமா?
If you write the word sugar and lick it, will it taste sweet?

சு.

3288. சுக துக்கம் சுழல் சக்கரம்.
Grief and joy are a revolving wheel.

3289. சுகத்துக்குப் பின் துக்கம் துக்கத்துக்குப் பின் சுகம்.
After joy grief, after grief joy.

3290. சுகத்தையாவது பெறவேண்டும் தவத்தையாவது பெறவேண்டும்.
We must either enjoy happiness or practise austerities.

3291. சுகத்தைப் பெற்றதும் அல்ல தவத்தைப் பெற்றதும் அல்ல.
He has neither obtained happiness, nor the fruit of austerities.

3292. சுகம் வந்தால் சந்தோஷப்பட்டுத் துன்பம் வந்தால் பின்வாங்குவானேன்?
If when prosperous you rejoiced, why draw back when adversity supervenes?

3293. சுகவாசி உடம்பு கழுதைப் பிறப்பு.
A man of luxurious habits is an ass.

3294. சுக்கிர உதயத்தில் தாலி கட்டி, சூரிய உதயத்திற்குள் அறுத்தாள்.
She who was married when Venus rose, was denuded of her marriage symbol at sunrise.

3295. சுக்கிரீவ ஆக்கினையாய் இருக்கிறது.
It is the infliction of Sugriva.

Sugriva, a monkey, the ally of Ramachandra.

3296. சுக்கு அறியாத கஷாயம் உண்டா?
Is there any decoction without dried ginger?

3297. சுக்குத் தின்று முக்கிப் பெற்றால் தெரியும் பிள்ளை அருமை.
The preciousness of children is known to her who has eaten dried ginger and borne one.

It is common when a woman is confined, to give her a preparation of dried ginger and other spices.

3298. சுக்குக் கண்ட இடத்திலே முக்கிப் பிள்ளை பெறுவாளா?
Will she bring forth as soon as she sees the dried ginger?

3299. சுக்குக் கண்ட இடத்தில் பிள்ளை பெற்றுச் சூரிய நாராயணன் என்று பெயர் இடுவாள்.
As soon as she sees the dried ginger, she will bring forth a child, and call it Suryanarayana.

The name being the expression of her joy.

3300. சுக்கும் பாக்கும் வெட்டித் தாறேன் சுள்சுள் என்று வெயில் எறி.
Shine out brilliantly, I will give you dried ginger and arica-nut.

3301. சுங்கம் மாறினால் சுண்ணாம்பும் கிடையாது.
If taxes are heavy, even chunambu cannot be had.

3302. சுங்கமும் கூழும் இருக்கத் தடிக்கும்.
Taxes and gruel become heavier by being kept.

3303. சுடர் விளக்காயினும் தூண்டு கோல் ஒன்று வேணும்.

Though it may be a bright burning lamp, a splinter is required for raising the wick.

3304. சுடலை ஞானம் திரும்பி வருமட்டும்.

The solemn thoughts occasioned by the funeral pyre, last till each one returns home.

3305. சுடுகாடு போன பிணம் திரும்பாது.

The corpse that has gone to the place of incremation will not return.

3306. சுடுகாட்டுப் புகையைப் பார்க்கும் கொம்பேறி மூக்கன்.

The tree snake looks anxiously for the smoke of the funeral pyre.

It is said that snakes enjoy the odour of a burning body.

3307. சுடு கெண்டைக்காக ஏரியை உடைக்கலாமா?

May one burst the bund of a tank in order to get fried fish?

3308. சுட்ட கரியை நாய் புரட்டுகிறாப்போல.

As a dog rolls burning charcoal.

3309. சுட்ட சட்டி அறியுமா அப்பத்தின் சுவையை?

Does the baking pan appreciate the flavour of a cake?

3310. சுட்ட சட்டியும் சட்டுவமும் கறிச் சுவை அறியுமா?

Do the chatty and ladle know the flavour of curry?

3311. சுட்ட மண்ணும் பச்சை மண்ணும் ஒட்டுமா?

Will burnt and moist earth unite?

3312. சுண்டைக்காய் கார்ற் பணம் சுமைகூலி முக்கார்ற் பணம்.

The price of the chundakai is a quarter of a fanam, its carriage three quarters of a fanam.

3313. சுண்டைக்காய் அளவிலே, சாப்பிடுகிறது பாதியா, வைக்கிறது பாதியா?

Of the food about the size of a chundaikkai, am I to eat half and leave half?

3314. சுண்ணும்பில் இருக்கிறது சூக்ஷமீ.

The speciality or charm of-*arica-nut and betel*-is in the chunambu.

3315. சுத்த விலங்கோடு சுத்த விலங்குதான் சேரும்.

A clean beast will join a clean beast.

3316. சுத்த வீரனுக்கு உயிர் துரும்பு.

To the real hero life is a mere straw.

3317. சுமைதாங்கி சுங்கம் இறுப்பது இல்லே.

No toll at a resting block.

3318. சும்மா அறுக்கிறுய் என்னடா சொத்தைக் களாக்காயை?

Why waste your time in cutting the rotten kalákkai?

3319. சும்மா கிடக்கிற தாரையை ஊதிக் கெடுத்தான் அம்மான்.

By blowing the unused trumpet my uncle spoiled it.

3320. சும்மா கலம் சுமக்கமாட்டான் நனேந்து முக்கலம் சுமப்பான்.

In fair weather he will not carry one kalam *of grain*, in foul weather, when drenched with rain, he carries three.

3321. சும்மா போகிறவனேப் பிடிப்பானேன், இராத்திரி எல்லாம் கிடந்து பிதற்றுவான் ஏன்?

Why seize one going along, and lie groaning all the night!

3322. சும்மா இருந்தால் சோறு ஆமா வாடா சித்தா கால் ஆட்ட.

Will boiled rice come of itself! Come along Chitta, let us shake our legs.

3323. சும்மா இருந்த அம்மையாருக்கு அரைப் பணத்துத் தாலி போதாதா?

Is not a marriage symbol worth half a fanam, a gain to the matron who is worth nothing?

3324. சும்மா கிடைக்குமா சோணுசலன் பாதம்?

Can one approach the feet of Chonachalan without effort?

3325. சுய காரிய துரந்தரன் சுவாமி காரியம் வழவழ.

He who is intent about his own affairs will not mind the things of God.

3326. சுய காரிய துரந்தரன் பரகாரிய பராமுகன்.

Intent about his own affairs, he turns from others.

3327. சரிகுழல் மனது சரி நடப்பது ஆர் ?

Who can act so as to please a woman ?

3328. சுருட்டை சோறு இடும் பம்பை பால் வார்க்கும்.

Curly hair will give rice, dishevelled hair will pour out milk.

3329. சுருதி சுகானுபோகம் இரண்டும் ஒத்தால் முத்தி.

When religious precepts and physical enjoyment are in harmony, happiness is the resultant.

3330. சுருதி குரு சுகானுபவம் மூன்றும் ஒத்தது மெய்ப்பொருளாம்.

When the vedas, the priest and enjoyment meet together, there is real wealth.

3331. சுரைப் பூவுக்கும் பறைப் பாட்டுக்கும் மணம் இல்லை.

The flower of a bottle-gourd is not fragrant, the song of a pariah is not chaste.

3332. சுவருக்கும் காதுகள் உண்டு.

Even a wall may have ears.

3333. சுவரை வைத்துக்கொண்டு அல்லவோ சித்திரம் எழுதவேண்டும் ?

You must first build the wall, must you not, and then adorn it with figures ?

3334. சுவர்க்கத்திலே தோட்டியும் சரி தொண்டைமானும் சரி.

In the paradise of Indra a scavenger and a Vellala of the Tonda country are equal.

3335. சுவர்க்கத்துக்குப் போகிறபோது கக்கத்திலே மூட்டை ஆமா ?

When on your way to heaven, do you carry a bundle under your arm ?

3336. சுவர்க்கத்திலே போகிறபொழுது கக்கத்திலே ராட்டினமா ?

When on your way to heaven, do you carry a spinning-wheel under your arm ?

3337. சுவர்க்கத்திற்குப் போகிறபோது பக்கத்திலே ஒரு கூத்தியாரா?

Is one expected to take his concubine along with him to the paradise of Indra?

3338. சுவாமி வரம் கொடுத்தாலும் முன்னடியான் வரம் கொடான்.

Though God may grant a boon, the devotee in his presence will not.

3339. சுள்ளாப்பு எல்லாம் பொல்லாப்பு.

Every bitter sneer leads to evil.

3340. சுள்ளைச் சுட்டுக்கொண்டு கள்ளைக் குடிக்கிறது.

To grill dried fish and drink toddy.

3341. சுற்றத் துணியும் இல்லை நக்கத் தவிடும் இல்லை.

No cloth to wear, no bran to lick.

3342. சுற்றத்திற்கு அழகு சூழ இருத்தல்.

It is the beauty of friendship to be surrounded-*by friends.*

3343. சுற்றத்தமரைப் பற்றி இரு.

Live close by your relations.

சூ.

3344. சூடு கண்ட பூனை அடுப்படியிற் செல்லாது.

A burnt cat shuns the fire-place.

3345. சூடு மிதிக்கிற மாட்டின் வாயைக் கட்டலாமா?

Is it proper to tie the mouth of the ox that treads out the corn?

3346. சூட்சத்திலே இருக்கிறது மோட்சம்.

Important ends are attained by comparatively insignificant means.

3347. சூடசாதி சூட்சத் துல்லிபன்.

The great contriver who is inscrutable.

3348. சூதபலத்தைச் சுகமுகத்தினால் அறி.

Know the efficacy of mercury by the glow of health on the cheeks

3349. சூதனுக்கு நீதி இல்லை.

The cheat is void of justice.

3350. சூதன் கொல்லையிலேதான் மாடு மேயும்.

The ox will graze in the field of the intriguing.

3351. சூதானத்துக்கு அழிவு இல்லை.

Circumspection leads not to ruin.

3352. சூதினால் வெல்வது எளிது.

It is easy to overcome *an enemy* by intrigue.

3353. சூதும் வாதும் வேதனை செய்யும்.

Gambling and boasting end in sorrow.

3354. சூது விரும்பேல்.

Desire not gambling.

3355. சூத்திரவேதன் சாஸ்திரம் பார்ப்பான்.

A stringed brahman observes the shasters.

3356. சூத்திரப் பாவைபோல நடிக்கிறான்.

He dances like a puppet.

3357. சூரியன்கீழே தோன்றினது எல்லாம் மாயை.

All under the sun is vanity.

3358. சூரியனைக் கையால் மறைத்ததுபோல.

Like hiding the sun with the hand.

3359. சூரியனைக் கண்ட இருள்போல்.

Like darkness that has seen the sun.

3360. சூரியனைக் கண்ட பனிபோலே நீங்கும்.

It will vanish as the dew before the sun.

3361. சூரியனுக்கு முன் மின்னாம்பூச்சிபோல.

Like a fire-fly before the sun.

3362. சூரியனைக் கண்டு உலகம் விளங்கும்.

The earth is illumined by the sun.

3363. சூரியனைக் கிரகணம் பிடித்ததுபோல் உன்னைச் சனி பிடித்தது.

Saturn has seized thee as the eclipse seizes the sun.

3364. சூரியன் எழுமுன் காரியம் ஆடு.

Form your plans before sunrise.

3365. சூரியனுடைய பிரகாசத்துக்குமுன்னே மின்மினி விளங்க மாட்டாது.

Fire-flies *do not* shine in the presence of the sun.

3366. சூரியனைப் பார்த்து நாய் குலைத்ததுபோல.

As the dog barked at the sun.

3367. சூரியனைக் கல்லால் அடித்ததுபோல.

Like striking the sun with a stone.

3368. சூலாகு மீன்கள் ஒன்றை ஒன்று மோந்துகொள்ளும்.

Like chula fish kissing each other.

3369. சூலி சூலி என்று சோற்றைத் தின்று மலடிவாயில் மண்ணைப போடுகிறதா?

Do you eat up the rice yourself on the plea of pregnancy, and put earth into the mouth of the barren!

3370. சூழ ஓடியும் வாயிலாலே.

Though you run round, you will have to enter by the gate.

செ.

3371. செக்கு உலக்கையை விழுங்கினவனுக்குச் சுக்குக் கஷாயம் மருந்தாமா?

Is a decoction of dried ginger a specific for him who has swallowed the pestle of an oil press!

3372. செங்கோலுக்குமுன்னே சங்கேதமா?

Will conspiracy against a just administration avail?

3373. செங்கோல் ஓங்குவன் திரித்துவ தேவன்.

He who holds the sceptre is the triune God.

3374. செங்கோல் கோண எங்கும் கோணும்.

If the sceptre turn aside, its effect will be felt every where.

3375. செடியிலே வணங்காதது மரத்திலே வணங்கும்?

If it would not bend as a sapling, will it bend as a tree?

3376. செட்டிக்கும் மட்டிக்கும் சென்மப் பகை.

The merchant and the farmer cherish innate hatred towards each other.

3377. செட்டிக்கு வேளாண்மை சென்மப் பகை.

The merchant has a natural aversion to agriculture.

3378. செட்டி கூடிக் கெட்டான் சேணியன் பிரிந்து கெட்டான்.

The Chetty was ruined by taking a partner, the weaver by separating from one.

3379. செட்டி போன இடம் எல்லாம் வட்டம் காற் பணம்.

Wherever the merchant goes there is a discount of a quarter fanam.

3380. செட்டி பணத்தைக் குறைத்தான், சேணியன் காலைக் குறைத்தான்.

The merchant reduced the money, the weaver lessened the width *of the* cloth.

3381. செட்டி படை வெல்லுமா, சேற்றுத் தவளை கடிக்குமா?

Can merchants disperse an army, can a toad inflict a wound?

3382. செட்டி சிங்காரிக்கிறதுக்குள்ளே பட்டணம் பறிபோகிறது.

While the Chetty is adorning himself, the city is besieged.

3383. செட்டியாரோ செட்டியாரோ என்றால், சீரகம் பணஎடை முக்காற் பணம் என்கிறார்.

When I *respectfully* call him Chettiyar, he says that a fanam weight of cumin is sold for three fourths of a fanam.

3384. செட்டி வீட்டிற் பணம் இருக்கிறது, ஆலமரத்தில் பேய் இருக்கிறது.

Wealth is in the houses of merchants, demons are in banyan trees.

3385. செட்டிகள் மாடு மலை ஏறி மேயுமா?

Will the oxen of Chetties ascend and graze on the mountains?

3386. செட்டியாரே வாரும் சந்தையை ஒப்புக்கொள்ளும்.

Chettiyar, come and take charge of the bazaar.

3387. செட்டியை நீலி தொடர்ந்ததுபோல.

As Níli-*a cruel woman*-followed the Chetty.

3388. செட்டிக்கு இறுத்துப் பைக்கும் இறுத்தேன்.

I paid the Chetty and also his bag.

3389. செட்டுக்கு ஒரு தட்டு, சேவகனுக்கு ஒரு வெட்டு.

A slap for the merchant, a sword cut for the warrior.

3390. செத்த நாய் திரும்பக் கடியாது.

The dead dog will bite no more.

3391. செத்தவன் வீட்டிற் கெட்டவன் ஆர்?

Who was ever ruined in a house whose owner was dead?

3392. செத்தவன் வாயிலே மண், இருந்தவன் வாயிலே சோறு.

Earth in the mouth of the dead, and rice in the mouth of the living.

3393. செத்த மாடு புல்லுத் தின்னுமா?

Can a dead cow eat grass?

3394. செத்தவன் கண் செந்தாமரைக் கண், இருந்தவன் கண் நொள்ளைக் கண்.

The eye of the dead is a red lotus, that of the living a sightless orb.

3395. செத்தபின் எப்படிப் போனாலும் என்ன?

No matter what becomes of one after his death!

3396. செத்தவன் தலை கிழக்கே இருந்தால் என்ன மேற்கே இருந்தால் என்ன?

What matters it whether the head of a corpse be towards the east, or west?

Most Hindus, and some Native Christians even, are very particular about the position in which they lie down to sleep. The head should be towards the south. The north is the region of Yama. The west is avoided because the person so lying down may not rise again.

3397. செத்த பிணத்திற் கடை உற்றார்க்கு உதவாதவன்.

He that does not help his friends or relations is worse than a corpse.

3398. செத்த ஆடு காற்பணம் சுமைகூலி முக்காற் பணம்.

The dead sheep is worth a quarter of a fanam, and three fourths of a fanam are required to remove it.

3399. செத்த பிணத்தைச் சுற்றித் திரிந்தாற்போல.

As they walk round a corpse.

This may refer to the custom of a relative going round a corpse three times at the place of incremation.

3400. செத்தவன் பெண்சாதியை இருந்தவன் கைக்கொண்டாற் போல.

As the surviver took the wife of the deceased.

3401. செத்த பாம்பை ஆட்டுகிறான்.

He is charming a dead snake.

3402. செத்தவன் கையிலே வெற்றிலை பாக்குக் கொடுத்த சம்பந்தம்.

Like putting betel and arica-nut into the hand of the dead.

The giving of betel and nut is one of the marriage ceremonies.

3403. செத்த மாட்டை அறுக்காத கத்தி சொத்தைக் கத்தரிக்காயை அறுக்கும்.

A knife that will not cut a dead cow, will cut a blighted brinjal.

3404. செத்த பாம்பு சுற்ற வருகிறதே அத்தை நான் மாட்டேன் என்ருற்போல.

As if one should say, aunt, I will not, the dead snake comes to coil round *my leg*.

3405. செத்த பிணத்துக்கு அருகே இனிச் சாகும் பிணம் அழுகிறது.

Those who will hereafter die weep by the body of the deceased.

3406. செத்த பிணத்துக்குக் கண் ஏன், சிவசிவ ஆண்டிக்குப் பெண் ஏன்?

Why an eye to the corpse, why a wife to the Saiva mendicant?

3407. செத்தால் தெரியும் செட்டியார் வாழ்வு.

The wealth of the Chetty will be known after death.

3408. செப்படி வித்தை எப்படிச் செய்கிருன்?

How dexterously he juggles!

3409. செப்பில்லாக் குடிக்கு அப்பாப் பட்டமா?

Is the title of Appa suited to a family that possesses no brass utensils?

3410. செப்பும் பந்தும் போல.

Like a box and a ball.

3411. செம்பரம் பாக்கத்தான் பெயர் பெற்ருன் மாங்காட்டான் நீர் பெற்ருன்.

Men at Champerempákum get a name, those at Mangadoo get water.

3412. செம்பால் அடித்த காசும் கொடான்.

He will not give even a copper coin.

3413. செம்பாலைக்குக் கரும்பு ஆலை வலிது.

Black wood is stronger than red.

3414. செம்பு நடமாடக் குயவன் குடிபோகிருன்.

Copper utensils being introduced, the potter removes.

3415. செம்மறி ஆடு வெளியே ஓடத் திருட்டு ஓநாய் உள்ளே.

The sheep is without, the thievish wolf is within.

3416. செயமுள்ள மட்டும் பயம் இல்லை.

While successful he knows no fear.

3417. செய்த வினை செய்தவர்க்கு எய்திடும்.

Every man's actions will cleave to him.

3418. செய்தார்க்குச் செய்வது செத்தபிறகோ?

Is it after death that benefits are to be requited?

3419. செய்யும் தொழில் எல்லாம் சீர்தூக்கிப் பார்க்கில் நெய்யும் தொழிலுக்கு நிகர் இல்லை.

When all occupations are duly weighed, that of weaving will appear unequalled.

3420. செய்வினை திருந்தச் செய்.

Do well, what you have to do.

3421. செருப்பால் அடித்துக் குதிரைக் கொடை கொடுத்தாற்போல.

Like giving a horse in compensation, to one who has been slippered.

3422. செருப்புக்கு அச்சாரம் துரும்பு.

The earnest paid for shoes is a straw.

3423. செருப்பின் அருமை வெயிலில் தெரியும் நெருப்பின் அருமை குளிரில் தெரியும்.

The value of shoes is appreciated when the sun is hot, the value of fire is known when the weather is cold.

3424. செருப்புக்காகக் காலைத் தறிக்கிறதா?

Is the foot to be cut off to try on the shoe?

3425. செருப்புக் கொள்ளுகிறது காலுக்கோ தலைக்கோ?

Is it for the feet or head, that one buys shoes?

3426. செலவிற் குறைந்த வரவானால் சேமப்படுகிறது எப்படி?

If expenses exceed income how can one thrive?

3427. செலவு அதிகம் வரவு போதாது.

Expenses exceed the income.

3428. செய்யும் எனச்சே எனக்கு இரண்டு என்கிறது.

On my saying do it, he replies give me two.

3429. செலவு இல்லாத சிங்காரம்போல.

Like ornamentation that costs nothing.

3430. செலவோடு செலவு கந்தப் பொடிக்குக் காற் பணம்.

A quarter fanam for sweet scented powder, over and above the expenses already incurred.

3431. செல்லம் சொல்லுக்கு அஞ்சுமா?

Will a spoiled child fear rebuke?

3432. செல்லம் சறுக்குதா வாசற்படி வழுக்குதா?

Does indulgence cause you to slip, or are the door-steps slippery?

3433. செல்லப் பிள்ளை சீலே உடாதாம் பிள்ளை பெறுமட்டும்.

A spoiled child will not put on clothes till it becomes a mother.

3434. செல்லாத காசு என்றைக்கும் செல்லாது.

A coin not current is always so.

3435. செல்லும் காசுக்கு வட்டம் உண்டா?

What discount for current cash?

3436. செல்லும் செல்லாததுக்குச் செட்டியார் இருக்கிறார்.

There is a Chetty who can say whether the coin is current or not.

3437. செல்வம் பரமண்டலம் செல்லாது, எல்லா மண்டலத்தும் செல்லும்.

Wealth goes anywhither but to heaven.

3438. செல்வம் உண்டாகும் காலம், செய்கை உண்டு, வல்லமை உண்டு.

In time of prosperity there is exertion and power.

3439. செல்வம் செருக்குகின்றது காசுக்கு வழி இல்லை.

He is proud of his wealth though he has not means to obtain a cash.

3440. செல்வப்பொருள் கொடுத்தால் குறையும், கல்விப்பொருள் குறையுமோ?

On giving, wealth diminishes, will learning also so diminish ?

3441. செலவம் செருக்குகின்றது வாசற்படி வழுக்குகின்றது.

Wealth makes one proud, the door-steps are slippery.

3442. செல்வர்க்கு அழகு செழுங்கிளை தாங்குதல்.

It is an honor to the wealthy to protect their relatives.

3443. செல்வன் சொலலுக்கு அஞ்சான், வீரன் போருக்கு அஞ்சான்.

The wealthy fear no orders, the hero is not afraid of war.

3444. செல்வம் நிலையில, சேட்டன் கீழ் இரு.

Wealth is impermanent, live in subjection to a superior.

3445. செவிடன் காதில் சங்கு ஊதினதுபோல.

Like blowing a conch in the ear of the deaf.

3446. செவிடனும் குருடனும் கூத்துப் பார்த்தாற்போல.

As the deaf and the blind attended a comedy.

3447. செவிடன் பாட்டுக் கேட்ட சம்பந்தம்.

As the deaf listened to a song.

3448. செவிடு இருந்தால ஊமை இல்லையா?

If one is deaf is he not dumb also ?

3449. சென்மக் குருடனுக்குக் கண் கிடைத்ததுபோல.

As one born blind obtained his sight.

3450. சென்ற காரியத்தைப் பார்த்து வரும் காரியத்தை அறி.

Learn the future by looking at things past.

3451. சென்ற இடம் எல்லாம் சிறப்பே கல்வி.

Learning distinguishes one whithersoever he goes.

சே.

3452. சேத நினைவிற்குப் பூதம் சிரிக்கும்.

A demon laughs at malevolent thoughts.

3453. சேம்பு கொய்யச் சிற்றரிவாள் ஏன்?

Why a small sickle to gather chémbu greens?

3454. சேர இருந்தால் செடியும் பகை, தூர இருந்தால் தோட்டியும் உறவு.

If too near even a shrub-*a worthless fellow*-is an enemy, if distant even a scavenger is a friend.

3455. சேரிடம் அறிந்து சேர்.

Associate with the agreeable.

3456. சேரியும் ஊரும் செல்வமும் கல்வியும்.

A hamlet, a country, wealth and learning.

3457. சேர்க்கை வாசனையா இயற்கை வாசனையா?

Is the habit natural or acquired?

3458. சேர்ந்தவர் என்பது கூர்ந்து அறிந்தபின்.

Regard those as friends whose sincerity has been carefully tested.

3459. சேலைமேற் சேலை கட்டித் தேவரம்பை ஆடினாலும், ஓலைமேல் எழுத்தாணி ஊன்றும் பெண் ஆகாது.

Though one wear cloth upon cloth, and is able to dance like a celestial, she is not to be desired if she can press a style on a palm leaf, i. e., *if she can write.*

A strong dissuasive against female education. The proverb is nevertheless in harmony with the sentiments of the majority of Hindus who have received high education in English.

3460. சேற்றிலே புதைந்த ஆனையைக் காகமும் குட்டும்.

Even a crow will peck an elephant when it is in the mud.

3461. சேற்றிலே செங்கழுநீர் பூத்தாற்போல.

As the water-lily blossoms in mud.

3462. சேற்றிலே நாட்டிய கம்பம்போல.

Like a pole set up in mud.

3463. சேற்றிலே கிடக்கிற எருமையைத் தூக்குவான் ஏன்?

Why lift up the buffalo that wallows in the mire!

3464. சேற்றால் எடுத்த சுவர்.

A wall of mud.

3465. சேனைக்குப் பட்டமோ சேனாபதிக்குப் பட்டமோ?

Are honorary distinctions bestowed on an army, or on its leader?

சை.

3466. சைகை அறியார் சற்றும் அறியார்.

Those who cannot take a hint know nothing.

3467. சைவ முத்தையாமுதலியார்க்குச் சமைத்துப்போட வள்ளுவப் பண்டாரம்.

The cook of the vegetarian Muttaiya of the Modelly caste, is a pariah mendicant.

சொ.

3468. சொக்கனுக்குச் சட்டி அளவு.

The *size of the* chatty is enough for the Chetty's attendant.

3469. சொக்கட்டான் விளையாட்டுப் பொல்லாத சூது.

The game of draughts is ruinous.

3470. சொட்டைவாளைக் குட்டி போல.

Like the young of a chottai válai fish.

3471. சொருகிக் கிடந்த அகப்பையும் சோறு அள்ளப் புறப்பட்டது.

Even the ladle th had been cast aside as useless, is again serving out rice.

3472. சொல்லச் சொல்லப் பட்டி பெண்ணைப் பெண்ணைப் பெற்றாள்.

Though again and again forbidden, Patti-*a strumpet*-brought forth only daughters.

3473. சொல்லச் சொலல மட்டி மண்ணைத் தின்கிறான்.

Though frequently forbidden, Matti-*a fool*-eats earth.

3474. சொல்லாமல் இருக்கிறவனே பண்டிதன்.

He who is of few words is a pundit.

3475. சொல்லிச் செய்வார் சிறியோர், சொல்லாமற் செய்வார் பெரியோர், சொல்லியும் செய்யார் கயவர்.

Inferiors may keep their word, the great do a thing without promising, but the wicked act not even after making a promise.

3476. சொல்லிக் கொடுத்த சொல்லும் கட்டிக் கொடுத்த சோறும் எத்தனைநாளைக்கு?

How long will the words put into one's mouth and the rice tied up *for a journey* avail us . .

3477. சொல்லுகிறது ஒன்று செய்கிறது ஒன்று.

Saying one thing, and doing another.

3478. சொல்லுக்கும் பொருளுக்கும் எட்டாதான் சோதிக்கும் சாதிக்கும் நடுவானான்.

He whom neither language nor wealth can influence, has come between God and man.

3479. சொல்லும் சொல் ஆக்கமும் கேடும் தரும்.

A word uttered may bring wealth as well as ruin.

3480. சொல்லும் பொருளும் தோன்றும் கல்வி.

Learning is conversant with words and things.

3481. சொல் வல்லனை வெல்லல் அரிது.

It is difficult to overcome the eloquent.

3482. சொல்வளம் இல்லார் நற்கதை சொல்லில் அதுவே துர்க்கதை.

A good story badly told, soon loses its effect.

3483. சொல்வது யார்க்கும் எளிது, அரியவாம் சொல்லிய வண்ணம் செயல்.

Saying is easy, but doing is difficult.

3484. சொல்வது இலேசு செய்வது அல்லவா பிரயாசம்?

It is easy to profess, but difficult to perform, is it not!

3485. சொலவார் சொன்னாலும் கேட்பாருக்கு மதி இல்லையா?

No matter what others say, have not those who hear, sense to judge for themselves!

3486. சொறிந்து தேயாத எண்ணெயும் பரிந்து இடாத சோறும் பாழ்.

Oil applied without rubbing *the head,* and boiled rice given with ill-will, are useless.

3487. சொறியாந் தவளையும் வேட்டை ஆடுகிறதாம்.

It is said that even toads go a hunting.

3488. சொற்பேச்சையும் கேளான் சுயபுத்தியும் இல்லை.

He has no sense, he will not listen to advice.

3489. சொற்றிறம் கூறல் கற்றவர்க்கு அழகு.

It becomes the learned to explain the force of words.

3490. சொன்னதைச் சொல்லும் கிளிப்பிள்ளை.

The parrot will utter what it is taught.

3491. சொன்னதைச் சொல்லடி சுணைகெட்ட மூளி.

Say what you are told, you senseless, deformed wretch.

3492. சொன்னது இருக்கச் சுரை பிடுங்குகிறாய்.

Neglecting what you were told to do, you pull up the beans.

3493. சொன்னபடி கேட்காவிட்டால் மண்ணை வெட்டி மாப் படைப்பேன்.

If you do not do as I say, I will make an offering of earth.

Addressed to a demon when driving him out.

3194. சொன்னால் வெட்கம் அழுதால் துக்கம்.

It is shameful to tell it, and painful to weep over it.

3195. சொன்னாற் பெரும்பிழை சோறென்றாற் பட்டினி.

As regards rice, he is famishing, but it would be a fault to say so.

சோ.

3196. சோம்பல் இல்லாத் தொழில் சோதனை இல்லாத் துணை.

Untiring service is reliable help.

3197. சோம்பலுக்குத் தொடர்ச்சி வறுமை, சும்மா இருத்தலுக்குச் தொடர்ச்சி மூடம்.

Indolence leads to poverty, inaction to ignorance.

3198. சோம்பலே சோறு இன்மைக்குப் பிதா.

Indolence is the parent of want.

3199. சோம்பேறிக்கு வாழைப்பழம் தோலோடே.

The sluggard eats his plantain, skin and all.

3500. சோழமண்டலமோ சூதுமண்டலமோ?

Is it the realm of Chola, or the realm of deceit?

3501. சோளியைப் பிடுங்கிக் கொண்டா பிச்சை போடுகிறது?

Is it after snatching away his bag one gives alms *to a beggar*?

3502. சோறு என்ன செய்யும் சொன்னவண்ணம் செய்யும்.

What can rice effect? whatever you like.

3503. சோறு சிந்தினால் பொறுக்கலாம், சுணை சிந்தினால் பொறுக்கலாமா?

If rice be spilt it may be picked up, but if one loses his sense of honour can he recover that?

3504. சோறு சிந்தினால் பொறுக்கலாம் நீர் சிந்தினால் பொறுக்கலாமா?

If rice be spilt it may be picked up, can water?

3505. சோற்றிலே கிடக்கிற கல் எடுக்கமாட்டாதவன் முகலைக்கல் எடுப்பானா?

Can he who would not pick a stone out of the rice, lift up the stone lintel of a temple gateway?

3506. சோற்றில் இருந்த கல் எடாதவன் சேற்றில் கிடக்கிற எருமையைத் தூக்குவானா?

Can he who will not pick a stone out of his rice, lift a buffalo out of the mud?

3507. சோற்றுக்கு வீங்கின நாயே மாட்டுப் பொங்கலுக்கு வாயே.

Thou dog, greedy of boiled rice, come to the *January* ox-festival.

3508. சோற்றுக்கு இல்லாத பூசணிக்காய் பந்தலிலே கட்டி ஆடவோ?

Of what use is a pumpkin which will not be available for food, is it to be suspended to a pandal swing?

3509. சோற்றுச் சுவையோடு தொத்தி வந்த கொள்ளை.

The blind that came drawn by the smell of rice.

3510. சோற்றுக்குக் கேடும் பூமிக்குப் பாரமுமாய் இருக்கிறான்.

He is a waste of rice, he is a burden to the earth.

3511. சோற்றைக் கொடுத்துக் கழுத்தை அறுக்கிறதா?

What, to cut one's throat after giving rice?

சௌ.

3512. சௌரியம் பேசேல்.

Boast not of your strength.

ஞா.

3513. ஞாபகம் இல்லை என்று எவனும் சொல்வான், ஞானம் இல்லை என்று எவனும் சொல்லான்.

Any may say I have forgotten, none says I have no sense.

3514. ஞாயப் பிரமாணம் இல்லாத குருக்கள் வீண்.
Teachers without moral rules are vain.

3515. ஞானமும் கல்வியும் நாழி அரிசியிலே.
Wisdom and learning are contained in a measure of rice.

3516. ஞானம் எல்லாம் ஒரு மூட்டை, உலகம் எல்லாம் ஒரு கோட்டை.
Collective wisdom is a bundle, and the whole world a fort.

3517. ஞானம் இல்லாச் சேயர்கள் ஆவின் கன்றிலும் அதிகமல்ல.
Ignorant children, are not better than calves.

3518. ஞானம் தனத்தையும் கனத்தையும் கொடுக்கும்.
Wisdom gives wealth and honour.

3519 ஞானிக்கு இல்லை இன்பமும் துன்பமும்.
The wise are not affected by pleasure and pain.

3520. ஞானிக்கும் மூடனுக்கும் சங்காத்தம் இல்லை.
A wise man and a fool do not associate.

த.

3521. தகப்பன் வெட்டின கிணறென்று தலைகீழாய் விழுவார்களா?
Will they fall headlong into the well because their father dug it!

3522. தகப்பனுக்கு இட்டது தலைச்சனுக்கு.
What was given to the father, will be entailed on his first-born.

3523. தகப்பனுக்குக் கட்டக் கோவணத்துக்கு வழி இல்லை, மகன் தஞ்சாவூர் மட்டும் நடைப்பாவாடை போடச் சொன்னானாம்.
Whilst the father is without waist-cloth, his son, it is said, asked him to spread cloth on the ground to walk on as far as Tanjore.

3524. தகப்பனைக் கொன்ற பாவம மாமியார் வீட்டில் ஆறு மாசம் இருந்தால் போகும்.
The murder of a father may be expiated by residing for six months in the house of one's mother-in-law.

The Hindus account it disgraceful in a son-in-law to live in the house of a mother-in-law at her expense. Bhárata when enumerating the various sins he would be guilty of, if he coveted the throne of his elder brother Ráma, mentions this as one.

3525. தகப்பன் பட்டம் பிள்ளைக்கு அல்லவா?

The title of the father descends to the son, does it not!

3526. தகப்பன் தேடக் கர்த்தன், பிள்ளை அழிக்கக் கர்த்தன்.

The father acquires wealth, the son destroys it.

3527. தகப்பன் பட்டத்தைப் பிள்ளைக்குக் கட்டினால் தகப்பன் சாஷ்டாங்கதண்டம் செய்யவேண்டும் அல்லவோ?

If the title of the father descend to the son, the father must prostrate himself before him, must he not!

3528. தக்கோன் எனத் திரி.

So live as to be reputed a deserving man.

3529. தங்கமுடி சூட்டினாலும் தங்கள் குணம் விடார் கசடர்.

Though crowned with gold, the base will not abandon their natural dispositions.

3530. தங்கச் சூரிக்கத்தியென்று அறுத்துக் கொள்ளலாமா?

May one cut himself with a knife because it is made of gold!

3531. தங்கத்தைக் குவிக்கிறேன் என்றாலும், தன் புத்தி விடுகிறது இல்லை.

Though I promised to give a heap of gold, he persisted in his own ideas.

3532. தங்கத்தூள் அகப்பட்டாலும் செங்கற்றூள் அகப்படாது.

Though gold-dust is procurable, brick-dust is not.

3533. தங்கத்தை உருக்கி விட்டதுபோல.

As fine gold was melted and poured out.

3534. தங்கம் தரையிலே தவிடு பானையிலே.

Gold scattered on the ground, bran in an earthen vessel.

3535. தங்கம் புடத்தில் வைக்கப்பட்டாலும் தன் நிறம் போகாது.
Though gold is put into the fire to be refined, its hue is not lost.

3536. தங்கம் தரையிலே, ஒரு காசு நாரத்தங்காய் உறியிலே.
Gold scattered on the ground, and a cash-worth of lemons placed on the swinging tray.

3537. தங்கம் எல்லாம் தவிட்டுக்கு மாறுகிறது.
To exchange all *his* gold for bran.

3538. தங்கைச்சி பிள்ளை தன் பிள்ளையானால் தவத்துக்குப் போவான் ஏன்?
If the child of his sister be his, why go to perform penance?

3539. தசை கண்டு கத்தி நாடவேண்டும்.
The knife should be applied where there is flesh.

3540. தச்சன் பெண்சாதி தரையிலே, கொல்லன் பெண்சாதி கொம்பிலே.
The wife of the carpenter is on the floor, and the wife of the smith is on the branch of a tree.

3541. தச்சன் பெண்சாதி அறுத்தால் என்ன, கொல்லன் பெண்சாதி கூலிக்கு அறுத்தால் என்ன?
What if the wife of the carpenter is bereaved of her husband? what if the wife of the smith is deprived of her hire?

3542. தச்சன் வீட்டிலே தயிரும் எச்சன் வீட்டிலே சோறும் எப்படிச்சேரும்?
Will curds be found in the house of a carpenter, or boiled rice in that of a niggard?

3543. தச்சன் வீட்டில் பாற்சோற்றை நத்தாதே வெள்ளாளா.
O! Vellala do not long for the rice and milk in a carpenter's house.

3544. தச்சன் அடித்த தலைவாசல் எல்லாம் உச்சியில் இடிக்க உலாவித் திரிந்தேன்.
I walked about in all the entrances where the carpenter had put up lintels, knocking my head against them.

3545. தஞ்சம் என்று வந்தவனை வஞ்சிக்கல் ஆகாது.

To cheat one that has come for protection is bad.

3546. தடவிப் பிடிக்க மயிர் இல்லை அவள் பெயர் கூந்தலழகி.

Not a hair to be felt; *yet* her name is the tressed beauty.

3547. தடவிப் பிடிக்கக் கை இல்லை அவன் பெயர் சௌரியப் பெருமாள்.

He has no hand to feel and seize *any thing,* his name is the notoriously strong.

3548. தடி எடுத்தால் எல்லாம் வேட்டைக்காரர்.

All are huntsmen who take up sticks.

3549. தடிக்கு மிஞ்சின மிடா.

A water pot too strong to be broken by a stick.

3550. தடிக்கு அஞ்சிக் குரங்கு ஆடினதுபோல.

Like a monkey dancing for fear of the stick.

3551. தடிக்கு மிகுந்த மிடாவானால் என்ன செய்யலாம்?

If the pot is too strong for the stick, what can be done?

3552. தட்டான் தாய்ப் பொன்னிலும் மாப்பொன் எடுப்பான்.

A goldsmith will pilfer the gold-dust even of his mother.

3553. தட்டானும் செட்டியும் கண் சட்டியும் பானையும் மண்.

The goldsmith and the Chetty have each two eyes, the chatty and the pot are of earth.

3554. தட்டானும் செட்டியும்போல.

Like the goldsmith and the merchant.

3555. தட்டானைச் சேர்ந்த தறுதலை.

The fool-hardy who associated with the goldsmith.

3556. தட்டான் தாழப் பறந்தால் தப்பாமல் மழை வரும்.

If a butterfly flies low, it is sure to rain.

3557. தட்டாரச் சித்து தறிச்சித்து வண்ணாரச் சித்துக்கு வராது.

The tricks of a goldsmith and of a weaver, are not equal to those of a washerman.

3558. தட்டானிடத்தில் இருக்கிறது, அல்லது கும்பிடுசெட்டியில் இருக்கிறது.

It is either in the possession of the goldsmith, or in his vessel.

3559. தட்டிப் பேசுவார் இல்லாவிட்டால் தம்பி சண்டப் பிரசண்டன்.

When there is none to contradict tambi is very fierce.

Tambi, a younger brother, is often used in a friendly way, when addressing a junior.

3560. தணிந்த வில்லுத்தான் தைக்கும்.

It is the bent bow that will shoot.

3561. தண்டிலே போனால் இரண்டில் ஒன்று.

When you go into the army, one of two-*life or death.*

3562. தண்டிற் போனால் இரட்டிப்புச் சம்பளம்.

Double remuneration to those who go into the army.

3563. தண்டு ஒன்று இலே மூன்று ஆரை அடா மந்திரி.

The arai plant, O minister, has one stalk and three leaves.

3564. தண்ணீரில் இருக்கிற தவளை குடித்ததைக் கண்டதார் குடியாததைக் கண்டதார்?

Who knows whether the frog in the water drinks, or that it does not drink!

3565. தண்ணீர் வெந்நீரானாலும் நெருப்பை அவிக்கும்.

Although cold water be heated, it will quench fire.

3566. தண்ணீரிலே விளைந்த உப்புத் தண்ணீரிலே கரையவேண்டும்.

Salt produced from water, must be dissolved in water.

3567. தண்ணீரில் அமுங்கின முட்டை உப்புப் போடக் கிளம்பும்.

An egg submerged in water will float, if salt be put upon it.

3568. தண்ணீரும் மூன்று பிழை பொறுக்கும்.

Even water will forgive a fault three times.

Referring to a person who rises to the surface three times after having fallen into deep water.

3569. தண்ணீர் குடித்த வயிறும் தென்னோலை இட்ட காதும் சரி.

The belly that has taken in water, and the aperture in the ear that has received a circlet of ola, are alike-*each enlarges as pressed.*

3570. தண்ணீரையும் தாயையும் பழிக்கலாமா?

May one abuse water, or one's mother!

3571. தண்ணீரில் இறங்கினால் தவளை கடிக்கும் என்கிறான்.

He says that the frog will bite him, if he descends into the water.

3572. தண்ணீரில் இருக்கிற தவளையைத் தரையில் எடுத்து விட்டது போல.

Like turning out, on dry land, a frog that lives in the water.

3573. தண்ணீரில் இறந்தவரிலும் சாராயத்தில் இறந்தவர் அதிகம்.

The number drowned in alcohol, is in excess of those drowned in water.

3574. தண்ணீரும் கோபமும் தாழ்ந்த இடத்திலே.

Water and anger *seek* low-*persons or places.*

3575. தத்துவம் அறிந்தவன் தவசி.

He is an ascetic who understands the philosophy of nature.

3576. தந்தை சொல் மிக்க மந்திரம் இல்லை.

There is no mantra superior to one's father's advice.

3577. தப்பில் ஆனவனை உப்பிலே போடு.

Put the illegitimate in salt.

3578. தப்பை அடித்தவன் தாதன், சங்கு ஊதினவன் ஆண்டி.

A Vaishnava mendicant beats a drum, and a Saiva mendicant blows a conch.

3579. தமிழுக்கு இருவர் தவத்துக்கு ஒருவர் ஆகும்.

In learning two, in austerities one.

3580 தம் இனம் தம்மைக் காக்கும் வேலி பயிரைக் காக்கும்.

One's own kin will preserve one, a hedge will guard a crop.

3581. தம்பி கால் நடையிலே பேச்சுப் பல்லக்கிலே.

My younger brother is on foot, and his talk is in a palanquin.

See proverb 3559.

3582. தம்பி பேச்சைத் தண்ணீரிலே எழுதவேண்டும்.

The sayings of the young man must be written on water.

3583. தம்பி பிடித்த முயலுக்கு மூன்றே கால்.

The hare my younger brother caught, has only three legs.

3584. தம்பி மொண்டது சமுத்திரம்போல.

The water my younger brother drew, is like a sea.

3585. தம்பி உழுவான் மேழி எட்டாது.

My younger brother can plough, but he cannot reach the handle of the plough.

3586, தம்பி பிறக்கத் தரைமட்டம் ஆயிற்று.

As soon as my younger brother was born, *the house* was levelled to the earth.

3587. தம்பி சமர்த்தன் உப்பில்லாக் கஞ்சி கலம் குடிப்பான்.

My younger brother is very clever, he can drink a kalam of kanji without salt.

3588. தம்பி சோற்றுக்குச் சூறுவளி வேலைக்கு வாராவழி.

My brother is like a whirlwind as a rice consumer, but very tardy at work.

3589. தயிருக்குச் சட்டி ஆதாரம் சட்டிகுத் தயிர் ஆதாரம்.

The chatty supports the curds, and the curds the chatty.

3590. தயிர்ப் பானையை உடைத்துக் காகத்துக்கு அமுது இட்டாற் போல.

Like breaking the vessel that contained the curds, and feeding the crows.

3591. தரத்தர வாங்கிக் கொள்ளுகிறாயா, தலையை முழுகிப்போட்டு போகட்டுமா?

Will you receive by little and little *what I owe*, or shall I bathe my head and begone?

3592. தருமத்தைப் பாபம் வெல்லாது.

Vice will not conquer virtue.

3593. தருமம் தலைகாக்கும் தலையை மயிர் காக்கும்.

Charity preserves the head, and the head the hair.

3594. தர்மமே தலைகாக்கும்.

Charity guards the head.

3595. தலை அளவும் வேண்டாம் அடி அளவும் வேண்டாம் குறுக்கே அள அடா படியை.

The measure of the head or foot is not wanted, you fellow, measure the cloth across.

3596. தலை இருக்கிற இடத்தில் கழுத்து வரட்டும் பார்த்துக் கொள்வோம்.

We will attend to the matter when the neck takes the place of the head.

3597. தலை இருக்க வால் ஆடுமா?

Will the tail wag as long as the head exists?

3598. தலை இடியும் காய்ச்சலும் தனக்கு வந்தால் தெரியும்.

When overcome by them, one learns what head-ache and fever are.

3599. தலை இடியும் சங்கடமும் தனக்கு வந்தபின் தெரியும்.

Head-ache and trouble are understood when actually experienced.

3600. தலை எழுத்துத் தலையைச் சிரைத்தாற் போகுமா?

Can you efface the letters of destiny, written on the skull, by shaving the head?

3601. தலை எழுத்தை அரியென்று சொல்லுவார் அதல்ல.

They call the writing on the head, Ari-*Vishnu*-it is not that.

3602. தலை கீழாய் இருந்து தபசு செய்தாலும் கூடுகிற காலந்தானே வந்து கூட வேண்டும்.

Though one perform severe austerities, standing on the head, a thing cannot be attained before the destined time.

3603. தலைக்கு மேற்பட்ட தண்ணீர் சாண் ஓடி என்ன முழம் ஓடி என்ன?

When the water flows over your head, what matters it whether it is a span or a cubit?

In either case death is inevitable without help.

3604. தலைக்குத் தலை பெரியதனம் உலைக்கு அரிசி இல்லை.

One is greater than the other, there is no rice to cook.

3605. தலைக்குத் தலை நாயகம்.

Each aims to be the head.

3606. தலைக்கு முடியோ காலுக்கு முடியோ?

Is it the head or the foot that is crowned?

3607. தலைக்கு ஏறினால் தனக்குத் தெரியும்.

If it ascend to the head, he will feel it.

3608. தலை சொறியக் கொள்ளி தானே தேடிக்கொண்டாய்.

You yourself have procured a firebrand to scratch your head.

3609. தலைச்சன் பிள்ளைக்காரிக்கு இடைச்சன் பிள்ளைக்காரி மருத்துவிச்சி.

The mother of a second child is midwife to the mother of a first child.

3610. தலைச்சன் பிள்ளைக்காரி இடைச்சன் பிள்ளைக்காரிக்குப் புத்தி சொன்னாளாம்.

It is said that the mother of a first child gave advice to the mother of a second child.

3611. தலைமாட்டிற்குக் கொள்ளி தானே தேடிக்கொண்டாய்.

You yourself have procured a firebrand for the head of your bed.

3612. தலைமுறை தலைமுறையாய் மொட்டை, அவள் பெயர் கூந்தலழகி.

Bald from generation to generation, and yet called the matron of beautiful tresses.

3613. தலை மேலே அம்பு பறந்தாலும் நிலையிற் பிரியல் ஆகாது.

It is not good to move when arrows are flying, *though* overhead.

3614. தலை மேலே தலை இருக்கிறதா?

Does a head exist above the head?

3615. தலை மேலே இடித்தாலும் தான் குனியான்.

Though his head strikes *the lintel*, he will not stoop.

3616. தலையாலே மலை பிளப்பான்.

He can split a mountain with *a blow of* his head.

3617. தலையில் எழுதி இருக்கத் தந்திரத்தால் வெல்லலாமா?

When destiny is written on the skull, can you avert it by artifice?

Writing on the head is another form of expression for destiny or fate, which is supposed to be written on the skull of every individual born into the world. Hence the Sanscrit proverb, Kapála, Kapála, Kapála múla. "The skull, the skull, the skull is the root of all." Kapála in Sanscrit means skull. The mundane history of all is determined by the actions of a former state of existence. This is one of the most prevalent doctrines of the Hindus. A man eats the fruit of his doings, not in our sense as the same individuated being, but as the same responsible agent who has previously been on the stage.

"Actions done, whether good or bad, must of necessity be eaten; if not, they will not wear away in millions of ages." *Smriti.*

The preordinations of Brahma, as supposed to be written on the skull, are regulated by the actions of former births. An elaborate shaster on this subject was published in Calcutta upwards of forty years ago by a Native gentleman, a Rajah of great learning.

3618. தலையில் வரும் மயக்கம் சருவ மயக்கம்.

When the head is crazed, all is wrong.

3619. தலையில் இடித்தால் தாழக் குனிவான்.

He will learn to stoop when the *lintel* strikes his head.

3620. தலையும் தலையும் பொருதினல் மலையும் வந்து பொறுக்கும்.

When one head fights with another, the mountains will come to bear them up.

3621. தலையை நனைத்து ஆச்சுது, கத்தியும் வைத்து ஆச்சுது.

The head has been already wet, the razor has been already applied.

3622. தலையோடு போகிறது தலைப்பாகையோடு போயிற்று.

That which would have gone with the head has gone with the turban.

3623. தலைவன் நிற்கத் தண்டு நிற்கும், தலைவன் மயங்கச் சர்வமும் மயங்கும்.

While the general is firm his army is so, but if the chief is perplexed all are so.

3624. தலை வலிக்குத் தலை அணையைத் தானே மாற்றிப் போட்டாற் போல.

As if one changed his pillow to cure head-ache.

3625. தலைவன் சொற் கேள், நன்னெறி தவறேல்.

Obey your superior, deviate not from the path of rectitude.

3626. தலைவெட்டிச் சமுத்திரமேற் போடலாமா?

May the head be severed and put on the sea?

3627. தவசே அணிகலன், தாழமையே மேன்மை.

Austerity is an ornament, humility is honourable.

3628. தவளை தாமரைக்குச் சமீபமாக இருந்தும் அதின் தேனை உண்ணாது. அதுபோல, அறிவீனர் கிட்ட இருந்தாலும் கற்றுக் கொள்ளார்கள்.

The toad living near the lotus drinks not its honey, the illiterate though they live near the learned remain ignorant.

3629. தவளை தன் வாயாற் கெடும்.

The frog perishes by its own mouth.

3630. தவிடு தின்பவனை அமுது தின்னச் சொன்னாற்போல.

Like requesting one who eats bran to feed on ambrosia.

3631. தவிடு தின்பவனை எக்காளம் ஊதச் சொன்னாற்போல.

Like telling one who is eating bran to blow a trumpet.

3632. தவிட்டை நம்பிப் போகச் சம்பா அரிசியை நாய் கொண்டு போயிற்று.

When *she* went out in expectation of fetching bran, her samba rice was carried off by a dog.

3633. தவிட்டுக்கு வந்த கை தனத்துக்கும் வரும்.

The hand that is ready to *steal* bran will be ready to steal money also.

3634. தழைத்த மரத்துக்கு நிழல் உண்டு, பிள்ளை பெற்றவளுக்குப் பால் உண்டு.

A flourishing tree has shade, a woman who has *recently* borne a child, has milk.

3635. தள்ளத் தள்ளத் தாழ்ப்பாளை, மெள்ள மெள்ள திறப்பாள் ஏன்?

Why open it gently again and again, when I am trying to bolt *the door*?

3636. தனக்குப் பிறந்தபிள்ளை தவிட்டுக்கு அழுகிறதாம் ஊரார் பிள்ளைக்குக் கூட்டுக் கலியாணம் செய்கிறானும்.

While his own child cries for bran, he is conducting the nuptials of his neighbour's child.

3637. தனக்குச் சந்தேகம் அடைப்பைக்காரனுக்கு இரட்டைப் படியாம்.

When uncertain regarding his means, he promises a double allowance to his betel-pouch bearer.

3638. தனக்கு அழகு மொட்டை பிறர்க்கு அழகு கொண்டை.

Touching one's own comfort a bald head, in respect to others luxuriant hair, is preferable.

3639. தனக்கு மிஞ்சினது தர்மம்.

That which is left belongs to charity.

3640. தனக்கு என்னவென்று இருக்கல் ஆகாது நாய்க்குச் சோறு இல்லையாயின்.

One must not be unconcerned, when there is no rice for his dog.

3641. தனக்கென்னச் சொன்னால் நாய் வெடுக்கென்னப் பாயும்.

If one speaks to a dog, it will jump *expecting* to get *something*.

3642. தனக்கு மூக்குப் போனாலும் எதிரிக்குச் சகுனப்பிழை வேண்டும்.

He is so intent on producing an ominous sign against his enemy that he is ready to give up his own nose.

He is willing to cut his own nose to spite an enemy: to meet one without a nose is a bad omen.

3643. தனக்கு என்றால் பிள்ளையும் களைவெட்டும்.

If his own crop, even a child may weed it.

3644. தனக்குத் தகாத காரியத்தில் பிரவேசிக்கிறவன் குரங்கு பட்ட பாடு படுவான்.

He who undertakes a matter not suited to him, will suffer as did the monkey.

3645. தனக்கு என்றால் புழுக்கை கலம் கழுவி உண்ணாது.

If for his own use a slave will not wash his plate before eating.

3646. தனக்குத் தகாத காரியம் செய்தால் ஆருக்கும் பிராண சேதத்தக்கு வரும்.

Whoever undertakes an affair unsuited to him will endanger his life.

3647. தனக்கு ஆகாத பானை உடைந்தால் என்ன இருந்தால் என்ன

What matters it whether an earthen vessel not required is broken or not?

3648. தனக்குப் பின்னால் அகம் இருந்து என்ன கவிழ்ந்து என்ன

What matters it whether one's house stands or falls after his death

---

3649. தனக்கு என்று ஒருத்தி இருந்தால் தலைமாட்டில் இருந்து அழுவாள்.

If he has a *wife* she will weep at the bed's head-*at his funeral.*

3650. தனக்குத் தவிடு இடிக்கத் தள்ளாது ஊருக்கு இரும்பு அடிக்கத் தள்ளும்.

He is unable to pound rice for himself, but he can beat iron for his neighbours.

3651. தனக்கு என்று அடுப்பு மூட்டித் தான் வாழும் காலத்தில் வயிறும் சிறுக்கும் மதியும் பெருகும்.

When the time comes for one to make his own fire and prepare his meals, then his stomach will become small and the judgment developed.

3652. தனி வழியே போனவளைத் தாரமென்று எண்ணாதே.

Do not regard her as your wife who goes out unattended.

3653. தன் இச்சையை அடக்காவிட்டால் அது தன்னையே வருத்தும்.

He who does not control his desires will thereby come to grief.

3654. தன் உயிரைப்போல மன் உயிர்க்கு இரங்கு.

Feel for others as you feel for yourself.

3655. தன் உயிரைத் தான் தின்கிறான்.

He himself consumes his own life.

3656. தன் ஊருக்கு அன்னம் பிற ஊருக்குக் காகம்.

A swan in his own village, a crow in the next.

3657. தன் ஊர்ச் சுடுகாட்டுக்கும் அயல் ஊர் ஆற்றுக்கும் அஞ்ச வேண்டும்.

In his own village one should fear the place of incremation, in an adjacent country, a river.

3658. தன் ஊருக்கு ஆனை அயல் ஊருக்குப் பூனை.

At home an elephant, abroad a cat.

3659. தன் ஊருக்குக் காளை அயல் ஊருக்குப் பூனை.

A bullock at home, a cat abroad.

3660. தன் காரியதுரந்தரன் பிறர் காரியம் வழவழவென்று விடுகிறவன்.

He who attends to his own affairs is indifferent about the things of others.

3661. தன் காரியம் என்றால் தன் சேலையும் பதைக்கும்.

If it is his own concern, even the folds of his garment will flutter.

3662. தன் காரியம் பாராதவன் சதைக்கு ஒரு புழு புழுப்பான்.

He who does not attend to his own affairs, will be tormented by worms at every pore.

3663. தன்காரியப் புலி.

In his own affairs *resolute* as a tiger.

3664. தன் கீர்த்தியை விரும்பாதவளைத் தள்ளிவிடு.

Abandon her who is careless of her own reputation.

3665. தன் குற்றம் பார்ப்பவர் இங்கு இல்லை.

No one on earth sees his own faults.

3666. தன் குற்றம் இருக்கப் பிறர் குற்றம் பார்க்கிறதா?

Do you condemn others when guilty yourself?

3667. தன் குஞ்சென்று வளர்க்குமாம் குயிற் குஞ்சைக் காகம்.

It is said that the crow nourishes the young of a cuckoo, under the impression that it is her own.

3668. தன் சோறு தின்று தன் புடைவை கட்டி வீண் சொல் கேட்க விதியா?

Am I destined to be unlawfully abused while eating my own rice and wearing my own cloth?

3669. தன் நிலத்தில் இருந்தால் முயல் தந்தியிலும் வலிது.

When in his own place a hare is stronger than a tusker-*an elephant.*

3670. தன் நோய்க்குத் தானே மருந்து.

The remedy of his disease is with himself.

3671. தன் பலம் கண்டு அம்பலம் ஏறவேண்டும்.

Having ascertained your own ability, display it in the assembly.

3672. தன் பணம் செல்லா விட்டால் தாதனைக் கட்டி அடிக்கிறது.

When his own coin will not pass, he ties up and beats the Vaishnava mendicant.

3673. தன் பல்லைப் பிடுங்கிப் பிறர் வாயில் வைக்கலாமா?

Can one take out his own teeth, and put them in another's mouth?

3674. தன் பல்லைக் குத்திப் பிறர் மூக்கில் வாசம் காட்டுகிறதுபோல.

Like picking the teeth and holding the tooth-pick to the nose of another.

3675. தன் பிள்ளைக்குப் பதைக்காதவள் சக்களத்தி பிள்ளைக்குப் பதைப்பாளா?

Can she who does not feel for her own child, feel for the child of her rival?

3676. தன் பிள்ளையைத் தான் அடிக்கத் தலையாரியைச் சீட்டுக் கேட்கிறதுபோல.

Like applying to the village officer for permission to punish his own child.

3677. தன் வாயாலே தான் கெட்டான்.

His own mouth ruined him.

3678. தன் வாயாலே தான் கெட்டதாம் ஆமை.

It is said that the tortoise perished by its own mouth.

3679. தன் வாய்ச் சீதேவி முன்வாயிலே.

The presence of the goddess of prosperity, will be evinced in the speech.

3680. தன் வினை தன்னைச் சுடும் ஓட்டப்பம் வீட்டைச் சுடும்.

His own actions will burn him, a false cake will burn the house.

3681. தன் வீட்டுக் கதவைப் பிடுங்கி அயல் வீட்டுக்கு வைத்தாற்போல.

As if one took down his door, and placed it in the house of his neighbour.

3682. தன் வீட்டு விளக்கென்று முத்தம் இட்டாற் சுடாதா?

If one kiss his lamp because it belongs to his own house, will it therefore not burn him!

3683. தன் வீடு தவிர அயல் வீட்டுக்கு மேட்டுவரி என்கிறான்.

He asserts that all houses are taxed but his own.

3684. தன் வீட்டுக் கதவைப் பிடுங்கி அயல் வீட்டுக்கு வைத்து விட்டு விடிகிற மட்டும் நாய் ஓட்டினதுபோல.

Like driving away dogs till break of day, because he had lent his door to a neighbour.

3685. தன்னாலே தான் கெட்டால் அண்ணாவியார் என்ன செய்வார்?

If a disciple is intent on his own ruin, what can his master do?

3686. தன்னைப் புகழாத கம்மாளனும் இல்லை.

There is no artificer who does not praise himself.

3687. தன்னை அறிந்தவன் தானே தலைவன்.

He who has studied himself is his own master.

3688. தன்னை அறியாத சன்னதம் இல்லை.

No excitement will make one forget himself.

3689. தன்னை அறிந்தவன் தலைவனை அறிவான்.

He who knows himself may know his maker.

3690. தன்னைக் காக்கிற் கோபத்தைக் காக்கவேண்டும்.

He who would keep himself must restrain anger.

3691. தன்னைக் கொல்ல வருகிற பசுவையும் கொல்.

You may kill even a cow that aims to kill you.

3692. தன்னைச் சிரிப்பாரைத் தான் அறியான்.

He knows not who laugh at him.

3693. தன்னைப் பெற்றவள் கொடும் பாவி, பெண்ணைப் பெற்றவள் மகராசி.

Despising his own mother as worthless, whilst holding his mother-in-law in high estimation.

3694. தன்னை அறிந்து பின்னைப் பேசு.

Know yourself before you begin to speak *of others*.

3695. தன்னைச் சிரிப்பது அறியாதாம் பல்லாவரத்துக் குரங்கு.

It is said that the monkey of Palaveram does not know that he is laughed at.

3696. தன்னைத் தானே தான் பழிக்குமாம் தென்னமரத்திலே குரங்கு இருந்து.

It is said that the monkey that mocks at the top of the cocoanut tree mocks itself.

தா.

3697. தாங்கித் தாங்கிப் பார்த்தால் தலைமேலே ஏறுகிறான்.

He mounts on the head by reason of continued indulgence.

3698. தாசரி தப்பு தண்டவாளத்துக்குச் சரி.

The tabret of the Vaishnava mendicant is like cast-iron.

3699. தாடிக்குப் பூச் சூடலாமா?

Can you wear a garland round your beard!

3700. தாடி பற்றி எரியும்போது சுருட்டுப் பற்றவைக்க நெருப்புக் கேட்டதுபோல்.

As one asked for fire to light his cigar when his beard was on fire.

3701. தாட்சிணியம் தனநாசம்.

Kindness leads to loss of wealth.

3702. தாட்டோட்டக்காரனுக்குத் தயிரும் சோறும், விசுவாசக்காரனுக்கு வெந்நீரும் பருக்கையும்.

The deceitful feasts on rice and curds, while the faithful feeds on warm rice and water.

3703. தாட்டோட்டக்காரனைக் கூடுவதிலும் தனியே இருப்பது நலம்.

It is better to be alone than to associate with the fraudulent.

3704. தாட்டோட்டக்காரனுக்குத் தயிரும் சோறும் கூட்டாட்டக்காரனுக்குக் கூழும் தண்ணீரும்.

The fraudulent enjoys curds and rice, while the honest man gets only gruel and water.

3705. தாதனும் பறையனும்போல.

Like a Vaishnava mendicant and a pariah.

3706. தாதன் கரத்தில் அகப்பட்ட குரங்கைப்போல் அலைகிறான்.

He moves about like a monkey in the hands of a juggler.

3707. தாது அறியாதான் பேதை வைத்தியன்.

He who does not know how to feel one's pulse is an empiric.

3708. தாதும் இல்லைப் பிராதும் இல்லை.

No cause, no complaint.

3709. தாபரம் இல்லா இளங்கொடிபோல.

As a tender creeper without a prop.

3710. தாமதம் தாழ்வுக்கு ஏது.

Delay will lead to ruin.

3711. தாமரை இலைத் தண்ணீர்போல் ததும்புகிறான்.

He trembles like a drop of water on a lotus leaf.

3712. தாம்பு அறுதல் தோண்டியும் பொத்தல்.

The cord is rotten and the water pot is fractured.

3713. தாயும் தகப்பனும் தள்ளிவிட்ட காலத்தில் வா என்று அழைத்த வங்காரவாசி.

A herb that welcomed a child cast off by its parents.

3714. தாயும் பிள்ளையும் ஆனாலும் வாயும் வயிறும் வேறே.

Though they are mother and child their mouths and bellies are diverse.

3715. தாயைக் கொன்றவனுக்கு ஊரிலே வாதி.

The prosecutor of a matricide is in *his own* village.

3716. தாயைச் சேர்ந்த உறவு ஆனாலும் அறுத்துத்தான் உறவு ஆட வேண்டும்.

Though related on the side of one's mother he must be treated as a relation after thoroughly ascertaining his connections.

3717. தாயைப்பார்த்துப் பெண்ணைக் கொள்ளு பாலைப் பார்த்துப் பசுவைக் கொள்ளு.

Before taking a woman in marriage ascertain the character of her mother, before buying a cow ascertain the quantity of its milk.

3718. தாயைப்போற் பிள்ளை நூலைப்போற் சீலை.

As is the mother such is the child, as is the yarn such is the cloth.

3719. தாயைப் பழித்து மகள் அபசாரி ஆடுகிறாள்.

The daughter reproached her mother and went astray.

3720. தாயைப் பார்த்து மகளைக் கொள்.

Look at the mother before you take her daughter in marriage.

3721. தாய் அறியாச் சூல் உண்டோ?

Is there any conception unknown to the mother?

3722. தாய் இல்லாப் பிள்ளையைத் தலையிலே தட்டலாமா?

Is it right to strike a motherless child on the head?

3723. தாய் உறவோ நாய் உறவோ.

A mother's attachment, a dog's attachment.

3724. தாய் எழுடி பாய்ந்தால மகள் எட்டு அடி பாய்வாள்.

If the mother leaps seven feet, the daughter leaps eight.

3725. தாய் ஒரு பாக்கு, தான் கமுகந்தோப்பு என்கிறாள்.

She says that her mother is only a nut, while she herself is a grove of arica-nut trees.

3726. தாய் கேட்டுப்பட்டி தகப்பன் காவடிப்பட்டி தங்கை மோருப்பட்டி தமக்கை சாதப்பட்டி.

The mother is wicked, the father vain, the younger sister a consumer of butter milk, and the elder sister a consumer of rice.

3727. தாய் கையில் இருக்கிற தனத்தைப் பார்க்கிலும் தன் கைத் தவிடே மேல்.

The bran in one's own hand is preferable to the wealth in the hand of his mother.

3728. தாய்க்கு உள்ளது மகளுக்கு.

That which is the mother's, is the daughter's.

This may refer to prosperity, temper, &c.

3729. தாய்க்குப்பின் தாரம்.

Next to one's mother, is his wife.

3730. தாய்க்கு ஒளித்த சூலும் உண்டோ?

Can the conception *of an unmarried daughter* be concealed from her mother?

3731. தாய்க்கு விளைந்தாலும் தனக்கும் விளையவேண்டும்.

It is not enough for one's mother's field to bear a crop, one's own field must also be fruitful.

3732. தாய்க்குச் சோறு இடுகிறது ஊருக்குப் புகழ்ச்சியா?

Does one acquire fame in a country because he feeds his mother?

3733. தாய்க்கு மூத்துத் தகப்பனுக்கு விளக்குப் பிடிக்கிறான்.

He carries a torch at his father's *second* marriage where the bride is younger than himself.

3734. தாய் செத்தால் மணம் மகள் செத்தால் பிணம்.

If the mother die, a marriage, if the daughter die, a corpse.

The wife is here called mother with reference to her children. In the event of her death the husband may marry again.

3735. தாய் செத்தாள், மகள் திக்கற்றாள்.

The mother is dead, the daughter is destitute.

3736. தாய் சொல் துறந்தால் வாசகம் இல்லை.

When one rejects the advice of his mother, no precept *can reform him.*

3737. தாய் தவிட்டுக்கு அழுகையில பிள்ளை இஞ்சிப் பச்சடி கேட்கின்றது.

While the mother is crying for bran, the child is crying for ginger chutny.

3738. தாய்தனக்கு ஆகாத மகள் ஆர்தனக்கு நல்லவள் ஆவாள்?

Who will approve of a daughter that is undutiful to her own mother?

3739. தாய் தூற்றினால் ஊர் தூற்றும், கொண்டவன் தூற்றினால் கண்டவன் தூற்றுவான்.

If a mother should spread evil reports, the village also will do so; if a husband should defame *his wife*, a stranger will.

3740. தாய் முகம் காணாத பிள்ளையும் மழை முகம் காணாத பயிரும் செவ்வைப்படமாட்டாது.

The child that has not seen the face of its mother, and the growing crop that has not seen rain, will not do well.

3741. தாய் முலைப்பாலுக்குப் பால்மாறினதுபோல.

As one complained that his mother's milk was insipid,

3742. தாய் வார்த்தை கேளாத பிள்ளை நாய் வாயிற் சீலை.

A child disobedient to her mother, is like a cloth in the mouth of a dog.

3743. தாரமும குருவும தலையில் விதி.

A wife and a Guru are preordained.

3744. தாராப் பெட்டைபோல.

Like a duck.

3745. தாராளந்தான் நெய், தண்ணீர் பந்தலில், நீர்ச்சோற்றுத் தண்ணீர் நெய்பட்ட பாடு.

Ghee is plentiful in his feasts, while cold rice water in the charity pandal is as scarce as ghee.

3746. தாலி அறுத்தவளுக்கு மருத்துவிச்சி தயவு ஏன்?

Of what use is the favour of a midwife to a widow?

3747. தாலி அறுத்தவள் ஏன் இருக்கிறாள்? தாரம் தப்பினவனுக்குப் பொங்கியிட.

Why does the widow survive her husband? that she may cook rice for a widower.

3748. தாவத் தஞ்சம் இல்லா இளங்கொடிபோல் தவிக்கிறான்.

He languishes like a tender creeper without a prop.

3749. தாழிபோல் வயிறும் ஊசிபோல் மிடறும்.
Pot-bellied and needle-throated.

3750. தாழ் குலத்திற் பிறந்தாலும் புத்தியினல் அலரிப்பூவைப்போல் பிரயோசனப்படுவார்.
Though low-born, they may by their good sense prove useful as an oleander flower.

3751. தாழ்ந்து நின்றால் வாழ்ந்து நிற்பாய்.
If humble thou shalt prosper.

3752. தாழ்ந்தது தங்கம் உயர்ந்தது பித்தளை.
Gold has become low *in estimation*, and brass high.

3753. தாழ்ந்து பணிதலே தலைமை ஆகும்.
The humble and obedient shall rise to eminence.

3754. தாழ்மை இல்லாத வாலிபன் வீண்.
An unsubmissive youth is useless.

3755. தாழ்விலே பெருமையும் வாழ்விலே தாழ்மையும் வேண்டும்.
In adversity, manly bearing; in prosperity, humility.

3756. தானத்தனத்தான் சகல சம்பத்தன்.
He is the wealthiest in the place, and possesses all in abundance.

3757. தானமது விரும்பு.
Desire to be charitable.

3758. தானுகவந்த சிதேவியைக் காலால் உதைத்துத் தள்ளலாமா?
When the goddess of prosperity unsought visits you, is it right to kick her out?

3759. தானும் உண்ணுன் பிறருக்கும் கொடான்.
He will neither eat himself, nor give to others.

3760. தானே கனியாத பழத்தைத் தடிகொண்டு அடித்தால் கனியுமா?
Can you mature a fruit by beating it with a stick when it does not ripen of itself?

3761. தானே தான் குருக்கள் என்பார் தனங்கள் வாங்கச் சதாசிவன் பேர் பூசை செய்வார்.

To get money they call themselves gurus, and perform pujas in honour of Sadasiva.

3762. தானே வளர்ந்து தவத்தால் கொடி எடுத்தவன்.

He has grown great and distinguished by his penance.

3763. தானே வாழவேண்டும் தலைமகளே அறுக்கவேண்டும் என்கிறாள்.

She herself desires to prosper, and wishes that her first-born daughter may become a widow.

3764. தான் அடங்கத் தன் குலம் அடங்கும்.

If he himself be under restraint, his race will be so.

3765. தான் அறியாச் சிங்களம் தன் பிடரிக்குச் சேதம்.

An attempt to speak a language not understood may lead to one's own hurt.

3766. தான் உள்ளபோது உலகம்.

While one lives, the world *subserves him.*

3767. தான் ஒன்று நினைத்தால் தெய்வம் ஒன்று நினைக்கும்.

If he thinks one thing, Deity thinks another.

3768. தான் கள்வன் பிறரை நம்பான்.

Himself a thief, he trusts not others.

3769. தான் கற்ற ஒன்றைத் தரிக்க உரை.

What you have learnt, teach *to others* impressively.

3770. தான் கெடுத்தது பாதி, தம்பிரான் கெடுத்தது பாதி.

Half was spoiled by himself, and half by his superior.

3771. தான் சம்பாதித்தால் தனக்கு உதவும், ஊர் சம்பாதித்தால் உதவமாட்டாது.

That which one acquires will be available, that which the country acquires will not be so.

3772. தான் சாக மருந்து உண்பார் இல்லை.

No one takes medicine with a view to death.

3773. தான் செத்தபின் உலகம் கவிழ்ந்து என்ன நிமிர்ந்து என்ன?

When one is dead, what matters it whether the world be overturned or not?

3774. தான் தளம்பல் பிறருக்கு ஊன்றுகோல்.

His tripping is as a staff to others.

3775. தான் திருடி அயல் வீட்டை நம்பாள்.

Being herself a thief, she trusts not her neighbours.

3776. தான் தின்கிற நஞ்சு தன்னைத்தான் கொல்லும்.

He who takes poison will destroy himself.

3777. தான் தின்னத் தவிடு இல்லை வாரத்துக்குப் பன்றிக் குட்டியா?

He has no bran to eat, why seek a young pig to rear for hire?

3778. தான் தின்னித் தம்பிரானாய் இருக்கிறான்.

In eating he has a monopoly.

3779. தான் தின்னி பிள்ளை வளர்க்காள், தவிடு தின்னி கோழி வளர்க்காள்.

A gluttonous mother will not feed her child, nor will one who feeds on bran keep fowls.

3780. தான் திருட்டுக் கொடுத்ததும் அல்லாமல் பயித்தியக்காரப் பட்டமும் கேட்டான்.

Besides suffering the loss of the property stolen, he acquires the title of a fool.

3781. தான் தேடாப் பொன்னுக்கு மாற்றும் இல்லை உரையும் இல்லை.

Gold not acquired by one's own exertions, has neither standard nor touch.

3782. தான் பத்தினி ஆனால் தேவடியாள் தெருவிலும் குடி இருக்கலாம்.

If a woman be chaste she may live in the street of the harlots.

3783 தான் பிடித்த முசலுக்கு மூன்றே கால் என்கிறான்.
He says that the hare he caught had three legs.

3784. தான் போனால் தாகத்துக்குக் கிடையாது, எழுதடா ஓலை நூறு குடம் தயிருக்கு என்கிறான்.
He says that if he go himself he cannot get *water* to quench his thirst, but if he sends written olas he can obtain a hundred pots of curds.

3785. தான் போகிற காரியத்துக்கு ஆட்போனால் ஒரு சொட்டு.
Faults will happen if another be deputed to do one's business.

3786. தான் போய் மோர் இல்லாமல் வந்தவன் தயிருக்குச் சீட்டு எழுதினானாம்.
It is said that he who went in person and could not obtain *even* butter-milk, sent a written order for curds.

3787. தான் போக வழியைக் காணாத மூஞ்சூறு விளக்கு மாற்றையும் கவ்விக்கொண்டு போனதாம்.
It is said that a musk-rat that was not able to find its way out, carried away the broom.

3788. தான்றிக் காயில் சனியன் புகுந்ததுபோல.
As if Saturn entered into the tánri fruit-*Terminalia Bellerica.*

தி.

3789. திகம்பர சந்நியாசிக்கு வண்ணான் உறவு ஏன்?
What has a naked mendicant to do with the friendship of a washerman!

3790. திகைப்பூடு மிதித்தவன் போல் அலைகிறான்.
He wanders about like one who has trodden on the tigai plant.

A plant whose touch is supposed to create aberration of mind and numbness.

3791. திக்கு அற்றவனுக்குத் தெய்வம் துணை.
God is the help of the destitute.

3792. திக்கு விஜயம் கொள்பவனுக்கு ஜெயம் அபஜெயகாலம் தெரியாது.

A successful conqueror does not regard times whether relating to victory or defeat.

3793. திங்களும் சனியும் தெற்கே நோக்க வேண்டும்.

Look south on Monday and Saturday *if leaving home.*

The direction given in this proverb is intended to convey a caution to those setting out on a journey on Monday or Saturday. It is based on the belief contained in a stanza of which the following is a translation.

Sangara, Siva, as the author of good, plants his trident on the earth in certain directions on particular days and at stated hours.

On Monday and Saturday in the east for eight náligais.*

On Thursday, in the south for twenty náligais.

On Friday and Sunday in the west, twelve náligais.

On Tuesday and Wednesday in the north, twelve náligais.

3794. திடமனப்படு தீம்பர்க்கருகில்.

Preserve your self-possession in the presence of enemies.

3795. திண்ணைக்குத் தேள் கொட்டிற்று தண்ணீர் மிடாவுக்கு நெறி கட்டிற்று என்றாற்போல.

As if one should say that the pial was stung by a scorpion, and the water pot *standing on it* became inflamed.

3796. திண்ணைக்கு விடிந்தால் வீட்டுக்கும் விடியும்.

If the sun rise on the pial, it will rise on the house also.

3797 திரவியத்தில் அழுத்தமானவன் செத்தாலும் கொடான்.

The miserly will not give though threatened with immediate death.

3798. திரள் எலி வளை எடாது.

Rats in large numbers do not burrow.

* Indian hour of twenty-four minutes.

3799. திரித்தவரையிற் கயிறு திரியாதவரையிற் பழுதை.

As far as twisted it is a rope, that not twisted is mere fibre.

3800. திரி மூர்த்திகளும் தேவரும் காணர்.

Neither the triad nor the *thirty-three crores of* supernals, are comparable to him.

3801. திரு உண்டானல் திறமை உண்டாகும்.

When there is wealth, there is power.

3802. திருகாணிக்கு வலுவும் பழஞ்சாணிக்குப் புழுவும் உண்டு.

A screw is strong, old cow-dung breeds worms.

3803. திருக் கண்ட கண்ணுக்குத் தீங்கும் காணலாயிற்றே.

Even those who have seen the holy one are not exempt from evil.

3804. திருக் கண்ட கண்ணுக்குத் தீங்கு இல்லை.

Those that have seen the holy one experience no evil.

3805. திருக்காவணப் பந்தலுக்கு நிழல் உதவி வேண்டுமா?

Does a marriage pandal require shading!

3806. திருடனைத் தேள் கொட்டினதுபோல.

As a scorpion stung the thief.

3807. திருடன் பெண்சாதி என்றைக்கும் கைம்பெண்சாதி.

The wife of the thief is always a widow.

3808. திருடனுக்குத் தெய்வமே சாட்சி.

The Deity is witness against the thief.

3809. திருட்டுப் பயலுக்குத் திரட்டுப்பாலும் சோறும் விசுவாசகாரனுக்கு வெந்நீரும் பருக்கையும்.

A rogue is fed with thick milk and rice, while the honest get nothing but warm water and rice.

3810. திருட்டு நாய்க்குச் சலங்கை கட்டினற் போல.

Like tying a string of bells round the neck of a thievish dog.

3811. திருட்டுப் பயல் கலியாணத்தில் முடிச்சு அவிழ்க்கிற பயல் பெரியதனம்.

At the marriage of a thief, the pickpocket is the chief guest.

Literally, the thievish fellow who unties a knot. Money or other valuables being often carried in the corner of the cloth worn as a dress, or in the corner of a handkerchief.

3812. திருட்டுப் பூனைக்குப் போடு திரட்டுப் பாலும் சோறும்.

Put thick milk and rice before a thievish cat.

3813. திருத்தி இல்லாத எசமான் வீண்.

A master whom it is hard to please is useless.

3814. திருநாளும் முடிந்தது எடுபிடியும் கழிந்தது.

The festival is over, the bustle has ceased.

3815. திருநாளுக்கு போகிறையோ தின்னுதலுக்குப் போகிறையோ?

Do you go to celebrate the holy day, or for the sake of food?

3816. திருநீற்றிலே ஒட்டாது கழற்சிக்காய்.

Holy ashes will not adhere to a killachi-kái.

3817. திருந்த ஓதத் திரு உண்டாமே.

The correct utterance of mantras secures the divine favour.

3818. திருப்பதிக்குப் போனாலும் துடைப்பம் ஒரு காசு.

Though taken to Tripati, a broom will fetch only a cash.

3819. திருப்பதியில் மொட்டை அடித்ததும் பற்றாதா, ஸ்ரீரங்கத்தில் சிரிப்பாய்ச் சிரித்ததும் பற்றாதா?

Is it not enough to have been shaven bald at Tirupati and disgraced at Shrírangam?

3820. திருப்பதியில் மொட்டைத் தாதனைக் கண்டாயா?

Did you see the baldheaded Vaishnava mendicant at Tripati?

3821. திருவன் கண்ட பச்சையாய்ப் போயிற்று.

It has become an emerald discovered by the king's jester.

3822. திரு வாசல் ஆண்டியும் ஒருவேளைக்கு உதவுவான்.

Even a religious mendicant at the temple gate will be of some use at times.

3823. திருவாசகத்திற்கு உருகாதார் ஒரு வாசகத்திற்கும் உருகார்.

Those who are unaffected by Tiruvasakam will not be moved by any other composition.

3824. திருவாக்குக்கு எதிர்வாக்கு உண்டோ?

Do the words of the great admit of contradiction?

3825. திருவிளக்கு இல்லா வீட்டில் பேய் குடியிருக்கும்.

Demons dwell in the house that is not illumined by a sacred lamp.

To smear a room with cow-dung, especially on Friday, and to keep a lamp burning through the night, are observances pleasing to the goddess of prosperity.

3826. திருவிளக்கு இட்டாரைத் தெய்வம் அறியும், நெய்வார்த்து உண்டாரை நெஞ்சு அறியும்.

The Deity knows those who place sacred lamps, and the mind knows who eats ghee and rice.

3827. திரை கடல் ஓடியும் திரவியம் தேடு.

Acquire wealth though compelled to cross the *stormy* ocean.

3828. தில்லுமுல்லும் திரியா வரமும்.

Lies and tricks.

3829. திறந்த கதவுக்கு திறவுகோல் தேடுவானேன்?

Why seek the key of an open door?

3830. திறந்த வீட்டிலே நாய் நுழைந்தாற்போல.

As if a dog entered an open house.

3831. தினத்தவ நிலையில் மனத்தை நிறுத்து.

Daily fix your mind on divine things.

3832. தினவுக்குச் சொறிதல் இதம்.

Scratching is agreeable where itching exists.

3833. தினவு எடுத்தவன் சொறிந்துகொள்ள வேண்டும்.

He whose *skin* itches will scratch.

3834. தினைப்பயறும் பாலும் தின்னாதிருந்தும், வினைப்பயனை வெல்லுவது அரிது.

Though one may abstain from *eating* millet-pulse and milk, he cannot escape from the effect of *his evil* actions.

3835. தினை விதைத்தவன் தினை அறுப்பான் வினை விதைத்தவன் வினை அறுப்பான்.

He who sows millet, reaps millet, he who sows evil deeds, must reap the same.

3836. தின்கிறதைத் தின்றும் தேவாங்குபோல் இருக்கிறான்.

Though well fed he is as lean as a sloth.

3837. தின்பது கொஞ்சம் சீவனம் நிலை இல்லை.

What one eats is little, human life is uncertain.

3838. தின்ற மண்ணுக்குத் தக்க சோகை.

Chogai *jaundice* proportioned to the earth eaten.

It is the opinion of some that jaundice is occasioned by eating sand or earth, a thing not uncommon.

3839. தின்ற நஞ்சு கொல்லும் தின்னாத நஞ்சு கொல்லுமா?

Poison taken kills; will the poison not taken, kill!

3840. தின்று கொழுத்தால் சும்மா இருக்க ஒட்டாது.

He who has grown fat will be inclined to mischief.

3841. தின்று உமிழ்ந்த தம்பலத்தைத் தின்ன நினைப்பார்களா?

Does any one desire to chew his betel over again!

3842. தின்னத் தின்னக் கேட்குமாம் பிள்ளைப்பெற்ற வயிறு.

A mother who is nursing a baby has a good appetite.

3843. *தின்னத் தெரியாமல் தின்பானேன்?*

Why eat, seeing that you know not how to eat *with moderation*?

3844. *தின்னா வீட்டில் தின்னி.*

One who takes food in a house in which he ought not.

தீ.

3845. *தீக் காய்ந்தாற்போல் இருக்கவேண்டும்.*

Act as one who warms himself-*do not burn yourself.*

3846. *தீக்குக் காற்று உதவியானதுபோல.*

As the wind assists fire.

3847. *தீங்கரும்பனுக்கு மாங்குயிற் கிள்வி.*

The notes of the kuyil bird to the sugar-cane-bowed *Cupid.*

3848. *தீட்டின மரத்தில் கூர்பார்க்கிறதா?*

Is the sharpness of the sword to be tried on the whetting board?

3849. *தீதுறும் பாவச் செய்கை அற்றவன் தேவன்.*

He who abstains from evil deeds is God.

3850. *தீபத்தில் ஏற்றிய தீவட்டி.*

A torch lit at a lamp.

3851. *தீப்பட்ட வீட்டிலே கரிக்கட்டை பஞ்சமா?*

Is there a lack of charred wood in a house on fire?

3852. *தீப்புண் ஆறும் வாய்ப்புண் ஆறாது.*

A burn is curable, but a wound occasioned by slander is not.

3853. *தீ மிஞ்ச வைத்தாலும் பகை மிஞ்ச வைக்கலாகாது.*

Though fire may be in excess, hatred may not.

3854. *தீமையை மெச்சுகிறவன் தீமையாளிதான்.*

He who approves evil is guilty of it.

3855. தீயாரைச் சேர்ந்து ஒழுகல் தீது, தீயார் பண் செய்வனவும் தீது.

To associate with the wicked is bad, to serve the wicked is also bad.

3856. தீயோரை விடுதலை ஆக்குகிறவன் நல்லோருக்கு நஷ்டம் செய்வான்.

He who liberates the wicked injures the innocent.

3857. தீரக் கற்றவன் தேசிகன் ஆவான்.

The thoroughly learned may become a religious guide.

3858. தீராக் கோபம் பாடாய் முடியும்.

Unrestrained anger will end in mischief.

3859. தீராக் கோபம் போராய் முடியும்.

Unrestrained anger ends in strife.

3860. தீராச் சந்தேகம் போருக்கு எத்தனம்.

Continued uncertainty leads to war.

3861. தீராச் செய்கை சீராகாது.

An unsettled affair is bad.

3862. தீராத நெஞ்சுக்குத் தெய்வமே சாட்சி.

God himself is the witness of the unquiet mind.

3863. தீரா வழக்குக்குத் தெய்வமே சாட்சி.

God is the witness in an undecided cause.

3864. தீரா வழக்கு நேராகாது.

An intricate case will never end satisfactorily.

3865. தீவினை செய்யில் பேய்வினை செய்யும்.

A demon does evil to him who does evil *to others.*

து.

3866. துக்கம் உள்ள மனதிற்குத் துன்பம் ஏன் வேறு?

Why additional pain to a mind already in grief?

3867. துஞ்சி நின்றான் மிஞ்சி உண்ணான்.

He that is addicted to sleep loses his appetite.

3868. துடியாப் பெண்டிர் மடியில் நெருப்பு.

Unsympathizing wives are like fire in the bosom.

3869. துடுப்பு இருக்கக் கை வேவானேன் ?

Why should the hand be burnt when there is a ladle !

3870. துடைப்பக் கட்டைக்குப் பட்டுக்குஞ்சம் கட்டினதுபோல.

Like tying a silk tassel to a broomstick.

3871. துஷ்ட நிக்கிரகம் சிஷ்ட பரிபாலனம்.

To the wicked, punishment, to the good, protection.

3872. துஷ்டப் பிள்ளைக்கு ஊரார் புத்தி சொல்வார்கள்.

The people of the village will reprove a wicked child.

3873. துட்டுக்கு ஒரு குட்டி விற்றாலும் துலுக்கக்குட்டி மாத்திரம் ஆகாது.

Though girls may be had at a pie a head, a Muhammadan girl is undesirable.

3874. துணிகிறவளுக்கு வெட்கம் இல்லை, அழுகிறவளுக்குத் துக்கம் இல்லை.

An impudent woman has no shame, a weeping woman has no sorrow.

3875. துணிந்தார்க்குத் துக்கம் உண்டா பணிந்தார்க்குப் பாடு உண்டா ?

Do the adventurous experience grief, or the humble, distress !

3876. துணிந்தவனுக்குத் துக்கம் இல்லை, அழுதவனுக்கு அகங்காரம் இல்லை.

The adventurous know not sorrow, the sorrowful know not anger.

3877. துணைபோனாலும் பிணைபோகாதே.

Though you may bear one company, do not become his security.

3878. துணையோடல்லது வழிபோகாதே.

Do not go on a journey without a companion.

3879. துப்பாக்கி வயிற்றில் பீரங்கி பிறந்ததுபோல.

As a cannon was born of a musket.

3880. தும்பர் அம்பலம்.

The wicked will be abandoned.

3881. துயரப்பட்டால் ஆறுதல் உண்டு, துன்பப்பட்டால் தேறுதல் உண்டு.

Grief leads to comfort, suffering to patience.

3882. துரியோதனன் குடிக்குச் சகுனிபோல.

Like Saguni to the family of Duryodhana.

Saguni was the maternal uncle of Duriyodhana, and had, like the latter, ninety-nine brothers. Duriyodhana was one of the kings whose exploits are narrated in the Epic Mahabharata. He imprisoned Saguni and his ninety-nine brothers. to prevent their combination against him, feeding them on gruel which was doled out from day to day. They all died of inanition excepting Saguni, who managed to secure sufficient nourishment to preserve his life. He afterwards became the counsellor of Duriyodhana and from sinister motives gave such advice as led to the ruin of his royal master, who lost his kingdom and also his ninety-nine brothers.

3883. துருக்க தெருவிலே திருவெம்பாவையா ஓதுகிறது?

Is it in a Muhammadan street that one should recite Tiruvemba?

3884. துரும்பும் கலத்தண்ணீர் தேக்கும்.

Even a fibre may help to fill up a kalam with water.

3885. துரும்பு நுழைய இடம் இருந்தால் ஆனையைக் கட்டுவான்.

If he find room for the insertion of a straw, he will tie an elephant.

3886. துரும்பு முற்றின கோபம் விசும்பு முட்டத் தீரும்.

Anger occasioned by a trifle may extend to the sky before it ceases.

3887. துரும்பு தூண் ஆனால் தூண் எவ்வளவு ஆகவேண்டும்?

If a straw become a pillar, how great the pillar must be?

3888. துரும்பைத் தூணாக்குகிறதா?

What, do you make a pillar of a straw!

3889. துரை சித்தம் கன சித்தம்.

The will of the ruler is weighty.

3890. துரோகத்தால் கொண்ட துரைத்தனம், குடிகளை வருத்தும் கொடுங்கோல்.

Power obtained by high treason, a sceptre that oppresses the subject.

3891. துரோபதையைத் துகில் உரிந்ததுபோல.

Like stripping off the cloth of Draupati.

Draupati was the common wife of the five sons of Pandu. When in captivity after the humiliation of the Pandavas, an attempt was made by Duriyodhana to strip off her cloth, as a punishment for laughing at him when he stumbled, she was however saved from dishonour, for as they drew away her cloth it was lengthned by divine interposition.

3892. துர்ச்சனனைக் கண்டால் தூர நில்.

Stand at a distance from the wicked.

3893. துலக்காத ஆயுதம் துருப் பிடிக்கும்.

A weapon not kept polished, will become rusty.

3894. துலாத்தில் வெள்ளி இருப்பதினால் உலாவிப் பெய்யும் மழை.

Venus being in Libra, there will be rain throughout the country.

3895. துலுக்க தெருவிலே தேவாரம் ஓதினதுபோல.

Like singing Dévaram in a Muhammadan street.

3896. துவிநாக்கு இடறும்.

A double tongue will slip.

3897. துழாவிக் காய்ச்சாதது கஞ்சியும் அல்ல, வினவிக் கட்டாதது கலியாணமும் அல்ல.

Kanji requires continued stirring while boiling, and marriage requires careful consideration before being entered on.

3898. துளசிக்கு வாசமும் முள்ளுக்குக் கூர்மையும் முளைக்கிறபோதே உண்டு.

The fragrance of the Tulasi and the point of a thorn are in the bud.

3899. துள்ளாதே துள்ளாதே குள்ளா, பக்கத்திலே பள்ளம் அடா.

Dwarf, do not jump, there is a ditch close by.

3900. துள்ளாதே துள்ளாதே ஆட்டுக்குட்டி என் கையில் இருக்கிறது சூரிக்கத்தி.

Do not leap about O lamb, the butcher's knife is in my hand.

3901. துள்ளின மாடு பொதி சுமக்கும்.

The restive or unruly bullock will carry its load.

3902. துள்ளித் துள்ளிக் குதித்தாலும் வெள்ளிப்பணமும் கிடையாக் காலத்தில் கிடையாது.

Though one may exert himself to the utmost, he cannot procure even a silver fanam when fortune does not smile.

3903. துள்ளித் துள்ளித் தொப்பென்று விழுகிறாய்.

By restlessness thou wilt throw thyself headlong.

3904. துள்ளுமான்குட்டி துரவில் விழுந்தது.

The springing young deer fell into a well.

3905. துறட்டுக்கு எட்டாதது கைக்கு எட்டுமோ?

Can that which is not reached by a long pole be seized by the hand?

3906. துறவறம் இல்லறம் மனதிலே

Ascetic and domestic virtues originate in the heart.

3907. துறவிக்கு வேந்தன் துரும்பு.

A king is but a straw before an ascetic.

3908. துன்பம் தருகிற காக்கையினது சத்தத்தினால் அதை விரட்டுவார்கள், இன்பம் தருகின்ற குயிலை விரட்டார்கள்.

Men scare away crows because their cries are a nuisance, but cuckoos they do not scare away.

3909. துன்பத்திற்கு இடம் கொடேல்.

Take care to keep off sickness.

3910. துன்பம் முந்தி இன்பம் பிந்தி.

Pain precedes, pleasure follows.

தூ.

3911. தூக்கணங்குருவி குரங்கிற்குப் புத்தி சொன்னாற்போல்.

As the hanging-nest bird gave advice to the monkey.

The story referred to is graphically told in, I think, Panchatantra. It is as follows: On a cold rainy day a monkey chilled by the inclemency of the weather approached a tree on the branches of which were hanging numerous nests of this ingenious bird. One of the inmates addressed his simian denizen of the forest expressing surprise that a creature endowed with limbs so well fitted for the purpose did not fabricate a suitable place of shelter. The monkey felt the reflection implied in the admonition, and unable to restrain his indignation, jumped into the tree and destroyed the residence of his innocent friend.

In my journeys on foot in various parts of this country I have frequently seen the nests of the pendulous bird. On a tree not many miles from Trincomalie on the eastern coast of Ceylon I once saw perhaps thirty or forty nests hanging from one tree not twenty feet high: they resembled large pears.

3912. தூக்கி நினைத்து நோக்கிப் பேசு.

Speak after deliberation and circumspection.

3913. தூக்கி வளர்த்த பிள்ளையும் துடையில வைத்துத் தைத்த இலையும் உருப்படாது.

A child brought up in the arms, and a leaf plate stitched when spread on the lap, will not be properly formed.

3914. தூக்கி நிறுத்தடா பிணக்காடாய் வெட்டுகிறேன்.

Lift me up you fellow, I will cut them down and convert the place into a burning ground.

3915. தூக்கி வினைசெய்.

Do a thing after due deliberation.

3916. தூக்கு உண்டானால் நோக்கு உண்டு.

Gravity inspires respect.

3917. தூங்காதவனே நீங்காதவன்.

The sleepless is the abiding one.

3918. தூங்காதவனுக்குச் சுகம் இல்லை.

He who does not sleep is not healthy.

3919. தூங்கினவனது கடாக்குட்டி, விழித்திருந்தவனது ஊட்டுக் குட்டி.

The weaned he-goat belongs to him who slept, the suckling to him who was awake.

3920. தூங்கினவன் கன்று கடாக்கன்று.

The calf of him who slept is a bull calf.

3921. தூங்கினவன் சாகிறதில்லை, வீங்கினவன் பிழைக்கிறதில்லை.

A *patient* who sleeps well will not soon die, one whose body is swollen will not live.

3922. தூண்டிற்காரனுக்குக் கண் எங்கே மிதப்பில் அல்லவோ?

Where is the eye of the angler? on the float, is it not?

3923. தூமத் தீயைப் பார்க்கிலும் காமத் தீ கொடிது.

The fire of lust is more fierce than a smoking fire.

3924. தூர இருந்தால் சேர உறவு.

Distance promotes close friendship.

3925. தூரத்துப் பச்சை கண்ணுக்குக் குளிர்ச்சி.

Green in the distance is cooling to the eye.

3926. தூரத்துப் பார்வைக்கு மலை மழமழப்பு, கிட்டப்போனால் கல்லும் கரடும்.

A mountain in the distance appears smooth, but as we approach it, the surface becomes rugged.

3927. தூரத்துத் தண்ணீர் ஆபத்துக்கு உதவாது.

Water at a distance is not available in an emergency.

3928. தூரப் போகவேண்டுமோ கீரைப் பாத்தியிற் கை வைக்க?

Must I go away that you may lay your hands on the bed of greens?

3929. தூர்ந்த கிணற்றைத் தூரவாக்காதே.

Do not empty a well that has been filled up.

3930. தூருன குடி நீறுகும்.

A profligate family will be reduced to ashes.

3931. தூற்றர் என்போர் சொல் எழுத்து உணரார்.

The slanderous are ignorant of letters.

3932. தூறறித் திரியேல்.

Do not go about slandering.

3933. தூற்றும் பெண்டீர் கூற்று எனத் தகும்.

A reproachful wife may fitly be called Yama.

தெ.

3934. தெண்டத்துக்குப் பணமும் திவசத்திற்குக் கறியும் அகப்படும்.

Money for fines, and greens for the anniversaries of the dead, are *readily* available.

3935. தெய்வ சித்தம் இருந்தால் செத்தவனும் எழும்புவான்

God being willing, even the dead may rise.

3936. தெய்வப் புலவனுக்கு நா உணரும் சித்திர ஓடாவிக்குக் கை உணரும்.

To a heaven-inspired poet, the tongue, to an artist, the hand are skilful.

3937. தெய்வம் துணைக்கொள் தேகம் அநித்தியம்.

Secure divine help,—the body is transient.

3938. தெரியாத் திணையே பிரியாத் துணை நீ.

O unconscicous earth, thou art my inseparable help.

3939. தெருளா மனதுக்கு இருளே இல்லை.

An unenlightened mind has no *sense of* darkeness.

3940. தெவிட்டாக் கனி பிள்ளை, தெவிட்டாப் பானம் தண்ணீர்.

A child is a fruit that does not nauseate, and water is a beverage that never cloys.

3941. தெளிந்த தண்ணீர் நீர் குடித்தீர் சேற்றைக் கலக்கி விட்டீர்.

Having drunk the clear water, thou hast stirred the mud.

3942. தெளிவுறும் பரதேவ தேசிகன்.

The illustrious, holy, divine teacher.

3943 தெள்ளிய திருமணி திருட்டுக்கு நவமணி.

In thieving he is a precious stone—one of the nine gems.

3944. தெறிக்க அடித்த தட்டானைப்போலே.

Like the goldsmith who beats off the gold in pieces.

3945. தெற்கத்தைக் குருவியை வடக்கத்தைக் குருவி தெற்றி அழைத்ததாம் சீகம்பழம் தின்னப் போக.

A northern bird induced a southern bird to feed on Sígampalam *fruit.*

3916. தெற்கே அடித்த காற்றுத் திரும்பி அடியாதா?

Will not the south wind blow again?

3947. தென் காசி ஆசாரம் திருநெல்வேலி உபசாரம்.

The manners of Tenkási, and the ceremoniousness of Tinnevelly

3948. தென்றல் முற்றிப் பெரும் காற்று ஆச்சுது.

The gentle southern breeze has increased to a gale.

3949. தென்னமரத்திற் பாதி என்னை வளர்த்தாள் பாவி.

I am half the height of a cocoanut tree, she who brought me up is a sinner.

3950. தென்னமரத்திலே தேள் கொட்டப் பனைமரத்திலே நெறி கட்டினதுபோல.

As when the scorpion stung the cocoanut tree, the palmyra tree had a glandular swelling.

3951. தென்னாலுராமன் பூனை வளர்த்ததுபோல.

As Tennáluráman reared a cat.

தே.

3952. தேங்காய் தின்றவன் தின்னக் கோம்பை சூப்பினவன் தெண்டம் இறுக்கிறதா?

While he who ate the kernal of the cocoanut escapes with impunity is he who sucked the fibre to pay the fine?

3953. தேசங்கள் தோறும் பாஷைகள் வேறு.

As countries differ, their languages differ also.

3954. தேடப்போன மூலிகை காலடியில் அகப்பட்டாப்போல.

As if a medicinal root he had gone to seek, was obtained at his foot.

3955. தேடித் திருவிளக்கு வை.

Prepare to place a sacred lamp.

3956. தேடித் தின்றவர் தெய்வத்தோடு ஒத்தவர்.

He who earns his own bread is like god.

3957. தேடிப் புதைத்துத் தெருவில் இரக்கிறதா?

What! begging in the street, after having acquired *wealth* and buried it!

3958. தேடிய பொருள் காலிலே தட்டினதுபோல.

As the thing one is in search of hits the foot.

3959. தேடின பூண்டு காலிலே மிதிபட்டது.

The plant one was looking for was being trodden under foot.

3960. தேடுவார் அற்ற பிணம் தெருவோடே.

No one being interested in its burial, the corpse lies in the road.

3961. தேம்படு பனையின் திரள் பழத்தொரு விதை.

A selected nut from a number of sweet palmirah fruit.

3962. தேய்ந்தாலும் சந்தனக்கட்டை மணம் போகாது.

Though worn by attrition, the sandal wood loses not its fragrance.

3963. தேய்ந்து மூஞ்சூறு ஆனீரோ கொம்புகள் உதிர்த்தீரோ?

Art thou worn out and become a musk-rat, hast thou cast thy horns?

3964. தேராச் செய்கை தீராச் சஞ்சலம்.

A thoughtless act occasions endless trouble.

3965. தேரைமோர்ந்த தேங்காய்போல.

Like the cocoanut smelt by a toad-*a blighted cocoanut.*

3966. தேரோடே நின்று தெருவோடே அலைகிறான்.

He wanders along the street with the temple car.

3967. தேர்ந்தவன் என்பது கூர்ந்து அறிவதனால்.

He is called intelligent because of his nice discrimination.

3968. தேவடியாள் தெரு கொள்ளைபோகிறதா?

Is robbery committed in a street of harlots?

3969. தேவடியாள் சிங்காரிக்குமுன்னே தேர் ஓடித் தெருவில் நின்றது.

Before the dancing girl had adorned herself, the car moved and came to a stand on the road.

3970. தேவடியாள் மகன் திவசம் செய்ததுபோல.

As the son of a harlot commemorated the death of his father.

3971. தேவடியாள் செத்தால் பிணம், தேவடியாள் தாய் செத்தால் மணம்.

When a harlot dies the body is a mere corpse, when her mother dies funeral rites are observed.

3972. தேவரைக் காட்டிப் பூதம் பணி கொள்ளும்.

Under pretence that gods require it, goblins exact service *from men.*

Goblins or ghosts of the kind referred to, are employed by magicians. They are supposed to haunt grave yards, places of incremation, buried treasure &c. Companies of them attend Siva, Ganésa &c.

3973. தேவர்கள் பணிவிடை செய்யு மேலவன் கர்த்தா.

He is the Lord whom the celestials serve.

3974. தேள் கொட்டப் பாம்புக்கு மந்திரிக்கிறதா?

When stung by a scorpion do you recite incantations as for a snake-bite?

3975. தேள் நெருப்பில் விழுந்தால எடுத்துவிட்டவனைக் கொட்டும்.

The scorpion, stings him who helps it out of the fire.

3976. தேனில் விழுந்த ஈ போலத் தவிக்கிறான்.

He flutters as a fly that has fallen into honey.

3977. தேனுக்கு ஈயைத் தேடி விடுவார் ஆர்?

Who cares to supply flies for honey?

3978. தேனும் தினைமாவும் தேவருக்கு அர்ப்பிதம்.

Honey *mixed with* tinai flour is offered to the gods.

3979. தேனும் பாலும்போல் இருக்கவேண்டும்.

Live in harmony, as honey and milk.

3980. தேனும் பாலும்போல் இருந்து கழுத்தை அறுத்தான்.

Pretending friendship as sweet as honey and milk, he cut my throat.

3981. தேனேபோலும் செந்தமிழ்க் கல்வி.

Mellifluous classical Tamil.

3982. தேனைத் தொட்டியோ நீரைத் தொட்டியோ?

Did you touch honey, or did you touch water?

3983. தேன் உண்டானால் ஈ தேடிவரும்.

Where there is honey there are flies.

3984. தேன் உள்ள இடத்தில் ஈ மொய்க்கும்.

Flies swarm where there is honey.

3985. தேன் எடுத்தவனுக்கு ஒரு சொட்டு, மாமன் மனையில் இருந்தவனுக்கு ஒரு சொட்டு.

A cuff for him who steals honey, a cuff for him who lives in the house of his father-in-law.

3986. தேன் ஒழுகப்பேசித் தெருக் கடக்க வழிவிடுவான்.

He speaks to him mellifluously, and accompanies him across the street-*in order to get rid of him.*

3987. தேன் ஒழுகப் பேசுவான்.

He speaks mellifluously.

3988. தேன் கூட்டிலே கல்லைவிட்டு எறியலாமா ?

May you throw stones at a bee-hive ?

3989. தேன் தொட்டார் கை நக்காரோ?

Will those who have touched honey not lick *their fingers* ?

3990. தேன் தொட்டவன் புறங்கை நக்காமற் போவானா?

When one has touched honey, will he not lick the back of his hand ?

3991. தேன் வார்த்து வளர்த்தாலும் காஞ்சிரம் தெங்கு ஆகுமோ ?

Will the gall-nut become as sweet as a cocoanut though watered with honey ?

தை.

3992. தை ஈனாப் புல்லும் இல்லை, மாசி ஈனா மரமும் இல்லை.

There is no grass that does not grow in January, nor tree that does not sprout in February.

3993. தைத்த வாயிலும் இருக்கத் தாணித்த வாயிலும் இருக்க எங்காலே போனீர் உப்பனாரே?

Whilst one gate is blocked up, and the other defended by artillery, O Uppanár how did you find your way in ?

3994. தை பிறந்தால் வழி பிறக்கும்.
If January come, roads come.

3995. தைப்புக்குத் தைப்பு மரம் பிடித்தாற்போல.
Like holding the lath as each nail is fastened.

3996. தையலும் இல்லான் மையலும் இல்லான்.
One who has neither wife, nor desire *to marry.*

3997. தையும் மாசியும் வையகத்து உறங்கு.
In January and February sleep under thatch.
Because dew is then excessive.

தொ.

3998. தொட்டால தோழன் விட்டால் மாற்றான்.
When together friends, if separated enemies.

3999. தொட்டிலிற் பிள்ளைக்கு நடக்கிற பிள்ளை நமன்.
A child that can walk, is as Yama to a child in the cradle.

4000. தொட்டியப் பேய் சுடுகாடு மட்டும்.
The demon of a wizard pursues one to the burning ground.

4001. தொட்டிலும் ஆட்டிப் பிள்ளையும் கிள்ளுவாள்.
She rocks the cradle and pinches the child.

4002. தொட்டிற் பழக்கம் சுடுகாடு மட்டும்.
Habits contracted in the cradle cleave to one till he goes to the burning ground.

4003. தொட்டுக் காட்டாத வித்தை சொட்டுப் போட்டாலும் வராது.
Without a preceptor an art cannot be attained.

4001. தொண்டர்கள் அன்பன் துணைக்கு நிற்பவன்.
He is the friend of his servants who helps them.

4005. தொண்டனெனப்படேல்.
Be not called a slave.

4006. தொண்ணூறு கடனோடே துவரம்பருப்புக் காற் பணம்.

With ninety debts, beans for a quarter of a fanam.

4007. தொண்ணூறு பொன்னோடே துவரம்பருப்பு ஒரு பணம்.

With ninety gold fanams, one for beans.

4008. தொத்துக்குத் தொத்துச் சாட்சி துவரம்பருப்புக்கு மத்தே சாட்சி.

A slave is a witness for a slave, a churn-staff is a witness for beans-*cytisus cajan*.

4009. தொழுதூண் சுவையின் உழுதூண் இனிது.

The food earned by the plough is sweeter than that obtained by serving others.

4010. தொழுவம் புகுந்த ஆடு புழுக்கை இடாமற் போமா?

When sheep are penned, will not dung be found in the fold?

4011. தொன்மை நாடி நன்மை விடாதே.

In your zeal for old forms neglect not what is really useful.

4012. தொன்மை மறவேல்.

Forget not your former condition.

4013. தொன்னிலம் முழுதும் தோன்றிய கல்வி.

Learning which is conspicuous to the whole world.

தோ.

4014. தோட்டக்காரன் வாழ்வு காற்று அடித்தால் போயிற்று.

The prospects of a gardener are destroyed by a gale.

4015. தோட்டத்தில் அந்தம்.

It ends in the garden.

4016. தோட்டத்து நரி கூட்டத்தில் வருமா?

Will the jackal of the garden come into the assembly?

4017. தோட்டம் முச்சாண் சுரைக்காய் அறுசாண்.

The garden is three spans square, the gourd *in it* is six spans *long*.

4018. தோட்டம் நிலைத்தல்லவோ தென்னம்பிள்ளை வைக்கவேண்டும்.

It is after laying out the garden plot, is it not, that cocoanut trees are planted.

4019. தோட்டிபோல் உழைத்தால் துரைபோலச் சாப்பிடலாம்.

If you work like a scavenger, you may eat like your master.

4020. தோணி போகும் துறை கிடக்கும்.

The ship goes, the port remains.

4021. தோண்டக் குறுணி தூர்க்க முக்குறுணி.

One kuruni for digging, three for filling up.

4022. தோல் இருக்கச் சுளை விழுங்கி.

He who can swallow the pulp while the peel remains intact.

4023. தோழனாவது துலங்கிய கல்வி.

Distinguished learning is a real companion.

4024. தோழனோடும் ஏழைமை பேசேல்.

Disclose not your defects even to a friend.

4025. தோளில் இருந்து செவியைக் கடிக்கிறதா?

What! seated on the shoulder and biting the ear!

4026. தோற்பது கொண்டு சபை ஏறுகிறதா?

Do you enter the assembly when sure of defeat!

4027. தோற்றின யாவும் தோற்றம் அற்று ஒழியும்.

All things that exist will vanish away.

தௌ.

4028. தௌவித் திரியேல்.

Do not romp about.

4029. தௌவையின் மனதுக்கு ஓவ்வுதல் இல்லை.

Nothing gives satisfaction to the goddess of misfortune.

ந.

4030. நகத்தாலே கிள்ளுவதைக் கோடரிகொண்டு வெட்டுகிறதா?

Do you use a hatchet when the nails would suffice?

4031. நகமும் சதையும்போலே வாழுகிறான்.

United like the nails and the flesh.

4032. நகரைக்குப் பெத்தை வழிகாட்டுகிறதோ?

Is a péttai-*a small fish* a guide to a nagarai fish?

4033. நகைக்கு மகிழ்ச்சி நட்புக்கு நஞ்சு.

Merriment is the poison of friendship.

4034. நகைச்சொல் தருதல் பகைக்கு ஏதுவாகும்.

Reproachful words lead to enmity.

4035. நகைத்து இகழ்வோனை நாயென நினை.

Regard him as a dog who laughs you to scorn.

4036. நக்குகிற நாய்க்குச் செக்கு என்றும் சிவலிங்கம் என்றும் தெரியுமா?

Does a dog addicted to licking, distinguish between an oil-press and a Siva linga?

The linga, the symbol of the Saiva worship, is anointed with oil.

4037. நக்குகிறபொழுது நாவு எழும்புமா?

Does the tongue rise when licking?

When eating the food of another reproachful language is not used.

4038. நக்கு உண்டார் நாவு எழார்.

Those who lick do not raise the tongue.

Those who have eaten the food of another man will not reproach him.

4039. நச்சு மரம் ஆனாலும் நட்டவர்கள் வெட்டுவார்களா?

Though a poisonous tree, will those who planted it cut it down?

4040. நஞ்சுக்குள் இருந்தாலும் நாகமணி மாணிக்கமே, குப்பைக்குள் இருந்தாலும் குன்றிமணி குன்றிமணியே.

Though associated with poison, the stone on a cobra's head is a gem; though it may be found in a dunghill, a kunrimani is still the same.

4041. நஞ்சு நாற்கலம் வேண்டுமோ?

Are four kalams of poison required?

4042. நடக்க அறியாதவனுக்கு நடுவீடு காதவழி.

To a person unaccustomed to walk, the middle of his house is ten miles off.

4043. நடக்கிறது நடக்கட்டும் தெய்வம் இருக்கிறது.

Let things take their course; there is a God.

4044. நடக்கும்கால் தவறுவதிலும் நா தவறுதல் கெட்டது.

A slip of the tongue is worse than that of the foot.

4045. நடந்த பிள்ளை தவழுதாம் தாயார் செய்த தவத்தால்.

It is said to be owing to the penance of the mother that the child that could walk has begun to crawl.

4046. நடந்தவன் காலிலே சீதேவி, இருந்தவன் காலிலே மூதேவி.

The goddess of fortune dwells in the feet of the industrious, the goddess of misfortune dwells in the feet of the sluggard.

The goddess of prosperity or fortune, and the goddess of adversity or misfortune, two sisters, mentioned in this proverb, exercise a mysterious influence over the minds of the vulgar. These remarkable beings are said to have been produced when the celestials, in search of ambrosia, churned the milky ocean. The opinion expressed in the proverb is also contained in a stanza of Nitinerivillakkam a poem on moral subjects, justly admired by the learned, for the terseness and beauty of its composition, as well as for the general purity of its moral sentiments. The poet says:—

"When the goddess of prosperity finds that her favours are not appreciated, she introduces her elder sister, the goddess of adversity, to the sluggard, and then takes her departure."

The goddess of fortune, whose presence is a guarantee for happiness and prosperity, is said to dwell in the face of a horse of superior caste,-with the wise and good,-in all fragrant flowers,-in the tree of paradise that bestows whatever it's votaries may desire,-in the beauty of a good and obedient wife,-in the ocean,-in the portal of a house where a marriage is being celebrated,-in a well governed country,-in grain,-in brilliant lamps and flaming torches,-in the words of the great,-with truth-speaking men,-in the arrows of Cupid,-and in vessels of milk.

The goddess of misfortune is said to have her habitation with the glutton,-the irascible,-with liars and other abandoned characters,-with those clothed in rags,-with vicious women,-in a flock of sheep,-and in the face of the dead.

4047. நடந்தால் நாடு எல்லாம் உறவு, படுத்தால் பாயும் பகை.

The whole country is friendly to one who is active, his own mat is at enmity with the sluggard.

4048. நடபடி உண்டானால் மிதியடி பொன்னாலே.

If allowance for a journey is provided, gold sandals will be used.

4049. நடவுக்குத் தெளி நாலத்தொன்று.

The yield of rice is a fourth part of that planted.

4050. நடு உழவிலே நுகத்தை தெறித்ததுபோல.

Like the snapping of the yoke tie when the plough has done half *its work.*

4051. நடு ஊரில் நச்சுமரம் பழுத்து என்ன?

Of what use is the ripening of the fruit of a poisonous tree in the middle of a village?

4052. நடுக்கடற் போனாலும் மறுப்படாமல் வரக்கடவீர்.

Though you go to the middle of the sea, return uninjured.

4053. நடுத்தெருப் பிச்சைக்கு நாணயம் பார்க்கலாமா?

Can one retain self-respect who receives alms in the middle of the road?

4054. நடுத்தரமானவருடைய தாங்கல் பொன்னின் பிளவு போலப் பற்றவைத்தால் மாறும்.

A fracture in gold vanishes when exposed to the fire; in like manner the anger of the good passes away.

4055. நடுவு நிலைமை உடையவர்க்குச் செய்த உபகாரம் கொஞ்சக்காலத்திற்கு நிற்கும்; அதுபோல, தாமரையில் விழுந்த மழைத் துளி நிற்காமல் மறையும்.

A benefit conferred on the indifferent is remembered for a short time, so a drop of rain on a lotus leaf vanishes soon.

4356. நடை சிறிதாகில் நாள் ஏறும், படை சிறிதாகிற் பயம் ஏறும்.

If one's pace be slow he will be long on the way, if an army be small, its anxiety will be great.

4057. நஷ்டத்துக்குப் பலர் நயத்துக்கு ஒருவனோ?

Is one to have the gain, and many to share the loss?

4058. நஷ்டத்துக்கு ஒருவன் நயத்துக்கு ஒருவன்.

One loses, one gains.

4059. நட்டாற்றிலே கைவிடுகிறது நன்மையா?

Is it kind to abandon one in the middle of a river?

4060. நட்டுவன் பிள்ளைக்கு முட்டடிக்கத் தெரியாதா?

Does not the child of a drummer know how to drum?

4061. நட்டுவன் பிள்ளைக்குக் கொட்டிக் காட்டவேண்டுமா?

Does the child of a drummer require a preceptor?

4062. நண்டுக் குடுவையை நடுத்தெருவில் உடைத்ததுபோல.

Like breaking in the middle of the street a pot containing crabs.

4063. நண்டு கொழுத்தால வளையில் இராது.

The crab will not remain in its hole when it becomes fat.

4064. நண்டைச் சுட்டு நரியைக் காவல் வைத்ததுபோல.

Like setting a jackal to watch a roasted crab.

4065. நண்பொருள் கொடுத்து நன்ருய் ஓது.

Pay the teachers fee, and learn well.

4066. நத்த வாழையிலே நித்தம் காற்பணம்.

A village plantain leaf always costs a quarter fanam.

4067. நத்தை வயிற்றில் முத்துப் பிறந்தது.

Pearls are produced in the belly of an oyster or snail.

4068. நந்த வனத்து ஆண்டிக்கும் முயல் வேட்டைக்கும் எத்தனை தூரம்.

How distant are the occupations of the mendicant of the grove, and of the hare-hunter.

4069. நபாப் அத்தனை ஏழை புலி அத்தனை சாது.

Poor as a Nabob, and gentle as a tiger.

4070. நமது தலைமயிர் அவன் கையில் அகப்பட்டுக்கொண்டது.

The hair of the head is seized by his hand.

4071. நமனுக்கு நாலு பிள்ளை கொடுத்தாலும், உற்ருருக்கு ஒரு பிள்ளை கொடுக்கமாட்டான்.

Though he may give four children to Yama, he will not give one to his relatives.

4072. நமன் எடுத்துக்கொண்டு போகும்பொழுது நழுவி விழுந்தவன்.

He slipped and fell when Yama was carrying him off.

4073. நமன் அறியாத உயிரும் நாரை அறியாத குளமும் உண்டோ ?

Is there a soul that Yama knows not, is there a tank unknown to the crane?

4074. நம்ப வைத்துக் கழுத்து அறுக்கலாமா ?

May you cut a man's throat after ingratiating yourself in his confidence?

4075. நம்பின பேரை நடு ஆற்றில் விடலாமா ?

May you leave in the middle of the river, those who have confided themselves to your care ?

4076. நரி ஊரைவிட்டுப் புலி ஊருக்குப் போனேன் புலி ஊரும் நரி ஊராயிற்று.

Leaving the region of jackals I went to that of the tigers, and that became a region of jackals.

4077. நரி ஒரு சாலுக்கு உழப்போனது.

The jackal is gone to plough.

4078. நரி கூப்பிட்டுக் கடல் முட்டுமா?

Will the howling of the fox reach the sea?

4079. நரி கூப்பிடு கடல் முட்டிப்போகும்.

The howling of the jackal will reach the ocean.

4080. நரி கொழுத்தால் வளையிலே இராது.

If the jackal becomes fat it will not remain in its hole.

4081. நரி கொழுத்து என்ன காஞ்சிரம் பழுத்து என்ன?

What if the jackal becomes fat, or the gall-nut ripen?

4082. நரிக்குட்டிக்கு ஊளை பழக்கவேண்டுமோ?

Is the young jackal to be trained to howl?

4083. நரிக்குப் பெரியதனம் கொடுத்தால் கிடைக்கு இரண்டு ஆடு கேட்கும்.

If the jackal gains the mastery, he will demand two sheep from every flock.

4084. நரி நாலு கால் திருடன் இடையன் இரண்டு கால் திருடன்.

The jackal is a quadraped thief, the shepherd is a biped thief.

4085. நரிமுன்னே நண்டு கரணம் போட்டதுபோல.

As the crab made somersaults before a jackal.

4086. நரியின் கையிலே குடல் கழுவக் கொடுக்கிறதா?

Are viscera to be given into the hands of a jackal to be washed?

4087. நரிவாலைக் கொண்டு கடல் ஆழம் பார்க்கிறதுபோல.

Like measuring the depth of the ocean with the tail of a jackal.

4088. நரை திரை இல்லை, நமனும் அங்கு இல்லை.

He is not grey nor wrinkled; Yama is not there.

4089. நல் இணக்கமல்லது அல்லற் படுத்தும்.

Evil communications will bring distress.

4090. நல் இனத்தில் நட்பு வலிது.

Friendship is stronger than close relationship.

4091. நல்ல உயிர் நாற்பது நாள் இருக்கும்.

A good man's life may continue forty days.

4092. நல்ல எழுத்து நடுவே இருக்கக் கோணல் எழுத்துக் குறுக்கே போட்டது என்ன?

A good letter-*destiny*-being in the middle, how were the crooked letters put in?

4093. நல்ல அமைச்சு இல்லாத அரசு விழி இன்றி வழிச்செல்வோன் போலாம்.

A king without a good counsellor, is like a wayfarirg man who is blind.

4094. நல்லது கெட்டால் நாய்க்கும் வழங்காது.

When the good becomes bad, even a dog will not use it.

4095. நல்லதுக்கு ஒரு பொல்லாதது, பொல்லாததுக்கு ஒரு நல்லது.

A good husband may have a bad wife, and a bad husband may have a good wife.

4096. நல்ல குடிக்கு நாலத்தொரு பங்காளி.

One who holds a fourth share in a prosperous family.

4097. நல்லது செய்து நடுவழியே போனால் பொல்லாது போகிறவழியே போகிறது.

If you do good and walk in the middle of the road, the evil will find its own way.

4098. நல்லது நாற்கலம், ஊத்தை ஒன்பது கலம்.

Of the good only four kalams, of the bad nine kalams.

4099. நல்ல நாளையில் நாழிப் பால் கறவாதது கன்று செத்துக் கலப் பால் கறக்குமோ?

In its best days the cow gave scarcely a measure of milk, will it yield a kalam after its calf is dead?

This proverb may refer to the fact that milch, cows in this part of India and in Ceylon refuse to give their milk in the absence of the calf. The cow when going to a neighbouring house to be milked, is accompanied by its calf which is often muzzled like a dog. When the milkman is about to draw the milk he allows the calf to suck for a few moments and then tying it to the fore leg of the mother, he draws the milk, while she stands quiet licking her offspring. Cows do sometimes allow their milk to be taken when the calf is absent but it not infrequently happens that the cow refuses to give her milk, and the calf is fetched from the homestead to encourage the mother.

If a calf die, its skin may be dried and stuffed. The cow deceived by the device licks the effigy of her calf and yields her milk.

4100. நல்ல நினைவை அனுசரித்தலே கெட்ட நினைவை நீக்கல்.

Entertaining good thoughts, is *in fact* leaving evil thoughts.

4101. நல்லபாம்பு ஆடியது கண்டு நாகப்பூச்சி ஆடியதுபோல.

As the earth-worm imitated the graceful movements of the cobra.

4102. நல்ல மரம் நச்சுக் கனியைத் தராது, நச்சு மரத்திலே நல்ல கனியும் வராது.

A good tree yields not poisonous fruit, nor a poisonous tree good fruit.

4103. நல்ல மரத்தில் முளைத்த புல்லுருவிபோல.

Like a mistletoe growing on a good tree.

4104. நல்ல மாடு ஆனால் உள்ளூரில் விலை ஆகாதா?

If the cow be a good one, will it not find a purchaser in its own village?

4105. நல்ல மாட்டிற்கு ஒரு அடி, நல்ல பெண்ணுக்கு ஒரு சொல்.

A good bullock requires but one blow, and a good woman only one word.

4106. நல்லவர் கண்ணில் நாகம் பட்டாலும் கொல்லார்.

Though it is before them the virtuous will not kill even a cobra.

4107. நல்லவன் என்று பெயர் எடுக்க நாட் செல்லும்.

Time must elapse before one can get a good name.

4108. நல்லவர்கள் ஒரு நாள் செய்த உபகாரத்தை மறவார்; அது போல, பனை ஒரு நாள் விதைத்துத் தண்ணீர் விட்டவனுக்கு பலன் கொடுக்கும்.

The good never forget a benefit; in like manner a palmyrah tree yields its produce to him who planted and watered it.

4109. நல்லவன் ஒருவன் நடுவே நின்றால் அறாத வழக்கும் அறும்.

If there be but one good man present in a suit, the greatest difficulties will be solved.

4110. நல்ல வார்த்தை சொல்லி நாடியைத் தாங்கினான்.

He spoke conciliatory words, and touched my chin *cringingly*.

4111. நல்ல இளங்கன்றே துள்ளாதே.

My good young calf, dont be frisky.

4112. நல்லறம் உள்ளது இல்லறம்.

Domestic virtue is excellent.

4113. நல்ல வேலைக்காரன் ஆற்றோடே போகிறான்.

He is a good servant, but the river carries him away.

4114. நல்ல உடலுக்கு இளைப்பாற்றி கொடாவிட்டாலும் நாவிற்குக் கொடு.

Though you may not give rest to your body, give rest to your tongue.

4115. நல்லவர்கள் சங்காத்தம் நல்ல மணலில் விழுந்த நீர்போல உதவு.

The friendship of the good will prove useful like water falling on good soil.

4116. நல்லாரைக் கண்டால் நாய்போல, பொல்லாரை பூனைபோல.

If he sees the good, a dog, if he sees the wicked, a cat.

4117. நல்லாரை நாவு அழியப் பேசினால் பல்லாலே பதக்குப் சொரியும்.

If one abuses his tongue by slandering the virtuous, maggots will drop from his teeth.

4118. நல்லாரும் நல்ல பாம்பைப்போலத் தங்கள் வலிமையை அடக்கி மறைந்திருப்பார் சில வேளை.

The good, like the cobra, sometimes restrain their power and conceal themselves.

4119. நல்லாரை நாவில் உரை, பொன்னைக் கல்லில் உரை.

Test the good by the words of the tongue, and gold on a touchstone.

4120. நல்லார் பொல்லாரை நடக்கையால் அறியலாம்.

The good and the bad may be known by their conduct.

4121. நல்லோர் ஒருவருக்குப் பெய்யும் மழை எல்லாருக்கும் ஆம்.

The rain that falls on account of one virtuous person is beneficial to all.

4122. நல்லோர் நடக்கை தீயோருக்குத் திகில்.

The acts of the virtuous are a terror to the wicked.

4123. நல்லோன் என வளர், நாட்கள் பாரேல்.

Grow up virtuous, observe not days.

4124. நற்குணமே நல்ல ஆஸ்தி.

A good disposition is the best treasure.

4125. நற்பெண்டிர் நல்லதைக் கண்டால் நமது நாயகனுக்கு என்பார்.

When a faithful wife finds a good thing, she will *keep* it for her husband.

...னைத்துச் சுமக்கலாமா?

Would you wet your burden?

...27. நனைந்த கிழவன் வந்தால் உலர்ந்த விறகுக்குச் சேதம்.

If the old man arive wet, there will be a consumption of dry fire wood.

4128. நன்மை செய்தார் நன்மை பெறுவார், தீமை செய்தார் தீமை பெறுவார்.

Those who do good, obtain good; and those who do evil receive evil.

4129. நன்மை செய்யத் தீமை விளையாது.

Evil will not spring from well-doing.

4130. நன்மையானதைக் கெடுத்தால் நஷ்டத்திலும் நஷ்டம்.

It is the greatest loss to destroy that which is good.

4131. நன்மையும் தீமையும் இம்மையிலே தெரியும்.

Good and evil are apparent in the present state.

4132. நன்மையைப் பெருக்கித் தீமையைக் குறைத்தல் நன்னெறி.

To promote good and to diminish evil is the right way.

4133. நன்மை கடைப்பிடி.

Persevere in that which is good.

4134. நன்றாய் இருந்ததாம் நல்லிசுட்ட பணிகாரம்.

The cakes prepared by Nalli are said to be excellent.

4135. நன்றி மறவேல்.

Forget not a benefit.

4136. நன்றி செய்த கீரிப்பிள்ளையைக் கொன்ற கதைபோல.

Like the story of killing a mungoose that had done well.

The tale is-a mungoose seeing a deadly snake approach a sleeping infant, killed it. When the mother returned from the well she saw blood on the animal, and imagining that it had bitten her child she killed it.

நா.

4137. நா அசைய நாடு அசையும்.

When the tongue moves, the *whole* country moves.

The allusion is to a despotic ruler whose word is law.

4138. நா என்னும் அட்சரம் நாதன் இருப்பிடம்.

The letter ந is the seat of God.

4139. நாக்குக்கு எலும்பு இல்லை எப்படிப் புரட்டினாலும் அப்படிப் புரளும்.

The tongue having no bone will turn any way.

4140. நாக்குப் புரட்டர் போக்குப் புகல்வர்.

Promise-breakers make excuses.

4141. நாங்களும் கங்கணம் கட்டினது உண்டு கழுத்துக்குக் கங்கணம் கட்டினது இல்லை.

We too tied coloured cords about our arms, but not a halter on the neck.

4142. நாச்சியாரும் ஒன்றைப்பற்றி வார்க்கிருள் நானும் ஒன்றைப்பற்றிக் குடிக்கிறேன்.

The mistress pours it out with one design, and I drink it wiht another.

4143. நாச்சியாரைக் காணாத இடத்திலே முறுமுறுப்பதுபோல.

Like murmuring in the absence of the mistress.

4144. நாடிய வரம் எல்லாம் நல்கும் நாயகன்.

A master who bestows all desired blessings.

4145. நாடு அறிந்த பார்ப்பானுக்குப் பூணூல் வேண்டுமோ?

Is a sacred thread necessary for a brahman, who is known throughout the country?

4146. நாடு எங்கும் வாழ்ந்தால் கேடு ஒன்றும் இல்லை.

If the whole country prospers, no evil will happen.

4147. நாடு ஏர்ப்பன செய்.

Do what is agreeable to the community.

4148. நாடு காடாயிற்று காடு கழனி ஆயிற்று.

The country has become a jungle, and the jungle has become a fruitful field.

4149. நாட் சென்ற கொடை நடைகூலி ஆகும்.

A delayed gift becomes the hire for walking *to receive it.*

4150. நாட்டாள் பெற்ற குட்டி நாகரிகம் பேச வல்ல குட்டி.

The child of the peasant is able to speak elegantly.

4151. நாட்டாளுக்கு ஒரு நீட்டாளோ?

Does a boor require a page?

4152. நாட்டுக்கு நல்ல துரை வந்தாலும் தோட்டிக்குப் புல் சுமை போகாது.

Though the country has a good ruler, the scavenger ıs not relieved of his burden of grass.

4153. நாட்டுக்கு ஒரு மழை நமக்கு இரண்டு மழை.

The country has received one downpour of rain, we have received twc i., e., too much.

4154. நாணமும் இல்லை மானமும் இல்லை.

No shame, no sense of honour.

4155. நாணம் இல்லாத வாத்திக்கு நாலு திக்கும் கூத்தி.

Concubines on all sides to a shameless teacher.

4156. நாணம் இல்லாத கூத்திக்கு நாலு திக்கும் வாசல்.

A shameless harlot has entrances on four sides.

4157. நாணம் இல்லாத பெண் நகைப்புக்கு இடம் வைப்பாள்.

An impudent woman gives occasion to be laughed at.

4116. நல்லாரைக் கண்டால் நாய்போல, பொல்லாரைக் கண்டால் பூனைபோல.

If he sees the good, a dog, if he sees the wicked, a cat.

4117. நல்லாரை நாவு அழியப் பேசினால் பல்லாலே பதக்குப் புழுச் சொரியும்.

If one abuses his tongue by slandering the virtuous, maggots will drop from his teeth.

4118. நல்லாரும் நல்ல பாம்பைப்போலத் தங்கள் வலிமையை அடக்கி மறைந்திருப்பார் சில வேளை.

The good, like the cobra, sometimes restrain their power and conceal themselves.

4119. நல்லாரை நாவில் உரை, பொன்னைக் கல்லில் உரை.

Test the good by the words of the tongue, and gold on a touchstone.

4120. நல்லார் பொல்லாரை நடக்கையால் அறியலாம்.

The good and the bad may be known by their conduct.

4121. நல்லோர் ஒருவருக்குப் பெய்யும் மழை எல்லாருக்கும் ஆம்.

The rain that falls on account of one virtuous person. is beneficial to all.

4122. நல்லோர் நடக்கை தீயோருக்குத் திகில்.

The acts of the virtuous are a terror to the wicked.

4123. நல்லோன் என வளர், நாட்கள் பாரேல்.

Grow up virtuous, observe not days.

4124. நற்குணமே நல்ல ஆஸ்தி.

A good disposition is the best treasure.

4125. நற்பெண்டீர் நல்லதைக் கண்டால் நமது நாயகனுக்கு என்பார்.

When a faithful wife finds a good thing, she will *keep* it for her husband.

4126. நனைத்துச் சுமக்கலாமா?

Would you wet your burden!

4127. நனைந்த கிழவன் வந்தால் உலர்ந்த விறகுக்குச் சேதம்.

If the old man arive wet, there will be a consumption of dry fire wood.

4128. நன்மை செய்தார் நன்மை பெறுவார், தீமை செய்தார் தீமை பெறுவார்.

Those who do good, obtain good; and those who do evil receive evil.

4129. நன்மை செய்யத் தீமை விளையாது.

Evil will not spring from well-doing.

4130. நன்மையானதைக் கெடுத்தால் நஷ்டத்திலும் நஷ்டம்.

It is the greatest loss to destroy that which is good.

4131. நன்மையும் தீமையும் இம்மையிலே தெரியும்.

Good and evil are apparent in the present state.

4132. நன்மையைப் பெருக்கித் தீமையைக் குறைத்தல் நன்னெறி.

To promote good and to diminish evil is the right way.

4133. நன்மை கடைப்பிடி.

Persevere in that which is good.

4134. நன்றாய் இருந்ததாம் நல்லிசுட்ட பணிகாரம்.

The cakes prepared by Nalli are said to be excellent.

4135. நன்றி மறவேல்.

Forget not a benefit.

4136. நன்றி செய்த கீரிப்பிள்ளையைக் கொன்ற கதைபோல.

Like the story of killing a mungoose that had done well.

The tale is—a mungoose seeing a deadly snake approach a sleeping infant, killed it. When the mother returned from the well she saw blood on the animal, and imagining that it had bitten her child she killed it.

4158. நாணும்கால் கோணும் நடக்கும் கால் இடறும்.

The foot of diffidence deviates, that of activity stumbles.

4159. நாதமும் கீதமும் ஒத்திருப்பது போல, வேதமும் போதமும் ஒத்திருக்க வேண்டும்.

As a melody and a song are in harmony, so must instruction be in harmony with the Veda.

4160. நாம் ஒருவருக்குக் கொடுத்தால் நமக்கு ஒருவர் கொடுப்பார்.

If we give to others, some one will give to us.

4161. நாம் ஒன்று நினைத்தால் தெய்வம் ஒன்று நினைக்கிறது.

When we think of one thing, the deity designs another.

4162. நாய் அறியுமா ஒருசந்திப் பானை?

Does a dog know which are sacred vessels?

4163. நாயின் பீயை மிதிப்பான் ஏன், நல்ல தண்ணீர் வார்த்துக் கழுவுவான் ஏன்?

Why tread on the dung of a dog, and waste good water to wash it off?

4164. நாயும் களிச்சட்டியும்போல.

Like a dog with a chatty of thick gruel.

4165. நாயும் சரி நாவியும் சரி உனக்கு.

A dog and a civet cat are both alike to you.

4166. நாயும் தன் நிலத்துக்கு ராஜா.

Even a dog is king in his own place.

4167. நாயும் பூனையும்போல.

Like dogs and cats.

4168. நாயும் வளர்த்து நரகலும் வாருவானேன்?

Why keep a dog and clean up its filth?

4169. நாயேன் சொல் அம்பலத்துக்கு ஏறுமோ?

I am but a dog, will my word reach the assembly?

4170. நாயை அடிப்பான் ஏன் பல் இழிவு பார்ப்பான் ஏன்?

Why beat a dog, why make it grin!

4171. நாயை அடிப்பானேன் பீயைச் சுமப்பானேன்?

Why beat a dog and carry away his filth!

4172. நாயை ஏவ, நாய் வாலை ஏவுகிறது.

When you command a dog, he commands his tail.

4173. நாயைக் கண்டால் கல்லைக் காணோம், கல்லைக் கண்டால் நாயைக் காணோம்.

If we see a dog, there is no stone, and if we see a stone, there is no dog.

4174. நாயைக் குளிப்பாட்டி நடுவீட்டில் வைத்தால் வாலைக் குழைத்துக்கொண்டு பீ தின்னப் போகும்.

If you wash a dog and place him in the middle of the house, he will wag his tail and go out to eat filth.

4175. நாயைக் கொஞ்சினால் வாயை நக்கும்.

If you caress a dog, he will lick your mouth.

4176. நாயைக் கொழுக்கட்டையால் எறிந்ததுபோல.

Like pelting a dog with cakes.

4177. நாய் இருக்கிற இடத்தில் சண்டை உண்டு.

Where there are dogs, there is quarreling.

4178. நாய் ஒரு சிறு எலும்புக்குச் சந்தோஷிக்கும்; அதுபோல, சிறியோர் சொற்ப காரியத்தை முடித்தாலும் சந்தோஷம் அடைவார்.

A dog is pleased with a bone, in like manner the low are pleased with their own little acts.

4179. நாய் கடித்ததற்கும் செருப்பால் அடித்ததற்கும் சரி.

The biting of a dog and the slippering of the wound *to effect a cure* are alike, *painful.*

4180. நாய் குலைத்து நத்தம் பாழ் ஆகுமா?

Will the village be ruined by the barking of a dog!

4181. நாய் குலைத்து விடியுமா, கோழி கூப்பிட்டு விடியுமா?

Does the day dawn because the dog barks, or because the cock crows!

4182. நாய் கெட்டகேட்டுக்கு மாமரத்து நிழல், அது கெட்ட கேட்டுக்குப் புளியிட்ட கறி.

Mean as the dog is, he has the shade of a mango tree,—his curry is flavoured with acid.

4183. நாய் கெட்ட கேட்டுக்குத் தேங்காய்ப்பாலும் சோறுமா?

Is a miserable dog to be fed with cocoanut milk and rice!

4184. நாய் கொண்டுபோன பானையை ஆர் கொண்டுபோனால் என்ன?

What matters it who takes away the vessel that the dog had carried off?

4185. நாய் கோவிலுக்கு போவான் ஏன் கோயில் காத்தவன் தெண்டம் இறுப்பான் ஏன்?

Why should a dog go to a temple, or why the keeper of a temple pay a fine?

4186. நாய்க்குக் கடிவாளம் பூட்டினாற்போல.

Like putting a bridle in the mouth of a dog.

4187. நாய்க்குத் தெரியுமா கொக்குப் பிடிக்க?

Does a dog know how to catch a crane!

4188. நாய்க்குத் தெரியுமோ தோல் தேங்காய்?

Does a dog appreciate an unhusked cocoanut?

4189. நாய்க்கு நறுநெய் இணங்காது.

Good cow ghee is not agreeable to a dog's stomach.

4190. நாய்க்கு இரும்புக்கடையில் அலுவல் என்ன?

What business has a dog in an iron bazaar!

4191. நாய்க்கு முழுத் தேங்காய் தக்குமா?

Will a whole cocoanut suit a dog!

4192. நாய்க்கு வேலையும் இல்லை, இருக்க நேரமும் இல்லை.

A dog has nothing to do, and no time to rest.

4193. நாய்க்கு மூத்தால் தாய்க்கும் ஈயாள்.

If she becomes older than a dog, she will not be kind even to her mother.

4194. நாய்க்கு ஏன் தேங்காய், நடுவீட்டுக்குள் போட்டு உருட்டவோ?

Why give a whole cocoanut to a dog, that he may roll it about the house?

4195. நாய்க்குப் பெயர் முத்துமாலை, அதற்கு ஆக்கிப் படைக்கிறது வரகந்தவிடு.

The name of the dog is garland, its food is bran.

4196. நாய் சந்தைக்குப் போனதுபோல.

As a dog went to the market.

4197. நாய் சமுத்திரத்திலே போனாலும் நக்குத் தண்ணீர்.

Although a dog may go to the sea, the water must be lapped.

4198. நாய் சிங்கத்துக்குப் பட்டம் கட்டுமா?

Can a dog invest a lion with a title?

4199. நாய நக்கிச் சமுத்திரம் குறையுமா?

Will the ocean be diminished by the lapping of a dog?

4200. நாய் பட்ட பாடு தடிக்கொம்புக்குத் தெரியுமா?

Are the sufferings of a dog known to the stick, *with which he was beaten*?

4201. நாய் வாய்ப்பட்ட தேன் நல்லது ஆகுமா?

Is the honey, defiled by a dog, fit for use?

4202. நாய் வாலிலே தேன் வைத்தால் ஆருக்குக் கூடும்?

Who will benefit by the honey placed on the tail of a dog?

4203. நாய் வாசலைக் காத்து என்ன, கை இல்லாதவன் பணக்காரனைக் காத்து என்ன?

What avails the waiting of a dog at the door, or the expectations of one who, having no hands, waits on the rich!

4204. நாய் வாலைக் குணக்கு எடுக்கலாமா?

Can you change the shape of a dog's tail?

4205. நாய் வாலைப் பற்றி ஆற்றில் இறங்கலாமா?

May you descend into a river holding on by a dog's tail?

4206. நாய் வாழ்ந்து என்ன, பூனை தாலி அறுத்து என்ன?

What though a dog prosper, or a cat be bereft of her táli!

4207. நாய் வேஷம் போட்டால் குலைக்கவேண்டும்.

If you assume the guise of a dog, you must bark.

4208. நார் அற்றால் கூடும் நரம்பு அற்றால் கூடுமோ?

If a fibre snap it may be united, if a tendon break can it be united?

4209. நாலாம் தலைமுறையைப் பார்த்தால் நாவிதனும் சிற்றப்பனாவான்.

If relationship be traced to the fourth generation, even a barber may become an uncle.

4210. நாலாவது பெண் நாதாங்கி முளைக்கும் திக்கு இல்லை.

A fourth born girl will not afford means even to procure a staple for a bolt.

4211. நாலு ஆறு கூடி ஒரு பாலாறு ஆயிற்று.

If four rivers unite, the stream will be equal to the Pálár.

4212. நாலு பிள்ளை பெற்றவளுக்கு நடுத் தெருவிலே சோறு.

A woman who has borne four children, eats her rice in the middle of the street.

4213. நாலு பேர் கூடினது சபை.

The meeting of four persons is an assembly.

4214. நாலும் இரண்டும் சொல்லுக்கு உறுதி, ஆலும் வேலும் பல்லுக்கு உறுதி.

Náladiyár and the distichs of Valluvar are terse in construction, the twigs of the banian tree and the Acacia are good for the teeth.

The tender fibre of the banian and Acacia are said to cure a gum-boil, and therefore they are used for cleaning the teeth.

4215. நால்வரோ தேவரோ?

Are they the four, or are they celestials?

4216. நால்வர் வாக்குத் தேவர் வாக்கு.

The testimony of four persons has the authority of a divine oracle.

4217. நாவில் பிறக்கும் நன்மையும் தீமையும்.

The tongue produces good and evil.

4218. நாவுக்கு இசைந்தால் பாவுக்கு இசையும்.

If agreeable to the tongue, it will be metrical.

4219. நாழி அரிசி சோறு உண்டவன் நமனுக்கு உயிர் கொடான்.

He that can eat a measure of rice may defy even the regent of the dead.

4220. நாழி நெல்லுக்கு ஒரு புடைவை விற்றாலும் நாயின் அரை நிருவாணம்.

Though a cloth is sold for a measure of rice, the dog goes naked.

4221. நாழி பணம் கொடுத்தாலும் மூளிப் பட்டம் போகாது.

Though one give a measure of fanams, his ill fame will not be removed.

4222. நாழி முகவாது நானாழி.

One measure cannot contain four measures.

4223. நாள் ஆற்றுகிறது நல்லார் ஆற்றார்.

Time effects that which the virtuous cannot achieve.

4224. நாளைக்குத் தின்கிற பலாப்பழத்திலும் இன்றைக்குத் தின்கிற களாப்பழம் நல்லது.

Better is the kala berry eaten to day, than the jack fruit in prospect for to-morrow.

4225. நாறத் தூற்றல் நரிக்குக் கொண்டாட்டம்.

The jackal is pleased with drizzling rain.

4226. நாறல் மீனைப் பூனைப் பார்ப்பதுபோல.

As the cat looks at the fish which has become putrid.

4227. நாறல் சாணியை மிதிப்பான் ஏன் நல்ல தண்ணீர் வார்த்துக் கழுவுவான் ஏன்?

Why tread on filth and waste good water in washing it off!

4228. நாறற் சோற்றுக்குப் பதம் பார்ப்பான் ஏன்?

Why inquire if the rice is properly boiled, seeing that it is unfit for food!

4229. நாறற் சடலம் நலம் இல்லா மட்பாண்டம்.

A fetid body, a useless earthen vessel.

4230. நாற்கலக் கூழுக்கு நானே அதிகாரி.

I have the command of four kalams of gruel.

4231. நாற்பது சென்றால் நாய்க்குச் சரி.

Like a dog, if over forty.

4232. நானிலம் தன்னில் நாயகம் கல்வி.

Learning is a gem when compared to the four kinds of soil.

They are the hilly,-forest,-agricultural and maritime tracts of a country.

4233. நானும் நரைத்து நரைமண்டை ஆனேன் காடு நடக்கக் கண்டது புதினம்.

I have lived long and become grey-headed, but I have not seen a moving jungle.

4234. நானும் அறியேன் அவளும் பொய் சொல்லாள்,

I indeed do not know; nor will she tell a lie.

4235. நான் இட்ட மருந்தும் போக ஒட்டாது நன்னாரி வேரும் சாக ஒட்டாது.

The medicine I gave, *as a charm*, will not allow him to go; the sarasparilia, an *ingredient*, will not suffer him to die.

The proverb relates to charms, in which, as in magical arts generally, the Hindus in every part of India and Ceylon, have great faith. Servants have recourse to this device, and lovers also, for the purpose of influencing the affections and will of those whose favour or compliance they desiderate.

The usual method, as indicated in the proverb, is to administer in the food of the party the ingredients that are fitted for the purpose contemplated; of course the preparation is surreptitiously added to the food of which it is known the individual is about to partake.

A gentleman of my acquaintance recently dismissed all his servants and took into his service a person in whom he appeared to place the greatest confidence. The neighbours and the discarded servants believe that the gentleman acted under a charm.

Some of the things used for certain purposes as charms, may not be mentioned here. The brain of a male child &c., are considered very potent.

Professional magicians are employed when stolen property or buried treasure is sought. The magician uses a black preparation, a small quantity of which is placed on a betel leaf and put into the hands of an attendent boy, who is directed to look steadily at it, aided by the light of a lamp, while the magician invokes the presence and aid of certain deities. When the boy announces a phenomenon, say a tree, a monkey or a dog or a goblin, he is told to do obeisance to it to encourage further discoveries. The earth may cleave asunder and reveal the thing wanted, or a scene, including a house and certain persons going and coming, water &c., may appear, when the boy proceeds to describe the objects before him, as an earthen pot, or a bangle &c., &c., as the case may be.

To discover a thief among suspected persons sometimes dry grain as rice may be given to be eaten. The person whose mouth secretes no moisture for mastication is supposed to be the thief.

4236. நான் ஒன்றை எண்ண விதி ஒன்றை எண்ணிற்று.

While I expected one thing, destiny ordained another.

4237. நான் நட்டேன் நாதன் பயிர் ஆக்கினான்.

I planted; god caused it grow.

4238. நான் பிடித்த முயலுக்கு மூன்று கால்.

The hare that I caught had three legs.

நி.

4239. நிசம் ஒன்று பல தீங்கு நீக்கும்.

One thing ascertained will remove many evils.

4240. நிசாம் அல்லி தண்டில் நிசார்க்காரனைக் கண்டது உண்டா?

Was any trousered sepoy seen in the army of Nizam Aly?

4241. நிஷ்டூரன் கண்ணைத் தெய்வம் கெடுக்கும், நீதிமான் கண்ணைப் பரிதானம் கெடுக்கும்.

God will destroy the eyes of an oppressor, and a bribe will destroy the eye of an upright man.

4242. நித்தம் சாவார்க்கு அழுவார் உண்டா?

Do any weep when deaths are of daily occurrence?

4243. நித்தம் போனால் முற்றம் சலிக்கும்.

If you continually go thither, even the court-yard will be weary of you

4244. நித்தியக் கண்டம் தீர்க்க ஆயுசு.

Constant trouble, long life.

4245. நித்தியம் கிடைக்குமா அமாவாசைச் சோறு?

May new moon fare be expected daily?

The proverb refers to the ceremonies which are performed, at the period of the new moon, in honour of deceased ancestors. On these occasions the household eat only once during the day, but the food is of a superior kind and prepared with great care in cooking utensils that are kept for sacred purposes. If a brahman be present he offers oblations of sesamum grain and water to the manes of the dead, naming each in order as far back as the third generation.

In some parts of India ceremonies supposed to affect the state of the dead are performed no less than ninety-six times every year. The ceremonies of the Ancient Romans of like kind are hinted at by Virgil and Horace as is known to the classical student.

4246. நித்திரை சத்துரு.

Sleep is an enemy.

4247. நித்திரை சுகம் அறியாது.

Sleep is unconscious of enjoyment.

4248. நிந்தனை சொல்லேல், நீதி கைப்பிடி.

Speak no reproachful words, do justice.

4249. நிமிஷநேரம் நிற்கும் இன்பம் சிற்றின்பம்.

Momentary pleasure is inferior pleasure.

4250. நிமிஷ நேரம் நீடிய இன்பம்.

A pleasure that lasts but a moment.

4251. நிமித்தம் பார்க்கிறவன் இரண்டகக்காரி மகன், பொருத்தம் பார்க்கிறவன் பொல்லாங்கன் புத்திரன்.

He who consults omens is the son of a deceitful woman, he who enquires into the fitness of *persons for marriage* is the son of a vicious man.

4252. நிமிர்ந்து போட்டது என்ன குனிந்து எடுத்தது என்ன?

What is lost by an erect posture, and what gained by stooping!

4253. நிமைப் பொழுதேனும் இல்லை நீச உடல்.

The vile body will not endure even for the twinkling of an eye.

4254. நிருவாண தேசத்தில் நீர்ச்சீலை கட்டினவன் பைத்தியகாரன்.

It were an act of folly to wear clothes in a country where all go naked.

4255. நிலத்தில் எழுந்த பூண்டு நிலத்தில் மடியவேண்டும்.

Plants decay on the ground from which they sprung.

4256. நிலத்திற்குத் தகுந்த கனியும் குலத்திற்குத் தகுந்த குணமும்.
Fruit appropriate to the soil, and quality agreeable, to one's rank.

4257. நிலம் கடக்கப் பாயலாமா?
Can you clear the earth at a leap?

4258. நிலவுக்கு ஒளித்துப் பரதேசம் போனதுபோல.
Like going to another country to escape from moonlight.

4259. நிலை இல்லான் வார்த்தை நீர்மேல் எழுத்து.
The words of the unstable are letters on water.

4260. நிலையிற் பிரியேல்.
Swerve not from rectitude.

4261. நிலையை விட்டால் நீச்சு.
When out of your depth, swimming.

4262. நில்லாத காலடி நெடும் தூரம் போகும்.
Ceaseless walking accomplishes great distances.

4263. நில்லாது ஏதும் நிலையே கல்வி.
Learning alone is enduring, all else is evanescent.

4264. நிழலுக்கும் களவுக்கும் ஒத்தது ஆக்கை.
The body may be compared to a shadow, and to theft.

4265. நிழல் அருமை வெயிலில் தெரியும்.
The salubrity of shade is realized in sunshine.

4266. நிழல் நல்லது முசிறு பொல்லாதது.
The shade is good, the ants are bad.

4267. நிறைந்த ஆற்றிலே பெருங்காயம் கரைத்ததுபோல.
Like dissolving assafœtida in a flooded river.

4268. நிறை பொதியிலே கழுதை வாய் வைத்தாற்போல.
As an ass put its mouth into a full sack.

4269. நிறையக் குறுணி வேண்டாம் தலை தடவிக் குறுணி கொடு.
I do not want a kuruni heaped up, give me a kuruni of grain level with the brim.

4270. நினைக்குமுன் வருவான் நினைப்பதும் தருவான்.
He will come before you think of him, he will give what you intend applying for.

4271. நினைத்த நேரம் நெடுமழை பெய்யுமா?
Will heavy rain fall as we may wish?

4272. நினைத்தது இருக்க நினையாதது எய்தும், நினைத்தது வந்தாலும் வந்து நேரும்.
When one thing is expected another may come, and that which is thought of may possibly come.

4273. நின்ற மரத்தில் நெடு மரம் போனால் நிற்கும் மரமே நெடு மரம்
When the lofty trees are felled, the remaining trees look tall.

4274. நின்ற வெள்ளத்தையும் வந்த வெள்ளம் கொண்டுபோயிற்று.
The flood that was, has been swept away by the flood that followed.

4275. நின்றால் நெடு மரம் விழுந்தால் பனைமரம்.
When standing, a tall tree, when fallen, a palmyrah tree.

4276. நின்றாற்போல் விழுந்தால் தலை உடையும்.
If you fall as you stand, your head will be broken.

நீ.

4277. நீசரானவர் நிலைபெறக் கல்லார்.
The base do not persevere in study.

4278. நீட்டு வித்தை ஏறாது.
Boasted learning will not avail.

4279. நீண்ட கை நெருப்பு அள்ளும்.
The stretched hand will lade out fire.

4280. நீண்ட தச்சும் குறுகிய கொல்லும்.

Length to the carpenter, shortness to the smith.

The former can easily shorten wood by cutting,-the smith can lengthen iron by heating.

4281. நீண்ட புல் நிற்க நிழலாமா ?

Will long grass afford a shade ?

A ready affirmation would answer this in central Africa.

4282. நீதி அற்ற பட்டணத்தில் நிறைமழை பெய்யுமா ?

Will sufficient rain fall in a city where justice cannot be obtained ?

4283. நீதி கேளாமல் தலே வெட்டுவார்களா ?

Will they cut off the head without judicial proceedings ?

4284. நீதிமான் தீவினை செய்யிற் பிழைப்பானு, நீதி இல்லாதவன் நீதி புரிந்தால் மரிப்பானு ?

Will a virtuous man escape *death* if he do evil, will the unjust die if he do justice ?

4285. நீ நீராலே விலகினுய் நான் நெருப்பாலே விலகினேன்.

You have escaped an accident by water, I have escaped one by fire.

4286. நீந்தமாட்டாதவனை ஆறு கொண்டுபோகிறது.

The river carries away him who cannot swim.

4287. நீ பிறர்க்கு உதவி செய்தால் தெய்வம் உனக்கு உதவி செய்யும்.

If you help others, God will help you.

4288. நீரகம் பொருந்திய ஊரகத்திரு.

Live in a village where there is a good supply of water.

4289. நீரில் எழுத்தாகும் ஆக்கை.

The body is an inscription on water.

4290. நீரிற் குமிழி சரீரம்.

The body is a bubble on water.

4291. நீரும் கொல்லும் நெருப்பும் கொல்லும்.
Water kills, and fire also kills.

4292. நீரை அடித்தால் வேறுமா?
Can water be divided by a stroke?

4293. நீரைச் சிந்தினையோ சீரைச் சிந்தினையோ?
Did you spill water, or did you spill your character?

4294. நீர் ஆழம் காணலாம் நெஞ்சு ஆழம் காணப்படாது.
The depth of water may be ascertained, but not the depth of the heart.

4295. நீர் உயர நெல் உயரும்.
As the water rises, the rice plant rises.

4296. நீர் உள்ள மட்டும் மீன்குஞ்சு துள்ளும்.
The young fish will sport as long as the water lasts.

4297. நீர் என்று சொன்னல் நெருப்பு அவியுமா?
Can fire be quenched by pronouncing the word water?

4298. நீர் என்று சொல்ல நெருப்பாய் முடிந்தது.
When it was said to be water, it turned out to be fire.

4299. நீர்க்குட் பாசிபோல் வேர்க்கொள்ளாது.
As moss in water, it will not take root.

4300. நீர் போனல் மீன் துள்ளுமா?
When the water goes, will the fish leap about?

4301. நீர்மேற் குமிழிபோல் நிலை இல்லாக் காயம்.
The body is unstable as a bubble on water.

4302. நீர் விளையாடேல்.
Do not play in water.

4303. நீலத்துக்குக் கறுப்பு ஊட்டவேண்டுமோ?
Is black dyed in blue?

4304. நீலம் கட்டுப்படப் பேசுகிறது.

To speak so as to confine the blue dye *to the skirts of the cloth.*

4305. நீலிக்குக் கண்ணீர் நிமையிலே.

A termagant has her tears in the eyelids.

நு.

4306. நுட்ப புத்திமான் திட்ப சித்திவான்.

The shrewed are successful.

4307. நுண்ணிய ஞானம் உரைப்பார்கள் சொன்னதில் ஒன்றும் நடவார்கள்.

They give wise counsels, but they themselves walk not according to any one of them.

4308. நுண்ணிய கருமமும் எண்ணித் துணி.

Although a small thing, do it after due thought.

4309. நுண்பொருள் கொடுத்து நுண்ணியராவர்.

They become possessed of discrimination by imparting instruction on abstruse subjects.

4310. நுண்மை நுகரேல்.

Be not particular in food.

4311. நுரை ஒத்ததுவே தரையிற் பவுஷு.

The affluence of this world is as froth.

4312. நுரையைத் தின்றால் பசிபோகாது.

Hunger cannot be satisfied by eating froth.

4313. நுழை விட்டு செய் நூல் கற்று அடங்கு.

Build a house with an entrance, acquire learning and be humble.

4314. நுளையன் அறிவானா ரத்தினத்தின் பெருமை?

Does a fisherman understand the value of gems?

4315. நுளையன் பேச்சு அம்பலம் ஏறாது.

The words of a fisherman will not reach the assembly.

4316. நுனிக்கொம்பில் ஏறி அடிக்கொம்பு வெட்டுவார்களா?

Having ascended to the extremity of the bough, will they sever it from the tree?

நூ.

4317. நூல் இல்லாமல் மாலை கோத்ததுபோல.

Like making a garland of flowers without a string.

4318. நூல் கற்றவனே மேலவன் ஆவான்.

The learned only will gain eminence.

4319. நூறு ஆண்டு ஆகிலும் கல்வியை நோக்கு.

Though a hundred years old, diligently acquire knowledge.

4320. நூறு குற்றம் ஆறு பிழை கொண்டு பொறுக்கவேண்டும்.

A hundred offences must be forgiven as if only six faults.

4321. நூறுநாள் ஓதி ஆறுநாள் விடத் தீரும்.

The learning acquired in a hundred days, will be lost by six days neglect.

4322. நூறோடு நூறு ஆகிறது நெய்யிலே சுட்டு பணிகாரம்.

Though *the debt* may increase to another hundred, bake the cakes in ghee.

4323. நூற்றுக்கு இருந்தாலும் கூற்றுக்கு அரிகிளை.

Though a hundred years old, he is only a young plant to the regent of the dead.

4324. நூற்றுக்கு இருப்பார் ஐம்பதில் சாகார்.

Those who will live to be a hundred, will not die at fifty.

4325. நூற்றுக்குமேல் ஊற்று, ஆயிரத்துக்குமேல் ஆற்றுப்பெருக்கு.

After a hundred a spring, after a thousand a flooded river.

4326. நூற்றுக்கு ஒரு பேச்சு ஆயிரத்துக்கு ஒரு தலை அசைப்பு.
When he is worth a hundred, a word, when a thousand, a mere nod.

4327. நூற்றைக் கெடுத்தது குறுணி.
One measure *of chaff* spoiled a hundred *of grain.*

4328. நூன்முறை தெரிந்து சீலத்தொழுகு.
Ascertaining the rules of the Veda, live virtuously.

நெ.

4329. நெஞ்சு அறியப் பொய் சொல்லலாமோ?
May one tell a lie knowingly?

4330. நெஞ்சை ஒளித்து ஒரு வஞ்சகம் இல்லை.
There is no deceit which can be concealed from the mind.

4331. நெடியார் குறியாரை ஆற்றிலே தெரியும்.
It will be known in the river, who is tall and who is short.

4332. நெடும் கடல் ஓடியும் நிலையே கல்வி.
Though you may cross the broad sea your learning will remain with you.

4333. நெடும் பகலுக்கும் அஸ்தமனம் உண்டு.
Even a long day has a sunset.

4334. நெய்கிறவனுக்கு ஏன் குரங்குக் குட்டி?
What has a weaver to do with a young monkey!

4335 நெய்க்குடத்தில் எறும்பு மொய்த்ததுபோல.
As the ants swarm on a ghee pot.

4336. நெய்க்குடம் உடைந்தால் நாய்க்கு விருந்து.
If the ghee pot is broken, the dog has a feast.

4337. நெய்க்குடம் உடைந்தது நாய்க்கு வேட்டை.
The breaking of the ghee pot, is a hunting excursion to the dog.

4338. நெய்யை உருக்கித் தயிரைப் பெருக்கிச் சாப்பிடவேண்டும்.

Use ghee after melting, and curds diluted.

4339. நெருஞ்சி முள் தைத்தாலும் குனிந்து அல்லவோ பிடுங்க வேண்டும்?

Though it be but a thistle that has entered your foot, you must sit down, must you not, to pull it out?

4340. நெருப்பில் ஈ மொய்க்குமா?

Will flies swarm in fire?

4341. நெருப்பினும் பொல்லாது கிப்பின் வாதை.

The distress of famine is worse than that of fire.

4342. நெருப்பிலும் பொல்லாச் செருப்பு.

Shoes worse than fire.

4343. நெருப்பிலே புழுப் பற்றுமா?

Will worms breed in fire?

4344. நெருப்பு ஆறும் மயிர்ப் பாலமும்.

A river of fire, and a bridge of hair.

4345. நெருப்பு இல்லாமற் புகை புகையுமா?

Will there be smoke where there is no fire?

4346. நெருப்பு நின்ற காட்டிலே ஏதாவது நின்றாலும் நிற்கும், நீர் நின்ற காட்டில் ஒன்றும் நிற்காது.

Something may possibly remain in a forest after a fire, but nothing remains after a flood.

4347. நெருப்பு என்றால் வாய் வேகுமா?

By pronouncing the word fire, will the mouth be burnt?

4348. நெருப்பைக் கண்டு மிதித்தாலும் சுடும், காணமல் மிதித்தாலும் சுடும்.

Whether you tread on fire wittingly or unawares, it will burn you.

4349. நெருப்பைச் சேர்ந்த யாவும் அதன் நிறமாகும்; அதுபோல, பெரியோரைச் சேர்ந்தவரும் ஆவார்.

Things put into fire partake of its colour, in like manner will it happen to those who join the great.

4350. நெருப்புச் சிறிது என்று முன்றானையில் முடியலாமா?

May you tie fire in the skirt of your cloth because a mere spark?

4351. நெருப்பைத் தலை கீழாய்ப் பிடித்தாலும் அதின் சுவாலை கீழாகுமா?

Although you carry fire head downwards, will the flame burn in that direction?

4352. நெல் எடுக்கவும் புல் எடுக்கவும் ஆச்சோ?

Am I destined to carry both paddy and grass?

4353. நெல்லும் உப்பும் பிசைந்து உண்ணக் கூடுமா?

Will a mixture of paddy and salt be agreeable to the palate?

4354. நெல்லு வகை எண்ணினாலும் பள்ள வகை எண்ணக் கூடாது.

Though one may enumerate the various kinds of rice, he cannot enumerate the varieties of the palla caste.

4355. நெல் விளைந்த பூமியும் அறியாய், நிலா எறித்த இடமும் அறியாய்.

You do not know a rice crop, nor a moonlight space.

4356. நெறி தப்புவார்க்கு அறிவிப்பது வீண்.

It is useless to teach those who diviate from rectitude.

4357. நெற்பயிர் விளை.

Cultivate rice.

நே.

4358. நேத்திர மணியே சூத்திர அணியே.

The apple of the eye, is an ingenious piece of mechanism.

4359. நேயமே நிற்கும்.

Love alone will abide.

4360. நேரா நோன்பு சீர் ஆகாது.

Fasting without a vow is not good.

4361. நேர்ந்து நேர்ந்து சொன்னாலும், நீசக் கசடர் வசம் ஆகார்.

Though repeatedly told, the base take no heed.

4362. நேர்பட ஒழுகு.

Behave evenly or agreeably.

4363. நேற்று வந்த மொட்டைச்சி நெய் வார்த்து உண்ணச் சிணுங்குகிறாள்.

The bald headed woman who came but yesterday, is whining for ghee to eat with her rice.

4364. நேற்று வந்தானாம் குடி அவன் தலையில் விழுந்ததாம் இடி.

It is said that he took up his abode only yesterday, and he has been struck by lightning.

நை.

4365. நைஷதம் புலவர்க்கு ஔஷதம்.

Naishadha is a cordial to poets.

4366. நைபவர் எனினும் நொய்ய உரையேல்.

Speak not roughly even to a beggar.

4367. நையக் கற்றினும் நொய்ய நன்கு உரை.

Though mollified by learning, speak effectively.

4368. நைவினை நணுகேல்.

Go not near that which is pernicious.

நொ.

4369. நொடிப்போதும் வீணிடேல்.

Lose not even a moment of time.

4370. நொண்டி நொண்டி நடப்பானேன் கண்டதற்கு எல்லாம் படைப்பானேன்?

Why walk limping, and why offer oblations, to every *god* you see?

4371. நொண்டிக் குதிரைக்குச் சறுக்கினது சாக்கு.

To slip is the excuse of the lame horse.

4372. நொந்த கண் இருக்க நோகாக் கண்ணுக்கு மருந்து.

Applying medicine to the sound eye, instead of to the one diseased.

4373. நொந்து அறியாதவர் செந்தமிழ் கற்றோர்.

Those who are well versed in classical Tamil know not want.

4374. நொய் யரிசி கொதி பொறுக்குமா?

Will *bruised* rice bear boiling!

4375. நொறுங்கத் தின்றோர்க்கு நூறு வயது.

Those who masticate their food, live a hundred years.

நோ.

4376. நோகஃது உணர்வோர் கல்வியை நோற்பார்.

Those who study unmindful of the pains *attending it* are devoted to learning.

4377. நோகாமல் அடிக்கிறேன் ஓயாமல் அழு.

I will beat you without giving pain, set up an unceasing cry.

4378. நோக்கத்தொதுங்கு.

Be careful *to secure* your object.

4379. நோக்க நோக்குவ நோக்காமுன் நோக்குவன்.

He whom we seek to see, has already seen us.

4380. நோயற்ற வாழ்வே வாழ்வு குறைவற்ற செல்வமே செல்வம்.
Freedom from sickness is true happiness, and competence is true riches.

4381. நோயாளிக்கு ஆசை வார்த்தை சொன்னாற்போல.
Like uttering soothing words to a sick person.

4382. நோயாளி விதியாளி ஆனால் பரிகாரி பேராளி ஆவான்.
If destiny favours the patient, his doctor will obtain fame.

4383. நோயாளிக்குத் தெரியும் நோயின் வருத்தம்.
The sick person knows the intensity of his suffering.

4384. நோய் கொண்டார் பேய்கொண்டார்.
The sick are *like those* possessed of demons.

4385. நோய்ஞ்சற் பூனை மத்தை நக்குமாபோலே.
As a lean cat licks the churnstaff.

4386. நோய்தத புலி ஆகிலும் மாட்டுக்கு வலிது.
Though the chetah is sick, it is stronger than on ox.

4387. நோலாமையினால் மேலானதுபோம்.
By neglecting religious austerities supreme good will be lost.

4388. நோவு ஒரு பக்கம் இருக்கச் சூடு ஒரு பக்கம் போட்டாற் போல.
Like branding the side that is not affected by disease.

4389. நோன்பு என்பது கொன்று தின்னாமை.
Not to take life for the purpose of eating, is to fast.

நௌ.

4390. நௌவித் தொழில் நலம்.
Youthful education will prove beneficial.

4391. நௌவியிற்றானே தெய்வறிவைக் கல்.
Know God when you are young.

4392. நௌவியும் முதுமையும் நடுவு மற்றவன்.

He who is without youth, old age, or manhood.

4393. நௌவியும் வாழ்க்கையும் அழகல்ல, நற்குணம் ஒன்றே அழகு.

Youth and affluence do not form one's beauty, goodness alone does.

ப.

4394. பகலிற் பக்கம் பார்த்துப் பேசு, அர்த்தராத்திரியில் அதுதானும் பேசாதே.

By day, look round and speak, at midnight do not utter a word.

4395. பகலிற் பசு தெரியவில்லை இரவில் எருமை தெரியுமா?

Not being able to distinguish a cow by day, how can he distinguish a buffalo by night?

4396. பகிடிக்குப் பத்துக் காசு திருப்பாட்டுக்கு ஒரு காசு.

Ten cash for a comedy, one cash for a sacred song.

4397. பகிடியைப் பாம்பு கடித்ததுபோல.

As the snake bit the jester.

4398. பகுத்தல் இல்லாத துணிவு பாரம் இல்லாத கப்பல்.

Daring without prudence, *is as* a ship without ballast.

4399. பகுர்த்து அறியாமல் துணியாதே படபடப்பாகச் செய்யாதே.

Attempt nothing without consideration, and do nothing hastily.

4400. பகைக்கச் செய்யேல் மறு ஜெனனப்படு.

Do not create enemies, act discreetly.

4401. பகையாளி குடியை உறவாடிக் கெடுக்கவேண்டும்.

You must ruin the family of your enemy by feigned friendship.

4402. பகைவர் உறவு புகை எழு நெருப்பு.

The friendship of foes is like fire concealed in smoke.

4403. பங்காளி குடி கெடுக்க வெங்காயம் குளிபோடச் சொன்னது போல.

Like advising his partner to plant onions in order to effect his ruin.

4404. பங்காளி வீடு வேகிறது சுங்கான்கொண்டு தண்ணீர் விடு.

The house of my partner is on fire, pour water with a pipe.

4405. பங்காளியும் பனங்காயும் பதம்பார்த்து வெட்டவேண்டும்.

Observe the proper time for cutting a partner and palmyrah fruit.

4406. பங்குனி என்று பருப்பதும் இல்லை, சித்திரை என்று சிறுப்பதும் இல்லை.

It wont grow larger because it is Panguni,-*March*-nor smaller because it is Chittarai-*April.*

4407. பங்குனிமாதம் பகல்வழி நடந்தவன் பெரும்பாவி.

He that goes abroad in the day time in March, is a great sinner.

4408, பசி இல்லாதவனுக்குக் கரிப்பு மயிர் மாத்திரம்.

He who is not hungry cares not a hair about famine.

4409. பசி ஏப்பக்காரனும் புளி ஏப்பக்காரனும் கூட்டுப்பயிர் இட்டது போல.

As two men, one belching through hunger, and the other by indigestion, were associated in joint tillage.

4410. பசு ஏறுவாலும் எருது கூழைவாலும்.

A cow with a long tail, an ox with a short one.

4411. பசிக்குக் கறி வேண்டாம், தூக்கத்துக்குப் பாய் வேண்டாம்.

When hungry curry is not needed, nor a mat when sleepy.

4412. பசிக்குப் பனம் பழம் தின்றால் பித்தம் பட்ட பாடு படட்டும்.

Eat palmyrah fruit to satisfy hunger, no matter about the bile.

Palmyrah fruit is believed to be very bilious.

4413. பசி தீர்ந்ததானால் பாட்டு இன்பமாம்.

Songs are pleasant after refection.

4414. பசித்த பறையனும் குளித்த சைவனும் சாப்பிடாது இரார்.

A hungry pariah and a saiva that has bathed, must have eaten first.

4415. பசித்தவன் தின்னாததும் இல்லை, பகைத்தவன் சொல்லாததும் இல்லை.

There is nothing *edible* which the hungry will not eat, there is no reproach which the malevolent has not uttered.

4416. பசித்தவன்மேல் நம்பிக்கை வைக்கலாமா ?

Can confidence be placed in a hungry person ?

4417. பசித்த செட்டி பாக்குத் தின்றானும்.

It is said that a hungry merchant chewed betel and arica-nut.

4418. பசித்தவன் பயற்றை விதைக்கட்டும்.

Let the hungry sow peas.

4419. பசித்தவன் பழம் கணக்கைப் பார்ப்பதுபோல்.

As a hungry man looks at his old accounts.

4420. பசித்தார் பொழுதும் போம் பாலுடன் அன்னம் புசித்தார் பொழுதும் போம்.

The sun goes down on the hungry, and also on those who eat their rice and milk.

4421. பசியாமல் மருந்து கொடுக்கிறேன் பழையது இருந்தால் போடு என்பதுபோல.

Like saying, put before me some old rice if there be any, and I will give you medicine that will prevent your hungering again.

4422. பசி ருசி அறியுமா நித்திரை சுகம் அறியுமா ?

Does hunger appreciate flavours, or sleep enjoyment ?

4423. பசி ருசி அறியாது, நித்திரை சுகம் அறியாது.

Hunger is ignorant of flavours, sleep is ignorant of enjoyment

---

4424. பசி வந்திடில் பத்தும் பறந்துபோம்.

Hunger dissipates the ten.

The ten, are the five senses and their organs.

4425. பசுகறுப்பென்று பாலும் கறுப்பா?

Because the cow is black, is her milk also black?

4426. பசுச் சாதும் பார்ப்பான் ஏழையும் உண்டா?

Are there any gentle cows, or poor brahmans?

4427. பசுத் தோல் போர்த்துப் புலிப் பாய்ச்சல் பாய்கிறது.

To wear a cow skin, and spring like a tiger.

4428. பசுப்போலே இருந்து புலிப்போலே பாய்கிறாய்.

Gentle as a cow, you spring as a tiger.

4429. பசு மரத்தில் தைத்த ஆணிபோல.

Like a nail driven into a green tree.

4430. பசு விழுந்தது புலிக்குத் தாயம்.

The falling of the cow, is a gain to the tiger.

4431. பசுவுக்கு இரை கொடுத்தால் மதுரமான பால் கொடுக்கும். அதுபோல, நல்லவர்களுக்குச் செய்கிற உபகாரம் பலன் அளிக்கும்.

When a cow is fed she yields sweet milk, so the favours shewn to the good will bring a reward.

4432. பசுவைக் கொன்றால் கன்று பிழைக்குமா?

If you slaughter a cow, will its calf live?

4433. பசுவைக் கொன்று செருப்புத் தானம் செய்தது போல.

Like killing the cow and giving shoes made of its hide.

4434. பசுவை அடித்துப் புலிக்குத் தானம் கொடுக்கிறதா?

Do you kill a cow, and make an offering of it to a tiger?

4435. பசுவை விற்றால் கன்றுக்கு வழக்கா?

Having sold the cow, is there a dispute about the calf?

4436. பச்சடி கண்டால் ஒட்டடிமகளே.

Daughter, if you find him rich, cling to him.

4437. பச்சிலையும் கிள்ளப்படுமோ பராபரமே!

O God, is a tender plant also to be cut off!

4438. பச்சை கொடுத்தால் பாவம் தீரும் வெள்ளை கொடுத்தால் வினை தீரும்.

If raw provisions are given, the sins of the present birth will be removed, if white *cloths* are given, the sins of former births will be cancelled.

4439. பச்சைச் சிரிப்புப் பல்லுக்குக் கேடு தூவு பருக்கை வயிற்றுக்குக் கேடு.

Feigned laughter is bad for the teeth, and scattered grains of *boiled* rice are bad for the stomach.

4440. பச்சை நெல்லுக்குப் பறையனிடத்திற் சேவிக்கலாம்.

You may serve a pariah for paddy.

4441. பச்சை மண்ணும் சுட்ட மண்ணும் ஒட்டுமா?

Will moist and burnt clay unite?

4442. பச்சை மரம் படப் பார்ப்பான்.

He can stare so as to make a green tree decay.

4443. பச்சை மரத்திற்கு இத்தனை என்றாற் பட்டமரத்திற்கு எத்தனை?

If so much to the green tree, how much to the dry!

4444. பஞ்சம் இல்லாக் காலத்தில் பசி பறக்கும்.

In the absence of famine hunger flies away.

4445. பஞ்சம் போம் பஞ்சத்திற் பட்ட வசை போகாது.

The famine will end, but a scar then made will not pass away.

4446. பஞ்சானும் குஞ்சும் பறக்கத் தவிக்கிறது.

The little ones starve excessively.

4447. பஞ்சாங்கம் போனாலும் நட்சத்திரம் போகாது.

Though astrological calculations prove false, the stars will not.

4448. பஞ்சு படிந்த பழம சித்திரம்.

An old picture covered with dust.

4449. பஞ்சப் பொதியில் நெருப்புப பட்டதுபோல.

Like fire touching a bale of cotton.

4450. பஞ்சப்பொதியிற் பட்ட அம்புபோல.

Like an arrow striking a bale of cotton.

4451. பஞ்சும் நெருப்பும் ஒன்ருய்க் கிடக்குமோ?

Can cotton and fire be placed together?

4452. பஞ்சும் நெருப்பும்போலே.

Like cotton and fire.

4453. பஞ்சை பணிகாரம் சுட்டதும், வீங்கல் விசாரப்பட்டதும்.

The poor baked the cakes, the greedy longed for them.

4454. படி ஆள்வார் நீதி தப்பிற் குடி ஆர் இருப்பவர் குவலயத்தில்?

If rulers err, who can abide on the earth?

4455. படிக்கு ஆசான் இருந்தால் குடிக்குச் சேதம் இல்லை.

If the giver of the daily allowance be alive, no loss to the family.

4456. படிக்கிறது திருவாய்மொழி, இடிக்கிறது பெருமாள் கோவில்.

To read Tiruváymoli, and to break down the temple of Vishnu.

4457. படிக்கிற பிள்ளை பாக்குப் போட்டால் நாக்குத் தடிப்பாய்ப் போம்.

If a school boy chew betel, his pronunciation will be spoilt.

4458. படித்து முட்டாளாய் இருக்கிருன்.

He is a learned fool.

4459. படித்தவனுக்கும் படியாதவனுக்கும், கொக்குக்கும் அன்னத்துக்கும் வித்தியாசம்போல.

The difference between the learned and the unlearned, is as great as that of a crane and a swan.

4460. படுகளப்பட்ட பன்றைடை.

A palm network driven in a battle-field.

4461. படுகளத்தில் ஒப்பாரியா?

Do they sing elegies in a battle-field?

4462. படுக்கைச் சுகம் மெத்தை அறியாது.

The comfort of the bed is not experienced by the mattress.

4463. படுவது பட்டும் பட்டத்துக்கு இருக்கவேண்டும்.

Whatever hardships he may have to endure, he must have the rank to which he is entitled.

4464. படை கெட்டு ஓடுகையில் நரை மயிர் பிடுங்குகிறதோ?

When an army is routed, are grey hairs pulled out?

4465. படைக்கு ஒருவன் கொடைக்கு ஒருவன்.

One to fight, and one to give.

4466. படை மிகுத்தால் அரண் இல்லை.

If an army be large, a fortress is not required.

4467. படை முகத்திலும் அறிமுகம் வேண்டும்.

An acquaintance is necessary even in a battle-field.

4468. படையாது படைத்த மருமகளே உன்னைப் பறையன் அறுக்கக் கனாக் கண்டேன்.

O, my daughter-in-law, who art entertaining me sumptuously, I dreamt that thou wast being dissected by a pariah.

4469. பட்சி பசித்தாலும் எட்டிக்கனியைத் தின்னாது

Though a bird is hungry, it will not eat poisonous berries.

4470. பட்ட காலிலே படும், கெட்ட குடியே கெடும்.

It will hit the foot already injured, the decayed family will be ruined.

4471. பட்டணத்தாள் பெற்ற குட்டி பணம் பறிக்க வல்ல குட்டி.

A young one born of a city mother is clever at thieving.

4472. பட்டணத்து வாசலைப் படலாலே மூடுகிறதோ?

Can you cover up a city gate with a hurdle?

4473. பட்டணத்து வாசலைப் பட்டாலே மூடி இருக்கிறதா?

Is the gate of the city veiled with silk!

4474. பட்டடை வாய்த்தால் பணி வாய்க்கும்.

If the anvil is good, the work will be good.

4475. பட்டவர்க்கு உண்டு பலன்.

Those who have taken pains will *enjoy* the gains.

4476. பட்டவளுக்கு பதவி உண்டு.

She who suffered will attain advantage.

4477. பட்டால் அறிவான் சண்டாளன், மழை பெய்தால் அறிவான் வெள்ளாளன்.

A rogue is wise when punished, the farmer when it rains.

4478. பட்டினத்து நரியைப் பனங்காட்டு நரி ஏய்த்ததாம்.

It is said that the jackal of the palmyrah grove cheated the city fox.

4479. பட்டிக் காட்டுக்குச் சிவப்புத் துப்பட்டிப் பீதாம்பரம்.

In a common village, a red garment is regarded as a sumptuous garment.

4480. பட்டு அறி கெட்டு அறி பத்து எட்டு இறுத்து அறி.

Be wise by suffering, by poverty, and by paying ten and eight *fines*

4481. பட்டு குலைந்தால் பொட்டு.

When silk thread is untwisted, it becomes useless.

4482. பட்டுக் கத்தரித்ததுபோலப் பேசவேண்டும்.

You must speak *carefully* as silk is cut by the scissors.

4483. பட்டுக் கோட்டைக்கு வழி எங்கே என்றால், கொட்டைப்பாக்கு விலை நூற்றைம்பது என்கிறான்.

When he was asked which was the way to Pattucotta, he said, the price of arica-nuts is a hundred and fifty *fanams*.

4484. பட்டுக்கு அழுவார் பணிக்கு அழுவார் வையகத்தில் பாக்குக்கு அழுத பாரதத்தைக் கண்டது இல்லை.

There are who cry for a silk cloth, and there are who cry for ornaments; I never saw any one in the world cry for betel nut.

4485. பட்டுப் புடைவை இரவல் கொடுத்து மணை எடுத்துக்கொண்டு திரிவதுபோல.

Like lending a silk cloth to another, and wandering about carrying a seat with her.

4486. பட்டும் பட்டாவளியும் பெட்டியில் இருக்கும் காற் காசுக் கந்தை ஓடி உலாவும்.

The silk and the velvet are kept in a box, while a rag not worth a cash walks about the street.

4487. பட்டைக்குத் தக்க பழம் கயிறு.

An old rope suited to the well-bucket.

4488. பணக்கள்ளி பாயில் படாள்.

A niggardly woman will not lie on a mat.

4489. பணக்காரன் பின்னும் பத்துப் பேர், பயித்தியக்காரன் பின்னும் பத்துப் பேர்.

Ten follow after a moneyed man, and ten after a fool.

4490. பணத்துக்குப் பெயர் ஆட்கொல்லி.

Money is called a man-slayer.

4491. பணத்துக்கு ஒரு அம்பு கொண்டு பாழில் எய்கிறதுபோல.

Like buying arrows at a fanam each, and wasting them.

4492. பணத்தைக் கொடுத்துப் பணிகாரத்தை வாங்கிப் பற்றைக்குள்ளே இருந்து தின்னவேண்டுமோ ?

Is it necessary for you to hide yourself in a bush, and eat the cakes for which you have paid !

4493. பணம் இருந்தால் பாச்சா, பணம் இல்லாவிட்டால் பக்கிரி.

If I have money, Páchcha; if not money, Pakkiri.

4494. பணம் இல்லாதவன் பிணம்.

He who has no money is a corpse.

4495. பணம் என்றால் பிணமும் வாய் திறக்கும்.

If the word money be uttered, even a corpse will open its mouth.

4496. பணம் என்ன செய்யும் பத்து விதம் செய்யும்.

What can money effect? it can do ten kinds of things.

4497. பணம் என்ன பாஷாணம், குணம் ஒன்றே போதும்.

Why money? it is poison; a good disposition is enough.

4498. பணம் குலம் ஆகும், பசி கறி ஆகும்.

Money, is rank; hunger, is curry.

4499. பணம் பந்தியிலே குலம் குப்பையிலே.

Money at the festive board, and rank on the dunghill.

4500. பணிகாரமோ சிலுசிலுப்போ?

Is the sound that of baking cakes, or is it mere frizzle?

4501. பண்டாரம் பிண்டத்துக்கு அழுகிறான், லிங்கம் பால் சோற்றுக்கு அழுகிறது.

The religious mendicant is crying for a mouthfull of food, the linga, he worships, for rice and milk.

4502. பண்டை பட்ட பாட்டைப் பழங்கிடுகில் போட்டுவிட்டுச் சம்பா நெல்குத்திப் பொங்கல் இடுகிறாள்.

Having put aside her former troubles on an old cadjan, she husked chamba rice and boiled it.

4503. பண்ணப் பண்ணப் பல விதம் ஆகும்.

The more he makes, the more varied the forms.

4504. பண்ணிய பயிரில் புண்ணியம் தெரியும்.

A man's merit may be seen in the grain he grows.

4505. பதறாத காரியம் சிதறாது.

A thing done without haste never fails.

4506. பதறிச் செய்கிற காரியம் சிதறிக் கெட்டுப்போகும்.

A hasty proceeding will go to ruin.

4507. பதினாறும் பெற்றுப் பெருவாழ்வும் வாழவேண்டும்.

May you bear sixteen *children*, and live very prosperously.

4508. பத்தி கொள்பவன் முத்தி உள்ளவன்.

The devout attain heaven.

4509. பத்தியத்துக்கு முருங்கைக்காய் கொண்டுவரச் சொன்னால் பால் தெளிக்க அகத்திக் கீரை கொண்டு வருவான்.

When requested to bring murunga fruit for diet, he brings coronilla grandiflora leaves for the milk-sprinkling ceremony.

See note under proverb 4584.

4510. பத்தி இல்லாப் பூனை பரமண்டலத்துக்கு ஏறுமா?

Will an ungodly cat ascend to heaven?

4511. பத்தி இல்லாத புத்தி அசேதனம்.

Reason without devotion is folly.

4512. பத்தி உண்டானால் முத்தி உண்டாம்.

If there be piety, there will be final happiness.

4513. பத்தியோடே பாகற்காய் சட்டியோடே தீயுது.

Pagal fruits in clusters are being charred in the chatty.

4514. பத்திலே விழுந்த பாம்பும் சாவாது.

Even a snake that has fallen among ten, will not die.

4515. பத்திலே பசலை இருபதிலே இடும்பு.

At ten childishness, at twenty arrogance.

4516. பத்தினியைத் தொட்டதும் துரியோதனன் பட்டதும்.

By touching the virtuous woman, *Dropati*, Duriyodhana was ruined.

4517. பத்து இறுத்தபின் பாரச் சந்தேகம் தீர்ந்தது.

After I paid a fine of ten, doubt was removed.

4518. பத்து அரிசியும் வேகவில்லை, பாவி பிராணனும் போகவி ல்லை.

Ten grains of rice wont boil, the life of the wretch wont go.

4519. பத்துக்கு மேலே ஒரு பறையனுக்கும் தள்ளவேண்டும்.

After ten years of age, a girl should be affianced if even to a pariah.

4520. பத்துப் பணம் கொடுத்தாலும் இத்தனை பதைப்பு ஆகாது.

Though you give ten fanams, such haste is bad.

4521. பத்துப் பேரிலே பதினொராம் பேராய் இருக்கவேண்டும்.

Of the ten, you must pass as the eleventh.

4522. பத்து வராகன் இறுத்தோம், என்றாலும் சந்தேகம் நிவிர்த்தி ஆயிற்றே.

We were fined ten pagodas, however our doubts were removed.

4523. பத்து விதத்திலும் பறையனை நம்பலாம் பார்ப்பானை நம்பக்கூ டாது.

In ten ways a Pariah is trustworthy, but a brahman is not.

4524. பத்து ஏர் வைத்துப் படைமரமும் தோற்றேன் எத்தனை ஏர் வைத்துக் கோவணமும் தோற்றாய்?

Possessed of ten yoke of oxen I lost the plough share; how many yoke did you possess before you lost your waist cloth?

4525. பந்தம் சொன்னார் படைக்காகார்.

Those who regard relationships are unfit for military service.

4526. பந்திக்கு முந்தவேண்டும் படைக்குப் பிந்தவேண்டும்.

Be first at a feast, and last at the fight.

4527. பந்தியிலே வேண்டாம் என்றால் இலை பொத்தல் என்கிறாய்.

When rejected at the feast, thou sayest that the leaf is torn.

4528. பயணக்காரன் பயித்தியக்காரன.

A man about to set out on a journey, is a fool.

4529. பயித்தியமோ பண்டாரமோ வென்றால் இப்போதுதான் தொ டருகிறது என்றான்.

When I ask him whether he is mad or a mendicant, he says, it is just following.

4530. பயித்தியம் மாறிப்போச்சு உலக்கைத்தடி கொண்டுவா கோவ ணம் கட்ட.

My madness is gone, bring me a pestle to tie round my waist.

4531. பரணி அடுப்புப் பாழ்போகாது.

A fireplace made on the second lunar day will not be deserted.

4532. பரம்பரை ஆண்டியோ பஞ்சத்துக்கு ஆண்டியோ?

Is he a hereditary mendicant, or a mendicant, because of the famine?

4533. பரிகாரி உறவு தெருவாசல் மட்டும்.

The friendship of the doctor ends at the threshold.

4534. பரியத்துக்கு அஞ்சிக் குருட்டுக் கண்ணியைக் கொண்டது போல.

Like marrying a blind woman to avoid paying the nuptial present.

4535. பரிவு இல்லாப் போசனத்திற் பட்டினி நன்று, பிரியம் இல்லாப் பெண்டிற் பேய் நன்று.

Hunger is preferrable to eating food given without good feeling, a demoness is better than an unkind wife.

4536. பருத்திக் கடையிலே நாய்க்கு அலுவல் என்ன?

What can a dog have to do in a cotton bazaar?

4537. பருத்திக்காடு உழுகிறதற்கு முன்னே பொம்மனுக்கு ஏழு முழ ம் திம்மனுக்கு ஏழு முழம்.

Ere the cotton fields are ploughed, Pomman asks for a cloth of seven cubits, and Timman wants one of the same length.

4538. பருத்தி புடைவையாய்க் காய்த்தது.

The cotton tree produced cloth.

4539. பருத்திப் பொதிக்கு ஒரு நெருப்புப் பொறிபோல.
As a single spark to a bale of cotton.

4540. பருப்பிலே நெய் விட்டதுபோல.
As ghee was poured on beans.

4541. பருமரத்தை அண்டிய பல்லியும் சாகாது.
If sheltered near a large tree even a lizard will not die.

4542. பல உமி தின்றால் ஒரு அவிழ் தட்டும்.
If one consume plenty of husks, a grain may turn up.

4543. பல சரக்குக்காரனைப் பயித்தியம் பிடித்ததுபோல.
As the vendor of curry stuff was seized with madness.

4544. பல தீட்டுக்கு ஒரு முழுக்கு.
One ablution for many defilements.

4545. பல துளி பெரு வெள்ளம்.
Many drops make great flood.

4546. பருவத்தே பயிர் செய்.
Cultivate in due time.

4547. பரோபகாரமே பெரிது.
Benevolence is indeed great.

4548. பலத்தவனுக்கு மருந்து சொன்னால் பிடுங்கிக் கொடுத்துத் தீர வேண்டும்.
If you prescribe medicine for the strong, you must procure the medicinal plants yourself.

4549. பலத்தவன் கைக்கு இளைத்தவன் துரும்பு.
The feeble is a straw in the hands of the powerful.

4550. பலநாளைத் திருடன் ஒரு நாளைக்கு அகப்படுவான்.
An old thief will one day be caught.

4551. பல பாவம் தீர ஒரு புண்ணியம் ஆகிலும் பண்ண வேண்டும்.
One virtuous deed at least, is required to expiate numerous sins.

4552. பல மரம் கண்ட தச்சன் ஒருமரம் வெட்டமாட்டான்.
The carpenter who is acquainted with various sorts of wood, is not able to fell a tree.

4553. பல முயற்சி செய்யினும் பகவன் மேல் சிந்தை வை.
After making every effort, fix your mind on God.

4554. பல வீட்டுப் பிச்சை ஆறாய்ப் பெருகும்.
The alms of many houses may flow as a river.

4555. பலன் இல்லாப் பல நாளிலும், அறம் செய் ஒரு நாள் பெரிது.
One day spent in alms giving is greater than many spent in doing nothing.

4556. பலா உத்தமம், மா மத்திமம், பாதிரி அதமம்.
The jack tree is the best, the mango is good, the pathri tree is indifferent.

4557. பல் ஆடப் பசி ஆறும்.
As the teeth move hunger is appeased.

4558. பல்லக்கு ஏற யோகம் உண்டு உன்னி ஏறச் சீவன் இல்லை.
He has a palanquin, but is not able to mount it.

4559. பல்லக்குக்கு மேல்மூடி இல்லாதவனுக்கும், காலுக்குச் செருப்பு இல்லாதவனுக்கும் விசாரம் ஒன்றே.
He whose palanquin has no top, and he who has no shoes for his feet are equal.

4560. பல்லு விழுந்த புடையன்.
A snake without fangs.

4561. பல்லு விழுந்த புடையனுக்கு கிருதா?
Is the rage of a fangless snake *dangerous* ?

4562. பவுசு கெட்ட பாக்கட்டிக்கு இரண்டு பக்கமும் தீவட்டியாம்.
A torch on either side of a lump of worthless sugar.

4563. பழக பழகப் பாலும் புளிக்கும்.
By constant use even milk will taste sour.

4564. பழங்கால் தூர்க்கவேண்டாம் புதுக்கால் வெட்ட வேண்டாம்.

Do not fill up an old channel; do not cut a new one.

4565. பழத்திலே பழம் மிளகாய்ப்பழம்.

The chief of berries is the chilli.

4566. பழத்தேங்காயிலே தான் எண்ணெய்.

Old cocoanuts yield oil.

4567. பழம் நழுவிப் பாலில் விழுந்ததுபோல.

Like fruit slipping and falling into milk.

4568. பழம் புண்ணாளி பாதிவைத்தியன்.

He who has an old sore is half a doctor.

4569. பழிக்கு ஆனோர் சிலர் பழி படுவோர் சிலர்.

One hasty commits the crime, and another suffers the penalty.

4570. பழிப்பான கல்வி பாவத்தின் ஊற்று.

Despicable learning is a fountain of sin.

4571. பழிப்பன பகரேல்.

Utter no reproach.

4572. பழுது செய்ததை அறிக்கை இடல் பாதி நிவிர்த்தி.

The confession of a fault removes half its guilt.

4573. பழுத்த ஓலையைப் பார்த்துக் குருத்து ஓலை சிரிக்கிறதாம்.

It is said that the young palm leaf is laughing at the dry leaf because it is falling off.

4574. பழுத்த பழம் கொம்பில் இராது.

Ripe fruit does not remain on the branch.

4575. பழைய கறுப்பன் கறுப்பனே பழைய மண்கிண்ணி மண்கிண்ணியே.

My name old Karuppan is still my name, and my earthen basin is still my eating dish.

4576. பழைய குருடி கதவை திறவடி.

O thou bliud old woman, open the door.

4577. பழையது மீந்த இடம் காணியாட்சி.

The place where one gets plenty of cold rice is the right one.

4578. பள்ளம் இறைத்தவன் பங்கு கொண்டுபோகிறான்.

He who irrigated the low ground takes his share *of the produce.*

4579. பள்ளம் உள்ள இடத்திலே தண்ணீர் நிற்கும்.

Water will stand in a hollow.

4580. பள்ளிக் கணக்குப் புள்ளிக்கு உதவாது.

Accounts learnt at school will not be practically useful.

4581. பள்ளிக் குப்பத்துக்கு அம்பட்ட வாத்தியார்.

A barber school master for a village inhabited by Pallis.

4582. பள்ளி பாக்குத் தின்றால் பத்து விரலும் சுண்ணாம்பு.

If a Palli chews betel, his ten fingers will be smeared with chunam.

4583. பள்ளிப் பிள்ளை என்றால் செல்வம் குறையுமா?

If you admit that you are a school boy, will your wealth decrease!

4584. பள்ளிக்கு வைக்காமற் கொள்ளிக்குக் குறைத்து வைத்தார்.

My father not only neglected to put me to school, but left me to bear the expenses of the fire brand.

Under this proverb a general note on funeral rites may not be out of place. The particulars given relate to Hindu families generally, not to brahmans.

When a person dies, the grief of the females in the family bursts out into loud lamentations. On its being made known by a conch-blower that a death has occurred, the neighbouring females go to the house, add the expression of their sympathy, and all unite in one general wail. Frequently one of the company, the mother, or it may be a professional person, breaks out into an ascription of praise regarding the deceased uttering a sort of elegy in measured cadence. In this case when a climax is reached, all join in a chorus of grief, and some may smite their breasts and tear their hair In such elegies, which are often of a touching kind, the personal beauty, the talents, the learning and the prowess of the deceased are dwelt on.

The body being taken out is bathed and dressed as in life. In the case of females the gold and pearls and precious stones, if she possessed them, will be put on. The sectarial marks will be added. The chárpoy on which the corpse has been laid out is then carried into the house. Again the females seat themselves around it and pour forth a torrent of grief, or at any rate make a loud noise. A kinsman whose business it is to attend to the customary observances spreads a cloth on the chárpoy to hold rice, called,-rice for the mouth. The females of the family take a little of the grain and put it on the corpse near the mouth. The same ceremony is performed by the male members of the family at the place of cremation. The family barber appropriates the remaining rice. At the burning ground the kinsman who conducts the ceremonies carries a pot of water round the pyre and the conch-blower follows him and makes an incision in the pot with his conch, when the barber puts four bits of sandal or other wood into the hands of the kinsman and points out the places in the pyre where they are to be inserted. The leaking pot is then taken by the barber to be broken near the head of the corpse. The kinsman hastens away that he may not hear the noise of the pot when broken, nor see the burning pyre. Then the barber receives permission to break the pot and to ignite the pyre.

On the next or on an early day the male friends of the deceased assemble at the place of cremation. The skull, the breast-bone and the bones of the hands having been abstracted from the ashes and deposited in a convenient place covered with a plantain leaf, are by the nearest of kin smeared with oil, ghee and honey and covered with flowers, whilst a priest recites appropriate incantations in the presence of the relatives. A pot of milk having been provided for this ceremony, the relatives take a sprig of *coronilla grandiflora* and having dipped it in the milk, sprinkle the relics, which are then put into an unburnt earthen vessel, covered with cloth to be cast into a sacred stream or bestowed on the ocean wave. Of course these elaborate rites are dispensed with by the poor.

I have seen Hindus, not by any means in abject circumstances, convey a corpse to the seaside, where a grave had been hastily dug, take off the cloth and ornaments, wrap the body in a common mat, and bury it with the burial of a dog.

In the year 1830 when travelling in Bengal I saw, on the bank of the Damooda, a sorrowing brahmanical father with two or three attendants dispose of a corpse with but little ceremony. The father himself who was much affected ignited the pyre.

4585. பள்ளி ஒளித்திரான் பார்ப்பான் குளித்திரான்.

A palli does not like to be secluded, nor does a brahman fast after bathing.

4586. பறக்கிற பறவைக்கு எது தூரம்?

What is distance to a bird on the wing

4587. பறக்கும் காகம் இருக்கும் கொம்பு அறியாததுபோல.

As a crow on the wing knows not on what branch it will alight.

4588. பறக்கும் குருவிக்கு இருக்கும் கொம்பு தெரியாது, பரதேசிக்குத் தங்கும் இடம் தெரியாது.

A bird on the wing knows not the branch on which it may alight, a stranger knows not his halting place.

4589. பறந்துபோகிற எச்சிற் கல்லைமேல் கல்லைத் தூக்கி வைத்தாற்போல.

Like one placing a stone on a flying leaf that has been used for a rice-plate.

4590. பறப்பான் பயிர் இழந்தான் அறக்காஞ்சி பெண்டு இழந்தான்.

A hasty man loses the produce of his field, and the jealous man his wif.

4591. பறித்த காட்டுக்குப் பயம் இல்லை.

No *further* fear in a jungle, where one has been *already* robbed.

4592. பறைச்சி பிள்ளையைப் பள்ளிக்கு வைத்தாலும் பேச்சிலே அய்யே என்னுமாம்.

Though a pariah child be sent to school, he will still call his father ayyè.

4593. பறை தட்டினாற்போல.

Like striking grain to the level of the measure.

4594. பறைத் தெருவிலே வில்வம் முளைத்ததுபோல.

As a vilva tree sprang up in a pariah street.

4595. பறைப்பாட்டுக்கும் பறைப்பேச்சுக்கும் சுரைப்பூவிற்கும் மணம் இல்லை.

A pariah's song, his dialect, and a surai flower, have no fragrance in them.

4596. பறையனும் பார்ப்பானும் போல.

Like a pariah and a brahman.

4597. பறையன் பொங்கல் இட்டால் பகவானுக்கு ஏறாதோ?

If a pariah boil rice as an offering to God, will it not be accepted?

4598. பறையை பள்ளிக்கு வைத்தாலும் துறைப்பேச்சுப் போமா?

Though a pariah is schooled, will his vulgar brogue be altered?

4599. பறைவேலை அரைவேலை.

The work of a pariah is only half done.

4600. பனங்காட்டு நரி சலசலப்புக்கு அஞ்சுமா?

Will the jackal of the palmyrah grove tremble at the rustling of leaves?

4601. பனிக்கண் திறந்தால் மழைக்கண் திறக்கும்.

If there be dew, there will be no rain.

4602. பனி பெய்து கடல் நிறையுமா?

Will the sea be filled by the falling dew?

4603. பனி பெய்து குளம் நிரம்புமா?

Will the falling dew fill the tank?

4604. பனி பெய்தால் மழை இல்லை, பழம் இருந்தால் பூ இல்லை.

When there is dew there is no rain, when fruit is ripe there is no blossom.

4605. பனிப் பெருக்கிலே கப்பல் ஓட்டலாமா?

Can you sail a ship in heavy dew?

4606. பனியை நம்பி ஏர்ப்பூட்டினதுபோல.

Like beginning to plough depending on the dew.

4607. பனை ஏறியும் பாளைதொடாது இறங்கினாற்போல.

Like descending from a palmyrah tree without touching the flower-spathe.

4608. பனை ஏறி விழுந்தவனைக் கடா ஏறி மிதித்ததுபோல.

Like a buffalo trampling on a person who has fallen from a palmyrah tree.

4609. பனை மரத்தின் கீழே பாலைக் குடித்தாலும் கள் என்று நினைப்பார்.

Though what you drink in a palmyrah grove be milk, every one will believe it to be toddy.

4610. பனைமரத்திற்கு நிழல இல்லை பறையனுக்கு முறை இல்லை.

A palmyrah tree *casts* no shade, a pariah has no rules.

4611. பனைமரம் ஏறுகிறவனை எதுவரையும் தாங்கலாம்?

How far can you support a man who is climbing a palmyrah tree?

4612. பனையின் நிழலும் நிழலோ பகைவர் உறவும் உறவோ?

Is the shadow of a palmyrah tree a shade, is the acquaintance of an enemy friendship?

4613. பனையில் இருந்து விழுந்தவனைப் பாம்பு கடித்ததுபோல.

Like a snake biting one who has fallen from a palmyrah tree.

4614. பனை வெட்டின இடத்திலே கழுதை வட்டம் போட்டது போல.

Like an ass going round a place where a palmyrah tree had been felled.

4615. பன்றிக்குட்டிக்கு ஒருசந்தி ஏது?

Does a young pig observe fasts?

4616. பன்றிக்குட்டி ஆனை ஆமா?

Will the young pig become an elephant?

4617. புன்றி பட்டால் அவனோடே, காட்டானை பட்டால் பங்கு.
If a hog be shot he takes the whole, if an elephant be shot I shall have a share.

4618. பன்றி பல குட்டி, சிங்கம் ஒரு குட்டி.
The sow has many young ones *at a time*, the lioness only one.

4619. பன்றி பல குட்டி போட்டு என்ன?
What, if a sow has a numerous litter!

4620. பன்றியோடு கூடிய கன்றும் மலம் தின்னும்.
A calf that goes with a pig will eat excrement.

4621. பன்னக்காரன் பெண்டில் பணியக் கிடந்து செத்தாளாம்.
It is said that the wife of a mat-maker died on the bare ground.

4622. பனனிப் பன்னிப் பழங்கதை படியாதே.
Do not tell old stories with affectation.

பா.

4623. பாகற் கொட்டை புதைக்கச் சுரைக் கொட்டை முளைக்குமா?
Will a bottle gourd spring from a págal seed?

4624. பாசம் அற்றவன் பரதேசி.
He who has no ties is like a foreigner.

4625. பாடகக்காலி வாழ்ந்தால் பத்து எட்டுச் சனம் பிழைக்கும்.
If the foot-ringed lady prosper, eight or ten people may be supported thereby.

4626. பாடம் ஏறினும் ஏடு கைவிடேல்.
Though you have learnt your lesson, do not throw away your book.

4627. பாடிப் பாடிக் குத்தினாலும் பதரில் அரிசி இல்லை.
Though pounded with a song, chaff will not yield rice.

4628. பாடு என்றால் பாணனும் பாடான்.
When pressed to sing even the professional singer refuses.

4629. பாடு படாமற் போனல் பலன் இல்லாமற் போகும்.
Where there is no labour, there is no profit.

4630. பாடும் புலவர் கையிற் பட்டோலை ஆனேனே.
I am become an ola in the hand of a poet.

4631. பாடை ஏறினும் ஓடு கைவிடேல்.
Though you may ascend the bier, forsake not your alms-dish.

4632. பாணம் தொடுத்தாற் போலப் பேசுகிறான்.
He speaks as if arrows were darting forth.

4633. பாதகர் பழக்கம் பாம்பொடு பழகல் போல.
Friendship with the wicked, is like playing with snakes.

4634. பாதிச் சுரைக்காய் கறிக்கும் பாதிச் சுரைக்காய் விதைக்குமா?
Can you take half a churaikáy for curry, and use the other half as seed?

4635. பாத்திரம் அறிந்து பிச்சை இடு, கோத்திரம் அறிந்து பெண் கொடு.
Give alms to the worthy, and your daughter to one of a good family.

4636. பாப்புக்கு மூப்பு இல்லை.
Brahmans have no chiefs.

4637. பாமணி ஆற்றிலே பல்லை விளக்கு, முல்லை ஆற்றிலே முகம் கழுவு.
Begin to clean your teeth at Pámani river, wash your face in Mullai river.

4638. பாம்பாட்டி பரம்பிலே, கள்ளன் களவிலே.
A snake charmer understands snakes, a thief understands thieving

4639. பாம்பிலும் பாம்புக்குட்டி விஷம் அதிகம் வீரியமும் அதிகம்.
A young snake is more poisonous and vigorous than an old one.

4640. பாம்பின் குட்டி பாம்பு அதன் குட்டி நட்டுவாக்காலி.
The young one of a snake is a snake, and its young one is a scorpion

4641. பாம்பின் வாய்த் தேரைபோல.

Like a toad in the jaws of a snake.

4642. பாம்புக்கு மூப்பு இல்லை.

Snakes have no chiefs.

4643. பாம்பு கடிக்கத் தேளுக்குப் பார்க்கிறதோ?

When bitten by a snake, will the incantations suited to scorpion bites avail aught?

4644. பாம்புக்கு இராசா மூங்கில் தடி.

A bambu stick is king to a snake.

4645. பாம்புக்குச் சத்துரு பஞ்சமா?

Are the enemies of snakes few?

4646. பாம்புக்குத் தலையைக் காட்டி மீனுக்கு வாலைக் காட்டி.

Showing the head to snakes, and the tail to fish.

Spoken of a two-faced person, in allusion to an eel that shows its serpent-like head to snakes, and its fish-like tail to fish.

4647. பாம்புக்குப் பால் வார்த்து வளர்த்தாலும் விஷத்தைக் கொடுக்கும்.

Though you feed a snake with milk, it will yield poison.

4648. பாம்புக்குப் பால் வார்த்ததுபோல.

Like pouring out milk to a snake.

4649. பாம்பும் கீரியும்போல.

Lik a snake and a mungoose.

4650. பாம்பும் கீரியும்போலப் பல காலம் வாழ்ந்தேன்.

I lived a long time *with him or her* as a snake with a mungoose.

4651. பாம்பு தன் பசியை நினைக்கும் தேரை தன் விதியை நினைக்கும்.

The snake has regard to its hunger, the frog thinks of its fate.

4652. பாம்பு பசிக்கில் தேரையைப் பிடிக்கும். அதுபோல, சிறியோர் சிறிய காரியங்களையே செய்வார்.

When a snake is hungry it will catch a frog, so the vile perform only mean acts.

4653. பாம்பு தின்கிற ஊரிலே போனால் நடு முறி நமக்கு என்று இருக்கவேண்டும்.

If we go to a country of snake eaters, we must be prepared for the middle bit.

4654. பாம்பு பகையும் தோல் உறவுமா?

Is the snake hostile, and its skin friendly?

4655. பாம்புக்குப் பகை கருடன்.

The hawk is inimical to the snake.

4656. பாம்பும் நோவாமற் பாம்பு அடித்த கோலும் நோவாமல் இருக்கவேண்டும்.

So strike that neither the snake, nor the staff with which you strike, shall be hurt or injured.

4657. பாம்பு என்றால் படையும் நடுங்கும்.

Even an army will tremble at the word snake.

4658. பாம்பொடு பழகேல்.

Have nothing to do with snakes.

4659. பாய்கிற மாட்டுக்கு முன்னே வேதம் சொன்னாற்போல.

Like reciting a portion of the vedas, to a cow about to gore you.

4660. பாய்மரம் சேர்ந்த காகம்போல் ஆனேன்.

I have become like a crow on the top of a mast.

4661. பாய்மரம் இல்லா மரக்கலம்போல.

Like a vessel without a mast.

4662. பாரபுத்தி உள்ள பறவை பதரால் பிடிக்கப்பட்டது.

A wise bird has been caught with chaff.

4663. பாராத உடைமை பாழ்.

Property not looked after perishes.

4664. பாரைக்கு ஊடாடாப் பாறை பசுமரத்தின் வேருக்கு ஊடாடி விடும்.

The rock that resists a crowbar, gives way to the roots of a tender plant.

4665. பார் ஆளலாமென்று பால் குடிக்கிறாய்.

Thou drinkest milk, hoping to govern the world.

4666. பார்க்கக் கொடுதத பணத்துக்கு வெள்ளிக்கிழமையா?

Is Friday a sufficient excuse for not *returning* the coin given you to look at?

It is believed by many that, though it is fortunate to receive money on Friday, it is unfortunate to pay it.

4667. பார்க்கிற கண்ணுக்குக் கேட்கிற செவி பொல்லாது.

A listening ear, is worse than a seeing eye.

4668. பார்த்த கண்ணும் பூத்துப் பகலும் இரவு ஆயிற்று.

The eyes have failed by looking too long, and night has followed the day.

4669. பார்த்த முகம் எல்லாம் வேற்றுமுகம்.

All the faces we see are diverse from one another.

4670. பார்த்தாற் பசுப்போல, பாய்ந்தால் புலிப்போல.

In appearance like a cow, in action like a tiger.

4671. பார்த்திருக்கத் தின்று விழித்திருக்கக் கை கழுவுவான்.

Gazed at-*by starving beggars*-he eats and washes his hands.

4672. பார்த்திருந்தவள் பச்சை குத்தினாள், கேட்டிருந்தவள் வறுத்துக் குத்தினாள்.

She who had seen *the process* pounded it undried, she who had heard of it pounded roasted.

4673. பார்ப்பதற்கு அரிய பரப் பிரமம்.

It is impossible to comprehend the supreme Brahma.

4674. பார்ப்பாத்தி அம்மா மாடு வந்தது.

Brahman matron, the cow has come.

4675. பார்ப்பாத்தி உப்புக்கண்டம் போக்கடித்ததுபோல.

As a brahman woman lost her salted mutton.

4676. பார்ப்பார் சேவகமும் வெள்ளைக் குதிரைச் சேவகமும் ஆகாது.

The service of a brahman. and the care of a white horse are bad.

4677. பார்ப்பானுக்கு வாய்போக்காதே ஆண்டிக்கு அதுதானும் சொல்லாதே.

Do not waste your breath on a brahman, nor converse with a mendicant.

4678. பார்ப்பான் கறுப்பும் பறையன் சிவப்பும் ஆகாது.

A black brahman, and a fair pariah are not trustworthy.

4679. பார்ப்பான் ஏழையோ பசு ஏழையோ ?

Which is the more helpless, a brahman or a cow ?

4680. பாலருக்குப் பலம் அழுகை, மட்சத்துக்குப் பலம் உதகம்.

The strength of a child is crying, and that of fish is water.

4681. பாலர் மொழி கேளாதார் குழல் இனிது யாழ் இனிது என்பார்.

Those who have not heard the lisping of their own children say, that the flute is sweet, the stringed instrument is sweet.

4682. பாலான நெஞ்சு எல்லாம் பகை ஆக்கினன்.

He has made enemies of all whose hearts are pure as milk.

4683. பாலுக்கும் காவல் பூனைக்கும் தோழன்.

He is the guard of the milk, and also the friend of the cat.

4684. பாலுக்கு வந்த பூனை மோரைக் குடிக்குமா ?

Will the cat that has come for new milk, drink buttermilk ?

4685. பாலுக்குச் சீனி இல்லை என்றோர்க்கும் கூழுக்குக் கறி இல்லை என்றோர்க்கும் விசாரம் ஒன்றே.

The care of those who want sugar with milk, and of those who want curry for their rice, are the same.

4686. பாலுமாம் மருந்துமாம்.

It is of use both as milk and medicine.

4687. பாலும் பதக்கு, மோரும் பதக்கோ?

Is the rate of fresh milk that of buttermilk?

4688. பாலும் வெள்ளை மோரும் வெள்ளை.

Milk is white and buttermilk is also white.

4689. பாலை ஊட்டுவார்கள் பாக்கியத்தை ஊட்டுவார்களா?

They may feed him with milk; can they feed him with good fortune?

4690. பாலைக்குடித்தவனுக்குப் பால் ஏப்பம் வரும், கள்ளைக் குடித்தவனுக்குக் கள் ஏப்பம் வரும்.

He who has drank milk will belch milk, and he who has drank toddy will belch toddy.

4691. பாலைப் பார்க்கிறதா பானையைப் பார்க்கிறதா?

Do you examine the milk or the vessel containing it?

4692. பாலோடு கலந்த நீரும் பாலாகும்.

Water mixed with milk looks like milk.

4693. பாலோடாயினும் காலம் அறிந்து உண்.

Though with milk, take your meals at the proper time.

4694. பால் ஆரியனுக்கு, பசு ராமநாதசுவாமிக்கு.

Milk to an Aryan, and a cow for Rámanádaswámi.

4695. பால் இருக்கிறது பாக்கியம் இருக்கிறது, பாலிலே போட்டுக் குடிக்கப் பத்துப் பருக்கைக்கு வழி இல்லை.

There is milk and money, but no means for procuring ten grains of rice.

4696. பால் தொட்டுப் பால் கறக்கவேண்டும்.

One must draw milk after moistening the fingers with milk.

4697. பால் நக்காத பூனையும் பரிதானம் வாங்காத பிராமணனும் உண்டா?

Is there a cat that will not lap milk, or a brahman that will refuse a bribe?

4698. பால் பசுவைக் கன்றிலே தெரியும், பாக்கியவான் பிள்ளையை முகத்திலே தெரியும்.

The milch cow is known by its calf, and the child of the wealthy by its face.

4699. பால் வார்த்து முழுகுவான்.

He will bathe after applying milk to the head.

Intimating that a person inimical has been got rid of.

4700. பாவட்டம் பூப்போல நரைத்தும் புத்தி இல்லை.

Though as grey as a pávattam flower, he has no sense.

4701. பாவத்திற்கு இடம் கொடாதவன் பாவத்தைச் செயங்கொள்வான்.

He who does not give place to sin, will conquer it.

4702. பாவம் செய்யாதிரு, மனமே!

O my heart, do not sin!

4703. பாவலர் அருமை நாவலர் அறிவார்.

The ability of a poet is best known to the learned.

4704. பாவியார் போன இடம் எல்லாம் பள்ளமும் திட்டியும்.

Whithersoever the simple go, they meet with ups and downs.

4705. பாவியைப் பிடித்துப் பாம்பு ஆட்டுகிறது.

Seizing a simpleton and making him dance like a snake.

4706. பாவில் இருக்கிறது பார்த்தும் இருக்கிறது.

That which is described in poetry is also seen *in nature*.

4707. பாழாய்ப் போகிறது பசுவின் வாயிலே.

That which is spoiled is *put* in the mouth of a cow.

4708. பாழ் ஊருக்கு நரி ராஜா.

The jackal is king in a deserted village.

4709. பானையில் உண்டானால் அகப்பையில் வரும்.

If in the pot, it will come into the spoon.

4710. பானையிலே பதக்கு நெல் இருந்தால் மூலையிலே முக்குறுணி தெய்வம் கூத்தாடும்.

If there be a pathaku of rice in the pot, three kurunies of gods will dance in the corner.

பி.

4711. பிசினி தன்னை வசனிப்பது வீண்.

It is useless to extol a miser.

4712. பிச்சன் வாழைத் தோட்டத்திலே புகுந்ததுபோல.

As a madman entered the plantain grove.

4713. பிச்சைக்காரனுக்குப் பயப்பட்டு அடுப்பு மூட்டாமல் விடுகிறதா?

Through fear of beggars do you refrain from lighting your fire?

4714. பிச்சைக்காரனை அடித்தானும் சோளியைப்போட்டு உடைத்தானும்.

It is said that he beat the mendicant and broke his alms-dish.

4715. பிச்சைக்காரன் சோற்றிலே சனீச்சுரன் புகுந்ததுபோல.

As Saturn entered into the rice of the mendicant.

4716. பிச்சைச் சோற்றிலும் எச்சிற் சோறு?

What! scrupulous about leavings in rice got by begging?

4717. பிச்சைக்காரன்மேலே பிரமாஸ்திரம் தொடுக்கிறதா?

Is an enchanted arrow discharged at a mendicant?

4718. பிச்சைக்கு வந்தவன் பெண்ணுக்கு மாப்பிள்ளையா?

Do you propose giving your daughter in marriage to one who came to ask alms?

4719. பிச்சைக்கு மூத்தது கச்சவடம்.

Merchandize is a little better than begging.

4720. பிச்சைச் சோற்றிலும் குழைந்த சோறு?

Is rice offered in charity refused because it is overboiled?

4721. பிச்சைச் சோற்றிற்குப் பஞ்சம் உண்டா?

Is rice given in charity ever scarce?

4722. பிச்சை போட்டது போதும் நாயைக் கட்டு.

The alms given are sufficient; tie up the dog.

4723. பிச்சை புகினும் கற்கை நன்றே.

Learning is good even when one is reduced to begging.

4724. பிச்சை இட்டுக் கெட்டவனும் உண்டா?

Has any one been ruined by giving alms?

4725. பிச்சை இட்டுக் கெட்டவனும் இல்லை, பிள்ளை பெற்றுக் கெட்டவனும் இல்லை.

None is ruined by giving alms; none is ruined because he has a family

4726. பிச்சை எடுத்தும் சத்துருவின் குடி கெடு.

Though you have to beg, destroy the family of your enemy.

4727. பிடாரம் பெரிதென்று புற்றிலே கை வைக்கலாமா?

Relying on the efficacy of the prescribed remedy, will you put your hand in a snake hole?

4728. பிடாரனுக்கு அஞ்சிப் பாம்பு எலிக்கு உறவு ஆச்சுதாம்.

It is said that a snake afraid of the charmer, sought the friendship of a rat.

4729. பிடாரியாரே கடா வந்தது.

O, demon, the bull has come.

4730. பிடாரி வரம் கொடுத்தாலும் ஓச்சன் வரம் கொடுக்கிறது அரிது.

Though a pidári may grant a favour, it will be difficult to obtain it through the priest.

4731. பிடி அழகி புகுந்தால் பெண் அழகி ஆவாள்.

If a woman ornamented with jewels enter, she will be regarded as a beautiful woman.

4732. பிடிக்குப்பிடி நமசிவாயமா.

Are incantations to be used again and again.

4733. பிடித்த கொம்பும் விட்டேன் மிதித்த கொம்பும் விட்டேன்.

I have left the branch I had seized, and also the one on which I was standing.

4734. பிடித்த கொம்பும் ஒடிந்து மிதித்த கொம்பும் முறிந்தாற்போல் ஆனேன்.

I have become as helpless as if the branch I seized and the one I stood upon, both broke *at the same time.*

4735. பிடித்தாற் கற்றை, விட்டாற் கூளம்.

If tied, a bundle; if loose, bits of straw.

4736. பிக்ஷாபதியோ லக்ஷாபதியோ?

Is he the prince of beggars, or the first as possessing lacs?

4737. பிணத்தை மூடி மணத்தைச் செய்.

Bury the corpse, and then celebrate the marriage.

4738. பிணம் போகிற இடத்தே துக்கமும் போகிறது.

Sorrow goes away to the place whither the corpse has gone.

4739. பிணைப்பட்டுக் கொள்ளாதே பெரும்பவத்தை உத்தரிப்பாய்.

Do not stand security, it will lead to endless evils.

4740. பிண்டத்துக்குக் கிடையாதது தெண்டத்துக்கு அகப்படும்.

That which cannot be obtained for sustenance, will be found to pay a fine.

4741. பித்தம் பத்து விதம்.

Madness is of ten kinds *i. e.*, many kinds.

4742. பித்தளை நாற்றம் அறியாது.

Brass is innocent of its own odour.

4743. பித்தர்க்குச் சில புத்திகள் சொன்னால் பேச்சைக் கேட்பாரா?

If advice be given to fools will they listen to it!

4744. பித்தனுக்குத் தன் குணம் நூலினும் செவ்வை.

The madman thinks his own character straighter than a line.

4745. பிரமசாரி ஓடம் கவிழ்த்ததுபோல.

As the brahmàchàri upset the boat.

4746. பிரமா நினைத்தால் ஆயுசுக்குக் குறையா?

If Brahma wills it, is there any chance of your life being short?

4747. பிழைக்கப்போன இடத்திலே பிழைமோசம் வந்ததுபோல.

As a grave occurrence befell one in the place to which he had gone for a livelihood.

4748. பிள்ளைக்காரன் பிள்ளைக்கு அழுகிறான் பணிசெய்வோன் காசுக்கு அழுகிறான்.

The parent weeps on account of his child, the servant weeps for his hire.

4749. பிள்ளைக்கு விளையாட்டுச் சுண்டெலிக்குப் பிராண சங்கடம்.

That which is sport to the child, is death to the mouse.

4750. பிள்ளை பதினாறு பெறுவாளென்று எழுதி இருந்தாலும், புருஷன் இல்லாமல் எப்படிப் பெறுவாள்?

Though it were written in the horoscope that she would have sixteen children, how could that be without a husband!

4751. பிள்ளை பெற்றவனுக்கும் மாடு படைத்தவனுக்கும் வெட்கம் இல்லை.

A parent and a cowherd know no shame.

4752. பிள்ளை பெற்றவளைப் பார்த்துப் பெருமூச்சு விட்டு ஆவது என்ன?

What if you look at her who has borne a child, and sigh?

4753. பிள்ளை அருமை மலடி அறிவாளா?

Does a barren woman understand the endearments of a child?

4754. பிள்ளையாருக்குப் பெண் கொள்வதுபோல.

Like obtaining a wife for Ganésha.

4755. பிள்ளையாரைப் பிடித்த சனி அரசமரத்தையும் பிடித்தது போல.

As Saturn who had seized Ganésha seized also the tree-*ficus Indica*.

4756. பிள்ளையார் கோவிலில் திருடன் இருப்பான், சொன்னாலும் கோள்.

The thief has taken refuge in the temple of Pillaiyár, it would however be a slander to mention it.

4757. பிள்ளையார் பிடிக்கக் குரங்காய் முடிந்தது.

The attempt to form *an image of* Ganésha, ended in the formation of a monkey.

4758. பிள்ளை இல்லா வீட்டில் கிழவன் துள்ளி விளையாடுகிறானாம்.

It is said that in the house in which there are no children, an old man plays like a child.

4759. பிள்ளையும் புழுக்கையும் சரி, பிள்ளைக்கும் புழுக்கைக்கும் இடம் கொடாதே.

A child and a slave are alike, be not indulgent to a child or a slave.

4760. பிள்ளையும் கிள்ளித் தொட்டிலும் ஆட்டுகிறதா?

Do you rock the cradle, while pinching the child?

4761. பிள்ளையைச் சாக்கிட்டு பூதம் விழுங்குகிறது.

Pretending to feed the child, the goblin swallows it.

4762. பிள்ளை வரத்திற்குப் போய் புருஷனைப் பறிகொடுத்ததுபோல.

Like losing her husband, when she went to ask the gift of offspring.

4763. பிள்ளைவருத்தம் பெற்றவளுக்குத் தெரியும் மற்றவளுக்குத் தெரியுமா?

A mother knows the pain of travail, is it known to others?

4764. பிள்ளைவீட்டுக்காரர் சம்மதித்தால் பாதி விவாகம் முடிந்தது போல.

If the family of the bridegroom consent, half *the ceremony of* marriage is over.

4765. பிறக்கிறபொழுதே முடம் ஆனால் பேய்க்கு இட்டுப் படைத்தால் தீருமா?

If a person be a cripple from his birth, can he be cured by offerings made to demons?

4766. பிறந்த பிள்ளை பிடி சோற்றிற்கு அழுகிறது, பிறக்கப்போகிற பிள்ளைக்குத் தண்டை சதங்கை தேடுகிறார்களாம்.

It is said that they are making silver bells for the child about to be born while the child on the lap is crying for a handful of rice.

4767. பிறந்தவன் இறப்பதே நிசம்.

It is certain that he who is born will die.

4768. பிறந்தன இறக்கும் தோன்றின மறையும்.

Those who are born will die, what is visible will vanish.

4769. பிறந்த அன்றே இறக்கவேண்டும்.

The day of birth *leads* to death.

4770. பிறந்த ஊருக்குச் சேலைவேண்டாம், பெண்டு இருந்த ஊருக்குத் தாலிவேண்டாம்.

A sumptuous cloth is not required in one's native village, nor a tàli where one is known as a wife.

4771. பிறர் பொருளை இச்சிப்பான் தன் பொருளை இழப்பான்.

He who covets the property of others, will lose his own.

4772. பிறர்மனைத் துரும்புகொள்ளான் பிராமணன் தண்டுகொண்டான்.

He who would not carry off a rush belonging to another's roof, robbed a brahman *his master* of his staff.

4773. பிறவிச் செவிடனுக்குப் பேசத் திறமுண்டா?

Are there any clever of speech who were born deaf?

4774. பிறவிக் குருடனுக்குக் கண் கிடைத்ததுபோல.

As one born blind received sight.

4775. பிறன் மனை புகாமை அறம் எனத் தகும்.

Not going to another man's house, deserves to be called virtue.

4776. பின்னாலே வரும் பலாக்காயினும் முன்னாலே வரும் களாக்காய் நலம்.

A kalàkkày is better in hand, than a jack fruit in prospect.

4777. பின்னை என்பதும் பேசாதிருப்பதும், இல்லை என்பதற்கு அடையாளம்.

By and by, and silence, are tantamount to a refusal.

பீ.

4778. பீரம் பேணி பாரம் தாங்கு.

Preserve your strength and bear the burden.

4779. பீறின புடைவை பெருநாள் இராது.

A ragged cloth will not wear long.

4780. பீற்றற் பட்டைக்கு அறுதற்கொடி.

A broken cord, and a ragged *basket* (well-bucket.)

பு.

4781. புகழ்ச்சியானுக்கு ஈந்தது பூதக்கண்ணாடி.

That which was given to the praise-worthy, is a microscope.

4782. புகழ்ந்தாரைப் போற்றி வாழ்.

Defend those who acknowledge your merit.

4783. புகைக்கினும் காரகில் பொல்லாங்கு எழாது.

Though eaglewood produces smoke, it will do no harm.

4784. புங்கப்புகழே தங்கத்திகழே.

The contempt of riches is the highest praise.

4785. புண்ணியத்துக்குக் கிணறு வெட்டப் பூதம் புறப்பட்டதுபோல.

As a demon came out of a well that had been dug as an act of religious merit.

4786. புண்ணியத்துக்கு உழுத மாட்டைப் பல்லைப் பிடித்துப் பார்த்ததுபோல.

Like looking at the teeth of a bullock that is ploughing for nothing.

4787. புண்ணியம் பார்க்கப் போய்ப் பாவம் பின்னே வந்ததாம்.

It is said that evil followed the man who attempted a kind act.

4788. புண்ணியம் இல்லாத வழிகாட்டி வீண்.

A leader not virtuous is worthless.

4789. புண்ணிலே கோல் இட்டதுபோல.

Like thrusting a stick into a wound.

4790. புண்ணிலே புளி பட்டதுபோலே.

As if a sore had become acidified.

4791. புண்ணுக்கோ மருந்துக்கோ விசம்?

Whether calls for immediate action, the sore or its remedy?

4792. புதிய காரியங்களிற் புதிய யோசனை வேண்டும்.

New things require fresh consideration.

4793. புதிய வண்ணானும் பழைய அம்பட்டனும் தேடவேண்டும்.

Employ a new washerman, but an old barber.

4794. புதிய வண்ணான் பொந்துகட்டி வெளுப்பான்.

A new washerman will wash with great care.

4795. புதியாரை நம்பிப் பழையாரைக் கைவிடலாமா?

Is it right to forsake old friends in reliance on new ones?

4796. புதுக் குடத்திலே வார்த்த தண்ணீர்.

Water poured into a new pot.

4797. புதுப் பானைக்கு ஈ சேராது.

Flies do not swarm on a new pot.

4798. புதுப் பெண்ணே புதுப் பெண்ணே நெருப்பு எடுத்துவா, உனக்குப் பின்னாலே இருக்கிறது செருப்பு அடி.

O bride, O bride bring some fire, what awaits you is slippering.

4799. புதுமையான காரியம் தான் இந்தக் கலியுகத்தில்.

Certainly it is a strange occurrence in kaliyuga.

4800. புதுமைக்கு வண்ணான் பறை தட்டி வெளுத்தான்.

The washerman inaugurated his washing by beat of tomtom.

4801. புதையல் எடுத்தவனைப்போலே.

Like one that has discovered buried treasure.

4802. புத்தி கெட்ட ராஜாவுக்கு மதி கெட்ட மந்திரி.

A foolish king and an ignorant minister.

4803. புத்தி அற்றோரும் தூங்கினர், புத்தி உற்றோரும் தூங்கினர்

Both the foolish and the wise slept.

4804. புத்திமான் பலவான்.

An intelligent man is strong.

4805. புத்தி முற்றினவர்க்குச் சித்தியாதது ஒன்றும் இல்லை.

There is nothing in which the mature in judgment fail.

4806. புத்தி உறப் புகழ்.

As soundness of judgment increases, praise will follow.

4807. புத்தி அற்றவர்கள் பத்தியாய்ச் செய்வதும் விபரீதமாம்.

E[illegible] that which fools perform earnestly is wrong.

4808. புத்தி ஈனர்கள் குளிக்கப் போய்ச் சேற்றைப் பூசிக்கொள்வார்கள்.

When the foolish go to wash, they will daub themselves with mud.

4809. புரட்டிப் புரட்டிப் உதைக்கிறபோதும், மீசையில் மண் படவில்லை என்கிறான்.

Even when kicked about and rolling in the dust, he affirms that his mustache did not touch the earth.

4810. புருஷன் அடிக்கக் கொழுந்தன் கோபித்ததுபோல.

Like the younger brother of the husband, rebuking him for beating his wife.

4811. புருஷனுக்கு ஏற்ற மாராப்பு.

The cloth covering the breast suited to the rank of her husband.

4812. புருவத்திற் பட்டால் கரிக்குமோ கண்ணிற் பட்டால் கரிக்குமோ?

When does *acid* cause smarting, when it is applied to the eye-brow or the eyes?

4813. புலி அடிக்குமுன்னே கிலி அடிக்கும்.

Struck with fear before struck by the tiger.

4814. புலிக்குப் பிறந்து நகம் இல்லாமற் போகுமா?

Being born a tiger, will it be without claws?

4815. புலிக்குத் தன் காடு என்ன வேற்றுக்காடு என்ன?

What matters it to the tiger whether he is in his native jungle or another?

4816. புலிக்குப் பிறந்து பூனையாய்ப்போகுமா?

Being born a tiger, will it become a cat?

4817. புலிக் கூட்டத்தில் மான் அகப்பட்டதுபோல.

As the deer was caught among tigers.

4818. புலி செவி திருகிய மத களிறு.

An elephant in rut whose ears w ere wrung off by a tiger.

4819. புலி நகம் படாவிட்டாலும், அதன் மீசை குத்தினாலும் விஷம்.
Though one may escape the claws of the tiger, even the pricking of its whiskers will prove malignant.

4820. புலி பசித்தால் புல்லுத் தின்னுமா?
When the tiger is hungry, will he eat grass?

4821. புலி பதுங்குவது பாய்ச்சலுக்கு இடம்.
The crouching of the tiger is the prelude to a spring.

4822. புலிப் பால் குடித்தவன்போல் இருக்கிறான்.
He is like one fed on tiger's milk.

4823. புலியைப் பார்த்து நரி சூடு இட்டுக்கொண்டதுபோல.
As the jackal branded itself in imitation of the stripes of a tiger.

4824. புலையனுக்கு வாக்குச் சுத்தியும் ஆணையும் இல்லை.
The base do not talk decently, nor do they heed oaths.

4825. புலையும் கொலையும் களவும் தவிர்.
Avoid lies, murder and theft.

4826. புல் உள்ள இடத்தில் மாட்டை ஆட்டை மேய ஒட்டாது.
It will not allow either sheep or cows to graze where there is grass.

4827. புல்லும் பூமியும் உள்ளமட்டும்.
As long as vegetation and the earth exist.

4828. புல்லும் பூமியும் கல்லும் காவேரியும் உள்ளமட்டும்.
As long as vegetation, earth, rocks and the Cauvery exist.

4829. புல்லு விற்கிற கடையிலே பூ விற்கிறது.
Selling flowers in a grass market.

4830. புல்லைத் தின்னும் மாடுபோலப் புலியைத் தின்னும் செந்நாய் உதவுமா?
Will the red dog that eats tiger's flesh prove as useful as the cow that eats grass?

4831. புழுக்கை கலம் கழுவித் தின்னாது.

The low-born does not eat from a washed plate.

4832. புழுக்கை ஒழுக்கம் அறியுமா பிண்ணாக்குச் சட்டி பதம் அறியுமா?

Does the low-born appreciate good manners, does the oil cake pan know when *the cake* is baked !

4833. புழுக்கை ஒழுக்கம் அறியாது பித்தளை நாற்றம் அறியாது.

Menials are ignorant of manners, brass is unconscious of its ill odour.

4834. புழுக்கைக்குப் புத்தி பிடரியிலே.

The sensibility of menials is in the neck.

4835. புழுங்கிப் புழுங்கிப் மா இடித்தாலும் புழுக்கைச்சிக்கு ஒரு கொழுக்கட்டை.

Though the slave girl who pounds rice labours so as to perspire, her share is only a cake.

4836. புழுத்த சரக்குக்குக் கொழுத்த பணம்.

Fat money for rotten articles.

4837. புளியமரத்தில் ஏறினவன் பல் கூசினால் இறங்குவான்.

He who has climbed a tamarind tree will come down when his teeth are set on edge.

4838. புளியம் பழத்துக்குப் புளிப்புப் புகுத்தவிட வருகிறாயோ?

Do you come to infuse acidity into the tamarind fruit !

4839. புளுகினாலும் பொருந்தப் புளுகவேண்டும்.

Even when boasting do it so as to secure belief.

4840. புள்ளிக் கணக்கன் பள்ளிக்கு ஆவானா?

Is a practical arithmetician fit to teach the theory of arithmetic ?

4841. புறக்கடை மருந்து கவைக்கு உதவாது.

The medicinal plant in the backyard will not avail in an emergency.

4842. புறக்குடத்துத் தண்ணீர்போல.

Like water on the outside of a pot.

4843. புற்றிலே ஆந்தை விழிப்பதுபோல.

Blinking like an owl on an ant-hill.

4844. புற்றிலே ஈசல் புறப்பட்டதுபோல.

Coming forth like a swarm of winged white ants from an ant-hill.

4845. புற்றிலே கிடந்த புடையன் எழும்பினதுபோல.

Rushing as a beaver snake from its hole.

4846. புற்றிலே ஈசல் புறப்பட்டாலும், மண்ணிலே கறையான் கூடினாலும் மழை வரவே வரும்.

When winged white ants issue out of a hole, and white ants swarm, it will certainly rain.

பூ.

4847. பூ அரசு இருக்கப் பொன்னுக்கு அழுவானேன்?

Why weep for gold while you have the tulip tree!

4848. பூசணிக்காய் அத்தனை முத்துக் காதில் ஏற்றுகிறதா மூக்கில் ஏற்றுகிறதா?

If a pearl be as large as a pumpkin, where is it to be worn, in the ear or in the nose?

4849. பூசணிக்காய் எடுத்தவனைத் தோளிலே காணலாம்.

If one has taken a pumpkin, its mark may be seen on his shoulder.

4850. பூசணிக்காய் அழுகினதுபோல.

Like a decayed pumpkin.

4851. பூசப் பூசப் பொன் நிறம்.

The more you gild it, the more like gold will it appear.

4852. பூசாரி பூ முடிக்கப் போனானும், பூ ஆலங்காடு பலாக் காடாய்ப் போச்சுதாம்.

The priest began to wear flowers, and the flower garden became a grove of jack trees.

4853. பூசை முகத்திலே கரடியை விட்டு ஓட்டினதுபோல.

Like driving a bear among those engaged in worship.

4854. பூச்சி மரிக்கிறதில்லை, புழுவும் சாகிறதில்லை.

Insects do not perish, nor do worms die.

4855. பூட்டிப் புசிக்காமல் புதைப்பார் ஈயைப்போல் ஈட்டி இழப்பார்.

Those who lock up their treasure and refuse to enjoy it will be deprived of it, as bees are deprived of their honey.

4856. பூட்டும் திறப்பும்போல.

As a lock and *its* key.

4857. பூதலம யாவும் போற்று முச்சுடர்.

The three lights which the whole world extol.

4858. பூத்தானமான பிள்ளை ஆத்தாளைத் தாலி கட்டிற்றாம்.

It is said that an indulged child tied a tali on his mother.

4859. பூத்துச் சொரியப் பொறுப்பார்கள் பூட்டிக் கட்டக் கலங்குவார்கள்.

They can endure seeing their tree shedding its blossoms, but will be disquieted at seeing others string and wear them.

4860. பூமி அதிர நடவாத புண்ணியவான்.

A virtuous person under whose footsteps the earth trembles not.

4861. பூமி திருத்தி உண்.

Till the soil, and enjoy *its produce.*

4862. பூராடக்காரனோடு போராட முடியாது.

One cannot strive with one born under the star purádam.

4863. பூரியோர்க்கு இல்லைச் சீரிய ஒழுக்கம்.

The base are void of good manners.

4864. பூர்வோத்தரம் மேரு காத்திரம்போல் இருக்கிறது.

His pedigree is weighty as *mount* Meru.

4865. பூலோகமுதலியார் பட்டம், புகுந்து பார்த்தால் பொட்டல்.

His title is lord of the world, but when examined he is found empty.

4866. பூ விற்கும் கடையில் புல் விற்பதுபோல.

As grass is sold in a flower market.

4867. பூ விற்ற கடையில் புல் விற்கலாமா?

May grass be sold in the flower market?

4868. பூ விற்ற காசு மணக்குமா புலால் விற்ற காசு நாறுமா?

Is the money obtained from the sale of flowers fragrant, does that obtained from the sale of flesh stink?

4869. பூ விற்றவனைப் பொன் விற்கப்பண்ணுவேன்.

I will enable him who sold flowers to sell gold.

4870. பூவுடன் கூடி நாரும் மணம் பெற்றதுபோல.

As a fibre *used for stringing* flowers partook of their fragrance.

4871. பூவுள் மங்கையாம் பொற்கொடியாம் போன இடம் எல்லாம் செருப்படியாம்.

It is said that she is Lackshmi residing in flowers, and she is a golden creeper, yet whithersoever she goes she is slippered.

4872. பூனை உள்ள இடத்திலே எலி பேரன் பேர்த்தி எடுக்கிறது.

The rat lives to see its grand-sons and grand-daughters in a place where there is a cat.

4873. பூனை கட்டும் தொழுவத்தில் ஆனை கட்டலாமா?

Can you tether an elephant in a place suited for tying up a cat?

4874. பூனைக்கு இல்லை தானமும் தவமும்.

Alms-giving and penance are not prescribed to cats.

4875. பூனைக்குக் கொண்டாட்டம் எலிக்குத் திண்டாட்டம்.

Amusement to the cat, and agony to the rat.

4876. பூனைக்குச் சிமாளம் வந்தால் பீற்றற்பாயில் புரளுமாம்.

It is said that if a cat be merry, she will roll about on an old mat.

4877. பூனை பால் குடிக்கிறதுபோல.

As a cat drinks milk.

4878. பூனைபோல் அடங்கினான் புலிபோல் பாய்ந்தான்.

He was quiet as a cat, and sprang like a tiger.

4879. பூனையைக் கண்ட கிளிபோலப் புலம்பி அழுகிறான்.

He cries as a parrot encountered by a cat.

4880. பூனையைத்தான் வீட்டுப் புலியென்றும், எலி அரசனென்றும் சொல்வார்கள்.

A cat is called a domestic tiger, and the king of rats.

பெ.

4881. பெட்டியிற் பாம்புபோல் அடங்கினான்.

He was as quiet as a snake in a box.

4882. பெட்டி பீற்றல் வாய்க் கட்டுத் திறம்.

The basket is torn, but the rim is strong.

4883. பெட்டைக் கோழி கூவியோ விடிகிறது?

Does the day break at the crowing of a hen?

4884. பெட்டைக் கோழி தட்டிக் கூவுமா?

Can a hen flap her wings and crow *like a cock*?

4885. பெண் என்றால் பேயும் இரங்கும்.

Even a demon will pity a woman.

4886. பெண்ணாசை ஒரு பக்கம் மண்ணாசை ஒரு பக்கம்.

Love of women on the one hand, and love of property on the other.

4887. பெண்சாதி இல்லாதவன் பேயைக் கட்டித் தழுவினதுபோல.

As the man who had no wife embraced a demoness.

4888. பெண்சாதியைத் தாய் வீட்டில் விட்டவனுக்கு ஒரு சொட்டு.

A cuff for the man who left his wife at her mother's.

4889. பெண்சாதி காற்கட்டு, பிள்ளை வாய்க்கட்டு.

Fettered with a wife, and muzzled with a child.

4890. பெண்டாட்டி கொண்டதும் திண்டாட்டம் பட்டதும் போதும்.

Enough of taking a wife and suffering the consequences.

4891. பெண்டிர்க்கு அழகு பேசாதிருத்தல்.

Not to remonstrate *with her husband* is an ornament in a woman.

4892. பெண்டுகள் குந்துக்குப் புரிமணை.

A straw twist for women to squat on.

4893. பெண்டுகளுக்குப் பெற்றார் இடத்திலும் பிள்ளைகள் இடத்திலும் மூப்பு இல்லை.

Women have no influence over parents and children.

4894. பெண்டுகள் சோற்றுக்குத் தண்டம் இல்லை.

Women are not in danger of forfeiting their rice.

4895. பெண்ணரம்பைக் கூத்துக்குப் போய்ப் பேய்க் கூத்து ஆச்சுதே.

The going to a dance of celestials ended as a dance of devils.

4896. பெண்ணின் குணம் அறிவேன் சம்பந்தி வாய் அறிவேன்.

I know the character of the bride, and the boisterousness of her mother-in-law.

4897. பெண்ணுக்குப் பொன் இட்டுப்பார், சுவருக்கு மண் இட்டுப் பார்.

Look at a woman after adorning her with jewels, and at a wall when you have plastered it with mud.

4898. பெண்ணுக்கும் பொன்னுக்கும் தோற்பு உண்டா?

Is any one ever tired of women and wealth?

4899. பெண்ணுக்குப் போய்ப் பொன்னுக்குப் பின்வாங்கலாமா?

Having gone to take a wife, can you turn back because marriage is expensive?

4900. பெண்ணுக்கு மாமியாரும், பிள்ளைக்கு வாத்தியாரும்.

For a wife, a mother-in-law, for a boy, a tutor.

4901. பெண்ணைக் கொடுத்தவளோ கண்ணைக் கொடுத்தவளோ?

Did she give one a wife, or did she give one her eye?

4902. பெண்ணைப் பிழை பொறுக்கப் பெற்றதாய் வேண்டாமோ?

Are you content to lose your mother in order to pardon your wife?

4903. பெண்ணைக் கொண்டு பையன் பேயானான், பிள்ளை பெற்றுச் சிறுக்கி நாயானாள்.

Having married a wife the boy has become a fool, having given birth to a child the damsel has become mean in appearance.

4904. பெண்ணை வேண்டும் என்றால் இளியற் கண்ணை நக்கு.

If you want the woman, lick her bleared eyes.

4905. பெண் புத்தி கேட்கிறவன் பேய்.

He who listens to the advice of women is a fool.

4906. பெண் புத்தி பின்புத்தி.

The thoughts of women are after-thoughts.

4907. பெண் வளர்த்தி பீர்க்கங்கொடி.

The growing of women is that of a gourd creeper.

4908. பெரியாரைத் துணைக்கொள்.

Secure the good will of the great.

4909. பெரியோர் எல்லாம் பெரியரும் அல்லர்.

All who are high in stature are not great.

4910. பெரியோர்முன் தாழ்ந்து பேசில், நாணலைப்போல் நிமிர்ந்து கொள்வார்கள்.

When speaking submissively to the great, they preserve an erect posture like a reed.

4911. பெரியோர் முன் எதிர்த்துப்பேசில், வெள்ளத்திற்குமுன் மரங்களைப்போல் விழ்வார்கள்.

If they should contradict the great, they will fall like trees before a flood.

4912. பெருங் கயிறு முடி அழுந்தாது.

A tight knot cannot be formed in a thick rope.

4913. பெருங்காயம் இருந்த பாண்டம்.

An earthen pot in which assafœtida was kept.

4914. பெருங் காற்றில் பீளைப்பஞ்சு பறக்கிறதுபோல.

Flying like cotton before a gale of wind.

4915. பெருங் குலத்தில் பிறந்தாலும் புத்தி அற்றவன் கரும்புப் பூப் போல.

Though born in a high family, a fool is like a sugar-cane flower.

4916. பெருங் கொடை பிச்சைக்காரருக்குத் துணிவு.

Beggars presume on large gifts.

4917. பெரு நெருப்புக்கு ஈரம் உண்டா?

Will moisture *affect* a great fire.

4918. பெரு மரத்தைச் சுற்றிய வள்ளிக்கொடிபோல.

Like a creeping plant-*Dioscorea sativa*-round a large tree.

4919. பெரு மழை விழுந்தாற் குளிராது.

No feeling of cold in a heavy fall of rain.

4920. பெருமாள் இருக்கிற வரையில் திருநாள் உண்டு.

As long as Perumal exists, holy days will be observed.

4921. பெருமாள் என்கிற பெயரை மாற்றப் பெரிய பெருமாள் ஆச்சுது.

The name Perumal being changed has become great Perumal.

5922. பெருமானைச் சேர்ந்தோர்க்குப் பிறப்பு இல்லை, பிச்சைச்சோற்றிற்கு எச்சில் இல்லை.

Those who have attained union with God are not subject to future births, rice given in alms is not refused because it is refuse.

4923. பெருமான் நினைத்தால் வாழ்வு குறைவா, பிரமா நினைத்தால் ஆயுசு குறைவா?

If God is pleased, will there be any lack of prosperity, if Brahma favour, will one's life be short?

4924. பெருமைதான் அருமையை குலைக்கும்.

Pride will diminish *one's* worth.

4925. பெருமையான தரித்திரன் வீண்.

Pride in a poor man is vain.

4926. பெருமை ஒரு முறம் புடைத்து எடுத்தால் ஒன்றும் இல்லை.

When a sieve, full of pride, is sifted, nothing remains.

4927. பெருமையும் சிறுமையும் வாயால் வரும்.

The great and the little come from the mouth.

4928. பெருமைக்கு ஆட்டை அடித்துப் பிள்ளை கையில் காதைச் சுட்டுக் கொடுத்தான்.

He killed a sheep to show his greatness, and gave the ear to his child after roasting it.

4929. பெரு ரூபத்தை உடையவரும் பிரயோசனமாய் இருக்கமாட்டார். அதுபோல, பனை விதை பெரிதாய் இருந்தும் நிழல கொடுக்கமாட்டாது.

The great are not *always* helpful, the lofty palmyrah casts no shade.

4930. பெரு வயிறு கொண்டது அறியாமல் சீமந்தத்திற்கு நாள் இட்டுக்கொண்டான்.

Not knowing that his wife is affected with dropsy, he has fixed upon a day for the performance of her simantham ceremony.

A ceremony relating to the first pregnancy, including bathing, the parting of the hair in the middle of the forehead, putting on jewels, &c., &c.

4931. பெற்ற தாய் இடத்திலோ கற்ற வித்தை காட்டுகிறாய்?

Do you practise your arts on your mother?

4932. பெற்ற தாய் செத்தால் பெற்ற அப்பன் சிற்றப்பன்.

If a mother dies, the father becomes uncle.

4933. பெற்ற தாய் பசித்திருக்கப் பிராமண போஜனம் செய்தது போல.

Like feeding brahmans when one's mother is starving.

4934. பெற்றது எல்லாம் பிள்ளையா இட்டது எல்லாம் பயிரா?

Are all that are brought forth children, is all that is sown available for use?

4935. பெற்றது எல்லாம் பிள்ளையோ வனைந்தது எல்லாம் குசக்கலமோ?

Are all that are brought forth children, is all earthen ware perfect that is fashioned by a potter!

4936. பெற்ற மனம் பித்து, பிள்ளை மனம் கல்லு.

The mother's heart is soft, that of her child is as a stone.

4937. பெற்றோர்க்கு இல்லைச் சுற்றமும் சினமும்.

The wise are not moved by relationship or anger.

பே.

4938. பேசப் பேச எந்தப் பாஷையும் வரும்.

Any language may be learnt by continual speaking.

4939. பேசாதிருந்தால் பிழை ஒன்றும் இல்லை.

No fault arises if nothing is spoken.

4940. பேசில் அபலம் பேசாக்கால் ஊமை.

When he speaks it is to no purpose, when he does not speak *he is accounted* dumb.

4941. பேச்சுக் கற்ற நாய் வேட்டைக்கு ஆகாது.

A noisy dog is not fit for hunting.

4942. பேச்சுக்கு இராவணன் பின்பு கும்பகர்ணன்.

In speech he is Ravana, but he turns out to be Kumbhakarnaan.

4943. பேச்சுக்குப் பேச்சுச் சிங்காரமா?

Is contradiction becoming?

4944. பேச்சை விற்றுக் காய்ச்சிக் குடிக்கிறான்.

He sells his words, and cooks and drinks.

4945. பேடி கையில் இருந்த ஆயுதம்போல.

Like a weapon in the hands of a hermaphrodite.

4946. பேடி கையில் வாள்போலே.

Like a sword in the hands of a hermaphrodite.

4947. பேதம் அற்றவர் நீதம் உற்றவர்.

He who is impartial is just.

4948. பேதைகள் வெள்ளத்திலே நின்றும் தாகத்திற்குத் தண்ணீருக்கு அலைவார்கள்.

Fools in the midst of a flood will wander about for water to drink.

4949. பேதைமை என்பது மாதர்க்கு அணிகலம்.

Simplicity is the ornament of a woman.

4950. பேயானாலும் தாய், நீரானாலும் மோர்.

Though like a demon she is a mother, though mere slop, it is butter-milk.

4951. பேயும் சிலது ஞாயம் பகரும்.
Even a demon will have some reason *to assign.*

4952. பேய் ஆடிய கம்பம்போல.
Like a pole on which a demon dances.

4953. பேய் கொண்டாலும் பெண் கொள்ளல் ஆகாது.
One may take a demon, but not take a wife.

4954. பேய்க்குக் கள் வார்த்ததுபோல.
Like pouring out toddy to a demon.

4955. பேய்க்கு வேப்பிலைபோலே.
As margosa leaves before a demon.

4956. பேய்க்கு வேலை இட்டதுபோல.
Like setting a demon to work.

4957. பேய்க்கூத்தும் ஆமணக்கும் ஆள்போனால் ஆள் தெரியாது.
A devil dance is a garden of castor oil plants, if one gets in he is not seen again.

4958. பேய் சிரித்தாலும் ஆகாது அழுதாலும் ஆகாது.
If a demon smiles it is bad, and if he weep that too is inauspicious.

4959. பேய் பிடிக்கவும் பிள்ளை பிழைக்கவுமா?
Will a child struck by a demon survive?

4960. பேய் போய்ப் புளியமரத்தில் ஏறினதுபோல.
As a demon ascended a tamarind tree.

4961. பேராசைக்காரனைப் பெரும்புளுகால் வெல்லவேண்டும்.
The avaricious must be overcome by notorious lies.

4962. பேராசை பெரிய நஷ்டம்.
Avarice ends in loss.

4963. பேர் இல்லாச் சன்னிதி பாழ், பிள்ளை இல்லாச் செல்வம் பாழ்.
The presence of one without reputation does no good, wealth without a child is useless.

பை.

4964. பைசாசைப் பணியேல்.

Yield not to a demon.

4965. பைந்தமிழ்ப் புலவோர் பாட்டுக்கு ஏற்றவன்.

He is worthy to be sung by poets.

4966. பையச் சென்றால் வையம் தாங்கும்.

If *you* walk gently, the earth will bear *you*.

4967. பைய மிதித்தது வேடன் அடி, பதறி மிதித்தது பன்றி அடி.

The light footstep is that of the hunter, the firm footstep is that of the hog.

4968. பைய மென்றால் பனையையும் மெல்லலாம்.

If masticated slowly even a palmyrah tree may be chewed.

4969. பையிற் கட்டிவைத்த பொருள் பறிகொடுக்கப்பட்டது.

The wealth tied up in a bag was lost.

பொ.

4970. பொக்கவாய்ச்சி மெச்சினளாம் பொரிமாவை.

It is said that a toothless dame appreciated the rice flour.

4971. பொங்கும் காலம் புளி பூக்கும், மங்கும் காலம் மா பூக்கும்.

In times of plenty the tamarind tree blossoms, in times of scarcity the mango bears *in abundance.*

4972. பொதி அளக்கிறதற்குமுன்னே சத்தத்திற்கு அளக்கிறதா?

Am I to measure out the hire, before measuring out the load!

4973. பொதியை வைத்து விட்டுப் பிச்சைக்குப் போனான், அதையும் வைத்து விட்டுச் செத்துக் கிடந்தான்.

Having loaded his bullock, he went abegging; the product he put on one side, and died.

4974. பொதி வைக்கிறதற்கு முன்னே சத்தத்திற்கு அளக்கிறதா?
Am I to measure out the hire before adjusting the load?

4975. பொத்தைச் சுரைக்காய்போலே.
Like a fleshy gourd.

4976. பொய் இருந்து புலம்பும் மெய் இருந்து விழிக்கும்.
Falsehood will never cease to weep, truth will ever be conspicuous.

4977. பொய் உடை ஒருவன் சொல் வன்மையினால் மெய்போலும்மே மெய்போலும்மே.
The falsehood of a liar by reason of its force, may appear like truth may appear like truth.

4978. பொய் சொன்ன வாய்க்குப் போசனம் கிடையாது.
The mouth accustomed to lies will be deprived of food.

4979. பொய் சொன்ன வாய்க்குப் பொரியும் கிடையாது.
The mouth accustomed to lies will be deprived of even parched corn.

4980. பொய் சொல்லி வாழ்ந்தவனும் இல்லை, மெய் சொல்லிக் கெட்டவனும் இல்லை.
No one ever prospered by telling lies, no one was ever reduced to poverty by speaking truth.

4981. பொய் மெய்யை வெல்லுமா?
Will falsehood conquer truth?

4982. பொய்யான பொருளாசை மெய்யான அருளாசையை விலக்குகிறது.
The false love of money, will take away the real love of divine grace.

4983. பொய்யும் ஒரு பக்கம் பொறாமையும் ஒரு பக்கம்.
Falsehood on one side, and envy on the other.

4984. பொய்யைச் சொன்னாலும் பொருந்தச் சொல்லவேண்டும்.
Though you tell lies, do so consistently.

4985. பொருடனைப் போற்றிவாழ்.

Preserve your substance and live.

4986. பொருளாசையும் மனச்சாட்சியும் பொருந்துமா?

Will covetous desires and conscience agree?

4987. பொருளும் கொடுத்துப் பழியும் தேட.

Giving one's wealth and incurring censure.

4988. பொருளும் போகமும் கூடவராது புண்ணியமே கூடவரும்.

Wealth and pleasure will be separated from us, but virtue will abide.

4989. பொருள் போன வழியே துக்கம் போம்.

Whithersoever wealth goes, sorrow follows in the same path.

4990. பொல்லாத மனம் கேளாது.

The wicked heart resists reproof.

4991. பொல்லாங்கு என்பவை எல்லாம் தவிர்.

Avoid whatever is evil.

4992. பொல்லாத காலம் சொல்லாமல் வந்தது.

Inauspicious times come without giving notice.

4993. பொல்லாதவர்கள் சினப்பட்டால் கல்லின் பிளவுபோல ராசியாகமாட்டார்கள்.

The anger of the wicked is like a fracture in a stone, they are not easily reconciled.

4994. பொல்லாத குணத்துக்கு மருந்து உண்டா?

Is there any medicine for a bad temper?

4995. பொல்லாதவர்கள் சங்காத்தம் உப்பு மணலில் வீழ்ந்த நீர் போல.

The friendship of the wicked is as bitter as water in brackish soil.

4996. பொல்லாப் பிள்ளையில் இல்லாப் பிள்ளை.

A bad child is worse than none.

4997. பொழுது பட்ட இடம் விடுதி விட்ட இடம்.

Halting where the sun sets.

4998. பொழுது விடிந்தது பாவம் தொலைந்தது.

The day has dawned, sin is ended.

4999. பொறி வென்றவனே அறிவின் குருவாம்.

He alone who conquers his senses is a teacher of wisdom.

5000. பொறுதி என்பது கடலினும் பெரிது.

Forbearance is greater than the ocean.

5001. பொறுத்தல் கசப்பாய் இருந்தாலும் பொறுக்கப் பொறுக்கத் தித்திப்பு.

Although suffering may be bitter, continued endurance will make it sweet.

5002. பொறுத்தார் பூமி ஆள்வார்.

Those who put up with injuries may rule the earth.

5003. பொறுத்தார் அரசாள்வார் பொங்கினர் காடாள்வார்.

They who endure will reign as kings, the irascible will wander through the jungles.

5004. பொறுமை புண்ணியத்திற்கு வேர் பொருளாசை பாவத்திற்கு வேர்.

Patient endurance is the root of religious merit, avarice is the root of sin.

5005. பொற் கலம் ஒலிக்காது வெண் கலம் ஒலிக்கும்.

A gold vessel does not sound, a brass one does.

5006. பொற் காப்புக்கு ஆசைப்பட்டுப் புலியின் கையில் அகப்பட்டது போல.

Like one whose desire for a gold bracelet, hurried him into the claws of a tiger.

5007. பொற் பூவின் வாசனையும் முருக்கம் பூவின் வாசனையும் சரி.

The smell of a flower of gold and that of the murukku flower are alike.

5008. பொற் பூ வாசிக்குமா?

Does a golden flower diffuse fragrance!

5009. பொன் ஆபரணத்தைப் பார்க்கிலும் புகழ் ஆபரணமே பெரிது.

The ornament of reputation is greater than ornaments of gold.

5010. பொன் இரவல் உண்டு, பூ இரவல் உண்டா?

Gold may be lent, can flowers!

5011. பொன் என்றால் பிணமும் வாய் திறக்கும்.

If the word gold be uttered, even a corpse will open its mouth.

5012. பொன்கத்தி என்று கழுத்து அறுத்துக்கொள்ளலாமா?

May one cut his throat with a knife because it is made of gold?

5013. பொன் காத்த பூதம்போலே.

Like the demon that guarded treasure.

5014. பொன்செருப்பு ஆனாலும் காலுக்குத்தான் போடவேண்டும்.

Though golden slippers, they must be put on the feet.

5015. பொன்மணி அற்றவளை அம்மணி என்பானேன்?

Why should a woman who has no gold beads be called Ammani?

5016. பொன்முடி அல்லது சடை முடி வேண்டும்.

One should wear either a gold crown, or matted hair.

5017. பொன்னம்பலம் உண்டானால் என்ன அம்பலம் கிடையாது?

If one has a golden house, what house can he not get?

5018. பொன்னம்பலத்துக்கும் புவனகிரிப் பட்டணத்துக்கும் என்றைக்கும் உண்டான இழவு.

The golden hall of-*Chidambaram*, and the town Puvanagiri, are always in trouble.

5019. பொன்னாங்காணிக்குப் புளி விட்டு ஆக்கினால் உண்ணாக்கு எல்லாம் தித்திக்கும்.

If acid be mixed with ponnánkáni-*Illecebrum sessile*-its flavour will be agreeable to the whole palate.

5020. பொன்னாங்காணிக்குப் புளி விட்டு ஆக்கினால் உண்ணாப் பெண்ணும் ஒரு உழக்கு உண்ணும்.

The compound of ponnánkáni greens-*illecebrum*-and tamarind, will enable a girl who has lost her appetite to eat an ulak of rice.

5021. பொன்னான மனதைப் புண்ணாக்குகிறான்.

He ulcerates the golden mind.

5022. பொன்னாலே கலம் உண்டானாலும் மண்ணாலே சுவர் வேண்டும்.

Though one may possess vessels of gold, the wall *of his house* must be of mud.

5023. பொன்னாலே மருமகளானாலும் மண்ணாலே ஒரு மாமி வேண்டும்.

Though the daughter-in-law is made of gold, she must have a mother-in-law made of earth.

5024. பொன்னின் கலப்பை வரகுக்கு உழப் போனதாம் வரகு சேருக்கு வரகு பட்டதாம்.

Golden ploughs were used for the cultivation of the millet, and the crop was less than the seed-corn.

5025. பொன்னின் குடத்திற்குப் பொட்டு இட்டுப் பார்க்க வேண்டுமா?

Must a royal mark be inscribed on a golden pot, that it may appear the more beautiful!

5026. பொன்னின் குடம் உடைந்தாற் பொன் ஆகும் என்ன ஆகும் மண்ணின் குடம் உடைந்தாக்கால்?

Though broken to pieces a golden pot will still be gold, of what use is an earthen pot when broken?

5027. பொன்னை வைக்கிற கோயிலிலே பூவையாவது வைக்கவேண்டும்.

Flowers, at least, must be offered in a temple in which gold is offered.

5028. பொன்னை எறிந்தாலும் பொடிக் கீரையை எறியலாமா?

Although you may throw away gold, you may not throw away edible herbs!

போ.

5029. போகா ஊருக்கு வழி கேள்.

Inquire the way to the village whither you are not going.

5030. போகாத இடத்திலே போனால் வராத சொட்டு வரும்.

If you go where you ought not, you will receive a cuff that might have been avoided.

5031. போக்கணம் கெட்டவன் ராஜாவிலும் பெரியவன்.

An impudent person is greater than a king.

5032. போக்கு அற்ற நாய்க்கு போனது எல்லாம் வழி.

A hungry dog finds a way wherever he goes.

5033. போசனம் சிறுத்தாலும் ஆசனம் பெருக்க வேண்டும்.

Though one's food be slight, the dish must be large.

5034. போதகர் சொல்லைத் தட்டாதே, பாதகர் இல்லைக் கிட்டாதே.

Obey *your* religious teacher, approach not the house of the wicked.

5035. போதகருக்கே சோதனை மிஞ்சும்.

A religious teacher meets with many temptations.

5036. போதும் என்ற மனமே பொன் செய்யும் மருந்து.

A contented mind is a specific for making gold.

5037. போரில் ஊசி தேடின சம்பந்தம்.

Akin to seeking a needle in a heap of straw.

5038. போரைக்கட்டிவைத்துப்போட்டுப் பிச்சைக்குப் போவானேன்?

Having stacked your corn, why go abegging!

5039. போரோடு தின்கிற மாட்டுக்குப் பிடுங்கிப் போட்டுக் கட்டுமா?

When an ox is accustomed to eat at a heap, will it be satisfied with a handful!

5040. போர்த்தொழில் புரியேல்.

Do not practise the art of war.

5041. போர் பிடுங்குகிறவர்கள் பூரக்களம் சாடுகிறவர்களை மாட்டுகிறார்களாம்.

It is said that those who steal from a corn-stack, will frighten those who glean *stealthily*.

5042. போலைக்கு ஒரு பொன்மணி கிடைத்ததாம், அதைத் தூக்கக்கண்ணில் தொட்டுத் தொட்டுப் பார்த்ததாம்.

It is said that the hollow-headed woman obtained a gold bead, and that she examined it when she was sleepy.

5043. போலை பொறுக்கப் போச்சாம் பூனை குறுக்கே போச்சாம்.

It is said that the destitute went out to gather orts, and a cat went across *the path*.

5044. போனகம் என்பது தான் உழைத்து உண்டல்.

That which one eats as the fruit of his own labour, is *properly* called food.

5045. போன சுரத்தைப் புளி இட்டு அழைத்ததுபோல.

Like inviting a fever that has subsided, by giving acids.

5046. போனதை நினைக்கிறவன் புத்தி கெட்டவன்.

He lacks sense who broods over the past.

5047. போன மாட்டைத் தேடுவாரும் இல்லை, மேய்த்த கூலி கொடுப்பாரும் இல்லை.

There is no one to seek the lost cow, none to pay the hire of the cowherd.

பௌ.

5048. பௌவத்து எழில்கோள்.

Be graceful as the moon.

5049. பௌவப் பெருமை தெய்வச் செயலே.

The greatness of the ocean *shows* the work of God.

5050. பௌவம் உற்றது ஆக்கை, செவ்வை அற்றது வாழ்க்கை.

The body is like a bubble, one's *present* existence is not lasting.

ம.

5051. மகதேவர் ஆடு இடித்துப் பேயும் ஆடுகிறது.

When butted by a ram of Mahadévar, even the demon shakes its head.

5052. மகளுக்குப் புத்தி சொல்லித் தாய் அவசாரி போனாளாம்.

The mother, having given advice to her daughter, played the harlot.

5053. மகள் செத்தாள் தாய் திக்கு அற்றாள்.

The daughter is dead, the mother is become destitute.

5054. மகள் செத்தாற் பிணம் மகன் செத்தாற் சவம்.

If the daughter die her remains are regarded as a pinam; if the son, his corpse is a savam.

5055. மகன் செத்தாலும் சாகட்டும் மருமகள் கொட்டம் அடங்கினாற் போதும்.

No matter if my son should die, it will suffice if the arrogance of my daughter-in-law is checked.

5056. மகாமகம் பன்னிரண்டு வருஷத்திற்கு ஒரு விசை.

Mahámaham festival is celebrated every twelfth year.

5057. மகா மேருவைச் சேர்ந்த காகமும் பொன்னிறமாம்.

Even a crow if it arrive at Mahaméru is said to assume a golden hue.

5058. மகா ராஜாவின் கலியாணத்தில் நீராகாரம் நெய் பட்ட பாடு.

At the marriage feast of the Maha Rajah, even cold rice water is rare as ghee.

5059. மகா லட்சுமி பரதேசம் போனதுபோல.

As Maha Lakshmi went on a pilgrimage.

5060. மகிமை சுந்தரி கதவை ஒஞ்சரி.

Illustrious beauty, leave the door ajar.

5061. மகிமைக்கு அஞ்சிய மருமகனே எருமைக் கன்றைக் கொல்லாதே.

Thou modest son-in-law, do not kill the young buffaloa.

This was said to a man by his mother-in-law. Wishing to appear to her a small eater he stinted himself at his ordinary meals, and yet appeared to flourish. Casting about for a solution of the mystery her attention was called to the ill condition of a young buffaloa. Suspecting that her son-in-law was the cause of this, she resolved to watch his movements. The following night she saw him emerge from his room and proceed to the buffaloa, whose milk he exhausted, and returned to his own quarters. On the morrow when he took his food she addressed him in the language of the proverb.

5062. மகிமைப்பட்டவனுக்கு மரணம், மாட்டுக்காரப்பையனுக்குச் சரணம்.

Death to the distinguished, homage to the cowherd.

5063. மகிமையிலே ஒரு பெண் குவளையிலே வாழுகிறாள், அதில் ஒரு பெண் அறுத்துவிட்டு அழுகிறாள்.

One matron flourishes in the water-lily, and one weeps bereft of her marriage symbol.

5064. மக்கள் களவும் வரகு பதரும் சரி.

The dishonest tricks of children, and the husks of varagu are alike.

5065. மக்கள் சோறு தின்றால் மகிமை குறையும்.

To be fed by children is a disgrace *to parents*.

5066. மக்காவுக்குப் போய்க் கொக்குப் பிடித்ததுபோல.

Like going on a pilgrimage to Mecca, and catching a crane.

5067. மங்கமாரி வந்தார் தங்க மழை பெய்தது.

Montgomery came, and it rained fine gold.

5068. மங்கும் காலம் மாங்காய் பொங்கும் காலம் புளியங்காய்.

In time of scarcity, mangoes, and in a season of plenty, tamarind fruit, are abundant.

5069. மங்கை தீட்டானால் கங்கையிலே முழுகுவாள் கங்கை தீட்டானால் எங்கே முழுகுவாள்?

If the damsel is polluted she may be cleansed by the ganges, but if the ganges be polluted whither can she go?

5070. மச்சத்தின் குஞ்சுக்கு இப்படி என்றால், மாதாவுக்கு எப்படியோ?

If such be the condition of the young fish, what will be that of the mother?

5071. மச்சானைப் பார்க்க உறவும் இல்லை, மயிரைப் பார்க்கக் கறுப்பும் இல்லை.

No friendship superior to that of a cousin, nothing blacker than hair.

The word மச்சான் is used for a brother-in-law, and also for a maternal uncle's son.

5072. மச்சான் செத்தால் மயிர் போச்சு கம்பளி மெத்தை நமக்கு ஆச்சு.

If my brother-in-law die I care not a hair; his cumbly mattress will be mine.

5073. மச்சை அழித்தால் குச்சுக்கும் ஆகாது.

If the roof be destroyed, the house will not answer for a hut.

5074. மஞ்சனமும் மலரும் கொண்டு துதிக்காவிட்டாலும் நெஞ்சகத்தில் நினைப்பதே போதகம்.

Though one may not worship *god* by bathing him, and scattering flowers on him, we are taught to keep him in mind.

5075. மடக்கிழவனிலும் புத்தி உள்ள வாலிபன் அதிகம்.
A prudent youth is superior to a stupid old man.

5076. மடக் கேள்விக்கு மாறுத்தரம் இல்லை.
A stupid question needs no answer.

5077. மடப் பெருமையே தவிர நீராகாரத்துக்கும் வழி இல்லை.
Besides a choultry, there is nothing,—not even water.

5078. மடம் பிடுங்கிக் கொண்டு போகும்போது நந்தவனத்துக்கு வழி எங்கே என்கிறான்.
After the choultry has been destroyed, he asks the way to the flower garden.

5079. மடி மாங்காய் போட்டுத் தலை வெட்டலாமா?
Are you about to behead one upon whom you have forced mango fruit?

5080. மடியிலே கனம் இருந்தால் வழியிலே பயம்.
If you have money in your waist-cloth, you may be afraid on the way.

5081. மடியைப் பிடித்துக் கள்ளை வார்த்து மயிரைப் பிடித்துக் காசு வேண்டுகிறதா?
Having forced one to take toddy, do you seize him by the hair and demand payment?

5082. மட்டான போசனம் மனதிற்கு மகிழ்ச்சி.
Moderation in eating exhilerates the mind.

5083. மட்டி எருக்கலை மடல் மடலாய்ப் பூத்தாலும், மருக்கொழுந்து வாசனை வருமா?
Though the erukkalai bears bunches of flowers, has it the fragrance of southern-wood-*artemisia austriaca*?

5084. மட்டு இல்லாமற் கொடுத்தாலும் திட்டுக் கேட்கல் ஆகாது.
Though he gives liberally, it is not right to hear his abuse.

5085. மட்டைக் கரியையும் மடப்பள்ளியாரையும் நம்பப்படாது.
Palm-stem charcoal and Madappallis are not to be trusted.

5086. மணலின்மேல் விழுந்த மழைத்துளி உடனே மறையும்; அது போல, பொல்லாதவர்களுக்குச் செய்த உபகாரம் மறைந்து போம்.

Drops of rain falling on sand will instantly disappear, in like manner favours shewn to the wicked will be soon forgotten.

5087. மணற் சோற்றில் கல் ஆய்வதுபோல.

Like picking out stones when eating a dish of sand.

5088. மணி நா அசையாமல் இராச்சியபாரம் பண்ணுகிறது.

So to govern a kingdom as not to move even the tongue of a bell.

5089. மண் குதிரையை நம்பி ஆற்றில் இறங்கலாமா?

May one descend into a river relying on a mud horse?

5090. மண்டைக்குத் தகுந்த கொண்டை போடவேண்டும்.

The knot of hair must be proportioned to the size of the head.

5091. மண்டையில் எழுதி மயிரால் மறைத்ததுபோல.

Like writing on the skull and covering it with the hair.

5092. மண்டை உள்ளவரையில் சளி போகாது.

As long as the head remains phlegm will abide.

5093. மண்ணுயினும் மனை ஆயினும காப்பாற்றினவர்களுக்கு உண்டு.

They may have house and grounds *who know how* to take care of them.

5094. மண்ணுங்கட்டி மாப்பிள்ளைக்கு எருமுட்டைப் பணிகாரம்.

Dried cow-dung is the proper form of wedding cake, when the bridegroom is made of sand.

5095. மண்ணால் ஆனாய் மண்ணாய் இருக்கிறாய்.

Made of earth, thou art earthy.

5096. மண்ணின்மேல் நின்று பெண் ஓரம் சொல்லாதே.

Whilst on earth pervert not judgment, in the case of a woman.

5097. மண்ணைத் தின்றாலும் மறையத் தின்.

Though what you may eat be sand, eat it in a secluded place.

5098. மண்ணோடே பிறக்கலாம் உன்னோடே பிறந்ததில்.

It were better to be born of the earth, than to be your brother.

5099. மண் பறித்து உண்ணேல்.

Do not live by extortion.

5100. மண்பிள்ளை ஆனாலும் தன் பிள்ளை.

Though earthen, one's own child is precious.

5101. மண் பூனை ஆனாலும் எலிப் பிடித்தால் சரி.

Though the cat is made of mud, if it catch rats, it is enough.

5102. மண்வெட்டி கூதல் அறியுமா?

Is a hoe sensible of cold!

5103. மண்வேலையோ புண்வேலையோ?

Are you engaged in making earthen ware, or sores!

5104. மதலைக்கு இல்லைக் கீதமும் அறிவும்.

A child has neither the power of singing nor discretion.

5105. மதன மலைக்கு ஒப்பிடலாம்.

He is comparable to Mathana mountain.

5106. மதாபிமானம் சுசாதிமானம் தேசாபிமானம்.

Love of father, caste, and country.

5107. மதியாத வாசலில் மிதியாதிருப்பதே உத்தமம்.

It is not well to tread even on the threshold of a house in which you are not respected.

5108. மதியும் உமது விதியும் உமது.

Thy purpose and thy destiny.

The settled judgment, and the decrees of God, are in harmony.

5109. மதியை மீன் சூழ்ந்ததுபோல.

As the stars surround the moon.

5110. மதில்மேல் இருக்கிற பூனைபோல் இருக்கிறான்.

He is like a cat on a wall.

Spoken of one who makes the most of his position.

5111. மது பிந்து கலகம்போல் இருக்கிறது.

Like the uproar of a honey drop.

5112. மதுரைக்கு வழி வாயில் இருக்கிறது

The way to Madura is in the mouth.

5113. மந்திரம் கால் மதி முக்கால்.

The incantation is one fourth, and common sense three fourths.

5114. மந்திரத்தில் மாங்காய் விழுமா?

Will mangoes fall by a charm?

5115. மந்திரம் இல்லான் பூசை அந்தி படுமளவும்.

Religious ceremonies not regulated by a form, will continue till sun-set.

5116. மந்திரிக்கு அழகு வரும் பொருள் உரைத்தல்.

It is the attribute of a minister to foretell things likely to occur.

5117. மந்திரி இல்லா யோசனையும் ஆயுதம் இல்லாச் சேனையும் கெடும்.

Decisions without councillors, and troops without arms, will perish.

5118. மந்தையிலும் பால் வீட்டிலும் தயிரா?

Do you expect milk in the fold, and curds at home?

5119. மயிர் உள்ள சீமாட்டி வாரி முடிக்கிறாள்.

The damsel who has a fine head of hair, combs and dresses it.

5120. மயிர் ஊடாடாத நட்புச் சிறிதுபொருள் ஊடாடக் கெடும்.

Friendship so close that a hair cannot be introdued between the parties, will be destroyed if money matters interpose.

5121. மயிர் சுட்டுக் கரியாகிறதா?

Can charcoal be formed by burning hair?

5122. மயிர் பிளக்க வகைதேடினாற்போல.

Like seeking means to split a hair.

5123. மயிலாப்பூர் ஏரி உடைத்துப்போகிறது என்றால், வருகிற கமிட்டிக்கு ஆகட்டும் என்றாற்போல.

Like saying it may be deferred to the next committee, on hearing that the Mylapore tank has given way.

5124. மயிலே மயிலே என்றால் இறகு கொடுக்குமா?

If you exclaim O peacock, O peacock, will it give you its feathers!

5125. மயிற் கண்ணிக்கு மசக்கை, மாப்பிள்ளைக்கு அவஸ்தை.

The peacock-eyed bride is phrensied, her bridegroom is in anguish.

5126. மரணத்திலும் கெட்ட மார்க்கத்துக்குப் பயப்படு.

Be more afraid of a vicious course than of death.

5127. மரணத்திற்கு வழி மட்டில்லை.

There are endless ways that lead to death.

5128. மரத்தில் இருந்து விழுந்தவனை மாடு மிதித்ததுபோல.

As an ox trampled under foot a man that had fallen from a tree.

5129. மரத்துப் பழம் மரத்து அடியிலே விழும்.

The fruit of a tree will fall at its foot.

5130. மரத்தை இலை காக்கும் மானத்தைப் பணம் காக்கும்.

Leaves cover a tree, money covers one's nakedness.

5131. மரநாயிலே புழுகு வழிக்கலாமா?

Can you obtain musk from a polecat!

5132. மரம் தன்னை வெட்டுகிறவனுக்கு நிழல் கொடுக்கும்.

The tree affords shade to the man who is felling it.

5133. மரம் வெட்டுகிறவனுக்கு நிழலும், மண் தோண்டுகிறவனுக்கு இடமும் கொடுக்கும்.

The tree affords shade to him who fells it, the earth supports him who digs it.

5134. மரம் ஏறிக் கை விட்டவனும், கடன் வாங்கிக் கடன் கொடுத்தவனும் கெட்டான்.

He who let go his hold after climbing a tree, and he who borrowed money to lend, came to grief.

5135. மரம் வைத்தவன் தண்ணீர் வார்ப்பான்.

He who planted the tree will water it.

5136. மரியாதை இல்லாதான் மகிமை அற்றான்.

He who was not respectful lost his reputation.

5137. மரியாள் குடித்தனம் சரியாய்ப்போச்சு.

Mary's domestic life has come to an end.

5138. மருண்டவன் கண்ணுக்கு இருண்டதெல்லாம் பேய்.

To a gloomy eye all obscure things are demons.

5139. மருத்து மாவுக்குச் சயிக்கினை, மடங்காக் குதிரைக்குச் சவுக்கடி.

A sign to a fleet horse, whipping to an obstinate one.

5140. மருந்து கால் மதி முக்கால்.

Medicine one fourth, common sense three fourths.

5141. மருந்தும் விருந்தும் மூன்று நாள்.

Three days for testing a medicine, and for a feast.

5142. மருந்தே ஆயினும் விருந்தோடு உண்.

Though the quantity be little, like medicine, distribute before eating it.

5143. மருமகனுக்கென்று சமைத்ததை மகனுக்கு இட்டு வயிறு எரிந்தாளாம்.

It is said that what she cooked for her son-in-law she gave to her son, and was distressed about it.

5144. மருவில் தின்ற சாப்பாட்டை லங்கணத்தில் நினைத்துக்கொண்டதுபோல.

Like remembering, when hungry, the food of the marriage feast.

5145. மலடிக்குத் தெரியுமா பிள்ளையைப் பெற்ற அருமை?

Does the barren woman understand the pains of parturition?

5146. மலடி அறிவாளா பிள்ளை அருமை?

Does the barren woman know the endearments of children?

5147. மலடியைப் பிள்ளை பெறச் சொன்னால் பெறுவாளா?

If the barren woman be asked to bring forth a child, will she do so?

5148. மலரில் மணமும், எள்ளில் எண்ணெயும், உடலில் உயிரும் கலந்ததுபோல.

All pervading, like fragrance in a flower, oil in sesamum seed, and life in the body.

5149. மலிந்த பண்டம் கடையிலே வரும்.

When commodities are abundant, they come to market.

5150. மலை அத்தனை சுவாமிக்குத் தினை அத்தனை புஷ்பம்.

A flower, as small as a millet-seed, is dedicated to an idol as large as a mountain.

5151. மலை அத்தனை சுவாமிக்கு மலை அத்தனை புஷ்பம் போடுகிறார்களா?

Do they dedicate flowers as large as mountains, to idols as large as mountains?

5152. மலை இலக்கானால் குருடனும் எய்வான்.

If a mountain be the target, even a blind man may shoot.

5153. மலை உச்சியில் கல் ஏற்றுதல் அரிது.

It is difficult to roll a stone to the top of a hill.

5154. மலை ஏறினாலும் மைத்துனனைக் கை விடாதே.

Though you ascend the mountains, do not leave behind your brother-in-law, or the *son of your maternal* uncle.

5155. மலைத்தேன் முடவனுக்கு வருமா?

Will mountain honey come to the lame man?

5156. மலை நெல்லிக்காய்க்கும் கடல் உப்புக்கும் உறவு செய்தவர் ஆர்?

Who created the affinity between the mountain nelli fruit, and sea-salt?

5157. மலைபோலப் பிராமணன் போகிறானாம், பின்குடுமிக்கு அழுகிறாளாம்.

It is said that when a brahman who was equal to a mountain was dying, his wife was weeping for his tuft of hair.

5158. மலைபோல வந்ததெல்லாம் பனிபோல நீங்கும்.

All that has come upon thee like mountains, shall pass away as dew.

5159. மலை முழங்கிச் சுண்டெலி பெற்றதுபோல.

As a mountain amidst thunder brought forth a mouse.

5160. மலைமேல் இருப்பாரைப் பன்றி பாய்வது உண்டா?

Can the wild hog rush on those who are on the mountain top?

5161. மலையில விளைந்தாலும் உரலில் மசியவேண்டும்.

Although produced on the mountains, *the rice* must be prepared for use in a mortar.

5162. மலையே மண்ணாங்கட்டி ஆகிறபோது, மண்ணாங்கட்டி எப்படி ஆகும்?

When a mountain becomes a sod, what will the sod be like?

5163. மலையே விழுந்தாலும் தலையே தாங்கவேண்டும்.

Should a mountain fall, the head must bear it.

5164. மலையைக் கல்லி எலி பிடித்ததுபோல.

Like excavating a mountain and catching a rat.

5165. மலையைச் சுற்றி அடித்தவனைச் செடியைச் சுற்றி அடியேனா?

After having chased and beaten him round a mountain, will it be difficult to do so round a bush?

5166. மலையைத் துளைக்கச் சிற்றுளி போதாதா?

Is not a small chisel sufficient to perforate a rock?

5167. மலையைத் துளைக்க வாச்சி உளி வந்தாற்போல.

As if an adze and chisel came to perforate the rock.

5168. மலையைப் பார்த்து நாய் குலைத்தால் மலைக்குக் கேடோ நாய்க்குக் கேடோ?

If a dog bark at a mountain, will the mountain be injured or the dog?

5169. மலையை மலை தாங்கும் மண்ணாங்கட்டி தாங்குமா?

A rock supports a rock, can a sod do so?

5170. மலை விழுங்கி அம்மையாருக்குக் கதவு சுண்டாங்கியா?

Will a door be a difficulty to *my* aunt who has swallowed a mountain?

5171. மலை விழுங்குதற்கு மண்ணாங்கட்டி பச்சடியா?

Is a sod used as a chutney, to swallow a mountain?

5172. மல்லாந்து உமிழ்ந்தால் மார்மேலே.

When one spits lying on his back, the spittle will fall on his breast.

5173. மவுனம் மலையைச் சாதிக்கும்.

Silence may defy a mountain.

5174. மவ் இடப் பவ் ஆயிற்று.

ம being elided, ப has appeared.

5175. மழைக்கால் இருட்டானாலும் மந்தி கொம்பு இழந்து பாயுமா?

Even in the darkness of the rainy season, will a monkey when leaping, miss the branch?

5176. மழைக்குத் தண்ணீர் மொண்டு வார்ப்பவர் ஆர்?

Who draws and pours water into the clouds?

5177. மழைக்குப் படல் கட்டிச் சார்த்தலாமா?

Can you put up a hurdle to keep out the rain?

5178. மழைக்கோ படல், இடிக்கோ படல?

Is the hurdle to keep out rain, or the thunderbolt?

5179. மழை பெய்து நிறையாதது மொண்டு வார்த்தால் நிறையுமா?

Can that be filled with a watering pot which cannot be filled by the rain!

5180. மழை முகம் காணாத பயிரும், தாய் முகம் காணாத பிள்ளையும்.

Vegetation without rain, a child without a mother.

5181. மழையும் பிள்ளைப்பேறும் மகா தேவருக்கும் தெரியாது.

Even Mahadéva does not know when it will rain, nor when a child will be born.

5182. மழை விட்டும் தூவானம் விட இல்லை.

Though the rain has ceased, the drizzling has not.

5183. மறந்த உடைமை மக்களுக்கும் ஆகாது.

An article forgotten is not good even for one's children.

5184. மறந்து செத்தேன் பிராணன் வா என்றால் வருமா?

If one say, I died through forgetfulness, will life return?

5185. மனக்கசடு அற மாயை நாடேல்.

Seek not empty pleasures to purify the heart.

5186. மனக் கவலை பலக் குறைவு.

Mental anxiety will diminish one's strength.

5187. மனச்சாட்சி குற்றுமேல் மறுசாட்சி வேண்டாம்.

If the conscience condemn, other evidence is unnecessary.

5188. மனதிலே பகை உதட்டிலே உறவு.

Enmity at heart, friendship on the lips.

5189. மனதில் இருக்கும் ரகசியம் மதிகேடனுக்கு வாக்கிலே.

A secret that should be concealed in the mind is uttered by a fool.

5190. மனதிற்கு மனதே சாட்சி, மற்றதற்குத் தெய்வம் சாட்சி.

The heart is its own witness, God is the witness of the rest.

5191. மனது அறியாப் பொய் உண்டா?

Can a mind be ignorant of its own falsehood!

5192. மனத்துயர் அற்றோன் தினச்செபம் உற்றோன்.

He who utters prayers daily has no anxiety of mind.

5193. மனம் கொண்டது மாளிகை

That which is agreeable to the mind is a palace.

5194. மனம் தடுமாறேல்.

Be not confused.

5195. மனம் இருந்தும் சற்று வகை அற்றுப்போவான்.

Although willing he will lack means.

5196. மனிதர் காணும் பொழுது மவுனம், இராதபொழுதில் உருத்திராக்ஷப்பூனை.

Silent in the presence of men, in their absence a beaded cat.

5197. மனிதன் மறபபான், குறைபடுவான், மாறுவான், போவான்.

Man forgets, is reduced in circumstances, changes and vanishes.

5198. மனுஷன் தலையை மான் தலை ஆக்குகிறான் மான் தலையை மனுஷன் தலை ஆக்குகிறான்.

He can transform a man's head into the head of a deer, and he can make a man's head out of a deer's head.

5199. மனையாள் விடியுமுன் எழுந்து வீட்டுப் பண் செய்வாள்.

A wife gets up before day-break and looks after her domestic affairs.

5200. மனையாளுக்கு உற்றது ஒன்றும் சொல்லவேண்டாம், மாற்றானை ஒரு நாளும் நம்பவேண்டாம்.

Do not disclose your secrets to your wife, nor trust an enemy at any time.

5201. மனோ வியாதிக்கு மருந்து உண்டா?

Is there any remedy for mental sickness!

5202. மன்னவர்கள் செத்தார்கள், மந்திரிகள் செத்தார்கள் முன் இருந்தோர் எல்லாம் முடிந்தார்கள்.

Kings have perished, their prime ministers have perished, and all who lived before, are dead

5203. மன்னவர்கள் ஆண்டது எல்லாம் மந்திரிகள் ஆண்மை.

The government of kings depends on the vigor of their councillors.

5204. மன்னவர்க்கு அழகு செங்கோன் முறைமை.

A sceptre of justice is the beauty of a king.

மா.

5205. மா இருக்கிற மணத்தைப்போல் அல்லவோ கூழ் இருக்கிற குணம்.

As is the flour so is the gruel.

5206. மா உண்டானால் பணிகாரம் சுடலாம்.

If there be flour, cakes may be baked.

5207. மா ஏற மலை ஏறும்.

The accretion of a particle to a mountain increases its size.

5208. மாடு திருப்பினவன் அர்ச்சுனன்.

He who drove back the cows was Arjuna.

5209. மாடு தின்னிக்கு வாக்குச் சுத்தம் உண்டா?

Is a beef-eater accustomed to decent words?

5210. மாடு முக்கிவர வீடு நக்கிவரும்.

When cows return fatigued the household will suffer want.

5211. மாடு மேய்க்காமற் கெட்டது, பயிர் பார்க்காமற் கெட்டது.

Without pasture cows die; without care vegetation perishes.

5212. மாட்டின் வாழ்க்கை மூட்டையிலே.

A bull's term of existence is in his sack.

5213. மாட்டுக்குப் பெயர் பெரிய கடா என்று.

A cow is otherwise called a large he-goat.

5214. மாட்டைப் புல் உள்ள தலத்திலும், மனுஷனைச் சோறு உள்ள தலத்திலும் இருக்க ஒட்டாது.

I will not allow the cow *to be content* in its pasture, nor a man with his boiled rice.

5215. மாட்டை மேய்த்தானும் கோலைப் போட்டானும்.

It is said that he tended the cows and threw away the goad.

5216. மாணிக்கக் காலுக்கு மாற்றுக்கால் இருக்கிறது.

There is a spare leg, for the one made of a ruby.

5217. மாதம் காதவழி மானைத் துள்ளுவான்.

He will leap like a deer, ten miles in a month.

5218. மாதா செய்தது மக்களுக்கு.

The faults of a mother are visited on her children.

5219. மாதா மனம் எரிய வாழாள் ஒரு நாளும்.

Whilst her mother's heart is wounded, she will not prosper even for a day.

5220. மாத்திரை தப்ப மிதித்தால், கோத்திரம் கூறப்படும்.

If one exceed his limit, his ancestry will be exposed.

5221. மாப் புளிக்கிறது எல்லாம் பணிகாரத்துக்கு நலம்.

The more the flour is leavened the better for the cakes.

5222. மாப் பொன் இருக்க மக்களைச் சாவக் கொடுப்பேனா?

Whilst I possess a particle of gold, will I allow my children to die?

5223. மா மறந்த கூழுக்கு உப்பு ஒரு கேடா?

Does the absence of salt spoil gruel made without flour?

5224. மாமி ஒட்டினாலும் பானை ஒட்டாது.

Though a mother-in-law may be reconciled, the broken pieces of an earthen pot cannot be reunited.

5225. மாமியார் உடை குலைந்தால் வாயாலும் சொல்லக்கூடாது, கையாலும் காட்டக்கூடாது.

If the dress of a mother-in-law be out of order, it must not be spoken of, or pointed at by the hand.

5226. மாமியார் உடைத்தால் மண்கலம், மருமகள் உடைத்தால் பொன்கலம்.

If broken by the mother-in-law it is an earthen vessel, if by the daughter-in-law, it is a golden vessel.

5227. மாமியாரைக் கண்டு மருமகன் நாணுகிறதுபோல.

As the son-in-law is embarrassed in the presence of his mother-in-law.

5228. மாமியார் செத்த ஆறும் மாதம் மருமகள் கண்ணில் கண்ணீர் வந்ததாம்.

It is said that six months after the death of the mother-in-law, a tear came into the eye of the daughter-in-law.

5229. மாமியார் செத்து மருமகள் அழுகிறதுபோல.

Like the wailing of a daughter-in-law, on account of the death of her mother-in-law.

5230. மாமியாரும் சாகாளோ மனக்கவலையும் தீராதோ?

Will my mother-in-law never die, will my sorrows never end!

5231. மாமியார் வீடு மகா சௌக்கியம்.

The house of the mother-in-law is very comfortable.

5232. மாயக்காரர் எல்லாம் பாதகர், மாறுபாட்டுக்காரர் எல்லாம் சாதகர்.

All impostors are perfidious villains, all double-dealers are practically so.

5233. மாயக்காரன் பேயிற் கடையே.

A hypocrite is worse than a demon.

5234. மாரி அல்லது காரியம் இல்லை.

Without rain nothing can be effected.

5235. மாரி காலத்தில் பதின் கல மோரும், கோடை காலத்தில் ஒரு படி நீரும் சரி.

Ten kalams of buttermilk in the wet season, are worth one measure of water in the hot season.

5236. மார் அடித்த கூலி மடிமேலே.

The hire for beating *their* breasts is at once on the lap.

5237. மார்பு சரிந்தால் வயிறு தாங்க வேண்டும்.

If the breasts be pendent, they must be supported by the stomach.

5238 மார்பைத் தட்டி மனதிலே வை.

Touch your breast, and keep it in your mind.

5239. மாலை குளித்து மனையில் புகும், தன் மனையில் ஆரையும் சேர்க்காது.

In the evening a crow bathes before it goes to its nest, and will not admit a stranger.

Many Natives attribute to the crow five peculiarities of which that indicated in this proverb is one. The peculiarities, or habits are as follows:—(*a*) Going forth very early of a morning. (*b*) Never being seen to pair. (*c*) Eating together. (*d*) Bathing before going to their nest. (*e*) Warning their companions of apparent danger.

5240. மாலை சுற்றிப் பெண் பிறந்தால் மாமனுக்கு ஆகாது.

For a girl to be born with a garland round her neck is ominous to her maternal uncle.

This மாலை may be either the navel-string or a thin membrane that covers the head, and which, sometimes decends like a ring, to the neck, it is then called மாலை, if otherwise முக்காடு a veil.

5241. மாலை சுற்றிப் பிறந்த பிள்ளை மாமனுக்கு ஆகாது.

If a child be born with its navel string round its neck, it is ominous to its uncle.

5242. மாவிலும் ஒட்டலாம் மாங்காயிலும் ஒட்டலாம்.

A share in the dough, a share in the mangos.

5243. மாவுக்கு தக்க பணிகாரம்.

Cakes proportioned to the flour.

5244. மாவைத் தின்றால் அப்பம் இல்லை.

If you eat the dough you will not get your *share of* cake.

5245. மாற்றிலே வளைவது மரத்திலே வளையுமா?

Will the tree be pliable because the sapling was so?

5246. மாற்றானுக்கு இடம் கொடேல்.

Yield not to a foe.

5247. மானத்தின்மேலே கண்ணும் மாப்பிள்ளைமேலே சிந்தையும்.

The eye is on the heavens, the mind is on the bridegroom.

5248. மானத்தை வில்லாய் வளைப்பான் மணலைக் கயிறாய்த் திரிப்பான்.

He is able to bend the sky as a bow, and he can twist ropes of sand.

5249. மானம் அழியில் உயிர் காவலா?

When honour is perishing, is life worth preservation?

5250. மானம் பெரிதோ, சீவன் பெரிதோ?

Is honour great, or is life?

5251. மானிலம் சிலரைத் தாங்கேன் என்னுமோ?

Does the spacious earth refuse to uphold any one?

5252. மானுக்கு ஒரு பள்ளி ஏறி என்ன, குறைந்து என்ன?

What matters it whether the deer has more or fewer spots?

5253. மானுஷியம் இல்லாதவன் மனுஷப்பதர்.

Among mankind one destitute of humanity is as chaff.

5254. மான் கண்ணிலும் அழகு வினாவிலும் விரைவு.

More beautiful than the eye of a deer, more rapid *than its* speed.

5255. மான் கூட்டத்தில் புலி புகுந்ததுபோல.

As the tiger sprang on a herd of deer.

மி.

5256. மிகுதி ஆசை அதிக நஷ்டம்.

The greater the inordinate desire, the greater the loss.

5257. மிகுதி உள்ளவனுக்கும் வஞ்சனைக்காரனுக்கும் பகை, வேதக்காரனுக்கும் உலகத்திற்கும் பகை.

Enmity exists between the wealthy and the hypocrite, and between a religious man and the world.

5258. மிகுந்தும் குறைந்தும் நோய் செய்யும்.

Both, excess and want, lead to disease.

5259. மிகைபடச் சொல்லேல்.

Do not exaggerate.

5260. மிஞ்சினது கொண்டு மேற்கே போகல் ஆகாது.

It is not good for one to go westward carrying refuse.

5261. மிஞ்சிய கருமம் அஞ்சச் செய்யும்.

A thing done through *inadvertence* may produce fear.

5262. மிடி இதயங்கொள் மீளாக் கதி தொடர்.

Be humble, and seek unfailing bliss.

5263. மிடிமையிலும் படிமை நன்று.

The habiliments of an ascetic are to be preferred before poverty.

5264. மிடுக்கன் சரக்கு இருக்க விலைப்படும்.

The haughty sells his goods sitting.

5265. மிதித்தாரைக் கடியாத பாம்பு உண்டா?

Are there any snakes that will not bite those who tread on them?

5266. மிருகங்களில் ஆனைபெரிது, அதிலும் சிங்கம் வலிது.

Among beasts an elephant is the biggest, and a lion the strongest.

5267. மினுக்கு உள்ள அம்பு துன்பம் செய்யும். அதுபோல, அந்தம் உள்ளவர்களும் துன்பத்தைத் தருவார்கள்.

A shining arrow will occasion pain, in like manner, those who are handsome in person may produce pain.

5268. மினைக்கெட்ட அம்பட்டன் பூனையைச் சிரைத்தானாம்.

It is said that a barber who had nothing to do, shaved a cat.

5269. மின்மினிப்பூச்சி வெளிச்சத்துக்கு இருள்போமோ?

Does a fire fly dispel darkness ?

5270. மின்னலைப்போல் பல்லை விளக்கானும், மினுக்கிக் கொள்வானும் பதர்.

He who will not clean his teeth so as to shine like lightning, and he who is fond of show, are chaff.

5271. மின்னாமல் இடி விழுமா?

Does the thunder-bolt fall without previous lightning ?

5272. மின்னாமல் மழை பெய்யுமா?

Does it rain without previous lightning!

5273. மின்னாமல் முழங்காமல் இடி விழுந்ததுபோல.

As a thunder-bolt fell without lightning and thunder.

5274. மின்னுவதெல்லாம் பொன் அல்ல.

All that glitters is not gold.

5275. மின்னுக்கு எல்லாம் பின்னே மழை.

Lightning is always followed by rain.

மீ.

5276. மீகாமன் இல்லா மரக்கலம் ஓடாது.

An unpiloted vessel will not sail.

5277. மீதூண் விரும்பேல்.

Be not gluttonous.

5278. மீந்த சுண்ணும்பையும் மெலிந்த ராஜாவையும் கைவிடல ஆகாது.

The remains of chunambu, and an enfeebled king, should not be renounced.

5279. மீனை மீன் விழுங்கினாற்போல.

Like a fish swallowing a fish.

5280. மீன் குஞ்சுக்கு நீச்சுப் பழக்குகிறதா?

Are young fish taught to swim?

5281. மீன் குழம்போ தேன் குழம்போ?

Fish curry or honey curry?

மு.

5282. முகக் கோணலுக்குக் கண்ணாடி பார்த்தால் தீருமா?

Will the distortion of the countenance be removed by looking into a mirror?

5283. முகத்துக்கு முகம் கண்ணாடி.

One face is a mirror to *another* face.

5284. முகத்துக்கு அஞ்சி மூத்தாரோடு போனால் குலத்துக்கு எல்லாம் ஈனமாம்.

If a *woman* elope with her husband's elder brother out of personal regard for *him*, it will be a disgrace to the whole family

5285. முகம் ஆகாதிருந்தால் கண்ணாடி என்ன செய்யும்?

If the face be ugly, what can the mirror do?

5286. முகம் சந்திர பிம்பம், அகம் பாம்பின் விஷம்.

A face like the moon, a mind of deadly poison.

5287. முக்காட்டுக்குள் சமுதாடா?

What! a dagger under a veil?

5288. முக்காட்டுக்குள்ளே கைக்காட்டா?

What, is it to make signs under a veil?

5289. முக்காதம் சுமந்தாலும் முசல் கைத்தூக்குத்தான்.

Though carried thirty miles, a hare is carried in the hand.

5290. முக்காலம் காகம் முழுகிக் குளித்தாலும் கொக்கு ஆகாது.

Though a crow bathe three times a day, it will not thereby become a white crane.

5291. முக்காலம் காகம் முழுகிக் குளித்தாலும் கொக்கு ஆகுமா?

Will a crow by bathing three times *a day* become a crane?

5292. முக்கூட்டுச் சிக்கு அறாது.

A triparty business is always involved.

5293. முசலை எழுப்பி விட்டு, நாய் பதுங்கினதுபோல.

Like a dog crouching after starting a hare.

5294. முடப்புல் முக்கல நீரைத் தடுக்கும்.

Crooked grass prevents the flow of six kalams of water.

5295. முடவனுக்கு நொண்டி சண்டப்பிரசண்டன்.

A lame man is very boisterous before a cripple.

5296. முடவன் கொம்புத் தேனுக்கு ஆசைப்பட்டதுபோல.

As a lame man longed for the honey that hung from a branch.

5297. முடவன் சந்தைக்குப் போனாற்போல.

Like a lame man going to market.

5298. முடிக்காதவனே படிக்காதவன்.

He who does not accomplish his object lacks training.

5299. முடிச்சுப் போனதும் அல்லாமல் இளித்தவாய்ப்பட்டமும் கூடக் கிடைத்தது.

You have not only lost the bundle *of money*, but also incurred a reproachful name.

5300. முடிய முடிய நட்டால் கோட்டை கோட்டையாய் விளையுமா?

If you plant bundles, will heaps be produced?

5301. முடியும் வகை யோசியாமல் முயற்சி கொள்ளாதே.

Never undertake a matter without due consideration as to how it is to be accomplished.

5302. முடி வைத்த தலைக்குச் சுழிசுத்தம் பார்க்கிறது, கொண்டு குலம் பேசுகிறதுபோல் இருக்கிறது.

Examining the circlets of hair in a crowned head, is like discussing the tribe of a girl after marrying her.

5303. முட்ட நனைந்தவனுக்கு ஈரம் இல்லை, முழுதும் கெட்டவனுக்குத் துக்கம் இல்லை.

When completely drenched one does not feel wet, when entirely ruined one feels no sorrow.

5304. முட்டரோடாடிய நட்புக் கருங்காலிக் கட்டை ஊடாடிய கால்.

Friendship with the rude is like the foot of a *traveller* among stumps of ebony.

5305. முட்டற்ற பெண்ணுக்கு இரட்டைப் பரியமா?

What double dower to a worthless woman!

5306. முட்டாளுக்கு இரண்டு ஆள்.

Two persons for one fool.

5307. முட்டாளுக்குக் கோபம் மூக்கின்மேலே.

The wrath of a fool is on his nose.

5308. முட்டிகைபோல முனியாது வைகலும், கொட்டி உண்பாரும் குறடுபோற் கைவிடுவார்.

Even those who like a pair of pincers uphold *their dependants* and daily feed them, will leave them like a pair of tongs.

5309. முட்டி ஊட்டின கன்று முதர்க் கன்று.

A calf that drains the udder is almost weaned.

5310. முட்டுக்கு முட்டல்ல மூடக் கதவும் அல்ல, சன்னிதிவாசலுக்குச் சார்த்தக் கதவும் அல்ல.

It is neither an obstruction, nor a door to shut, nor even a screen to the temple gateway.

5311. முட்டுப்பட்டும் ஜெயம் வருமானால் குட்டுப்பட்டாற் குறை என்ன ?

If victory comes by being pressed with want, what matters a cuff on the head !

5312. முதலில் எடுத்துச் செலவிடாதே.

Do not spend on *your* capital.

5313. முதலிலே கெட்டிக்காரன் முடிவிலே சோம்பேறி.

Clever at the beginning, indolent at the end.

5314. முதலுக்கு மோசமாக இருக்கிறது இலாபத்துக்குச் சண்டை போடுகிறதா ?

When the principal is in danger, do you quarrel about the interest ?

5315. முதலே தூர்ப்பலே அதிலே கர்ப்பிணி.

Already weak, and withal pregnant.

5316. முதலைக்கு இல்லை நீச்சும் நிலையும்.

A crocodile cares not whether the water is deep or shallow.

5317. முதலை தன் இடத்து, மலை ஒத்த ஆனையையும் இழுத்துச் செல்லும்.

In his own element, the alligator will carry off an elephant as big as a mountain.

5318. முதலை வைத்துப் பெருக்காத வணிகரைப்போல.

Like merchants who do not increase the capital they invest.

5319. முதல் இல்லார்க்கு ஊதியம் இல்லை, மதலையாம் சார்பில்லார்க்கு நிலை இல்லை.

Those who have no capital have no gain, those who have no sons to lean on, have no support.

5320. முதல் இல்லார்க்கு ஊதியம் இல்லை.

Those not possessed of capital, have no gains.

5321. முதல் எடுக்கும்போதே தப்பட்டைக்காரன் செத்தான்.

When the funeral procession was moving forward, the tomtom beater died.

5322. முதல் எழுத்திலே வெள்ளெழுத்தா?

What, dim-sighted at the beginning of the Alphabet!

5323 முதற் கோணல் முற்றும் கோணல்.

If crooked at fisrt, it will be so throughout.

5324. முதுகிலே புண் உண்டானால் செடியிலே நுழையப் பயம்.

If one has a wound on his back, he will fear to pass under a bush.

5325. முத்தால் நத்தை பெருமைப்படும், மூடர் எத்தாலும் பெருமைப்படார்.

A snail is precious by reason of its pearl, fools have naught wherewith to attain greatness.

5326. முத்திலும் சொத்தை உண்டு, பவழத்திலும் பழுது உண்டு.

Flaws may be found in pearls and also in coral.

5327. முந்தி வந்த செவியைப் பிந்தி வந்த கொம்பு மறைத்ததாம்.

It is said that the ears which came first, were covered by the horns which sprung up afterwards.

5328. முந்தினோர் பிந்தினோர் ஆவர் பிந்தினோர் முந்தினோர் ஆவர்.

The first shall be last, and the last first.

5329. முந்தின சோற்றைத் தட்டினால் பிந்தின சோறு பீயும் சோறும்.

If the first food be rejected, worse may be offered.

5330. முந்நாழி கறக்கிற பசுவானாலும் இறப்பைப் பிடுங்குகிற பசு ஆகாது.

Though a cow yields three measures of milk, it is not desirable if it pulls down the roof.

5331. முப்பதிலே மூர்க்கம், நாற்பதிலே நாகரீகம்.

Obstinacy at thirty, civility at forty.

5332. முப்பது பணம் கொடுத்தாலும் மூளிப்பட்டம் போகாது.

Though one may give thirty fanams, the nickname, crop-eared, will not be removed.

5333. முப்பதிலே வாழ்ந்தவன் மூடன், முன்னும் பின்னும் தெரியாத வன் குருடன்.

He is a fool who prospered at thirty, he is blind who does not see before and behind.

5334. முப்பணி இட்ட பெண்ணுக்குக் கொப்பு ஒன்றுதான் குறை.

To the woman adorned with three jewels, the ear ornament is the only want.

5335. முப்பது வருஷம் வாழ்ந்தவனும் இல்லை, முப்பது வருஷம் தாழ்ந்தவனும் இல்லை.

None ever continued to prosper or decay for thirty years.

5336. முப்பொருள் ஆதி மூலமானவன்.

He is the triad who is the first and the last *of all*.

5337. முயற்சி உடையார் இகழ்ச்சி அடையார்.

The industrious will never be put to shame.

5338. முரட்டுப் பெண்ணும் சுருட்டுப் பாயும்.

A stubborn wife, a mat rolled up.

5339. முருக்குப் பருத்து என்ன தூணாகப் போகிறதா?

What if the murukku tree grow large, will it do for a pillar!

5340. முருங்கைக்காய் என்றால் பத்தியம் முறியுமா?

Will the mention of the murungai fruit affect a prescribed diet!

5341. முலைகொடுத்து வளர்த்தவள் மூதேவி, முன்றானை போட்டவள் சீதேவி.

The one that nursed and brought up the child is Múdévi, the wife is Shridévi.

5342. முலைக் குத்துச் சவலைப் பிள்ளைக்குத் தெரியுமா?

Is the pain in the breast of the nurse, known to the suckling?

5343. முழங்கையிற் பட்ட சுகம்போல.

Like the pleasure experienced when the elbow is struck.

5344. முழுகி முப்பது நாளாச்சு, இறங்கி உப்பு அள்ளக்கூட இல்லை என்கிறான்.

It is thirty days since he bathed, and he says that he is so clean that touching salt would defile him.

5345. முழுக் கட்டி பெயர்க்கிற பன்றிக்குக் கொழுக் கட்டி விட்டது போல.

Like arming a hog in the snout with a ploughshare, that can tare up the ground without it.

5346. முழுச் சோம்பேறி முள்ளு உள்ள வேலி.

A perfect sluggard is like a hedge of thorns.

5347. முழுப் பங்குக்காரனுக்கு முந்திரிப் பங்குக்காரன் மிண்டன்.

He whose share is only one three hundred and twentieth part, is more persistent than he who has a whole one.

5348. முழுப் பூசணிக்காயைச் சோற்றிலே மறைக்கிறதுபோல.

Like attempting to conceal a whole pumpkin in a plate of rice.

5349. முழு மணிப் பூணுக்குப் பூண் வேண்டுமோ?

Does a gemmed ferrule require an ornamental rim?

5350. முளைத்த மயிர் மூன்று அதிலும் இரண்டு புழுவெட்டு.

His beard consists of three hairs, of which two are rotten at the root.

5351. முளையில் கிள்ளாததை முற்றினால் கோடரிகொண்டு வெட்ட வேண்டும்.

That which was not nipped in the bud will have to be felled with an axe when matured.

5352. முள்ளாலே முள்ளை எடுக்கவேண்டும்.

Thorns are extracted by thorns.

5353. முள்ளுக்குக் கூர்மையும் துளசிக்கு வாசனையும் இயற்கை.

By nature the thorn is sharp, and the tulasi fragrant.

5354. முள்ளுக்கு முனை சீவி விடுவார்களா?

Who sharpens the point of a thorn?

5355. முள்ளுமேல் சீலை போட்டால் மெள்ள மெள்ள வாங்கவேண்டும்.

If a cloth be spread on a thorn bush, it must be taken off with great care.

5356. முறத்தடி பட்டாலும் முகத்தடி படலாகாது.

Though one may endure being struck with a sieve, he cannot endure being brow-beaten.

5357. முற்பகல் செய்யிற் பிற்பகல் விளையும்.

What is done in the forenoon will result *in good or evil* in the afternoon.

5358. முற்றும் நனைந்தவர்களுக்கு ஈரம் ஏது?

Do those who are drenched complain of being wet?

5359. முனைமுகத்து நில்லேல்.

Do not stand in the face of a battle.

5360. முன் அளந்த நாழி பின் அளக்கும்.

The same measure that was used before, must be used afterwards.

5361. முன் ஒன்று ஓதிப் பின் ஒன்று ஆடேல்.

Do not say one thing and do another.

5362. முன் கை நீண்டால் முழங்கை நீளும்.

If the fore-arm be stretched, the elbow will be so also.

5363. முன் கோபம் பின் இரக்கம்.

Anger first, and pity afterwards.

5364. முன் விட்டுப் பின் நின்று கழுத்து அறுக்கலாமா?

Having given one the lead, will you follow and cut his throat?

5365. முன்னவனே முன் நின்றால் முடியாத பொருள் உளதோ?

If the eternal be with you, will anything be impossible?

5366. முன்னேபோனால கடிக்கிறது பின்னேபோனால் உதைக்கிறது.

Biting before, and kicking behind.

5367. முன்னே பார் பின்னே பார் உன்னைப் பார் என்னைப் பார்.

Look before, look behind, look at yourself, look at me.

5368. முன்னே போனால் சிசுவத்தி பின்னே போனால் பிரமததி.

When you go before you arε guilty of infanticide, when you follow you are guilty of brahmanicide.

5369. முன்னேரம் கப்பற்காரன் பின்னேரம் பிச்சைக்காரன்.

In the forenoon a ship owner, in the afternoon a beggar.

5370. முன்னே வந்த காதைப்பார்க்கிலும் பின்னே வந்த கொம்பு பலம்.

The horn that came after, is stronger than the ear that came before.

மூ.

5371. மூக்கிலிக்குக் கண்ணாடி காட்டினதுபோல.

Like showing a noseless man a mirror.

5372. மூக்கறையனுக்கு வாழ்க்கைப்பட்டால் முன்னும் போகவிடான் பின்னும் போகவிடான்.

If a woman is married to one whose nose is rent, he will not allow her to go before or after him.

5373. மூக்கு அறுபட்ட கழுதை தூவானத்திற்கு அஞ்சாது.

A crop-nosed ass does not fear driving rain.

5374. மூக்குப் புண்ணாளி அல்லவோ தாசரி ஆகவேண்டும்?

A man with a sore nose ought to become a Vaishnava mendicant, ought he not !

5375. மூக்கு மயிர் பிடுங்கினதுபோல வருத்தம் வரும்.

The pain will be felt as keenly as when the hair in the nose is plucked out.

5376. மூக்கு மயிர் பிடுங்கினால் ஆட் பாரம் குறையுமா?

Will a person's weight be diminished by pulling the hair out of his nose?

5377. மூக்கைப் பிடித்தால் சீவன் போகிறது.

If the nostrils be closed, life will depart.

5378. மூக்கைப் பிடித்தால் வாய் ஆ வென்னத் தெரியாது?

He knows not how to open his mouth when one closes his nostrils

5379. மூங்கிற் பாயும் முறட்டுப் பெண்டாட்டியும்.

A bamboo mat, and an obstinate wife.

5380. மூங்கில் இலைமேலே தூங்கு பனி நீரே.

Thou art a dew drop depending from the leaf of a bamboo.

5381. மூடரோடு ஆடிய நட்புக் கடுவழியிற் கட்டை ஊடாடிய கால்.

The friendship of fools is as the feet that have travelled by a jungle path covered with stumps of trees.

5382. மூடர் முன்பு மூர்க்கம் பேசாதே.

Speak not harshly before fools.

5383. மூடர்கள் சேர்க்கையால தப்பாமல் கெடுதி வரும்.

The companionship of fools invariably leads to loss.

5384. மூடர் கூட்டு உறவு முழுதும் அபாயம்.

Danger attends the friendship of fools.

5385. மூடனாய் இருக்கிற பிள்ளையினாலே எப்போதும் நஷ்டமே வரும்.

One always sustains loss if he has a stupid child.

5386. மூடனுடைய பங்கு தரித்திரமும் இகழ்ச்சியும்.

Adversity and disgrace form the lot of fools.

5387. மூடன் சண்டை மூட்டுப் பிரிக்கும், மோர்க்கடன் வீட்டைத் தொடும்.

The quarreling of fools will break friendship, debt on account of buttermilk will affect one's house.

5388. மூடின முத்து மூன்று லோகம் பெறும், மூடாத முத்து முக்காற் காசும் பெறாது.

A pearl concealed is worth the three worlds, one that is uncovered wont fetch three quarters of a cash.

5389. மூட்டைக்காரனுக்கு முழங்காலிலே புத்தி.

A porter's sense is in his knees.

5390. மூத்தது மோழை இளையது காளை.

The first-born is a hornless animal, the younger is a bull.

5391. மூத்தோர் சொல் வார்த்தை அமிர்தம்.

The utterances of elderly persons *are* ambrosia.

5392. மூப்பினும் தருமம் செய்தல் முயற்சிதான்.

The charitably disposed exert themselves even in old age.

5393. மூப்பு ஏன் பிடிப்பது, மூதேவி வாசத்துக்கு அடையாளம்.

Why does one grow old ? it is a sign that he is under the influence of the goddess of misfortune.

5394. மூர்க்கனும் முதலையும் சரி.

The stubborn and crocodiles are alike.

5395. மூர்க்கன் முகத்தில மூதேவி குடி இருப்பாள்.

The goddess of misfortune dwells in the face of the stubborn.

5396. மூர்க்கனைச் சேர்ந்தவன் வாழான், மூடனைச் சேர்ந்தவன் படியான்.

He who associates with the angry will not prosper, and he who associates with fools will not learn.

5397. மூர்க்கம் உள்ள ராஜாவும் மூட மந்திரியும் அழிவார்கள்.

A king that is easily provoked, and a prime minister wanting discretion, will come to ruin.

5398. மூர்க்கரோடு இணங்கேல்.

Associate not with the angry.

5399. மூலிகை அறிந்தால் மூன்று உலகமும் ஆளலாம்.

He who is acquainted with botany may govern the three worlds.

5400. மூன்றும் கட்டு அவிழ்த்தால் தெரியும்.

It will be clear if you loose the third knot.

5401. மூன்று முழமும் ஒரு சுற்று, முப்பது முழமும் ஒரு சுற்று.

A cloth of thirty cubits is put on with as much ease as one of three cubits.

5402. மூன்று வீட்டுக்கு முக்காலி நாலு வீட்டுக்கு நாற்காலி.

A three legged seat to three houses, and four legged seat, to four houses.

5403. மூன்று பெயர் வழிக்குத் துணை, இரண்டு பெயர் பிணையல் மாடு, ஒருவன் போனால் பரதேசி.

Three may help one another on the way, two are like a yoke of oxen, one is like a pilgrim.

5404. மூன்று பொருளையும் தேடு முதிர்வயதில் ஊன்றுகோல் ஆகும்.

Secure the three things *virtue, wealth and happiness*, they will serve as a staff in old age.

5405. மூன்றே முக்கால் நாழிகைக்குள் முத்து மழை பெய்தது, வாரி எடுக்குமுன்னே மண்மாரி பெய்தது.

It rained pearls for three and three fourths of a náligai, but before they could be gathered it rained earth.

மெ.

5406. மெத்தப் படித்தவருக்குச் சோறு வெல்லம்.

To the profoundly learned rice is sugar.

5407. மெத்தப் படித்தவன் பையித்தியக்காரன்.

He who is very learned, is a fool.

5408. மெத்தப் பரிவாம் உள்ளே எரிவாம்.

Externally sympathising, internally envying.

5409. மெத்தெனப் படுத்தல் நித்திரைக்கு அழகு.
A soft bed is favourable to sleep.

5410 மெய்கொண்டு விழிக்கிறது பொய்கொண்டு பொரிகிறது.
Shining with truth, burning with lies.

5411. மெய் சொல்லி வாழாதான் பொய் சொல்லி வாழ்வானா?
Will he who cannot prosper by truth, prosper by falshood!

5412. மெய்த் தொழில் என்றும் மெய் பயக்கும்.
Honest occupation always secures substantial results.

5413. மெய்ப்பொருள் கல்வியே கைப்பொருள்.
Learning is real wealth.

5414. மெய் மூன்றாம் பிறை, பொய் பூரண சந்திரன்.
Truth is the crescent of the third day, falsehood is the full moon.

5415. மெய்மை சாற்ற வையம் ஏற்றும்.
When you speak truth, the world will honour you.

5416. மெய்யது நன்றி இடும்.
Truth is beneficial.

5417. மெய்யான சத்தியன் வேதவாசகன்.
He is the truthful man who knows the vedas.

5418. மெய்யுடை ஒருவன் சொல்லமாட்டாமையால் பொய்போலும்மே பொய்போலும்மே.
Truth in one who cannot speak easily, may appear like falsehood.

5419. மெலிந்தவனுக்கு மெத்தப் பெலன், மேனி மினுக்கு இட்டவளுக்கு மெத்தக் கசம்.
A lean woman is strong, a gaudy woman is consumptive.

5420. மெல்லப் பாயும் தண்ணீர் கல்லையும் குழியப் பாயும்.
Gently flowing water will hollow even a rock.

5421. மெல்லியாடோள்சேர்.
Live with your wife.

5422. மெழுகின வீட்டிலே நாய் புகுந்ததுபோல.

As a dog entered a house whose floor was smeared with cow-dung

மே.

5423. மேட்டிமைக்காரருக்கு எதிர்த்து நிற்கவேண்டும், மெத்தனக் காரருக் கிருபை அளிக்கவேண்டும்.

Submit not to the haughty, and to the humble shew pity.

5424. மேட்டுக்காகப் பயமாம், வீதி வழியில் திகிலாம்.

It is said that he is afraid, of the hill, and alarmed at the high road.

5425. மேயப் போகிற மாடு கொம்பிலே புல்லைக் கட்டிக்கொண்டு போகிறதா?

Do cattle going to graze, carry grass tied to their horns!

5426. மேய்கிற மாட்டை நக்குகிற மாடு கெடுத்தாற்போல.

As the cow that grazes is interrupted by the one that licks it.

5427. மேய்கிற கழுதையைக் கூவுகிற கழுதை கெடுத்ததாம்.

It is said that the braying ass interrupted the ass that was grazing.

5428. மேய்க்கும் மேய்ப்பனை வியக்கும் வாயன்.

He who praises the cowherd.

5429. மேய்த்தால் மைத்துனியை மேய்ப்பேன் இல்லாவிட்டாற் பரதேசம் போவேன்.

If I am to rule I must rule over my sister-in-law, otherwise I shall go on a pilgrimage.

5430. மேய்த்தாற் கழுதை மேய்ப்பேன் இல்லாவிட்டால் பரதேசம் போவேன்.

I will tend the donkeys, or go on a pilgrimage.

5431. மேலாம் மினுக்கியைக் கொண்டவன் கெட்டான், மேட்டிலே பயிரிட்டவன் கெட்டான்.

He who marries a woman of great beauty will be ruined, he who sows on hilly ground, will be impoverished.

5432. மேலைக்கு வாழ்க்கைப்படுகிறேன் கழுத்தே சும்மா இரு.

I will marry some time hence; be still *till then*, my neck.

5433. மேலைக்கு உழுவார் கூழுக்கு அழுவார்.

Those who plough late will cry for want of food.

5434. மேழிச் செல்வம் கோழைபடாது.

The wealth of the plough is unfailing.

5435. மேனி ஒறுப்பே ஞானி நினைப்பு.

Sages are intent upon self-denial.

5436. மேன்மக்கள் சொற் கேள்.

Listen to the words of the great.

5437. மேன்மையின் மேன்மையன் மேலாம் பதவியன்.

The most excellent is the possessor of the highest state of bliss.

மை.

5438. மை கரையாமல் முதுகு ஆட்டு.

Rub your back without spoiling the paint.

5439. மைவிழியாடனைக் கையகன்றொழுகு.

Live far removed from prostitutes who paint their eye-lids.

5440. மைவிழியார் மனையகல்.

Avoid the house of a prostitute.

மொ.

5441. மொட்டைத் தலைக்கும் முழங்காலுக்கும் முடி இட்டதுபோல.

Like joining a bald head and the knee, by tying a knot *of hair*.

An impossibility.

5442. மொட்டைத் தலையில் பட்டம் கட்டி ஆள வந்தானோ?

Has he come to reign with a crown on his bald head!

5443. மொட்டைத் தலையில் பேன் சேருமா?

Will lice attach themselves to a bald head!

5444. மொட்டைத் தலையிற் பேய் வருமா?

Will a demon come on a bald head!

5445. மொட்டைத் தலையிற் பேன்போல.

Like a louse on a bald head.

5446. மொட்டைத் தலையன் போருக்கு அஞ்சான்.

A bald-headed man fears not to fight.

5447. மொட்டைத் தலைக்கு ஒரு கொட்டுக் கூடை, மோழைத் தலைக்கு ஒரு தாற்றுக் கூடை.

To a bald head, a cup-shaped basket, to a hornless head, a basket of goads.

5448. மொட்டைத் தலையன் முழு மோசக்காரன்.

A bald-headed man is a perfect cheat.

5449. மொட்டைச்சிக்குத் தகுந்த மூக்கறையன்.

A noseless man, fit for a bald woman.

5450. மொண்டு ஆளுகிற வீட்டில் கொண்டு ஆண்டால் நிறையுமா?

Will an affluent household be content to live from hand to mouth?

5451. மொத்தைச் சோற்றுக்கு மேளம் அடிக்கிறான்.

He beats a tomtom to get a mouthful of rice.

5152. மொழி தப்பினவன் வழி தப்பினவன்.
A promise breaker is in the wrong way.

5453. மொழி தவறாதான் வழி தவறாதான்.
He who is true to his word, swerves not from rectitude.

5454. மொழிவது மறுக்கின், அழிவது கருமம்.
If one break his promise, his undertaking will fail.

5455. மொழிவது அற மொழி.
Speak decisively.

மோ.

5456. மோகத்தை முனி.
Renounce lust.

5457. மோகம் முப்பது நாள் ஆசை அறுபது நாள்.
Lust continues thirty days, desire sixty days.

5458. மோகனக் கல் ஆனாலும் பளு ஏறினால் உடையாதா?
Will not even a door-step break under excessive pressure!

5459. மோசம் பாய் போட்டுத் தூங்குகிறது.
Danger slumbers on a mat.

5460. மோந்துகொள்வதுபோல கடிக்கிறது.
To bite when apparently kissing.

5461. மோருக்குப் போகிறவருக்கு முட்டி பிறகாலேயோ?
When going for buttermilk why carry the pot concealed behind you!

5462. மோருக்குப் போய் மொந்தையை ஒளிப்பான் ஏன்?
Why conceal the vessel when going for buttermilk!

5463. மோரோ என்கிறவன் கழுத்தில் லிங்கம் கட்டினதுபோல.
As a linga was tied to the neck of a buttermilk seller.

5464. மோனம் என்பது ஞானவரம்பு.

Silence is the bulwark of wisdom.

மௌ.

5465. மௌனம் கலக நாசம்.

Silence puts an end to quarrels.

5466. மௌனி குடியைக் கெடுப்பாள்.

A reserved woman will destroy her family.

யா.

5467. யாதி முற்றினல் வியாதி.

Matured meditation ends in disease.

5468. யானை கறுத்தால் ஆயிரம் பொன் பெறும், பூனை கறுத்தால் என்ன பெறும்?

A black elephant is worth a thousand gold peices, what will a black cat fetch?

5469. யானைக்கு அறுபது அடி, அருங் குள்ளனுக்கு எழுபது அடி.

Sixty feet from an elephant, seventy from a dwarf.

5470. யானை தன் தலையிலே மண்ணை வாரிக் கொட்டிக்கொள்கிறது போல.

As an elephant throws sand on its head.

5471. யானை தின்ற விளாங்கனிபோல.

Like a blighted wood-apple.

5472. யானை மிதிக்கப் பிழைப்பார்களா?

Will they survive who have been trampled on by an elephant?

5473. யானைமுன்னே முயல் முக்கினதுபோல.

As a hare strained itself before an elephant.

5474. யானைமுதலான பெரிய ஜெந்துக்கள் தாழ விழுந்தால் பிழைக்கா; அதுபோல, பெரியோர் கீழே விழுந்தால் தேறமாட்டார்.

Large beasts such as elephants &c., when they fall down from a high place, live not, so are the great.

5475. யானையை ஆயிரம் பொன்னுக்கு வாங்கி இருப்பு அங்குசத்திற்கு ஏமாந்து நிற்பான் ஏன்?

Having bought an elephant for a hundred pieces of gold, why hesitate to buy its iron goad?

5476. யானையைத் தேடக் குடத்துக்குட் கை வைத்ததுபோல.

As one put his hand into a jar when he was seeking an elephant.

யு.

5477. யுகமுடிய மழை பெய்தாலும் ஓட்டாங்கிளிஞ்சில் கரையுமா?

Suppose it rain to the end of the Yuga, will a potsherd be thereby dissolved?

ர.

5478. ரண்டாட்டில் ஊட்டின குட்டியாய்த் தீர்ந்தது.

It turned out to be a kid that had sucked two dams.

ல.

5479. லங்கணம் பரம ஔஷதம்.

Abstinence is the best medicine.

லோ.

5480. லோபிக்கு இரு செலவு.

Double expense to the niggard.

வ.

5481. வங்கணக்காரன் புளுகு வாசற்படி மட்டும்.

The lies of a paramour reach as far as the door.

5482. வங்கம் தின்றால தங்கம், வங்கம் கெட்டால் பங்கம்.

When lead is eaten it becomes gold; when it is spoiled it becomes useless.

5483. வங்கிஷம் வார்த்தைக்கு அஞ்சும், புழுக்கை உதைக்கு அஞ்சும்.

The high-born are afraid of reproach, a menial is afraid of kicks.

5484. வசனம் பண்ண உபாயம் காரணம்.

In framing rules tact is required.

5485. வச்சநாபியிலே புழுத்த புழு.

A worm produced in poison.

5486. வச்சநாபியை உப்புப் பார்க்கலாமா?

Is arseric to be tasted to ascertain its flavour?

5487. வச்சத்துக்குமேலே வழி இல்லை, பிச்சைக்குப் போகச் சுரைக் குடுக்கை இல்லை.

There is no way beyond Vachham, there is no gourd-shell to beg alms.

5488. வஞ்சகர்க்கு என்ன நேசம் காட்டினாலும் நெஞ்சு நேசம் கொள்ளார்.

No matter what love is shown to the deceitful, it will not affect the mind.

5489. வஞ்சர் உறவை வழுவி விலகு.

Relinquish intercourse with the deceitful.

5490. வஞ்சர் பால் ஊட்டினாலும் நஞ்சாய்விடும்.

Even milk given by the deceitful becomes poison.

5491. வஞ்சித்து நெடும் காலம் வாழ்தலில் மரணம் அடைவதே நலம்.

It is better to die than to live long in a deceitful course.

5492. வடகாற்று அடிக்க வந்தது மழையே.

As the wind veered to the north it began to rain.

This is generally true as regards Madras.

5493. வடக்கத்தியானையும் வயிற்று வலியையும் நம்பல் ஆகாது.

You must not be heedless of a northman, or of the belly-ache.

5494. வடக்கே கறுத்தால் மழை வரும.

Darkening in the north betokens rain.

5495. வடக்குப் பார்த்த மச்சுவீட்டைப் பார்க்கிலும் தெற்குப் பார்த்த தெருத்திண்ணை நல்லது.

A pyal facing south is preferable to a terraced house with a northern aspect.

The following *rules* relating to the building of a house will illustrate this proverb.

Having selected a site, the frontage must be divided into nine equal parts five being assigned to the right, and three to the left, the fourth division being reserved for the door-way. The enumeration begins on the left, and thus the fourth section is in the mansion of Mercury. The occupant of such a house may become as wealthy as Kubéran.

A person born under Gemini, Cancer or Leo must build his house on a line stretching east and west, the entrance being placed easterly.

A person born under Virgo, Libra or Scorpio, must build on a line running north and south, the door-way being southerly.

One born under Sagitarius, Capricorn or Aquarius must build west and east placing the entrance westerly. If born under Pices, Aries or the Twins, he must build south and north the door being placed northerly.

A family occupying a house built contrary to these rules will be ruined.

5496. வடலியை வெட்டி ஆள், எருமையைக் கட்டி ஆள்.

Trim the young palmyrah, and tie up the buffaloe.

5497. வடலி வளர்த்துக் கள்ளைக் குடிக்கிறதா?

Is it in expectation of toddy that you plant a palmyrah tree?

5498. வடுகனும் தமிழனும் கூட்டுப் பயிர் இட்ட கதை.

The story of a Telugu man and a Tamil man, cultivating jointly.

5499. வடுகன் தமிழ் அறியான் வைக்கோலைக் கசு என்பான்.

A Telugu man does not understand Tamil, he will call vaikól kásu

5500. வடுகு கொழுத்தால் வறை ஓட்டிற்கும் ஆகாது.

If a Telugu man prosper, he is of no use to any one.

5501. வடுகு பொடுகாச்சு வைக்கோற் போர் நெல் ஆச்சு.

The slave has become small, the corn-stack is thrashed into paddy.

5502. வடையைத் தின்னச் சொன்னளா துளையை எண்ணச் சொன்னளா?

Did she tell you to eat the cakes, or to count the holes in them?

5503. வட்டம் சுற்றியும் வழிக்கு வரவேண்டும்.

Although you go round, you must come in by the entrance.

5504. வட்டி ஆசை முதலைக் கெடுத்தது.

Excessive desire after interest, destroyed the capital.

5505. வட்டிக்கு வட்டி எதிர் வட்டியா?

Is compound interest uncommon?

5506. வட்டி ஓட்டம் விழ ஓட்டத்திலும் அதிகம்.

The speed at which interest accumulates is greater than that of a car.

5507. வட்டுவத்தின்மேல் சொட்டுப் போட்டால் வட்டுவத்திற்கு மாத்ரமா படும்?

Will a slap on a betel-pouch, affect the pouch only!

5508. வணங்கின வில் தீங்கை விளைக்கும்.

A bent bow will do mischief.

5509. வணங்கின முள் தைக்காது.

A pliant thorn will not penetrate.

5510. வணிகர்க்கு அழகு வாணிபம் செய்தல்.

To trade is the beauty of merchants.

5511. வண்டி ஓடத்தின் பெயரில் ஓடம் வண்டியின் பெயரில்.

A cart may be seen on a boat, and a boat on a cart.

5512. வண்டு தூரத்திலே பூவின் வாசனையை அறியும்; அதுபோல, கற்றோர் தூரத்திலேயே ஒருவன் நடத்தையை அறிந்து கொள்வார்கள்.

As beetles smell at a distance the fragrance of flowers, so the learned understand one's character when he is at a distance.

5513. வண்டு ஏறாத மரம் இல்லை.

There is no tree that cannot be bored by a beetle.

5514. வண்ணத்துக்குக் கிண்ணம் பாடுகிறான்.

He sings an unmelodious tune.

5515. வண்ணானுக்கு நோய் வந்தால் கல்லோடே.

If a washerman is sick, he gets better at the washing stone.

5516. வண்ணானுக்கும் நிருவாணிக்கும் உறவு என்ன?

What friendship has a washerman with one who wears no clothes !

5517. வண்ணானுக்கு வண்ணாத்திமேல் ஆசை, வண்ணாத்திக்குக் கழுதைமேல் ஆசை.

The washerman longs for the washer-woman, and the washer-woman's desire is fixed on her donkey.

5518. வண்ணான் கையில் மாற்றுச் சும்மா.

A change of garments in the hands of the washerman.

5519. வண்ணான் கையில் சேலையைப் போட்டுக் கொக்கின் பின்னே போகிறதா?

Having put your clothes to the washerman, do you chase the crane?

5520. வண்ணான் பிள்ளை செத்தால் அம்பட்டனுக்கு மயிர் போயிற்று.

If the washerman's child die, the barber cares not a hair.

5521. வண்ணான் துறையில் முயல்போல.

Like a hare at the washerman's washing place.

5522. வண்ணானுக்குப் போனான் வண்ணாத்திக்கு வந்தான்.

To the washerman, his name was "gone;" to the washer-woman, "come."

This proverb is explained as follows:—a washerman engaged a servant who gave his name as Pónán, *he is gone*. In the absence of her husband he told the washer-woman that his name was Vandán, *he is come*.

The washerman wanting the man called him by name,-Pónán. At the same moment the wife called the man by his other name Vandán. The washerman thereupon concluded that the servant had gone to his wife. Again he called as before, and his wife also called. As the servant did not come to him, the washerman became angry and went to his wife when an altercation took place. The matter being explained, they suspected that something was wrong, and soon found that the man had made off with their savings, and that he had given the two names to serve his secret purpose.

5523. வதுவை செய்து வாழ்.

Get married and live prosperously.

5524. வஸ்திராபரணம் விசேஷமோ, அன்னம் விசேஷமோ?

Which is more important, dress or food?

5525. வந்த காலோடு பந்தற் காலைக் கட்டிக்கொண்டு இருக்கிறாய்.

Thou standest embracing the pillar of the pandal, having walked a long way.

5526. வந்த சண்டையை விடுவதும் இல்லை வலியச் சண்டைக்குப் போவதும் இல்லை.

The quarrel that has ensued is not relinquished, nor is another causelessly sought.

5527. வந்தவர் எல்லாம் சந்தையில் குடியா?

Do all that come to market reside there?

5528. வந்த வினை போகாது வாரா வினை வாராது.

The evil that has betided one will not go, that which has not, will not come.

5529. வந்த அளவிலே சிறுக்கி பந்தடித்தாள், வரவரச் சிறுக்கி சோர்ந்து போனாள்.

The damsel played at ball as soon as she came, in the course of time she became indolent.

5530. வந்தாரை வாழ வைக்கும், மண்ணில் பிறந்தாரைத் தூங்க வைக்கும்.

It will cause strangers to flourish, and natives to decay and sink.

5531. வந்தாலும் சரி, போனாலும் சரி.

It is all the same whether he comes or goes.

5532. வந்தாற் சும்மா வரும் வராமற்போனால் ஒன்றும் வராது.

When *good things* come, they do so unsolicited ; when they do not come, not one of them appears.

5533. வம்பான வார்த்தை மனதுககு அருவருப்பு.

Bad words are an abomination to the mind.

5534. வம்புத் துரைத்தனத்தாரைக் கும்பிடத் தகுமோ?

Is it p oper to make obeisance to a government, that rules with severity !

5535. வயதுக்கோ நரைத்தது மயிருக்கோ நரைத்தது.

Does the becoming grey ari-e from age or from the hair.

5536. வயல் முயற்சியில் தானியம் உண்டாம்.

The labour of the field brings grain.

5537. வயித்தியன் தலைமாட்டில் இருந்து அழுததுபோல.

As the physician wept at the head of the bed.

5538. வயித்தியன் கையைப் பார்த்து வாக்கிட்டதுபோல.

As the physician, after feeling the pulse, gave his opinion.

5539. வயித்தியன் கைவிட்டதுபோல.

As given up by a physician.

5540. வயித்தியனுக்கு மோக்ஷம் இல்லை, உவாத்திக்கு மோக்ஷ வழி உண்டு.

A physician does not attain heaven, a teacher may.

5541. வயிராக்கியத்துக்கு அம்பட்டக் கத்தியை விழுங்குகிறதா?

Will enthusiasm induce one to swallow a razor?

5542. வயிறாரப் போசனமும் அரையாறப் புடைவையும் இல்லை.

No food for the stomach, nor cloth to for the waist.

5543. வயிறு நிரம்பினால் பானை மூடாள்.

She will not cover the rice-pot if her belly is full.

5544. வயிற்றைக் கீறிக் காண்பித்தாலும் மா இந்திர ஜாலம் என்பார்.

If one should cut open his belly *to prove his innocence,* even then they would attribute it to jugglery.

5545. வயிற்றுச் சோற்றுக்காக வயித்தீசுவரன் கோவில்மட்டும் நடப்பான்.

He will walk as far as Vaidiswaran kovil, if he can get a meal.

5546. வயிற்றுக் குடலைக் காட்டினாலும் வாழை நார் என்கிறான்.

Although the entrails be shown to him, he says they are only the fibre of tne plantain tree.

5547. வயிற்றுப் பிள்ளையை நம்பி மாடு மேய்க்கிற பிள்ளையைப் பறி கொடுத்தாற்போல.

As if one suffered herself to be deprived of her son, who was tending cattle, in anticipation of a child in the womb.

5548. வயிற்றுப் பாம்புக்குக் கடுகும், வளைப் பாம்புக்கு வெந்நீரும் இடு.

Take mustard to *kill* the maw-worm, and pour hot water to *kill* a snake in a hole.

5549. வரப்போ தலைக்கு அணை வாய்க்காலோ பஞ்சு மெத்தை.

The ridge of the field, his pillow; the channel, his cotton mattress.

5550. வரம்பு உயர நீர் உயரும், நீர் உயர நெல் உயரும், நெல் உயரக் குடி உயரும், குடி உயர முடி உயரும்.

As the ridges rise the water will rise; as the water rises the paddy will grow, as paddy flourishes, the population will increase; as that increases the crown will rise.

5551. வரம்பு உயர்ந்தால் நெல் உயரும், நெல் உயர்ந்தால் சொல உயரும்.

When the fields are full of water, paddy will rise, when paddy rises the *farmer's* authority will rise.

5552. வரவச மாமியார் கழுதைபோல் ஆனாள்.

In the course of time the mother-in-law became a donkey.

5553. வரவுக்குத் தகுந்த செலவு.

Expense according to one's income.

5554. வரவு கொஞ்சம் வலிப்பு மெத்த.

The income small, the labour great.

5555. வரி போடேல் கேட்டைத் தேடேல்.

Do not impose taxes, do not cause evil.

5556. வரிசையும் இல்லை, அரிசியும் இல்லை.

Neither respect nor rice.

5557. வருகிறபோது எல்லாம் வலிய வரும், வந்தபின் போகிறபோது எல்லாம் போம்.

When coming, all comes unsought, and having come, all goes at once.

5558. வருணன் சிலரை வகுத்துப் பெய்யுமோ?

Will clouds shower on a select few?

5559. வருந்தினால் வாராதது ஒன்று இல்லை.

Nothing is unattainable when steadily pursued.

5560. வருந்தி வருந்திப் பார்த்தாலும் வருகிறபொழுதுதான் வரும்.

Though one labours never so hard, the desired good will only be obtained in its time.

5561. வருமுன் காப்பவன் சொன்ன புத்தியை வந்தபின் காப்பவன் தள்ளினதுபோல.

As the after-wise, rejected the advice of the fore-sighted.

5562. வருவது சொன்னேன் படுவது படு.

I predicted the consequence, suffer what you have to suffer.

5563. வருவது வந்தது என்றால் படுவது படவேண்டும்.

If that which was to come is come, endurance is necessary.

5564. வருவான் குருடன் விழுவான் கிணற்றிலே.

The blind man will come and he will fall into the well.

5565. வலிமைக்கு வழக்கு இல்லை.

Power admits of no disputes.

5566. வலியப் பெண் கொடுக்கிறோம் என்றால் குலம் என்ன கோத்திரம் என்ன என்பார்கள்.

If a girl be offered in marriage unsolicited, they will enquire after her family and after her tribe.

5567. வலிய வந்த சீதேவியைக் காலால் உதைத்துத் தள்ளலாமா?

Should the goddess of prosperity who came to you spontaneously, be kicked and turned out?

5568. வலியவன் எடுத்தது வழி.

The strong man's way is the way.

5569. வலிய உறவாடி வாசலிலே வந்தாலும், பொய் உறவாடிப் போய் வா என்று சொல்லுகிறான்.

When I go to his door in a friendly way, he feigns friendship, but bids me go away.

5570. வலியவன் வெட்டினதே வாய்க்கால்.

That is the channel which was cut by the strong man.

5571. வலையிற் சிக்கிக்கொண்ட மான்.

An ensnared deer.

5572. வல்லடி வழக்கைச் சொல்லடி மாமி.

Mother-in-law, give an account of the violent quarrel.

5573. வல்லவன் ஆட்டிய பம்பரம் மணலிலும் ஆடும்.

The top thrown by the strong will spin even in sand.

5574. வல்லமை பேசேல்.

Boast not of thy power.

5575. வல்லவனுக்குப் புல்லும் ஆயுதம்.

Even a blade of grass is a weapon to the strong.

5576. வல்லவனுக்குப் புல் ஆயுதம்.

Grass is a weapon to the strong man.

5577. வல்லவனுக்கு வல்லவன் வையகத்தில் உண்டு.

Every powerful man in the world has his rival.

5578. வல்லார் இளைத்தால் வந்து இளைப்பாறும் என்று சொல்லாநிரார்கள் சுத்த வீரர்கள்.

When the powerful fail, the brave will surely welcome them.

5579. வல்லார் கொள்ளை வாழைப்பழம் ஆகும்.

The spoils of the strong will soon go to waste as a plantain.

5580. வல்விலைக் கூறையும் மெலவிலைக் காளையும் ஆகாது.

A dear-bought cloth, and a low-priced bull are useless.

5581. வவ்வால் வீட்டுக்கு வவ்வால் வந்தால் நீயும் தொங்கு நானும் தொங்கு.

When one bat visits another, *the host will say*, you hang, and I will do the same.

5582. வழிகட்டிப் பறிக்கிறவன் திருடன், வரதராஜனு ஏறுகிறதே கருடன்.

He who waylays and plunders is a thief, the vehicle of Vishnu is the hawk.

5583. வழிநடை வார்த்தை வாகனம்போல.

Conversation on a journey is equal to a conveyance.

5584. வழியிலே கண்ட குதிரைக்கு வைக்கோற் பழுதை கடிவாளம்

A straw rope is the bridle for a stray horse.

5585. வழியிலே கிடக்கிற கோடாலியை எடுத்துக் காலின்மேல் போட்டுக்கொள்வானேன்?

Why should a man meddle with a hatchet lying in the road and cut his foot?

5586. வழியே ஏறுக வழியே மீளுக.

Go by the way, and return by the way.

5587. வழியே போய் வழியே வந்தால் அதிகாரி செங்கோல் என்ன செய்யும்?

If a man go and come by the highway, what can the sceptre of the chief do to him?

5588. வழியே போகிற சனியனை வாரத்துக்கு வாங்கினாற்போல.

Like hiring Saturn whom one met on his way.

5589. வழி வழியாய்ப் போகும்போது விதி விதியாய் வருகிறது.

As each goes on his way, destiny accompanies him.

5590. வழுக்கி விழாத குதிரை வளமான குதிரை.

The horse that does not stumble is the best horse.

5591. வழுவழுத்த உறவைப் பார்க்கிலும் வைரம் பற்றிய பகை நன்று.

Inveterate hatred is better than fickle friendship.

5592. வளரும் காய் பிஞ்சிலே தெரியும்.

The future fruit may be known when it nits.

5593. வளர்த்த கடா மார்பிற் பாய்ந்ததுபோல.

As the trained ram flew at the breast.

5594. வளர்த்த நாய் முகத்தைப் பார்க்கிறதுபோல.

As a trained dog looks at the face.

5595. வளர்ப்பு வக்கணை அறியாது.

A hanger on does not understand politeness.

5596. வளவன் ஆயினும் அளவு அறிந்து அளித்து உண்.

Though possessed of abundant wealth, be moderate in giving and eating.

5597. வளைந்த மூங்கில் அரசன் முடிமேல், வளையாத மூங்கில் கழைக் கூத்தர் காலின்கீழ்.

A bent bamboo above the king's crown, a straight one under the feet of pole-dancers.

5598. வறியோர்க்கு அழகு வறுமையிற் கேண்மை.

Decency in adversity is commendable in the indigent.

5599. வறுத்த பயறு முளைக்குமா?

Will parched peas germinate?

5600. வறுமை கண்டவர் வையத்தில் அநேகர்.

There are many in the world who are accustomed to poverty.

5601. வறுமை வந்தால் பத்தும் பறந்துபோம்.

When poverty comes, the ten *vital airs* will fly off.

5602. வறுமைக்கு மூதேவியும் செல்வத்திற்குச் சீதேவியும்.

Adversity is attended by the goddess of misfortune, prosperity by the goddess of fortune.

5603. வனாந்தரத்து நுழைநரிகள இடையர்களின் தீர்க்க விரோதிகள்.

The sly jackals of the wilds, are inveterate enemies to shepherds.

5604. வன்சொல் வணக்கத்திலும் இன்சொல் வணங்காமை நலம்.

Better is gentle resistance, than submission with rough words.

வா.

5605. வாகனம் உள்ளவன நடைக்கு அஞ்சான், பால் உண்டான் பந்திக்கு அஞ்சான்.

He who has a conveyance will not be afraid of moving, he who is fed on milk will not care to attend a feast.

5606. வாகை இளம்பிஞ்சு கண்டவர்கள் இல்லை, வாகான தென்னம்பிள்ளை கண்டவர்கள் இல்லை.

None ever saw the tender fruit of the *Mimosa flexuosa*, nor a straight young cocoanut tree.

5607. வாகை இளம் பிஞ்சு கண்டவர்கள் உண்டோ?

Has any one seen the tender fruit of the Mimosa?

5608. வாக்கினால் கெட்ட கழுதையைப் போக்கிலே விடுங்கள்.

Let the ass go that brought evil on itself by braying.

5609. வாங்கின கடனைக் கொடாத வல்லாளகண்டன்.

A mighty cheat who never pays his debts.

5610. வாசற்படி இட்டு விடிகிறதோ மகாதேவர் இட்டு விடிகிறதோ?

Does the sun rise by the permission of the threshold, or by the permission Mahadéva?

5611. வாணாளுக்கு ஏற்ற வயிற்று எரிச்சல்.

Sorrow suited to the present life.

5612. வாணாள் உடையான் வலுப்பட்டுச் சாகான்.

He who is destined to live long, is not liable to die by accident.

5613. வாணிபம் செய்யிற் காணியும் குறி.

In matters of trade, note down the smallest fraction.

5614. வாணியக்கட்டை வயிரக் கட்டை தேயத்தேயத் துடைப்பக் கட்டை.

The pestle of an oil-press is tough, when worn away it may become a broom-stick.

5615. வாணியன் ஆசை கோணியும் கொள்ளாது.
A gunny bag will not hold the excessive desires of the oil merchant.

5616. வாணியர்கள் ஆடும் செக்கை வளைய வரும் எருதுகள்போல.
Like the oxen that go round the oil-man's press.

5617. வாதத்து இயல்பு எடேல்.
Do not indulge in rheumatic humour.

5618. வாதம் கெடுத்தது பாதி வண்ணான் கெடுத்தது பாதி.
It was destroyed partly by the wind, and partly by the washerman.

5619. வாதம் ஊதி அறி, வேதம் ஓதி அறி.
Learn alchemy by experiment, and the vedas by recitation.

5620. வாதி கண்ணுக்கு மட்டம் எட்டு மாற்று.
To the eye of an alchemist, common gold appears as standard gold.

5621. வாதுக்கு ஆடின தேவடியாள் வயது சென்றால் கழுதை மேய்ப்பாள்.
When a distinguished dancing girl becomes old, she may tend asses.

5622. வாதுமுற் கூறேல்.
Do not begin a quarrel.

5623. வாயாடி வார்த்தை மட்டில்லா ரவை.
The words of a babbler are fine dust.

5624. வாயாலே தின்று வாயாலே கக்கும் வௌவாலைப்போல்.
Like a bat that feeds and ejects by the mouth.

5625. வாயாலே கேட்டால் வாழைக்காய்ப் பிஞ்சும் கொடான், தாய் புருஷன் வந்தால் தாரோடே கொண்டு போவான்.
Though you entreat, he will not give even an unripe plantain; but if the keeper of his mother comes, he will produce a whole bunch.

5626. வாயாலே கேட்டால் வாழைப்பிஞ்சும் கொடான் தண்டித்துக் கேட்டால் தாரோடே கொடுப்பான்.
When entreated he will not give an unripe plantain, but when punished he will give a whole bunch.

5627 வாயிலே உறவு மனதிலே பகை.

Friendship in the mouth, and hatred in the mind.

5628. வாயிலே உண்டு வழி.

The way is in *one's* mouth.

5629. வாயைப் பார்த்து ஆளை ஏய்த்தான்.

Seeing the man's inability to speak, he cheated him.

5630. வாய் இருந்தால் வங்காளம் போகலாம்.

If possessed of a mouth. one may find his way to Bengal.

5631. வாய் இல்லா விட்டால் நாய் கொண்டு போய்விடும்.

If you had no mouth, a dog would carry you away.

5632. வாய் இல்லாவிட்டால நாய்கூடச சட்டை செய்யாது.

If not possessed of a mouth, even a dog will not take notice of him.

5633. வாய் இருந்தால் பிள்ளை பிழைக்கும்.

If the child have a mouth, it will live.

5634. வாய் உள்ள பெட்டிக்குத் தூர் இலலை.

The box that has a mouth, has no bottom.

5635. வாய் காய்ந்த புலி ஆள்மேலே விழுந்ததுபோல.

As a hungry tiger fell on a man.

5636. வாய்க்கொழுப்புச் சீலையில் வடிகிறது.

His arrogance oozes through his cloth.

5637. வாய்க்கு உண்டோ வாதம்?

Does rheumatism affect *one's* mouth?

5638. வாய் சர்க்கரை கை கொக்கரை.

Sugar in his mouth, and the very opposite in the hand.

5639. வாய் சொல்லும் பிடரி கும்பிடும்.

The mouth will resist, the nape of the neck will worship.

5640. வாய்தான் இருக்கின்றது வாய்க்கு அரிசிக்கு வழி இல்லை.
He has a mouth, but no means of procuring rice for it.

5641. வாய் திறக்கப் பொய் திறக்கும்.
When the mouth opens, lies come forth.

5642. வாய்த் தவிடும் போய் அடுப்பு நெருப்பும் போனதுபோல.
Like losing bran from the mouth, and fire from the hearth.

5643. வாய் நல்லதானால் ஊர் நல்லது.
When the mouth is good, the village is good.

5644. வாய் பார்த்தவள் வாழ்வு இழந்தாள் அம்பலம் பார்த்தவன் பெண்டு இழந்தான்.
She who was looking at the mouth, became a widow: and he who watched the house, lost his wife.

5645. வாய் புளித்ததோ மாங்காய் புளித்ததோ?
Which is sour, the mouth or the mango?

5646. வாய் மதத்தால் வழக்கு இழந்தான்.
He lost his suit by the haughty words of his mouth.

5647. வாய் மதத்தால் வாழ்வை இழந்தான்.
He lost his fortune by the arrogance of his mouth.

5648. வாய் வாழைப்பழம் கை கருணைக்கிழங்கு.
Plantain fruit in the mouth, and karanai roots in the hands.

5649. வார்த்தை இருந்துபோம், வழி தூர்ந்துபோம்.
Words will endure, ways will fall into disuse.

5650. வாலிபத்திலே முதிர்ந்த புத்தி குறுகின வயதுக்கு அடையாளம்.
Premature genius foretokens a short life.

5651. வால் நீண்ட கரிக்குருவி வலம் இருந்து இடம் போனால், கால் நடையாய்ப் போனவர்கள் கனக தண்டிகை ஏறுவார்கள்.
If a long tailed blackbird fly from right to left, those who went on foot will, on their return, mount palanquins wrought with gold.

5652. வால் போனாலும் போகிறது எனக்குத் தோல் வேண்டும்.

It does not matter if the tail is lost, I want the skin.

5653. வாழாத பெண்ணுக்கு மை ஏண்டி, பொட்டு ஏண்டி, மஞ்சள் குளி ஏண்டி?

Of what use are paint, the marriage symbol, and turmeric water, to a woman who refuses to become a wife?

5654. வாழுகிற வீட்டில் மரநாய் கட்டினதுபோல.

As a polecat was tied up in a house occupied by a prosperous family.

5655. வாழும் பிள்ளையை விளையாட்டிலே தெரியும்.

The future prosperity of a person may be known when he is playing as a child.

5656. வாழை அடி வாழை.

The sucker of a plantain tree becomes another tree.

5657. வாழைப்பழத்தில் ஊசி ஏறுவதுபோல.

Like a needle penetrating a plantain.

5658. வாழைப்பழம் தின்னாத குரங்கு இல்லை.

There are no monkeys that will not eat plantain fruit.

5659. வாழைப்பழம் கொண்டுபோனவள் வாசலில் இருந்தாள், வாய் கொண்டுபோனவள் நடு வீட்டில் இருந்தாள்.

She that took the plantains sat at the entrance, she that took her mouth, seated herself in the middle of the house.

The one who trusted her power of address obtained a better place than the one who sought recognition by a gift.

5660. வாழை வடக்கு ஈனும் வான் கமுகு தெற்கு ஈனும்.

Plantain trees put forth their bunches to the north, and arica-nut trees, on the south.

5661. வாழ்கிற பெண்ணைத் தாயார் கெடுத்ததுபோல.

As a mother ruined a girl that was settled in life.

5662. வாழ்கிற வீட்டில் வன்குரங்கு வைத்ததுபோல.

Like placing a monkey in a family.

5663. வாழ்கிற வீட்டுக்கு இது ஒரு வன்குரங்கு.

He is as a monkey in a house.

5664. வாழ்கிற வீட்டுக்கு வாழை வைத்துப்பார்.

Ascertain the future of a family by putting down plantain trees.

It is said that plantains naturally put forth their bunches to the north. Should the fruit appear otherwise, it is considered ominous to the homestead.

5665. வாழ்க்கை கொடுத்தவன் கையில் வாணுளும்.

Length of days is in the hands of him who gave prosperity.

5666. வாழ்ந்தது கெட்டால் வறு ஓட்டுக்கும் ஆகாது.

When that which flourished decays, it is not worth even a potsherd.

5667. வாழ்ந்தவன் வறியவனுனல வறை ஓட்டிற்கும் ஆகான்.

If a prosperous person suffer reverses, he will not be worth a black potsherd.

5668. வாழ்ந்த மகள் வந்தால் வணணத் தடுக்கு இடு, கெட்டமகள் வந்தால் கிழிந்த தடுக்கு இடு.

When the daughter who lives in affluence pays a visit, let her be seated on a fine mat; when she who is reduced to poverty comes seat her on an old mat.

5669. வாழ்வாருக்குச் சிதேவி வாயிலே.

The goddess of fortune is in the mouth of the prosperous.

5670. வாழ்வும் சிலது காலம் தாழ்வும் சிலது காலம்.

Prosperity for a time, and adversity for a time.

5671. வாளுக்கு ஆயிரம் தோளுக்கு ஆயிரம் சம்பாதித்தாலும் மட டாய்ச் செலவிடு.

Though you may acquire thousands of wealth by dexterity, and physical strength, be frugal.

5672. வாளுக்கு ஆயிரம் தோளுக்கு ஆயிரம்,

A thousand by his sword, a thousand by his arm.

5673. வானத்துக்குக்கீழ் இருந்து மழைக்குப் பயப்படலாமா?

Living under the conopy of heaven, may we be afraid of rain?

5674. வானமும் பூமியும் கொள்ளாதான் மரத்திலும் கல்லிலும் இருப்பானோ?

Will he whom heaven and earth cannot contain, dwell in wood and stone?

5675. வானமே ஈன்றது பூமியே தாங்கிற்று.

The heavens produced, and the earth sustained.

5676. வானம் பார்க்கப் போயும் இடைஞ்சலா?

When you go to gaze at the heavens, do you find any impediment?

5677. வானம் சுரக்கத் தானம் சிறக்கும்.

When it rains abundantly, liberality will abound.

5678. வானம் சுருங்கிற் றானம் சுருங்கும்.

When drought prevails charity fails.

5679. வான் செய்த உதவிக்கு வையகம் என்ன செய்யும்?

What can the world do in return for the favours of heaven?

வி.

5680. விசும்பிற் றுளி வீழினல்லால் பசும்புற் றலை காண்பது அரிது.

If the sky withholds rain, not a blade of grass can be seen.

5681. விசுவாசக் கொக்கு நடமாடிச் செத்ததாம்.

It is said that a devout crane died from wandering about.

5682. விசுவாசம் இருந்தால் வேசியும் பிழைப்பாள், நிசம் இருந்தால் நீசனும் தழைப்பான்.

If she be faithful, even a harlot will prosper; if he be honest, even the low-born will flourish.

5683. விசுவாசப் பூனை கருவாட்டைத் தூக்கிக்கொண்டு போகிறதாம்.

It is said that a devout cat carried away the dried fish.

5684. விஷத்தைக் குடிக்கப் பாலாமா?

Will poison when drunk turn into milk?

5685. விஷத்தின் மேல் விஷம், விஷம் போக்கும்.

Poison is the medicine of poison.

5686. விஷம் தின்றால் கொல்லும்.

If poison be swallowed, it will kill.

5687. விஷம் குடித்தவன் மிளகுநீர் குடிக்க வேண்டும்.

He who has swallowed poison must take pepper water.

5688. விஷம் குடித்தாலும் சாகார் விசுவாசிகள்.

Though they may take poison, the faithful will not die.

5689. விஷம் பெரிதோ பாவம் பெரிதோ?

Which is the more destructive, poison or sin?

5690. விஷம் தீர வைத்தியன் வேண்டும், பாவம் தீரத் தெய்வம் வேண்டும்.

A physician is necessary to counteract poison, and God, to remove sin.

5691. விஷ்ணு பெரியவர் என்று ஸ்ரீரங்கத்தில் பார்க்கவேண்டும்.

You must go to Srírangam to understand that Vishnu is great.

5692. விஷ்ணுவைப் பெரிது என்பார் ஸ்ரீரங்கத்தில், சிவனைப் பெரிது என்பார் அருணாசலத்தில்.

The inhabitants of Srírangam say that Vishnu is great, those of Arunasalam, say that Siva is great.

5693. விஷ்ணுவே சமஸ்தம் என்பார் சிலர், சிவனே பெரிது என்பார் சிலர்.

Some profess that Vishnu is all in all, while others maintain that Siva is the greater *of the two*.

5694. விடாச்சுரத்துக்கு விஷ்ணுகரந்தை.

Vishnukarantai-*Sphœranthus Indicus*-is a specific remedy for fever.

5695. விடாத மழை பெய்தால் படாத பாடு படவேண்டும்.

Should it rain unceasingly, intolerable suffering would follow.

5696. விடாத மழையால் இல்லி ஒழுக்கு அடைபடும்.

Unceasing rain stops leaks.

5697. விடிந்தால் தெரியும் மாப்பிள்ளை குருடும் பெண் குருடும்.

It will be known at day-break whether the bridegroom or the bride is blind.

5698. விடிந்தும் பெண்ணுக்கு முட்டாக்கோ?

Does the woman require a veil even after sunrise?

5699. விடிய விடியக் கதை கேட்டு இராமனுக்குச் சீதை என்ன வேண்டுமென்று கேட்டதுபோல.

As one asked what relationship existed between Ráma and Síta, after listening to their history till day-break.

5700. விடியற்காலம் கலியாணம், பிடி அடா தாம்பூலம்.

The marriage will take place at dawn, thou fellow, take betel.

5701. விடியா மூஞ்சிக்கு வேலை அகப்பட்டாலும் கூலி அகப்படாது.

Though the unfortunate may find work, he will not get his hire.

5702. விடியுமட்டும் இறைத்தவனும் விடிந்தபின்பு சாலை உடைத்தவனும் சரி.

He that draws water till day-break, and he that breaks his bucket at day-break, are on an equality.

5703. விடியுமட்டும் மழை பெய்தாலும் ஓட்டாங்கிளிஞ்சில் முளைக்காது.

Though it may rain till day-break, a potsherd will not germinate.

5704. விட்டிற்பூச்சியைப்போல் பறந்து திரிகிறான்.

He flits about like a grass-hopper.

5705. விட்டு விட்டுப் பெய்கிற மழையிலும் விடாமற் பெய்கிற தூவா னம் நல்லது.

Unceasing driving rain is preferable to intermitted showers.

5706. விட்டுதடா ஆசை விளாம் பழத்து ஓட்டோடே.

The pleasure of the wood-apple ceases with the shell.

5707. விண் காட்டப் போனவன் கண் காட்ட வந்தானும்.

It is said that he who went to point out the heavens, returned to shew his eyes.

5708. விண்ணணம் எங்கே, கின்னரம் எங்கே?

What is become of your ostentation, and where is your guitar?

5709. விண்ணுமாலைக்குக் கலியாணம் விழுந்து கொட்டடா சாம் புவா.

O, thou tomtom beater, Vinumal is to be married, fall down and beat your tomtom.

5710. விண்ணேறு தப்பினும் கண்ணேறு தப்பாது.

One may escape a thunderbolt, but he cannot escape *the effects of* an evil eye.

5711. விண்தொடு கொடிமுடி மேருவும் வீறளி தென்திசைக் கிரியும்.

Meru whose summit reaches to heaven, and the merit giving mountain on the south.

5712. விண் பொய்த்தால் மண் பொய்க்கும்.

If the sky fail, the earth will fail.

5713. விண் வலிதோ மண் வலிதோ?

Which is the more powerful heaven or earth?

5714. விதி போகிற வழியே மதி போகும்.

The mind will follow destiny.

5715. விதி முடிந்தவனைப் பாம்பு கடிக்கும்.

A viper will bite him whose prescribed term of life is at an end.

5716. விதியை மதியால் தடுக்கலாமா?

Can destiny be averted by prescience?

5717. விஸ்தாரக்காரன் செத்தால் பிழைக்கான்.

A boaster if he die, cannot return to life.

5718. வித்து இல்லாச் சம்பிரதாயம் மேலும் இல்லைக் கீழும் இல்லை.

Out of nothing, nothing comes, whether above or below.

5719. வித்துவானுக்கு எது பரதேசம்?

What country is foreign to a man of learning?

5720. வித்துவான்களுக்கு எது பெரிது?

What is difficult to the learned?

5721. வித்தைக் கள்ளி மாமியார் விறகு ஒடிக்கப் போனாளாம் கற்றா ழை முள்வந்து கொத்தோடே தைத்ததாம்.

The sapient old mother-in-law is said to have got foul of the thorny cactus, when she went to gather firewood.

5722. வித்தை அற்றவன் அழகு வாசனை இல்லா முருக்கம் பூப் போல.

The beauty of the unlettered, is like the inodorous Muruku flower.

5723. வித்தை விரும்பு.

Desire learning.

5724. வித்தைக் கள்ளி, விளையாட்டுக் கள்ளி, பாகற்காய் விற்ற பழங் கள்ளி.

She is a hypocrite, and idle;—she is that old thief that sold págal fruit.

5725. வித்தையடி மாமி விக்குதடி பணிகாரம்.

O thou pretending mother-in-law, cakes stick in my throat.

5726. வித்தையில் எளியது சூனியம், பன்னத்திலே எளியது நீற்றுப் பெட்டி.

Of arts sorcery is the easiest, of textures the pastry boiling basket.

5727. விதந்தை அடிக்கிற கோழிக்கு விலாவில் இருக்கிறதாம் பித்து.

It is said that an hypercritical hen has its bile in its chest.

5728. வித்தையுள்ளவன் பெரியவன்.

He who is learned, is truly great.

5729. விநாசகாலே விபரீத புத்தி.

Bent on destruction by a strange fatality.

5730. வியாச்சியம் சேற்றில் நட்ட கம்பம்.

Litigation is a pole planted in mud.

5731. வியாதிக்கு மருந்து உண்டு விதிக்கு மருந்து உண்டா?

Medicine may be had for a disease,—is there any for destiny!

5732. வியாதியிலும் மருந்து கொடிது.

The medicine is worse than the disease.

5733. விரதத்திலும் பெரிதோ ஒரு சந்தி?

Is fasting more meritorious than penance!

5734. விரதம் கெட்டாலும் சுகம் தக்கவேண்டும்.

Though the penance may prove ineffectual, one must have regard to his comfort.

5735. விரலுக்குத் தக்க வீக்கம்.

The swelling will be proportioned to the *size of the* finger.

5736. விரல் உதவி விருந்தினர் உதவார்.

Guests are not as serviceable, as are one's fingers.

5737. விரல் உரல் ஆனல் உரல் என்ன ஆகும்?

If the finger *swell* to the size of a rice mortar, how large will the mortar be when that swells!

5738. விரல் போகாத இடத்தில் உரல் போமா?

Can a mortar pass through an opening which is not large enough to admit a finger!

5739. விரிந்த உலகில் தெரிந்தவர் சிலர்.

There are few on the face of the wide world who are wise.

5740. விருது கூறி வந்து செடியில் நுழையலாமா?

Anxious for fame, may one crawl under bushes?

5741. விருதுக்கோ வேட்டை ஆடுகிறது?

What, hunting, to acquire fame!

5742. விருத்தாசலம் போனால் திரட்பாவம் போகும்.

Pilgrimage to Viruttáchalam will expiate great sins.

5743. விருந்து இட்டுப் பகை தேடுகிறது.

Seeking enemies by means of hospitality.

5744. விருந்திலோர்க்கு இல்லைப் பொருந்திய ஒழுக்கம்.

The inhospitable are destitute of agreeable manners.

5745. விருந்து இல்லாச் சோறு மருந்து.

Food without hospitality is medicine.

5746. விருந்தைப் பண்ணிப் பொருந்தப் பண்ணு.

Win *your enemy* by hospitality.

5747. விருந்தும் மருந்தும் மூன்று பொழுது.

Hospitality and medicine must be confined to three days.

5748. விருப்பத்தினால் ஆகாதது வீம்பினால் ஆகுமா?

Can that which is unattainable by ambition, be attained by mere boasting?

5749. விரை ஒன்று போடச் சுரை ஒன்று முளைக்குமா?

Will the bottle gourd spring up when a different seed is sown!

5750. விலக்கக் கூடாத துன்பத்திற்கு விசனப்படாதே.

Do not fret about disagreeables that cannot be averted.

5751. விலங்கை விட்டுத் தொழுவில் மாட்டிக்கொண்டதுபோல.

Like being put in the stocks after liberation from chains.

5752. விலை மகட்கு அழகு தன் மேனி மினுக்குதல்.

It befits a harlot to make her person shine.

5753. வில் அடியால் சாகாதது கல் அடியால் சாகுமா?

Will that which resisted the stroke of a bow, die by the pelting of stones?

5754. வில் இல்லாதவன் அம்பு தேடுவான் ஏன்?

Why should a man without a bow seek arrows?

5755. வில்லம்போ சொல்லம்போ?

Is it an arrow or sarcasm?

5756. வில்லுக் குனியாது எய்தால், விலகாது எதிர்த்த பகை.

If you shoot *an arrow* when the bow is not sufficiently bent, the enemy will not retreat.

5757. வில்லுக்கு விஜயன் பரிக்கு நகுலன்.

In archery Vijaya, in horsemanship Nakula.

5758 வில் வளைந்தால் மோசம் தரும்.

The bending of a bow is dangerous.

5759. வில்வப்பழம் தின்பார் பித்தம் போக, பனம்பழம் தின்பார் பசி போக.

They eat vilvam fruit to remove biliousness, and palmyrah fruit to appease hunger.

5760. விவேகத்தின் மேன்மை அவிவேகத்தை ஒழித்தல்.

It is the excellence of discretion to avoid indiscretion.

5761. விழலுக்கு இறைத்த நீர்.

Water drawn for *coarse grass*.

5762. விழித்தவன் கன்று நாகுகன்று தூங்கினவன் கன்று கடாக்கன்று.

The calf of the man who watched is a female; that of him who slept is a male.

5763. விழுகிற சுவரிலே கை வைப்பான் ஏன்?

Why put your hand on a tottering wall?

5764. விழுங்கின ரசம் வயிற்றில இராது.

Swallowed mercury will not remain in the stomach.

5765. விழுந்த பிள்ளையை எடுக்க நேரம் இல்லை.

No time to lift up the child that has fallen down.

5766. விழுந்தாலும் மீசையில் மண் ஒட்டவில்லை என்கிறான்.

Though he has fallen down, he says that his mustache is not soiled with dust.

5767. விளக்குமாற்றுக்குப் பட்டுக் குஞ்சமா?

What, a silk tassel for a broom!

5768. விளக்கெண்ணெய்க்குக் கேடே தவிரப் பிள்ளை பிழைப்பது இல்லை.

The child did not survive,—it was only waste of oil.

5769. விளக்கெண்ணெயைத் தடவிக்கொண்டு ஆற்று மணலில் புரண்டாலும் ஒட்டுகிறதுதான் ஒட்டும்.

Though one roll himself in sand, after applying oil to his body, he cannot make a larger quantity of sand adhere to his body.

5770. விளக்கெண்ணெயாம் தலைக்கு எண்ணெய்.

It is said that what he uses for the head is lamp-oil.

5771. விளக்கைப் பிடித்துக்கொண்டு கிணற்றில் விழுகிறதா?

What, falling into a well with a lighted lamp in the hand!

5772. விளக்கைக் கொளுத்திக் கீழே வைப்பார் உண்டோ?

Does any one place a lighted lamp on the floor?

5773. விளக்கை வைத்துக்கொண்டு நெருப்புக்கு அலைகிறதுபோல.

Like wandering abroad for fire, while there is a lighted lamp in the house.

5774. விளக்கு ஒளிக்கு ஆசைப்பட்ட விட்டில்போல.

Like a grass-hopper fascinated by a lighted lamp.

5775. விளங்கா மடையன் விறகுக்குப் போனால் விறகு கிடைத்தாலும் கொடி கிடையாது.

If a simpleton go for firewood, though it be found, a creeper to bind it into a bundle will not be found.

5776. விளையாட்டுப் பிள்ளை விஷத்துக்கு அஞ்சாது.

A playful child will not fear venomous reptiles.

5777. விளையாட்டாய் இருந்தது வினையாய் முடிந்தது.

Originating in playfulness it ended seriously.

5778. விளையாட்டுப் பண்டம் வீடு வந்து சேராது.

Things prepared by playful children never come home.

5779. விளையும் பயிர் முளையிலே தெரியும்.

The future crop is known in the germ.

5780. விறகு கட்டுக்காரனுக்கு நாரை வலம் ஆனால் ஒரு பணம் விற்கிறது ஒன்றேகாற்பணம் விற்கும்.

If a crane cross a firewood man from left to right, what he sells ordinarily for a fanam, will fetch a fanam and a quarter.

If a crow fly on the right of one going out of his house, he is sure to meet with success. If on the left, he will not obtain what he seeks.

5781. விறகு கோணலானாலும் நெருப்புப் பற்றாதா?

Will firewood not ignite, because crooked?

5782. விற்ற குண்டைக்குப் புல் போடுவான் ஏன்?

Why feed a bullock after it is sold?

5783. வினைக்காலம் வரும் காலம், மனை வழியும் தெரியாது.

When times are inauspicious, one does not know his way home.

5784. வினை விதைத்தவன் வினை அறுப்பான் தினை விதைத்தவன் தினை அறுப்பான்.

He who sows actions will reap actions, he that sows millet will reap millet.

வீ.

5785. வீக்கமோ தூக்கமோ?

Is it the effect of swelling or of sleep?

5786. வீக்கம் கண்டால் தூக்கமாம்.

Swelling is followed by languor.

5787. வீங்கலுக்கு விஷம் அதிகம்.

Looking at the swelling, the inflammation is excessive.

5788. வீசம் இறுத்த குடி நாசம்.

The payment of a sixteenth is a loss to a family.

5789. வீசி நடந்தால் வெள்ளி வீசம் குறையும்.

Silver *ornaments* are injured by swinging the arms when walking.

5790. வீச்சு என்றாலும் விடுவேனா, வீர புத்திர அம்பலகாரா?

Thou son of the violent Ambalakáran, shall I let thee go because thou squeakest?

5791. வீடு அசையாமல் தின்னும் யானை அசைந்து தின்னும்.

A house consumes standing still, an elephant when moving.

5792. வீடு எல்லாம் குருடு, வாசல் எல்லாம் கிணறு.

The inmates of the house are all blind, and there are wells all over the yard.

5793. வீடு கட்டுகிறது அரிது, வீடு அழிக்கிறது எளிது.

To build a house is difficult, to destroy one is easy.

5794. வீடு கட்டுமுன்னம் கிணறு வெட்டவேண்டும்.

Before building a house dig a well.

In a Sanscrit work on architecture I saw some years ago, the advice here expressed is given as the first thing to be attended to, when selecting a site for a house.

5795. வீடு தருவோன் மேலும் தருவோன்.

He who gives a house may give more than that.

5796. வீடு நிறைந்த விளக்குமாறு.

A house full of brooms.

5797. வீடு போ என்கிறது, காடு வா என்கிறது.

The homestead says go, the place of cremation says come.

5798. வீடு வெறு வீடு வேலூர் அதிகாரம்.

His house is empty, but *he acts as if he* were the chief of Vellore.

One of the Nabob's palaces was at Vellore.

5799. வீடு வெறுவீடாய் இருந்தாலும் மணியம் ஏழு ஊர்.

Although his house is empty, he is the manager of seven villages.

5800. வீட்டில் அழகு வேம்பு அடியாகும்.

The shade of a margosa tree is good for a house.

5801. வீட்டில் அடங்காதவன் ஊரில் அடங்குவான்.

He who is not obedient in the house will obey in the village.

5802. வீட்டுக்கருமம் நாட்டுக்கு உரையேல்.

Do not make known abroad the affairs of the homestead.

5803. வீட்டுக்கு இருந்தால் வெண்கலப் பெண்டாட்டி, வீட்டுக்கு இல்லாமற் போனால் தூங்கற் பெண்டாட்டி.

If in the house she is bell-metal wife, if she goes abroad, she is a slumbering wife.

5804. வீட்டுக்கு அலங்காரம் பெரிய குடி.

A large family *gives* beauty to a house.

5805. வீட்டுக்குச் சோற்றுக்கு இல்லை சிவன் அறிவான், நாட்டுக்குச் செல்வப்பிள்ளை நான் அல்லவோ?

Siva knows that I have no rice at home, yet am I not regarded abroad as a wealthy person!

5806. வீட்டுக்கு அலங்காரம் விளக்கு.

A lighted lamp *gives* beauty to a house.

5807. வீட்டுக்கு வீடு மண் அடுப்புத்தான்.
An earthen hearth is the rule in all houses.

5808. வீட்டுக்கு அலங்காரம் மனையாள்.
A wife *gives* beauty to a house.

5809. வீட்டுக்கு அலங்காரம் வேளாண்மை.
Grain gives beauty to a house.

5810. வீட்டுச் செல்வம் மாடு, தோட்டச் செல்வம் முருங்கைக்காய்.
A cow is house-wealth, and murungai fruit is garden-wealth.

5811. வீட்டுச் சோற்றைத் தின்று வீண் சண்டைக்குப் போவானேன்?
Why go and quarrel causelessly when eating your own rice!

5812. வீட்டுச் சோற்றைப் போட்டு வீண் பேச்சுக் கேட்பானேன்?
Having given his own rice why should one hear abuse!

5813. வீட்டுப் பாம்பு காட்டுக்குப் போனால் அதுவும் காட்டுப் பாம்பு ஆகும்.
If a tamed snake go to the jungle, it will become a wild one.

5814. வீட்டு வேலை வெளி வேலை பார்த்துக் காட்டு வேலைக்குக் கட்டோடே போகலாம்.
After finishing house work and out door work, one should go to that of the jungle with due preparation.

5815. வீட்டுப் பிள்ளையும் வெளிப் பிள்ளையும் வித்தியாசம் அறியாது.
Children in one's own house and strange children make no difference.

5816. வீட்டு மூதேவியும் காட்டு மூதேவியும் கூடி உலாவுகிறது.
The house-goddess of misfortune, and one of the wilds are walking together.

5817. வீட்டுக்குப் புகழ்ச்சியோ நாட்டுக்குப் புகழ்ச்சியோ?
Is it fame to a family or to the country!

5818. வீட்டுக்காரியம் பாராதவன் நாட்டுக் காரியம் பார்ப்பானா?
Will he who cannot manage his *own* household affairs, attend to the management of a country?

5819. வீட்டுக்காரி என்று பெண்சாதிக்குப் பெயர்.

Another name for a wife is the mistress of the house.

5820. வீட்டுக்கு வீரன் காட்டுக்குக் கள்ளன்.

At home, a hero, abroad, a coward.

5821. வீட்டுக்கு வீடு எதிர் வீடு ஆகாது.

The *door-ways* of opposite houses must not be over against each other.

5822. வீட்டுக்கு ஏற்றின விளக்கு விருந்துக்கும் ஆகும்.

A lamp lit in a house for the inmates may answer for a feast.

5823. வீட்டுக்கு வாய்த்தது எருமை, மேட்டுக்கு வாய்த்தது போர.

A buffaloa makes a house prosper, a corn-stack makes high ground conspicuous.

5824. வீட்டுக்கு ஒரு வாசற்படி, பூட்டுக்கு ஒரு திறவுகோல்.

One step as an entrance to the house, and one key tc a lock.

5825. வீட்டுப் பெண்சாதி வேம்பும் காட்டுப் பெண்சாதி கரும்பும்.

The wife is a margosa tree, the mistress sugar-cane.

5826. வீட்டைக் கட்டிக் குரங்கைக் குடி வைத்ததுபோல.

Like building a house, and allowing a monkey to dwell therein.

5827. வீட்டைக் காத்து அருள், பாட்டைப் பார்த்து அருள்.

Watch your house, and manage your affairs.

5828. வீட்டைக் கட்டிப் பார், கலியாணம் செய்து பார்.

Enjoy the convenience of a house after building it, and the happiness of the conjugal state, after marrying a wife.

5829. வீட்டைப் பிடுங்கி விறகாய் எரித்தாலும் வீணுதிவீணனுக்கு ஐந்து பணம் எப்படி வரும்?

Although he may pull down his house and use it for firewood, a notorious idler can never get five fanams!

5830. வீட்டைக் காத்த நாயும், காட்டைக் காத்த நரியும், வீண் போகாது.

The expectations of a dog in a house, and a fox in the jungle are not vain.

5831. வீட்டைக் கட்டி ஓட்டைப் போடு.

Build the house, and then tile it.

5832. வீட்டைக் கட்டு, அல்லது காட்டை அழி.

Either build the house, or destroy the jungle.

5833. வீட்டை ஏன் இடித்தாய் மூட்டைப்பூச்சிக்குப் பயந்து?

Why pull down the house, for fear of bugs?

5834. வீட்டை எல்லாம் வெல்லத்திற்கு மாறினான்.

He gave the whole house in exchange for sugar.

5835. வீணருக்குச் செய்தது எல்லாம் வீணும், கடற்கரையில் காணும் மணல்மேல் எழுத்துக்காண்.

Favours shewn to the worthless are vain, they are like writing on the sand of the sea-shore.

5836. வீணாய் உடைந்த சட்டி வேண்டியது உண்டு என் தலையிற் பூணாரம் பூண்ட புதுமைதனைக் கண்டது இல்லை.

There are plenty of pans uselessly broken, I have scarcely ever seen my head adorned with jewels.

5837. வீணுக்கு உழைக்கிறவன் வீணன்.

He who labours for no purpose is a fool.

5838. வீண் இழவுக்கு மார் அடிக்கிறதா?

Am I to smite my breast on account of the death of a stranger?

5839. வீண் இழவுக்கு வீட்டைக் கட்டிப் பார இழவிற்குப் பந்தல் போடு.

Build a house for the use of a stranger, and put up a pandal for the same purpose.

5840. வீண் விபரீதத்தால் பேதையர் வீண் செலவு செய்ய உடன் படுவார்கள்.

Fools are extravagant through mere perverseness.

5841. வீம்புக் குப்பையில் விளையும் வீண் செடி.

A useless shrub growing on a rubbish-heap of ostentation.

5842. வீம்புக்கு வேடம் கொள்ளாதே.

Do not assume a garb for mere show.

5843. வீம்பு பேசுகிறவன் அழிவான், வீரியம் பேசுகிறவன் விழுவான்.

A boaster will be ruined, he who talks as a hero will fall.

5844. வீரம் பேசிக்கொண்டு எழுந்த சேவகன் வெட்டும் களம் கண்டு முதுகிடலாமா?

May a soldier who defiantly rose to the combat, retreat in sight of the battle field!

5845. வீரன் கேண்மை கூர் அம்பாகும்.

The friendship of a hero, is a sharp arrow.

5846. வீரியம் பெரிதோ காரியம் பெரிதோ?

Which is the greater boasting or acting?

வெ.

5847. வெங்கண்ணை வாங்கு உன் கண்ணைக் கொடுத்து.

Give your eyes in exchange for white-eyed fish.

5848. வெகுஜன வாக்கியம் கர்த்தவ்வியம்.

The sayings of the many involve duty.

5849. வெச்செனவுக்கு அன்றி வெண்ணெய் உருகுமா?

Can butter be melted without heat?

5850. வெட்கம் கெட்டாலும் கெடட்டும் தொப்பையில் இட்டால் போதும்.

It matters little if his honour is at stake, it is enough if his paunch be filled.

5851. வெட்கத்தால் ஒல்காதவள் குலஸ்திரிக்குப் போகாது.

She who is not restrained by modesty, is not a woman of superior birth.

5852. வெட்கம் அற்ற பெண்பிள்ளை வீண்.

A woman without shame is worthless.

5853. வெட்கப்படுகிற வேசியும் வெட்கம் கெட்ட சமுசாரியும் உதவாதவர்கள்.

Shame in a prostitute, and want of modesty in a wife, are equally out of place.

5854. வெட்கமே கெட்டு வெளிப்பட்ட முண்டைக்கு முக்காடு ஏது?

What signifies a veil to a widow who goes about without shame!

5855. வெட்கத்துக்கு அஞ்சினவன் சசசரவு செய்வானா?

Will he who is afraid of disgrace quarrel?

5856. வெட்கத்துக்கு அஞ்சினவன் கடனுக்கு அஞ்சுவான்.

He that is afraid of disgrace is afraid of running into debt.

5857. வெட்கத்தை விற்றுக் கக்கத்திலே கொண்டுபோகிறான்.

Having sold his sense of shame, he carries *its price* under his arm.

5858. வெட்கம் கெட்டவனுக்கு மேனி எல்லாம் அழுக்குத்தான்.

The whole body of the shameless, is dirty.

5859. வெட்டப் பலம் இல்லை வெட்டிக்குப் போக மனம் இல்லை.

He is too weak to cut, and unwilling to go out.

5860. வெட்ட வெளியிலே வையாளி விடுகிறதா?

Would you let loose a frisky calf in an open plain?

5861. வெட்டிக்கு இறைத்து விழலுக்குத் தண்ணீர் கட்டினதுபோல.

Like irrigating for no purpose.

5862. வெட்டிக் கொண்டுவா என்றால் குத்திக் கொண்டுவருகிறான்.

When he is told to reap and bring, he pounds and brings.

5863. வெட்டிவேரில் விசிறியும், விலாமிச்சை வேரில் தட்டியும பண்ணு.
Make a fan of the cuscus root, and a tat of sweet scented grass root

5864. வெட்டின இடத்தில் சலம் ஊறும், வீடு கட்டின இடத்தில நடை ஏறும்.
Where the ground is dug water will spring, where a house is built there will be an entrance.

5865. வெட்டி எல்லாம் தண்ணீர், மண் கட்டி எல்லாம் புல் நாற்று.
There is water all over the path, young grass all over the sod.

5866. வெட்டிவெட்டிப் பார்த்தாலும் முட்டக் கரிக்காசுதான் அகப்படும்.
Though you may examine by continued digging, you will get only coin of coal in abundance.

5867. வெட்டிக்குப் பெற்று வேலியில் எறிந்தார்களா ?
Did they give birth to me in vain, and throw me at a hedge !

5868. வெட்டியானும் பிணமும் கட்டிக்கொண்டு அழட்டும்.
Let the Vettiyan and the corpse embrace each other, and weep.

5869. வெட்டின குளத்திலும் தண்ணீர் குடியாது கட்டின வேலியும் தாண்டமாட்டாது.
It neitner drinks in an artificial reservoir, nor leaps an artificial hedge.

5870. வெட்டினவனுக்கு ஒரு கேணி வீணுதி வீணனுக்குப் பல கேணி.
He that has sunk a public well has only one, a notorious idler has many.

5871. வெட்டு ஒன்று கண்டம் இரண்டு.
One cut, two slices.

5872. வெட்டென உரையே துட்டர்கள் அறைவர்.
The wicked speak harshly.

5873. வெட்டெனப் பேசேல்.
Do not speak harshly.

5874. வெண்கலக் கடையில் யானை புகுந்ததுபோல.

As an elephant entered a brass vessel bazaar.

5875. வெண்டலைக் கருடன் வந்திடுமானால் எவர் கைப்பொருளும் தன் பொருள் ஆகும்.

When a brahmany kite crosses one *from right to left*, he may become possessed of the wealth of all.

5876. வெண்ணெய்யை வைத்துக்கொண்டு நெய்க்கு அழலாமா ?

Having butter, would you weep for ghee !

5877. வெண்ணெய் திரளுகிறபோது தாழி உடைந்தாற்போல.

As the churn broke just as the butter was forming.

5878. வெண்ணெய் உருக்குகிறதற்குள்ளே பெண்ணை ஆற்றிலே தண்ணீர் வருகிறது.

Ere butter can melt, freshes appear in the Pennar.

5879. வெந்த சோற்றைத் தின்று வந்தது எல்லாம் பிதற்றுகிறான்.

He eats his rice, and talks at random.

5880. வெந்த சோற்றைத் தின்று விதி வந்தால் சாகிறது.

Eating one's rice, and dying when the time comes.

5881. வெந்ததுபோதும் முன்றானையிலே கொட்டு.

It is boiled enough, put it into the end of my cloth.

5882. வெந்ததைப் போடு முன்றானையிலே.

Put what is boiled into my cloth.

5883. வெந்த புண் வினை செய்யாது.

No evil consequences can arise from a burn.

5884. வெந்தயம் இட்ட கறிக்கு சந்தேகம் இல்லை.

A curry with vendayam in it needs not be questioned.

5885. வெந்தயம் போடாத கறியும் கறி அல்ல, சந்தை இல்லாத ஊரும் ஊர் அல்ல.

A curry made without vendayam-*Trigonella Fœnum Græcum*-is not a curry, a village without a market is not a village.

5886. வெந்தால் தெரியும் வெங்காயம் மணப்பு.

The flavour of an onion will be known after it is boiled.

5887. வெந்நீரிலே வீடு வேகுமா?

Can a house be burnt down with hot water?

5888. வெய்யிலிலே போட்டாலும் உலரான், தண்ணீரிலே போட்டாலும் கரையான்.

He will not dry in the sunshine, nor dissolve in water.

5889. வெய்யோன் வெயில் முன் எரி தீபம்போல.

Like a burning lamp in sunshine.

5890. வெல்லப் படை இல்லை, தின்னப் படை உண்டு.

No army to conquer, though there are enough to consume.

5891. வெல்லப் பானையை எறும்பு மொய்த்ததுபோல.

As the ants swarmed on a pot of sugar.

5892. வெல்லப் பானையை ஈக்கள் மொய்த்துக்கொண்டதுபோல.

As the flies swarmed on a pot of sugar.

5893. வெல்லம் சாப்பிடுகிறவன் ஒருவன் விரலைச் சூப்புகிறவன் ஒருவன்.

One eats the sugar, another licks his fingers.

5894. வெல்லப் போனான் ஒரு செல்லப்பிள்ளை மெலலப் போனான் ஒரு அமுங்குத் தலையன்.

A pet child went to conquer, a flat-headed fellow *followed* him *slowly*.

5895. வெல்லாது உங்கள் படை செல்லாது பாண்டியன்முன்.

Your army will not conquer, nor even oppose Pandya.

5896. வெளிச்சம் இருள் ஆனால் இருள் என்னவாம், மெய்ஞ்ஞானி துர்மார்க்கனானால் அஞ்ஞானி எப்படி ஆவான்?

If light become darkness, what will the darkness be; if a wise man becomes wicked, what a great fool he will be?

5897. வெளிச்சீர் உட்சீரைக் காட்டும் கண்ணாடி.

The exterior is the mirror of the interior.

5898. வெளுத்தது எல்லாம் பால் கறுத்தது எல்லாம் தண்ணீர்.

Every thing white is milk, and every thing black is water.

5899. வெளுத்து விட்டாலும் சரி சும்மா விட்டாலும் சரி.

It will be all the same whether he is punished or let go.

5900. வெள்ளம் பள்ளத்தை நாடும் விதி புத்தியை நாடும்.

The flood inclines to a hollow, fate follows the intention.

5901. வெள்ளம் வருவதற்குமுன் அணை கோலிக் கொள்ளவேண்டும்.

One should raise the dam before the flood comes.

5902. வெள்ளரிக்காய் விற்ற பட்டணம்.

The city where cucumbers were sold.

5903. வெள்ளாடு நனைகிறது என்று வேங்கைப்புலி விழுந்து விழுந்து அழுகிறதாம்.

It is said that the tiger is fallen down and crying for grief because the goat was wet.

5904. வெள்ளாடு குழை தின்றதுபோல.

As the goat crops leaves.

5905. வெள்ளாட்டிக்குச் சன்னதம் வந்தால் விழுந்து விழுந்து கும்பிட வேண்டும்.

If a servant girl, be possessed of a devil, all must fall down before her.

5906. வெள்ளாட்டி பெற்ற பிள்ளை விடியற்காலம் செத்துப் போயிற்று.

The child brought forth by a servant girl, died at sunrise.

5907. வெள்ளாட்டியும் பெண்டாட்டியும் சரியா?

Are a maid servant and a wife, on an equality!

5908. வெள்ளாளன் மரபே மரபு கள்ளர் திருட்டே திருட்டு.

Of all ranks that of the Vellala is foremost, of thefts that of the Kallar is notorious.

5909. வெள்ளாளன் கெடுக்காவிட்டாலும் வெள்ளோலை கெடுக்கும்.

If the Vellala did not procure your ruin, his white olas will destroy you.

5910. வெள்ளாளன் மினுக்குப்பண்ணிக் கெட்டான், வேசி சளுக்குப் பண்ணிக் கெட்டாள்.

The Vellala was ruined by adornment, the harlot by finery.

5911. வெள்ளாளன் கிரந்தமும் பார்ப்பான் தமிழும் விழல் விழலே.

The Sanscrit of a Vellala, and the Tamil of a brahman, are equally faulty.

5912. வெள்ளாளர் செய்யாத வேளாண்மை வேளாண்மை அல்ல.

Agriculture not performed by Vellalas, is no agriculture.

5913. வெள்ளாளர் குடிக்கு ஒரு கள்ளாளர் குடி

A Kallála family in a Vellála house.

5914. வெள்ளிக்கு எதிரே போனாலும், வெள்ளாளனுக்கு எதிரே போகலாகாது.

One may go before an *evil* star, but not before a Vellalan.

5915. வெள்ளிக்குப் போட்டதும் கொள்ளிக்குப் போட்டதும் சரி.

Money laid out on silver ornaments, and that spent for firewood are equally *a loss.*

5916. வெள்ளி போட்ட காலுக்கு வெறுங்கால் அடிமையா ?

Is a naked foot, the slave of a foot wearing silver ornaments ?

5917. வெள்ளி வட்டிலும் வேண்டும் விளிம்பிலே பொன்னும் வேண்டும்.

I must have a silver platter with a rim of gold.

5918. வெள்ளெருக்குக்கும் வெள்ளாட்டுப் பாலுக்கும் கள்ளக் கரு மேகம் காணமற் போம்.

The disease which blackens the skin, will be thoroughly cured by the white species of erukku and goats milk.

5919. வெள்ளை கொடுக்க வினை தீரும்.

One's sins will be expiated by giving cloth to the destitute.

5920. வெள்ளைக்குக் கள்ளம் இல்லை.

White is faultless.

5921. வெள்ளைக்கு இல்லை கள்ளச் சிந்தை.

The out-spoken are free from deceit.

5922. வெறுங்கைத் தட்டான் இரும்பு ஊதிச் செத்தான்.

A money-less goldsmith died by blowing iron.

5923. வெறிகாரன் குடியை விடான் வீண் புத்திக்காரன் பாவத்துக்கு அஞ்சான்.

A drunkard will not forsake drinking, a fool is not afraid of evil deeds.

5924. வெறிகொண்ட யானை மிதந்து திரிகிறப்போலே.

As an elephant in rut wanders about *unrestrained.*

5925. வெறிக்கிட்டு அழியேல்.

Squander not by drinking.

5926. வெறு நாய் சந்தைக்குப் போனல் வெள்ளிக்கோலால் அடிபட்டு வரும்.

A dog which goes alone to the market, will be beaten with the steelyard.

5927. வெறும் கை முழம் போடுமா ?

Can the arm measure a cubit, when there is nothing to be measured !

5928. வெறும் சட்டி தாளிக்கிறன்.

He flavours an empty chatty.

5929. வெறும் புளி தின்றால் பற் கூசும்.

Tamarinds if eaten alone, will set the teeth on edge.

5930. வெறும் பானையில் ஈ புகுந்ததுபோல.

As flies entered an empty pot.

5931. வெறும் பயலுக்கு ஏற்ற வீறுப்பு.

Arrogance suited to one's worthlessness.

5932. வெறும்பிலுக்கு வண்ணான் மாற்று.

Finery borrowed from a washerman.

5933. வெறுவாய்க்கு இலைகெட்டவன் விறகுக்குப் போனால் விறகு கிடைத்தாற் கொடி கிடையாது கொடி கிடைத்தால் விறகு கிடையாது.

If a worthless fool go out to gather firewood, he cannot procure a creeper, when he gets a creeper, he can find no firewood.

5934. வெறுவாய் மெல்லுகிற அம்மையாருக்கு நாழி அவல் அகப்பட்டதுபோல.

As a measure of bruised dried rice *given* to an old dame, who had nothing to chew but an empty mouth.

5935. வெறு வாயைத் தின்றவனுக்கு வெள்ளை அவல் கிடைத்தது போல.

As one who had nothing to eat but an empty mouth obtained bruised rice.

5936. வெற்றி பெற்றவன் சுத்த வீரன்.

He who has conquered is a perfect hero.

5937. வெற்றிலைக்குத் தண்ணீரும் வேசைக்கு மஞ்சளும்போல.

Like water to the betel creeper, and saffron to a prostitute.

5938. வெற்றிலைபோல் இருக்கும் மிகுந்த மரம் ஆகி விடும் புத்தி உள்ள பூமரத்துக்குப் பூவிரண்டு வக்கணையாம்

Its leaf is like betel leaf, it grows to a large tree, this intelligent tree has two flowers.

வே.

5939. வேகத்தில் நாலுவிதம் உண்டு.

Of speed there are four kinds.

5940. வேகப் பொறுத்தது ஆறப் பொறுக்கக் கூடாதா?

Having been patient *till the food* was boiled, can you not wait till it cools?

5941. வேகாத வீட்டில் வேகும் கட்டை காமம்.

Lust is a burning block of wood in a house, not on fire.

5942. வேகாத சோற்றுக்கு விருந்தாளிகள் இரண்டு பெயர்.

There are two guests for the insufficiently boiled rice.

5943. வேகிற வீட்டில் பிடுங்குகிறது லாபம்.

Whatever is snatched from a burning house is an advantage.

5944. வேகிற வீட்டுக்கு வெட்டுகிற கிணறு.

To dig a well to put out a house on fire.

5945. வேகிற வீட்டிற்குக் கணக்குப் பார்ப்பார் உண்டோ?

Are there any who waste time in casting up the cost of a house when it is on fire?

5946. வேகிற வீட்டை அவிக்காமல் இருப்பார் உண்டோ?

Will not men extinguish the fire, when a house is on a blaze?

5947. வேசி உறவு காசிலும் பணத்திலுந்தான்.

The friendship of a prostitute is in the money she gets.

5948. வேசி காசு பறிப்பாள்.

A prostitute knows how to deprive one of his money.

5949. வேசியரும நாயும் விதிநால் வைத்தியரும் பாசம் அறறு [illegible]பது கண்பார்.

See how harlots, dogs, and physicians, are at variance.

5950. வேடக்காரனுக்கும் ஆடக்காரனுக்கும் பகை, வேசிக்கும் தாசிக்கும் பகை.

Enmity exists among dancing masters and among harlots.

5951. வேடக்காரா வேடம் விடடா, ஓடக்காரா ஓடம் விடடா.

Thou hypocrite, quit thine hypocrisy, thou boatman, steer the boat.

5952. வேடத்தில் நாலு விதம் உண்டு.

Of disguises there are four kinds.

5953. வேடத்தினால் என்ன, வெண்ணீற்றினால் என்ன?

What avail special forms, what avails white ashes!

5954. வேடமோ தவவேடம் மனதிலோ அவவேடம்.

In appearance an ascetic, at heart a cheat.

5955. வேடம் மூன்று வகை.

There are three forms of disguise.

5956. வேடம் அழிந்துபோம்.

Disguises will perish.

5957. வேடம் கூடமும் கொள்ளாது.

His pretence is such that a room cannot contain it.

5958. வேடருக்கு அருமையான வேடடை முசல் வேட்டை.

Foresters' favourite sport is hare hunting.

5959. வேடருக்கு தேன் பஞ்சமா, மூடருக்கு அடி பஞ்சமா?

Is honey rare among foresters, or chastisement to fools!

5960. வேடர் இல்லா ஊரில் யாவும் குடி இருக்கும்.

In a village where there are no hunters, all *kinds of beasts* may be found.

5961. வேடர்களில் மலைவேடர் விசேஷம்.

Of hunters those that inhabit hill tracts, are the most distinguished.

5962. வேடர் கையில் அகப்பட்ட தேன் கூண்டுபோல்.

As a bee-hive in the hands a forester.

5963. வேட்டை ஆடிச் சிங்கம் தின்னும்.

The lion lives by hunting.

5964. வேட்டையில் பெரிய வேட்டை பன்றி வேட்டை.

Hog-hunting is the most exciting of sports.

5965. வேட்டையில் பிரியமான வேட்டை சிக்காரி வேட்டை.

The most favourite of sports is that of the huntsman.

5966. வேண்டாத பெண்டாட்டியின் கைபட்டாற் குற்றம் கால் பட்டாற் குற்றம்.

A wife not liked offends, whether she touches with the hand, or with the foot.

5967. வேண்டாத பேருக்கு ஈந்து என்ன, வேலையில் ஆற்றுத்தண்ணீர் விழுந்து என்ன?

What is the good of giving to those who are not in want, and what is the good of a river flowing where work is being done!

5968. வேண்டி வினை செயேல்.

Do not act from selfish motives.

5969. வேண்டி வேண்டிக் கொடுத்தாலும் வேண்டாம் என்றாற்போல.

Like refusing to accept *a thing* when requested again and again.

5970. வேண்டுமென்றால் வீடு வேண்டாம் என்றால் காடு.

Domestic or ascetic life just as he pleases.

5971. வேண்டும் என்று நூற்றால் வெண்ணெய்க் கொடிபோல.

If one spins for her own benefit, the thread is as smooth as butter.

5972. வேதத்தில் நாலு விதம் உண்டு.

Of Vedas there are four kinds.

5973. வேதத்திற்கும் விக்கிரகபத்திக்கும் பகை.

The Vedas are opposed to idolatry.

5974. வேதத்தை அறியாத கிழவன் வீண்.

The old man that knows not the Vedas, is worthless.

5975. வேதத்திற்கு உலகம் பகை உலகத்திற்கு ஞானம் பகை.
The world is at enmity with the Vedas, and wisdom with the world.

5976. வேதம் ஆய்ந்து ஓதல் போதகர் முறைமை.
It is the duty of religious teachers to study the Vedas before teaching them.

5977. வேதம் பொய்த்தாலும் வியாழம் பொய்யாது.
Though the Vedas may fail, Jupiter will never fail.

5978. வேதம் கேட்டவரை வேதம் கேட்டவர் என்பான் ஏன்?
Why call those Védiar, who have heard the Vedas?

5979. வேதம் ஏன் நாதம் ஏன் விஸ்தாரக் கள்ளருக்கு?
What need has a widely known hypocrite of the Vedas or the special forms of worship?

5980. வேதம் ஒத்த மித்திரன்.
A friend whose conduct is consistent with the precepts of the Vedas.

5981. வேதம் ஓதிய வேதியர்க்கு ஓர் மழை.
One rain (in a month) for the brahmans that expound the Vedas.

5982. வேதாரணியத்தில் பாம்பு கடிக்கிறதும் இல்லை, வேதாரணியத்தில் பாம்பு குறைகிறதும் இல்லை.
At Védaranyam snakes do not bite, nor do they cease to abound.

5983. வேதியர்க்கு அழகு வேதமும் ஒழுக்கமும்.
The Vedas and virtue, form the beauty of the brahmans.

5984. வேதியர்க்கு அழகு வேதம் ஓதுதல்.
It is the office of brahmans to expound the Vedas.

5985. வேந்தனும் பாம்பும் சரி.
A king and a snake are alike.

5986. வேந்தன் சீறில் ஆந்துணை இல்லை.
No help if the king is angry.

5987. வேப்பெண்ணெயும் ஆபத்துக்கு உதவும்.

Even margosa oil will avail on an emergency.

5988. வேப்பெண்ணெய் விற்ற காசு கசக்குமா?

Will the money obtained by the sale of margosa oil be bitter?

5989. வேப்பெண்ணெய் விருந்து எண்ணெய் அல்ல, மருந்து எண்ணெய்.

Margosa oil is not used in entertainments; it is medicinal.

5990. வேம்பில் தேனை விட்டால் கசப்பு நீங்குமா?

Will the bitterness of margosa be removed by infusing honey into it?

5991. வேம்பும் கரும்பாச்சே வெற்றிலையும் நஞ்சாச்சே.

The margosa has become sugar-cane, and betel has become poison.

5992. வேம்புக்குப் பல் அழகு, வேலுக்குப் பல் இறுகும்.

When cleaned with a margosa stick the teeth look beautiful, when cleaned with a vél stick-*Acacia arabica*-they are made firm.

5993. வேம்பும் சரி வேந்தனும் சரி.

The margosa and a king are alike.

5994. வேம்பும் சரி பாம்பும் சரி.

A margosa tree and a snake are alike.

5995. வேம்பை விரும்ப விரும்பக் கரும்பு.

Constant use makes even margosa sweet.

5996. வேரைக் கல்லி வெந்நீர் வார்த்த கதை.

The story of digging up a root, and pouring out hot water.

5997 வேர் களைந்த மரம் பிழைப்பது எங்கே?

How can a tree deprived of its roots live?

5998. வேர் நின்றால் மரம் நிற்கும், வியாபாரம் நின்றால் செட்டி நிற்பான்.

Trees endure as long as their roots are undecayed, merchants will maintain their social position if their trade continues.

5999. வேர் மூலிகை, மரமூலிகை, காய் மூலிகை.

Roots, wood, and fruit are all drugs.

6000. வேலமரத்து முள்ளும் ஆலமரத்துக் கனியும் ஆனேன்.

I am become a thorn of the vél,-*Acacia arabica*-and a fruit of the banyan.

6001. வேலமரத்திற்கு நிழல் இல்லை, வெள்ளாளனுக்கு உறவு இல்லை.

The vél tree casts no shade, the Vellala has no friendships.

6002. வேலம் பட்டை மேகத்தை நீக்கும், ஆலம் பட்டை பித்தத்தை அடிக்கும்.

The bark of the vél cures venereal heat, that of the banyan removes bile.

6003. வேலி ஒன்றுக்குப் பன்னிரண்டு கலம் விரைப்பாடு.

Twelve kalams of seed corn for one *veli* of land.

A veli is nearly equal to five acres.

6004. வேலி ஒன்றுக்குப் ஈரணை மாடும், இரண்டு ஆளும் வேண்டும்.

For every veli two yokes of oxen and two ploughmen are required.

6005. வேலிக்கு ஓணான் சாட்சி, வெந்ததுக்குச் சொக்கன் சாட்சி.

The chamelion is the witness of the hedge, the cook boy will testify to the food being well boiled.

6006. வேலிக்குப் போட்ட முள் காலுக்கு வினையாச்சுது.

The thorns collected for a hedge, have proved injurious to the feet.

6007. வேலி பயிரை மேய்ந்தால் விளைவது எப்படி?

If the hedge consume the crop, how is the harvest to be obtained?

6008. வேலிலும் நாலு பலன் உண்டு.

Even a vél tree is useful in four ways.

6009. வேலிவைத்துக் காப்பாற்றாத கன்றும் ஆலைவைத்து ஆட்டாத வாணியனும் சரி அல்ல.

Plants not protected by a hedge, and an oil-monger who does not work a press, are out of place.

6010. வேலை அற்ற அம்பட்டன் பூனையைப் பிடித்துச் சிரைத்தானாம்.

It is said that a barber who had nothing to do, got hold of a cat and shaved it.

6011. வேலை அதிகம் சம்பளம் கொஞ்சம்.

The labour is excessive, the pay little.

6012. வேலை இல்லா ஊருக்கு ராஜா ஏன், பாம்பு இல்லா ஊருக்குக் கீரிப்பிள்ளை ஏன்?

What need is there of a king in a country where there is no work. or of a mongoose where there are no snakes?

6013. வேலை இலலாதவனுக்குச் சாப்பாடு என்னத்திற்கு, எச்சிசோற்ற்றுக்காரனுக்கு டம்பம் என்னத்திற்கு?

Why food to him who does no work, why display to him who lives on offal?

6014. வேலை இல்லாத அம்பட்டன் ஆட்டைச் சிரைத்தானாம்.

It is said that a barber who had no work, shaved a sheep.

6015. வேலை ஏன், பிள்ளை ஏன், வேலை இல்லாருக்குச் சாப்பாடு ஏன்?

Why work, why child, why food to those who are destitute of energy?

6016. வேலைக்கள்ளிக்குப் பிள்ளைமேல் சாக்கு, வெட்கம் கெட்டநாறிக்கு அகமுடையான்மேலே சாக்கு.

An idle woman pleads her child in excuse *for her faults*, a shameless woman, her husband.

6017. வேலைக்கள்ளிக்கு வேளைக்குக் காற் படி, வீண் கட்டைக்கு வேளைக்கு அரைப் படி.

To a shuffling woman a quarter measure for a meal, to a worthless block half a measure.

6018. வேலைக்கள்ளிக்குப் பிள்ளைமேலே சாக்கு.

A lazy woman neglects her work, and lays the blame on *her* child.

6019. வேலைக்காரியாய் வந்தவள் வீட்டுக்காரியானால் அவள் அதிஷ்டம்.

If a maid servant becomes the mistress of a house, it is her fortune.

6020. வேலைக்காரி என்று வேண்டிய பேர்கள் கேட்டார்கள், குடித்தனக்காரி என்று கொடுக்கமாட்டோம் என்றார்கள்

Many asked her *in marriage* thinking that she was skilful in domestic affairs, but they refused on the plea that she was a married girl.

6021. வேலைக்குத் தக்க கூலி, விருப்பத்துக்குத் தக்க கூர்மை.

Hire suited to the work, sharpness equal to the desires.

6022. வேலைக்கோ சம்பளம், ஆளுக்கோ சம்பளம்?

Is the hire for the labour, or the labourer !

6023. வேலை செய்தாற் கூலி, வேஷம் போட்டாற் காசு.

If the work be completed, hire ; if the character has been sustained, a fee.

6024. வேலை செய்யாத பிள்ளையைக் கையில் வை, வேலை செய்கிற பிள்ளையைக் காலில் வை.

Carry in arms the child that does no work, and the child which works, place on your legs.

6025. வேலை மினக்கெட்ட அம்பட்டன் பெண்டாட்டி தலையைச் சிரைத்தானாம்.

Being without work, the barber is said to have shaved his wife's head.

6026. வேலை மினக்கெட்டு அம்பட்டன் பூனைக்குட்டியைச் சிரைத்தானாம்.

It is said that a barber wasted his time by shaving a kitten.

6027. வேலை முத்தோ பிள்ளை முத்தோ?

Is the work a pearl, or the child a pearl !

6028. வேலையைப் பார்த்துக் கூலி கொடு.

Look at the work before you pay the hire.

6029. வேலையைப் பார்த்துப் பெண்ணை எடு, சாலையைப் பார்த்து ஊருக்கு நட.

After ascertaining her domestic skill take a girl in marriage, proceed to your village taking care not to miss the road.

6030. வேல் வைத்துப் பயிர் ஆக்குவோர் இல்லை.

No one cultivates the vél-*Acacia arabica*-tree.

6031. வேழத்தை ஒத்த வினை வந்தால் தீர்வது எப்படி?

When a monstrous evil betides *one*, how can it be removed?

6032. வேழத்திற்குச் சிறிதும் பெரிதாய்த் தோன்றும்.

To an elephant small objects appear great.

6033. வேழம் முழங்கினாற்போல.

Like the thundering of an elephant.

6034. வேளை அறிந்து பேசு, நாளை அறிந்து பயணம் பண்ணு.

Speak opportunely, set out on a journey on an auspicious day.

6035. வேளைக்கு அரைக் காசு ஆயிரம் பொன் ஆகும்.

Half a cash at a time will, in the long run, amount to thousands of gold.

6036. வேளைக்கு உதவாத பிள்ளை தாழங்காய்க்குச் சரி.

A child who does not help in an emergency is like the fruit of the screw-pine.

6037. வேளையோ அவவேளை வீட்டிலோ அன்னம் இலலை.

The time is unfavourable, at home there is no rice.

6038. வேறே வினை தேவை இல்லை, வினையாத்தாள் கோவிலுக்குப் போகவேண்டியதில்லை.

There is no need of another evil, it is not necessary to go to the temple of the goddess of misfortune.

6039. வேனலுக்குக் கன மழை வரும், வேந்தனுக்குக் கன சனம் சேரும்.

Excess of heat foretokens a heavy fall of rain, *the presence of a* king attracts a multitude of people.

6040. வேனிற் காலத்திற்கு விசிறி ஆன காலத்திற்கு ஆச்சாவும் தேக்கும்.

In the hot season a fan *is useful*, in prosperous times acha-*ebony*-and teak wood.

வை.

6041. வை என்ற எழுத்தே பெயரும் வினையும் ஆகும்.

The letter வை is both a noun and a verb.

6042. வைகறைத் துயில் எழு.

Rise at dawn.

6043. வைகாசி மாதம் ஆற்றில் தண்ணீர்.

The river is in flood in May.

6044. வைகுண்டம் என்பது திரு மா நகரம்.

That which is called Vaikundam is a very great city.

6045. வைகை ஆற்றுத் தண்ணீர் வேகம் அதிகம்.

The current in the Vaigai is great.

6046. வைகை ஆற்று வெள்ளத்தில் பாலம் நிலைக்கிறது இல்லை.

When the Vaigai is in flood, its bridges do not escape uninjured.

6047. வைகை ஆறு தாமிரபருணிக்கு மத்திமம்.

The Vaigai is smaller than the Tamravarni.

6048. வைக்கத் தெரியாமல் வைக்கோற்போரிலே வைத்தானும்.

It is said that he unwittingly placed it in a stack of straw.

6049. வைக்கத் தெரியாமல் வைத்துவிட்டு வந்தவரை எல்லாம் கேட்கலாமா?

Having inserted it by mistake, may he ask every one that comes by *to help him out of the straits*?

6050. வைக்கோற்கட்டுக்காரனை ஒப்புக்குக் கட்டி அழுதாற்போல.

As one embraced a straw carrier and pretended to weep.

6051. வைக்கோற்பட்டடையில கட்டின நாய்

A dog tied by a stack of straw.

6052. வைக்கோல் பஞ்சமா வறட் பசு பஞ்சமா?

Which is the more scarce, straw or a barren cow?

6053. வைக்கோல் தின்னும் குதிரை வீட்டுக் கூரையையும் பிடுங்கும்.

A horse which eats straw will also pull down the thatch of the house.

6054. வைக்கோல் தின்கிற மாட்டுக்குப் பால் கொஞ்சம், மதுரம் அதிகம்.

The cow that eats straw gives a small quantity of milk but it is very sweet.

6055. வைக்கோல் தின்கிற குதிரைக்கு வேகம் அதிகமா?

Is the horse that feeds on straw uncommonly fleet?

6056. வைக்கோற் கூரையிலும் விழற் கூரை வெகு நாள் இருக்கும்.

A reed roof lasts longer than a straw roof.

6057. வைக்கோற் கூளமும் ஒரு வேளைக்கு உதவும்.

Even old straw may be of use sometime or other.

6058. வைசியரும் சூத்திரரும் இருந்து அல்லோ பிராமணரும் க்ஷத்திரியரும் வருவார்கள்.

It is from Vaisyas and Sudras who must have existed previously, is it not, that Brahmans and Kshatris must *have come.*

6059. வைசியர்களில் பூவைசியர் சிரேஷ்டம்.

Of the Vaisyas the agriculturists are the chief.

6060. வைசூரி வந்தவர்கள் அம்மா என்று கூப்பிட வேண்டும்.

Those who are attacked with small-pox must call it the goddess.

6061. வைதாரை வாழவைக்கும் வாழ்ந்தாரைத் தாழவைக்கும்.

It will confer on calumniaters prosperity, and reduce the affluent to poverty.

6062. வைதிகர் என்றால் பார்ப்பாருக்கு பெயர்.
The term vaidikar is another name for brahmans.

6063. வைதீகம் லௌகிகம் இரண்டும் வேண்டும்.
The sacred and the secular are both indispensable.

6064. வைதீகம் என்றால் தெய்வ சமயம்.
Vaidikam means the divine religion.

6065. வைதீகம் ஆய்ந்து அறி.
Arrive at a knowledge of religion by studious investigation.

6066. வைத்தது உண்டானால் கெட்டதும் உண்டாம்.
If its being put there be true, its being lost may also be true.

6067. வைத்தது கண்டது சொல்லாதே.
Tell not what has been kept or what you saw.

6068. வைத்தால் குடுமி சிரைத்தால் மொட்டை.
If *the hair is* left to grow, kudumi, if shaved, bald.

6069. வைத்தியன் பெரிதோ வாத்தி பெரிதோ?
Which is greater, a physician or a schoolmaster?

6070. வைத்தியனுக்கும் வாத்திக்கும் பேதம் இல்லை.
A physician and a schoolmaster never disagree.

6071. வைத்தியன் எல்லாருக்கும் பொது.
A physician is common to all.

6072. வைத்தியம் வேண்டாதார் உலகில் இல்லை.
There is no one on earth who does not require the services of a physician.

6073. வைத்தியம் வாயாடிக்குப் பலிக்கும்.
A loquacious doctor is successful.

6074. வைத்தியம் எல்லாம் நம்பிக்கையாற் பலிக்கும்.
Faith in medicine makes it effectual.

6075. வைத்தியனுக்கும் அஞ்சவேண்டும், வம்பனுக்கும் அஞ்சவேண்டும்.

One must fear a doctor as well as a traitor.

6076. வைத்தியமோ பைத்தியமோ?

Is it medical skill or madness?

6077. வைத்தியன் சொன்னது எல்லாம் மருந்து.

Whatever a physician prescribes is a remedy.

6078. வைத்தியனுக்குத் தன் அவிழ்தம் பலிக்காதாம்.

It is said that a physician cannot cure himself.

6079. வைத்தியன் தகப்பன் போல.

A physician is like a father.

6080. வைத்தியனே பெரிது என்பார் சிலர், வாத்தியே பெரிது என்பார் சிலர்.

Some will say that a physician is greater than a schoolmaster, and others, that a teacher is greater than a physician.

6081. வைத்தியன் பாராத நோய் தீருமா?

Can a disease be cured without treatment?

6082. வைத்தியன் பிள்ளை நோயினால் அல்ல, மருந்தினால் சாகும்.

A doctor's child dies, not by disease, but by medicine.

6083. வைத்தியனுக்கு ஊரார் யாவரும் சினேகிதர்.

The whole town is friendly to a physician.

6084. வைத்தியத்தில் இரண வைத்தியமும், வயதில் யௌவனமும் நல்லது.

As regards medical science, surgery—in regard to age, youth are preferable.

6085. வைத்தியனே உன்னையே குணமாக்கு.

Physician, heal thyself.

6086. வைத்தியம் செய்தவன் எல்லாம் வைத்தியன்.

6087. வைத்தியம் கொஞ்சமாகிலும் தெரியாத பேர்கள் இல்லை.

There is none that does not know, at least, a little of medicine.

6088. வைத்தியன் மருந்திலும் கைமருந்தே நலம்.

Domestic medicine is preferable to that of a physician.

6089. வைத்தியன் பெரிதோ மருந்து பெரிதோ?

Which is greater, a physician or his medicine?

6090. வைத்தியன் பேச்சு நாலில் ஒரு பங்கு.

But a fourth part of a quack's pretensions *proves to be true.*

6091. வைத்தியனுக்கு வந்தது அவன் தலையோடே.

The malady of a physician cleaves to him till death.

6092. வைத்திய சாஸ்திரம் சாஸ்திரங்களில் விசேஷம்.

Medical science is the most important of all sciences.

6093. வைத்தீசுரன் கோவிலுக்குப் போயும் வயிற்று வலி தீர இல்லை.

His belly-ache is not cured even after going on a pilgrimage to Vaidisvaran's temple.

6094. வையகத்து உற்றவன் மெய்யகம் உற்றவன்.

In all the world, he who is sincere is a friend.

6095. வையகத்துக்குத் துணை வரதன் கழல் இணை.

At the ankled feet of the giver of all good is *found* the refuge of the world.

6096. வையகம் ஒழியும் வான் ஒழியும் வல்லவர் வசனம் ஒழியாது.

Earth and heaven will perish, but the words of the mighty will endure.

6097. வையகத்தில் எல்லோரும் ஒரு போக்கு அல்ல.

All the world do not follow the same course.

6098. வையகத்தில் பொய் சொல்லாதவன் இல்லை.

There is no one in the world who has not uttered a falsehood.

6099. வையத்துள் நீதி செய்யத்தக்கது.

It is proper to do justice in the world.

6100. வையத்தில் உயர்ந்தோர் சிலர் தாழ்ந்தோர் பலர்.

In the world some are high, and many are low.

6101. வையத்தில் உயர்ந்தோர்க்கு இரை தாழ்ந்தோர்.

In the world the low are the victims of the high.

6102. வையத்தில் உப்புக்கு ஏமாறின பேர் உடம்புக்கும் ஏமாறுவார்கள்.

On earth those who are disappointed of salt will meet with disappointment as regards their body also.

6103. வையத்தில் உப்பில்லாத பேர்க்கு உடம்பு இல்லை.

On earth those who have no salt have no body.

6104. வையத்தில் உடம்பு இல்லாதபேர்க்கு உப்பு வேண்டாம்.

Those on earth who have not a body, have no occasion for salt.

6105. வையத்தில் உப்பும் வேண்டும் உடலும் வேண்டும்.

While on earth salt, and a body, are indispensable.

6106. வையத்தில் உடம்பு இல்லாவிட்டாலும் உடைவேண்டும், பணம் இல்லாவிட்டாலும் கனம் வேண்டும்.

Though destitute of personal beauty, clothing is needful, though destitute of money reputation is necessary.

6107. வையத்தில் வாழ்வாங்கு வாழ்பவன் தெய்வத்துள் வைக்கப்படும்.

He who lives as he ought in this world, will be ranked with the gods.

6108. வையத்தில் மேலான பேர்க்குத் தாழ்மையான மனது இருக்கவேண்டும்.

The great in the world must be distinguished by a humble mind.

6109. வையத்தில் நல்லோர் ஒருவரைக் கண்டது இல்லை.

In all the world none really good, has been seen.

6110. வையத்தில நெல்லுக்கு இறைத்த நீர் புல்லுக்கும் பாயும்.

Water drawn for the rice crop, benefits the grass also.

6111. வையத்தில் நெல் அரிசி வேண்டாதாரும் உண்டு, புல அரிசி சிக்காதாரும் உண்டு.

In the world there are those who do not care for rice, as well as those who can scarcely procure even the seeds of grass.

6112. வையத்தில் சைவனுக்குச் சைவன்மேல.

As a rule one saiva regards himself superior to another.

6113. வையத்தில் வைஷ்ணவனுக்கு வைஷ்ணவன் மேல்.

One vaishnava thinks himself superior to another vaishnava.

6114. வையத்தில் தந்தையிலும் தாய் விசேஷம்.

On earth a mother is more serviceable than a father.

6115. வையத்தில் தெவிட்டாத பொருள் அன்னமும் தண்ணீரும்.

While on earth the things which do not cloy, are rice and water.

6116. வையத்தில் நல் வினையால் ஆகாதது தீவினையால் ஆகுமா?

May that which cannot be accomplished by good deeds, be accomplished by evil deeds?

6117. வையத்து மனிதர் நாலு வகை.

There are four kinds of men in the world.

6118. வையம் தோறும் தெய்வம் தொழு.

Worship God through all the world.

6119. வையம் ஏற்றின் ஐயம் இல்லை.

When the whole world applauds one, his merit is unquestionable.

6120. வையம் ஒத்தால் ஐயம் இல்லை.

If the world agree, there is no question *about the matter.*

6121. வையம் புகழ்ந்தால் ஐயம் இல்லை.

When the *whole* world praise one, his *character* is unimpeachable.

6122. வையம் பெரிதானாலும் வளம் உள்ள இடம் கொஞ்சம்.

Though the earth is of vast extent, the space adapted to the wants *of man* is limited.

6123. வையம் பெரிது அதில் வருத்தமும் பெரிது.

The world is great, and its anxieties are also great.

6124. வையம் கெட்டால் ஐயம் இல்லை.

If the world be destroyed, almsgiving will cease.

6125. வைய வைய வைரக்கல், திட்டத் திட்டத் திண்டுக்கல்.

The more abused the more durable, the more despised the more hardened.

6126. வைரத்தை வைரம்கொண்டே அறுக்க வேண்டும்.

A diamond must be cut with a diamond.

6127. வைரம் மனதில வையாதே.

Harbour not malice.

6128. வைரம் கொண்டவன் வைரப்பொடி தின்று சாகிறான்.

He who purchases diamonds will die by swallowing the particles

6129. வைராக்கிய சதகம் சதகங்களில் விசேஷம்.

The most distinguished of satakams is that or self control.

A satakam is a poem of a hundred stanzas.

6130. வைராக்கியம் பகை முதலிய துர்க்குணங்களில் விசேஷம்.

Malice is of all forms of hatred the most pernicious.

6131. வைவார்க்கு இன்பம் இல்லை, பொறுத்தார்க்குத் துன்பம் இல்லை.

The abusive have no happiness the forbearing, have no misery.

6132. வைராவி துறவிகளில் விசேஷம்.

Among ascetics the vairávi is the most distinguished.

வௌ.

6133. வௌவாலுக்கு ஒரு கனிக்கு நூறு கனி நஷ்டம்.
For every fruit consumed by a bat, a hundred are spoiled.

6134. வௌவாலுக்கு மரமே கதி, அதன் குஞ்சுக்கு அதுவே கதி.
Trees are the asylum of bats; bats are the refuge of their young.

6135. வௌவாலுக்கு எது தூரம்?
What place is too remote for a bat!

6136. வௌவாலுக்கு இரவில் கண் தெரியும்.
Bats can see in the dark.

6137. வௌவாலுக்கு நீளவும் தெரியும் குறுகவும் தெரியும்.
Bats know how to extend or contract the body.

6138. வௌவாலைத் தின்றாலும் அணிலைத் தின்னல் ஆகாது.
Though one may feed on bats, he may not feed on squirrels.

6139. வௌவாலைக் கொன்றாலும் பிடியை விடாது.
A bat will not let go its hold though killed.

6140. வௌவாலைப் பட்சி என்னலாமா?
May a bat be called a bird!

6141. வெள்வாலோடு அணிற்பிள்ளை சேருமா?
Do squirrels mix themselves with bats!

6142. வௌவாலோ சிறிது அதன் அடியோ வலிது.
Small as the bat is, its stroke is powerful.

6143. வௌவால் அடித்துத் தின்னும், அணில் கடித்துத் தின்னும்.
Bats devour by striking, squirrels by nibbling.

6144. வௌவால் அடிக்குப் பயப்படலாமா?
May one fear the stroke of a bat!

6145. வௌவால் கூட்டம் கூட்டமாக இருக்கும்.
Bats are found in companies.

6146. வெளவால் தலை நரித் தலைபோல்.
The head of a bat resembles that of a jackal.

6147. வெளவால் தின்னாத பழம் இல்லை.
There is no fruit that a bat does not eat.

6148. வெளவால் போலத் தொங்குகிறான்.
He hangs like a bat.

6149. வெளவால் அடித்த பழமும் அணில் கடித்த பழமும் தள்ளுபடி ஆகுமா?
Is fruit knocked off by bats, or nibbled by squirrels, rejected?

6150. வெளவால் அடைகிற வீட்டில் குடி இருப்பது எப்படி?
How can one dwell in a house frequented by bats?

Some suppose that bats in a house foretoken the speedy removal of the resident family.

6151. வெளவி அணில் தொத்துகிறதுபோல.
As a squirrel ascends by clinging.

6152. வெளவிச்சேர்த்த பேர்க்குப் பொருள் உண்டு.
They have wealth who amassed it by plunder.

6153. வெளவில் குடி இருக்கலாமா?
May one continue to dwell among those whom he robs?

6154. வெளவி வெளவிச் சேர்த்தாலும் மற்றவர்க்கு வைத்து ஒழிவான்.
Though he may have amassed wealth by continued rapine, he will leave it for others when he dies.

6155. வெளவின பேர்க்கு முடிவது சுருக்கு.
The rapacious end their days in the halter.

6156. வெளவிய கருமம் எண்ணித் துணி.
Carefully persevere in what you undertake.